Candida Royalle

and the

Sexual Revolution

Candida Royalle

and the

Sexual Revolution

A HISTORY FROM BELOW

Jane Kamensky

W. W. NORTON & COMPANY
Independent Publishers Since 1923

Frontispiece: *Candice and her Olympus, circa 1978.* Candice, c1978, CRP 55.1va

For information about permission to reproduce selections from this book, write to
Permissions, W. W. Norton & Company, Inc., 500 Fifth Avenue, New York, NY 10110

For information about special discounts for bulk purchases, please contact
W. W. Norton Special Sales at specialsales@wwnorton.com or 800-233-4830

Manufacturing by Lakeside Book Company
Book design by Beth Steidle
Production manager: Anna Oler

ISBN 978-1-324-00208-6

W. W. Norton & Company, Inc., 500 Fifth Avenue, New York, N.Y. 10110
www.wwnorton.com

W. W. Norton & Company Ltd., 15 Carlisle Street, London W1D 3BS

1 2 3 4 5 6 7 8 9 0

For my sister, Ann
And in sisterhood, to Judith, Elise, Jill, and Sue

Sex, a great and mysterious motive force in human life, has indisputably been a subject of absorbing interest to mankind through the ages; it is one of the vital problems of human interest and public concern.

−Justice William J. Brennan, *United States v. Roth*, 1957

Growing up female in America. What a liability!

−Erica Jong, *Fear of Flying*, 1973

Contents

A Note on Spelling

LET ME JUST PUT IT OUT THERE: Candice Vadala, like most people at most times in modern history, was a lousy speller. I have left her unique spellings intact in portions of this book centered on her girlhood. She sounds like a kid, and that's how we need to encounter her in that crucial and vulnerable stage of life. But I have silently corrected her spelling as an adult, to save the reader a stream of [*sic*], and to treat my subject with the respect she deserves, the limits of her formal education notwithstanding.

Candida Royalle

and the

Sexual Revolution

Prologue
Personal Appearances

"**E**ach time I know I have to go on stage soon I feel like screaming and crying," Candice Vadala wrote in her journal in November 1980.[1] It was Election Day, the dawning of what Ronald Reagan, the landslide victor in the presidential race, would later declare to be morning in America. But night still hung thick in the places where Vadala made her personal appearances, in embattled strip clubs in struggling industrial cities around the United States. The blinking lights on the marquee always used her professional name, Candida Royalle. She had chosen it six years before, in San Francisco, for her work in underground theater. She might have known, from her Catholic girlhood, that *Candida*—derived from the Latin *candidus*—meant white, pure. It meant what *Candice* meant, but it looked fancier, more upper-class, especially when paired with *Royalle*. "I thought it sounded like a rich French dessert," she later wrote.[2]

She'd worked the live-show circuit for a year or so, on and off, gigs tucked between films and romances and writing assignments. She played Chicago, Detroit, Washington, D.C. She played Bridgeport, Connecticut, and New York's Times Square. The bookings lasted several days, sometimes a full week. She'd done a show in Toronto in the dead of winter, a few days before her wedding.[3]

The contracts her agent brought her always sounded so promising, one more sign that Royalle's name was "getting big & respected," she wrote. The money seemed good: as much as $250 a night—about $750 in today's money. It was more than she made by writing an article for a men's magazine, roughly equal to her day rate for shooting a film. Sometimes, a club's owner even paid her travel and hotel. Royalle's "star status" also meant she could set her own limits on the circuit: "No sleazy crotch shots or anything."

The first time she readied for the road, Candice had relished the anticipation: picking numbers to lip-sync during her striptease, pairing the vampy siren song "Whatever Lola Wants," from *Damn Yankees*, with the Blockheads' throbbing postpunk anthem, "Hit Me with Your Rhythm Stick." Assembling costumes—fishnets and garters, always. A sheath that looked like the half-ravaged tiger-skin of a porno Wilma Flintstone, or a gamine nightdress that called to mind a dirty Doris Day, or a bodystocking made entirely of string, a cross between '70s macramé and the dawning '80s bondage fashion. She was keen to use her dance and vocal training, and to flaunt her personal style, which evoked the movie stars of the '40s and '50s.[4] She thought she might have found her "true calling in life: to bring back burlesque the way it was meant to be! To prove that excitement can be generated by sheer electricity rather than just sheer cunt!"[5]

The audience wanted sheer cunt.

The first time Candice had strutted onstage, at the Hi-Way in Chicago in September 1979, she had felt like a silver-screen star—like "Mae West with her young strapping bodyguards by her side, signing autographs, posing for pictures." The club's owner had produced *Hot and Saucy Pizza Girls*, one of Candice's favorites among the forty-plus pornographic films in which she'd appeared. Ads for her live show in the *Sun-Times* touted "Pizza Girl in Person! She Sings! She Dances! She Delivers!" The Hi-Way's staff waited on her hand and foot: "Would you like your water now Miss Royalle?" She had always been a sucker for any hint of luxury, a princess awaiting her prince and her castle. It had taken a couple of days, and a boost from some hash, but she managed to "warm up and get loose & sexy" on the club's stage, really "cookin'," she wrote, feeling the kind of energy she got from singing jazz or doing theatre.[6]

But then, in Detroit, disappointment set in, as if they'd turned up the houselights to reveal the kinds of theaters that played 16mm hardcore for the raincoat crowd, places managed by people she called "low life sleazoids" or "hillbilly slobs" who exploited their customers, the "strange & sometimes retarded little men" who came to watch Candida Royalle dance, hoping for a feel or even a taste, bringing her "odd little gifts," telling her how much they admired her early work, in silent peep-show loops, the cheapest, lowest form of sex film, the stuff that had embarrassed her even on the days she made those horrible one-act wonders, sometimes two in the course of a single morning. Yet the adoring customers Candice both pitied and despised also complained to the management: Royalle gave them too much burlesque and too little beaver. She scribbled in the spiral notebook she used as a makeshift diary an angry poem:

> *They pull up in front of the blinking marquis*
> *Park their pickup trucks and pay the fee—*
> *They're all set for an hour of fun*
> *Watching girls' pussies pretending to come*
> *They'd like it if I shoved my pussy in their face*
> *They'd like me to be an awful disgrace. . . .*
> *Ya wanna see me writhe on the floor*
> *You wanna see me . . . act like a whore*
> *I dare ya!*[7]

She dared them, but still she danced, and the men kept paying, and she kept wriggling, and now, fourteen months after her debut in Chicago, she was opening in Pittsburgh, "live on stage" at the Casino Royale, in the failing steel city's fallen downtown, sandwiched between adult bookstores, blue-movie theaters, and massage parlors. Liberty Avenue was the kind of place where someone might sell you a fix and then pull you into the alley with a knife at your throat.[8] "Maybe there's something to be said for expecting the worst," Candice wrote shortly after she checked out the club. When the curtain went up, she was relieved to spy "a couple of genuinely good-looking guys" amidst the toads.[9]

The Pittsburgh gig ran for a week, four shows a day, plus a midnight special on Friday and Saturday. Sunday's performances started at noon, right after church.[10] When the engagement was nearly done, a friend flew out from New York to bring her some heroin. Candice sniffed rather than shot it now, only when she really needed a bump to get her through. "Stoned I hardly felt the anguish," she wrote in her journal.[11]

Unchained by the dope, she lost herself in the dance, her beauty reflected back to her in the onlookers' gazes. "They shrieked! They were at the edge of their seats panting," she wrote after the show. The friend who brought the heroin took pictures: Candida with her hair tied in ribboned pigtails, wearing a filmy pink baby-doll nightie, dancing to Cole Porter's "My Heart Belongs to Daddy," with "the mood," as she later put it, "definitely little girl." Candida tearing off the nightie to reveal a demure pink satin push-up bra. Candida stripped to her G-string, head thrown back, one arm hooked behind her. Candida on her knees, fully nude, still singing. The club was dark, and the pictures are blurred, but you can see the men, all white, some in coat and tie, their faces rapt, surrounding the runway on three sides, near enough to touch the writhing star if their hands weren't busy in their laps. They were crestfallen when she finished: "screams—yells," Candice wrote. She left the stage "laughing, sweating, panting, having just worked myself up into an explosive ending. I looked like I was coming—I felt like I was."[12]

Then she flew home to Brooklyn and found that she couldn't stop crying, the tears "dragging long black streams of makeup down my face."[13]

Candice insisted she felt no shame, though Reagan had won the election and not only his family-values conservatives but also many of her onetime sister-feminists were out on the barricades, marching against porn. "I don't suffer guilt," she wrote in her diary. "I find erotic entertainment valid & necessary." Still, the appearances gutted her. On film sets, she'd been surrounded by other performers, women and men who'd faced the same chances and made the same choices she had. How different it felt to stand before the "men that actually go & get off watching me."

She knew that her work in hardcore film hadn't been "wrong," wasn't "sin." But that didn't make porn the hill she wanted to die on. "I don't even care about any 'cause,'" she wrote. In fact, she hadn't voted in the big election. "I don't even live like most people fighting for sexual freedom," she wrote. "I am sexually free. And I'm also old fashioned."[14]

One of those things was true.

She turned thirty right after the Pittsburgh gig. She had begun to ponder how she had fallen into her line of work, and whether she might yet get out. She thought about telling her story; having kept a diary for eighteen years, she'd "become a pretty good writer!" She pitched an essay about the personal-appearance circuit to editors at *New York* and other mainstream magazines, promising to offer their readers "understanding into the mind behind the body. Women in the sex industry have long been misunderstood & put down," she said. "I would like to help change that."[15]

She began to imagine a full-dress memoir. *Candida Royalle, Porn Queen* would be the story of a generation, and of the "different experiences & choices we all make every day of our lives—we women trying & needing to prove ourselves." She had lived those experiences and choices "more extremely than others," and so her tale was more "telling of what we all go through."[16] About this, and much else, she was surely right. Her life, despite or indeed because of its extremes—its literal bareness—embodies both the promise and the perils of her times, and their aftermath.

She pored over her diaries and letters, highlighting passages to feature, softening rough and bigoted language, smoothing over flaws. She pondered existential questions: how did Candice Vadala—"a nice middle-class" kid, supplied with "ballet lessons, girl scouts, all those ingredients that go into making a nice wholesome American Girl"— end up as Candida Royalle, Porn Queen?[17] And to what extent would she succeed in the project she set for herself in the '80s: creating feminist porn, writing a different ending to her own life in the process?

She made outlines. But she got busy, and then she got sick, and finally, in 2015, she died, too young, without producing a draft.

———

CANDICE VADALA LONG WANTED to share the story of her life. I never expected that I would be the one to write that history—at once the book she never managed, and nothing like it.

In the fall of 1981, nearly a year after Candida Royalle's Pittsburgh show, I started college. The most explicit images I had ever seen were the drawings illustrating my parents' copy of *The Joy of Sex*, which they hid, under blankets, in the back of a bureau drawer. Those pencil sketches wouldn't do for a thoroughly modern coed. Sometime that year, or the next, I saw a pornographic movie in the company of a group of friends. The VCR was still novel; just over 1 percent of American households had one.[18] Dorm rooms certainly didn't. Students watched *cinema*, programmed by film societies, in campus spaces. My porno, as I recall it, was screened in the auditorium of the Yale Law School, where, by day, I attended a popular course in Soviet history. Maybe some First Amendment principle was involved? Not for me or my friends, heaven knows. For us, the outing represented at least four parts dare to one part lust. I'm sure I laughed in the crowd in the dark.

The relationship of pornography to misogyny loomed large in the American women's movement at the time, yet I was only dimly aware of the internecine feminist conflict that would soon become known as the sex wars.[19] Subjects like women's history and feminist theory were just making their way onto campus. I scarcely was taught by a female professor, and never confronted a female protagonist who lived beyond the pages of a Victorian novel.

Candice Vadala's aversion to "cause" notwithstanding, she wound up enlisting in the sex wars, a conflict that, among its many other ironies, enlarged the cultural cachet of adult actresses and filmmakers. As Candida Royalle, she played an unpredictable role that scrambled the division of feminist sensibilities into anti-porn and pro-sex sides. Royalle was a stealth fighter, an insurgent, a mercenary. She rejected both the victimology and the criminology of anti-pornography feminism. But she also knew, and sometimes spoke to, darker sides of the sex industry, which belied the facile hedonic sex-positive arguments made by those who worked sex only on paper.

Shortly before Reagan's second landslide victory, Candice turned the camera around and got behind it. Her production company, Femme, made explicit movies she considered to be, and touted as, feminist. In the last decades of the American century, Femme films— eighteen in all—raised the temperature in countless marriages. They carried the imprimatur of the sex- and family-therapy industry. By the turn of the millennium, when "the pedagogic enshrinement of porn" became "an established fact," as James Atlas wrote in *The New Yorker*, the films Royalle directed were not just screened but taught on elite college campuses. "Sex is now seen as the motive force of our beings," one pioneer of the genre of porn studies told Atlas.[20]

Just as Royalle settled into the director's chair, I graduated from college and moved to Manhattan. The sex wars were raging, and the toll of the AIDS epidemic was increasing exponentially. *Time* magazine had run a cover story entitled "Sex in the 80s: The Revolution Is Over."[21] Since the Carter years, Congress had debated numerous bills attempting to curb explicit materials, chiefly in the name of child protection. Early in Reagan's second term as president, he directed his attorney general to produce a doomsday book documenting the impacts of pornography. Edwin Meese's Commission on Pornography held its first hearings the month I got to New York.

The feminist anti-pornography movement was then entering what turned out to be its last major domestic phase. Campaigns to pass local ordinances allowing people who claimed to be harmed by pornography to sue those who made or sold or displayed it had failed in Minneapolis, Los Angeles, and Cambridge, Massachusetts; the courts had turned back the strategy's one legislative success, in Indianapolis. Still, anti-porn's feminist warriors fought on, sometimes in concert with Meese's evangelical coalition. I remember seeing, on streetcorners around the city, activists displaying enormous reproductions of an infamous *Hustler* magazine cover, on which a nude woman is fed, headfirst, through a meat-grinder, reduced to a pile of ground chuck, misogyny made flesh. A young person from a mostly middle-class life—Girl Scouts, ballet lessons—I was stunned to witness such enormous hatred in the world upon which I sought to make my mark.

One day after work, I picked up, from a table on the sidewalk in Morningside Heights selling books said to have been stolen from Columbia University's library during the student uprisings of the '60s, a fading copy of Andrea Dworkin's fierce and fearless *Woman Hating* (1974). Dworkin knew the depths of misogyny and saw pornography as both its root cause and its native tongue. Images like that *Hustler* cover were not aberration but essence. "Pornography, like fairy tale, tells us who we are," she wrote. "It is the structure of the male and female mind, the content of our shared erotic identity, the map of each inch and mile of our oppression and despair."[22] It is an exaggeration, though

Women Against Pornography demonstration, c1979.

not much of one, to say that the power of Dworkin's pain and the gut-punch of her prose sent me to graduate school.

I didn't know then that *Hustler*'s meat-grinder cover, blown up on those curbside easels, had been published seven years earlier, shortly after the magazine's publisher, Larry Flynt, was shot and paralyzed while standing trial for obscenity. I didn't know that, Dworkin's synecdoche notwithstanding, the image wasn't in fact typical of porn, nor even of *Hustler*, much less that it had been a satire: a poke in the eye of feminists who said that such magazines treated women like pieces of meat. Published in the wake of Flynt's conversion to Christianity, the image may also have contained elements of self-critique, as some defenders said.[23] Anti-pornography feminists' use of the *Hustler* cover, like many weapons in many culture wars, was a carefully curated piece of propaganda, and a bit of moral jujitsu too.

I knew even less of the feminist arguments *against* anti-pornography, arguments that cast women as desiring subjects rather than as victimized objects, that foregrounded sexual freedom and sexual difference, and that saw far greater danger in the powers of the state than in even the most misogynist images. Nor could I have then anticipated the ways that the bill for the sex wars would come due: the cost of a generation of revolutionary intellect and organizing squandered in stalemate while our democracy went through the meat grinder.

The more I learned, the more I came to equivocate on the question of porn.

––––––

DECADES PASSED. I became a historian of the United States and taught university courses on a range of topics in American history, mostly centered on the nation's founding era. I wrote books, several of them combining history and biography, field and figure, times and life. Though trained in the history of women and families, I had largely left the twentieth century, and with it, the feminist sex wars, behind.

And then, in the fall of 2015, I started a new job, which combined a professorship in history at Harvard with the directorship of Radcliffe's Schlesinger Library on the History of Women in America, the most comprehensive research archive of its kind in the world. Days after my appointment began, the *New York Times* noted Candice Vadala's death, headlining a half-page obituary with her *nom de porn* and lauding the movies she "infused with plots, passion, seduction and even romance," as well as her work as a founder of Feminists for Free Expression, "a so-called sex-positive organization" that had challenged efforts to censor pornography from left and right alike.[24]

The Schlesinger holds the papers of Andrea Dworkin and those of her frequent collaborator Catharine A. MacKinnon, as well as the records of Women Against Pornography, among many other collections centered on sexual violence and women's liberation. But even the capsule biography of Royalle in the *Times* obituary revealed an individual life, and a *kind* of life and work, that remained underdocumented.

That lacuna impoverished not only the library's vaults, but also the accounts scholars could assemble of the complex issues to which Royalle's experience spoke.

And so I wondered whether it was even remotely possible that Candice Vadala/Candida Royalle had documented her own life, and whether those papers, if they existed, might find an institutional home.

It seemed, for all sorts of reasons, improbable. But she had, and they did.

Candice's impulse to archive surfaced even before she began her nearly continuous run of diaries, at the age of twelve. By her early twenties, she had developed a sense of her own intrinsic importance that would never fail her, no matter how many times she got knocked down. That conviction was both personal and generational, part of an inward turn among those born after World War II that the journalist Tom Wolfe called a Third Great Awakening, cresting in "the 'Me' Decade" of the '70s. "The old alchemical dream was changing base metals into gold," Wolfe wrote in 1976. "The new alchemical dream is: changing one's personality—remaking, remodeling, elevating, and polishing one's very *self*. . . and observing, studying, and doting on it. (Me!)"[25]

Candice's commitment to self-knowing and self-making deepened her commitment to her archive, and vice versa. By the time she turned thirty, she had called more than twenty places in six cities home. And still she kept her collection close. She had to. As she'd told her diary at age fifteen, "I'd never throw you out! You've sort of become a part of me, my inner self. . . . you *are* me in a sense."[26] In the '80s, when Candice kicked heroin and co-founded Femme, and when the sex wars burst the narrow confines of academic debate and gave Candida Royalle a national stage, she began to think not just about the inherent interest of her life—her biography—but also about its broader significance—her relationship to History. She realized she should "be sure to preserve all of it carefully." Her husband suggested looking into microfilm.[27]

The cartons holding Royalle's papers began to arrive at the Schlesinger in late 2016, just as the *Washington Post* published a leaked audiotape in which the Republican candidate for president of the United States bragged that he could "Grab 'em by the pussy."[28] Now processed, the Papers of Candida Royalle span 106 file boxes; 109 folders of photographs; 209 videotapes; three archived websites; tens of thousands of emails, posters, costumes, and more: evidence of a life as overexamined as it was overdetermined. In that sense, the collection, as Candice sometimes recognized, was at once a savior and a trap, leading her inward and leaving her there.

Yet the Royalle Papers are also an archive of immeasurable, even revelatory, potential: the remains of a profoundly, uniquely twentieth-century American life, a life like no other, and also like every other—a biography and a history. The parlor drama of a family and its failures unfolds against the epic of cultural transformation in postwar America, shot through with the ironies of feminism and its foibles, and psychology and its discontents. Just as Candice Vadala, born in 1950, was forged in the crucible of the Cold War, Candida Royalle was a product of the sexual revolution, her persona made possible, if not inevitable, by the era's upheavals in demography, law, technology, and ideology. Her life could not have unfolded as it did in any place but the United States, or in any time but the one in which she lived.

As Candice Vadala would have been the first to argue, she also shaped her times. Her having done so is perhaps less remarkable than her insistence on documenting that impact. People like her—working-class, physically and sexually abused, psychologically battered, and sidelined to the sex trades—have rarely told the stories of their own lives. Scholars have glimpsed them, across centuries, through a series of objectifying gazes: the patriarchal gaze of pornography and the disciplining gazes of moral reformers, including anti-pornography feminists. Royalle's papers flip the point of view, seizing the camera and insisting that she be treated as a thinking subject, creating as well as created by. Historians have had few tools with which to probe the mainstreaming of pornography in American culture, and especially to understand it from the inside out. Candice Vadala's life, and her extraordinary record of that life, lays that machinery bare.

In its broadest contours, then, this book is a study of the ways ordinary individuals make history even as history makes them. Specifically, it offers a wholly new history of the origins, course, and consequences of the so-called sexual revolution.

IN 2017, I taught, with a colleague, a research seminar on the vexed history of feminism and pornography, rooted in the Schlesinger's collections on the subject, including Royalle's papers. My colleague and I had lived through the sex wars, I as an observer and she as a combatant. To us, they still felt raw and present. But to our students, those battles of the '70s and '80s appeared remote, sepia-tinted, further from their lives in college than World War II had been from mine.

Had a student asked me, that semester, when the sex wars ended, I would have said they sputtered to a draw in the '90s. Leading anti-pornography feminists had made enduring institutional alliances, and so their arguments lived on in laws governing hate speech, domestic violence, even war crimes. But in the broader culture, the sex-positive side had triumphed. As evidence to support that claim, one might cite: Pretty much any episode of pretty much any series on pretty much any premium cable channel. Or the annual campus bacchanals that fly under the name of Sex Week, which began at Yale in 2002 and continue decades later in many universities, including my own.[29] Or the evolution of the Take Back the Night march into the SlutWalk.[30] Or, I suppose, the very existence of our course at Harvard.

At moments that term, some students sensed a tension between aspects of their theoretical feminism—rooted in narratives of victimization and trauma, with remedies that foregrounded punishment—and their lived sexual ecology—an alcohol-fueled, no-holds-barred, tits-out free-for-all. Still, on the whole, it was the antis whose work and worldview seemed strange to them. Reading Catharine MacKinnon felt a bit like reading Mary Wollstonecraft: once a bracing and righteous message, now desiccated and curled, sealed in a bottle and left on the shelf.

But late that autumn, the #MeToo movement ignited, its fires fed by the familiar American tension between liberty and equality. The sex wars, it turned out, had been buried, half-alive, in a shallow grave. Old arguments roared back in new covers, like the pulsing red paperback anthology of Andrea Dworkin's essays, bearing the Gen-Z-friendly title *Last Days at Hot Slit*, issued in 2019.[31] Books meditating on the ambiguous achievement of sexual freedom for women—works whose titles include words like *rethinking* or *unfinished* or *lost*—have brought the voices of the '70s and '80s to bear on a vastly different moment, in which core aspects of women's lives remain stubbornly unchanged.[32] In 1986, in the midst of hearings on pornography held by the National Organization of Women, the president of NOW's Portland chapter had asserted, confidently, that the "elimination of pornography is more basic than reproductive freedom."[33] Nearly forty years later, it is painfully clear that feminists secured neither goal.

The authors of these rueful new works, young intellectuals who came of age amid the rubble of the sex wars, grapple, inconclusively, with difficult truths common to most if not all such conflicts: Both sides were wrong. Neither fully captured the complexities of pleasure or danger, let alone of women's full humanity. The sexual revolution was a war. And as in all wars, nobody won anything without also losing something.

These were realities Candice Vadala was already living, unknowingly, when she started her long run of diaries, on New Year's Day in 1963. Almost two decades later, Candida Royalle held such bitter truths in her very marrow, when she stepped off the runway in Pittsburgh, sweaty and shaken, to begin again.

PART I

Normal

I don't think I've ever had quite a "normal" childhood. . . . What is normal?
—Candice Vadala, 1969

My childhood was as normal as anybody else's.
—Candida Royalle, *How to Tell a Naked Man What to Do*, 2004

1 Home

"Jim, Peg, Me in Lap," c1950.

Candy grew up hearing that her mother, the former Peggy June Thompson Hume, had delivered her at home, in the master bedroom, while her father, Louis, sat in the living room listening to his wife scream.[1] *Home* was a trim brick colonial on Claflin Boulevard, in Franklin Square, a neighborhood at the western edge of the town of Hempstead, in Long Island's Nassau County, which bordered the New York City borough of Queens.

Hempstead was an ancient settlement, far older than the United States. As late as 1940, it had remained an agricultural town. During the 1940s, Grumman Aircraft built bombers for the war effort there, and the aerospace industry grew apace. As soldiers returned, flush with federal money to buy the homes their families had yearned for through the long, lean years of Depression, Hempstead became one of the first places in the country to reinvent itself as a car suburb. In the years just before Candy's birth, in October 1950, the fields around Hempstead rang with the sounds of chainsaws and bulldozers and cement mixers, pouring the concrete slabs on which to set the cookie-cutter boxes that held American dreams.[2]

The house on Claflin Boulevard, one of the Franklin Homes, went up early in the suburban boom: in 1941, the year the United States entered the war. The development marched along a grid of newly built streets, four houses in models A through D, cul-de-sac, repeat. By 1950, the community numbered nearly 5,000—more than seven times its size a decade before. Most heads of household were men in gray flannel suits: office workers, salesmen. Virtually all were white and either Catholic or Jewish, the children of immigrants leaving the city to make good.[3] The Vadalas' family snapshots center on a big backyard that yields to open space just over the fence. Candy would spend her whole wild and roaming life trying to reclaim this suburban ideal.

Candy's paternal grandmother, Marion Vadala, seems to have found the house on Claflin Boulevard for her son Louis and his bride some time before their first daughter, Cynthia (now Cinthea), was born, in 1948. Until then, Louis and Peggy and Peggy's toddler son, Jimmy, had all bunked with her in Brooklyn. Marion wasn't rich—far from it. But she was canny. She "had it figured out," Cinthea says.[4]

Born Marianna Passantino in Palermo, Sicily, Marion had arrived in the United States at the turn of the century and settled with her family in the dense Italian Catholic wards of Brooklyn. She finished eighth grade and went out to work, like all the other girls in the neighborhood. She married at the age of twenty-two, late by the standards of the day; her husband, Pasquale Vatala, Americanized as Charles Vadala, was a Brooklyn native, though his parents, too, were Sicilian.[5]

By 1920, Marion and Charles owned a brownstone on President Street, in Carroll Gardens, where they lived with their young sons, Charles Jr., aged three, and baby Louis, born the year before. The house was imposing if no longer elegant, standing four stories high and three bays across, big enough that the Vadalas rented rooms to boarders. Charles caulked ships at the piers along the East River. In time, he moved into white-collar work, as a collector for the growing insurance industry. Once the kids could fend for themselves, Marion got a job, weaving straw bonnets in a hat factory, working at a frenzied pace each year from October until the Easter Parade.[6]

Charles kept a second family on the side. Periodically, the other woman wrote to Marion and begged her to let her husband go. She refused. Charles went anyway, around the time of Candy's birth. But Marion knew how to take care of herself, and by then, her sisters had husbands, one of them a medical doctor: only in America. They helped. Marion kept her house and her peace, but she held a grudge. Years later, she would bequeath her wandering rogue of a husband a dollar to buy a rope to hang himself.[7]

Between her job, her network of kin, her knack for frugality, and the good fortune of the President Street house, which grew valuable over the years, Marion had probably squirrelled away enough to manage the $524 down payment on the colonial in Hempstead. But she didn't in fact buy it for her son and his new wife; Louis and Peggy rented the place.[8] Maybe Marion helped them to cover the monthly costs, which stretched his modest pay as a drummer gigging for jazz bands. Peggy stayed home with Cindi and her older toddler, Jimmy, and soon with baby Candy, whose middle name, Marion, honored her grandmother. There was a dog, too, a collie named Melody, a nod to Louis's calling.[9]

Peggy Thompson Hume Vadala adored that little brick-faced colonial. The year before she delivered Candy there, she wrote to tell her brother Johnny all about her "very nice house in a good community." She had painted the nursery herself, in both pink and in blue, since Cindi and Jimmy shared it. "We have a maple dinette set," she bragged. "We have a real big yard with flowers and plants and in the back a big tree."

Peggy hoped her brother would come to live with them when he mustered out of the service. Louis would teach him the drums. Maybe Johnny could date some of Louis's cousins, real lookers. Peggy was nuts about New York, where opportunity abounded. Even so, she got "home sick every once in a while when I don't hear from any body that I know." Nobody back in St. Louis answered her cards or thanked her for the presents she sent. Not even Johnny, who she'd always thought was different from the rest.[10]

————

CANDICE LATER BOASTED that her arrival, at home, was unusual "at a time when babies were delivered by doctors in hospitals as mothers were knocked out & made oblivious by heavy duty drugs."[11] About this, she was right. By 1950, only 5 in 100 American babies were born outside a hospital. And there were so very many births: across the United States, maternity wards, built earlier in the century as delivery left the home for the clinic, grew crowded with the fruits of the baby boom. The surge in U.S. birthrates began before the war ended and accelerated afterward. For the first time in decades—in generations—American women married younger and had more children than their mothers or even their grandmothers had. And they gave birth to them, almost exclusively, in hospitals, which promised, not always accurately, healthier outcomes for mother and child alike.[12]

But not Peggy, not this time.

Candy understood the circumstances of her arrival as a sign of Peggy's preference for "natural childbirth." This was rosy post-Lamaze hindsight. There is no hint that Peggy and Louis were among the vanguard who read the British obstetrician Grantly Dick-Read's *Childbirth without Fear: The Principles and Practice of Natural Childbirth* (1944), or even its condensation in *Reader's Digest* in 1947, the year of their marriage.[13] Cindi had been born in hospital, in crisis: on their way to the delivery ward, a cab broadsided Peggy and Louis's car, injuring Peggy and endangering the baby. The bills—for Peggy's "operation," for Cindi's birth, the whole medical kit and caboodle—had cleaned the Vadalas out.[14] Giving birth at home this second time would have been cheap, but also risky in its way. Writing later in life, after many years of therapy centered on the damage her parents had inflicted, Candice took that choice as evidence that Peggy "was not an ordinary woman." This was one of her rare understatements.[15]

Peggy had every reason to relish the house in Hempstead. Hers had been a knockabout life. Born in rural southeastern Missouri in 1928, she had moved by the time she turned two into St. Louis, where her family rented a tumbledown place up the road from the Anheuser-Busch factory and the railroad yards. The census takers valued the home at $18. Peggy's father drove long hauls for a trucking company.[16] In time, he took up with a new woman on the road, a rural version of Charles Vadala's adulterous arrangement.

Peggy's mother, Helen, told the government she was a widow, maybe to get some benefits. Around 1940, she moved Peggy and her other children to another flat in the city, down the block from a rooming house. Their neighbors came from all over the country, part of the great human tide set in motion by dust and Depression. They were waitresses, janitors, carpenters, domestics, factory workers, and the odd salesman. None of them had finished high school. Helen worked long hours for low wages as a machine operator in a clothing factory, each year pulling in about a quarter of what Marion Vadala made in six months at the hat factory in Brooklyn.[17]

Everyone on Peggy's block told the census taker they were white. Yet race is always a fiction and sometimes a lie. The Thompsons whispered about "Indian blood," from an ancestor in the Oklahoma Territory. "Cherokee—Peggy always said," Candice jotted, decades later.[18] Peggy had no truck with the color line; Candice would learn that her mother's last husband was Black. But the talk of Native ancestry seems to have been a family romance. Maybe playing Indian felt more authentic—nobler—than being poor and rural and white. A photograph taken shortly before Peggy's father left shows a raven-haired family in worn and ill-fitting clothes. Everyone is grinning broadly, but for Peggy, who stares straight ahead, as if scanning for the exit.

She found it in January 1945. Three months after her sixteenth birthday, Peggy married Theodore Frank Hume, whose family lived around the block. The Humes were better off than the Thompsons; Ted's father worked in the steel mills, for a steady wage, which meant that his mother didn't work for pay at all. But Ted and his brother were hooligans, the kind of kids who provoked a national panic over juvenile delinquency. Ted left school after the eighth grade and found jobs as a metalworker, a useful trade for a blossoming car thief. At seventeen, he was sentenced to a two-year stint at the local "training school" for wayward boys.[19] The army called him up in the spring of 1943,

Thompson Family, 1938. Peggy is standing, second from left.

along with all the other eligible young men still left in the neighbor-hood, as the war cleaned out the bars and honky-tonks for miles around. Private Ted Hume lasted a bare six months in uniform, per-haps because he stole another car while still stationed stateside.[20] Then he came home and took up, again or afresh, with Peggy, who was brash and glamorous in equal measure, with pin curls and paste jewelry and penciled-on eyebrows: a young Joan Crawford of the prairie.

They married in Arkansas, just over the state line. Peggy, who was young to marry even by the standards of her day, gave herself an extra two years on their application for a license. If anyone at the courthouse sensed the lie, they didn't care enough to halt the proceedings.[21]

In April 1945, less than four months after the wedding day, likely before Peggy even knew she was pregnant, Ted Hume went back to prison: his seventh arrest and his second incarceration, this time at the state reformatory in Osage.[22] That summer, she buried her mother and moved out of the marital home in St. Louis. In October, as her belly swelled, Peggy Thompson Hume, still a minor, asked the City Court to appoint a "special friend"—a kind of guardian—to enter her petition for divorce, on grounds of cruelty, saying that her husband had beaten her and threatened her life. The marriage was dissolved in February 1946, when little Jimmy, who had never met his father, was about six weeks old.[23]

Then Louis Vadala came to town.

2 Hepcat in Squaretown

Louis Vadala in Brooklyn, c1950.

I 'm a cat who gets a solid kick from digging squares and characters," Louis Vadala told *Yank: The Army Weekly* in late 1942. Private Vadala played drums with a five-man army band, a "solid little outfit," he said. "It's really too much to dig these plowboys who try to jump to our 52nd Street jive." It was a cushy gig, a "terrific life." But still he pined: "WHERE ARE THE WOMEN?"[1] Louis loved being highly sexed, but he didn't always know where to turn his attentions, which would come to haunt him, and even moreso his family, later in his life.

He had been called up in the spring of 1941, before Pearl Harbor. Tapped for his talents. A bandsman, which was better than bullets. But still, the army. What "a drag. . . . What a bringdown!" When the draft board found him, he had been making his way as a musician. A musician! Unlike his older brother, Charles, who took a sensible job in a shoe factory, Louis Vadala had joined Louis Prima's jazz ensemble fresh out of high school. (He'd graduated, though, first in the family to do so.) By day, he lived with his mother and father in Brooklyn. At night, he held court with Prima's band at dance clubs in Midtown.[2]

Prima's ancestors, like Vadala's, came from Sicily. By the time his band roared into New York from the Bayou, he had begun to overlay a New Orleans jazz sound with distinctly Italian accents. Novelty songs like "Angelina," "Felicia No Capicia," and especially his breakout 1945 hit, "Just a Gigolo /I Ain't Got Nobody," brought Sicilian idioms into American living rooms, creating a goombah vogue that would culminate with Frank Sinatra.[3] Prima set Louis Vadala's world to music. He told *Yank* that Vadala was "one of the greatest, most promising young drummers on the swing horizon."[4]

And then Uncle Sam came knocking. Prima had a knee injury that kept him out of the war, but Vadala seemed a decent specimen, though perhaps not quite so fine as he thought himself. The army clocked him at 5'5", 142 pounds, but he strutted taller.[5] He spent months posted to

Fort Snelling, in Minnesota, "digging the fine musicians at Mitch's Cafe" at night, only to answer "those Squaretown boys prancing the barracks floors" each dawn at reveille.[6] A picture taken there shows Louis in deeply pleated pants, with his thick black hair slicked back, more jazzman than GI.[7]

In the spring of 1944, Private First Class Vadala crossed the Pacific. When the Allies liberated the Philippines in the spring of 1945, Louis kept time for the regimental band that played in celebration. Come August, it was over. By October, Louis was stateside, awaiting discharge.[8] And then he was back in civvies, back in Brooklyn, with his mother nagging and his sticks twitching, dying to get out of squaretown before the music stopped.

————

LOUIS VADALA WAS AN ARTIST, "free thinking," he later told his daughter: one of the "few and far between," the "strays" who refused to join "the herd."[9] Still, he needed a job. A guy he'd jammed with in the army—"one of the finest cats"—had returned to Raymond Scott's orchestra.[10] Scott, who pioneered a brand of novelty jazz infused with classical melodies and vaudeville gimmicks, had lately settled into a safer, more commercial big-band sound.[11] It wasn't the hottest jazz, but the cash was cool. When Louis followed his army buddy into Scott's group, he traded the waterfront for wanderlust. Soon they were crisscrossing the country and jamming on the radio.

Scott and his boys stormed St. Louis at least five times in late 1946 and early 1947. On Easter Sunday, they mugged for the cameras, appearing through the new miracle of television on the four hundred "receiving sets" in living rooms around the city.[12] And somewhere, in the clubs or at the shops or on the streets, was Peggy June Thompson Hume.

Peggy had turned eighteen. She was alone with one-year-old Jimmy; Ted Hume would be locked up for years yet.[13] Maybe her sister minded the baby so Peggy could kick up her heels now and then. Maybe she drank with the band, like those "chicks . . . in the Twin Cities" who had grooved with Louis and his quintet back at Fort

Snelling.[14] Family story has it that Peggy earned her keep in a Laundromat.[15] The band members worked up a sweat when they were jamming; maybe she washed and folded their clothes. How cosmopolitan he would have seemed, this drummer from the metropolis who spoke some Italian and had seen the world.

One way or another, Peggy met Louis. And then she was free of her marriage and out of St. Louis and on to New York City, all just like that.

In August 1947, a Monday, in the middle of the afternoon, Peggy Thompson married Louis Vadala at a JP's office in Yonkers. It is hard to imagine a ceremony with less ceremony: no priest, no incense, no scripture, no relatives. A friend of Louis's witnessed the vows with his fiancée. Maybe they also looked after little Jimmy while the judge pronounced Louis and Peggy man and wife. Peggy gave herself four extra years on the marriage license, calling herself twenty-two, perhaps an age that seemed more suited to a bona fide divorcée.[16]

After she and Louis tied the knot, Peggy sent a telegram to her sister in Missouri. A year and a new baby later, she was still waiting to hear back.[17]

PLAYING HOUSE WAS FUN for a while. Painting the nursery and papering the bedroom and pruning the roses and walking the dog. Bundling Jimmy off to school, where he went by the name Vadala.[18] Hosting the relatives: the few pictures that survive from Claflin Boulevard show an army of Vadalas and Passantinos in their Sunday best, the men with starched shirts and Brylcreemed hair, the women in neat, patterned dresses. Beside them, Louis several times appears shirtless, having a smoke or flexing on the lawn with his stepson and his lithe new bride. The relatives look at Louis. Peggy looks at Jimmy. Nobody looks at Peggy in her two-piece gingham swimsuit, the style that had just gotten the name bikini.

Marriage—for young Peggy, this second marriage—was supposed to make it all come out right. Already during her short lifetime, the ideal American marriage had been transformed, the bar raised from stolid stick-to-itiveness to never-ending bliss. Magazines, advice manuals, and an ever-growing army of therapists touted that golden ring as the one, necessary ingredient of a happy life, the key not just to economic security but also to friendship and personal growth and sexual fulfillment.

Yet the more that middle-class Americans expected of their marriages, the less satisfied they found themselves. Responding to a survey of the nation's mental health conducted in 1957, some 45 percent of women said their marriages "had problems," for which wives mostly blamed themselves.[19] As cultural critic Paul Goodman declared in the bestselling *Growing Up Absurd*, published when Candy was nine, "A dispassionate observer of modern marriage might sensibly propose, Forget it; think up some other form of mating and child care."[20] Even the magazines that taught teenage girls to prepare their trousseaus for that day of days carried stories about the ever-present threats to wedded harmony, from affairs to simple ennui. Perfection required practice. Pastors, priests, and rabbis, along with exponents of the still new profession of marriage counseling, rushed into the breach, training couples in the hard work of happiness. The idealized postwar marriage felt to many as arduous as it was essential.[21] "Show me the married woman who can loll about and eat cherry bonbons!" wrote journalist Helen Gurley Brown in her runaway 1962 bestseller, *Sex and the Single Girl*. "Hourly she is told by every magazine she reads what she must do to keep her marriage from bursting at the seams."[22]

The seams came apart on Claflin Boulevard.

"It was all my fault!" Louis later told Candice. He had been too "wrapped up" in his art to carry his weight at home. "I should never have married anyone."[23]

Probably not, but it wasn't all his fault. The relatives had been pitiless from the start. Louis had married out of the clan, the class, the faith. Most of the Brooklyn kin cut Peggy dead. Maybe Marion quoted the Sicilian proverb: *Qual è chidda nor chi voli beniri a la sògirra:* show me what daughter-in-law likes her mother-in-law.[24] Cinthea thinks that Peggy had dreamed of finally getting a big, close-knit family, after her years of fragment and fracture, only to find "they would have nothing to do with her." She spent so much time alone. Louis worked nights in the city while she languished in the still-treeless suburbs, with Jimmy and then Cindi to care for.

When Cindi was a year old, Peggy took the kids and left.

Louis wooed her back, and soon another baby was on the way. Peggy pitched herself down the stairs of the little brick house in hopes of triggering a miscarriage. But Candy came anyway, and then there were three.

A few months after Candy's birth, Peggy cleared out the pink-and-blue nursery, parked the infant with her godmother, packed up Jimmy and Cindi, and left a second time. A second time Louis reeled her back in, with whatever combination of sweet talk and shouting had worked before.[25]

The third try was well and truly splitsville. Jimmy, who was nearly seven at the time, later told Candice he remembered violence: that he'd walked in to find Peggy pinned to the couch, with Louis whaling on her, and had run for help from the policeman who lived a couple houses away, to no avail.[26] Cinthea tells a different story: that Peggy drove a bargain. Something like, *"If you give me $500, I'll give you the girls and go away."*[27]

Which is what happened. In May 1952, Louis published in the *New York Times*, probably on the advice of a lawyer, the kind of public notice that shamefaced husbands of wayward wives had posted for centuries: "Peggy Vadala, having left me, not responsible for her debts." The following February, the courts made the separation official. Peggy got her $500 and gave up all future claims to Louis's support. He ceded her some of the stuff that made their house a home: "linens, blankets, doilies, and scarves," flatware and dishes, a vacuum cleaner and a mixer. Peggy kept Jimmy, who was hers alone, and who lost in the arrangement the only father he had ever known. Louis kept his daughters, with the court's proviso that he must maintain a home for them, "with his mother or other relative."[28] Most likely, that caveat demonstrates only the anomaly of a father granted full custody in the early 1950s, in the rabbit-hutch of the suburbs, rather than some special peril the lawyers had sensed in Louis, though later events would prove any such concern well placed.

Peggy's little brother drove East, loaded up the spoils, and spirited her and her boy back to St. Louis. They got caught in a blizzard; Jim Hume recalls being stuck in the car in the snow, eating licorice, for two days. Then Peggy found a job in a bar, and Jimmy landed "in foster." He learned that he had once had a different name, and a different father. One afternoon, the boy was sent for a visit with Ted Hume, who had gotten out of jail and remarried. Hume decided to keep his son. It would be two years before Ted was sent up again, and Jimmy found his way back to his mother. It had been, on the whole, a "tough lifestyle," he later told Candice.[29]

The divorce decree granted Peggy an afternoon a week with her daughters, plus a weekend each month, and a month every summer.[30] She never exercised any of these visitation rights. How could she have, really, with a thousand miles between them, and bills to pay, and Jimmy to reclaim, and Ted to contend with, and a life to assemble from grit and ashes?

Jim Hume says that Peggy kept the girls' pictures on a stand in the living room. But speaking of them was just too painful, for everyone.[31] So no one ever did, and Peggy buried the memory of New York, like some fleeting, far-off Atlantis.

Neither Candice nor Cinthea ever saw her again.

3 Peter Pan

Candy, age four, October 1954.

For her fourth birthday, in October 1954, the month her parents' divorce was finalized, Candy received a cap and matching purse emblazoned with a plastic bas relief of Peter Pan by way of Walt Disney. The wildly popular animated film version of J. M. Barrie's play and then novel about the boy who wouldn't grow up had hit theaters the month her parents' separation became official. Though Candy had in fact grown up a great deal, and not by choice, she looks, in a snapshot taken that day, healthy and well fed. Her party dress is clean and pressed, her anklets neatly folded, the toes of her Mary Janes scuffed as if from play. Parts of a man and a woman appear behind her in the frame. Marion's ample left hand still sports a wedding ring, though her husband had absconded even before Louis's wife checked out. A man, maybe one of Candy's many great-uncles, unbuttons his cuff. Behind them peeks just a sliver of an older, taller Cindi, in a starched white dress.

The scene plays out in Marion's house on President Street, where Louis and the girls have lived since Peggy took off.[1] Candy will remember that house all her life—will visit it during school breaks and summers, and revisit it in diaries and sometimes in nightmares. Its dark and somber dining room, with the heavy mahogany table and high-backed chairs covered in burgundy velvet. The Virgin Mary looming over the mantel in the parlor. A "funny indoor-outdoor plastic furniture set," perhaps in the kitchen, which was wallpapered in yellow plaid trellised with green vines. Marion and her sisters sit and cluck, "talking their sister stuff, sometimes shifting to Italian so the kids wouldn't know what they're saying." "Little Candy" perches "at the head of the table, eating saltines w/ butter, tomatoes, & oranges," listening to them chatter over the hit parade on the plastic radio.[2]

Much of the talk must have been about Louis: his broken vows and his shattered life. *Nessun perdono*—no forgiveness—from Marion. After a sharp spike when the war ended, U.S. divorce rates had paused their steady upward rise in the late 1940s and 1950s, making Louis's predicament all the more noteworthy. Not to mention, for these Catholics, a sin.[3]

And oh, those poor little girls. How could he hope to care for them—what could that judge have been thinking? What had Louis expected with that woman, anyway? "A tramp," Marion called Peggy, to anyone who would listen, no matter if the girls overheard. In later life, the word *tramp*—the essence of her grandmother's cruelty and her father's blinkered worldview—would make Candy weep and shudder. "He frowned upon women and sexuality," she wrote in her diary at the age of nineteen. Her father's disdain for sex was one-sided, of course: the hypocrisy of a broken family, the hypocrisy of an age.[4]

Marion blamed Louis nearly as much as Peggy. As the Sicilian proverb holds, *a lustru di cannila, nè fimmini nè tila:* neither women nor cloth should be chosen by candlelight. That was Louis, *che cazzo:* a creature of half-lit bars and half-wit choices. *Lu vinu, lu tabbacu, e li donni ruinanu l'omu:* wine, smokes, and women wreck a man. And wrecked he was.[5]

Louis would have seen it differently, no doubt. He was out of the suburbs and back on the town. And whatever these squares said, there were plenty of cats just like him: players, rovers, tramp-catchers. *Just a gigolo,* as Prima crooned. In December 1953—which is to say, after Louis's separation and before his divorce—*Playboy* magazine began its long, gleaming run at the newsstand. Louis must have dug Hugh Hefner's philosophy, in which hip singles—especially single men—enjoyed sex without consequences. Not only men, though: Alfred Kinsey's bestselling *Sexual Behavior in the Human Female,* which took flight the same year as *Playboy,* revealed that roughly half of American women had had sex before marriage. Condoms muted the fear of pregnancy, and penicillin, widely prescribed since the end of the war, cured the bite of disease.[6]

A hepcat like Louis could prowl and take his chances.

Sometime that year or the next, Louis started dating Helen Duffy, who worked as a cigarette girl and dreamed of being a lounge singer. Helen had all kinds of advantages over Peggy. Born in 1920, just a year after Louis, she was a grown-up, shifting for herself; they met on the job. She was Catholic, and from the area. She'd had a year of college. She knew, as Candy and Cindi now did, the pain of abandonment: when Helen was a girl, her mother had been institutionalized; her father, once prosperous, lost his money to the Depression and his senses to drink. Most important from Louis's perspective, Helen had never married. No husband, no kids, no complications.[7]

Helen Duffy was no pushover. Friends called her Tuffy.[8] Maybe Marion would simmer down, having met her match. As 1954 drew to a close, Louis must have had high hopes for the New Year.

Not so Candy and Cindi.

Marion had been happy enough to have them all under her roof—and not just because their abashed return had proved her right about Peggy. She watched over her granddaughters and lit prayer candles in their bedroom. Many years later, Candy could recall the votive's light "flickering across the entire ceiling above our bed all night."[9]

But Marion's health was shaky. She was sixty, and her life hadn't been easy. *La vicchiaja è pinitenza:* old age is penance.[10] Twice in the months after Marion took Louis in with his daughters, she suffered heart attacks that left her unable to look after the girls. Louis, who worked nights, knew he wasn't up to the job. The first time, Candy and Cindi had each bunked with one of Marion's siblings, split apart—"farmed around," Candice later recalled.[11] She had gotten the luckier draw: Aunt Nellie and Uncle Gene, the doctor, took her into their home in Rockaway. They adored the little girl and wanted to adopt her. But Marion recovered, and Louis brought his daughters back to the big, dark house on President Street.[12]

Then Marion was stricken again, just after Candy's Peter Pan birthday. This time, Louis refused to deepen his debt to the Passantino clan, who looked down on him no matter what he did. He put Candy and Cindi into a boarding home, "using us to hurt" his mother's relatives, Cinthea says. More than a decade later, when Candy began to write about this formative moment in her life, she blamed herself, at least in part: "Daddy didn't really want us, he did, but not really—we were a pain." So "as much as the relatives wanted us, Dad refused & put us in a stinken home."[13]

Accounts of their brief stay in the care of a Mrs. Hennessy read like folk tales: Snow White and Rose Red in Suffolk County. Six-year-old

Cindi can do no wrong. She's good at school. Mrs. Hennessy dotes on her. Four-year-old Candy can do no right. She's always in trouble. She needs some sense knocked into her.[14]

One day, while Cindi was off at school, two other boys consigned to the home climbed a cherry tree that Mrs. Hennessy had strictly forbidden them. When she caught them, they blamed Candy, who held her tongue. Mrs. Hennessy hauled them, one by one, into the basement, through the looking glass of the suburban dream, to the dark place where little girls, especially poor little girls, were as vulnerable as postwar society pretended they were venerated.

Candy's punishment came straight out of *Uncle Tom's Cabin*: a thrashing with a leather cat-o'-nine tails. That the gruesome sentence corrected her "for something I didn't do," as she later wrote, made it sting all the more.[15]

Mrs. Hennessy's teenage son wielded the whip while the other inmates, including the guilty climbers, looked on, riveted. Years later, Candice remembered being at the center of that shivering circle, "in front of all those people. All their eyes focused on me, I, the little girl who felt lost and disconnected, thrust into a strange house full of strangers & mean people who didn't like me. . . . I wailed."

But as vividly as she recalled the terror and the pain, she also felt, at least in retrospect, an unexpected thrill. "Now they got to watch me," she reflected in her diary in 1990. "My god, I'm the center of all their attention."[16]

———

AUNT NELLIE AND UNCLE GENE, the worldliest among the Passantino clan, went to Europe that winter. On a plane, on a lark. When they got back to the States, they had a present for Louis's girls: a gingerbread house carried all the way from Switzerland. They took that fairy-tale gift to the girls out at Mrs. Hennessy's and were shocked to find their once-bubbly Candy silent and withdrawn.[17] "Catatonic," as Candice later put it.[18] Gene, the doctor, knew he was seeing the aftereffects of something awful; he and Nellie sounded the alarm. *Voi sapiri la virità? Dumanna a li piccirdi*: if you want the truth, ask the children.[19] Marion, or Louis, or his girlfriend, Helen Duffy, swung into action. Louis and Helen were planning to get married anyway, so they moved the date up by a couple of months, to rescue the babes from the witch in the woods.

This was the family story, repeated often by Helen, its hero. It seemed to satisfy the girls, this Exodus tale in which Helen played the huntsman to Mrs. Hennessy's big bad wolf.[20] Though as Cinthea reflects now, in distant retrospect, it doesn't quite add up. "Why we weren't just taken out immediately, I do not know," she says. "This was the frustration of life back then."[21]

There would be no JP's office in Yonkers for Helen Frances Duffy. Her wedding to Louis Vadala, in May 1955, took place in Manhattan's St. Patrick's Cathedral. Helen's brother and his wife acted as witnesses, surely not the last time they scrutinized this divorced man with his young daughters and his legion of relatives and his bohemian job. Though perhaps the Duffys were grateful, too, that Louis had put a ring on Helen's finger. Women's median age at first marriage hovered just above twenty, its lowest point in a century.[22] The month after Helen traded vows with Louis, she turned thirty-five.

Helen Duffy and Louis Vadala wedding reception, May 1955.

In a photograph from their wedding reception, Louis looks gaunt. Helen is shiny and plump. A tipple—maybe sherry—sits near her manicured right hand, ready to toast the future. On the table just in front of them stands an Italian cream cake with two compact tiers: not many people at the reception, then. The plastic couple that tops it stands arm in arm, wrapped in cellophane, a keepsake, a promise, a relic.

———

LOUIS AND HELEN VADALA set up house in Astoria, at the northwestern tip of Queens, just past the Hell Gate Bridge, which spanned that section of the East River known as the Middle Ground. Middle ground it was. Not Brooklyn: Helen put some space between her fragile new family and the Sicilian swirl at Marion's. And not Hempstead: Louis was done with the picket fences and the Long Island Railroad. Now he could hop the BMT at Ditmars Boulevard and reach Swing Street in no time. A lot of jazz cats lived in Queens, where the rents were cheap. Better-known musicians—Coltrane, Goodman, Armstrong—lived in more central neighborhoods, like St. Albans and Forest Hills and Jamaica.[23] Personally, economically, and professionally, the margins suited Louis Vadala.

Candy's new home was a two-bedroom flat in a three-story, H-shaped brick building, one of twelve identical apartment houses overspreading four blocks of the enclave in which Norman Lear would later set *All in the Family*.[24] The Vadalas' neighbors were working people: laborers, secretaries. More than a quarter of them had been born overseas.[25]

Heavy industry edged the neighborhood. At the end of the Vadalas' block, a hulking Con Ed generating complex grew bigger by the year, eventually stretching almost to LaGuardia Airport, a mile away.[26] Candy would have heard the constant hum of the turbines from the bedroom she and Cindi shared. In summer, the breeze carried the stink of the rich, from the Ward's Island wastewater treatment plant, which sifted the sewage of Manhattan's Upper East Side.

A snapshot from April 1960 shows a sliver of the Vadala girls' room, tidy and spare, with a well-made twin bed—a detached bunk—and a

Candy, age ten, in her bedroom in Astoria, April 1960.

few curling photos tacked to the side of the wardrobe. Posing for the little Kodak Brownie that Cindi got for her birthday, Candy, not yet ten years old, looks like the older, riper girl she already wanted to be.[27]

The girls attended P.S. 122, a hop-skip from the apartment, even on spindly kid legs. Candy started there in kindergarten, and she excelled. Her fifth-grade teacher, Mrs. Sharkey, had the students fill out a worksheet titled "Something About You." Here are some things about ten-year-old Candy: she likes scary movies, and watches *Twilight Zone* and *Hitchcock Presents* on TV. Debbie Reynolds and Frank Sinatra are her favorite film stars. She isn't much of a reader, beyond the funnies and fanzines like *Teen Scream*. She goes to the public library a few times a year but owns no books of her own. She plays some piano and likes to draw and paint, even then a budding artist.[28]

A budding archivist too: young Candy likes to save things, to *curate* them, making a safe harbor in a stormy life. A valentine from her grandmother, with sweets attached, candy for Candy, with the girl's pencil scrawl on the back: "Grandma is very nice to me. I love her very much. 3rd grade 1959." Later that year, a birthday card from Helen to her "wonderful Daughter," annotated, in the same childish hand, "Mommy & daddy are very nice. I love them very much."[29] Collecting, labeling, making a family out of paper. Helen has become the only mother Candy will ever know, and she will call her Mommy or Mom all her life.

Candy is a bit of a romantic, too, with movie-star fantasies, courtesy of the glossies, and dreams of being spirited away. The sisters had a globe in their room, Cinthea remembers. They played a game where one of them would spin it, and the other would close her eyes and put her finger on a random spot. That became the destination to which their imaginary sea captain father—not their real father, who works nights and sleeps much of the day—would spirit them in his boat.[30]

At age fifteen, in 1966, Candy will tuck into her diary a poem with a stanza voicing herself as a child in Astoria:

I'm a little girl
Don't look at me
I'm just a little girl
I'm only six
I play with sticks
I'm just a little girl
But most of all, I'm innocent
No sex, no knowledge, no cares
I play, I play
I'm afraid of night—I love day.[31]

4 American Girl

First Grade, PS 122, 1956. Candy sits in the first row, third from right.

I n the picture of her first-grade class, Candy sits ramrod straight, hands clasped, neat as a pin: a front-row girl. She wears thick woolen tights; though it's November, most of her female classmates appear in anklets or in bobby sox. All of them wear dresses; girls will not be allowed to wear pants to public school in New York for a decade yet.[1] Most of the boys sport ties, and one has a tie clip: a mini *Man in the Grey Flannel Suit*. Behind them looms an enormous United States flag, with forty-eight stars, seven boys wide. When they pledge allegiance to that flag, they vouch safe "one nation under God," a phrase added to the century-old pledge just a couple years earlier.[2]

The Cold War was Candy's first culture war. Her class primped and posed for that picture in the season of the Suez Crisis and the Hungarian uprising against Soviet rule. That very month, President Eisenhower readied a request to Congress, to fund a vast new network of atomic fallout shelters.[3] Candy and her classmates practiced ducking and covering under their desks. The hot wars, proxy battles pitting the United States and its allies against the Soviet Union and its client states, took place a world away from Astoria. The Cold War, by contrast, was in every sense domestic, unfolding in American bedrooms and over dinner tables. The nuclear family of the Nuclear Age, in which father knew best and mother kept house, was a sudden and short-lived aberration: a radical innovation marketed, then and since, as tradition.[4]

The notion of an innocent childhood, free from work or want, lay at the center of the ideal '50s family. In his popular polemic, *The Organization Man*, published the year of Candy's first-grade picture, the sociologist William H. Whyte fretted over the fate of a country descended into "filiarchy": a society ruled by its children, who had more space and more time for play, not to mention more toys, than ever before. With marriage and birth rates soaring in tandem, suburbs like Hempstead and urban neighborhoods like Astoria teemed with kids. Twenty-seven six-year-olds packed into Candy's first-grade class in the aging Mamie Fay School. Rearing them up right was deemed crucial to sustaining the gossamer social fabric of the nation-under-God. In the wake of the Allies' victory over one brand of totalitarianism in World War II, and in the midst of the perilous confrontation with another in the Cold War, stable, well-adjusted children who would grow into stable, well-adjusted parents were cast as nothing less than the bedrock of a free world.[5] It was a terrible weight to bear.

Shortly before Candy and her classmates posed for their school picture under the American flag, *Parents* magazine ran a pair of how-to essays: "Raise Your Boy to Be a Husband," and "Raise Your Girl to Be a Wife." The mothers of girls were counseled to be "matrimony-minded" on their daughters' behalf. It was never too early, Constance Foster, the author of the girl-to-wife essay urged, to encourage "a feminine orientation toward life and the tender, caring-for feelings that go with it."[6] Of course, prescriptive literature always conceals its opposite: the instability that makes stern advice necessary. Such counsel to the mothers of baby girls responded to the shifts that had brought large numbers of middle-class white women into the labor force in the World War II era, thereby changing sex roles within households and roiling the ambitions of daughters. "Your daughter is born a female, but she has to learn how to be feminine," Foster explained. "And that's a big order in our present society where male and female roles are something confused."[7]

Foster was hardly alone in worrying about the "confusion" of American girls. The social survey was the method of the day, and the Girl Scouts of America interviewed a national sample of girls between ages eleven and eighteen in 1956, the year of Candy's first-grade picture. The study's goal was to reveal the crucial role of youth organizations, including the Scouts, to which Candy, like an increasing number of American girls, belonged.[8] The respondents, nearly 2,000 girls, testified to the widespread anxieties provoked by the "duality of the feminine role." The American girl was prodded to strive and to achieve but also to prepare to submerge herself in marriage. She needed to become "interesting," but not too interesting; she must avoid seeking to be overly "involved" in the world of work. The survey's young respondents dreamed of careers and college, men and money and marriage in equal proportions, setting up a collision course, as its authors worried, for later life.[9]

Desire itself was increasingly part of the public language of Americans in Candy's youth. Under the waving flag, under God, under the watchful eyes of censors and preachers and other moralists, frank depictions of sex burst forth in the marketplace and in the marketplace of ideas. In 1952, the year Peggy Vadala skipped town, the U.S. Supreme Court extended First Amendment protection to motion pictures, which spelled the gradual end of the Hollywood production code, which meant more sex on more screens, big and small.[10] In the fall of 1956, the season of Candy's first-grade picture, Elvis Presley played *The Ed Sullivan Show*. He swiveled his hips; CBS cut him off at the waist: a pyrrhic victory in a losing war.[11]

The following year, a U.S. Supreme Court led by California's Earl Warren and increasingly committed to the protection of individual liberties declared, in *Roth v. United States*, that obscenity would continue to fall outside the capacious umbrella of the First Amendment. Yet the justices also narrowed the definition of what counted as obscene. Acknowledging a crucial free-speech precedent guaranteeing the frank and free discussion of "*all matters of public concern* without previous restraint or fear of punishment," the court ruled that works with "even the slightest redeeming social importance" must have the "full protection" of the law. *Roth* also insisted, as associate justice William J. Brennan wrote for the majority, that "sex and obscenity are not synonymous." Indeed sex, Brennan said, was "a great and mysterious motive force in human life . . . a subject of absorbing interest to mankind through the ages" and thus "one of the vital problems of human interest and public concern."[12]

Human interest in sex proved robust. By 1960, a bare three years after the *Roth* decision, the number of "men's sophisticate" magazines had tripled: a "floodtide of filth" as a new anti-smut organization, Citizens for Decent Literature, put it.[13] The CDL was a purveyor of moral panic. But it was not wrong about the volume of explicit material newly available above the counter.

Pubescent girls were both battened down and sexed up by the growing frankness of popular and literary culture in the post-*Roth* era. In 1958, barely a year after *Roth*, an American edition of Vladimir Nabokov's *Lolita*, which had been published in Paris in 1955 but suppressed in the United States, was issued to wild acclaim and spent thirty-seven weeks on the bestseller list. The title character, whose given name was Dolores Haze, was twelve years old, "standing four foot ten in one sock": a nymphet, as the narrator, Humbert Humbert paints her. To spot the nymphet in a class picture, Humbert explained, "you have to be an artist and a madman, a creature of infinite melancholy, with a bubble of hot poison in your loins."[14] That same year, another tale of predatory men and sexy girls was published in London: lower-brow than *Lolita*, more pulp than prestige. The teenage heroine is pursued, relentlessly, by all manner of adults: her teachers, her doctor, her gardener, her uncle, and especially her father. The protagonist's name, and the title of the book, was *Candy*. Candy Vadala's nickname must have elicited snickers throughout her teenage years, given the book's success on the American market, beginning in 1964.[15]

Movies and pulp fiction depicted Cold War girls, especially teens, as both dangerous and endangered. Parents worried about bobbysoxer babysitters who ran wild with school friends while their young charges languished.[16] The FBI worried that innocent-looking bobbysoxers were themselves at risk. "How Safe Is Your Daughter?" J. Edgar Hoover had asked in an article published in *American Magazine* shortly after Louis married Peggy. "Sex fiends" were on the march, Hoover warned. "The nation's women and children will never be secure . . . so long as degenerates run wild." The threat, such literature emphasized, came from outsiders, strangers. A photograph of three little girls in pinafores and pigtails running for their lives as an enormous hand closes in from behind graces one page of Hoover's screed. An advertisement for chewing gum, hawked by a buxom pinup in a low-cut black bustier decorates another.[17]

If such threats were largely imaginary, a profound moral realignment was indeed under way. In the spring of 1960, as Candy finished fourth grade, the FDA announced that it had ratified the work of teams of scientists over many years to bring hormonal contraception to American women. Taken daily in tablet form, the newly approved medicine with the brand name Enovid, combining the hormones estrogen and progestin, severed intercourse from pregnancy. Within five years, nearly a quarter of married American women of childbearing age were using it.[18] The rapid adoption of Enovid, which soon came to be known simply as the Pill, is often treated as the opening salvo in the second culture war Candy would experience, one that came to be called the Sexual Revolution. But that narrative confuses cause and effect.

At the end of Candy's fifth-grade year, Helen and Louis decided to move the family out of Astoria. Candy told Mrs. Sharkey, who sent the girl home with a letter. "I shall think of you many times," the teacher wrote. "Your nice work, your fine manners, and your thoughtfulness to me and to your classmates as well made my days happy ones. May you find happiness in your new home, Candy, and may God keep you in the hollow of his hands."[19]

Probably it was a generic blandishment, from a teacher who took the time to write to each of her charges at the end of the school year. Or maybe Mrs. Sharkey had sensed, as teachers do, that Candy needed more or different care than she was getting.

5 Lock and Key

Candy as a pupil at Miss Jeffrey's Dancing School, June 1962.

At the age of eleven, in the summer of 1962, Candy penciled a letter to her future self, in careful cursive, titled "My Secret Desires"—a school exercise, it seems, to mark the beginning of junior high. "Right now I'm still a little girl that wants to grow up fast," she wrote. She imagines future occupations including college coed, mother, and "famous dancer."[1]

One of these dreams will come true.

Candy's fantasies of upward mobility were nourished by the New York City of the 1950s and early 1960s, when public investment in libraries, schools, colleges, hospitals, and transportation made it possible for myriad postwar New Yorkers to do better than their parents had. The Vadalas decamped from Astoria as Cindi reached middle school in order to ease their daughters' climb. The options in their stretch of Queens were "very rough," Cinthea recalls. "I was going to get my ass kicked if I stayed there any longer." And so, to Riverdale, "a sparkling little white community," where the Vadalas rented an apartment in a new building on Broadway, right across from the enormous, untamed expanse of Van Cortlandt Park.[2]

The family was still working-class, and their social geography showed it. They lived alongside the other ethnic Catholics at the foot of the steep rise that ascended to the leafier precincts above Riverdale Avenue. Down the hill, even today, Italian and Irish flags flutter from neat aluminum-sided houses. But more of their new neighbors had comfortable incomes; almost all of them had finished high school; many had some college under their belt. Overall, twice as many Riverdale children attended private school as public—the opposite proportions of Astoria. The fancier kids, from the western part of the village, went to places like Horace Mann, Fieldston, and the Country Day School. But even at PS 81, and then for junior high at JHS 141, Candy had college-bound classmates with professional parents.[3]

The Vadalas' apartment, with its beige living room and baby-blue bedrooms, the girls' with some flowers appliqued, was nothing grand.[4] But there was plenty of open space nearby, and headroom for the girls. Candy and her friend Susie pretended they were "French waitresses," or even "college teachers." Her friend Michelle's parents invited her to go to the opera with them, to see *The Barber of Seville*, which Candy would already have known from Bugs Bunny. Another friend took her along for a ski vacation. One Christmas, Helen gave her "the ballet record Swan Lake album." (Helen, Cinthea recalls, "had airs.")[5]

Very soon, Candy shed her baby fat and progressed in ballet, the most refined of feminine accomplishments. She yearned for toe shoes, like the ones her Barbie had. Though she sometimes felt "an inferiority complex" in Miss Jeffrey's Dancing School, she soon took on bigger roles, including Scheherazade, the princess who saved her life with stories.[6]

———

IN 1963, on New Year's Day, twelve-year-old Candy started her first diary. The little book, covered in red leatherette and embossed with gold foil, measures about four by six inches, smaller than a paperback and bigger than a deck of cards, easy to tuck out of sight. A miniature brass lock—made for a tiny key but easy enough to spring with a bobby pin—promises more privacy than it can deliver. *This Book Belongs To:* Candy filled in the lines carefully, in a practiced cursive, with her full name and her still-new address in Riverdale, as if the diary, probably a Christmas gift, might get lost and find its way back to her. From the first page, she addressed the book as a person, a *you*, to whom she said good night at the end of each entry. *Dear Diary* was a friend, a bedtime ritual, a form of prayer. On many nights, Candy concluded her entry with a labeled thumbnail sketch showing her outfit and her hairdo, like one of her Barbie dolls come to life. During the day, she would stash the little volume in a blue calico-covered cardboard box, to be joined by her 1964 and 1965 journals, along with poems, drawings, mash notes, and keepsakes, like a painted plaster heart stamped "T & C," from Tommy, or, after Tommy was over, a Confederate $5 bill with "Candy & Denny" written in ballpoint, encircled with a heart.[7]

Diaries were everywhere in the world Candy and her seventh-grade friends inhabited. Therapists and teachers, printers and preachers, popular magazines and moms all played their parts in launching the Great American Diary Project.[8] *Seventeen*, whose circulation topped 2 million, carried advertisements for beauty diaries and hope-chest diaries and bridal diaries, sold by soap companies and manufacturers of feminine hygiene products and brands hawking China and sterling.[9] "Are You Made for 'Fire and Ice'?" asked a quiz promoting Revlon's flaming new red lipstick. Question three: "Do you keep a diary under lock and key?" *Yes* meant you were the ultimate feminine paradox: "tease and temptress, siren and gamin, dynamic and demure."[10]

Fiction for girls and young women of Candy's generation often featured diarist heroines and sometimes took diary form. Louise Fitzhugh's *Harriet the Spy* (1964), centered on what one critic calls the "guerilla journal keeping" of its protagonist, was a touchstone for many on the younger end of Candy's cohort.[11] In Judy Blume's generation-defining *Are You There, God? It's Me, Margaret* (1970), the protagonist sounds uncannily like Candy. "I wrote to American Girl about not wearing a cup bra," she noted in early 1963. "Boy! I'm so frustrated. Sonia got her period Feb 3, she wears light grey stockings to school every day (unless they have runs) and she wears a 30-AA bra!"[12]

Like many American middle schoolers, Candy read the most celebrated diary of the era. First published in English in 1952 as *Diary of a Young Girl*, Anne Frank's journal, written in hiding from the Nazis, had become, by the time Candy encountered it twelve years later, a radio play, a Broadway drama, and a Hollywood feature film.[13] Candy compared her own story to Frank's and found it wanting. "Dear Diary ever since I've read Anne Frank I've realized that I should try to interest you. . . . If a reader ever took my diary they'd find it quite boring. But hers was so interesting—So I shall try to write interesting things from now on," she pledged in March 1964.[14] But only occasionally did Candy journal about events beyond herself or her neighborhood, and when she did, she felt an emotional connection. Like when President

Kennedy was killed and the funeral came into her living room on TV. ("Oooh I hate Texas.")[15] Or when the Beatles stormed New York. (Oooh, she loved George.)[16]

If diaries emulated and aspired, they also competed and seduced, especially within the domain of girls. In Candy's early journals, Jeff and Bobby and Harold and Tom and Mattie and Gino and Petey and a gaggle of other eager suitors peck at the margins of her world. "I hate boys! They're the most discusting [*sic*] & mean things," she wrote in May 1963. People whispered about *making out* and *going steady*, but it was all talk, much of it confusing. "No one really knows the meaning" of making out anyway, Candy admitted. She suspected that "it means to *go all the way!*"[17]

While grown-ups and boys hovered at the edges of these early diaries, at the center, in tight focus, were Candy's female friendships, intense and often physical. She and her friends "fell in love," but their alliances also had a tendency, after a great deal of drama, to "end in hate."[18] The Vadalas' jobs, with Helen working nights and Louis sometimes on the road, meant that Candy often slept over with friends.[19] There were baths with Liza and showers with Dianne and Cathy, who "wants me to spank her! Oh no!" There were pajama parties where Candy and Yvonne indexed their bodies against one another's: "She really has a lot of hair you know where!"[20] The girls' cruelty sometimes matched their passion. Dianne, long Candy's best and most vexing

Drawing tucked into Candy's 1964 diary.

friend, lived next door, and considered herself higher-class than the Vadalas. She told Candy her hair smelled. "I'd rather have my hair smell than my personality stink," Candy clapped back.[21]

Knowing that Dianne and the others might contrive to read what she had written about them was part of the thrill. "Dianne has this suit case & there's something in it. She yelled 'Don't open it!' Her diary's in it! (probably)," Candy wrote after playing dolls next door. "Dianne wanted to look at my Diary but she doesn't know she'll never look at it!" Dianne read all that and more when Candy showed her the diary several months later. Candy had also managed to read what Dianne had written about her: "she said I was flat & I thought all boys liked me." Both of these things were true.[22]

For all their intensity, diaries like Candy's were also a powerful form of discipline, a way to dampen desire by expressing it. *Woman's Day* pointed out that keeping a diary could "*ventilate your emotions. . . . you can blow off steam in a diary with as much vehemence and violence as you please. . . . As a famous psychiatrist once said, a diary can be a lightning rod that will conduct explosive emotions harmlessly to the ground.*"[23]

———

THE NORTHERN PART of the thousand-acre expanse of Van Cortlandt Park, up near Candy's apartment, was an urban wild, less lawn than forest. Proximity to the park actually reduced rents. Dense thickets crisscrossed only by bridle paths stretched from Broadway to the Saw Mill River Parkway, nearly a mile to the east. That bramble could hide any secret. Teenagers went into the woods to settle scores and sneak smokes and make out. You could wander in those woods, or even picnic, like the Vadalas did one warm spring Sunday. But you might also venture in on a dare. Once some boys marched the kids Candy was babysitting into the woods, so she'd have to traipse after them, and then they could run after her. Another time, in the fall, she and a boyfriend went into the woods "and decided to lie down in a pile of leaves," just talking and staring at the changing colors.[24]

All that came later, after Candy better understood the secrets those woods kept. In the fall of 1963, she was twelve and still, she later wrote, looked "more like ten."[25] The incident takes up a whole page in her first diary, the entry for September 28:

Dear Diary—The most terrible thing happened to me. In the woods I was attacked by a man. He had no underpants on—His zipper was open. He tried to take my close [sic] down. I had my liatard on thank god! It's horrid riding in a police car! I just thank god for helping me! Love, Candy

In the little drawing Candy made below the entry, she sketches herself with a high ponytail, wearing a purple skirt and a black-and-white plaid vest over that momentous leotard.[26]

The attack she describes took place on a Saturday, too early in the fall for the leaves to be changing. What was there to see in the park? Maybe she went to meet an older boy—one of the swarm who asked her to "go steady" or "fool around." She had felt, before the attack, increasingly womanly, even sexy. "Now I am really getting hips," she wrote earlier that month. She had started, each day, to draw the underwear beneath her outfits.[27]

Whatever the reason, Candy, like some Riverdale Red Riding Hood, said she had strayed into the woods, where she had surely been told, by every fairy tale ever written, if not by her feckless parents, never, ever to wander alone. She drew a kind of power from the story she lived to tell. "It made her feel strong," Cinthea says. She "took pride in being the kind of person that could fight back."[28]

Candy wrote about the attack many times in the ensuing years: about the "policeman . . . who comforted me as I cried into his uniform."[29] (No police record survives.[30]) About her assailant, who melted back into the thicket like a phantom. She conjured him in her mind's eye: he had looked, she recalled, not a bit like her father.[31] "No one will ever find him," she wrote several months later as she mused about the tangled relationship between dreams and reality. "I think he was an angel from God warning me not to go in woods."[32]

But the wolf was already inside the house.

When the police brought Candy home, Helen slapped her silly. Louis just stood there, watching.[33]

———

HELEN DRANK AND SWORE and wept and cursed her lot. "Mom was crying today. She's so unhappy—I try to be good with her Dear Diary but I just can't!" Candy wrote in February 1963. "I really feel so sorry for her. But it's so confusing!" Helen gave the girls the silent treatment one day and woke up "in a real good mood" the next. She could be violent, raging at Candy in front of her friends, once throwing her against a wall for eating a candy bar before dinner. Then she'd turn up with a gift, "a gorgeous dress! . . . rayon or silk."[34] Or she'd give first and take away later, bringing home something pretty from Lord & Taylor, only to return it if Candy stepped out of line.[35] Or she'd fly into a "shit fit" and storm out, refusing to make supper. "Dad had to go to work and he didn't even have any dinner!" Candy wrote.[36]

Louis seethed and pouted. "Dad feels unhappy because of us," Candy decided.[37] But that wasn't the whole story. "This nagging, sort of cancerous burning inside of me to just live a life of music in all its forms—an artist's life—has been the cause of all the mistakes I've made," he later told Candy.[38] However hot he burned, he couldn't manage to keep the fire lit. Louis was slipping, sliding, stumbling down the ladder of success. For a while, he had a regular gig in Manhattan with Lester Lanin, the society bandleader, keeping time for the businessman's bounce and the debutante's dip. Even if it wasn't real jazz, the Lanin sound, like the Biltmore Clock and Grand Central Station, was part of what made midcentury New York shimmer.[39] But then Louis pulled an old drummers' gag, messing with the count, and Lanin sacked him. Louis grabbed the next rung down, searching for club dates at the union hall, dragging his drum kit here one weekend, there the next. He started offering lessons to make ends meet. "Feels like a failure, and just keeps drinking," Candy wrote in her diary.[40]

Helen and Louis battled constantly, often, as Candy understood it, over his daughters. Helen grounded them; Louis let them go out.

When school visits rolled around, Helen suggested, "*Dad* can come," the *real* parent, when everyone knew she did all the work. Candy felt she "wouldn't be so much on Dad's side" if Helen "didn't always get drunk, criticize our family," and nag and needle and slap.[41] In March 1964, Helen told Louis "she couldn't stand being with him another year!" Candy heard it, of course. The apartment was a fishbowl. Sometimes the fights were loud enough to bring the neighbors. "I think the end's really coming! She's not a very good mother." Even so, Candy felt sorry for Helen. "I hate to see someone suffer so much," she wrote.[42]

Sometimes, it seemed as if it were all Cindi's fault. She was the older one, sweet sixteen in May 1964. She had a boyfriend, when thirteen-year-old Candy was still begging Helen for permission to start shaving her legs and longing for the onset of her period, which she told her friends she'd already gotten. "I wish I was dead!" Candy confessed to her diary. "I'm so ugly! I have no figure at all."[43] Meanwhile, Cindi, who went by Cynthia now, looked every inch a woman, with long chestnut hair and smart dresses that flattered her hourglass shape. She looked, in fact, quite like the mother whom neither of the girls could remember—Peggy, with the eyes that lit up her face. Bedroom eyes, the racier women's magazines called them.[44] Cynthia grew beautiful while Candy strained for cute, freckle-faced. "Pug nose," one boy jeered.[45]

Everyone fussed over Cynthia. Whenever Candy went to Brooklyn to visit her grandmother, Marion nagged her "about poor Cynthia!" Whenever Candy got weepy, Helen told her she had "better not get like Cynthia." To Candy, it felt as if the Vadalas torqued their meager lives around her blossoming, struggling sister. She resented it. So when Cynthia's boyfriend, Kenny, came over, Candy "fooled around" with him behind her sister's back. Candy thought things were generally better when Cynthia stayed with Marion, but also noted that Louis was "very grouchy" when she was out of his sight.[46]

For all the tension between them, Candy and Cynthia really did try to make a go of it as allies in their unpredictable family. They took dance lessons together at Miss Jeffrey's. They shared their Beatles fandom. Cynthia had a George Harrison doll and Candy, a John Lennon hat. Candy said she hated her sister, but Cynthia told her, "You can't hate anyone unless you loved them." The sisters traded taunts and secrets and presents. For Christmas 1963, Candy gave Cynthia the next year's diary.[47]

———

LOUIS HAD BEEN WATCHING Cynthia for years. Since around the time she turned twelve, prime Nabokovian nymphet territory, back in the spring of 1960.

Helen worked nights at the Waldorf—a "glamorous job," as Cinthea remembers it—and left Louis "home babysitting" for the two girls, "a nightmare for him." So promising, so thwarted, the hepcat neutered and slowly dying in the Bronx. As he sat and stewed, his older daughter, the one who looked like Peggy, the one who was ripening by the day, became an object of his longing. While Helen was off snapping photos of the revelers in the ballroom, Louis and the girls watched TV in the living room. Positioning himself with his back to Candy, he exposed himself to Cynthia, like the man Candy said had importuned her in the park. When Louis tucked Cynthia in at night, he'd ask her, "Do you want a Daddy kiss or a lover kiss?" She learned not to kiss him at all.[48]

Everyone knew, and no one talked. Grandmother Marion knew to fret about her granddaughter, always so ineffably blue. "I've seen the way he looks at you," Cinthea recalls her saying. Candy knew enough to feel an inchoate jealousy. Her sister was "such a bitch!" she wrote in April 1964, right before their secrets burst into plain view. Helen knew to feel sorry for herself, whining to anyone who would listen that nobody wanted or needed her. She also knew just enough to buy the girls a TV for their bedroom, a luxury a family like theirs could scarcely afford.[49]

At which point, Louis started lurking outside the girls' room at night, the door open "just a few inches," stroking himself while he watched Cynthia sleep. She would wake in the wee hours and sense the door moving. Once, when Candy spent the night at a friend's house, Louis crawled into bed with Cynthia, quickly recovering himself and slinking out.[50] The next time Candy headed to a sleepover while Helen was working nights, Cynthia came along with her little sister. "Because daddy was home alone with her & he was like in a certain mood," Candy wrote.[51]

All the while, Cynthia filled the diary that Candy had gotten her for Christmas with the stuff of girl-world: clothes and music and boys, boys, boys, especially Kenny, who kept trying to "feel her up," even while he sneaked kisses from Candy on the side.[52]

The little brass lock on a young girl's diary was no match for a father without scruples. Louis popped the catch and read what Cynthia had written about Kenny's roving hands, and it excited him, and he scrawled in the margins in pencil. He erased his proposition, but he had a heavy hand, and his clumsy printing left an impression, one Cynthia could feel with her fingertips. She shaded over what Louis had erased until his words revealed themselves. She showed it to Candy, who wrote in *her* diary that her father had scribbled, "'Let's fuck & neck' or something like that!" Then Cynthia razored out Louis's comment and showed the slip of paper to Helen, to explain why she'd been afraid to stay home with her father.[53]

———

HELEN VADALA REFUSED to believe that the husband who had rescued her was preying on the stepdaughter she disliked. She wanted more evidence than the sliver cut from Cynthia's diary, so she sneaked a peek at Candy's, where she read the same story, and much else besides. "I really loved you Candy—I wish you loved me!" Helen said after reading it.

Then she gave the stepdaughter she favored five dollars and fled to her mother's in Gulfport, Florida, abandoning the girls to their fates.[54]

That was June 1964. Candy went quiet for weeks. "I haven't written because of many misfortunes," she jotted in August. She had spent the summer shuttling among her relatives in Brooklyn and Rockaway and a neighbor's house in Riverdale. Cynthia had gone, as long planned, to upstate New York with a friend's family, but when she threatened to run away from there, Marion brought her back to President Street. Which probably felt even worse than rural exile for a teenager since, as Candy said, Gram was "a big nagger." Marion's kin stirred the pot too. Uncle Gene—the doctor, who had wanted to adopt four-year-old Candy—urged the girls to remain in Brooklyn, telling Candy that if she didn't "stay at Gram's" she "would be very sorry!" Cynthia also voted for President Street. But Candy would have nothing but Riverdale. "I had a hard time getting to go home," she wrote. Everyone had called her "the spoiled brat, thinking only of myself, and all that." But she held out, and she prevailed. Come fall, Louis's girls went back to him and the Bronx. Candy resumed her dance lessons, dreaming of toe shoes.[55]

Years later, she reflected that staying in Brooklyn would have been "ghastly—like taking 15 steps down the social ladder," which was the wrong way to climb.[56]

HELEN WROTE OCCASIONALLY: a birthday card, a letter here and there. She was waiting tables at a drive-in, trying to scrape some cash together. She said she was glad Candy had "stuck to [her] guns and stayed with Daddy." She hoped everything was all right and asked the

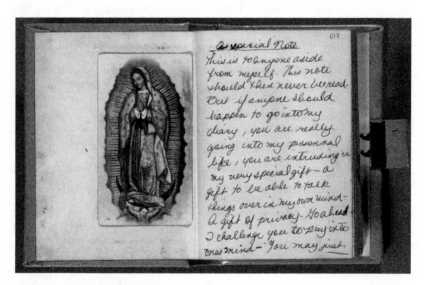

Frontispiece, Candy's 1965 Diary.

girls to "write more often so I will be reassured." She wondered who was doing the cooking, and how the cats were faring. "Did you get my bed?" she asked. Cynthia got a three-word postscript.[57]

By December, Candy had resigned herself to the fact that "Mom is gone for good." The holidays were hard. Gram pestered. Louis sulked. "It really didn't seam [*sic*] like Christmas," Candy wrote. "Cindi & I both cryed a little but that's how it is."[58]

The family's exchange of presents, at Marion's, felt desultory. Helen sent Candy a pink-and-green mohair sweater, which was cute, but no substitute for a mother, even a lousy one. Louis gave her Milton Bradley's insanely popular board game, The Game of Life, which must have felt like a bad joke.[59] Cynthia got her a new diary, at the front of which Candy affixed a *"special note,"* addressed to anyone who "should happen" to breach the lock, as Helen and Louis had each so disastrously done in their turn the previous spring:

> You are really going into my personal life, you are intruding in my very special gift—a gift to be able to talk things over in my own mind—A gift of privacy—Go ahead. I challenge you to pry into one's mind—You may *just* Consider yourself trying to take the place of God. . . . . *STAY OUT!!.* . . . If you do read this— when you close the book, why not go look in the mirror. Are you proud of what you see?[60]

Candy wrote the year's first entry on New Year's Day, which proved eventful: "Today Mom came back. In a way I'm happy & in a way not." On balance, she thought it was "better" to have Helen home. All the same, she knew she would "miss being a little spoiled."[61]

6 Help!

Candy and Cyn, 1965. Candy's hat is modeled on the one John Lennon wore in Help!

I saw the movie Help! It was great," Candy wrote in September 1965, shortly after she started high school. Though Helen worried that listening to rock 'n' roll "infects the brain," the film's title song could have served as the Vadala family's anthem.[1] *Won't you please, please help me!* But who, and how? Where were the Vadalas to turn and to understand what was happening in their home on Broadway?

Louis seems to have decided to bootstrap the family's problems. After Helen returned, he declared that he would henceforth run the household "like the army." Aping the drill sergeants who had whipped him into shape years before at Fort Snelling, he grew strict with the girls, especially Cynthia. Early in 1965, he threw her out for a few days, for "being very disrespectful."[2] She went to Marion's house.

Church was another traditional answer. The Brooklyn relatives must have been lighting candles and crossing themselves, praying for Louis's family—his second, tenuous try at a family—to right itself. Candy had her own pieties. Back in May, the month of Marian devotions, right before their troubles leapt off the pages of her and Cynthia's diaries, she had written to the "Blessed Mother" as if to Santa Claus, acknowledging "all the bad things" she'd done, and promising to "be good," if the Madonna would only make her breasts grow.[3] She prayed for bigger boobs and better boys.[4] But by the summer after the Vadalas' fall, Catholicism had come to seem mostly pap. Candy admitted that her faith had faltered. "I love God—but don't know if anything else is true."[5]

Where Louis hearkened to the army, and Marion Vadala might have sought out a priest, Helen called instead upon the kind of help that so many midcentury Americans thought would enable them to conquer their demons and perfect themselves: psychoanalysis and its intellectual kin, psychiatry and psychology, whose practitioners had multiplied during and after the war. Between 1940 and 1960, membership in the American Psychological Association grew sixfold. Freud's influence receded as new modalities of treatment downplayed warring drives and focused instead on personal growth. Everyone was flawed, and everyone could get better, through some combination of talking and striving. Many tried; a national survey conducted in 1957 found that roughly one woman in six, and one man in ten, had sought some kind of counseling. More than twice as many said they should have or might yet.[6]

With or without therapists of their own, ordinary Americans encountered psychological concepts in song lyrics, or at the movies, or in the magazine aisle at the supermarket. *Ladies' Home Journal* offered a quiz: "How Neurotic Are You?"[7] *Cosmopolitan* ran "An Analyst's Diary," while *Parents* published a primer entitled "This Is the Way Psychotherapy Works."[8] An expanding number of analytically flavored self-help books by experts, ranging from the pediatrician Benjamin Spock to the evangelical minister Norman Vincent Peale, crowned the bestseller lists. Even comic books took to the couch. In the graphic serial *Psychoanalysis*, a superhero analyst with Freud's iconic beard and glasses defeats enemy neuroses.[9] Candida Royalle's first full-length pornographic movie, whose plot turns on the concept of repression, would take the punning title *The Analyst* or, in some editions, *Back-Door Therapy*.[10]

By the age of thirteen, more than a decade before appearing in *The Analyst*, Candy was already fluent in the psychological concepts that suffused her world. She had read about the emotional roller coaster of adolescence. She wondered, in her diary, whether her stepmother had "heard of stages." Such knowledge was vital. "When you're a teen you *must* go through stages," Candy explained.[11] She felt sure she didn't "have a complex," not even about her figure, still a girl's. Yet she worried that her "subconscience" sometimes made her to do or say things she didn't plan. She wrote down her dreams and scoured their imagery for hidden meanings. "Going in & out of water," for instance: "going in means getting Fucked—coming out means having a baby," she told her friend Liza.[12] She also read magazine articles on topics like divorce and alcoholism, which she felt spoke "directly to our problems."[13]

Helen already had a counselor, whom she saw in secret, perhaps even before the girls' revelations about Louis cracked her brittle veneer. The doctor "must have been a devout follower of Freud," Candice later supposed: when Helen repeated what Cynthia had said Louis was up to, the therapist declared that the girl had imagined it all, a classic seduction fantasy. Helen clearly didn't think Cynthia was telling tales; she fled to Florida on the strength of her stepdaughter's story. But perhaps she convinced herself it was make-believe after all, because she came back.[14]

In any case, little that Helen might have read or heard, from her doctor or a priest or a lawyer or a neighbor or a teacher or anyone else, would have classed the family troubles as sexual abuse, much less have found fault with Louis. The clinical literature of the day ignored domestic violence in general and concluded that father-daughter incest, in particular, was exceedingly rare.[15] And if it *had* happened? Well, then it was Helen's fault, and Cynthia's. The alluring daughter and her frigid, often-absent mother: these were the stock figures of everything from academic treatises on the family to the proliferating genre of men's magazines. When the Vadala family needed it most, the feminist rediscovery of domestic violence and family sexual abuse still lay years in the future.[16]

By 1967, Cynthia had a therapist too. "And she really needs it!" wrote Candy, who thought she'd probably get one for herself soon as well. "Everyone is just so damned neurotic!" Helen was manic, re-covering the furniture as if to upholster her scars. But nothing could disguise her "inner feeling of rejection from us . . . she'll always feel like an outsider," Candy supposed. Louis was "terribly neurotic" and Cynthia, "obviously neurotic!" Candy was tired of being "the 'normal' one." She didn't know how long she could hold out. "This family can make you sick," she said.[17]

Professionals of the day agreed: the family, that alpha and omega of postwar American culture, was a psychosocial pressure cooker. And nowhere was the home more fraught than along the fault line between fathers and their teenage girls. In the years following World War II, academic psychologists, playwrights, novelists, and screenwriters developed a "complex," as Candy might have said, about the charged relationship between American dads and their bobbysoxer daughters.[18]

Experts felt great sympathy with fathers of Louis's vintage: men who confronted a rapidly changing role. "Grandfather knew that he was captain of the domestic ship," said the authors of *Making the Grade as Dad*, a guidebook for fathers published the year Candy was born. But a generation later, dictators had become "as suspect in the American home as on the political scene."[19] Deprived of many of the traditional markers of paternal power—physical prowess, martial discipline, a family wage—postwar patriarchs were steered toward what historian Rachel Devlin has called "the subtle, psychological power of erotic attraction" as their daughters came of age.[20] As *Making the Grade* explained, an "affectionate father" gave his daughter a firm "foundation . . . for getting on with men later in life." A good father praised his growing daughter's femininity. His blushing, befuddled appraisal of her form, her dates, and her dawning desires became a staple not only of psychoanalytic and sociological theory but also of film, fiction, and television, from *Father of the Bride* (1950) to *Father Knows Best* (1954–1960) and beyond.[21] It couldn't last, of course. Fathers needed to steel themselves to pass their daughters on to the next man, shaking hands with the groom at the altar, proud or at least resigned, if a little teary-eyed.

That was the script, anyway. But sometimes the plot got tangled, and fond fathers crossed the blurry line between appreciation and lechery. Some of the period's most esteemed fiction pivoted on father-daughter incest plots. So did one of the century's most popular novels; Candy was an avid fan of both the TV and movie versions of Grace Metalious's *Peyton Place*.[22]

The Oedipal investments of postwar American culture didn't make Louis Vadala a predator. He accomplished that all on his own. But the culture taught him his lines and helped the other members of the Vadala family to build their roles in turn: Louis powerless before his urges. Helen mute and raging. Cynthia blossoming yet fragile.

And Candy? She wandered in the wings while her sister took center stage. Louis thought women had only one purpose: to gratify men.

And Candy had fallen short of even that; her father had chosen Cynthia. Several years later, with a therapist of her own, Candy, by then Candice, would find herself wondering, "why not me?"[23] The question itself was troubling, as she would later acknowledge: "could I be that sick that I would be jealous of that sort of attention?"[24]

But at the time, all she knew was that she'd been written out of the drama. "I wonder how I'm supposed to grow up a normal, happy-go-lucky kid, when I haven't even got normal parents," she mused, "Or how am I going to be able to trust myself as a life-long companion to some man and be good mother and wife, when I've had this kind of an example of marriage shown to me?"[25]

If Candy wanted a different life, she knew she would have to save herself.

———

"I'M A WOMAN!" Candy crowed, just a few days before the Vadalas saw *Help!* She had, at long last, gotten her period, just in time: high school started in a few days. That meant leaving Riverdale for Manhattan, if not quite in the style she intended. She had set her heart on the School of Performing Arts, the city's elite public academy for music, theatre, and dance. But the jurors there had found her ballet audition wanting, not to mention her grades. (Louis told Candy he'd find her "a better dance school.")[26]

She landed, instead, at the High School of Art and Design, or A&D, a technical arts school on the east side of Manhattan, pursuing a major in fashion illustration, which might make a business out of her years of doodling outfits in the margins of her diaries. It wasn't as refined as Cynthia's placement, in the fine-arts-focused High School of Music and Art. But A&D's building was "*modern* and beautiful," Candy wrote. And she'd noticed, during her audition, that the halls were filled with "hunky boys" in "black leather jackets."[27]

Candy hoped that high school would mean leaving childhood behind. Like many girls then and since, she seemed to mature from the outside in. "Since I'm slightly new to me, I seem to look out of proportion to myself," she noted that summer, just before she found blood in her panties. But she was proud of her new bra size, and relieved to "fit [her] bathing suit almost completely with only the tip (the very tip) not filled up!" She swapped her ponytail for a shoulder-length flip, like Marlo Thomas in the hit TV comedy *That Girl*. "I dismissed myself from being cute little Candy when I cut my hair," she wrote.[28]

To become a woman meant figuring out what kind. "I'm finding myself sort of different than the common teenager," Candy wrote on the first day of 1966. A new year meant a new diary, this one a gift from Cynthia, who inscribed the flyleaf with the wish that "each page be filled with more happiness than the last." By the time Candy reached the journal's end, she'd be a high school junior, sixteen years old. She felt in no hurry. "I can wait, unlike many other girls," she wrote. Because "I have an older sister, I've seen it's no different if not worse than these past frustrated years!"[29]

If it was a particular agony to ripen toward adulthood in the Vadala household, the plight of adolescents was also part of a national conversation then reaching a fevered pitch. Teenagers—their music and their mores, their "baffling conflicts and contradictions"—were a particular focus of surveys and bestsellers in the 1950s and '60s.[30] Marketers courted their purchasing power. Teen boys dreamed of cars, but girls outspent them, doling out their allowances and babysitting nickels on clothes and lipsticks.[31] Culture mavens both fretted over and lionized what had just come to be called the "generation gap." Some of it inhered to the species. "There is a very general psychological basis for some tension between generations, which is not unique to this decade or to our culture," wrote John D. Black, director of Stanford University's Counseling and Testing Center, in November 1966, shortly after Candy turned sixteen. But other experts worried that the chasm between those born after World War II and their parents, who had endured the Depression, *was* unique. And the Vietnam War was already making the gap political.[32]

In the Vadalas' apartment in Riverdale, Louis and Marion and especially Helen hovered and hectored, just as it happened in TV sitcoms and young adult novels. Candy complained, in typical teenage fashion, about her grandmother's nagging and her stepmother's tendency to turn a little backtalk into a "revolutionary war." But for the most part, the grown-up Vadalas couldn't be bothered to learn their roles. "My parents have so little interest in us it's pathetic," Candy wrote as she counted down the days before high school started. "Daddy treats everything for me like a chore," while Helen lurched between neglect and drunken rage. "She blames my growing up on me," Candy fumed.[33]

Grow up she did. The High School of Art and Design was, at least by Riverdale standards, permissive. Girls could wear makeup and slacks and soon even jeans. There was a terrace where students were allowed to smoke. The classes were easy. "We hardly do anything," Candy wrote; "students rule the teachers."[34]

Her real classroom was Manhattan. Her classmates at A&D came from all over the five boroughs, and some of her friendships, for the first time, crossed the color line. On occasion, she still expressed inherited prejudices, against "Spanish boys," or Jews, or "fairies." More often she embraced the people, places, and experiences that smacked of what she called "the city life . . . Go go, discos & everything!"[35] She and her friends checked out folk clubs like the Night Owl, in the West Village, and danced at pulsing new *discotheques*, including the Cheetah, on West Fifty-Third, where the psychedelic musical *Hair* debuted before heading to Broadway. The Doors had once played live at Ondine, on East Fifty-Ninth, where Candy and a date drank Singapore slings and Champagne cocktails, and she let loose on a dance floor no bigger than a large living room. These were new venues, not the staid hotel ballrooms her dad had played, but former industrial spaces where psychedelic light shows ricocheted off metallic walls. The crowd got high, and you might catch a glimpse of a downtown celebrity, like Andy Warhol or Edie Sedgwick. Candy drank a little, but she never smoked pot, not even when people teased her about it.[36]

Every now and again, Candy looked out past the mirror and the city and toward the world around her. There was a war on, escalating by the day. Every so often, a Riverdale boy went into the service and came back in a body bag. The more she thought about the United States and its mythos, the less she believed in it. "All that seems important is winning countries, ruling people, making them your worshippers, and reaching the moon!" People like her elders sat numb in their churches and synagogues, "little guinea pigs" bowing to a god they pretended could hear them. In the spring of 1966, nearing the end of her sophomore year, as American troop levels in Vietnam neared the 200,000 mark, she wrote a poem:

> *America, America*
> *Land of opportunity*
> *A story book made up by fools.*
> *Is all it really means to me*
> *It promises a good career*
> *And a chance to open your door*
> *As long as you follow every rule.*[37]

THE RULES THAT MATTERED most to Candy governed boys. For years, they had buzzed her, before she budded or bled or knew if she liked the attention, before she could figure out whether she was the spider or the fly. Boys pressed against her in elevators. Grown men propositioned her from cars.[38] Once at the Central Park Zoo, she and her friend Sue were watching the animals and Candy felt something behind her; she turned to find a man masturbating against her "backside." On a Saturday night that same spring, her last in middle school, she and some girlfriends had walked down to Fordham Road to hang out and watch people. "I'll list all the things that were said to us," Candy wrote in her diary:

1. Hey you're cute. "Wanna go buy some ice cream with us?"
2. Hi Doll!
3. We got about 8 kisses.
4. You're surrounded.

There were others she couldn't remember.[39]

Men taught boys to revel in their impunity, and girls like Candy learned to accept their vulnerability. They were to hide, not to seek. To be prey, never predators. Yet as she said she had learned in Van Cortlandt Park, they allowed themselves to be caught at their own peril.

For years, Candy had worried that the sexual attention she wanted would saddle her with "the reputation of being a sort of runaround."[40] Yet she also found herself dreaming of "making out"—with Michael and Julio, with Jeff, and Gary, and Nicky. "Oh I'm so ashamed!" she confessed to her diary on waking. "What's wrong with me!" She resented boys who acted as if it was her "duty to be felt up!" Yet she also worried that she might be "dreaming these things because I'm afraid of sex!" Was she a "runaround" or a "prude"? Who had the power to decide, and why did there seem to be no other choices? It was enough, as she wrote, to give a teenager a "terrific complex."[41]

What did it mean for a girl to flip the script: to yearn, to hunger, to hunt? Candy's ninth-grade boyfriend, Gary, was an octopus of a guy, hands everywhere, always out of sync with whatever she herself might be feeling, when she knew what she felt, which was rarely. Just before starting high school, she had read an article in *Seventeen*, by a psychologist who proclaimed that girls were "lucky to be growing up in a time when sex has emerged from its cover of shame and secrecy." Candy took notes: "Boys either like a girl to show their maleness because they get an erge [*sic*] for sex—Or it's true love. Just for her." Gary, she decided "just wanted to show his maleness," but maybe also "liked just me—(Love)." Then he left her. "I'm almost afraid I might become an old maid," she wrote.[42]

Gary was back in the fall, pressing Candy for more than she wanted to give while offering her less than she wanted to get. "Boy! Gary's nothing but a little Sex fiend who likes to get his thrills using girls for enjoyment!" she fumed. Yet she found herself "getting hot too," as if she had urges of her own. Where she had once been sure sex was "dirty and horrible," she felt, by the spring of her sophomore year, increasingly "mixed up" about it. "In fact, now that the boys in school have cooled down a bit, I sometimes feel as though I crave it! . . . It's taking me a lot to admit this," even to her diary, but sometimes she couldn't wait for boys "to start fooling around and touching me." She hoped it might be "normal for a teenage, adolescent girl of my age." She wondered if sex gave her "a feeling of importance," especially around the "top" boys at

A&D. Maybe she was "afraid of rejection." Fooling around and "getting fresh" meant the boys would "at least know I'm there."[43]

They knew she was there.

A couple months later, in a stairwell at school, two of her male friends pinned her arms and started to untie her wraparound denim skirt, shouting, "let's rape her!" They ran away when a teacher happened by. "Boy was that a close call!" Candy wrote.[44]

The next fall, her junior year, Candy turned "Sweet Sixteen": a beacon, a portent. "Don't expect too much from sixteen," Cynthia warned. For her birthday, her uncle Charlie—Louis's much-favored older brother—and aunt Lucy gave her some embroidered linens for her bridal trousseau. Candy thought she was still "too young to get serious." She filled out a computer dating profile from a magazine, a novelty then. Men in their twenties and thirties responded, grownups "with marriage on their minds already!" Which sent her back to the schoolyard.[45] A friend tutted that boys only wanted Candy "for sex appeal," which sounded unfair, though maybe true. And was that necessarily so wrong? "Things are beginning to wake up now," she wrote at year-end. "Because after you don't make out or anything for a while—Boy! That can really make you feel sex starved! And I felt it!"[46]

What was a girl—a good Catholic girl from a "good neighborhood" who wanted one day to be a "good mother and wife"—to do with her yearning for "sexual satisfaction"? The script said the boy was the engine and the girl, the brakes.[47] She was supposed to "control" her date, because "once he starts, there's no stopping him," and not stopping was for marriage. But what if Candy wanted neither to stop nor to marry? "Marriage seems like a drag to me," she wrote on the first day of 1967. "It's more fun living a challenging life." The next month, the venerable *Good Housekeeping* magazine asked its readers: "Should Birth Control Be Available to Unmarried Women?" Nearly two-thirds of survey respondents said no.[48]

After junior year ended, during what the papers were calling the Summer of Love among the colorful hippies in faraway San Francisco, Candy decided to give up on the TV-fueled dream of "summer romance" and play the field. Friends set her up on blind dates. She went out with Glenn, who was terribly "sexy looking," with his "tanned skin" and his "bedroom eyes," not to mention his "high class bracket, which is above me." One night, while she was staying out in Rockaway with her cousins, she and Glenn fooled around, with the sea air blowing through the curtains, and Candy knew, all of a sudden, "why people like sex!! I have never been so excited in my life!" Glenn felt her up, "but luckily, didn't get far enough!" She came away with a sense of mastery: "I was getting him so excited too! . . . And even though it's wrong, I was kind of proud of myself." But then day broke, and she "felt so cheap!" The next time a boy tried to slip his hand into her blouse, she stopped him cold, with a "sneer and [a] crooked smile," explaining that she had "the right to be respected."[49]

Louis backslid that June, staggering home drunk and standing, once again, at the bedroom door watching Cynthia, on Father's Day no less. He knocked over a fan in the hallway, and the girls woke up. Candy, who had "never wanted to take it seriously before," had to own that it was all real. "I have a sick father," she wrote. "He's very, very

Candy at her grandmother's house on her seventeenth birthday, October 1967.

mixed up! And no one can help him." Helen was talking separation, again; sometimes she said she'd spirit Candy away with her. Cynthia got herself out a couple weeks later, moving with a group of friends to a ratty apartment off the Grand Concourse, in the East Bronx.[50]

Candy turned seventeen in October 1967, shortly before *Newsweek* reported that "old taboos are dead or dying," and a "new, more permissive society is taking shape."[51] Candy was glad to be done with "sweet sixteen" but already "afraid of getting old." Her friends at A&D—they were seniors now—sometimes passed a joint around at parties, but she never took a hit. The boys were still mashing on her, particularly with a little dope in them, because "pot stimulates you," Candy wrote. They were so clumsy, grinding against her, or "humping on my knee," which "turned me off completely." Yet she decided on the first day of 1968, as she reflected on yet another unsatisfying New Year's Eve spent fending off yet another horny teenage lothario, that the problem was hers: she wasn't "that open or sex minded."[52]

Later that month, following an antiwar march in Washington, a liberationist group called New York Radical Women pronounced traditional womanhood—wherein men called the shots and women faced the consequences—dead at the ripe old age of three millennia. Kathie Amantiek, who would soon rechristen herself Kathie Sarachild, delivered a mock eulogy at Arlington National Cemetery, urging American women to recognize that their debilities were "social, not merely personal." The sexual double standard that bounded the life of every mother and daughter was "interlocked with the other problems in our country," including "the very problem of war itself."[53]

This would have seemed quite shocking to young Candy Vadala of Riverdale, in her last semester of high school and still trying to figure it out on her own: why necking in the backseat of a car made her feel "cheap at times" and turned on at others; whether letting a guy get to second base really was all "that terrifically bad." She remained confused about who was in charge. When a date soldiered on after she "tried to pull away," she felt she "couldn't be mad because I knew that I brought it on," by letting him unbutton her winter coat. When the boundaries seemed blurry, she re-chalked the lines and cautioned herself to "remember my principles."[54]

"I always seem to be getting myself into these 'uncomfortable situations,'" Candy wrote after a thrillingly frustrating date in February 1968. "I'm very proud of myself because it really felt great, but I wouldn't let him."[55] There was a certain brinksmanship to it all, not so unlike an increasingly hot Cold War. Positions must be held, and a great deal of firepower was required to defend them, long after anyone remembered exactly why. When would American women declare that they'd had enough of the quagmire?

PART II

Wide Open

I have such a wide open range of activities to choose from.
—Candice Vadala, 1973

7 Freedom

Candy and Joe Kovacs, c1969.

Candy graduated high school in 1968, marching across the stage of A&D and into the headwinds of a revolution. In March, Lyndon Johnson had shocked the nation by declaring he wouldn't stand for reelection. In April, the Reverend Martin Luther King Jr. fell to an assassin's bullet. Cities across the country exploded in agony and rage. New York's mayor, John V. Lindsay, a dashing liberal Republican tipped as a presidential hopeful, walked the streets of Harlem and called for calm, which helped to contain the neighborhood's despair.[1] Then in June, shortly before Candy received her diploma, Robert F. Kennedy was murdered in Los Angeles.

That spring, college campuses from coast to coast roiled in protest. Student radicals occupied the administrative offices at Columbia, bringing the university to a standstill. Women activists who felt sidelined by the Students for a Democratic Society and other New Left organizations, boys' clubs all, organized their own movement around kitchen tables. A Chicago-based women's group titled its mimeographed six-page newsletter *voice of the women's liberation movement*, all lowercase, for equality's sake. New York Radical Women published a longer and partially typeset annual, *Notes from the First Year*, a name that evoked the French Revolution.[2] The *New York Times* gathered these ripples into a "wave," in a splashy story in the Sunday magazine, declaring that "feminism, which one might have supposed as dead as the Polish Question, is again an issue."[3] Sometimes, it was clearer what the radicals were against than what they were for. James Kunen, a Columbia student who participated in the student takeover of administrative offices that spring—he wrote a book about it that Candy read—recalled hearing the Rascals' anthem, "People Got to Be Free!" on the radio during that long, hot revolutionary summer. "And it hit me, what the hell does it mean? Free? Free to do what? Free from what?"[4]

These were Candy's questions, too, as she launched into her adult life. Her desires remained, in many ways, conventional: dreams of the still-lingering '50s. She felt proud, before leaving A&D, of having ascended the student pecking order, finally reaching the "inner crowds." She decided to continue her study of illustration at Parsons School of Design, which had tight connections to the fashion houses on Seventh Avenue. Like most of the college girls she knew, Candy would commute from home, which would save money. Parsons was a private school, but at $850 per semester (about $6,000 in today's money), its tuition was relatively modest. Students could work their way through doing odd jobs in the industry, like modeling and sewing.[5] When Candy imagined her life after graduation, she pictured herself as a "cosmopolitan," living on the Upper East Side, "meeting Mr. Right and marrying around the age of 26"—some five years later than the national average—and working as a fashion illustrator, well paid and much in demand.[6]

Before starting her freshman year at Parsons, Candy took a part-time job at Bergdorf Goodman, the elegant department store on Fifth Avenue, across the street from the Plaza Hotel. In her diary, she spelled it "Bergdoff," which must have been how she said it: the girl from the Bronx making good. Like the Miss Bergdorf ads that ran in the *Times*, Candy's aesthetic was "cute" and "modely," featuring backcombed hair, false eyelashes, and other feminine war paint. She bought clothes with her employee discount: *Seventeen* en route to *Town & Country*. Some of her skirts may still have required crinolines. Her signature scent was Replique, which advertised in ladies' magazines as "the perfume with a language all its own," but whose French name meant *replica*.[7]

The summer after graduation, Candy got up to all manner of PG-rated hijinks. She and her friend Dianne presided over "a week of splendor" in Dianne's apartment, with her parents away. Dianne's Joe and Candy's Steve and a pair of other recently graduated couples played house. The boys stayed overnight, as Dianne's parents had worried they might. But in Candy's telling, the scene plays more like an outtake from *The Pajama Game* (1953) than from *Valley of the Dolls* (1966). There was lots of flirting and cuddling, but only the ambiance of sex: pillow fights instead of pillow talk. The company sprayed each other with shaving cream. The boys provisioned, and the girls made fancy dinners: "tiny frankfurters, cold cuts, potato chips, and salad with russian dressing" one night, lamb chops another. They drank cheap wine and mixed screwdrivers. Sometime later in the summer, Candy smoked pot for the first time, "finally," she wrote.[8]

Come fall—after the violence at the Democratic nominating convention in Chicago was broadcast live from coast to coast, and the protests by women's liberationists against the Miss America pageant in Atlantic City generated spurious headlines about bra burning—some of Candy's friends plunged headlong into the burgeoning drug scene. One of the boys from July's "splendid week" at Dianne's house nearly drowned in a bathtub during an intense acid trip. This frightened, even disgusted, Candy. She wasn't "a drug user" and so didn't "fit in with the so-called 'hippies.'" Nor could she stomach the flower child's studied squalor. Yet she worried that she relished fancy clothes "simply for impressiveness. I have this embedded belief that in order to be respected, you must prove to have money."[9]

This concern with what others saw and thought, and the lingering fear that she remained, somehow, "inferior," loomed large among the "hang-ups," "weaknesses and complexes" Candy still yearned to shed. She had grown to disdain the "typical little jewy Riverdalians" who peopled her youth. While she knew that no religion held a monopoly on "materialistic values," which were as American as apple pie, Candy thought such views especially common "amongst the Jewish people." They cared about appearances, where she sought the essence of things. Like a latter-day Salinger character, Candy abhorred "shallow, simpleminded, and superficial people with their phony sentiments," even as she worried she might be one of those phonies herself. She realized "the importance of self-appreciation and individuality," joining her generation's mass pursuit of uniqueness. "i'm finally finding myself and reaching out to my own identity," she wrote on the eve of her eighteenth birthday, giving up on capital letters. "i'm finally trying just to be me."[10]

———

JOE KOVACS ENTERED Candy's life much as several other boys already had, and other men later would: he belonged to somebody else.

During that flirty week of innocent bliss in July 1968, Joe had been Dianne's date, firmly claimed. Candy found Joe "cute" but "not outstandingly gorgeous," and decided he "simply wasn't my type." But it turned out that he was, not least because "he was paying much more attention to me than to Dianne!" Joe called to ask Candy out the day after the slumber party ended. Candy sought Dianne's permission, and offered to cool it, for a month or so. She started up again with Richie, from the old neighborhood, who was handsome and fun, "but his speech is terrible and he's quite illiterate as a result of living in Brooklyn and going to a bad school," and there was no future in that. When Joe called again, Candy agreed to a date. He took her to the Yonkers Raceway, and they were off.[11]

Joe was in many ways like Candy, a kid from the Bronx, the son of Hungarian Jewish immigrants. He recalls that he and his friends called themselves lower-middle-class but were really working-class. The Kovacses were a stable family, close-knit, quite unlike the Vadalas. Joe's parents cared, which would come to matter. He went to SUNY–Stony Brook, lived on campus, and did well enough there to be ambitious about his future. Both he and Candy, at the time, were "sort of preppy," he recalls. Candy's early sketches of Joe depict a bookish boy, his hair neatly parted and trimmed above his ears. The wild mop of curls and the cowboy mustache came later.[12]

After the Raceway came an evening at the Palisades, on the other side of the Hudson, at the end of which Joe and Candy parked in front of the Vadalas' apartment building for "an extended goodnight kiss." Louis spied them out the window and grumbled that he'd caught Candy "making hanky panky." Helen, who was drunk, told Candy her father thought she was "a tramp." Some of Candy's friends, and Cynthia, too, worried that Joe was "only using" her.[13]

The date Joe planned for Candy's eighteenth birthday, in October, convinced her he was serious. She wrote about it with a breathlessness that sighs from the diary page: how he picked her up at Bergdorf's dressed in a three-piece suit. How he took her to the Sheraton in Midtown ("so beautiful and exquisite"), where a harpist serenaded them in the dining room ("quite spooky"). How they ordered soup made with cherry wine, and Long Island duckling ("Oh, that meal!"). How he whisked her off to Philadelphia to hear Dionne Warwick. Candy was dazzled, not least by the amount of cash Joe had lavished on the evening. (She totted up the prices.) Joe was "just the kind of boy" Candy thought she needed: "One with a strong upper hand."[14]

Barely three months after Candy and Joe started dating, she began picturing their wedding, even as she held the prospect at arm's length. "If I were about 21, I would probably really be thinking about him as a prospective husband," she wrote, though it gave her "kind of a weird feeling to think that if I were to marry Joe, I would never go out with another boy or man. It would be as if I really missed out on something—like he stole part of my life away." But then she thought about "how many girls do get married at eighteen! And so many of my friends are getting married to their present beaus." It was all so romantic and so confusing: a "fingerpainted dream dressed in lace," she called it in a letter to Joe, whose absence, out in Stony Brook, made Candy's heart grow fonder.[15]

And Candy's heart, of course, was attached to her body, which was where things got complicated. After the birthday extravaganza, Candy "engaged in sex with him, and farther than with any other boy." What she called "sex," which was petting, at least seemed proportional to their commitment. "No other boy ever meant what Joe means to me!" Joe, whom Candy figured was "much more experienced," took her to see Franco Zeffirelli's lush film *Romeo and Juliet*. Afterward, they made out for a while, and Joe suggested that they go up to his room. "But, would you die? I said no!" She supposed that if she kept seeing Joe "for a very long time, I may not remain a virgin! But I hate to talk about sex in this book because although this book is only for me, you never know what snoop might go through it." (She knew all too well.)[16]

Before Thanksgiving, Joe and Candy contrived a weekend together in his Stony Brook dorm. Lynn and Bobby, another of the couples from Dianne's pajama party, would be there too. The university, a major rock 'n' roll venue at the time, was hosting a concert with some of the most exciting artists of the day: folkie Richie Havens, who sang a newly electric blues; and Big Brother and the Holding Company, fronted by Janis Joplin, her raspy alto swooping and plunging at the edge of control, a glass of Southern Comfort in her hand as she belted out "Down on Me."[17]

They all got high before the concert, and Candy and Lynn made a show of readying for bed afterward. Candy donned her Stony Brook nightshirt, "of course way shortened!" Joe kept his underwear on and ground against her, and "did everything" before she was even "warmed up." After so much anticipation about spending a weekend "like 2 married couples," the reality left Candy "absolutely unsatisfied." At least she hadn't done anything untoward. Out with Joe at a Chinese restaurant a couple weeks later, Candy got a fortune that read, "YOU BETTER PREPARE YOUR HOPE CHEST." She tucked the slip of paper into her diary.[18]

In December, Joe took his Candy to see *Candy*, the film based on Terry Southern's 1958 novel. John Astin, iconic as Gomez of TV's *The Addams Family*, played a double role as Candy's father and her equally lecherous uncle, "thus torn between incest of varying degrees," as a fizzy feature in the *Times* quipped. The book ended with Candy in flagrante beneath the Buddha, crying out in her honeyed girlish voice, "GOOD GRIEF—IT'S DADDY."[19] A big-budget romp with as much nudity as the law allowed, *Candy* must have seemed to Joe the ultimate date movie. Candy Vadala was disgusted. They walked out in the middle.[20]

Just before Christmas, Joe asked Candy "something kind of shocking." Tired of making out in his car, he wondered, as casually as he could, if she'd mind going to a hotel with him. She was stunned, "because the first thing that came to my mind was the thought of going all the way," which "really frightened" her. She supposed "there wasn't anything wrong with going all the way as long as you both really loved each other." But it had only been four months. The answer, for now, was no. "Damn these stupid Christian upbringings," Candy jotted as the revolutionary year of 1968 wound down.[21]

"I DO HAVE new and different morals, and feel I am part of the sexual revolution," Candy wrote in February 1969, less than two months after rebuffing Joe's request to get a room.[22] Like most unmarried American women of her generation, she remained a virgin. Despite a great deal of hand-wringing about youth morals and teen pregnancy, surveys suggested that only a quarter of college girls had engaged in intercourse, a percentage that hadn't budged much since the '50s. As Gael Green joked in *Cosmopolitan*, the raciest of the supermarket women's magazines, "Even in the Permissive Sixties, girls still suffer through the virginity crisis."[23]

Candy, not yet nineteen, was, like an increasing number of girls her age, exhausted by manufactured sexual agony. She had spent another night out at Stony Brook, for another concert—Arlo Guthrie this time. When Joe pulled down her panties and rolled on a condom, she felt so "terrified" she "almost started crying." So "he never did it." Which was a relief, but also a worry: she wondered "just why he didn't go all the way after all," with or without her. She sneaked a peek inside the condom box and felt heartened to find only one rubber gone. She figured she shouldn't be "angry if more were missing since he's got to release his urges."[24]

And then, on the train home, Candy noticed Allen, a handsome soldier in uniform. He was returning from a weekend with his reserve unit. A blizzard raged. Buses to the Bronx looked chancy. Candy and Allen wound up at her friend Thea's apartment on Forty-Fifth Street, with some others. They smoked a little grass, just enough to loosen them up. Candy and Allen tumbled into bed. They traded back rubs and made out, and he climbed on top of her, and he stayed there, and she liked it. In a flash, "aha—breakdown of the old belief—I can only get excited by one I like—what shit!" Then she decided that while Allen "turned me on sexually, he turned me off otherwise," so they didn't have intercourse. Even so, the experience had been enough to "lift the black veil off of sex":

> Love is love, and sex is sex. Sex and love don't go together. You can have a very nice night in bed with someone and should be able to say goodbye in the morning and that's that. According to

the old double standard it's O.K. for a man to do that but the girl is always left stranded. It should be just as permissible for a girl to say goodbye and leave. Sex is a wonderful thing. Something not to be so emphasized—love is an emotion and sex is a feeling. . . . if you do feel like having sex with someone, you should, there's nothing wrong with it. It's only a natural part of life and living. The only reason we think it's wrong is because we were taught to think that, and it's an old puritanical belief that you should only have sex with someone you love.

Candy woke up feeling "proud—like, I'm really of a new breed & belief." Enough of yesterday; "everything should be changed to today." She wrote a poem:

Changing world
old ideas discarded . . .
A new time
A new life
A new me.

She wasn't sure Joe would be able to follow her. In revolutions, things moved fast, and people got left behind.[25]

———

TO CANDY, it felt as if the sexual revolution began that night in February 1969. She was barely an adult: a college freshman with a decreasing commitment to her studies, still living in a cramped apartment with her parents. But in fact, the sexual revolution was, by the time it reached her, old news, with an increasingly broad array of critics.

Even during Louis and Helen Vadala's childhoods, in the '20s, the sense that "New Women," along with the new science of psychiatry, augured a radical transformation of sexual mores had been sufficiently commonplace to inspire a bestselling spoof, E. B. White and James Thurber's *Is Sex Necessary?* (1929). New York had then been "the capital of the sexual revolution," as "young ladies from the South and from the Middle West whose minds were not quite made up about sexual freedom" flocked there, Thurber wrote.[26] A decade later, the Austrian émigré psychoanalyst and sexologist Wilhelm Reich treated the proposition that a revolution in mores was or should be under way more seriously. First published in English in 1945, Reich's *The Sexual Revolution* argued for "sexuality as the core of a life-affirmative culture" that would free society as well as individuals from neurosis.[27] Reich's attempts to bolster his patients' "orgastic potency" by sitting them naked inside a telephone booth–sized "orgone accumulator" ran afoul of the law, on the twin grounds of obscenity and fraud. In 1956, FDA agents in New York incinerated six tons of Reich's books.[28]

But by then, the phrase "sexual revolution" had entered the American vernacular. Those who worried about changing standards could see the evidence in towns as well as cities, in parks and on campuses as well as at newsstands. Ordinary young people born a decade or so before Candy and Cynthia Vadala were redefining morality on the ground, sometimes literally.[29] Alfred Kinsey's volumes on male and female sexual behavior were selling widely, and William H. Masters and Virginia E. Johnson embarked on a twelve-year-long empirical study of human sexuality. The Pill was being tested in Puerto Rico. Early battles of a gathering culture war over sexual license were being waged in the courts and by grassroots organizations like Charles H. Keating's Citizens for Decent Literature, based in Cincinnati, which sought to rally the good and decent people of the American heartland against "perversion for profit."[30]

Around the time that Candy started keeping diaries, mass media began to spread the story that these skirmishes portended a full-fledged moral transformation. "Sexual intercourse began / In nineteen sixty-three," the English poet Philip Larkin quipped in "Annus Mirabilus."[31] Larkin's comic verse mocked the very idea of a big bang for the sexual revolution, yet it also had a basis in fact. In the spring of 1963, the popular talk-show host David Susskind taped a two-hour panel discussion on "The American Sexual Revolution" for his weekly television program, *Open End*.

"You want teen-agers to have sexual relations without marriage?" Susskind, the father of teenage daughters, asked one of his expert panelists, Albert Ellis, the author of the popular compilation *Sex without Guilt.*

"I certainly do," answered the psychologist.[32]

The network pulled the plug before the segment aired. Susskind cried censorship. The ensuing controversy made good copy. *Mademoiselle* magazine published the full transcript of the "banned program" in October, as Candy turned thirteen.[33]

By 1964, *Time* was ready with a 6,000-word cover story on this "Second Sexual Revolution," chronicling an epidemic of casual affairs in suburban cul-de-sacs. "The atmosphere is wide open," said one minister.[34] The venerable *Ladies' Home Journal* hopped on the sexual revolution bandwagon, with a cover story on the topic by Nobel Prize–winning novelist Pearl S. Buck, an aging paragon of middlebrow respectability. "The change is so abrupt, so far-reaching, that we are all dazed by it," Buck wrote. She, too, bemoaned the decoupling of sex and love.[35] "What is sex when it is nothing but release or sport?" Buck asked in a follow-up article in *Family Weekly*. The Pill, she fretted, could become "even more devastating than the nuclear bomb."[36]

Changing sexual behavior and frank depictions of sex profoundly distressed a new breed of conservatives, strongest in the country's booming sun belt, who pushed opposition to sex education, premarital intercourse, and abortion toward the forefront of political discourse. In April 1967, Lyndon Johnson's Department of Justice endorsed a Democratic congressman's proposal to study the effects of the proliferation of sexually explicit material.[37] The commission's charter deemed "the traffic in obscenity and pornography to be a matter of national concern." Moderates and liberals predominated in its ranks, which would include jurists, psychiatrists, clergymen, publishers, schoolteachers, film industry executives, and social scientists, tasked with surveying the landscape, determining "whether such materials are harmful to the public, and particularly to minors," and proposing "advisable, appropriate, effective, and constitutional means" to stem the tide.[38]

Conservative reaction to the shift in American mores was predictable. But by the time Candy Vadala signed on to the sexual revolution, other critiques had also begun to emerge. During 1967's "Summer of Love," while Candy was still in high school, *Seventeen* had published the results of its national survey on "Teenagers and Sex," which found that the consequences of premarital intercourse still weighed heavily on young women. Condom use required negotiation, and the Pill remained more often the subject of "brave talk" than the stuff of preventive action. It could be obtained only from a physician, and its access by unmarried people would not be constitutionally guaranteed until 1972. What's more, fewer than half the girls who answered *Seventeen*'s questionnaire reported feeling "contented" after crossing the threshold of intercourse. Nearly as many "felt guilty or ashamed."[39]

In late 1968, as Candy was falling for Joe, Dana Densmore, a computer programmer at MIT, published an essay, "On Celibacy," in a new journal of "female liberation," *No More Fun and Games*, one of the first feminist arguments against what passed for sexual revolution. "Sexual freedom is the first freedom a woman is awarded and she thinks it is very important because it's all she has; compared to the dullness and restrictiveness of the rest of her life it glows very brightly," Densmore wrote. But in fact, sex was merely a pacifier: "a minor need, blown out of proportion" by advertisers hawking goods and Romeos trying to get laid.[40] Densmore would soon call on her fellow feminists to declare "independence from the sexual revolution." Sex, she wrote, was "forced down our throats. It's the great sop that keeps us in our place." Women who fell for this thin version of self-determination played narrow roles, long on display and short on substance. Their freedom was an illusion. "When men say to us, 'But aren't you already liberated?' what they mean is, 'We *said* it was okay for you to let us fuck you . . . that chaste makes waste; you're already practically giving it away on the street, what more do you want or could you stomach?'"[41]

This vexed question of *wanting*, at once so shallow and so vast, would consume the movement for decades to come.

———

WHEN CANDY GOT BACK from her snowy night with Allen, in February 1969, she poured her triumph into her diary. "Liberation of the female! Being able to have one-night stands and the girl saying bye!"[42]

Two weeks later, Joe's parents went away, and he and Candy stayed in the Kovacses' apartment, and she offered up what was left of her chastity. After so much build-up, the event proved tense, painful, and sad: in every way, an anticlimax. Candy described intercourse as something that had happened *to* her: "I expected him to go all the way," she wrote, a passenger on her own journey. He had. And it was "just so horrible." She felt "like screaming or crying," but had "stayed cool." And she "felt like telling him to get it out" but stayed mum, while he kept it in, for as long as it took. "I asked him to go slowly," she wrote the next morning, "but boys come so fast." There had been no way for her to catch up.

Writing about the Act after so much prologue, Candy sounds both proud and gutted. "I just can't understand why I'm so upset," she said. "After all, it wasn't like I was let down." Except that she had been. "In the morning he did it again—and it wasn't quite as painful."[43] Which seemed like revolution enough. For now.

8 Liberation

Candy, c1969.

"**M**y course in life has made a gradual but sudden change," Candy wrote in March 1969, a canny description not only of her own mad sprint, helter-skelter in every direction, but also of the mood of the United States as a whole. "The center was not holding," Joan Didion had written, paraphrasing Yeats.[1] And Candy's center had been so fragile to begin with. Within weeks of committing herself to sexual revolution, she found herself drawn toward nearly every other social transformation within view.

She turned on. Having first dared pot only the summer before, she tried opium. "Quite an experience—literally!!" she wrote, as if taking up the invitation Jimi Hendrix had wailed on the title cut of his 1967 debut album, *Are You Experienced?*[2] Now she was, joining the growing ranks of young Americans trying hard drugs. The number of people who reported using hallucinogens more than doubled between 1968 and 1971. Heroin use was increasing, too, though not as rapidly. And the mean age of first turning on dropped slightly, to right around Candy's own.[3] After a weekend during which she got high both nights—hash this time—Candy decided that drugs really did "change you. I've all of a sudden become more daring in a sense—not afraid to search my soul. Not afraid of making decisions that I previously would have been too precautious to make." It helped with sex too. Still, Candy wasn't "hung up on drugs," not like some of her friends who dropped acid all the time, or were "off & on the needle & . . . in & out of the hospital."[4]

She tuned in, cultivating a new level of political engagement. She packed relief supplies for the victims of famine in Biafra. She woke to the "horror and realness of terror" in Vietnam. In April, she and Joe marched for peace, in one of a coordinated set of mass demonstrations held in cities on both coasts. "I guess the march doesn't do anything," she admitted, though it had felt good, and showed "how many people are against this damned, inhuman war!" She was proud of her dawning consciousness. "I used to be completely oblivious to events around me," she wrote. "But now I have such a thirst. All I want to do now is read—keep up with the changing times."[5]

She thought about dropping out. She had come to dread her classes at Parsons, not least because Helen held the cost of tuition over her head. She had also come to hate the fashion world and thought she might prefer "a small village school for painting, figure drawing, & photography." Maybe dancing again too. And guitar. Her freshman spring, Candy decided she wouldn't go back to Parsons in the fall. "I think I really have found definite direction somewhat," she wrote.[6]

That Candy loathed her job went almost without saying. Work and money, stuff and status: she had come to hate "this society full of money grabbers and capitalists." She needed an income, yet she also feared that "working for money is only giving in to the way of life I'm against."[7] When school prevented her from working the hours Bergdorf's wanted, Candy felt liberated from "a disgusting situation." She picked up a couple of shifts modeling for "men in a photography club," at first finding the gig "unreal—and *so* flattering!" But then her boss started hitting on her, offering her a hundred dollars "just for a long kiss! That's sick!" she wrote. "Did he actually think I was so damned materialistic . . . ?! The next thing you know he'd be asking me to make love to him for $200!"[8] Which was, in relative terms, a lot of money—a sizeable fraction of a semester's tuition, or several months' rent.

There was not much recourse for a woman pressured for sex on the job in 1969. Though Title VII of the Civil Rights Act of 1964 had prohibited discrimination "on the basis of sex"—a provision so outlandish that it had been added to the bill as a poison pill by its Southern enemies—feminist organizations had had, to date, little success mobilizing the law in the workplace. The passage of Title IX, part of the Education Amendments of 1972, lay three years in the future. The concept of sexual harassment would come later still; the phrase was coined only in 1974, and elaborated on by the feminist legal scholar and anti-pornography advocate Catharine A. MacKinnon several years after that.[9]

So Candy confronted the options available to the vast majority of working women in her day: to grin and bear it, or to quit. She quit, and gave in to the grind of an office job, as the private secretary of "the highest man there who's only 25 years old—And I can't believe it—He liked me out of so many others!" she wrote, plainly impressed with her boss and herself. "There are many things that bother me like—office girl—secretary? Me?! And the responsibility of work every day?" But she was making a decent salary, and so she kept at it, disdain for capitalism going only so far.[10]

The job gave Candy the means to begin therapy. She started seeing a psychiatrist in July 1969, sometimes twice a week. Like most forays into depth psychology, treatment seemed at first to hurt more than it helped. Sessions with Dr. Galanter sometimes gave her "a feeling of relief" but also made her "more depressed," because they dragged up "all the hell [she'd] gone through." She stared at Peggy's picture and wondered if being abandoned had determined the course of her life. She feared that she'd been "too infected and disturbed throughout childhood" to have an honest and equal relationship with Joe, or anyone else.[11]

While Candy mined her past, the Vadalas continued their slow-motion collapse. Cynthia had left home because Louis was preying on her again. Helen wanted to leave him, but worried about her ability to support herself. At various points, she tried to enlist Candy in a fantasy of moving to Manhattan together. Candy was flattered, but also thought it was "too late for Mom & I. . . . Because now I consider her almost as sick as the others." She worried about her father too; she thought he'd "probably kill himself" if she and Helen followed Cynthia out the door.[12]

Shortly before she started seeing Dr. Galanter, Candy had packed up her clothes and her childhood belongings, including her precious diaries. She moved into Cynthia's apartment, on the fifth floor of a dingy yellow-brick walk-up on Field Place, with bars on the windows and a floor-mounted police lock reinforcing the door. The security was not just for show; the neighborhood felt "unsafe at 1:00 in the afternoon." The apartment itself was cramped, roach-infested, and dark. It backed on an airshaft. But Candy and Cynthia—Cyn, now—made the place over in their images, painting the door cranberry, the trim teal, and the walls red and purple. They scavenged furniture and made art. An upside-down peace sign graced the front door.[13]

A rotating cast of roommates lived with them communally: a collection of "freaked out dopers and artists" who became the Vadala sisters' found family. They were "flower children in a neurotic city," with "no flowers—just lots of free opiated hash," Candy recalled a couple years later, when strains of Jim Morrison singing "Light My Fire" on the radio brought Field Place flooding back to her: gathering friends at their salvaged table for Christmas, tripping on mescaline in glorious neons while the "grayness of the bronx . . . lingered like a layer of film over our walls."[14]

Louis and Helen could not help but ruin even the girls' exodus. They took off too—suddenly, and together, still, despite all Helen's talk of having had enough—moving to Gulfport, Florida, where Helen's mother lived, and turning Candy's escape into yet another abandonment. Her "mixed up, broken up, frustrated family" was "split up now—For good," she wrote in September 1969. Louis and Helen even left behind the family dog, a shaggy poodle named Anopheles, called Noph, who pops up in photos from Field Place. Save for Noph and Cyn, nineteen-year-old Candy was on her own.[15]

She decided to go back to school, to CUNY's City College, to earn a bachelor's degree, an ambition outsized to her upbringing. She knew she would have to retake some high school courses. But seeing Joe and his friends at Stony Brook "learning & working toward a goal" inspired her. "I feel I have the drive I need now," she wrote. She told Louis and Helen that CCNY's SEEK program (Search for Education, Elevation, and Knowledge), "for poverty stricken, underprivileged students" who needed remedial work to succeed in college, might be able to subsidize her if they submitted a statement of their income. "You have to sound really poor," Candy said, which she figured "won't be too hard since you're both not working now."[16]

Helen's reply was predictably disappointing. "I think it is wonderful that you want to further your education and we would do anything we could to help you," she said, doing exactly nothing to help. Life in Florida remained tenuous; she and Louis were living in a motel. He was looking for work as a salesman, a great relief to Helen, who said she'd "give anything if he could be something besides a musician." She was sorry she hadn't talked to Candy on her nineteenth birthday; the pay phone ate her dime. She didn't mention the paperwork for SEEK.[17]

While Candy loathed Parsons, and her jobs, and capitalism, and the war, and while she mourned her family, she remained a dedicated student of love and sex, and an explorer of the rocky territory in between. For her as for many of her generation, the self and especially the body seemed like the seat of human liberation. "I hate work but I love Joe," she doodled over and over again on a page of her sketchbook from Field Place.[18] Their relationship grew richer and more complex, "a real love now," she said. The sex got better—not good, but better— and she tried her best to be less "possessive and prudish."[19]

Candy's efforts to become less prim were in step with American constitutional law, which was gradually decriminalizing sexual materials of all kinds. She and Joe went to see *I Am Curious—Yellow*, an explicit Swedish film that had been seized for obscenity in Boston, only to be rescued by the U.S. Court of Appeals. Vincent Canby, in the *Times*, pronounced it "a good, serious movie about a society in transition," insisting that scenes in which the protagonists "effect sexual congress in a tree, on a balustrade in front of the royal palace . . . and in other locations, indoors and out, are explicit, honest and so unaffectedly frank as to be nonpornographic." Candy, by contrast, deemed the movie "pretty shit."[20]

Sometimes she wanted more from their relationship than Joe did, sometimes, less. Increasingly aware of her own sexual magnetism, she felt "the urge to 'spread my wings.'" Initially part of her path to liberation, Joe now seemed to require her to choose "between fun & love." The more urgent that choice became, the less obvious Candy found the answer. "Now that things have opened up for me and I'm able to run around more—And all of a sudden there are all these groovy guys— I've just got to let it all out," she wrote.[21]

The groovy guys multiplied. A neighbor, an older man, invited Candy to visit his photo-retouching business. When she got to the studio, he brought her a cocktail, showed her his erotic paintings, and talked to her about the "ridiculousness of the old morals." Then he asked her to model nude. She was caught up short, but she checked herself. "I realize that it shouldn't be so shocking, because the body is a natural & beautiful thing, and we shouldn't be so ashamed & inhibited," she wrote. She told herself it was "time to see if I'm a doer or talker." She chose doer.[22] She sits naked, at the edge of a couch or bed, her hair long and wet, arranged to cover her nipples, her legs pressed tight together and defiantly unshaven, her stare unyielding.

The clock was ticking on monogamy, whether Joe knew it or not. Suitors from A&D resurfaced, and new ones from Parsons emerged. They were so persistent, and Candy liked so much to be wanted. She fooled around with this one and that, all the while wondering whether Joe was not quite enough, or too much, or maybe both. He was "the only one who can and is helping me," and who would "allow me to lead a normal, happy life full of the love I want to give him," she wrote just before beginning treatment with Dr. Galanter. A month later, she had decided the relationship was "terribly superficial" and couldn't imagine spending the rest of her life with Joe.[23]

But she couldn't quite imagine anything else either. So they kept on. Candy got a prescription for the Pill and was thrilled to indulge in "a full night of sex" with "no protection." She said she "felt like such a woman afterwards . . . so full & so satisfied," though she had yet to experience orgasm, with Joe or anyone else. Months later, she reported she had still only gotten "very close." Yet she made herself lusty in a letter to Joe, joking that he had "totally corrupted what was once a pure & innocent, virtuous young girl." And what's more, that she had liked it.[24]

They reveled in their freedom and in each other that summer, dancing nude on the beach and fucking in the woods. They went to hear Phil Ochs and Joan Baez, artists singing for their lives, against the war. They drove up to Bethel for the Woodstock Music and Art Fair and found among those hundreds of thousands of revelers in the mud of Max Yasgur's farm a "community of people" who rejected the "struggle for money, status, recognition" which defined the straight world. At the end of August, to mark their one-year anniversary, Joe gave Candy a pair of front-row seats to see Peter, Paul & Mary in Forest Hills. Afterward, they drove up the Hudson and skinny-dipped in the Croton Reservoir, a storybook day.[25]

And then, in the fall, Dianne, who had been dating Joe when he and Candy met, decided to marry Bobby, in "an ultra-bourgeois wedding." Candy was tapped to be maid of honor—Dianne's attempt to make her jealous, she supposed. If so, it backfired. "I guess I'm just not the typical young girl whose main dream is marriage & a suburban home," she wrote. "I feel stifled right now as it is." Stifled by her job and by the ruins of her family, stifled in her own skin. Stifled by everything holding her back from what she really wanted to do: "Run!"[26]

———

THE MOVEMENT FOUND CANDY the way it found so many women in the late '60s and early '70s: with a mimeographed leaflet and a meeting and a "click" of recognition. She had been scrambling, once again, for just enough of a job to make rent. Her most recent post, in the showroom of a company that made swimsuits in the Garment District, had lasted only hours. Her duties had included trying on sample bikinis, much to her bosses' delight. "I don't like the 2 men, nor their forced immodesty," she wrote shortly after she interviewed. Her first morning on the job, one of them hung around while she changed, and then ran his hands through her hair and offered her a drink. She bolted before lunch. On her way home, she stopped at Lehman College, CUNY's campus in the Bronx, to check out the job listings. Somebody handed her a flyer for a women's liberation meeting. She'd been interested in the topic for a while. But the group met during the day, better for college girls than working girls. So they referred her to the Women's Liberation Collective of the Bronx Coalition, which met at night, in her neighborhood.[27]

Candy was an instinctive feminist well before her first meeting with the collective, in March 1970. Even in junior high school, she'd developed a keen awareness that boys had more latitude than girls in matters of love and sex. Since her own epiphany about the sexual revolution the previous year, she'd tried to fashion a committed, unfettered, and egalitarian relationship with Joe. In January, they had decided that they'd spend much of the summer apart, no strings binding either of them. "He has accepted the refusal of the double standard," Candy wrote, even as she lamented that she had not yet reached orgasm after a year of trying.[28]

In therapy, Candy was striving to free herself from the tyranny of the male gaze. A breakthrough came when she confessed that she felt "inferior toward Dr. Galanter because he hasn't responded sexually to me!" Unpacking this psychoanalytic transference offered a stunning revelation: "I don't really want Dr Galanter's approval & affection, and sexuality, I want daddy's!" But to her father, the only thing that made women count also made them "tramps," a word whose very utterance during one therapy session made Candy cry "uncontrollably." She realized that the "feeling of being a tramp has been with me for a very long time and has affected many things I do." A couple days later, she picked up the women's liberation flyer at Lehman.[29]

This tense and solitary feminism carried Candy to the collective, and she was buoyed by what she found there. "The main purpose is to raise your consciousness as a woman & become aware of your capabilities—what you can do as a woman—without the aid of men!" she discovered. The women who gathered for meetings seemed like a "pretty good group," and she hoped she might soon be "making friends instead of conquests."[30]

Candy joined the women's movement not only at a heady time in her own coming of age but also at the moment "women's lib" went mainstream. The year 1970 was a tipping point. A CBS poll taken that summer revealed that some 80 percent of adults in the United States knew about women's liberation. They could hardly avoid it; magazines as diverse as *Esquire*, the *Saturday Review*, and *Newsweek* ran cover stories about "Women in Revolt."[31] Activists and theorists whose works had been available only in mimeograph released big books with mainstream publishers. Kate Millett, who took her doctorate from Columbia just as Candy joined the collective, published her dissertation, *Sexual Politics*, with Doubleday four months later. The book landed Millett on the cover of *Time* in August, right after the national Women's Strike for Equality, which marked the fiftieth anniversary of the passage of the Nineteenth Amendment declaring that the right to vote could not be abridged on account of sex.[32]

That fall, as Millett's literary analysis of the patriarchy climbed the bestseller lists, two other major books emerged from the hothouse of New York Radical Women: Shulamith Firestone published *The Dialectic of Sex* with William Morrow, and Random House launched *Sisterhood Is Powerful*, Robin Morgan's anthology of feminist essays, many of which had previously appeared in underground publications. The *Times* grouped these and other women's-rights titles under the headline "Adam Takes a Ribbing; It Hurts."[33] In the paper's *Book Review*, Marilyn Bender quipped, "Isn't it ironic that the book publishing industry which has always underpaid, underrated, and underemployed the second sex, should now be gallantly courting the women's liberation movement?"[34]

Candy was hungry for ideas for when she joined the collective. She also yearned for community and purpose in a life of rupture and drift. Just as she started attending meetings, Dr. Galanter told her he was leaving New York and would soon need to terminate their therapy, an abandonment Candy termed "traumatic." For all these reasons, she took to the group with the zeal of an acolyte.[35]

By the time Candy found the movement, a wide variety of thought and action sheltered under the capacious umbrella of feminism. Liberal standard bearers like the National Organization for Women, established in 1966, sought to level the existing playing field, and so concentrated their energies on sex-based discrimination in employment and law. More radical groups wanted to reinvent the game. They imagined a revolution in gender roles from the inside out and the bottom up. New organizations coalesced, grew, exploded, and reconstituted with a shocking rapidity. Vivian Gornick, a veteran of several such formations, joked in the *Village Voice* that "if five feminists fall out with six groups, within half an hour they'll all find each other (probably somewhere on Bleecker Street), within 48 hours a new splinter faction will have announced its existence, and within two weeks the manifesto is being mailed out."[36]

In addition to leafletting and litigating, feminists sought to make change by raising consciousness. Kathie Sarachild of New York Radical Women claimed to have coined the phrase. At the First National Women's Liberation Conference, near Chicago, in late 1968, she had urged women to "share our feelings and pool them." Those feelings would then "lead us to our theory, our theory to our action, our feelings about that action to new theory and then to new action."[37] Consciousness-raising, or C-R, challenged the distinction men on the New Left drew between therapy and politics. Therapy taught women to adjust to their rotten circumstances. "Women are messed over, not messed up!" NYRW's Carol Hanisch wrote. "We need to change the objective conditions, not adjust to them," she insisted. As women testified, and as their stories echoed and chimed, they came to know that their individual travails stemmed from structural inequalities—that "personal problems are political problems," as Hanisch put it.[38]

The Bronx Coalition's women's group engaged in C-R, but also in other actions and practices, many of them with a materialist spirit directed firmly at reforming society more than the self. A community organization, the coalition grew out of New Left campaigns to end the war in Vietnam and included members who emerged from radical student groups like SDS. Though racism was a central focus of the coalition, its membership was predominantly white. Yet the coalition ranged widely across lines of age, class, and gender, which was atypical in the muscular New Left.[39] The diverse group tackled a broad array of issues. Some were intensely local: "faulty subways and clogged expressways, worn-out buildings . . . filthy streets." Others were national (freeing the Black Panthers and reforming drug laws); international (ending the war, liberating the peoples of the third world); or even planetary (a global ecology project). The coalition's newsletter, *CrossBronx Express*, offered counsel on everything, from where to find birth control to how to resist the draft to the number to call to "Dial-a-Poem."[40]

Like many feminist groups, the Women's Liberation Collective was born in internal dissent, when female members of the coalition felt sidelined. Unusually, the coalition's men embraced the feminist critique. One male member describes the "reeducation program" that the Women's Collective devised as a "life-changing experience."[41] In addition to assigning a program of readings to inform (and reform) the awareness of its members, the Women's Liberation Collective faced outward, toward a wide range of community problems. Their politics were personal, but they were also structural, even practical. As an essay published in *CrossBronx Express* the month Candy joined explained, women's liberation meant

> bringing together all oppressed people in this society to fight for
> a different society where we can live together as equals. It's about

creating cooperative child-care for all our children, cooperative laundries, kitchens, stores, and play areas where we can share house-work and child-raising not only with each other, but with men too. . . . Together we are developing ideas about changing the ways we are forced to live, and together we are . . . launching the struggle to liberate ourselves by changing this society.[42]

Compared to collective's vision of root and branch liberation, mere sexual revolution was thin gruel. Nothing had "fundamentally changed for women sexually," argued an article in *CrossBronx Express* whose title punned "Freedom Is a Long Time Coming." "What used to be a 'wifely obligation' is now a 'revolutionary duty,'" the author wrote. "Nothing has changed because the relations people have with each other (their most intimate and vulnerable) are still power relations."[43]

As Candy worked through the collective's reading list—which included everything from advertisements and nursery rhymes that sexualized girls, to excerpts from sex manuals that peddled libertinage as liberation, to Black feminist writings that explored the intersections of racial and gender-based oppression—she came to share this view. "I may be liberalizing myself sexually, but I'm also becoming one of those women who do it as a duty," Candy wrote after Joe convinced her to try a "weird position" that he thought hilariously "perverted" but which Candy found demeaning. In fact, she realized, "We didn't fuck—he fucked me!!"[44] In her sketchbook, she drew her anger, quoting Bertrand Russell on marriage as slavery, and caricatured the slavish "all-American" woman, who holds a sign saying "We . . . support our wonderful (masters) husbands," and looks like the conservative activist Phyllis Schlafly.[45]

Candy remade her body according to her readings. The sexist underpinnings of the consumer culture in general, and of the beauty industry in particular, had been targets of feminist ire at least since *The Feminine Mystique*. In solidarity with her sisters in the collective, Candy found herself "working very hard on trying to recondition, or rather, take away all that conditioning I've had." Out went the false eyelashes and the conical bras and the teasing comb and the lipstick and the Replique. In came long, flowing skirts and loose cotton shifts and hair hanging lank to her waist. "I'm really getting away from that need to be *pretty*," she wrote, adding, "I've managed to keep my weight."[46]

Fat was the feminist issue that eluded Candy's dawning consciousness. She was horrified when a female therapist took over for her beloved Dr. Galanter. "I never could have worked with her," she wrote upon quitting after a couple of sessions. "She represented just about everything I would never want to be—Fat, dumpy, and self-conscious—plus being a woman!"[47] And Candy felt almost proud of attracting yet another of Cyn's boyfriends. "I didn't ask to be thinner than her, and I didn't ask for some guys to like me rather than her," she wrote in her diary.[48] Sisterhood rarely began at home.

If Candy's views on the members of her own sex were still evolving, she reported that her "women's lib beliefs" had quickly made her "skeptical & suspicious of men," especially the many who propositioned her. She tried turning the tables. In July, while Joe was out in San Francisco, she picked up a guy on the Upper West Side and had sex with him. Breaking the frame of the one-man woman came as a great relief. "I honestly don't feel guilty," she wrote. Warren was older, handsome, and educated—a med-school dropout—so his interest had been "quite an ego booster." It proved less of a boost in September, when Candy discovered her first case of gonorrhea. She thought Joe, who had sex with three other women while they were apart, seemed the likelier conduit than the ever-considerate Warren. But whichever man gave her the clap, she was the one who wound up in agony in the emergency room, another casualty of a limited revolution.[49]

Candy's political awakening broadened in the fall of 1970. She started at CCNY, which had just committed to a policy of open admissions to distribute the benefits of higher education as widely as possible. The students who entered City College under SEEK's auspices, as she had, were almost entirely Black and Puerto Rican. She felt, from the first, somewhat alien to the mainstream of student politics, which centered on the Black and Chicano freedom movements, and left her feeling like "an intruder."[50] She recommitted to her own struggle, growing more deeply involved with the collective. She lamented the "fucken chauvinists" she met everywhere. Even Joe had not fully shed his "male chauvinism." He tended to "get furious" when she talked about women's liberation. He grew jealous when Candy talked about other men but thought nothing of praising the "fine chicks" he saw at a party. Perhaps worst of all, he had read her diary. "He has no respect for me and my right to privacy," she wrote.[51]

By 1971, Candy was flirting with feminism's separatist strain.[52] "I'm finally seeing women as people & feeling really comfortable around them," she wrote that January, as she worked on the collective's health initiative, provisioning poor women with free pap smears. In March, the collective sponsored a women-only party for International Women's Day, which Candy pronounced "one of the best if not the best parties I've ever been too. It's incredible to think that at one time the idea of an all girl party was absurd . . . and only for girls who couldn't get guys." She and her sister-members got high, ate "health wheat germ cookies," watched films on the suffering of the Vietnamese people, and danced to Hebrew folk music." In April, Candy decided to "discontinue all relations with men—at least for a while. I realize what a drastic thing this is but I feel I need time to grow and build up my strength"— "strength to tell a guy I don't want to sleep with him or even go out with him!" She was sick of sympathy fucking, sick of shrinking herself to fit the miniskirt. Plus, Steve, a friend's boyfriend with whom she'd been hooking up, had offered her "a head start on . . . refraining from sex": another case of the clap.[53]

Celibacy proved better in theory. In May, Candy slept with the psychologist who led a two-day "sensitivity group" she attended. He told her she was so highly evolved that she could only be attracted to the leader of the group. Then came Ralph, who was "forceful & mechanical." She felt proud of these short-lived affairs, in which she maintained "the upper position." Yet her therapy and her newly raised consciousness taught her that her flickering hostility to men was political as well as personal. "I believe my father's actions had very great social significance," she wrote. "Sure he was perverted & disturbed & took his feelings & actions to a sick degree. But in essence he was saying I have a penis & a power over you." She couldn't help noticing how often men "take advantage of their strength."[54]

WHEN SHE FIRST JOINED, Candy had expressed relief that the collective was "not a 'castrate all men' type of thing full of lesbians," which countered the stereotypes she had heard about women's lib and assuaged the prejudices she brought to organized feminism.[55] In her youth, she had shared the attitudes of her parents, making casual references to "fairies" and "fags" if ever a man or a boy strayed even minutely from the narrow path of conventional gender norms. Her passionate and sometimes physically intimate relationships with girls had never required a label beyond friend.[56]

But at Field Place, the closet door cracked open. Joe Merlino, who lived in the neighborhood and hung out with the Vadala sisters a lot, was gay, or maybe bisexual—Candy meant to find out. She was a bit in love with him, maybe because Cyn was too. Her own Joe, Joe Kovacs, had an older cousin, John, who was gay and living in the Bay Area. A lesbian mom who lived in the building became a fixture in the talking and tripping circle in the Vadala sisters' apartment.[57] As Candy worked in her therapy on her disordered relationships with men, she experienced "dreams of a slightly lesbian nature," which led her to realize she sometimes used sex with men "as a defense."[58]

This awakening to the broader spectrum of sexual experience owed as much to the moment as to Candy's psyche. Gay liberation and second-wave feminism grew up in tandem, if not always in harmony. The "next two big movements are going to be the women and then homosexuals," predicted one New York publisher who was betting big on feminist books in 1970.[59] He was right, though the trajectory wound up more braided and less sequential than he imagined. The Stonewall uprising, in New York's Greenwich Village in June 1969, the same month Candy moved out of her parents' home, is often used to mark the genesis of the modern gay-rights movement, which actually began a good deal earlier, in California. But if Stonewall's singularity is overstated, those riots on Christopher Street catalyzed a new chapter of gay liberation.

Lesbian activists occupied an uneasy middle ground, hamstrung on one side by the patriarchy of gay liberation, and on the other by the implicitly heterosexual framework of the feminist mainstream. Even though several of its founders were lesbians, liberal organizations like NOW worried that the taint of homosexuality would harm the movement. In 1969, the year of Stonewall, Betty Friedan had decried the "lavender menace" as a threat to the feminist advance.[60] The following spring, as Candy joined the Bronx Women's Liberation Collective, lesbian activists mutinied at the Second Annual Congress to Unite Women, bursting into the auditorium sporting purple T-shirts reading "Lavender Menace."[61] Calling themselves Radicalesbians, the group distributed copies of a manifesto, "The Woman-Identified Woman," which pronounced lesbianism as much a political as a sexual orientation: less an erotic preference than the purest distillation of feminism.[62] As one movement leader put it, "Feminism is the theory; lesbianism is the practice."[63]

The language of Candy's diaries suggests that she read "The Woman Identified Woman," and other writings praising the moral integrity of political lesbianism.[64] But none of Candy's homework quite prepared her for Phyllis Rabine.

———

SHE STARTED HANGING OUT with Phyllis in the spring of 1971, when the term at CCNY ended, and right as she decided to use her full name, to mark the distance "between the Candy of Riverdale and the Candice of now." "I've been getting closer to my collective sisters," she wrote, after a bike ride with some of the Field Place crew and several collective members, including Phyllis and her husband, Larry. Phyllis had joined the collective later than the rest, after the others had already bonded as a group. But Candice hadn't grown especially close to any of the sisters, not individually, until "Phyllis came in and we found one another."[65]

Phyllis was only a little older than Candice, but already married and a mother. She lived near Field Place and spent her days in a baby-minding fog. "I could feel the spark in me drifting out," she recalls. Then she started reading: Friedan, Greer, Firestone. She felt the famous "click" of recognition. She found the collective, meeting weekly, in an empty storefront in the neighborhood. They read and talked about everything. They planned to change the world, from the inside out. "We did acid together, all kinds of things to look further into ourselves." Sisterhood was powerful. "Life-changing," Phyllis says. "The women's movement saved me." Her marriage unraveled, in that particular way that movement marriages sometimes did. "Change was the word of the day," Phyllis recalls. She began to realize she preferred women.[66]

Phyllis fell in love with Candice: with her warmth and strength, with her beauty, which radiated from "her whole self," not merely her face or body. Candice was "*magnetic*," Phyllis says. The friends grew closer than Candice planned, though less intimate than Phyllis hoped.[67]

Given the example her family had set, Candice wondered how she could "ever relate normally to men." Roseanne, a roommate and a collective sister, asked the obvious question: "why do we have to relate?" Why indeed? When she was honest with herself—and god knows, she always tried—Candice realized she was "most comfortable & happy with Women & happiest relating warmly to a group of people," even if she still found herself "looking at men like pieces of meat & prospective lovers."[68] Phyllis was "beautiful & strong," with a wild mane of black curls and, Candice wrote, "the very insatiable warmth only women had." Phyllis was also needy. Candice, she says, was her "saving grace."[69]

But Candice felt incapable of saving anyone but herself. And so, in June, she stuffed her things into a backpack and took off with Joe Kovacs for Europe. In Amsterdam, which Candice found "spoiled," not least by its "horrible red-light district with all of its sex shops," they met up with Joe Merlino. He carried letters from Cyn and Phyllis.[70] When they hitchhiked south, to Italy, Candice found herself staving off the advances of a rapacious truck driver, whose unwanted attention made her "understand why women are turning to women—Why I'm turning to women." She poured her emotions into a letter to Phyllis. Phyllis felt overwhelmed by Candice's letter, which she told her was "the most precious gift I've ever received. I keep it with me—on my body daily."[71]

While Phyllis was back in the Bronx, pressing Candice's letter to her body, Candice was in Marseille, pressing herself against Joe Merlino. "Wow—I guess he sure isn't homosexual," she wrote, though she also noted that he "went soft" as soon as he climbed on top of her. This she took as evidence of "what society has done to men." She wasn't sure she'd ever actually been "turned on to a man," so much as by the fantasy of being "an innocent girl . . . unwillingly seduced." She blamed her father. But still, the body wanted what it wanted.[72]

When she got home, Candice broke up with Joe Kovacs. "For 3 years one man was the center of my life," she wrote. Now she was on her own. Cyn had left, decamping to a macrobiotic commune near Ithaca.[73] Field Place was desolate. And Phyllis was ready, waiting.

"Love is a very, very inadequate word," she told Candice.[74]

"I don't think I'm that attracted to Phyllis physically," Candice noted in her diary.

Candice supposed that, if she "were to relate to women physically I would probably get into long, thin women. It probably has a lot to do with the desire to be long & thin myself—a vicarious fulfillment." She thought "bisexuality . . . a desired point" for her to reach. But she couldn't get there on demand, just because feminism said it was more evolved, just "because someone wants to be your lover."[75]

Phyllis had no such reluctance. "When I touch you and you respond it's like we've just spoken—communicated at the deepest level I know of," she wrote to Candice that fall. She hoped they would soon "stop living our lives on the borders." That they would "get out of this skeleton city." That they would not come "so close & throw away so much."[76]

The letter stayed sealed, tucked into Candice's diary, until an archivist slit it open decades later.

———

IN DECEMBER 1971, the Women's Liberation Collective of the Bronx Coalition, like many radical feminist cells, succumbed to a potent combination of the strenuousness of its philosophy and the laxity of its members.[77] Phyllis's soon-to-be-ex-husband was sleeping with two of the collective sisters and hitting on four more. That was conditioning for you, Candice wrote: "even being in Women's Liberation, they will assume an allegiance & a relationship with a man over their sister." And while much of what she had read and learned felt like a key to open locked doors, the collective's body politics had always felt like a corset. "I am a woman. I am Candice Vadala. I feel full of rushes; full of beauty," she wrote one night while tripping on mescaline. She loved the long shiny hair cascading down her back. She went back to "bright red nail polish," to dresses, to lipstick, the movement be damned.[78]

When the collective came apart, Candice forecast that her "last association with the serious political world and feminism" had ended. She was not surprised. "I knew it was going to," she wrote. "I knew that it was time to take a look at my honest feelings . . . about men regardless of theory & ideal." That was the problem of feminism, and perhaps of "all political movements": they were all theory and no practice, all mind and no body. "I actually want & need men & their approval," she confessed. "I actually have a lot of anger and dislike for women." She was sick of trying to transcend the male gaze. She was done with "strong willed, revolutionary, dungaree clad, scrubbed, t-shirted women," done with trying to make herself want to fuck them, much less to *be* them. She loved "thin, muscular bodies with grace, and I like decorating them and I like being aware of my body and looking at it and feeling it move smoothly and feeling the muscles firm and the skin soft and apricot."[79]

Feminists—the capital-F kind—had other priorities when it came to women's bodies. "Let it all hang out," urged Robin Morgan, one of the founders of New York Radical Women, which, like the collective, had imploded. Women must allow themselves to be "bitchy, catty, dykey, frustrated, crazy . . . , nutty, frigid, ridiculous, bitter, embarrassing, man-hating, libelous, pure, unfair, envious, intuitive, lowdown, stupid, petty, liberating"—in short, to be *"the women that men have warned us about."* Morgan urged her readers to say goodbye to the male Left. "Goodbye to the dream that being in the leadership collective will get you anything other than gonorrhea. . . . Goodbye to Hip Culture and the so-called Sexual Revolution, which has functioned toward women's freedom as did the Reconstruction toward former slaves—reinstituted oppression by another name." Goodbye, goodbye, *goodbye to all that*, as Morgan titled her germinal essay.[80]

Candice was just steadying herself to say hello.

9 The Golden West and the Golden Age

"The Journey," September 14, 1972.

San Francisco was the end of the line, the last frontier of the self, "America's most excited city," Jack Kerouac had written in 1957.[1] It was a site of "pilgrimage," as one underground paper put it a decade later: the magnet pulling tens of thousands of young people across the country to harvest a Summer of Love from a winter of discontent. A service called the Switchboard offered "'hippie' travelers" information about free pads and free meals, though they "could not give out information on free drugs over the phone."[2] By 1968, San Francisco had become the eye of the storm, the place "where the social hemorrhaging was showing up," as Joan Didion wrote. Haight-Ashbury teemed with teen runaways crowned with wilting flowers. Homeless trippers waked from drugged dreams, begging alms to underwrite their visions.[3]

San Francisco was also the whipping post of a rising conservatism focused on family, faith, and marriage: the place whose mores the movie star Ronald Reagan ran against in his successful bid to become California's governor. He was sworn in on January 2, 1967, less than two weeks before a Human Be-In at Golden Gate Park drew thousands of seekers and believers, would-be citizens of a "new nation . . . grown inside the robot flesh of the old," as the event's press release promised.[4] San Francisco was Eden and Sodom and Gethsemane, all rolled into one fat, sticky spliff, smoked naked among the boulders at Ocean Beach.

Candice was a New Yorker born and bred and till now, bound. In her youth, for all her talk of running, she had left the tri-state area only to visit her stepmother's mother in Florida; her plane flight there, in 1967, had felt impossibly exotic. Yet she had read about the hippies and had listened to the pop song urging members of "new generation" to head to San Francisco with flowers in their hair, and had hungered after California as early as 1969, when a friend of hers, a draft resister, moved to Berkeley.[5] She got there the following summer to meet up with Joe Kovacs, who was spending the school break in the Bay Area with his cousin. Joe sent her a postcard: "The beauty of nature and the beauty of love are true experiences no human being should miss." Candice boarded a 747—"terribly big"—to see for herself. She loved "the young hip people. . . . So friendly and warm," and thought the whole scene "much greater" than filthy, failing, falling-apart New York. She bought a ring from a shop called the House of Today. She took yoga classes and ate bean sprouts. She felt "much freer sexually"—joyously "uninhibited," like the rest of the town.[6]

San Francisco's liberties seemed wholesome, political, even spiritual—unlike the "decadent and disgusting type of fun" Candice found on offer in Las Vegas, where she and Joe stopped overnight on the long drive back east, and which she "immediately hated": "tits & asses all over the walls—showgirls, fucken chauvinists . . . such a nightmare!" But oh, California. "If I could I would run—away from 114 Field Place in the Bronx of awful New York City," she wrote, still dreaming, a year later, amidst the roaches and the crumbling plaster. "I would run very far away, perhaps out to sunny California. And I would leave all of you behind." She paraphrased Joni Mitchell, whose album *Blue* was playing in the background, wishing for "a river I could float away on." She stared out her grimy apartment window, imagining "the golden west."[7]

In January 1972, after the Women's Liberation Collective of the Bronx Coalition disbanded, Candice realized there was nothing tying her to New York. "I don't have a job, i'm not going to CCNY any longer next term, and I don't have anyone here to really keep me," she wrote. She may have flunked out of her fall classes; no transcript for that semester survives. She was twenty-one, with a year of design school and two years of remedial college courses—slender credentials for stable, white-collar employment. She didn't have a job or a home or family in the west, either, but she figured that "at least there's sun in California."[8]

Joe had already made the move. After graduating from Stony Brook, he had returned to San Francisco to work on a scheme with his cousin John: they would turn a derelict synagogue near the iconic Fillmore auditorium into a concert venue called the House of Good, a pun on its origins as a house of God. Joe and Candice were sort of back together; she could crash with him.[9] And she had some cash. Her grandmother Marion had died in 1970, leaving Candice and Cyn each a thousand dollars. When the estate cleared probate, Candice packed her bags.[10]

Four women crammed their clothes and their gear into a little red Toyota. The car belonged to Sherry Falek, two years older than Candice and a battle-hardened veteran of the Israeli Army, the SDS, and the collective, who remained "very militant": antiwar and anti-nonsense, dressed in boots and camouflage and ready for anything. Sherry found the other passengers. One woman lived across the hall from her; another was part of her feminist auto-repair class. And there was Candice, who showed up the morning they set off, wearing a floral-print dress and full makeup, "intellectually . . . a feminist, but in every other way a princess," Sherry recalls. Candice stood by the passenger-side door and waited for somebody to open it. She didn't know how to drive, which made her dead weight in a crew trying to cover a thousand miles a day.

They took a southern route. In North Carolina, nobody knew what to make of Candice's flowing costume and poppy-red lipstick. Locals asked Sherry if her friend might perhaps be a witch. In Tennessee, they stayed the night with friends of one of the other passengers, who served them brown rice and turned them on to some homegrown grass. They played guitar and talked politics late into the evening. Candice glimpsed "the beginning of the rest of my whole life—a different kind of life" opening before her. By the time they reached San Francisco, she sensed some hostile vibes in the car; the "negative feelings i've always had for women" had resurfaced. No doubt her fellow travelers agreed.[11]

Having visited only once before, Candice was a near stranger to San Francisco. But so was everyone else, or at least it felt that way. "Is she from here?" asks a character in Armistead Maupin's *Tales of the City*, a compilation of his wildly popular '70s columns in the *San Francisco Chronicle*. Comes the answer: "Nobody's *from* here."[12] You weren't from there until you were. And now she was.

The flowers had wilted by the time Candice arrived. In the years since the Summer of Love, the city's alternative scene had grown both more gay and more glamorous, as the Age of Aquarius yielded to what one chronicler calls the "Glitter Age." At the dance clubs, which would soon throb to the backbeat of disco, the chemical tang of poppers mixed with the earthier fug of pot and patchouli.[13] The old-timers Candice met—those who'd gone west all of three or four years before her—may have told her that had she missed the city's heyday. She knew she'd gotten there just in time.

YOU COULD DO or buy or see just about anything in the city's North Beach district, where sailors and soldiers and workers and traders and immigrants had mixed freely for more than a century. That wide-open reputation pulled the Beats there. They founded and haunted the City Lights Book Store, which in 1956 had published Allen Ginsberg's epic poem *Howl*—a Whitmanesque anthem to ass-fucking and peyote and the wharves. Just across the street from City Lights, Carol Doda danced topless at the Condor Club in 1964, fully two years before anybody risked it in New York.[14] Gay anti-discrimination protests began in San

"X-rated strip in North Beach, San Francisco, c1972."

Francisco the same year, half a decade before Stonewall. "There are, perhaps, 90,000 homosexuals in San Francisco," a municipal report estimated in 1971. "At anything close to that figure, they constitute a substantial proportion of the population, and an even larger percentage of potential voters." Faced with demands by homophile activists for full, unashamed gay citizenship, police began to ease off the arrests of consenting adults for having sex in quasi-public places.[15] The Sexual Freedom League staged public sex happenings, including naked swim-ins. Some of its members went into the adult film industry, pursuing profit as well as politics.[16]

At that point, the pornography industry remained relatively small. In its 1970 report, Lyndon Johnson's Commission on Obscenity and Pornography had estimated that fifty to one hundred film companies in the United States were producing sexual exploitation or "skin flicks," which aped but didn't actually show explicit sex. Their budgets rarely exceeded four figures, which meant that the "most expensive exploitation films cost far less than the lowest-budget general release films." Nationwide, fewer than three hundred theaters specialized in the sexploitation genre. Despite the reputation of coastal cities as the cutting edge of American licentiousness, Texas boasted the largest number of them, North Carolina the highest percentage, and the South, as a region, the greatest per capita concentration. The films yielded profits outsized to their costs, but their combined earnings remained small. The Adult Film Association of America, organized in 1969 as the first trade association for sex films, represented a sliver of the overall motion picture pie: less than $70 million of an estimated $1.1 billion in annual gross box office receipts, or about 6.4 percent of the total.

At the same time, mainstream Hollywood movies were growing steadily more explicit, especially after 1967, when the Swedish art films *I Am Curious, Yellow* (which Candice had seen with Joe) and *I Am Curious, Blue*, broke new standards for the showing of nudity. The commission discerned an overarching "trend toward highly sex-oriented motion pictures . . . across most of the industry," in R-rated as well as the limited number of X-rated general-release films (37 of them produced between 1968 and 1970) and sexploitation films (roughly 150 titles). What's more, borders separating these genres grew increasingly blurry. "No single element of theme or content serves to distinguish exploitation films from sexually oriented general release films," their report explained.[17]

The commission also noted the very recent arrival of what would come to be known as hardcore films: "an entirely new genre of sexually oriented motion picture," which "graphically depict actual sexual intercourse, an activity previously unknown to public theaters." In 1970, the national hardcore market had remained too tiny, or too well hidden, to measure.[18]

The City by the Bay was a pioneer in sex onscreen, as in so much else. In January 1971, a year before Candice got there, an article in the *New York Times Magazine* pronounced San Francisco "The Porn Capital of America." Some thirty adult movie houses showed nothing but hardcore. The North Beach district counted dozens of adult bookstores in addition to numerous topless dancing joints and several live sex shows. But what distinguished San Francisco was less the scope of its adult sector than its openness. Porn films were widely marketed, and many Bay Area hardcore theaters were "clean, comfortable, and staffed by attractive girls in miniskirts and polite well-groomed young men in business suits," William Murray explained in the *Times*. Arlene Elster, a former medical researcher, opened an erotic cinema on Sutter Street, in the central business district of Union Square. Her Sutter Cinema offered discounted tickets to couples and senior citizens, and gave out donuts and free coffee at every showing.[19]

Porn was not only respectable but also *political* in San Francisco in a way that was true nowhere else. A self-defined sexual liberationist, Arlene Elster cared about the depiction of female orgasm as well as about story and character.[20] She was the kind of activist, in other words, who might have understood Candice's devotion to pleasure as a core tenet of feminism.

San Francisco's hardcore scene also generated opposition, but efforts to harness the backlash generally proved fruitless. In 1970, Dianne Feinstein, an ambitious young member of the city's Board of Supervisors, explored amending the municipal code to outlaw the depiction of various forms of "aberrant sexual behavior," a proposal she thought would help her to court older white ethnic voters.

The gambit failed.[21] Lobbying for a statewide anti-obscenity initiative, Proposition 18, was heating up when Candice arrived in January 1972. But a poll taken in San Francisco that spring revealed that less than a quarter of respondents supported the proposed measure, and fewer than two percent said they considered pornography a pressing social problem. The ballot question went down to resounding defeat, much as a prior effort had done.[22] Most San Franciscans seemed to feel that the city's diverse and permissive sexual ecology strengthened the urban fabric, not least by drawing young people like Candice and her friends to remake their lives there.[23]

Residents' attitudes on other issues concerning sex and sexuality tracked their views on porn. A survey of local outlooks on "non-victim crime" discovered that over three-quarters of San Franciscans supported the decriminalization of prostitution and homosexuality. An astounding fifty-one percent agreed that "Homosexuals should be permitted to marry each other," an idea then so outlandish that the pollsters felt the need to explain: "That is, a man should be able to marry another man, and women should be able to marry each other."[24]

Sexual freedom and feminism seemed to nourish each other in San Francisco, and Candice may have imagined her newly adopted city as a place where she wouldn't have to choose between them. In many West Coast women's groups, the radical feminist commitment to consciousness-raising cross-pollinated with the counterculture's commitment to mind expansion, often with a chemical assist.[25] *Mushroom Effect: A Directory of Women's Liberation* (1970) listed more than two dozen feminist groups and women's centers in the Bay Area.[26] In addition to astrologers, tantric yoga studios, and gestalt therapists, *The People's Yellow Pages* (1972) offered pages of listings for drug-abuse treatment, birth-control clinics, and providers of abortion—legal, on a limited basis, since 1967, when the governor, Ronald Reagan, signed California's Therapeutic Abortion Act. Any woman overwhelmed by the sheer panoply of possibilities could turn to the Women's Freak-Out House—still "in the planning stages" when Candice got to town—which was to be "loosely based on R. D. Laing's theory that madness is therapeutic."[27]

SAN FRANCISCO MAY HAVE BEEN the Porn Capital of America in 1971. But the next year, the national discourse around pornography underwent a sudden shift. Gerard Damiano's *Deep Throat*, which opened in June 1972, changed the culture as well as the industry.

Deep Throat starred the freckle-faced young actress Linda Boreman, billed as Linda Lovelace.[28] Stitching together more than a dozen sex acts to sustain the barest outline of a plot over sixty-two minutes, *Deep Throat* departed only modestly from the grammar of the stag film, leavening classic pornographic tropes like the "wacky sex-mad doctor with a parody of the American fetish for the perfect orgasm," as one analyst wrote in 1977.[29] In a genre marked by low seriousness, *Deep Throat* dared to be self-mocking. The *Times* reported that "guffaws" often erupted during showings, a phenomenon "virtually unprecedented in porno movie houses."[30]

One way and another, the picture caught the national mood. *Variety* reported that its first day's receipts in Los Angeles, of roughly $7,000, had likely set a record "for sex houses."[31] (The film had cost roughly $22,000 to make; Lovelace was paid $1,200 for her performance, high by the standard of the day.) In New York, the long lines outside the New Mature World Theater, north of Times Square, "amazed even porno vets." Many credited a pre-release rave in *Screw*, the tabloid weekly Al Goldstein had begun publishing in 1968.[32]

Deep Throat quickly became one of the nation's highest grossing films, even though many newspapers refused to print its title. In July 1972, while the Democrats met to choose the candidate who would run against Richard Nixon that fall, *Deep Throat* was the second biggest box office draw in New York.[33] In September, the *Wall Street Journal* weighed in, offering "A Kind Word or Two about Smut," on libertarian grounds. "No one is forcing it upon those who don't like it," the columnist concluded. "So why can't we all just mind our own business?"[34] Come January, a jury in Binghamton, New York—no coastal elites—decided that the film did not lack redeeming social value, and thus failed to meet the key criterion for obscenity established in *Roth*.[35]

Deep Throat ignited a media as well as a box-office sensation. It was, as one writer noted in New York's *Daily News*, a "herd movie . . . the pace setters are running blindly to see it just so they won't feel left out at their next cocktail party."[36] Linda Lovelace appeared on *The Tonight Show*, joking with Johnny Carson and Ed McMahon, who professed himself a huge fan. In May 1973, she landed on the cover of *Esquire*, sporting a polka-dotted dress with a prim Peter Pan collar, and white gloves. Of course, that *Deep Throat* was legal and popular did not make it good. Six months after the film premiered, the *Times* film critic, Vincent Canby, finally weighed in; he deemed it "junk." Nonetheless, he reported, the film continued to attract remarkably "cheerful" mixed-sex audiences, with nary a raincoat in sight.[37]

It was this broader phenomenon that the *Times* labeled "Porno Chic" in a five-page Sunday magazine feature that nodded to Tom Wolfe's "Radical Chic," the pioneering New Journalism takedown of New York's liberal elite. Much like the Black Panthers whose wealthy supporters Wolfe had skewered two years earlier, *Deep Throat* had become "a premier topic of cocktail-party and dinner-table conversation in Manhattan drawing rooms, Long Island beach cottages and ski-country A-frames." Couples saw it on dates. Diplomats nipped across town from the UN, seeking a bona-fide taste of American culture. A sequel was in the works, as well as a tie-in "film book"; a record album was contemplated. In its first two years, *Deep Throat* would earn over $25 million, making it one of the most profitable movies in history. And that didn't count unreported cash receipts in Mafia-run adult theaters.[38]

Deep Throat and the ensuing wave of porno chic triggered a feminist gag reflex. Screenings drew sporadic protests from women's liberation groups in New York and on college campuses. Had Candice stayed in the Bronx, her collective might well have expressed disgust at its misogyny. Writing for the highbrow men's magazine *Esquire* in early 1973, Nora Ephron labeled the film "not just anti-female but anti-sexual as well." She had left the theater "muttering" about the "degrading" nature of the film. But she also worried about how her critique sounded. "I always cringe when I read reviews of this sort, crazy feminists carrying on, criticizing nonpolitical films in political terms." Ephron didn't want to come off like some "hung-up, uptight, middle-class, inhibited, possibly puritanical feminist who lost her sense of humor at a skin flick."[39] Indeed, most of those picketing *Deep Throat* belonged to church groups, which targeted the film not only for its explicitness but also for its endorsement of oral sodomy.[40] And those sorts of pickets only added to the frisson of naughtiness that drove the porno chic phenomenon.

The runaway success of *Deep Throat* made a new market for other feature-length hardcore movies. In San Francisco, Jim and Artie Mitchell, brothers who had cranked out hundreds of short, low-budget porn films to show in the theater they ran in the Tenderloin, created several months later a hit in the *Deep Throat* model, investing thousands to make millions. *Behind the Green Door* launched the porn career of Marilyn Chambers, a wholesome, girl-next-door blonde with a peaches-and-cream complexion whose face had appeared on boxes of Procter & Gamble's baby detergent, Ivory Snow. Like *Deep Throat*, it would enjoy a large theatrical audience nationwide.[41] Gerard Damiano's next major production, *The Devil in Miss Jones*, had not one scintilla more artistic value than its predecessor. But only nine months after the premier of *Deep Throat*, it debuted at the Lincoln Art Theater, across the street from Carnegie Hall and a world away from Times Square.[42]

GEORGE McGOVERN, the presidential candidate the Democrats selected shortly after *Deep Throat* premiered, proved to be no match for Richard Nixon, who began his second term in the White House the month the film's legality was affirmed. Nixon was both potty-mouthed and anti-porn. Rallies against the "growing menace of the smut peddler" had been key to his victories in the suburbs of Southern California and elsewhere.[43]

In October 1970, early in his first term, Nixon had denounced the report of his predecessor's Obscenity and Pornography Commission as soon as it landed on his desk, calling its conclusions "morally bankrupt." The Commission's recommendations notwithstanding, there would be "no relaxation" in his administration's crusade against explicit materials, for "if an attitude of permissiveness were to be adopted regarding pornography, this would contribute to an atmosphere condoning anarchy in every field." Nixon vowed not just to hold the line, but to reverse the tide. "Smut should not be simply contained at its present level; it should be outlawed in every state in the Union," he declared.[44]

Nixon, like many others in his party, had long decried the liberal leanings of the Supreme Court under Chief Justice Earl Warren, not least on the subject of pornography. When Warren announced his retirement in 1968, in the waning days of Lyndon Johnson's presidency, conservatives successfully torpedoed LBJ's nomination of Associate Justice Abe Fortas, because they considered Fortas soft on smut, which was both damning and true. Soon after taking office, Nixon began to remake the court, first with the selection of Warren Burger as chief justice, and then with the elevation of three conservative associate justices, including William Rehnquist, over the next two years.[45]

In the fall of 1972, at the peak of porno chic, the Burger court heard arguments on a suite of obscenity cases, five in all. Each offered the potential to revise an aspect of the standard set by *Roth* and to refine the right to view pornographic materials privately, in the home, that the justices had affirmed in *Stanley v. Georgia* (1969). Rulings in the cases were handed down in June 1973, all decided by a one-vote majority. Each narrowed the aperture for films like *Deep Throat*. The opinion in *Miller v. California*, the most significant of the five, established that the standards of a given state or locality, not those of some imaginary "national community," must prevail when obscenity was alleged. Topeka was not San Francisco. A fig leaf of merit would no longer suffice; a work could be judged obscene if, "taken as a whole," it was found, by ordinary people, to lack "serious literary, artistic, political, or scientific value." That the consumers of the material were consenting adults did not constitute sufficient defense, one of the allied cases established. Moreover, the zone of privacy established in *Stanley* did not extend beyond the home.[46]

In June 1972, the month *Deep Throat* premiered, a small group of political operatives working for Nixon's reelection campaign had broken into the offices of the Democratic National Committee in the Watergate Complex in Washington. The following summer, as the Burger court handed down its obscenity decisions, televised hearings on the Watergate break-ins and the ensuing cover-up convulsed the nation. *Washington Post* reporters had broken the story that would end Nixon's presidency.

Their cloak-and-dagger informant called himself Deep Throat.

———

CANDICE NEVER MENTIONED *Deep Throat* in her diaries. Though they passed the theaters where it played, her friends don't recall her seeing the movie; it was far too mainstream to interest those who favored the radical underground theater of the Haight over such blatant commercialism.[47] But whether or not she watched the film and its porno chic cousins, Candice came of age in the world that made *Deep Throat*, and that *Deep Throat* remade in turn. The movie's breakout success—and the possibilities and perils its success betokened—would set the table for her own life and work.

All that lay in the future. For now, Candice cared only that she had at long last arrived at the still point of the turning world, the best and only place to find herself, or help herself, or just to Be.

10 Becoming

Candice, June 1973.

"**J**eff asked me when I started being a people. Wow." Day three in San Francisco, and Candice could already feel herself growing, which meant "just being me . . . being a person which radiates me in such a real way. . . . Being a person & sharing that person with people." She was trembling, cracking, "shaking up that whole frame of reference that was with me for so many years." Losing Marion. Left by Helen and Louis. Leaving Cyn behind. Stepping away from her "game" of slinking and seducing and sometimes even "using women's liberation consciousness in certain ways," to get with guys, even when she wasn't sure she wanted them.[1] Giving up on Joe Kovacs, who had always wanted to be "all man," and now had another lady, too, and what was Candice supposed to feel when she heard them making love in the next room? Opening herself to Joe Merlino, a self-styled "freak with high-heeled old shoes and fitted kids' sweaters," sexually ambiguous and still back in New York. Maybe she loved him, even if he didn't want her, not exactly. Wasn't the spiritual plane the only reality anyway? Because "trying to be sexy and desirable takes away from my ability to be a person," and a person was the thing to be, and being was the job to have, the only real job there was. It was all so painful and exquisite, like labor pangs, she said. Like "giving birth to myself."[2]

Just being lay at the core of the hippie ethos that still suffused the Haight-Ashbury neighborhood when Candice pulled up in Sherry Falek's Toyota. *Being* offered an antidote to an American dream poisoned by Madison Avenue admen. Jobs, politics, society, even family had come to seem as bankrupt as the East Coast cities. Only the self—plumbed, freed, shared—could redeem the fallen world. "The point is to examine, examine, examine. Feel, feel, feel!" urged Tuli Kupferberg, poet-priest of the counterculture, in a 1969 paean to "catastrophic leisure."[3]

Examining and feeling, remaking and elevating comprised the authentic, necessary work of being. The nine-to-five, "consumer-conveyor-sit-in-a-slot-boom-boom-boom" was as dead as the gray flannel suit. Being remade time itself. "It's like sentences don't have so many periods," one hippie informant told a sociologist probing the differences between counterculture and "straight" ethics in 1972. "It's like getting more dashes and colons and commas and involutions."[4]

In her diaries, Candice traded periods for dashes and judgment for acceptance. She drew a matrix of aspirations and values, crossing out "GOOD" and "BAD" and circling "BE." She took up the hippie sense of style, rejecting the treadmill of fashion in favor of old velvets and lace and cameos that washed up in thrift shops on Haight Street. She cut her hair in a campy Prince Valiant style that seemed to hearken to an earlier century. In one photo, she sports a broad-brimmed hat with ribbon ties, the straw chipped and crumbling, the kind of thing her grandmother might have made for a long-ago Easter parade.[5]

Candice found a room in a house on Belvedere Street, a three-story Victorian down on its heels, painted a deep red, the trim picked out in white. Its bay windows faced west, and she loved the afternoon sun and the "red and moody" evenings, when she wrote and drew by candlelight. A couple blocks up the hill from Haight Street, the house sat far enough away to dampen the traffic noise but close enough that you could smell weed and turmeric if the breeze caught right. The hippie influx had whitened what was once a largely Black community. Travel agents touted the flower power of the neighborhood Hunter S. Thompson had called "Hashbury." Sherry Falek recalls the Japanese tour bus that rumbled down Belvedere Street every day. Sometimes she and Candice posed for photos.[6] The city was startlingly green when Candice got there, with eucalyptus in leaf and jasmine and magnolias in bud. Open space abounded. The panhandle—the eastern extension of Golden Gate Park—lay several blocks north. To the east, Buena Vista Park loomed, flat where it fronted Haight Street and then a wild tangle as the hill rose, secluded enough to serve as a popular gay cruising spot.[7]

Rented out cheaply, piece by piece, 144 Belvedere Street was part commune, part rooming house. Candice found herself surrounded by a revolving cast of "fine, mature, advanced people" embarked on similar journeys. The "Belveweird Freakos," they called themselves.[8] Don, "27, gay," had "done a lot of learning & experiencing." Peggy, another "fine mellow person," also in her late twenties, had a partner doing time in San Quentin, to whom she smuggled acid when she could. Renee was closer to Candice's age, but more cosmopolitan, having traveled the Americas. Jeff, in his mid-twenties, was into his body, and sometimes into Candice's. Bill Brown, who went by "Colias," had lived there before, and left. When he returned, Candice moved out of his room and into the living room. Don split for Morocco; Sherry took his room. Dan, who had been there before Candice, came back for a while, and then rambled up the coast to Seattle, his "home place." Eighteen-year-old Johny, whose "old man" in San Quentin knew Peggy's old man, showed up with her four-month-old son and a big, white sheepdog, which joined a wobbly puppy Peggy had found on the street. Johny needed "a lot of company and validation," Candice said. Then Don came back, which set Johny hunting for a new place for her and the dog and the baby. All between January and April.[9]

Candice staged her room like a set for her own dawning. She painted the walls mauve and covered her dresser with gold-fringed burgundy velvet, which went with threadbare drapes in a dusty rose satin. She hung a Star of David and a mirror and used an old oil lamp that Don left behind. Her bed was a mattress on the floor. She told a friend the place was "more beautiful" than other run-down Victorians around the city: "not just a typical hippie flat with indian prints and mattresses & incense."[10] She sketched the window bay, with an upright piano, a pair of salvaged Oriental rugs, and a cluster of floor pillows and beanbag chairs surrounding a "KLH stereo!"[11]

While the living room was lovely, Candice complained that the kitchen was often left a mess. Sherry recalls that Candice rarely washed a dish.[12]

———

BACK IN NEW YORK, Candice had used drugs, starting, like every other teenager, with secret swigs of her parents' booze, and then, after high school, layering in weed and then hash and then opium-laced cigarettes, all within a few months' time. A little speed now and then, maybe, and the occasional flight on mescaline or mushrooms. Things

"What Can She Do to Free Her Soul?" c1972–73

had gotten heavy at Field Place during the summer of 1969, "a summer of total confusion and disorder," when her parents left and she dropped out of Parsons. She had turned on almost daily then, "never . . . anything really hard," but everything too often.[13] But even as she wrote about those dissolute months, Candice had pulled back, plowing her energies into the collective and into school and especially into therapy.

On Belvedere Street, Candice traded psychotherapy for psychedelics, one kind of mind mapping for another. The shrink she left behind in New York had seen it coming. "California is not a substitute for therapy," Margo Machida warned in a six-page typed summary of their work together shortly before her patient left New York. "The only advantage of California is that it is 3,000 miles away from home. If you do decide to stay there, then it is really necessary for you to get into therapy—you really need it because you still carry your parents around in your head."[14] This was something of an understatement.

Candice had at least one phone session with Dr. Machida right after she got there, talking through her dreams. But there were so many other roads pointing toward wisdom that finding a credentialed counselor didn't feel urgent. She tried a class that blended tantric yoga with energy work. She brought her existential questions to a woman named Pineapple, who sought answers in a deck of tarot cards. She reread her journals, "hundreds of times in desperation," using her past diary-keeping as a form of auto-therapy. She searched within: "I am my teacher. I learn from myself," she wrote.[15]

Candice was tripping often now, sometimes every day. San Francisco was advanced that way. "No offense, but New York is about two years behind," Ken Kesey, acid prophet and arch prankster, had told Tom Wolfe in the late '60s.[16] LSD had been legal, studied by government and university psychology labs, when Kesey and his Merry Pranksters started the happenings that took the drug to a broader recreational public. Some of his "acid tests" were enormous affairs. The Trips Festival, in January 1966, brought 2,400 dancers and dreamers to the Fillmore auditorium, on Geary Street, where the Grateful Dead played, and a bathtub filled with acid-laced punch sat in the middle of the dance floor.[17] A couple months later, *Life* ran a cover story on "The Mind Drug that Got Out of Control," depicting emergency rooms overflowing with "panic-stricken young people" on bad trips. Fears about the drug's dangers spread. The state of California acted that fall, making the possession of LSD a misdemeanor and its sale a felony. President Richard Nixon called Timothy Leary, the defrocked Harvard psychology professor who had told the nation's youth to turn on, tune in, and drop out, "the most dangerous man in America." In the Controlled Substances Act of 1970, Congress classified LSD as a schedule one drug, placing it in the same category as heroin.[18]

And yet, when Candice got to San Francisco in early 1972, LSD and its psychedelic cousins, mescaline and MDMA, remained no harder to get than groceries—and in the Haight maybe easier, because food cost money. "We never had to buy our own drugs, ever," Sherry says. What they didn't grow they were given, "for the pleasure of our company" on the journey. She remembers a cocktail of other substances that modulated the Belveweirds' near-daily trips: uppers to power you back to reality, homegrown dope, from the little backyard, to mellow you out. They fried it up in the morning, in that kitchen that Candice never cleaned.[19] There were harder drugs by then too. Speed flowed into the neighborhood, and crime came with it. There was angel dust around—PCP, a powerful chemical hallucinogen— and they all did it, and it sometimes got "pretty heavy," says Jorgé Socarras, who moved in with the Belveweirds in late 1972 or early 1973. Addicted vets limping home from Vietnam brought their heroin habits with them, and supply followed demand. Candice may have dabbled as early as 1972; a drawing she made that summer shows a poppy oozing out of a roll of aluminum foil.[20]

Candice thought her psychedelic trips—on acid, mushrooms, peyote, and mescaline—heightened the natural beauty of her new city. She tripped on the beach and danced in the tides. She saw "tangerine dawns and purple sunsets and marshmallow mornings"; she felt herself "made into mirrors." She drew her visions in precise pen and ink washed with watercolor, or sometimes in smudged pastels. Skin melts. Flowers dance. Borders liquefy. The walls of the Belvedere house dissolve as the windows shimmer, floating free.[21] But she did not seem to experience the ego dissolution touted by many proponents of psychedelic experience. What Candice once called her "high consciousness" remained Technicolor self-consciousness. She lettered a mantra, surrounded by hearts and vines: "put the I in place of the eye and then you will begin to know."[22]

As Candice tripped more, she wrote less. "now I think in images," she said that first San Francisco June, inking a pointillist, pixilated nude beneath her words. Sometimes, not even images came, and all she could say was "wow." Or writing was too neat, too straightforward, and "what I have to say is too complex" for a lined page. Or she felt despondent—maybe suicidal—and "writing doesn't even help . . . when I really want to yell & scream." In November 1972, she decided that she was "in a new depression." Not writing was like not talking had been, back at Mrs. Hennessy's, when she was four. "Here I am in silence again. It's the only way I know to let someone know i'm freaking out." In a letter that month, Cyn addressed her sister as "Candle Flame Vadala," burning at both ends.[23]

Everything in San Francisco was frenetic, disorienting, "a wild scene," Joe Kovacs remembers. Some of the self-styled freaks in Candice's set—young women and men with stronger families, or less damage, or richer connections to the world beyond themselves—gave up on the experiment. The drug scene grew too intense for Sherry, who began to look for a way home. Joe's parents flew out from the Bronx and urged him to walk away from a life that "wasn't something to make your folks proud." Sometime late that year, he packed up a van and headed east. Sherry drove with him, back to the straight world. Joe went to law school. Sherry went into nursing.[24]

Toward the end of that first year, Candice dialed back the constant tripping and joined a Transactional Analysis group. A stripped down and scaled up version of psychotherapy, "TA" promised fast transformation through interpersonal confrontation. Leary had been an early proponent, but it was Thomas Harris's *I'm OK, You're OK* (1969) that turned the practice into a phenomenon, especially in California, where groups sprang up in prisons, hospitals, and community centers. Harris's book was issued as a mass-market paperback in 1972, and Candice and Cyn both read it. Like psychoanalysis, and indeed like LSD, TA promised a scouring of the self, though with a stronger element of forward momentum and much less depth work, more coach than couch.[25]

For Candice, TA seemed grounding. In January 1973, she assured a worried sister from the collective days that her "highs now come from marijuana, dancing, drawing till early in the morning, live sensational music, and being with lots of new people." Some of her letters had concerned the friends and family she had left behind. "I'm not understood," she wrote in her diary. "People from my past are becoming just that—part of my past." They had let her down, and she figured she should let them go.[26]

That was the best face. But it was a mask. In a sketchbook, she drew herself melting into a plot of earth, just hair and lips and one hand still visible above ground. She labeled it, "the goddess who is trying not to drown."[27]

———

CANDICE WAS DROWNING in sex as well as drugs. As the counterculture entered the " 'Me' Decade," sex was becoming "a religion," a "theology" that rendered orgasm "a form of spiritual ecstasy," Tom Wolfe quipped.[28] Sex promised deep, authentic knowledge of self and Other. It was the throbbing core of the human condition. The Belveweirds, like many others in San Francisco, believed, passionately, urgently, that you could fuck your way to freedom.[29] They called it "relating."

At first, Candice found herself "relating very intensely" to her housemates Don and Jeff, and "non-relating to joe k," who was busy relating to Renee.[30] She also related to Joe Merlino, "both his mind and body." On his first visit to Belvedere Street, before he moved west for good, Joe told her he'd always wanted the two of them to "make love." They hadn't, though; Candice supposed it was because they were "both going through changes about where our sexual identity lies."[31] But whether Joe loved boys or girls hardly mattered. "We didn't really ask if someone was gay or straight," Candice's friend Jorgé says. "We just went for it." On any given night, twenty people might be living and relating, in pairs or trios, in an apartment with only two or three names on the lease.[32]

In March, Candice "related to Randy"—a near stranger—twice. She was trying to "actually just follow my honest desires," which proved hard to locate. "the fact that I feel led into it without my own choice is what allows for all the negativism," she supposed. She resolved not to "make love to someone when I don't feel like it," and hoped that would keep her "from feeling controlled & used and might lead to discovering how I truly feel about sexuality." But the principle was easier to write than to uphold. In April, she related to Dan, another of her erstwhile housemates. He couldn't bring her to orgasm, but nobody else could either. Relating often seemed to involve more performance or even politics than it did pleasure, which, for Candice, lay in a darker place. What most excited her was to play-act being "unwillingly forced" into sex. She worried a lot about these rape fantasies, which she connected to the double bind her father had woven around her: tramp if she wanted it, prude if she didn't. It was hard to choose neither—hard, in fact, freely to choose at all.[33]

Randy and Dan couldn't make Candice come, but one of them made her pregnant, a high price to pay for what she called "a Romeo in a fantasy that lasted one week." The IUD she'd had implanted in late 1970—"No more pills!"—had failed her.[34] She ended the pregnancy quickly and legally, one of a growing number of American women to choose that option in the growing number of states that permitted it. The CDC's Abortion Surveillance Report for the year Candice had her procedure documented that the number of licit abortions had increased twenty-five-fold between 1969 and 1972, when nearly 600,000 terminations were performed in the twenty-seven states from which the Center collected data. Roughly a quarter of those occurred in California alone. Nationwide, the abortion ratio—measuring terminations to live births—approached twenty percent. In California, it was more than double that, though the statistic is somewhat misleading, since many women came there from out of state to end pregnancies.[35]

Candice just headed down the street, to Golden Gate Community Hospital. She went by herself, which made her realize "the severity of how alone I am. There was no one going through it with me. Not even the father": Randy, she thought. It's not clear that she told him, or even that she could have found him had she wanted to. She called the procedure her "first abortion," as if assuming others would follow. (They did.) Nonetheless, both the pregnancy and its end unnerved her. "I was pregnant. I had the beginnings of a human being growing in my uterus—my body," she wrote in her diary, her vague new naturalism mingling with what remained of her Catholic girlhood. On the back of her discharge instructions, she drew herself naked, eviscerated, beside a ghostly fetus in a half shell, like the Virgin. She captioned it: "i can't bring another life in when my own waivers on the border of extinction." She was twenty-one, an age by which many American women were married and expecting. But she knew she wasn't ready. "i'd probably fuck it up so badly. I'd want it for 'my own'—for my security; for my play pal; to make up for how I was neglected," she wrote. She felt depressed for a while after the procedure and began, for the first time, to "think about actual ways I could kill myself."[36] She was careful not to perseverate, lest she make those fleeting ideations concrete.

"I Can't Bring Another Life In . . ." April 1972.

Come summer, Candice was relating again, to a tall handsome man who went by James Neon. He was "into S&M and bondage," which she hoped might turn her tortured fantasies of submission into a sexy costume drama, but she still couldn't climax, "except by myself of course." With James, she found herself back in her "little girl role," a persona she had perfected in junior high and then abandoned. That felt fun, until it felt lousy. She worried that she was still making men the "super figures" in her life. And the wrong men, at that: so many of the beautiful creatures who surrounded her in San Francisco were sexually fluid or gay. She lived with gay men, and danced with gay men at clubs like the Stud, on Thirteenth and Folsom, in the Leather District, where she and her friends dressed up in '50s drag and did the Lindy or the jitterbug till they cleared the floor. "I like gay men because they're safe," she decided. Their lack of interest in her wasn't personal, and her desires for them weren't sexual, and so didn't make her a tramp, though she felt left out when the men she was dancing with headed into the night together.[37] Living in a house dominated by gay men sometimes made her "feel like I must either be a lesbian or one of the boys." She was pretty sure she was neither, though she was willing to "give everyone and everything a chance."[38]

Phyllis Rabine flew out from New York in November, and spending time with a deep and true friend made Candice realize that months of tumbling in and out of bed had left her fundamentally alone. In a culture that was supposed to be so radically open, she had "become so closed—to expressing myself—to loving," even "to needing sexual enjoyment." Just a month past her twenty-second birthday, she felt like "a dried [up] prune."[39] Phyllis and her daughter moved into the house on Belvedere Street. "It was a very exciting time, of letting loose for everybody," Phyllis recalls. "Music was always blasting," but the soundtrack of Candice's life had changed. Field Place had strummed gently to Carole King's *Tapestry*. Belvedere Street was wilder, louder, electrified. Unable to "take that scene" for more than a month or so, Phyllis brought her daughter back to the Bronx.[40]

After Phyllis left, Candice finally related to a woman, a new housemate named Jane. "I guess I've always wanted to," she wrote, which would have been bitter news to poor, pining Phyllis. "It was very exciting. . . . It shouldn't matter what sex your partner is as long as you derive & bring pleasure to one another." Candice hoped the experience with Jane had "freed" her from the "preconditioned stimuli" that had primed her to "only get off on one sex." When in fact she couldn't get off with a partner of any gender. "I have an incredible time trying to reach orgasm. I just can't flow with it," she wrote.[41] Relating, premised on the politics of pleasure, sounds like awfully hard work.

Candice decided that "experimenting" was her best hope for discovering the authentic desire that she understood as a political as well as a personal project. She spent a couple nights with "an Okie who's an artist & musician"; she started "to get it on with a black dude";

she experienced her "first Orgy." She swore off bi and gay men as lovers, and wished she had close women friends nearby, for the kind of intense, non-sexual relating she'd found in the Bronx Collective. Her TA group proved a poor substitute. The "head bitch" told Candice she had "distorted thoughts," while the others made her feel as if everything she said was wrong. She kept at it, though, peppering her diary with potted TA affirmations: "I am an absolute gift of nature." "I am a star." "I am all the things I ever wanted to be. . . . I love me—I am OK and everyone else is also OK."[42]

Candice rang out the night she turned twenty-three, in October 1973, by bringing home a "very pretty blond" she met at a party—a "birthday prince" who slipped away before she woke the next morning. The winsome birthday prince turned out to be the musician Patrick Cowley, who would come to play a significant role in her artistic life. More fleeting relationships followed. At a party that "turned into a nudie crowd & a wonderful orgy," she "made it" with two men "and had orgasms with both of them!" A breakthrough. That week, she slept with a different guy "every single night," men she "liked & chose to be with."[43]

In December, she "finally got it on" with Danny Isley, a bass player she knew through friends. He was rangy and wild, a rock-'n'-roller, with haunting, wide-spaced blue eyes. Danny slept with everyone; he often had "a little thing" going on with gay guys who wanted him more than he wanted them. Candice got a kick out of him, but she thought he was "neurotic" and "undependable," both of which would prove correct. But not for a while. Right after their first night together, he landed in jail, "for the tacky job of ripping off an old lady's purse" to support his heroin habit. And so that, for then, was that.[44]

"Oh well. My search goes on," Candice wrote, after nearly two years in the Belveweird house. San Francisco—"freakland U.S.A.," as she fondly called it—was at once fertile and rocky ground for a straight woman hell-bent on mastering the relating game. Too often, Candice found herself with a cold, empty bed. "Where is my prince anyway goddamit!" asked the freelover who had not yet given up on fairy tales.[45]

She sounds so lonely and so sad, finding little solace in joyless sex and a relentlessly examined life. Still, she believed she'd made progress. She had become bolder, less fearful, and more selective. "I've only been with men I've wanted to be with," she wrote in late 1973. While she was with the men she chose—whether for a couple hours, a night, or a week—she allowed herself to "truly love them." She felt "so un-neurotic—so liberated."[46]

Candice had proclaimed herself part of the sexual revolution in 1969, on that snowy night on the way back from Joe's dorm at Stony Brook, when she discovered that women, too, could attempt guiltless one-night stands. Four years, five therapists, three thousand miles, two encounter groups, and countless mostly orgasmless fucks later, she had landed more or less where she began.

11 Making Art and Getting By

Candida Royalle (center, in polka dots) in Rickets: A Day in the Life of the Counter Culture, *1974. Left of her are Joe Morocco, Janice Sukaitus, Scrumbly, and Theresa McGinley. Lailani stands front right.*

I t seemed like everyone Candice met in the Haight was an artist of one kind or another. Jorgé Socarras, a New Yorker by birth, had trained at the School of Visual Arts as a painter. Joe Merlino, who finally moved in with Candice and the Belveweirds in late 1972, had gone to SVA too. He rechristened himself Joe Morocco, a nickname he'd picked up for peddling hash smuggled back from his North African travels. His stylized dress sometimes included a djellaba. Richard Koldewyn came to San Francisco to study piano and transformed himself into Scrumbly, one of the founding members of the Cockettes, an acid drag troupe that set out to deconstruct the norms of both theatre and gender in anarchic performances that spiraled to the edge of chaos. Scrumbly was classically trained, but you didn't really need an instrument or a script or a canvas or toe shoes or even a sketchpad to fancy yourself an artist in '70s San Francisco. The house on Belvedere Street was itself a kind of art project: a stage set for a performative life. Dress was Art. Sex was Art. The self was Art. Jorgé recalls Candice's "sense of theatricality about her femininity," not just on stage but every day, as she kitted up to go thrifting in the neighborhood, or dancing at the Stud.[1]

Like her father, Candice knew that she was, at the core of her being, an artist. But what kind? She excelled at illustration, and she had planned to return to art school when she got to San Francisco.[2] That first fall, she enrolled in a painting class at the Art Institute in Russian Hill and felt numb to it. But then she worked up a book of acid-fueled drawings that "freaks people out for its beauty." In early 1973, maybe at the Art Institute, she met the venerable film animator Jules Engel, one of the team who had drawn Disney's *Fantasia*. He looked at her book and offered to nominate her for a scholarship to his division at CalArts, in Southern California. "I'm too advanced for any more art training other than technical," Candice wrote in her diary.

But with Engel's nod, she began to picture herself as an animator, her "drawings moving and talking and dancing and living" as she paged through her sketchbook. She vowed to cast off old patterns of self-sabotage and failure. "I'm going to stop the Vadala sickness right now. I'm going to be a successful artist," she wrote.[3] It wouldn't be easy, as her father soon warned her: "In dealing with art, in any form, you are in a small, really unknown world."[4]

Sometime over the winter, she drafted an application essay describing her influences and ambitions. An artistic lineage beginning with her grandmother Marion, a self-taught pianist, and continuing through Louis, a "non-conforming jazz musician," and Helen, a sometime singer, made Candice a third-generation bohemian. "Hippiedom" and women's liberation had helped her discover an artistic "consciousness" devoid of "glamour and material desire." As an animator, she aspired to engage "every part of the film: the drawings, music, sounds, script," and camera work. There is no indication that the application went further than the pages of her diary.[5]

Instead, Candice discovered her voice. She worked up a repertoire of a dozen or so songs, ranging from top-forty pop (the Carpenters' "Close to You") to Broadway musical numbers ("Where Is Love," from *Oliver*; and "Sixteen Going on Seventeen," from *The Sound of Music*) to jazz standards ("The Shadow of Your Smile") to TV ditties (the theme song from *The Mickey Mouse Club*, sung breathlessly, like Marilyn Monroe's "Happy Birthday"). She taught herself to compose at the old upright in the living room. "I sat down and with both hands played my soul," she wrote. "It was like having my first orgasm." The first song she wrote, "The Little Tomato," a bluesy acapella number in the Peggy Lee style, would become her signature. Rhyming "flavor," "waiter," and "tomato," the San Francisco ditty retained a decided Bronx accent.[6]

Over the summer, Candice and Joe Morocco cobbled together a short set combining the "Little Tomato" and an old Louis Prima number, "Banana Split for My Baby." She made their costumes and choreographed a tap routine. They performed their numbers in a happening organized by the Angels of Light collective, a Cockettes splinter troupe that one member described as "a fusion of Gilbert

& Sullivan, Philadelphia's Mummer's Parade, the Cirque du Soleil, and Bertolt Brecht."[7] The Angels, most of them gay men who lived together in a commune on Oak Street, practiced a kind of ironic Maoism, at once winking—always in quotes, as Susan Sontag said of the camp aesthetic—and strenuous. They wrote their shows collectively and allowed no individual credits, least of all to female members, who labored behind the scenes. The performance at which Candice and Joe's debut took place, the *Kitsch-On* show, held at the University of California's extension campus in the Haight, had a food theme. Candice dressed as a tomato, sporting a cap of green felt leaves. For "Banana Split," Joe wore a yellow bikini and brown body and face paint: blackface whitewashed as chocolate syrup.[8]

Candice felt herself blossoming as a performer. "Dance, draw, sing, write songs & poetry, play an instrument—I am just so gifted—so special," she wrote in the argot of TA, in August 1973, around the time of the Angels show. A musical career felt increasingly within reach;

Candice as a tomato, Angels of Light's Kitsch-On *show, 1973.*

shortly after Christmas, she found a piano teacher.[9] With friends and lovers she formed short-lived groups that often petered out as organically as they had coalesced. Like the European music scene, Scrumbly says, or the constantly shifting constellation of Andy Warhol's Factory, according to Jorgé.[10] Candice and Patrick Cowley, the "birthday prince" who would become a disco and electronic music pioneer, experimented with synthesizers.[11] She and her friend Laurie Ann Detgen, an abused teenager from the Midwest who had run away to San Francisco, attracted appreciative stares when they busked on the streets; the two of them were rehearsing to open for the rock trio Rick & Ruby at a gig in Anchorage.[12]

With Patrick's housemates Janice Sukaitis, who wrote for the Angels of Light, Theresa McGinley, a college friend of Patrick's and yet another transplanted New Yorker, and several other women, Candice and Laurie Ann formed an all-female song and theatre troupe, White Trash Boom Boom. They were "a group of wayward feminists who've been performing their own brand of outrage," devoted to laying bare "the dilemmas of women on various spiritual and economic levels," as one flyer put it.[13] Janice, the group's leader and lyricist, remembers White Trash Boom Boom as a rejoinder to the misogyny of the Angels. Like that group, White Trash Boom Boom mixed high comedy and social criticism. In two musical skits, the first set in Little Italy and the second in the American West, the Boom Boom girls lampooned sexual inequality. Candice painted the sets for the Little Italy show, performed atop the bar at the Stud. The plot, Janice says, centered on "the double standards of female morality . . . the virgin vs. the whore." Candice's character, Anna, was the virgin, awaiting her wedding night. She modeled her dress and mannerisms on the beach movie songstress and former Mouseketeer Annette Funicello.

White Trash Boom Boom staged the western skit several times around San Francisco and at the state women's prison near Pomona. Audiotapes of some of their rehearsals recently surfaced in a Bay Area attic, having miraculously survived the chaos of their moment and the passage of decades. Patrick's synthesizer apes a fiddle and guitar, over which the Boom Boom girls warble in multipart harmonies, sometimes struggling to find their pitches in mock-tragic songs like "A Beer and a Pizza," in which a battered wife implores her abusive husband to stay.[14]

Candice also joined the Gospel Pearls, a group whose ironic relationship to Black praise music mirrored the ways the Boom Boom girls channeled Tammy Wynette. Its leader, Bobby Kent, had started as a Pentecostal singer in Redwood City before he got himself to San Francisco and turned glitter gay.[15] Kent impressed Candice, and he seems to have been taken with her; the Pearls featured her on "I'll Fly Away." "And I really do it up," she wrote. A photograph of the group shows nine singers, hands clasped, playing it straight in prim black choir robes, while Candice, the tenth, opens hers with a lewd wink to reveal a strapless sequined bodysuit.[16]

Scrumbly assembled a group he called Old Jazz, featuring Candice, Joe Morocco, and Candice's busking buddy, Laurie Ann, who had started going by the name Lailani. Scrumbly told Candice she sounded like the great Keely Smith, who had headlined with her husband, Louis Prima, in the '50s, when Louis Vadala played with Prima's band. She felt enormously flattered by the comparison. Old Jazz played private gigs, at restaurants and parties. Candice also joined another Scrumbly project that Christmas: a group of sixteen carolers who sang wry sendups of seasonal music as the "Humbug Cantata." The Cantata riffed on what Scrumbly calls the "love/hate relationship people have with Christmas," especially in a place like 1970s San Francisco, where so many queer artists had fled their natal families to form communities of choice and resistance. He arranged the music and Janice wrote the lyrics. On Christmas Eve, they sang their anti-carols at what Candice called "the hottest, most important house" in the Haight, the commune where Cockettes stars John Rothermel and Keith Blanton, who performed as Pristine Condition, lived with the fashion designer who costumed the group. Candice had been nervous, but the Cantata's numbers "knocked em dead," all those fabulous "music & show people!" They ended the night at the Stud, where they sang three of their "hot jazzy numbers" standing atop the bar.[17]

New Year's Eve topped even that. The Gospel Pearls played Bimbo's, a North Beach club featuring mostly gay acts, just up the road from City Lights bookstore. The gig, with its $10 cover charge, was to be the "gala event of San Francisco underground freak town," Candice said. Rothermel and Sylvester, a Cockette who had launched a gender-bending solo career as a disco star, were the main attraction; the Pearls sang between sets. The group was "truly excellent," outshining the headliners, the *Bay Area Reporter* gushed. When the Pearls took the stage, "the dance floor was so crowded all you could do was jump up and down in place," like some "tribal dance from 'King Solomon's Mines'" on acid.[18]

At four in the morning on the first day of 1974, after the last revelers stumbled home from Bimbo's, Candice filled the final page of the diary she had kept, in fits and starts, over three tumultuous years. She started the entry with a drawing of a shooting star, and described a fairy-tale night spent "glittering in the spotlight." She foresaw "many many smiles in the year ahead—and perhaps a little heart throb too." She wished herself "lust, love, laughter . . . and a bit of fame & spotlight to go along please." And then she signed off, using the new pseudonym she'd practiced nine times in several variations around the perimeter of the back flyleaf of that journal: "*xx Miss Candida Royalle.*"[19]

———

THE BIG QUESTION WAS how to make art pay. Except for party gigs like the ones Old Jazz did at Christmas, nobody made much money. The Angels were as committed to free theatre as they were to vegetarianism. The other groups were less dogmatic but scarcely more lucrative. Helen Vadala, who had done so very little to help her stepdaughters find their footing, worried about how Candice—her "Flower child of Love," her "Nature girl"—was eking out.[20]

But when it came to scraping by, San Francisco in the early 1970s had every advantage, even as the United States slid into the deepest financial downturn since the Depression. As one city booster famously put it, "The worst San Francisco can get is still better than any place else."[21] Violent crime was lower than in New York by an order of magnitude.[22] Housing remained abundant, much of it rent-controlled. In the fall of 1973, Joe Morocco moved out of Belvedere Street to seed a new group house near the Castro. They called the place the Ranch.

Jorgé moved to a studio.[23] Candice thought she might strike out on her own too. She scanned the listings for studios and one-bedrooms and jotted down a dozen or so to check out. The most expensive of them, in the middle-class neighborhood of Pacific Heights, went for $105 a month, less than $600 in today's money. Plenty of places asked half that or less. Dolores DeLuce, who was part of White Trash Boom Boom, paid less than $40 for a room in a big group house at Haight and Clayton.[24]

Which still left the question of earning enough to float even a modest lease. Unemployment rates were rising. Yet that meant relatively little to people like Candice and her friends, who retained the love generation's beliefs about work. Nobody she knew wanted an identity rooted in profession. "We never ask each other 'what do you *do*? In the sense of 'how do you make money?'" said one hip author.[25] From the flatlands of the Haight, you couldn't even see the city's business district, a couple miles to the east, where the straights in suits beavered away at their nine-to-fives. The hip made a fetish of craft and other soulful, independent ways of getting by. The goal was to work just often enough to live just well enough. In Haight-Ashbury, a neighborhood job co-op served as a clearinghouse for positions that might last hours or days, maybe a week or two.[26]

Candice associated the workaday world with "the ugliness and grayness" of New York, packed with "people busting their asses in crummy jobs for crummy little holes . . . in big cement buildings." In San Francisco, labor could take a backseat to life. She worked a variety of short-term posts to make rent. She served as a live model for the students in a figure-drawing class. She wore a lion costume to hand out flyers for a language school. She sold windowpane acid, which can't have been very profitable, given the glut sluicing through the neighborhood. She staffed a boutique on Polk Street, and then worked as a "girl Friday" for Lonely Ladies T-shirts. She looked for jobs where she could use her illustration talents, but nothing panned out. She thought her dance training probably qualified her to teach for Arthur Murray, but the hours were "so damned long" and the steps so dull that she didn't try.[27]

Her friends likewise cycled through low-commitment, low-pay jobs. Sherry recalls a position answering phones in the rectory of St.

Mary's, for which she had to run up a respectable outfit on her sewing machine, and to which she regularly showed up tripping. When she looks back at the schemes and contortions they went through to pull in just enough to get by, she wonders, "why didn't we all just *work*?" But the ethos of the counterculture early '70s, as Scrumbly points out, was to "take what comes" and make do. The tribe's existence at the margins of the cash economy at least had happy side effect of cushioning them against the runaway inflation of the late Nixon and Ford years.[28]

Performance was the realm where Candice and Scrumbly and their other artist friends invested their deep, authentic selves. The alternative theatre and music scene was arguably more vibrant in San Francisco than anywhere else in the United States. And Candice's visibility in that scene was growing. She had the goods to become a serious, professional performer, Scrumbly says: a strong voice with an amazing range, precise intonation, a lot of control, and a keen ear for harmony. You could hear her deep appreciation for the jazz and the American popular song traditions with which she'd grown up. *Miss Candida Royalle* had stage presence and humor too. "Go professional" figured as one of the "most important goals & loves" Candice listed for herself in the spring of 1974.

By then her calendar was chock-a-block with rehearsals, five days a week for six weeks, maybe more.[29] Scrumbly and Janice had cast her in an original musical, to be put on by a troupe called Warped Floors, which featured a number of former Cockettes, along with transplanted New Yorkers from the Belvedere house and other communes. Janice wrote the show's lyrics with the Cockettes' Martin Worman. Scrumbly created the music. *Rickets: A Day in the Life of the Counter Culture*, is set in an upscale department store, and dramatizes the agony of service jobs and the human price of corporate greed. Janice says the inspiration came from a newspaper article about a saleswoman who'd been let go, without a pension, after forty years of working in the same store.[30]

Unlike the Cockettes and the Angels, whose anarcho-drag productions were all but unrehearsed, *Rickets* was a structured show, with a book and songs and sets. Its harmonies are intricate and layered, the lyrics barbed and brainy, as if Tom Lehrer updated *The Pirates of Penzance*, stirring in Ella Fitzgerald and a microdose of LSD. Joe

Morocco, Jorgé, Janice, Pristine Condition, Lailani, and Theresa were also part of the ensemble—"the cream of the scene!" Candice said. She played Keely Over, a character whose name honored the jazz singer Keely Smith. With Rimsky Maladroit (Scrumbly), an uptight home entertainment system salesman, Keely sings "Whatdya Do for Laughs?" a flirty duet where he goes high and she digs deep, scatting and singing the praises of "playin' with the low-down folk."[31]

Rickets played for three nights that July, at the Village Theater in North Beach, a storefront playhouse near Bimbo's. Tickets cost $2.49 in advance and $3 at the door, barely enough to cover the space rental. But the show proved popular, and a reprise run opened in the fall, at the Montgomery Playhouse, a larger venue with a higher ticket price. The alternative press picked up the second run. The *San Francisco Phoenix* called the show "bright fun with plenty of clever musical show-stoppers." A photo of Candida as Keely Over illustrated the review.[32] The *Bay Area Reporter*, a gay tabloid, seemed baffled. "They were looking for drag queens," Janice quips. But if the *Reporter*'s critic panned *Rickets* as a "torpid testimonial to untalented trivia," he singled out Candida Royalle for showing "glimmerings of genuine talent."[33]

Candida had been noticed, then. But Candice remained uncertain about her own desires. Doing the play, putting everything into it for a season, left her wondering whether she'd rather be a "serious actress," or maybe "just a gypsy freak."[34]

———

IT WASN'T EASY to make a living as an actress, much less as a gypsy freak. But many San Francisco artists found support under the auspices of the Social Security Administration's Supplemental Security Income program called Aid to the Permanently and Totally Disabled, or ATD. After years of resistance from small-government conservatives, California had begun dispensing ATD in 1957. In the 1960s, the state's welfare system expanded, part of a strong public commitment to keeping the poor and disabled off the streets and out of institutions.[35]

Leaders of the counterculture encouraged fellow travelers to game the system. In *Steal This Book*—still hard to find on the shelves of a library—Abbie Hoffman proclaimed that it was so "easy to get on welfare that anyone who is broke and doesn't have a regular relief check coming in is nothing but a goddamn lazy bum!" He encouraged readers to "head on down to the Welfare Department in your grubbiest clothes," with "your heaviest story ready to ooze out. If you have no physical disabilities, lay down a 'mentally deranged' rap. . . . Keep bobbing your head, yawning, or scratching."[36] The *San Francisco Survival Manual* offered less cheeky guidance on local, state, and federal welfare programs, explaining that the S.S.I. defined "disability" as being unable "to perform gainful employment for a continuous period of at least 12 months." As the *Survival Manual* pointed out, that definition did not mean that a person approved for ATD was "actually incompetent." The underground filmmaker John Waters later called ATD "a grant . . . from the government, to continue your insane lifestyle in San Francisco."[37]

Most of Candice's friends either went on ATD or knew others who had. "Everybody did it," Theresa McGinley says. Scrumbly estimates that half of the people in the underground performance scene got welfare checks.[38] Don from the Belvedere house was on ATD when Candice got there. Cyn, who was planning someday to head west, meant to "apply for the thing Don gets" as soon as she got to town.[39]

Candice first sought assistance in late 1973, around when she started singing with the Gospel Pearls, Old Jazz, and the other groups. A nurse issued a diagnosis of "Depressive Neurosis," explaining that Candice experienced "periods of depression and inability to complete tasks that had been started."[40] (Her diaries bear this out.) At her benefits interview, Candice played up her "more quiet childlike self," a version of the little-girl act she sometimes used with men. She worried about what it meant to go on record as mentally disabled. But she wanted out of the Belveweird scene. Jorgé recalls that she was teased mercilessly by Joe Morocco and the others, as her sensibility edged toward sincerity and away from the corrosive irony of the house's "group ego."[41] "I've had it with camp," Candice wrote. "I'm ready for a bit of seriousness & real work & real lovers and warm girlfriends." If ATD would get her into an apartment of her own, she was willing to take the risk. In December, she received notice that her petition had been granted, with benefits of $181 each month, including allowances for housing, utilities, medical transportation, and "other basic needs." Food stamps and a California state allotment brought the total to $235, which made an apartment renting for $70 or even $80 a month affordable.[42]

Candice left Belvedere Street in January and couch surfed for a couple of months. In April, as *Rickets* began rehearsing, she moved into her own place, in a small brick apartment building at the corner of Vallejo and Laguna, on the northern edge of Pacific Heights. The new place felt "like having a gigantic piece of art to play with." And the neighborhood was filled with "young successful people—straight people" in both senses of the word. She liked walking down tree-lined streets, past neat, candy-colored houses, and feeling she'd come full circle, to a sparkling West Coast version of Riverdale. "I'm white and middle class bordering on the fringes of the upper half of the middle class by my desires for beauty and taste," she wrote that spring. She felt a little guilty about the government subsidy, and the "bit of illegal manipulation" she'd used to get it. She continued to imagine herself and her theatre friends dragged "in their tattered frivolous sequined garb" to a "work camp," all too easy to picture at a moment when battles over welfare had begun to dominate the political news.[43]

Mostly, though, she was exhilarated to be on her own, in what she called "the first glorious year of my rebirth living a healthy, rational life." She wanted love, but not marriage or children. She knew her life was "rather untraditional," yet thought she was also "somewhat representative of a new brand of woman in 20th-century western society."[44]

About this, she was surely right.

The day before Candice found her new place on Vallejo, she noted an appointment in her datebook: see "Bob about movie."[45] It may have been her first.

———

SOMEWHERE BETWEEN being and relating, among the bullshit jobs and subsidized impairments, opportunities to trade sex for money blinked on and off, like the rosy nipples on the neon sign at the Condor

Club in North Beach. By the end of the decade, some Bay Area activists would begin to use the umbrella term *sex work* to describe and dignify their embodied employment, as just one among many forms of physical labor for pay. " 'Sex work' has no shame, and neither do I," wrote Carol Leigh, aka Scarlot Harlot, who coined the phrase.[46] In some ways, sex work was *better* work than much of what was out there. Barriers to entry were low. There was more cash in it, and less hypocrisy. As Candice would later say, "you know what you are being paid for."[47] Many of her friends did a bit of it here and there.

By the time Candice moved west, sex work had begun to emerge from the shadows in San Francisco. The city's Committee on Crime advocated decriminalizing prostitution as early as 1971. Trying to wedge the blunt instrument of the law into what was "essentially a business transaction between a willing buyer and a willing seller" had proved as expensive as it was futile. While emphasizing that open solicitation should continue to be illegal, the committee recommended that "discreet, private, off-the-street prostitution should cease to be criminal."[48] The sex-worker rights organization COYOTE—an acronym for Call Off Your Old Tired Ethics—sought not just a blind eye but a public face for the trade. "Hookers of the World, Unite!" the *Chronicle* headlined an article about the new organization in May 1973. COYOTE's annual Hooker's Ball became a hot ticket among Bay Area celebrities and demimondaines. Candice attended for the first time in 1975.[49]

As enforcement eased, nude encounter parlors opened in North Beach and the Tenderloin. Customers could sit naked in a booth and talk to a man or woman who was also naked. Either party, or both, might masturbate, but no touching was allowed. The *Berkeley Barb* thought this was a rip-off, and ran an exposé in which Vicki, one of the booth girls (probably from Kitten's, a couple blocks from City Lights) expressed pity for the patrons. "You'd be surprised how hard it is to get men to open up," she said. Still, it was good pay for easy work. Vicki pulled in two or three hundred dollars in a decent week, which her fiancé appreciated.[50] Jorgé recalls that the nude encounter scene seemed like a fair way to make money; he, Lailani, and Candice each worked an occasional shift. The gig was "well suited to our theatrical natures," he says, noting that creative people have active libidos.[51]

Candice also did some exotic dancing, another brand of light sex work for which her years at the barre and her love of music suited her. In her diary, she cast her willingness to apply for one such job as a sign of the self-reliance she was gaining through TA. "I have the nerve to go to a night club that specializes in beautiful women. that wants to attract customers with beautiful, sexy women who dance beautifully—I have the nerve, the confidence to go there & say 'I am all those things.'" She got the job, "dancing semi-nude." She must have told her stepmother about it, because Helen wrote with questions: "What I didn't understand were your hours, and it sounded like you got paid more for dancing in the day time than at nite. Do they have entertainment like that in the daytime?"[52] Indeed they did.

Right before she left Belvedere Street, Candice went on some dates for pay. Five years earlier, she had quit a job when pressured by her boss to have sex in exchange for money. Now it felt different, maybe because she had become less inhibited, and was less economically resourceful, or maybe because sex *was* the job, and not a side hustle. In her diary, she cast the work as evidence of her own magnetism. She supposed such interactions represented a kind of liberty, in that she was "free to choose whether I actually want to use someone, a man, men, to my advantage, financially, materially, egotistically, sexually." Yet it felt cold to "take a man for a ride," and she hated "making love to someone that doesn't fill my soul with magic." That had been the problem with Gary, a thirty-four-year-old with whom she had some kind of contractual arrangement. He showered her with gifts and squired her around in his Austin-Healey. She loved going out "to eat filet mignon and snort cocaine and being told how great I am," though she didn't much care for "burnt out middle aged" drug dealers, and so cut it off after four evenings.[53]

Green-card marriages were like pay dates that pretended to last forever. Shortly after she left Belvedere Street, Candice flew to New York to embark on what she called "an illegal/legal? immigration marriage" with a Polish elevator operator named Tadeusz "Stanley" Puchacz, who lived in Queens. They tied the knot in February 1974, and Stanley's payment got her back to San Francisco and helped with the rent for her new apartment. That spring, she petitioned the INS to naturalize her long-distance husband.[54] Soon the marriage was under investigation; Cinthea—who had lately changed the spelling of her name on the recommendation of a numerologist—stood in for Candice at one interview. Candice flew back to Manhattan to appear with Stanley in November, making every attempt to look like her sister—which, as Stanley wrote, would not be "difficult to do." The proceeding went badly. He wanted to restart the process out in San Francisco, but Candice declined, and dissolved the marriage in Reno. By January 1975, she was, on paper, a divorcée.[55]

Candice also took a variety of nude modeling jobs. Some took place in an art school; she complained about long sessions in uncomfortable poses where she let her mind drift.[56] In other instances, she served as a photographer's model for skin magazines. She joked that she'd made "the big time in Tackyness culture" when her picture appeared in *Candid*, a small-circulation men's magazine out of Canoga Park, near Los Angeles. She was cast as a masseuse who "LOVES BIG TIPS!" She thought the photo spread was "great" and was proud her article had gotten "top billing!" The images must have been semiclothed; she sent a copy to her parents. "My first reaction was good for you & your liberation," Helen responded. "But I did not show it to Dad—I do not think he is as broad minded as you think." She warned her stepdaughter not to "let yourself go too far or become too involved" in that kind of work.[57]

Janice Sukaitis remembers being "shocked" when Candice made the "porno" turn.[58] But in fact it was more of a bend. Shooting hardcore was different, but not all that different, from dancing topless or posing for skin mags or going on dates for pay. The Belveweirds, the Cockettes and their spin-offs, the counterculture, the bathhouses: all preached a radical openness about sex, including communal sex and sex in public spaces. Their lives were in many ways porn-adjacent. Patrick Cowley, a fixture in the gay male bathhouse scene south of Market Street, wrote music for porn films as well as for alternative theatre.[59] Theresa, Sherry, and Scrumbly all had friends—male and female, gay and straight—who shot a little porn now and then: just another temp job for young people short on cash and inhibition. Porn "didn't seem out of bounds to any of us," Sherry says. She remembers a man asking her to appear in a film in 1972. She declined, but not out of any "judgment about it." Scrumbly gave it a whirl; he spent a couple hours filming in a motel on Market Street, where a housemate who was acting in a film dragged him along as an extra. "It was a disaster," he chuckles. But porn was nonetheless a "very welcoming profession," and its claims to map a frontier in personal and legal freedoms resonated with a lot of hippies and allied souls.[60]

Filmed pornography came looking for Candice well before she debuted her Candida Royalle persona. In the summer of 1972, the summer of *Deep Throat*, James Neon, a man she was relating to, said he was directing a "pornographic movie," and asked her to star. There's no evidence, however, that the film was ever made.[61] There seems to have been another movie project in late 1973: an underground production to feature Pristine Condition and several other Cockettes, as well as Candice and Lailani. "Cinthea says you are a movie star!" Helen wrote the following summer.[62] But though *Vector*, a San Francisco "homophile" monthly, ran a page of (clothed) stills from the "satire . . . currently in the final phases of casting," no trace of the film has survived. Janice and Scrumbly recall that it was never completed, if in fact it was begun.[63]

The "movie" Candice noted in her datebook in March 1974 was probably a loop—a ten- or twelve-minute recording of a single sex act, largely plotless, and typically silent.[64] Shot with a fixed camera, on one spool (400 feet) of 8mm or 16mm film, loops were fused end-to-end, to run continuously, most often in arcades. These short, transactional films are grainy and poorly lit, the scenes unframed, the plots unformed: pilot meets horny flight attendant, doctor cures horny nurse, handyman repairs horny customer, Santa gifts horny helper. Costumes are minimal; Candice's often consist of little more than a garter belt or knee socks. In one early loop, "Game of Lust," she has oral sex and intercourse with a paunchy, balding middle-aged man while a woman wearing a sequined beret masturbates. The camera zooms in so close that their buttocks look like rotting cantaloupes. Candice looks scarred, pale, and desperately bored. Some eight minutes in, the male player ejaculates: the conventional ending of every pornographic narrative. Such climaxes were difficult to achieve on demand, and so were often faked. This one almost certainly was. Candice ends the loop with a bright-white dollop of what looks like Elmer's glue pooling on her lower lip. "Autumn in New York" plays in the background.[65]

Royalle later called loops "the bottom rung" of the porn hierarchy. But the little films were amazingly profitable, costing as little as $15 to produce, with the potential to earn thousands each week, as the quarters pumped into peepshow machines piled up. The live models who served up their bodies to the viewer—"they are not dignified in the trade with the term 'actors,'" the *Washington Post* sniffed in 1971—earned $50 or $100 per film.[66]

Which was, after all, still a solid month's rent.

Candice made at least seven loops in 1975. One day that August, she shot two in the morning and still finished in time to meet her sister, who had recently moved to town, for lunch. That was also the month she acted in her first feature-length film, Jerry Abrams's *The Analyst*.[67] She plays Anita Gartley, a housewife whose brutal husband, Preston, pushes her to shed her "hang-ups," chiefly about anal sex. "Love, honor, and obey, dammit!" he shouts. The movie at once critiques and celebrates this cardboard caveman; Anita, not Preston, must be reformed. Psychotherapy liberates her lust. The male doctor— "Don't let the PhD scare you"—penetrates her anally while Preston watches and takes instruction. "You see sexuality and human relations are definitely a two-way street," the therapist tells Preston: the fig leaf of "redeeming social importance" the Supreme Court required.[68]

Candice filmed *The Analyst* in two days. She remembered it as her single worst experience in the industry. Her description, some years later in a letter to a friend, sounds almost dissociated: staring at the "tacky paisley furniture and fun fur rugs," "counting the minutes while sucking hard so I can get my money and run."[69]

One film led inexorably to the next. She landed a small role in *Femmes de Sade*, in a scene filmed at the Bay Area Bondage Club. Directed by Alex de Renzy, whom the *Times* had called the "Jean-Luc Godard of the *nouvelle vague* in porn," the film promised to break new ground for the range of kink on display. "For the serious enthusiast," ads warned.[70] Candice was unnamed and uncredited, appearing in what she called "a bizarre pornographic party scene." Though she was barely more than an extra, the part involved grueling, physical work: multiple sex acts filmed over two consecutive nights of shooting till dawn.

"It feels sooo good to be home," she scribbled on a piece of loose paper before crawling into bed after the second marathon shoot. She'd gone into the project "in my usual curious and unpresuming manner" and had had "some very interesting moments & experiences" along the way. But she found herself, during the final hours, just "wishing it were all over. Pornography is not my thing," she concluded. "Amen. It's been good for a few hundred."[71] She put down her pen and fell asleep, certain a brief chapter of her life had closed.

PART III

Shooting Star

The star that doubts flickers & goes out.
—Candice Vadala, 1977

12 Heartbreak

Candice and Danny Isley, c1975.

He turned up again, as such men do. It was August 1974, the day after Nixon resigned. They saw each other across a crowded room, at a party thrown by the Angels of Light. Danny smoldered. Candice trembled. They clung to each other, couldn't be parted for days.[1]

So much had happened since their night together the previous December, which felt like the start of something, until Danny's arrest for petty theft scotched it. Candice had found her voice and begun using it onstage. She had scraped some money together: a monthly ATD check, the payment from her green-card marriage. She had settled into the apartment on Vallejo Street, hanging an old army parachute, dyed red, over her bed to set the mood.[2] The neighborhood was made for some other kind of woman: a housewife, a "Polk Street baby," a female drone, Candice said. She felt out of place when she walked down Union Street in her '50s fashions, "all lit up in bright red," Betty Boop in a sea of beige Twiggies. She loved the view, with Mount Tamalpais in the distance, but found Pacific Heights a tough place for "an artist . . . an individual . . . a freak . . . a loner."[3]

While she relished her status as an artist and even a freak, Candice had grown oh so weary of being a loner. She was tired of "being a fag hag," tired of "dishing." Tired of feeling so frequently, systematically overlooked: her father's perverse sexual neglect all over again. And she was tired of the shallows, the cheap one-nighters, when a date soured into a mere "trick," whose only lasting trace was a "case of the crabs." She had grown bored with merely "having sex" and become eager to " 'fall in love,' " even if the idea of falling in love, in San Francisco in the mid-1970s, sounded so corny that it took scare quotes. Candice made bad choices in men, and she knew it. "I'm looking for a romeo . . . and romeo's are always played by actors," she wrote. She wanted something deep, with someone real.[4]

And then there was Danny, as free as Candice and nearly as beautiful. Their night together, followed by his lockup, took on a storybook quality. For months she conjured the memory of his touch.[5] Danny towered over her, draped himself around her, longing and languid. His gaze had the intensity of Jagger iced by the eeriness of Bowie. The year after they got together the second time, he was cast as the naïve heartthrob in a big-budget hardcore film, *Cry for Cindy*. He plays a tender, graceful lover with a dancer's body. To watch him, now long dead, is to glimpse some of what Candice saw in every inch of him.[6]

They cut a striking figure. A photo of the couple graced the cover of the *Bay Guardian* in late 1975, to illustrate the "Discomania" craze sweeping the city of the Grateful Dead. Danny wears velvet trimmed in fur, his jacket open nearly to the waist, tinsel twined around his neck like a boa. Candice sports a sequined bodysuit with flowing sleeves, her face painted with the tree of life. The song of the season was Donna Summer singing—groaning, grinding—"Love to Love You, Baby."[7] And they did.

Danny was sweet and hungry and more than a little hapless. He was fragile, broken in places Candice seemed whole, out of sync where she was balanced. Danny was needy. And oh, how Candice loved to be needed.[8]

Danny was also clever. He knew very well that the straight women of the avant-garde saw straight men—even more-or-less straight men—as almost magical creatures. In a world of painted queens and plaid-shirted machos, he would be Candice's dark knight, her satanic majesty, as the Rolling Stones put it. He sensed what Candice called her "great need of love and affection," and he satisfied it, just fully enough and just often enough to keep her hanging on.[9]

Danny Isley knew a good thing when he saw one. The month after their reunion, he moved his stuff into Candice's little apartment.[10]

———

DANNY WANTED CANDICE, lusted after her, unambiguously, which came as an enormous relief, after so many "faggots" and "closet case[s]," men who wanted to want her more than they actually did.[11] At the beginning, the sex was passionate, urgent. Janice Sukaitis remembers Danny and Candice coupling, at least once, in Scrumbly's rehearsal space, more or less in the open.[12] With Danny, Candice explored the kink she'd been hankering for too. "I never knew if I'd ever really find a guy who would get into my sado-masochistic fantasies & help me live them out. But it's happened. I couldn't ask for more," she wrote in September. Finally, an honest-to-god "boyfriend" after so many fleeting flings. Danny had a romantic streak; he sold his bracelet, the only valuable thing he owned, to buy presents for Candice's twenty-fourth birthday. They made music together, his electric bass beneath her sultry alto. It was a "strong and complex love affair," almost a "'marriage,'" she wrote after they had spent a few months together.[13]

Though theirs was a "heavy interpersonal relationship," and Danny could be possessive, they weren't exclusive, or at least he wasn't. By October, Candice had gonorrhea again. She half wanted to freak Danny out by sleeping with someone else, but the clap meant she couldn't. Candice sensed that Danny wanted her to be "his woman," to play the "lovesick wife 24 hours a day." But he also knew he was a "hot number," and he liked to flirt in front of her, and to fuck strangers when he felt like it. It agonized her, when she could muster the emotional energy to be jealous.[14]

———

CANDICE LOOKED AFTER DANNY, paying his rent and collecting his welfare checks. "He was her baby," Jorgé Socarras remembers.[15] Yet by some sleight of hand, Danny made it appear as if *he* was the one taking care of *her*. In a letter written during their first months together, he called her "Conceita Spoilall," the haughty killjoy cramping his fun. He doled out his love sparingly or lavishly, as the situation required. "Well one never knows when the ax might fall," he teased.[16] That was November 1974. Candice had gone to New York, to playact her pretend marriage for the INS. Danny missed her, and hoped she was coming back, not least because her landlord had balked at accepting his ATD voucher for the rent. All his letters are like that: *I love you, passionately, probably. And could you please, just this once, cough up some bread?* Read in hindsight, the push-me pull-you of Danny's affection feels planned, a program of catch and release and catch again. By year-end, Candice realized that the dynamic recalled her relationship to her stepmother.[17]

She asked Danny to pack his things. Then she mooned over her empty bed and her solitary toothbrush. She spent New Year's Eve alone and vowed that her "next romance" would be "based on a more realistic picture of who the person is."[18]

But Danny hadn't fully left, because he had no place else to go. "So he keeps his food & clothes here, feeds me as he gets 2 sets of food stamps, fucks me, & leaves when I ask him to for however long I ask," Candice told her friend Sherry in May. Their living more-or-less together had "gotten really smooth." Danny, she wrote, "sweet as ever, loves me to death."[19]

———

THE FIRST THING anybody who loved Candice and remembers Danny will tell you is that he was an unregenerate junkie. "He was a drug addict. That was easy for him to be," says Karen Dunaway, one of the White Trash Boom Boom Girls. Janice Sukaitis recalls watching him shoot heroin into his neck, near the jugular.[20]

Candice knew that Danny was an addict, and she knew that addicts were impossible to live with. By the spring of 1975, she had decided that there were only two "solutions" to the Danny dilemma: she could either convince him he had a serious problem and "hope that his love for me is stronger than his love for heroin," or she could end the relationship.

But there was, of course, a third way, which was to join him on the slide.

Candice was no drug virgin when she and Danny connected. Her tripping days were mostly behind her, but there were bar drugs: Quaaludes, cocaine, that sort of thing.[21] Sniffing "angel dudu"—PCP, originally developed as an anesthetic—was for spacing out completely. A potent cocktail of Valium and speed was good for "when you have tons to do and you want to lose weight," Candice wrote in her diary. She may have tried heroin, too, with Joe Morocco, who dabbled in it, or on porn sets.[22]

Danny was no dabbler. He shot and he nodded and he dealt, and then he shot some more. When money came in, he blew it on smack. Increasingly, he got too high for sex. Sometimes Candice did it too, getting high enough not to care. She remained ambitious but became less reliable. Musicians who liked her voice needed to depend on her for gigs. But by the middle of 1975, Scrumbly recalls, Candice was "a mess," and he had "pretty much written her off" as a collaborator.

More than a year and several not-quite-breakups later, Candice was still trying to free herself from him. "Danny is a vampire," she wrote.[23]

She had it backward. The problem was less what he sucked out of her veins than what he shot into them.

ALL THROUGH THOSE off-again, on-again years with Danny, Candice continued to work toward a career in the arts. Over Christmas in 1974,

Candice's drawing of the Heartbreak cast c1975. Divine is second from left, Candice second from right.

during that first sort-of breakup, she sang a second season with Scrumbly's Humbug Cantata. In the New Year, she thought about trying the "nightclub circuit" again, if she could get over her hang-ups about "the perversity of dancing topless in front of a bunch of creepy horny men." She jotted down the phone number for the Galaxie, a strip club in North Beach. She still drew, and once answered an ad seeking a painter who could create original illustrations on the side of trucks. Nothing panned out. By February, she was reeling again. She thought about why people killed themselves. "You'd have to be pretty stuck to just end it all—pretty miserable," she wrote, wondering if she was that stuck, that miserable.[24]

Sometime during those damp, cold months, Danny slunk back into her bed.

And then, shazam, it happened, just like in the movies. One night in April, Candice and Danny went out to a café. He stepped away from the table, and she started singing to herself to pass the time. A man sidled over and asked if he'd seen her the year before, in *Rickets*. He introduced himself as Eugene Babo, and said he'd found her performance as Keely Over memorable. He wondered if she might read for a new show he was writing with his partner Sebastian, a "paying play."

The venture was built around Divine, the San Francisco underground drag star turned cult movie sensation after his appearance in John Waters's *Pink Flamingos* (1972), proudly billed as "The Most Disgusting Movie Ever Made." Babo and Sebastian were "old Cockettes," Candice noted, which meant "old friends/enemies" of Danny, who had done an occasional show with the troupe, and had had, for a time, a Cockette boyfriend. She took the audition, "ended up knocking 'em dead," and snared the second lead. The gig paid union rates: $450 for six weeks of rehearsals, and then $150 per week for a projected ten-week run at the Kabuki Theater on Post Street. Shortly after Candice landed the role, she kicked Danny to the curb, or at least to the couch, again.[25]

The musical, called *The Heartbreak of Psoriasis*, mined territory adjacent to *Rickets*: the emptiness of a culture hollowed out by consumerism. The songs, like the musical's title, borrowed from the advertising jingles and product slogans that shaped the lives of its protagonists, the Dee family. Candice played the acne-pocked Connie

Dee, daughter of Divine's Deede Dee. Janice Sukaitis played Connie's brother. Patrick Cowley did the sound effects. But this was no White Trash Boom Boom put-up job. With a six-piece orchestra, three choreographers, and a professional publicity team, *Psoriasis* was meant as a star turn for Divine, the vehicle that would take him mainstream. Babo later estimated that the producers had put $75,000 into the show: nearly a half-million-dollar investment in today's terms.[26]

Candice called *Psoriasis* "the most wonderful work I've ever done." She loved even the grueling rehearsals. "If I can't do shows for the rest of my life, there's no other reason for me to be here," she wrote. She figured anything featuring Divine, for whom even the *New York Times* had a soft spot, was sure to succeed.[27] It is striking, given her track record in *Rickets* and other alternative shows, that she billed herself, in the *Psoriasis* program, as Candice Vadala, the first time her given name had appeared in print since her concerts with Miss Jeffrey's ballet troupe back in Riverdale.

Psoriasis opened on June 18 and was scheduled to run until Labor Day. The show flopped so epically that it was hard for the critics to publish their pans quickly enough to matter. The *Examiner* compared Divine's singing to "a muffled concrete mixer." The *Bay Area Reporter* singled out Candice Vadala as one of the performers who "fare a little better" than the rest of the cast, and a reviewer on local TV called her "a promising young actress," or at least that's how she remembered it.[28] But it wasn't enough. The producers pulled the plug after three performances. Janice recalls Divine saying, "Why rock the dead baby?"[29]

A month after the catastrophe, Babo and Sebastian told the actors they were broke, unable even to sell off the sets or the costumes, let alone the rights. They hoped "to pay all of our debts as soon as possible," especially to the cast and crew, "our favorite creditors."

It surprised exactly no one that the money never came.[30]

13 Porn, Inc.

Candice, c1975.

I n the summer of 1975, after *The Heartbreak of Psoriasis* closed, Candida Royalle began appearing in hardcore films on a more than occasional basis. To porn's boosters, that year would come to seem like the great takeoff point in "The History of Adult," as a promo reel from *Adult Video News* maintained. It was also the moment the industry's center of gravity shifted west, from New York to California, meeting Candice where she lived.[1]

Three years after the premier of *Deep Throat*, as the political upheavals of the 1960s receded like so many helicopters over the rooftop of the U.S. embassy in Saigon, pornographers operated more openly and more successfully than ever before, commanding a wider share of public attention. Sex without consequence was in, on the street and on the screen, its most obvious consequences held at bay. Medicine had vanquished most sexually transmitted infections. The Pill prevented conception cheaply and effectively, with as yet few recognized side effects. The Supreme Court's ruling in *Roe v. Wade* in early 1973 meant that a woman could legally terminate a pregnancy up to the edge of fetal viability anywhere in the United States. In 1974, the first post-*Roe* year, the number of legal abortions topped three-quarters of a million.[2]

Conservatives saw a full-blown cultural crisis, with porn at its center. "Pornography reinforces the view that a primary value of human life is sensual stimulation to the detriment of the values of individual dignity and respect that are basic to liberal democracy," warned a white paper from the American Enterprise Institute in 1974. The republic itself was at stake: "If the capacity for moral distinctions and self-governing is lost or dulled in a large number of citizens, then the democracy may well lose the capacity to govern itself according to moral principles."[3] Yet at the same time, some of pornography's critics sensed a turning point, when the swelling "floodtide of filth," which

Citizens for Decent Literature had long warned against, might at last be dammed.[4]

Though Nixon's presidency had not survived the unraveling that began with "Deep Throat's" revelations, the rightward tilt of his Supreme Court endured for decades. (The *Miller* test is still the operative standard for the adjudication of obscenity in the United States.) *Miller*'s more localized ecology of community standards meant that the legality of explicit materials would be determined in an endless array of skirmishes, fought town by town and state by state.[5] New space opened for the successful prosecution of publishers, filmmakers, and distributors. A Supreme Court ruling in 1974 affirmed the sentencing of William Hamling, a Chicago-based adult bookseller and publisher, to federal prison for trafficking obscene materials through the U.S. mails. At issue in *Hamling* was a pictorial edition of the Report of Johnson's Commission on Obscenity and Pornography. "THANKS A LOT, MR. PRESIDENT," ran Hamling's explicitly illustrated brochure for the explicitly illustrated text, promising "all the facts, all the statistics, presented in the best possible format . . . and . . . completely illustrated in black and white and full color," all for just $12.50. The volume carried an introduction from the ACLU. The Ninth Circuit had ruled that this First Amendment fig leaf was but "the facade through which clearly shines the (appellants') true and only purpose; that is the presentation of unmistakably hard core pornography." The Burger court narrowly agreed, and Hamling went to prison.[6]

Such convictions notwithstanding, a U.S. Customs official told *Forbes* magazine, "If I were a pornographer, I would not fear any city, state or federal authority."[7] The numbers supported him. Since 1970, when the Johnson Commission had counted sixty-two "men's sophisticate" titles selling a combined 41 million copies, the number of sex magazines sold "above the counter" in venues including supermarkets had exploded. New publications catered to seemingly every demographic and sexual niche.[8] The Customs Service continued to initiate obscenity proceedings every year, seizing thousands of explicit items. *Screw*'s Al Goldstein, one of porn's few millionaires, joked late in the decade that his "lawyers have made as much as I have." But if he lamented his legal bills, Goldstein and his industry colleagues also knew that the feds were playing cat and mouse, a game that the mice generally won through sheer profusion.[9]

Since the heyday of *Deep Throat*, the hardcore feature film market had begun to mature and level off. In 1976, roughly 100 feature-length hardcore films were released in the United States. Their audience comprised approximately 15 percent of movie ticket buyers.[10] A year later, *Forbes* estimated that adult theaters grossed more than $365 million: about ten times the size of the market the Johnson Commission documented. But their star was dimming. Explicit big-budget studio productions like *Last Tango in Paris* (1973) and the French import *Emmanuelle* (1974) claimed a share of the valuable couples' market *Deep Throat* had discovered.

Sexually explicit magazines had modestly larger revenues than films in the aggregate, though their earnings, too, had plateaued; *Playboy's* circulation had been shrinking since *Deep Throat* was released, and many of its competitors followed suit. The big money was in peep shows and loops, though *Forbes* predicted that the videocassette recorder—which debuted on the retail market in 1975—might one day "open up dazzling new prospects."[11]

Men like Al Goldstein, William Hamling, and Larry Flynt— who had begun publishing *Hustler* as a lowbrow alternative to *Playboy* in 1974—loved sticking a thumb in the eye of the government while they lined their own pockets. Still, their industry remained heavily stigmatized.[12] At the height of porno chic, Boston and Detroit had passed zoning ordinances to regulate adult entertainment. Detroit dispersed theaters showing explicit films around the city, to dilute their impact on the central business district. Boston chose the opposite tack, confining them to a neighborhood popularly known as the Combat Zone. In a 5–4 decision issued in 1976, the Supreme Court affirmed the constitutionality of segregating a dirty industry "to preserve the quality of urban life." Writing for the majority, Justice John Paul Stevens noted wryly that "few of us would march our sons and daughters off to war to preserve the citizen's right to see 'Specified Sexual Activities.' "[13]

That year, the General Social Survey reported that the number of Americans who thought pornography should be illegal in at least some instances outnumbered those who favored unfettered access by more than 10 to 1.[14] The "sex industry" was, as Candice later wrote to Cinthea, "a field looked down on by most conventional people."[15] Hardcore performers used noms de porn, not only for their camp value but also to shield their occupations from parents and friends, and to separate their authentic selves from their screen avatars. *Candida Royalle* was born as a proud underground theatre performer. In porn, the name became a disguise.

Writing for the majority in the *Miller* case in 1973, Chief Justice Burger had insisted on the continued necessity of separating the decent from the obscene. "One can concede that the 'sexual revolution' of recent years may have had useful byproducts in striking layers of prudery from a subject long irrationally kept from needed ventilation," he wrote. "But it does not follow that no regulation of patently offensive 'hard core' materials is needed or permissible." After all, he continued, "civilized people do not allow unregulated access to heroin because it is a derivative of medicinal morphine."[16]

———

THE HEARTBREAK OF PSORIASIS turned out to be the big break that broke Candice. She decided she "was a failure once & for all."[17] In her journal—now a pile of loose pages, scribbled on the backs of flyers, or on legal pads—she vowed: "No middle of the road bullshit anymore. If you're not gonna do straight legitimate theater you're gonna have to shock 'em."[18]

She needed money. Unemployment was surging, approaching 9 percent nationwide.[19] Both state and federal governments were looking to trim benefit costs; ATD was under threat. Many of Candice's friends—onetime revolutionaries—had more or less gone straight. Sherry was cutting hair in a department-store beauty salon in New York. Roseanne, from the Bronx Collective, was working for Goodwill. Another friend, Rhonda, had taken a post as a receptionist. "This job saved my sanity," she wrote, begging Candice to "start doing *any-thing* to occupy your time."[20]

Candice thought she was "too sensitive" for a job in an office.[21] Instead, she started working regularly in adult films. A beautiful young white woman of greater aspiration than discipline, her theatrical dreams dashed and her judgment increasingly impaired, she was a perfect fit for the industry. Over the summer and fall of 1975, she shot seven loops and two features.[22]

She had met some of her adult industry contacts on the set for *Cry for Cindy*, the feature-length production in which Danny starred.[23] She swore she wouldn't take up with him again. "No masochism for little cookie—I've had my share of that." She knew he was lying and using and dealing. "He's like a little child when it comes to his needs and I'm tired of playing mommy," she wrote. "Let this be the end."[24]

It was not the end.

The relationship appears to have grown violent. "Seen the police lately?" Rhonda asked, begging details "to feed my soap opera mentality."[25]

Candice reached out to both of her parents for counsel, surely a sign of growing desperation, as well as the paucity of sober adults around to offer a lifeline. Louis, alarmed enough by his daughter's letter than he took pains to "reply at once," offered a lengthy defense of the plight of the Artist. "Only people of your type understand you," he wrote, as much of himself as of Candice and her "many propensities." He explained his own failures in love. "Your mother was 19 & I was 28 when we married. Isn't it amazingly incredible for me to have been so immature at that age? And I'm sorry, oh so sorry, to say that I'm still almost the same way." Indeed. "I hope I've been of some help Candi," he closed.[26] (That seems unlikely.) Helen Vadala, for her part, said she understood what it was "to be fearful of someone close to you." Musicians, she warned, belonged to "a slightly different breed." She hoped her stepdaughter would turn away from "unnecessary heartache." (Helen had finally done so, filing for divorce from Louis the previous year.)[27]

Oh, how Candice tried to shake him loose! On the final day of 1975, she wrote in her datebook this resolution: "last day of my relationship with Mr. Isley."[28]

Three days later: "Get stoned with Danny!!"[29]

She slid fast that winter. She lost her apartment in Pacific Heights and started bunking with Joe Morocco at the Ranch on Haight Street, where she and Danny could "hang out & get high all day." She discovered she was pregnant and had her second abortion.[30]

Come summer, she moved into a tiny apartment on the second floor of a triple-decker a block from the Castro Theater. Her friend Karen Dunaway lived upstairs. Candice was using every day by then, and selling, too, heroin and speed. She grew proud of her prowess with the needle: a new skill, a new thrill, "something in the way of masturbation," she wrote.[31]

Candice shot more drugs and more films: six loops and seven features between May and December 1976.[32] Most of her roles were too small for the characters to merit names. She appeared as "ex-nurse" (*The Pony Girls*), or "dance student" (*Honey Pie*), or "Alan's secretary" (*Love Secrets*), and under a variety of pseudonyms (Mary Pearson, Candice Ball, Bettina Mia, as well as Candida Royalle), when she earned a credit at all. In *Easy Alice*, she played the furious, hollow-eyed "Girl in Laundromat" who suffers a rape at the hands of "Paul," a pornographic actor playing a pornographic actor out on a crime spree in North Beach. The scene is devastating, stripped of the usual porn convention in which rape ignites a survivor's latent desire. Her character's fear, her fight, and her ultimate resignation look all too real: Method porn.[33]

In August 1976, Danny hitched home to Illinois. He told Candice to "try and stay alive till I get back."[34]

"It's so strange how psychic you are at times," she replied. "You asked me to stay alive—Well only days after I received your letter I ended up in the hospital as an O.D. victim." The doctors had noted track marks on both arms, and "lectured" her about her choices. Cinthea rushed to her sister's side, and the hospital discharged Candice into her sister's care.[35]

Candice knew she was "deteriorating." Warning signs flashed everywhere. Not just the overdose, but disease: her friend Kirby Lowe, a bass player, had pulled up with hepatitis C, and she and others in their circle had shared needles with him. They all got tested, and she was clear. Miraculously, for now. She sounded breezy when she told her friend Karen that she had "decided it was time to do a little house cleaning and fact facing." "I didn't really fancy becoming a junkette," Candice wrote, though she was grateful the drugs had helped her to lose those "pregnancy puffs" and get back into a bikini.[36]

In her makeshift diaries, though, Candice was pitiless, plumbing the "streak of self destruction" she had inherited from Louis and Helen, both alcoholics, worrying she would sink even lower than they had. "I cannot let myself keep on this way," she wrote. "Am having awful visions of myself leading a very insignificant life full of unfulfilled dreams of grandeur."[37]

So much fear and so much hunger and so much grit. But on the other side of Libra's scales hung "the rush," she wrote on a piece of loose paper:

> warm tingly powerful—gasping—ohhhh—I want more & more—the evil lust—insatiable—once more is never enough! . . . It is my new romance—dependable and sure—the tiny prick of a needle will seduce me. . . . And the rush of a drug so frenetic and dizzying will serve the same release and pleasure as the rush of blood thru my body during climax.[38]

She was no match for this new romance. She lost the grip on her pen, and, for several years more, on her life.

———

"THIS YEAR HAS BEEN rock bottom for me," Candice wrote after the overdose. She would soon turn twenty-six. "25 years old and what's to become of me?" Three times, she copied the question into the spiral notebook she was using as a journal, like a naughty schoolgirl assigned to chalk sentences on the blackboard.[39]

It was partly a question of money. Life had gotten expensive, even as inflation eased from its double-digit highs. In November 1976, right after Jimmy Carter's election to the presidency, Candice moved to a larger place on the corner of Castro and Nineteenth, at the staggering cost of $225 a month. She must have been counting on her porn earnings. But two weeks later, she lost her ATD benefits, though she was

Candice, c1977.

arguably more disabled than ever before. "How can a drug dependent young woman re-enter the world of reality?" she wondered.[40] She had weaned herself from heroin several times since the summer, the first time in a clinical setting, likely with methadone, and the second time using her own cocktail of cures, from Quaaludes to whiskey. The ministrations of a devoted new man named Mark helped her through the worst of it. But then came "a month-long coke binge."[41] And on it went.

Candice had stumbled into a "very quick, easy, and successful dope business," but selling drugs only partly offset the cost of her habit. She continued her film work, booked some singing gigs that holiday season, and took "a crummy office temp job." She ended the year in debt to her friend Karen, to her dope connection, to the photographer who had taken some headshots to advance her performance career. On occasion, she went hungry.[42]

She soon discovered she was pregnant again, this time by Mark. The prospect of a third abortion—the second within a year—mortified her. As she waited to pick up the emergency Medi-Cal voucher that would pay for the procedure, she castigated herself for having failed to expend even the "little effort" a diaphragm required. She seemed touched, even amazed, that her boyfriend stayed with her at the clinic, telling Danny about the way Mark held her hand while they scraped out her uterus.[43]

She cleaned up again after that, for five days, the "longest span in ages." But then she relapsed, shooting morphine, shooting Demerol. She placed herself among "the league of . . . 'hard users' or 'hypos' as we're sometimes referred to." She found a steady new client, "a Saudi Arabian princess who's a skin & bones junky dyke," who lived in a lavish apartment on Telegraph Hill. Princess Jay was one of the youngest daughters of King Saud; Candice met her through friends who supplied the royal entourage with drugs. The dealer was ripping Jay off, Karen remembers, and so Candice became the princess's supplier, at what she deemed a fairer price.[44]

EVEN AS PORNO CHIC FADED, its afterglow lingered in the industry. *Deep Throat* had created what *Forbes* called a "porno star system."[45] A handful of actresses—Linda Lovelace and Marilyn Chambers and *The Devil in Miss Jones*'s Georgina Spelvin—had made a handful of producers and distributors very rich. As one adult-film veteran noted, "There is nothing as valuable as a girl who is innocent and beautiful— and who knows how to handle herself. It's worth the same in this world as a man who's been to graduate school for seven years."[46] *Innocent and beautiful* coded white as well as young; there were vanishingly few Black female performers. Innocence was tantalizingly vulnerable; it faded fast. One media studies scholar warned in 1977 that pornographic actresses tipped into "coarseness" almost overnight, "as if a Dorian Gray syndrome were operative." The industry's appetite for fresh, pale faces and bodies was insatiable. Nonetheless, the supply of women who thought they were liberated enough, or knew they were hungry enough, to pit themselves against the "final refuge of narcissism" more than met demand.[47]

As Candice battled debt and drug dependency, Candida Royalle's renown as a pornographic performer grew. In October 1976, she and her formerly homeless friend Laurie Detgen, aka Lailani, who was still barely of age, auditioned together for *Hard Soap, Hard Soap*, which Candice called "a high budget X-rated take off on *Mary Hartman, Mary Hartman*," Norman Lear's popular television sitcom, itself a spoof of soap operas. They snagged the two leading female roles. They'd each make a thousand dollars for four days of work—more than ten times what the office job paid, a month's rent in a day.[48] This was the big-time. Candice decided she and Lailani were now officially "porn queen beauties," like their "porno queen friend" Annette Haven, who had starred in several films, including the bicentennial-themed *Spirit of Seventy-Sex*, in which she played Martha Washington, giving blowjobs in a mob cap.[49]

The porn star was a recent arrival in the firmament of American celebrity. Neither "porn star" nor "porn queen" had appeared in books, newspapers, women's magazines, or entertainment industry periodicals until late 1972.[50] But just four years later, she was a familiar figure, her louche stardom burnished by television and personal appearances and sustained by the proliferating sex press. Big-name porn queens commanded somewhat higher fees than workaday actors, but their status remained precarious and their incomes insecure. Those who could branched out. Linda Boreman had reclaimed her birth name but called the company she helmed Lovelace Enterprises; it sold T-shirts and shampoo. Marilyn Chambers hit the nightclub circuit as a singer.[51] Andrea True, a relatively minor performer in some fifty sexploitation and hardcore films during the '60s and early '70s, was recast as a "porn queen star" when she released a disco single, the suggestively titled "More, More, More."[52]

The porn-star phenomenon resulted, in part, from a deliberate campaign for legitimacy by the group of directors, producers, publishers, and lawyers who, in the late '60s, had constituted themselves as an adult industry, with its own trade association, the Adult Film Association of America (AFAA). The AFAA, like Al Goldstein's *Screw* magazine, took shape in the immediate wake of Nixon's election to the presidency. Both policing and promoting the respectability of pornography, its leaders mounted an aggressive defense against the counterrevolution that threatened to supplant the sexual liberalism of the counterculture.[53] Modeled on the Motion Picture Association of America, the AFAA refused to lurk in the shadows, instead defending sexually explicit fare as part of a "new freedom born from enlightenment." "We're in a business we should not be ashamed of," one industry spokesman told the *Independent Film Journal* in late 1969.[54]

The AFAA's spotlight strategy meant that, by the time Candice was shooting hardcore regularly, ambitious 35mm pornographic films often launched with formal, openly advertised premiers. The year she filmed *Hard Soap, Hard Soap*, Candice attended a midnight preview of one of her earlier films, probably *Honey Pie*, at the Presidio Theater, which also hosted a well-publicized annual Erotic Film Festival.[55] She and Danny had gone to the premier of his film, *Cry for Cindy*, as well as a launch party for another of hers, likely *Baby Rosemary*, one of her two 1976 releases to earn a review in *Variety*.[56]

The reviews were generally lousy, and they didn't yet mention Candida Royalle or any of her other aliases, but the skin magazines came calling all the same. The growing number of explicit glossies—*slicks* in industry parlance—on offer at newsstands, and the increased space mainstream newspapers and trade magazines devoted to the adult film industry, meant more column inches to fill and more publishers seeking stories.[57] Shortly before Candice's audition for *Hard Soap, Hard Soap*, a reporter from *Hustler* contacted her. Being interviewed had made her "feel so special," she wrote, even as she worried that she wouldn't be able to show the article to her parents.[58]

Candice also considered writing and launching her story into a dawning age of memoir. In the '70s, the diary craze of Candice's girlhood yielded to new and less-private genres of feminine self-scouring and self-exposure, as if the therapist's couch had burst its stuffing all over the public sphere. Television talk shows, a genre that began with Phil Donahue in 1967, proliferated and grew increasingly intimate. In 1973, *An American Family*, a documentary series on PBS that prefigured the era of reality TV, riveted the nation with the miniature dramas of the Loud family, including one son's coming out. In 1974, *American Family*'s matriarch, Pat Loud, published a confessional detailing her experience with the television show, one among a spate of memoirs centered on the family traumas of relatively minor celebrities.[59]

Serious, sexually explicit feminist novels like Alix Kates Shulman's *Memoirs of an Ex-Prom Queen* (1972) and Erica Jong's *Fear of Flying* (1973) turned the standard male bildungsroman formula inside out, offering up the grist of consciousness-raising to a broad and passionate readership. Celebrity former sex workers published autobiographical tell-alls. Xaviera Hollander made headlines with *The Happy Hooker* in 1972; three years later Fanne Foxe, the Argentine stripper and mistress of disgraced Democratic congressman Wilbur Mills, used Hollander's ghostwriter when she published her own life story.[60]

In 1974, when Candice read Sylvia Plath's autobiographical novel *The Bell Jar* (1963), she had felt inspired "to immortalize" her "thoughts and adventures more closely" than she had done in recent diaries. At that point, she didn't think anyone else would ever read her words, because her life wasn't "quite entertaining enough." But by 1976, her life had changed. After devouring a titillating novel called *Inside Daisy Clover*, written in the form of a teenager's explicit diary, she thought again about the potential audience for her journals. "How many women can say they did an x-rated film up on a ranch in Northern California," Candice wrote of a film in which she "got it on with a real life 'professional' cowboy. . . . The scene was supposed to be of me & another guy fucking on a horse, but we simulated it." The ambiance, she said, had been "just like in the Misfits with Marilyn Monroe and Clark Gable." She figured a book based on her diaries, and featuring encounters like that one, would be "a best seller for sure."[61] That was vainglory. But Candice was right that the audience for her new style of stardom was growing. In October 1976, COYOTE asked Candida Royalle to be photographed, as a VIP, while entering the third annual Hookers' Ball, which crammed two thousand revelers into the San Francisco Hilton and made the front page of the *Examiner*.[62]

———

JOHN C. HOLMES WAS one of the biggest names in the porn business, renowned for the astonishing size of his penis, reputed to be over a foot long. When *Variety* called Holmes "a performer of lengthy credentials," it referred only partly to his filmography, which encompassed nearly three thousand appearances before Bob Chinn's *Hard Soap*, which would be Candice's breakout movie.[63] Erectile dysfunction provides *Hard Soap*'s running joke—inverting the more common *Deep Throat* or *Analyst* formula, in which the female protagonist must be cured of frigidity. But like those and many other golden-age porn films, *Hard Soap* has a therapeutic substrate. "Dr. Holmes" is a psychiatrist, the physician who cannot heal himself. Linda Lou (Candida Royalle) and Dr. Holmes's wife, Penny (Lailani) conspire to effect a cure. The unveiling of Holmes's erect penis is the climax of the movie.

Hard Soap has softer edges than the films Candice had made before it. Most of the action takes place in Penny's suburban home, where the two friends dish at the kitchen table, and sometimes on top of it. There's a lot of natural light, and the actors generally look healthy. (Chinn trained at UCLA film school.)[64] The score—which parrots the trembling organ melodies of midcentury soap operas (organ, get it?) and the iconic saxophone riffs of Blake Edwards's *Pink Panther* films— adds a note of camp. The opening credits feature the Liberty Bell, perhaps a wink to the bicentennial year in which *Hard Soap* was made.

The hours were long. Constraints of space and budget, as well as the schedules of crewmembers who held down straight day jobs, meant that adult features were often made by night or on weekends. (Union members—soundmen, camera operators—liked to moonlight on porn shoots because they were quick and typically local.)[65] Many skin flicks were shot in as little as three marathon sessions, and few directors could afford more than five. The work was physically arduous, especially for the female performers, who maintained awkward, even gymnastic poses, sometimes for hours, all the while striving to look as if they enjoyed it. Scripts that featured sexual violence were especially grueling. One actress told Stephen Ziplow, the author of a how-to guide for would-be porn directors, that she had found it "easier to be raped for real."[66] By comparison to her violent scene in *Easy Alice*, *Hard Soap* was short on pain and long on play.

At that point, porn typically paid performers by the day rather than by the sex act, though the deal memo with an actress generally contained a checklist of what she would and wouldn't undertake. In *Hard Soap*, "Candice Chambers" fellates four men—one while wearing a ski mask—and has vaginal intercourse with two. Each sex scene would have had to be filmed three times: first "MOS" or motor-only, without sound; then again with sound, but short of completion; and finally to capture the male orgasm, the temperamental proof-of-concept image known as the "money shot." (Ziplow recommended filming at least ten male climaxes, "to allow for some freedom of choice" in the editing room. He also suggested that directors "bring along a can of concentrated milk," or egg whites, milk and sugar, to confect a counterfeit ejaculate in a pinch.) Almost every sex scene also involved extreme close-ups of performers' genitals, known as "meat" or "medical shots." These images were like verbs, indispensable to the grammar of pornography. "The *meat shot* is the only *real* difference, outside of fellatio or cunnilingus, between the pornos and the simulated sex films," one adult director argued. To get those "anatomical" images in focus and properly lit, a gaffer or two was essential. On the set for a movie like *Hard Soap*, four or more crewmen swirled around the couple having sex in bed.[67]

At points in *Hard Soap*, Candice looks like she's having fun. She does not partner with the punishingly enormous Holmes onscreen, though she later recalled that one day during rehearsal, he led her into a back room and had intercourse with her, more or less consensually. Holmes liked "throwing his weight around," she said. Candice was booked to film a couple of loops for Jerry Abrams the week after *Hard Soap* wrapped, and she hoped those shoots would be brief, since she was "sure to be exhausted by then."[68] And no wonder.

Though she generally disliked seeing herself onscreen and complained that Chinn had caught all her "worst angles," Candice watched *Hard Soap* at least three times in theaters and kept a personal copy. (She hung on to only five of the fifteen feature-length films she made between 1975 and 1977.)[69] As her one-time co-star Howie Gordon points out, pornography is a genre of compromises. "In a porn film, if you are not too humiliated by what transpires between the sex scenes, then you may have yourself a rollicking success on your hands." The adult industry rewarded even modest professionalism, he says. "If you showed up on time and were sober and had your lines memorized, they treated you like you were Laurence Fucking Olivier."[70]

"I love professionalism," Candice had written after the *Psoriasis* debacle. And as in many of her films, she outshines the context and much of the cast of *Hard Soap*, with a big screen presence and a lot of style, courtesy of her own '50s fashions. She knows her lines, and she reads them with conviction. She had also learned, by then, the tricks of the hardcore trade: kiss with your tongue, not your lips, or your partner will wind up smeared with lipstick. Don't block his genitals with your face. Be ready for long pauses, which inevitably require the male player to recover his arousal. And especially, as she later wrote, "Never, never look into the camera. It breaks the fantasy for the viewer."[71]

A dedicated student of camp through her close observation of the Cockettes and her work with the Angels of Light and its offshoots, Candice brings a comic snap to Linda Lou's serial seductions of stock characters: the mooning milkman, the peeping paperboy. As Penny, Lailani, barely twenty, looks smacked-out and ethereal, her wide, pale, glassy eyes framed by pencil-thin eyebrows, Jean Harlow to Candice's Rosalind Russell. For much of the movie, the viewer is teased with the possibility that Linda Lou and Penny may eliminate the limp middle-man and head off to bed together. Their offscreen friendship is palpable. Candice and Lailani hold each other up, even though they never wind up lying down together.

———

DURING SOME SOBER MOMENT in late 1976 or early 1977, Candice sat down with a ballpoint pen and a yellow legal pad to reckon with her "new career as a porn queen." Her musings turned into a six-page essay, which she titled "Close Call with Male Power Game." In it, she recalled moving west, after "serving my time in the women's movement." At first, it had seemed like San Francisco would fulfill her feminism. She had managed to build her life "almost entirely with unoppressive men," which led her to "forget about the remaining 3/4 of the population of chauvinist pigs, a term I haven't used in many years."

But porn had brought her old feminist fury to the surface again. She had rationalized the work, which she took because she was "seriously broke"; hardcore was, as she said, "financially rewarding." She had "validated" her explicit roles by treating them "as an exercise in acting," whose mastery would further her "ultimate goals," the "stage & silver screen." She told herself that she was slaying the double standard.

And yet, none of those ways of justifying her choices had quite blunted the force of the work itself. "The world of pornography, from the simulated quickies to the higher budget feature films, is not at all concerned with what people have learned from women's or men's liberation, and in fact still bases its success on all the old traditional oppressive male attitudes toward sex," Candice wrote. She had tried to ignore the genre's "obvious insult to my intelligence" and "consciousness" by dwelling on the power of the performer over the "poor horny saps" that made up the bulk of hardcore's audience, men whom she never met and could scarcely imagine. She told herself they were "being fooled," cheated—that the porn queen had the last laugh. That mantra had helped her "overlook my own self-prostitution for something I absolutely did not believe in."

But she didn't, couldn't buy that script for very long. And so, for the second time, she decided she was done. "So much for the world of pornography," she wrote. "It was a brief flirtation with a male dominated industry."[72]

Had she held to this line, Candida Royalle might have traded her emerging status as a porn queen beauty for a role in the feminist anti-pornography organizations then taking shape in California.

14 Anti-Porn, Inc.

Take Back the Night, *performance by Suzanne Lacy and Leslie Labowitz
as part of the Take Back the Night march organized by Women Against
Violence in Pornography and Media, San Francisco, 1978.*

When Candice was a chauvinist-skewering, consciousness-raising, card-carrying feminist, in 1971, the movement had devoted scant attention to pornography. None of the twenty-four items on the reading list she worked through with her sisters in the Bronx Coalition's Women's Liberation Collective tackled the issue.[1]

Nor was there much on the topic they could have assigned themselves. Liberal feminist organizations tended to care more about the representation of women in law and political life than about their depiction in magazines or movies. Since its founding in 1966, NOW had concentrated its energies on securing passage of the Equal Rights Amendment, which, after kicking around Congress since the 1920s, finally roared out to the states for ratification, with overwhelming bipartisan support, in 1972, the same year Shirley Chisholm became the first Black woman to run for president. Devoted to a legislative and constitutional agenda that seemed essential to female equality, NOW had little time to think about porn, which was surely more symptom than cause of women's oppression. When NOW and other organizations of the "feminist establishment" tackled sex, they made the availability of contraception and the legality of abortion preeminent.[2]

Radical feminists had different priorities. Imagining a universal sisterhood that united women of all races, as a gendered caste, some of them saw heterosexual intercourse itself as a primary site of women's subordination. In the late '60s and early '70s, several radical feminist authors began to critique the sexual revolution as a thin and facile freedom that chiefly benefited men. In "'Sexual Liberation': More of the Same Thing," Roxanne Dunbar questioned the very notion that "sexuality is the source of human liberation." She was among the first to isolate pornography as a case in point, in which "the power motive" was literally "laid bare." Images of naked women served up for male pleasure looked, to Dunbar, like so many "corpses laid out" on slabs. She urged feminists to consider "what is *behind* pornography": employment that took women from the false "pedestal" of traditional marriage to "the very bottom" of the labor market. Tweaking her New Left brethren, who wanted their liberatory politics and their manly prerogatives, too, Dunbar mused that perhaps "fucking" itself was "doomed to die as property and power relations are changed" by the withering away of the state.[3]

Feminist critiques of the sexual revolution accumulated, and in 1970, when New York Radical Feminists staged a takeover of *The Rat*, Robin Morgan singled out the paper's "porny photos, the sexist comic strips, the 'nude-chickie' covers" for special opprobrium.[4] Yet Morgan's anthology *Sisterhood Is Powerful*, published that same year, contained an essay on "Madison Avenue Brainwashing," but none on pornography. In the inaugural issue of *Ms.* magazine, published in the spring of 1972, Anselma Dell'Olio distinguished women's liberation from the men's "More-Free-Sex-For-Us Revolution." But while Dell'Olio decried the compulsory sexualization of the "liberated" woman, she said nothing specific about porn.[5] When supermarket women's magazines tackled the topic, they focused on child protection, excepting the odd sassy piece in Helen Gurley Brown's *Cosmopolitan*, which suggested that porn might provide women with sex tips.[6] Sporadic feminist protests against *Deep Throat* notwithstanding, it remained possible, as late as 1975, for the Rutgers University–based Transaction Books to publish a volume entitled *The Pornography Controversy* without a single female contributor or any reference to the genre's impact on women who made, viewed, or were otherwise exposed to it.[7]

By then, some feminists had begun to target sexual violence as a taproot of female subordination. Rape was more than a category of felony; it was an organizing structure of society and a social epidemic, "the most frequently committed violent crime in America today," Susan Griffin had argued in *Ramparts* in 1971. "The fear of rape keeps women off the streets at night. Keeps women at home. Keeps women passive and modest for fear that they be thought provocative."[8] Rape also kept women married to their protectors, who were sometimes also their rapists.

Rape had long been classed as a kind of theft, a property crime against the tangible interests of husbands in their wives' fidelity, and of fathers in their daughters' chastity. Feminists set out to transform this understanding, casting rape as a crime against female humanity, rooted in violence and misogyny rather than sexual passion. They organized self-defense courses and founded rape crisis centers and battered women's shelters across the United States, hundreds of them by the mid-'70s. They pressured police departments and state legislatures to change the way assaults were defined and prosecuted.[9] As press attention to gender-based violence increased, and as women shared their personal histories in consciousness-raising circles, more victims reported assaults, and sex crime statistics worsened, dramatically.

The Presidential Commission on Obscenity and Pornography had refuted the claim, advanced mostly by conservatives, that explicit materials incited sex crime. The free availability of "erotic materials" in Denmark proved the inverse: more porn correlated with *fewer* rapes. And in the United States, the commission's social scientists found "no evidence to date that exposure to explicit sexual materials plays a significant role in the causation of delinquent or criminal behavior among youth or adults."[10]

But increasingly, feminists dissented from this view, merging critiques of the sexual revolution and of popular media with the burgeoning movement against rape and battery. In *Against Our Will* (1975), Susan Brownmiller codified the feminist analysis of rape and its relationship to pornography and other sex work. "The case against pornography and the case against toleration of prostitution are central to the fight against rape," she argued. Yet she admitted that it was difficult, as a Leftist, to advance such a claim. "Because the battle lines were falsely drawn a long time ago, before there was a vocal women's movement," she noted, "the anti-pornography forces appear to be, for the most part, religious, Southern, conservative and right-wing, while the pro-porn forces are identified as Eastern, atheistic and liberal."

A feminist analysis demanded "a totally new alignment, or at least a fresh appraisal," and Brownmiller steeled herself to offer it. "Pornography, like rape, is a male invention, designed to dehumanize women, to reduce the female to an object of sexual access," she insisted. "Pornography is the very essence of anti-female propaganda." And propaganda mattered. Just as antisemitic caricatures "gave an ideological base to the Holocaust and the Final Solution," just as the tropes of minstrelsy "gave an ideological base to the continuation of black oppression," so pornography organized the relations of the sexes. Its proliferation was a precondition for and, yes, a "causative factor in crimes of sexual violence," she argued. The genre could not be reformed. "There can be no 'equality' in porn, no female equivalent, no turning of the tables in the name of bawdy fun," Brownmiller insisted. It must be understood, not as mere speech but as a clear and present danger, nurturing "a climate in which acts of sexual hostility directed against women are not only tolerated but ideologically encouraged." Thus understood, it must be suppressed.[11]

Against Our Will brought the feminist argument linking pornography to sexual violence from scattered pages in mimeographed newsletters to the living rooms of middle America. In a front-page review, the *New York Times Book Review* called the study "chilling and monumental." Brownmiller barnstormed the country on a six-week, twenty-seven-city tour, during which she gave an average of eight interviews a day to television, radio, and print journalists.[12] There is no evidence that Candice saw Brownmiller's several appearances in San Francisco, or that she read *Against Our Will.* Had their paths crossed, Brownmiller might well have made her an object-lesson.

The *Times* named *Against Our Will* one of the dozen best books of 1975.[13] Read by a large national audience, Brownmiller's polemic elevated the work of her sisters in the nascent feminist anti-violence movement and transformed the definition of rape and public understandings of the consequences of pornography. An essay by Robin Morgan, published around the time of *Against Our Will,* labeled as rape "any time sexual intercourse occurs when it has not been initiated by the woman, out of her genuine affection and desire." Pornography, the "billion-dollar industry" founded on the fantasy of aggressive sex, was rape's handmaiden. The lurid films, the "degrading signs and marquees," the "sidewalk verbal hassler" were decidedly "*not* harmless," Morgan said. To the contrary. "Pornography is the theory, and rape the practice."[14]

BACK IN 1973, as the generally ecstatic reaction to *Deep Throat* threatened to legitimize pornography, whispers had begun to circulate about a new subgenre of hardcore in which a female performer was actually murdered onscreen. Such movies, called snuff films, were said to distill the soul-killing logic of porn, which was like that of drugs: users developed tolerances, and purveyors needed therefore to push ever more potent and extreme products. The rumors about snuff appear to have been part of a deliberate campaign, the work of Ralph Gauer, president of Citizens for Decent Literature (CDL). In an interview with *Adam*, a men's magazine, Gauer offered a non-denial denial of his involvement in the rumors. Neither he nor the "undercover guy" he had put on the case had ever seen such a film. Still, Gauer said he believed in the reality of snuff "because of what I know *does* exist."[5]

For a couple years, the whisper campaign stayed close to CDL, surfacing in the organization's fundraising mailers. In one such letter, Gauer urged supporters to press the FBI to begin an investigation. That may have been how the New York tabloids, the *Post* and the *Daily News*, got the scoop in October 1975, the same month *Against Our Will* caught fire.[16] Once the wire services picked up the *Post* and *Daily News* articles, the urban legend of "snuff" spread nationwide. "Reel Scene of Murder in Porno Proves Real," ran the headline in the Orlando *Sentinel Star*. "Porno Movie Murders Under Probe by FBI," screamed the *Cincinnati Enquirer*.[17] Whatever their headlines, the articles cited bureau and NYPD sources, men chasing mirrors who, like Gauer, remained fully convinced of the reality of something they'd never seen.

Indeed, *not* seeing became key to believing. "It's such a secret operation," New York detective Joseph Horman explained. He had received "dozens of tips," a few of which had nearly panned out when the trail ran cold: evidence that the film was being hidden. An editor at the *Hollywood Reporter* had phoned him to say that a producer out there was said to have purchased a script that called for "the real murder and dismemberment of an unwitting actress on screen." Nameless editor, nameless producer, nameless screenwriter, nameless actress—though everyone else on set was apparently in on the secret. Figures abounded: snuff films sold "for about $300." There were eight such movies in circulation. People paid up to $200 to watch them in "private screenings." And there was a location as well: "The information I had received said they were probably shot in Latin America," Detective Horman told the papers. "Argentina was the word I got." That Argentina was then descending into its decade-long dirty war, during which military death squads backed by the United States would "disappear" tens of thousands of citizens, added a frisson of verisimilitude, giving the rumor the kind of setting that had figured, as early as the beginning of the nineteenth century, in panics around "white slavery." After the wire-service stories blanketed the United States, Argentine federal police produced bodies to fit the headlines: three prostitutes had been murdered earlier in the year, in the Andean city of Mendoza. The stories about snuff offered a ready-made motive for these unsolved crimes, though "no firm connection had been established," as one unnamed official said.[18]

Pornography's appetite for misogynistic violence was real enough. Candice had just finished her work on *Femmes de Sade*—in which actresses playing prostitutes are whipped and beaten and left for dead—when the "snuff" news broke. But the snuff story was a fraud that inspired further swindles. It didn't take long for an entrepreneurial bottom-feeder to smell profit in the rumors. Allan Shackleton, whose production company specialized in grindhouse horror movies, bought a never-released film called *The Slaughter*, which had sat in the canister for five years, because even the people who made it deemed it too wretched to distribute. To this story of a violent Argentine cult led by a Manson-like figure, Shackleton appended a four-minute final scene purporting to depict—as if by the accident of hot mics and a still-rolling camera—the sexual torture and murder of one of *The Slaughter*'s actresses. He retitled the picture *Snuff* and advertised it with a tagline: "Made in South America, where life is cheap."

Variety called out the hoax before *Snuff* hit theaters.[19] But for Shackleton, the controversy was gold, and he did everything he could to prolong the murder mystery till the film's world premiere, in a Black neighborhood of Indianapolis, in January 1976. Almost nobody showed up, save for cops and reporters. In Wichita, more paying customers turned out, but the film provoked more laughter than screams. One viewer told *Boxoffice* that *Snuff* "should be rated R instead of X."[20]

There had been no pickets in Indianapolis, and only a handful in Wichita, but by the time *Snuff* arrived in major coastal cities, it had become, as *Boxoffice* said, "a real *cause celebre*." Dozens of "sign-carrying women" demonstrated in Philadelphia.[21] In New York, celebrity feminists including Gloria Steinem and Susan Sontag organized a petition demanding that Robert Morgenthau, the Manhattan district attorney, enjoin the film's showing. His investigation resulted in an official declaration that the murder was staged, "as is evident to one who sees the movie."[22] It hardly mattered. The protesters who converged on the Times Square venue screening *Snuff* were proud not to have seen it. One carried a placard emblazoned, "We Mourn the Death of Our Latin American Sister."[23]

Anti-violence feminists in California mounted a phone campaign to prevent the film from being shown. The newly formed Women Against Violence Against Women, or WAVAW, told volunteers to stress that their actions were "not censorship" but rather a form of "self-defense." It didn't matter whether the violence was real or staged, they argued, adapting the logic of Brownmiller and Morgan: "Studies have shown that movies like this encourage and foster similar behavior and acts of atrocities [*sic*] in reality."[24]

WAVAW succeeded in driving *Snuff* from Southern California, which turned out to be a Pyrrhic victory. Eithne Johnson and Eric Shaefer, the scholars who have probed the *Snuff* phenomenon most deeply, discovered from their careful study of box-office grosses that the film was "both a smash *and* a bomb." Critics panned it. Feminists organized against it. But across the country, the pattern was the same: more protests, more profits. The anti-pornography turn in feminism wound up cleaving the movement, but it was great for shock jocks like Arthur Shackleton. "Pickets sell tickets," he quipped. And he was right.[25]

———

WAVAW'S PROTESTS PROVIDED a durable model, and chapters of the group quickly opened around the country. The organization's toolkit—phone trees, fliers, pickets, a speaker's bureau, the occasional act of vandalism—would not sit idle, even as the furor around Shackleton's rotten film died down. The next major target of feminist organizing against violent images surfaced in June 1976, on the eve of the U.S. bicentennial, just as the effort to ratify the ERA began to stall. A billboard for the new Rolling Stones album, *Black and Blue*, went up in Los Angeles, along the Sunset Strip, showing a woman half-nude, bound, and bruised, over the caption, "I'm Black and Blue from the Rolling Stones and I Love It!" In response, WAVAW created a slide-show about media violence, which could be aired by women's groups coast to coast. The billboard came down almost immediately. But the group's protests against explicit and violent album covers were sustained for years, eventually forcing policy changes at Warner and other media companies.[26]

Where WAVAW's founders targeted a broad array of representations of sexual violence, its successor organizations put porn more squarely in their sights. In late 1976, Bay Area radical feminists singled out pornography as a target of special concern: a crucial link in a causal chain between media representation and sexual battery. After trying on a couple of other names, like the Women's Anti-Degradation Alliance, and Women Against Media Violence, they decided to put *pornography* in their association's title, the first feminist organization to do so.[27] Women Against Violence in Pornography and Media, or WAVPM, would insist, like Brownmiller, on a direct connection between the proliferation of hardcore and a rise in reported sex crime.

At the outset, WAVPM targeted violent pornography. The group's first major protest, in March 1977, was directed at the Mitchell brothers' San Francisco theater, where a space called the Ultra Room featured a dungeon. Candice had appeared in two of the films the Mitchells produced, including *Femmes de Sade*, which featured BDSM sequences that fit the WAVPM brief. But the protesters' second action, a stroll through the North Beach sex district on May Day, cast a looser net. Stickers reading, "This is a crime against women" were plastered on the windows of adult bookstores and dance parlors like the Galaxie, where Candice had auditioned to dance topless a couple years before.[28]

Working through a network of women's shelters and rape crisis centers to mobilize grassroots protests, WAVPM quickly succeeded in changing the advertising policies of major national newspapers, including the *Los Angeles Times*. (Though WAVPM staged a rally outside the *San Francisco Chronicle*'s building, where protesters carried signs reading "*Chronicle* Delivers Porn to Your Door," the paper of record in the porn capital of the United States refused to submit.) In November 1978, the organization hosted its first national conference, "Feminist Perspectives on Pornography," drawing scholars and activists from thirty states to San Francisco. The program featured a who's who of radical feminist orators, including the poet Adrienne Rich and the Black lesbian radical Audre Lorde as well as Susan Brownmiller.[29]

The writer and activist Andrea Dworkin, a brilliant rhetorician whose book *Woman-Hating* (1974) had acquired the status of scripture in the feminist anti-violence movement, was the last speaker of the day, charged with rallying protesters to embark on the nation's first Take Back the Night march. Her address, "Pornography and Grief," had the force of Medea, all keening rage. Pornography, she said, begat a vicious circle: it "exists because men despise women, and men despise women in part because pornography exists." It had to be toppled, smashed, extirpated. "Tonight, with every breath and every step, we must commit ourselves to going the distance: to transforming this earth on which we walk from prison and tomb into our rightful and joyous home."[30] With Dworkin's powerful words ringing in their ears, some three thousand activists surged through the streets of North Beach. Photographs show a sea of impassioned mourners, many of them young, most of them female, and almost all of them white. Symbolizing their cause was a spectacular float, designed by Suzanne Lacy and Leslie Labowitz, whose arts collective, ARIADNE, targeted violence against women. Perched atop a car studded with flowers stood a serene Madonna, cloaked in gold, fronted by an altar's worth of electric candles, like something out a feast day in Little Italy. Behind her was the carcass of a three-headed lamb, from whose body spilled a mound of pornographic images. She was virgin and whore, goddess and tramp:

an incarnation of the bifurcated view of women that filled the dreams of men like Louis Vadala and fueled the pornographic imagination.[31]

At the beginning of the decade, the *New York Times* had proclaimed San Francisco the unofficial "Porn Capital of America." By the late '70s, it had become the feminist *anti*-porn capital as well. But by then, Candice had begun to pivot southward, toward the film capital of the United States.

15 Project Los Angeles, U.S.A.!

Candice, c1977.

The first time Candice visited Los Angeles, over a weekend in 1974, she had pursued what turned out to be a "disgustingly disappointing affair" with a man who stood her up for lunch the next day. She left him a paper napkin signed "in turquoise ink, 'with love from Ms. Candida Royalle.'" L.A. was like that: city of lipstick traces and stage names and hazy sunsets, a "city of one night stands," Candice wrote.[1] She found it "visually and culturally starved, full of true tackiness." But L.A. was also packed with "interesting and ambitious people, good contacts, & opportunity." She filed those contacts away.[2] The opportunities she imagined lay in the world of mainstream performance, not in porn.

On her shoots in San Francisco, Candice met a lot of film technicians who held straight day jobs in the movie industry in Hollywood, and then loaded their equipment into vans and sped north, up Interstate 5, to shoot hardcore in San Francisco or Marin. In Los Angeles, the Motion Picture Association of America, tasked with defending the always-tenuous reputation of the movie business, was eager to police the blurry lines between mainstream studio films and pornography. The LAPD, as the industry's enforcer, was so energetic staking out and shutting down hardcore shoots and hassling the patrons of adult businesses that pornographers dubbed it the Pussy Posse; one printed the phrase on T-shirts and mailed a bunch of them to the vice squad.[3]

Pornographers complained that the LAPD went after porn shoots because they married low risk with high visibility. Nobody on a porno set ever pulled a gun on the cops. One director suspected that vice officers secretly hoped for a sexual bribe—that "some chick will talk them out of a bust with her bust, plus the rest of her." Regardless, breaking up a pornographic set, or "ring," as the newspapers always put it, made good copy.[4]

Though it remained hard to *make* porn in Los Angeles, the city hosted as much commercial sex as other large urban centers. The national trade in mail-order erotica had centered in L.A. County since the *Roth* decision. Scores of adult bookstores and theaters showing hardcore films operated on the northeastern edge of Hollywood, just past where the LAPD's jurisdiction stopped. The state attorney general's office estimated that Los Angelenos consumed $100 million worth of pornography— books, magazines, peeps, live sex shows, and movies—in 1976: the year of *Snuff*, the year of *Hard Soap*, the bicentennial year Larry Flynt broke a longstanding taste and even legal barrier by showing pubic hair, curling over an American flag bikini, on the cover of *Hustler*, the year Candice began to think in earnest of "trying [her] fate in L.A."[5]

What made L.A. distinctive was less the size of its sin market than the zeal of its anti-smut forces, which included not only Hollywood studio heads and civic leaders but also organized citizens' brigades, particularly in the suburbs of the San Fernando Valley and Orange County. Just beyond the borders of Los Angeles lay the heartland of a new conservatism forged by a coalition of housewives, Catholics, and evangelical Protestants, focused on moral issues. Their crusades against the roots and fruits of sexual liberalism—abortion, sex education, por- nography, prostitution, and homosexuality—often framed the issues around the safety of neighborhoods and the sanctity of households, thus uniting Nixon's law-and-order agenda with the emerging Reagan- ite focus on faith and family.[6]

Adult-industry professionals caught the cheap floral scent of hypocrisy in a town where would-be starlets were pressed to trade sex for acting jobs that somehow never materialized. "Hollywood is about dangling promises and hopes," said Jane Hamilton, who performed as Veronica Hart, and would soon become a close friend of Candice's. "The difference between the porn business and the straight business is that in porn you don't have to fuck anybody to get a job."[7]

———

"I'M FINALLY GOING TO L.A.," Candice wrote in February 1977, after her third abortion and just before the first WAVPM protests. She was sick of her "tired life" in San Francisco and eager to put the "Days of drugs & Danny" behind her. She moved out of her expensive apartment in the Castro and crashed with Cinthea, "in a remote area of town," farther from temptation. She devised a system to will herself clean: "I give myself a 'star' for each day I don't indulge—And each day brings me closer to being a 'star.'"[8] Sometimes it worked.

Now twenty-six years old, Candice wanted to see her name in lights. She had friends in Los Angeles to ease the transition. Karen Dunaway had recently moved with her husband to Venice, by the beach. In June, she told Danny goodbye, again. She lined up a ride, packed "a suitcase full of experiences," and cast herself in her latest role, the ingénue bound for the big-time:

> Hollywood—I'm going to Hollywood. Another princess with stars in her eyes and determination under her belt is about to hit the pavement of the city of the 'fallen Angels'—hoping with all her heart & soul to rise and soar thru the fluffy white clouds of mysterious expectation.[9]

She found a place to live. On a leafy street in West Hollywood, a Tudor mansion had been built in the Roaring '20s, for Charlie Chaplin. It was peeling now, but Candice called it "the castle." She leased what she described as a "little cottage in a courtyard": a stage set for a larger life.

The cottage was, in fact, Chaplin's long-ago car garage, with a drain in the middle of the concrete floor.[10]

That was the reality. But in Los Angeles, surfaces mattered most.

———

"I'M IN HOLLYWOOD, Los Angeles, California—southern California," Candice wrote in July 1977, soon after hauling her boxes into the garage apartment. She rhapsodized about the things that people who love Southern California love: the sun, the palms, the oranges, the movie stars. She sounds like she was pinching herself awake.[11]

Even so, she felt "ready to get down to serious business": figuring out a way to make a living. Pulling a "freak scene" at the SSI office in San Francisco before she left, she had managed to prolong her ATD benefits for six weeks. But shortly after she landed in L.A., they cut her off for good, pronouncing that she lacked the "degree of mental impairment or maladaptive behavior patterns of such severity as to preclude the claimant from all industrial suitability." Candice had told the interviewer she was eager to get back to work, and she set about it in earnest.[12]

As soon as she unpacked, she set about improving her gifts. She pored over newspapers and phone books, writing down addresses for voice coaches and acting studios. She jotted the name of a speech therapist; getting serious roles in serious pictures meant muting her Bronx accent. She joined a gym. She enrolled at Santa Monica Community College and signed up for classes in voice and commercial art. She found a piano teacher and a tap studio. She entered a drug-treatment program. One afternoon, she grilled hot dogs and poured lemonade for her fellow addicts at the methadone clinic's summer fair.[13]

She hustled for work as an extra. She pulled together a portfolio of illustrations. She threw a housewarming party, where she showed her artwork and played the demo tapes she'd made with Patrick Cowley. "That's what I came here for," she wrote, "to meet interesting & new people & good contacts—and get bigger & better breaks." She got some small ones. One new friend found her a couple of jobs recording children's books on cassette tapes. Another contact got her an assignment drawing figures for a film publicity campaign. She auditioned for TV commercials. "I'm setting my plan of action into motion & keeping my eye set on particular goals—I'm gonna do it baby," she wrote a month into her new life.[14]

She felt lonely—lonely enough to consider visiting Danny. But she kept focused, and she kept trying. The L.A. story she wanted for her own was the Tale of the Big Break. "Oh please work out, L.A. please please please work out for me," she prayed, like so many starry-eyed supplicants at the altar of Hollywood before her, and since.[15]

PORN STAYED IN THE MIX, if not in the plan. Candida Royalle pulled into Los Angeles at a pivotal moment for the adult industry and its quest for legal and cultural legitimacy. The year before, the Adult Film Association of America had joined Women Against Violence Against Women on the barricades against *Snuff*, decrying the film as "the greatest ripoff since Watergate." The trade group also enlisted in the fight against child pornography, another front in the battles against sexual violence that found conservatives, industry groups, and feminists allied.[16] As Royalle launched her "Project Los Angeles," the AFAA invited nominations for the first Erotica Awards, for adult movies. "The Oscars have a new Hollywood rival," a columnist in *Screen International* quipped, announcing that the "long rumored and often joked about notion of sex-film awards" was about to become "an annual reality."[17]

The rise of feminist anti-pornography, quite inadvertently, brought new opportunities to women in the adult industry, by making more Americans aware of and curious about porn, which in turn made more journalists eager to find industry spokespeople to interview. Women whose style and stories gave them a kind of mainstream respectability were especially sought after. Ann Perry, an actress in explicit films from the days of "nudie cuties" through the early years of hardcore, and more recently a director and producer of feature-length erotic films, knew that the pickets had helped her career. The first female member of the AFAA, Perry became, amidst the *Snuff* controversy, its first woman president. "It was good press, and it was great for the Women's groups," she later said of her election to the role. The association's male leadership may have taken her for a token, "sort of like a figurehead, sticking out there," but Perry was a seasoned executive with a vision of her own.[18]

It was Perry who dreamed up the Erotica Awards, designed, she said, "to elevate the industry" by rewarding better films. The annual gala would function as a coming-out party for hardcore. "Finally, the Victorian era is behind us, and every American can now honestly discuss and view that which has only been discussed and viewed surreptitiously in the past," one AFAA spokesman told a movie-industry broadsheet.[19] The first awards ceremony would take a long backward glance, to honor films produced in the early '70s, including a special prize for *Deep Throat*. As many publications noted, the award categories and the structure of the ceremonies aped the Oscars. "There is no word yet on statuettes . . . but batteries are not included," the *Philadelphia Inquirer* joked. "May we have the plain, brown, manila envelope, please?"[20]

Perry tapped Candice—she addressed her as "Candice Royalle"—to present an award, likely on the strength of her work in *Hard Soap, Hard Soap*, a notable picture though too recent to be considered for an Erotica. (*Femmes de Sade* was nominated, for costumes, which the newspapers found oxymoronic, but Candice had appeared only as an uncredited extra in that film.) She was still unpacking from her move to Hollywood when she got Perry's call and was thrilled by the recognition. Perry hoped the appearance would encourage Candice "to do your best, look your best and never feel ashamed of an industry that has so much to offer so many people."[21]

A profitable mix of performers, protesters, police, and press made their way to the ceremony at the Wilshire Ebell Theatre, a gilded old-time movie palace that had recently played host to the Warsaw String Quartet and the American Youth Symphony Orchestra.[22] Starlets arrived in "low-cut gowns and limousines," the *Los Angeles Times* reported. They were greeted by activists carrying signs reading "DIRTY MOVIES: BIG BUCKS AND WHORES!" or "THE BIBLE IS GOOD; SMUT IS BAD." Candice took her turn as a presenter among a roster of the biggest names in the business. A "Deep Throat Award" and a dance number called "Latin Sensuality" seemed poised to titillate. But the reporters wound up disappointed by the staid nature of the three-hour program, which included "erotic dances that could have passed the toughest censors at CBS," and film clips carefully edited, at the theater owner's request, to eliminate nudity.[23]

Even so, the combination of porn stars and golden statuettes in the studios' backyard made an irresistible subject. Newspapers as far away as the UK carried the story. A reporter from a local CBS television affiliate reached out to Candice for an interview. She wasn't sure she should do it, since her goal was to find television and straight film work. If she agreed to talk to him, no record of it remains.[24]

A few weeks later, Candice flew up to San Francisco to shoot a new adult movie, produced by Mike Esposito, who was rumored to be part of the Lucchese crime family. The production company comped her travel and hotel, for seven days. This impressed her; she noted the arrangement in her journal and her date book. But when she got there, she balked. "A very dreadful day—I was supposed to be in a film but blew it off royally," she wrote in her diary, without saying why. Esposito's company paid her kill fee, a hundred dollars, and flew her home. "I hate Porno!" she wrote. "It's an insult to my talents."[25]

———

"YOU CAN'T WRITE a story about L.A. that doesn't turn around in the middle," Eve Babitz wrote in 1977, in "Slow Days."[26] Candice learned Babitz's lesson almost immediately, as her narrative of cleaning up and getting ahead bent back on itself. "I'm not a drug head anymore," she wrote in her journal after a couple months in L.A.[27] But wishing it, writing it, did not make it so.

She was still dealing, flying up to San Francisco to meet her heroin connection and returning with a fresh supply for Princess Jay, who

"Me and My Camera," May 1979.

had moved to the canyon lands northeast of Beverly Hills. During the second half of 1977, selling smack to Jay was Candice's "main financial staple," as she put it. Throughout the following year, satisfying Jay's habit prevented Candice "from having to take on shit work," and allowed her to try things—a comedy workshop, singing gigs at clubs that paid in drinks—that she would otherwise have been "unable to do for lack of cash."[28]

But temptation lurked on all sides of every transaction. From her San Francisco connection, Joey, who always seemed ready to offer her a taste. From her friends, especially her fellow "porn queen" Lailani, who had a heavy habit of her own, and Karen Dunaway, who had introduced her to Jay in the first place, and who gave herself over to dope more fully and less fretfully than Candice. Candice saw a lot of Karen, especially after January 1978, when a man peeping into her apartment window prompted her to leave Charlie Chaplin's garage and move in with Karen's now-estranged husband, Dorsey, and Dorsey's boyfriend, Dean. Dorsey and Dean acted like "a honeymooning duo," Candice wrote. She felt "emotionally blank," but the two men provided "enough emotion around the house for eight people."[29]

Jay herself was uniquely alluring, a bona-fide princess to Candice's imaginary Cinderella. "My continental friend," Candice called her. Sometimes Jay sent a car for Candice, to have her "very jet settingly whisked" to her gated mansion in Benedict Canyon, near the house in which Charles Manson's followers had massacred Sharon Tate. Jay had done up the inside of the mansion as an Arabian fantasia, lining the first floor with a mirrored leather tent. Jay and her girlfriend were often taken advantage of by users and hangers-on, people like Vicki Morgan, the mistress of Ronald Reagan's close friend Alfred Bloomingdale, among others. The transactional nature of so many of Jay's relationships made her grateful for Candice's genuine affection—though their relationship, too, was ultimately one of seller and buyer. Karen says Jay more or less "adopted" the two of them. "It's amazing to me that one of my few everlasting friends is a princess from such a controversial country as Saudi Arabia," Candice wrote after a "stoned out evening" in the canyon. "I'm almost afraid to say it for fear that some CIA agent might come leaping out at me all of a sudden—But really, we're just good, ordinary ol' friends."[30]

Being good, ordinary ol' friends with Princess Jay meant shooting smack and smoking hashish until you could scarcely walk. Sometimes there was cocaine, purified with ether and smoked as freebase. Always, there were pills: Quaaludes, Tuinals. Jay once swallowed an entire jar. Everyone at Jay's overdid it, but at least once, Candice frightened them, shooting enough China white to wind up on the floor, unresponsive. She came to with Jay and Karen shouting her name, "wondering whether they had just done me in for good." Jay felt bad enough that she sent Candice home with some party favors: "a bunch of grade D smack" that kept her and Dorsey and Dean stumbling around their apartment for days.[31]

Copping for Jay usually involved heading to San Francisco, which meant that the Saudi Arabian Princess kept Candice in the orbit of the man she called her "prince Devil," who proved as tough to quit as junk. They continued to tumble in and out of each other's lives, in San Francisco or in L.A. In April 1978, she again swore off Danny and dealing. But by June, she was back to being "the girlfriend of a down-trodden strung-out punk."[32]

It was easy for Candice to attract men, but harder for her to judge their character, much less to sustain a relationship. "Been having an average of about 2 lovers a week," she wrote that spring. The sex was mechanical at best, for which she figured she was partly to blame. Occasionally, she found herself broke enough to go out for meals with strangers. "It's actually quite interesting," she wrote. "I don't go unless I want to. And I don't have sex—where is my sex drive?" (It was buried at the bottom of a pill bottle or a syringe.) Sometimes the dinner men gave her their business cards, and she meant to call, "and hit them up for jobs before they can hit me up for a lay." But then she'd feel "a quaalude blitz taking over."[33]

"I spend much of my time trying to think of 'constructive' ways of spending my time," she wrote. She was desperate to "burst forth in a flutter of color & excitement." But even in the crystalline southern light, life looked increasingly gray. She felt the days "roll by," like waves on Venice beach, without end, "meaning nothing." She sensed that somewhere on the road of life, she "took the wrong turn.[34]

Hollywood curdled. "This town is rough—very rough," Candice wrote.[35]

She began to imagine getting all the way out. She inked into her diary, sometime in the spring of 1978, a composition labeled "Suicide Note #1":

When life becomes a series of trials and disappointments—a constant worry of how to get the next month's rent—When each morning is as crummy as the last because you just don't want to get up, you don't want to get showered and dressed and hit the outside world. You begin to wonder how you're going to keep it going. And whether it's worth it.[36]

PORN MAY HAVE BEEN, as Candice said, an insult to her talents. But it was there to catch her when she fell.

Publicity still from Hot and Saucy Pizza Girls, *1978. Candice stands second from right, with Lailani behind her.*

By April 1978, after having stayed away from the industry for the better part of a year, Candice decided that it would be porn, again: "quick $ so that I can go after what I want." She thought about how her next role could be different. "I am quite natural in front of the camera, but no porn star," she wrote. She wanted better direction, and vowed, "my next film project is going to be taken much more seriously."[37]

The movie was *Hot and Saucy Pizza Girls*, a big-budget picture directed by Bob Chinn, who had worked with "Candice Chambers" on *Hard Soap*. For the first time, *Candida Royalle* appeared in newspaper advertisements, right beneath the top-billed John C. Holmes. A comic caper, *Pizza Girls* has the thinnest crust of a plot: Country Girl Pizza, managed by John Seeman (Holmes), serves as a front operation for a brothel on wheels. Three counterfeit cowboys, who run a competing operation, try to muscle Country Girl out of business. They send a masked bandit to terrorize the girls; the San Francisco Night Chicken spoofs the contemporary frenzy over the Hillside Strangler. Lailani played one of Candice's fellow pizza girls, and Danny (credited as Spender Travis) had a part as one the cowboys. Howie Gordon played another member of the hayseed trio. He got stage fright when the cameras rolled, and a "stunt cock" was brought in to finish the scene. When the double failed, too, the cowboy vignette wrapped as softcore.[38]

Pizza Girls was shot over five days in June, in multiple Northern California locations. One was a seedy motel, "spit balls on the ceiling and a splash of brown liquid on the walls," Candice wrote. Another was a business, Straw Hat Pizza in Oakland, which stood in for the Country Girl Pizza Parlor, until Chinn's crew mistakenly set it on fire. Other scenes were shot in a big, airy house in Marin County, with a pool and a sauna. Candice and the other talent tore the place up and got scolded: "no more frolicking in the pool area."[39] Tracking shots show the pizza girls skateboarding down some perilous hills; Candice learned to skate for the film and was proud of it.

Candice remembered *Pizza Girls* fondly, "for its sincere silliness." She even saved her costume.[40] There is little evidence of that delight on film, though. Her character, Gino, looks as rough as Candice's circumstances at the time suggest: sallow and slightly dazed. At climactic moments, "Gino" appears to be counting the minutes until her paycheck, or her next fix.

While filming *Pizza Girls*, Candice met a wealthy and accomplished man, the forensic psychiatrist Martin Blinder, who moonlighted as a jazz pianist and had served as mayor of the little town of St. Anselmo. Blinder's home there, dating from the late nineteenth century, was a rare piece of old California. The site became, he says, "a magnet" for companies scouting movie locations. Productions filmed in his home several times a month—everything from ads for Sherwin-Williams paints to major studio movies. Blinder estimates that hardcore films comprised about 20 percent of his rental business. One evening, he returned from work to find a crew wrapping a day's shoot. He heard a "terrific jazz singer" accompanying herself on the piano. He sat down and jammed with Candice, and then invited her out to sing with his quartet at its regular gig at the Dock, downtown. "She was a force of nature," Blinder recalls, an intuitive musician with what jazz folks call "big ears" for the way music unfolded around her.[41]

The doctor was smitten, and the two began a love affair. They jetted off for what Candice noted was an "all expenses paid trip" to Maui, where Blinder had a second office. "You haven't seen paradise until you've seen Hawaii," she wrote in her diary. Several months later, when her stepmother, Helen, visited her in L.A., they flew up to see Blinder in St. Anselmo, to "be shown around in style." Candice hoped Helen would be impressed by the doctor's grand home, and his Mercedes, and the way he paid the tab in fancy restaurants.[42]

Blinder's name would soon be all over the newspapers, for his work as an expert defense witness on behalf of Dan White, the San Francisco supervisor who gunned down the city's first openly gay mayor, Harvey Milk, in November 1978, shortly after *Pizza Girls* hit theaters. Blaming White's diet of junk food for worsening his depression, the doctor invented what would be derided as the Twinkie defense.[43]

———

WHEN CANDICE RETURNED to Hollywood after shooting *Pizza Girls*, her career took what she called, in her journal, "a quantum leap forward," toward "the beginnings of an established name and identity as a sexy porn star." She won her next role, in a film called *Hot Rackets*, within days of getting back to town. For the first time since *The Analyst*, Royalle was cast as the lead, alongside Lailani. She felt "beautiful and appreciated—sexy and talented," during the Bay Area shoot.[44] She wrote to Karen on the stationery of the Travel Lodge on Ellis Street, in the Tenderloin, drawing an arrow to the logo and noting, "this is where I had my own room for a week while staying in S.F. to film. I felt so important." She pledged to avoid "funny stuff"—no drugs, no Danny—so she could prove she was worth more than $200 per day.[45]

Royalle was nominated for an Erotica that summer, as best supporting actress in *Hard Soap*.[46] She also presented a statue at the awards ceremony, which had moved to the five-thousand-seat Hollywood Palladium, with an Oscars-style after-party at the fabled Brown Derby. At an after-after party in the Hollywood hills, John C. Holmes "of course started an orgy," Candice told Karen. She sat that one out, but then the British rocker John Mayall "kidnapped" her to a bedroom where the red satin sheets matched her red dress and red stockings. He showed her his shelves full of porn recorded on the new medium of videotape—"one of the world's largest collections," she said.[47]

The summer of 1978 glided on like that: parties where "liberated women go topless while they serve the dip." Quaaludes by the pool for the masses, a blizzard of Bolivian and angel dust in the " 'coke room' with the closed door" for the stars. The lad magazines—*Chic* and *Oui*—sponsored parties that turned into orgies, where Candida cut loose with B-list movie stars and A-list pornographers. "I made friends with Al Goldstein from *Screw*," she boasted to Karen.[48]

Candice brought the porn-star lifestyle home, cavorting on the pool deck of the apartment complex on Alta Loma until her landlady threatened action. "I have received many complaints about your friends, your bathing suit or lack of it and your carrying on," Mrs. Fox scolded. "Many of the tenants will not use the pool because of you." She warned: "Either act worthy of living in this apartment building or leave."[49]

In between visits to Blinder up north, Candice had some brief affairs that summer, "with sweet but mean" young musicians from the burgeoning L.A. punk scene, a guitarist here and a drummer there. She felt relieved to be "moving from 1 night's roll to a few nights, or whatever," still chasing the guiltless sex that had beckoned to her since 1969, and finding, if anything, less joy in it.[50]

Candice vowed that the next serious man in her life was "going to have to meet up to some pretty important standards." Cinthea had moved to L.A., where she was living with her boyfriend Tom's family; that fall, she gave birth to their son. "It's been very incredible getting to experience Cyn's pregnancy and birth with her. I've been very close to it, almost as if it were my own," Candice wrote that fall. She thought, for the first time since her first abortion, about having a baby.[51]

Instead, not long after Cinthea gave birth, Candice had sex with Tom. Her sister found out, as perhaps she was meant to do. In a long letter apologizing, much too late, for her "sheer stupidity and insensitivity," Candice swore it had all been a heedless mistake, not some insidious plot, though as she well knew, and as Cinthea had surely pointed out, such triangles reached all the way back to their childhoods. "There was nothing to prove," Candice insisted. "All I can say is that on quaaludes people get real dumb."[52]

Janice Sukaitis remembers the scene differently. One night, at an apartment near Venice Beach—maybe Tom's mother's place—she saw Tom and Candice emerge from the bathroom together, hair awry, clothes askew. She says Candice turned to her with a stage whisper, and maybe a wink, saying: *I got him.*[53]

Regardless of how and why it happened, the incident, and its exposure, opened a rift between the sisters that would take years to close. They revisited their terrible childhood. "I won't believe that because of Dad's sexual preference to you I developed the need to prove I could have men—or your men," Candice wrote in 1980, by which point the sisters' battle had raged for more than a year. "In fact," she continued, "if you'll excuse my show of confidence, if anything my biggest problem was getting rid of men or warding off male attention." Where Candice made a weapon of her beauty and her sex appeal, Cinthea used the arsenal at her disposal: she told Louis and Helen that their beloved younger daughter—the princess, the ballerina—was a junkie and a porn star. "I must say that was the most expensive lay I've had," Candice noted, acidly, of her desperate fling with Tom.[54]

"CANDIDA ROYALLE HAS come back to life after a few too many months into years in a dusty hatbox," Candice wrote shortly before the disastrous lapse with Tom. She felt like she was showing the folks back home what she was capable of: "guess what Aunt Rose and Aunt Nellie and Gram and all the rest of you whether you're dead or alive—I made it to TV!" she scrawled in her diary. Having grown up watching *The Dating Game* and fantasizing what it would mean to appear on a game show, she had made her "TV debut" as a contestant on *The $1.98 Beauty Show*, winning about $700. "Only in America would a dream like that come true!" she said.[55]

Candice's rediscovered porn-stardom drew tantalizingly close to the world of mainstream film. She went to a pool party at the home of Howard Ziehm, a hardcore pioneer who had hit the big-time with *Flesh Gordon* (1974), and who was rumored to be casting an R-rated picture. She got a job on the crew of a PG-rated film, *Rock and Roll High School*, directed by Roger Corman and starring the Ramones, a New York punk quartet whose music she loved. But she walked off the set after just one day, deeming the life of a technician beneath her. "Being known as a grip, marching around in army fatigues, no make-up, and dirt all over me, just doesn't make it with me. The image may have been a desirable one in my feminist days—but not for miss Candida Royalle, thank you." She needed to be "in front of the cameras, to entertain all the folks that'll pay to see me." Besides, the grip gig paid scale, by the hour, while Princess Jay and her new girlfriend were offering Candice a quick grand to make a dope run to the Bay Area.[56]

Oh, to be in Hollywood! "I've grown so accustomed to wearing my dark glasses while sipping breakfast tea in the morning inside our dimly lit dining room," Candice wrote, acting every inch the movie star. But she couldn't sustain the pose. "Oh this is all bullshit," she continued. "My time's almost up and I'm rambling on stoned." It was the eve of her twenty-eighth birthday. She'd swallowed a handful of Darvocet. ("At least I didn't shoot them.") She had the clap, again. "Can you imagine how rude it feels to have gonorrhea at my age and level of sophistication? And having to call the men I've been with and tell them?" There were a lot of calls to place.[57]

Candida Royalle made more than twenty films in the two years following *Pizza Girls*, the busiest season of her acting life. Porn became her career, no mere stopgap or sideline. As she told Karen, she had begun thinking of her films "as a potential artistic outlet." Her stage name appeared in public, if not always in lights, at least on the back pages of those newspapers that proved immune to pressure campaigns by WAVAW and WAVPM to cease accepting advertisements for pornographic films. Display ads for *Pizza Girls* even carried her picture. *Swank* and *Adam* called for interviews. She received her first invitations to dance on the personal-appearance circuit. She paid her dues, becoming a card-carrying member not of the Screen Actors Guild, but rather of the Adult Film Association of America.[58]

It was in her capacity as a standard-bearer for the adult industry that Candice got her first and only turn in front of the camera on an A-list Hollywood set, as an extra in Blake Edwards's movie *10*, which starred Julie Andrews and Dudley Moore, and made a global icon of the actress Bo Derek, her blond hair in cornrows, jogging down the beach in a beige swimsuit that matched her tanned skin, breasts heaving to the incantatory rhythms of Ravel's *Bolero*. A midlife-crisis-themed sex comedy, *10* flirted with the blurry line between R and X. It featured a softcore orgy: a raunchy pool party that Moore's character spied through his telescope and then rushed to join.

Candida Royalle was one of the twenty adult performers Edwards recruited for the scene. In January 1979, he put them all up for four nights at the downtown Ramada Inn and paid each $1,000, much like a porn shoot. The filming lasted two days, with no sex on camera: "not very much work" for the money, Candice said, having done more for less. The rest of the time, the porn stars did what porn stars do when they are "all revved up to work," she wrote. They ran up a huge bar tab and cut fat lines of Bolivian powder to spell out MGM, "a tribute to the company that had supplied our 'goodie' money." They cavorted in hotel rooms, in twos and threes and fours and more. When the gossip columnist Rona Barrett picked up the story, the Ramada Inn cut off their room service.[59]

Candice was dazzled by the money flowing through the production, whose $5 million budget was orders of magnitude beyond that of any film she'd worked on. Being on Edwards's "notorious set" was, she said, "another whole experience. No rushing, no yelling, pampered from head to toe—my hair done by one person, my face by another." She schemed to ensure she didn't get cut in post-production. "I was no fool to be the only one totally decked out in red," she noted in her journal. And because she'd been clothed in the shot, she could brag to her parents, although she figured that "even with nudity, Julie Andrews being there I'm sure would have caused them to be 'open minded' about it all."[60]

The orgy scene in *10* lasts less than two minutes. Candice's poppy-red halter dress flickers onscreen for roughly twelve seconds. Still, she thought the film had opened doors for her. "The work started pouring in and hasn't stopped," she wrote two weeks after the shoot. By then, she'd completed filming for two more hardcore movies, the comic *Pro-Ball Cheerleaders* and the dystopian *Ultra Flesh*, set in a techno future when excessive sugar consumption has rendered the once-virile men of the United States impotent. In the latter, she had been lowered by rope, her feet in stirrups, onto a nude male actor lying prostrate on the floor. It was thrilling, she later wrote. "I felt magnificent floating mid-air in a grand pose, all eyes fixed on me, a goddess descending from the stars to bring pleasure to a man waiting eagerly below."[61]

Still, Candice's role as "third female sex performer" had involved strenuous physical labor for modest pay and the most fleeting glory. She had begun to wonder what came next.

16 Ripe and Ready

Candice and Sherry Falek at Coney Island, summer 1979.

"I f only life were so simple for me. If only I didn't have such driving ambition," Candice wrote in early 1979. She had stuck it out for more than a year in Los Angeles, an "evil hard city." Increasingly, she thought about leaving. Jorgé was back in San Francisco, making music with Patrick. And Martin Blinder had hinted that he was "in the position to take care of me," Candice wrote.[1] After so many years of shifting for herself, the ease of being kept, in fine style, had a certain allure. But she wanted more.

Ambition, the most American of the seven deadly sins, was especially vexed for pornographic actresses, whose careers withered even as they bloomed. For the male viewer, a big part of the fantasy of pornography was novelty: the imaginary conquest of an ingénue for the price of a movie ticket. "The porno audience gets tired of seeing the same old faces time and time again," warned the *Film Maker's Guide to Pornography*. For male performers, orgasmic reliability was the gold standard, and could ensure a lifetime of work for those with the homeliest of faces. But for women, ripeness was all, and in the heat of the triple-X theater, ripeness quickly sugared into rot.[2] The publisher of *For Adults Only* magazine put it bluntly: "The sad fact is that porn stars age in dog years."[3]

By 1979, Candice's ambition had begun to collide with her exposure. "I feel I should leave this industry with people remembering who I am," she wrote in March. She was working to open new doors: drafting articles about her experiences onscreen and peddling them to men's magazines, taking meetings with industry executives who were exploring the still-new technology of videocassette, hanging out "with guys in the distribution end of the X industry." The money men had "flipped out so much over me," Candice wrote. "I'm described as beyond average into top ranking for my personality which involves beauty & intelligence," as well as a selling combination of "sleaze & class."[4]

But if producers and directors still sought out Candida Royalle, they gave her smaller roles. In *Olympic Fever*—one of the first movies Candice made in Southern California—her nameless character floats by as "Olympic Swimmer."[5] She played "Guest #19" in *The Tale of Tiffany Lust*, "Lesbian" in *Champagne for Breakfast*, and "Last Hooker into Cell" in *Taxi Girls*. Often, in 1979 and after, Royalle appeared in a single scene, sometimes as a kind of "sextra," or in a clothed cameo, as directors drew on a combination of her second-tier fame and her facility with dialogue. In *Sissy's Hot Summer*, a John C. Holmes vehicle, Candida Royalle acted "The Hostess," the equivalent of a character role in ballet: no leaps, only pantomime.[6]

Because adult movie audiences now knew the *nom de porn* Candida Royalle, producers sometimes called her out in advertisements, even when ticket-buyers would see her in only a scene or two, or only clothed, or both. CANDIDA ROYALLE was becoming a marquee attraction, too, at the venues where Candice made personal appearances, which she thought of as burlesque song-and-dance gigs, even though the customers wanted live-action pornography. She knew that her days in front of the camera were drawing to a close—that she was becoming, in industry parlance, "shot out," meaning that all the patrons who would ever want to masturbate to her image on celluloid had already done so. She tried to make light of her predicament. "After all," she joked in one of her early essays on the industry, "how long can you seek your fame sucking cock and screwing on yachts?"[7]

But in a later interview, she remarked on the gendered irony of "over-exposure": early on, the "typical line is something like we can't pay you a great deal of money because you're not a name yet. Then when they use you in every damn thing around and you become dependent on the income, they tell you we can't pay you very much because you're overexposed." She said young women entering the business should know that "directors are gonna grab them, chew them up, and spit them out real fast." Her own career had lasted six years, an eon for a woman in porn. She talked about "leaving with a big splash."[8]

———

Women Against Pornography March through Times Square, November 1979.

AS CANDICE CONTEMPLATED her departure from the blue screen, the adult film industry, after two decades of expanding rights and growing tolerance, found itself on the defensive. The legal net was still full of holes. But the feminist critique had grown too loud and too visible to be easily dismissed. Once an outlaw position, expressed in radical cells and underground papers, anti-pornography feminism was becoming a full-blown social movement, one that was increasingly bicoastal.

Shortly after the Take Back the Night march in San Francisco, feminist lawyers, theorists, and activists gathered on the other side of the country, at New York University, to wrestle with the challenge pornography posed to the First Amendment, and vice versa. If pornography was speech, several presenters argued, it was speech that silenced women. They envisioned new solutions that respected both civil liberties and women's lives. Susan Brownmiller pondered the use of libel prosecutions against pornographers who had graphically lampooned her, as *Screw* and *Hustler* had done. (*Hustler* publisher Larry Flynt, self-styled as one of the nation's most outrageous and least appealing free-speech crusaders, had been paralyzed by an attempted assassination several months before the NYU conference—shot in the back by a white supremacist outraged at the magazine's depiction of interracial sex.) Brenda Feigen Fasteau, a leader of the Women's Action Alliance, a feminist anti-discrimination organization, went further, envisioning a new type of tort, allowing "a class action to be brought by a group of women injured both mentally and physically by a particular movie or magazine." Such "civil rights of action," if carefully crafted, might be able to "eliminate works like the movie 'Snuff.'"[9]

By the time of the NYU conference, in late 1978, East Coast anti-violence feminists, with Brownmiller at their center, had begun to court WAVPM leaders in hopes of establishing a second bastion of anti-pornography activism in New York. In the first months of 1979, a group that started as a New York chapter of WAVPM grew into a distinct and more narrowly focused organization, which settled on the name Women Against Pornography, or WAP. WAP's founders—prominent white feminists including, in addition to Brownmiller, Gloria Steinem, Adrienne Rich, and Robin Morgan—had press connections and funding sources their San Francisco sisters could scarcely dream of.[10]

That spring, WAP opened an office in a storefront near the corner of Forty-Second Street and Ninth Avenue, in the heart of the Times Square sex district. That the location had, until WAP moved in, been what the *New York Times* called "a soul food restaurant and gathering place for transvestites and prostitutes" fittingly symbolized the racial and class outlines of the new organization, whose leaders quickly forged alliances with corporate and municipal groups seeking to "clean up," or gentrify the area. At their New York headquarters, and in a growing number of chapters around the country, WAP presented a slide show featuring a curated selection of graphic, violent images to dramatize their cause. Using tactics that echoed those of the temperance movement a century before, WAP also offered tours, leading shocked sympathizers into the brothels and peep parlors and live sex shows that surrounded the Ninth Avenue office. Over a thousand people—mostly women—paid to take the WAP tour in the second half of 1979 alone, gawking at prostitutes and heckling pimps.[11]

The slideshows and the porn tours lured the media. The daytime talk-show pioneer Phil Donahue featured three of WAP's founders on his program in July. A month later, *Time* magazine dubbed WAP's tours an "unlikely female sortie" in what was fast becoming "an all-out war against pornography." The conflict was heating up nationwide, *Time* explained; a Take Back the Night event in Minneapolis had recently drawn 4,500 marchers, while in tweedy Harvard Square, a local anarcho-feminist who had published a pamphlet entitled *Pornography: A License to Kill*, was charged with firing a gun into the ceiling of a bookstore that carried explicit titles.[12]

One activist from Cleveland told *Time*'s reporter she thought the war against porn might be "the one thing women can unite on," implying that American women were otherwise divided, which was true enough.[13] By the time WAP formed, issues related to gender roles, sex, and family had opened rifts not only within women's groups but also across American party politics more broadly. Opposition to abortion, sex education, and gay liberation became headline issues for a Republican Party increasingly responsive to evangelical Protestants in the sunbelt and Catholics in the Midwest, constituencies that linked shoring up the traditional family to containing the Communist menace.

The Equal Rights Amendment, whose passage had seemed certain when it cleared the Senate by a vote of 84 to 8 in 1972, was moribund, casualty of a sophisticated and energetic campaign led by Phyllis Schlafly and other conservative women. Rallying under the banner "S.T.O.P."—for Stop Taking Our Privileges—Schlafly and her followers defended distinct, complementary sex roles for women and men. New national conservative organizations like Focus on the Family, the Moral Majority, and Concerned Women for America, all founded between 1977 and 1979, enlisted hundreds of thousands of members in their grassroots battles. In his failed 1976 presidential bid, former California governor Ronald Reagan had championed "the values of the family" over the wisdom of government bureaucrats. By 1979, it was clear that Reagan meant to ride that hobbyhorse all the way to the White House.[14]

Anti-pornography feminists and family values conservatives tended to see the world very differently. Like others in the women's movement, most anti-porn feminists supported gay rights, sex education in the schools, and liberalized access to abortion. Many among the new breed of conservatives opposed those things. But both sides agreed that pornography was not only degrading but also posed a grave and growing danger to children, to women, and to families. Well before WAP had taken shape, the potential for what the journalist Molly Ivins called "peculiar alliances" between feminists and "traditional anti-smut groups" had become evident. And indeed, letters trickled into WAP's offices from religious women eager to combat premarital sex, egalitarian marriages, and sex education as well as pornography.[15]

Soon after opening its Times Square office, WAP began to organize a demonstration, to take place in October 1979. More than five thousand people showed up. Student groups caravanned from colleges along the East Coast. One contingent traveled all the way from Alaska. Steinem, Brownmiller, and Democratic congresswoman Bella Abzug led the line of march. Behind them, a sea of protesters—again largely young, white, and female—inched down Broadway from Columbus Circle to Times Square waving hand-lettered signs: PORN IS VISUAL ASSAULT. PORN IS THE MALE DEATH CULTURE. They chanted: "Two, four, six, eight, pornography is woman-hate." "Clean it up, shut it down, make New York a safer town." When they reached Forty-Second Street, the marchers turned east, for a rally in Bryant Park, with the hulking granite New York Public Library, a pillar of free-expression liberalism, rising behind the speakers. Susan Brownmiller called on President Jimmy Carter to empanel a new commission, a successor to Johnson's disappointing effort, "so we can get the real facts about the causality between pornography and violence."[16]

As the marchers filed by, customers continued to trickle into the peep parlors and hardcore theaters lining the demonstration route. Photographs show men standing at the edges of the march, jeering and grabbing their crotches. "I like pornography very much. It relaxes me and makes me feel good," a man standing in the doorway of the Pussycat Cinema told an AP reporter. "I think these women are crazy."[17]

———

CANDICE WAS IN MANHATTAN when WAP's marching multitudes closed Broadway. She had finished shooting her scenes in a film called

October Silk, and had interviews scheduled with the editors of various men's magazines, to pitch stories about her life in the industry. It's possible that she threaded her way to their Midtown offices through the protests.

She had been in the city, off and on, since July, visiting old haunts and making new scenes. The velvet ropes parted for her at Studio 54, where she danced alongside Halston and other famous habitués of the notorious cocaine-fueled discotheque. She much preferred the punk and new wave acts at the Mudd Club, in TriBeCa, where she heard Blondie and Robert Fripp. She'd gone back to her old neighborhood, near Field Place, to see *The Wanderers*, a film about the Bronx of her youth. One night walking down East Fifty-Ninth Street, she looked up to see a blinking marquee touting *Pizza Girls*. She and her friends— Joe Morocco, who had also moved back east, was with her—grabbed a couple slices and headed in to watch the movie. She felt "very much a NYC person again."[18]

It had been, Candice wrote, a "summer of romance," a bookend to the Summer of Love that had set in motion her pilgrimage to San Francisco. Martin Blinder was still smitten; he wanted to fly her to the Yucatán for ten days in October, to celebrate her twenty-ninth birthday. She wasn't sure she could stand to tear herself away from the whirl of men and movies in New York. She had started a "sweet, torrid affair" with Ron Sullivan, her director in *October Silk*. He was married, and what Candice called, in her diary, "the question of morality" gave her pause. But Sullivan treated her like a princess and not just a porn queen. When he pressed a hundred dollars into her hand for a splurge at Bloomingdale's, it felt like "a generous gift" rather than like sex for hire.[19]

In September, amidst her affairs with Martin on the West Coast and Ron on the East, Candice met Per Sjöstedt, who was working for director Chuck Vincent on a comic adult film, *That Lucky Stiff*. Per was, as she noted, "(very!) young": barely twenty, fresh out of military service in Sweden. He was also cosmopolitan, an international porn scion, raised in Sweden and Rome. Per's father, Sture Sjöstedt, had founded and still ran Saga Films AB, which one scholar calls "the most ambitious, prolific, and longest-running erotic filmmaking concern in

Scandinavia," arguably the adult filmmaking capital of the world.[20] At age nineteen, about a year before he met Candice, Per had acted—a sex role—in one of his father's films, *Fäbodjäntan* (*Come Blow the Horn!*). He had been a stand-in, pinch-hitting for an established actor who didn't show. Father and son agreed not to mention the performance to Per's mother, who would not have approved. (When I asked Per whether it had been weird having sex on camera in front of his father, he explained that he had seen *Deep Throat* in one of his dad's theaters when he was "like, six years old," and that Sture had gotten him his own wet bar when he turned eleven.) But then *Fäbodjäntan* became wildly successful, an almost *Deep Throat* level of notoriety, and the chance that somebody would recognize Per from the film grew, and it seemed prudent to get out of town.[21]

The elder Sjöstedt often invested in projects with American directors; he, Chuck Vincent, and Larry Revene had set up a New York–based joint venture, Lunarex. When Sture sent Per to the United States to work, he told him, "If you can survive in New York, you can survive anywhere." Just like the title song in Martin Scorsese's film, *New York, New York* (1977). Per started pouring coffee and lugging equipment on the sets of his father's friends. "I didn't really have any skills," he says. But porn directors weren't fixated on credentials. Hardworking and well connected, Per moved quickly up the ranks of the industry's production side.[22] By the time he met Candice, in Vincent's office, he was credited as an assistant director. Per was the one who cast her in what she called the film's "largest speaking role." When Candice told Per she wanted more money than her standard one-day rate, he offered to take her to dinner instead, and she agreed. "What an insufferable romantic I am!" she wrote.[23]

Soon afterward, Candice started a new journal in a spiral notebook, labeling it "Candy & Per," their names inside a heart, like a lovesick teenager's carving on a tree. She called Per "the prettiest, smartest, most sexy thing I've had the pleasure of being with in a very long time." She nicknamed him "my little 'Nazi'" because aside from his perfect blond, fair skinned Aryan look, which turns me on unbelievably," he also had "a strong firm commanding side to him." Their dates thrilled her: a "heavenly wicked weekend" in Canada, staying "at the

RITZ CARLTON." Lavish meals. Attending premieres of her movies together. "I'm not banking on being with Per forever. Who knows? It could end tomorrow," she reminded herself in early October. Yet they remained inseparable. "I hesitate to use the word love," she wrote. "It's like accepting a position you're still not sure you want to assume." But there was something real with Per, something that could last, a "glorious romance," the kind she'd dreamt of as a little girl.[24]

In November, she flew off to do a personal appearance in Detroit, in a seedy club with grabby men. But by then she had a plan. She returned to Hollywood and sorted through her things. Per joined her at the end of the month, while she shot a couple scenes in one more movie in Los Angeles: *Ball Game*, directed by Ann Perry, still one of the only female directors in the adult film business. She took a quick trip to San Francisco, where she stumbled around in an "opium haze" and said her farewells—not least to her younger avant garde self. Then she and Per piled her stuff into a moving truck and boarded a plane to New York: "home."[25]

———

CHRISTMAS LIGHTS and fairy-tale shop windows made the city a winter playground. Candice and Per toasted the season at a brunch with his parents at Windows on the World, perched on the 110th floor of the World Trade Center, the behemoth that opened after she went west. The building seemed to embody the resurgence of the metropolis that had teetered, mid-decade, on the brink of bankruptcy.[26]

Candice hadn't rented an apartment of her own; for now, she crashed with Joe Morocco and his boyfriend, Doug, who lived in a studio in the Ansonia Hotel, a fading Second Empire castle on Broadway. Earlier that year, Plato's Retreat—the notorious sex club co-owned by *Screw*'s Al Goldstein—had taken up quarters in the building's basement, moving into the space formerly occupied by the Continental Baths, perhaps the country's most famous gay bathhouse.

Upstairs in Joe's place, Candice and Per toasted the New Year with lines of cocaine and heroin. In a blissed-out haze, Candice jotted her dreams and fears for the '80s. She was barreling "toward the big one.

30." Would Per, nine years her junior, one day see her "as an old hag?" She hadn't yet told him her age.[27]

She looked back over the '70s—her twenties—imagining who she might be had she stayed the course at Parsons: "Candice Vadala becomes a fashion illustrator, marries Joe Kovacs, helps him get through law school, until he passes his bar and becomes a successful attorney and moves the two of them into a nice Manhattan apartment, eventually moving on to owning a lovely upper east side brownstone."

Maybe it didn't sound so bad?

But the Bronx Coalition's Women's Liberation Collective had shattered that domestic delusion. "There went it all. Now I was a hippy feminist."

Then came the migration west, to begin her "blossoming period," amidst the "very bizarre & colorful gay underground sect" of San Francisco.

Then Danny, and with him a long slide, now paused, but maybe not over.

Candice thought her stint in L.A. had raised her "level of toughness & sophistication" and allowed her to "sand down the rough edges from hippy, feminist, & freak influences."

And now here she was, "ripe and ready."[28]

But for what, exactly?

"When do my dreams begin changing more solidly into real life?" she asked, slowly shaking off New Year's Eve. Like so many other revelers staring red-eyed at the first day of 1980, she made a resolution: "This decade I will pull it all in together & make it work for me."[29]

PART IV

Finally Femme

Candida is a brilliant woman with killer timing.
—*Penthouse Letters*, 1988

In the '80s I rescued myself.
—Candice Vadala, 1990

17 A New Beginning

Candice and Per cut their wedding cake, 1980.

The bride wore black, a '50s number, thrifted, with a tight, boned bodice and a sweetheart neckline. The groom sported a black jumpsuit, tight in all the right places, topped by a bomber jacket, shiny, quilted, zippered. Just twenty, with the blond corona of a baby chick, Per looks barely old enough to shave. The maid of honor, Leslie Bovee, who had acted with Candice in a handful of adult pictures, showed up at Manhattan's City Hall in hot-pink Spandex. The ceremony was quick, civil: no priest, no prayers, no relatives. "Anyway—big weddings are a waste of time & money & a hazard to a decent relationship!" Candice later wrote.[1]

There were rings and vows and a sloppy kiss, but the piece of paper was the point. The bride and groom posed in front of the City Hall elevators holding the marriage certificate, which would keep Per in the country. He had been deported once already, for carrying pornographic material into the United States. Busted by Customs at JFK Airport, he recalls being escorted by armed guard onto a plane back to Stockholm. He returned to New York four days later, and this time he wasn't taking any chances.[2] The whole thing was "done in a very light-hearted way," Candice later told her father. Per "needed a green card to stay in the country and since we loved each other we decided to make it easy for him." She greeted her wedding day with bemused disbelief: after "all those other proposals," and "all those girlhood fantasies about when, where, with whom, why—Here I was—after only five months of bliss."[3]

In those scant months, Candice had expressed pride in her pretty young boyfriend. "Porn is reaching new dimensions—and he's already at the age of 20, helping to do it," she wrote, some weeks before the wedding, after they attended the premiere of Larry Revene's *Sizzle*, for which Per was credited as producer. Yet she had also felt a flickering wariness. At the end of January, she doodled a song with the chorus,

Rumblings of restlessness
Beating on my brain
Rumblings of restlessness
Will it be the same?
Rumblings of restlessness
Should I tell him now
I don't wanna be your
little house frau!

She titled the lyric "Fear of Wivery."[4]

The proposal came a few days after she wrote the song, over dinner at a Japanese steak house in Midtown. That night, Candice swooned in her diary about how perfect Per was: "Young & virile with a sexual appetite that won't quit, the blond Aryan look I so love, cultured with much class, schooled all over Europe, extremely bright, interesting, creative," with "just the right touch of craziness." He was also "very ambitious" and, she thought, "guaranteed to be in the money pretty soon."[5]

Shortly after Per and Candice announced their engagement, his parents, who had been in New York since December, returned to Sweden. His mother, Ann-Marie, was skeptical of the match. She looked down on her husband's industry, now also her son's, Per recalls. Pretty much the last thing she had ever wanted was for her baby to marry a porn star. Before she left New York, Ann-Marie ventured a warning: "She loves you now. But if she ever hates you, she can take all your money." Candice sketched the scene in her diary, joking, "I'm so sorry they won't be able to attend the wedding!"[6]

Between the Sjöstedts' departure, on Valentine's Day, and the trip to City Hall two weeks later, Candice flew to Toronto for a personal appearance, which gutted her; as usual, she self-medicated against her shame and fury. She had gained some control over her heroin habit, but she hadn't kicked it entirely. She sweated and shook and cramped through withdrawal, asking herself how she'd slipped, again. She hoped Per's "healthy non-abusive appetite for drugs" might rub off on her.[7]

And then she pulled herself together for "The Big Leap" she and Per would take on February 29: Leap Day.

After the ceremony, the newly minted Sjöstedts celebrated with their friends at the loft of Chuck Vincent, the adult film producer on whose set they had met. It was an airy space, filled with plants and books and midcentury modern furniture. A framed poster from a Gilbert and Sullivan performance at City Center hung next to one from Vincent's X-rated comedy *Bad Penny*. The photographer Candice and Per hired documented a small, low-key reception. Guests wear everyday clothes, nibble cheese wedges, and clink cans of Budweiser. Only a tiered cake clearly identifies the occasion.[8]

But if the wedding of Candice Vadala and her beau was an intimate affair, the marriage of Candida Royalle and Per Sjöstedt was also, as she noted, "an industry happening." Royalle was at least second-tier famous, and Per's father was porn royalty. Couples in the world of adult film rarely wed and were almost never monogamous. Candice knew she and Per were "forerunners to be getting married within the biz—'married?!'"[9] *High Society* sent a photographer, for whom the happy couple and their friends hammed it up in haute porn style. In those pictures, Candice's bodice flips down and her breasts pop out and Per bites her nipples and feels his way past the tops of her black seamed stockings. In those pictures, the guests toke and "cozy up" in groups of three or four, or steal off to "cop a feel" in the bathroom. "A veritable gallery of porn stars made the scene," the magazine crowed in a two-page photo spread entitled "The Bride Went Pink."[10]

Porn stars at home made for good copy, copy of a sort Candice was eager to try her hand at writing. But what were the chances it would make for a decent marriage? Sex work was full of intimacy, jealousy, and temptation. Sture Sjöstedt had had affairs with actresses, and Candice worried that Per would follow suit. There was hypocrisy, too: soon after the honeymoon, Candice learned that Chuck Vincent had cut her from a film to which her husband was attached, because he "felt it was morally wrong for me to have sex on the set with Per there since we were now married."[11]

Both of them meant to make the marriage real, and make it work. While it had started as a "marriage of convenience," Candice "came to realize [it] probably contained more love, and love of the purest, healthiest kind, than many legitimate marriages do." It wasn't easy,

Per recalls, to remain a "solid married couple in the middle of this storm": the maelstrom of the sex industry and its off-set expectations. He remembers nights out at clubs like Plato's Retreat, where friends headed for the back rooms while the newlyweds sat holding hands. They were monogamous because they "really loved each other," Per says. Candice treated their rented brownstone, on Sackett Street in Brooklyn, several blocks from her grandmother's place, "like a big doll house." She scoured antique shops; she revived the ancient grape arbor that edged their brick patio; she began fostering rescued cats. She loved bringing things "back to life," Per says.[12]

"And so, who knows," Candice wrote, the night of the small wedding and the big industry event. "If it lasts forever, we'll be very happy—if it ends in a year, we'll be happy for what we had. Right now, we're very much in love and happy to be husband & wife."[13]

———

CANDICE AND PER tied the knot at a moment of profound national anxiety about marriage, sex, and family. Abortion, sex education, divorce, and gay rights had moved to the very center of American politics and public life. Liberals and conservatives alike vied to attach themselves to a pro-family agenda.

"As you know, the American family is under unprecedented pressure," President Jimmy Carter had said the summer before, in a statement promoting the White House Conference on Families (WHCF), to be held in the spring of 1980. American families felt the sting of wrenching social transformations and the pinch of tough economic times. But American families also held the key to national renewal. "There is an old Yiddish proverb," said the evangelical Baptist president: "God gave burdens, but also shoulders." American families had big shoulders. "With strong families, I'm convinced, as I know you are, that our Nation's strength now and in the future will be assured."[14]

For Democrats, restoring the nation's strength meant mobilizing the resources of the federal government on behalf of families that took many forms. Carter charged the conference's large organizing committee to "reach out, not only to scholars and to experts but to many thousands of Americans around this country," to discover "what makes a family strong." During the scant six months between the beginning of Per and Candice's whirlwind courtship and their green-card/love-match/sex-press wedding, the WHCF's National Advisory Committee fanned out across the United States to listen. Ordinary people came forward by the tens of thousands to talk: about low wages and late nights, about taxes and childcare, about divorce and alcoholism and violence, about the endless pressures of making ends meet while helping children grow.[15]

A new breed of Republicans already knew what made the family strong, and government, in their view, had nothing to do with it. The White House conference was "a charade" with "a predetermined result: the demand that federal bureaucrats serve as Big Mama and Big Papa—of course, at a Big Price," wrote Phyllis Schlafly. She was skeptical even of the convening's name, alleging that the plural *families* had been adopted at Gloria Steinem's insistence, to endorse "alternate 'family' lifestyles."[16] Homosexuality, as well as equal rights, contraception, and especially abortion provoked heated debate and ultimately mass defections by conservative delegates to the WHCF convenings. "We have become a pitiful minority and we're walking out on principle," the head of the National Pro-Family Coalition told the *New York Times* at the June conference, held in Baltimore.[17]

During the final WHCF gathering, in Los Angeles in July 1980, just as Per and Candice's sexed-up wedding photos hit the news-stands, traditionalists held an enormous counterassembly, following the model that had proven so successful during the National Women's Conference in Houston three years before. Beverly LaHaye, whose Concerned Women for America organized the protest, addressed the gathering of some 7,000 activists, as did Schlafly, Dr. Mildred Jefferson of the National Right to Life Committee, and Charles H. Keating, whose Citizens for Decent Literature had been inveighing against pornography since the '50s. The WHCF had "jolted thousands more traditional Americans out of their easy chairs and 'evangelical ghettos'" and into the headlines, wrote Rosemary Thompson, an Illinois activist who worked closely with Schlafly. That same summer, representatives of some three hundred local conservative groups—many of them previously oriented to single issues like abortion or school prayer—took their fight to the capital in the American Family Forum, dubbed "the first national convention of the pro-family movement."[18]

Shortly after the Los Angeles WHCF concluded, Republicans gathered in Detroit to nominate Ronald Reagan as their candidate for president. The aging movie star had run twice before, in the revolutionary moment of 1968 and again in the bicentennial year of 1976, neither time reaching center stage. Despite Reagan's prodigious gifts as a communicator, his conservatism, in those earlier runs, had had fuzzy edges: anti-communism mixed with law and order mixed with an antipathy to regulation. Social issues took something of a backseat. During his California gubernatorial race in 1966, Reagan had railed against the hippies and their versions of free speech and free love. But then he also signed, in 1967, one of the nation's most liberal abortion bills.

In 1980, Reagan cast his candidacy in moral terms. He called abortion "murder" and sought to outlaw it in almost all cases. What North Carolina senator Jesse Helms called "a coalition of shared values," espoused by Catholics and Protestant evangelicals, helped to propel the Californian, finally, to the top of the ticket.[19] The priorities of this new Right, a disciplined and vocal minority, shaped the party's platform as well. Support for the ERA, a staple of every Republican platform since 1940, came out. The call for "a constitutional amendment to restore protection of the right to life for unborn children" went in, along with an affirmation of "the traditional role and values of the family."[20]

Several weeks later, at their convention in New York City, Democrats stood tall for ERA, for "family planning" and *Roe v. Wade*, for "adequately funded, comprehensive quality child-care" and other programs that served "the needs of the family, in all its diverse forms." The phrase "sexual orientation" appeared in a major party platform for the first time.[21] The sexual revolution would be on the ballot in November.

Bracing and sere, like the Santa Ana winds of his home state, Ronald Reagan exuded conviction. He promised a return to first principles, as stony and sure as Plymouth Rock. "Together, let us make this a new beginning," he said, accepting his party's nomination. In that address, and many times in the following months, Reagan distilled the core promises of his campaign into five warming words. *Family* was the first of them.[22]

———

PORNOGRAPHY WAS one of the only social issues about which Carter Democrats and Reagan Republicans often agreed. In 1976, some two-thirds of Americans polled thought that "the government should crack down more on pornography in movies, books and nightclubs." Carter's White House Conference on Families had urged the Federal Communications Commission to do more to restrict explicit and violent content. Congress considered some fifty-seven proposals regulating pornography between Carter's inauguration and Reagan's. Most of these were initiated by Republicans, whose growing anti-government and anti-regulatory fervor stopped short of materials that offended public morals. But several were co-sponsored by Democrats.[23]

At the ideological edges of the major political parties, radical feminists and evangelical activists alike abhorred pornography. Rev. Jerry Falwell, who was consumed with the issue, had incorporated the Moral Majority in July 1979, just as Women Against Pornography opened its offices in Times Square.[24] It can be hard to tell, on a blind test, which kind of activist said what. For instance: pornography is "a form of enslavement" which "degrades" women, turning them into "mere sex objects." Pornography is violence, its victims "tortured, devoured, and mutilated." Dworkin or Falwell?[25] "The pimps of pornography are hailed by leftists as saviors and savants." Falwell or Dworkin?[26]

Linda Lovelace's autobiography would fuel the anti-porn pyres on right and left alike. In the spring of 1980, with the presidential primaries in full swing, the star of *Deep Throat* published a memoir entitled *Ordeal*, issued under her *nom de porn*, in which she revealed that her ex-husband, Chuck Traynor, had beaten, raped, and held her captive at gunpoint. Her performances were hostage films; she likened herself to Patty Hearst. The signs of her distress should have been obvious to moviegoers, she wrote. And indeed, for all its lightheartedness, *Deep Throat* shows her speckled with bruises. The actress had earned little from her success; the contracts Traynor drew up left her with only 3 percent of her gross royalties, and almost nothing of her future earnings. She'd given pleasure to millions and known only fear and want in return. "I hope this book brings us some money," she wrote.[27]

Ordeal was uniquely useful to activists because it directly connected pornography to a lived experience of sexual terror. Anti-pornography feminists, some of them celebrities, picketed sites like the Frisco Theater on Seventh Avenue, where *Deep Throat* was *still* playing, some eight years after its release. WAP issued a press release, which generalized Lovelace's experience to "the slavery of thousands of women and girls trapped by poverty, violence, and fear in an industry that reaps four billion dollars a year from their degradation."[28]

No major newspaper reviewed *Ordeal*. Yet the demonstrations and the media coverage they attracted made the book a national bestseller, appearing on the nonfiction lists a few slots below *Free to Choose*, the bible of the new supply-side economics, by the University of Chicago monetarist Milton Friedman and his wife, Rose. The *Times* was sniffy about *Ordeal*'s success. "Linda Lovelace's 'Ordeal,' is in seventh place on the mass market paperback list despite the refusal of some distributors and many bookstores to handle it," ran a footnote to the bestseller list in March 1981, which further clarified: "Miss Lovelace was the heroine of the movie 'Deep Throat,' and her book explains, among other things, how she got the job."[29]

If both conservatives in the heartland and feminists in the cities were concerned with pornography, they worried about different things and spoke in different registers. Anti-pornography feminists rarely inveighed against filth or longed for decency. Anti-pornography conservatives rarely spoke about women's equality—or, indeed, about women at all. But both groups thought about the issue, increasingly, in terms of harm and victims. And both groups fretted, most of all, about the impacts of pornography on children. For with the rise of cable television and the video cassette recorder, sexually explicit programming began to migrate from the sin district to the suburban split-level.

Cable's ascent had begun in 1972, when the Federal Communications Commission declared that producing content for the "electronic soapbox" was a basic citizenship right. What's more, rules for what could be shown on cable channels, available by subscription, were more relaxed than those governing broadcast TV. The adult industry moved quickly into the new airspace; in 1975—the year Candice made her first pornographic movies—*Screw* publisher Al Goldstein began airing an explicit talk show, *Midnight Blue*, on public access cable in New York.[30]

Late that same year, SONY introduced its Betamax video cassette recorder, the first such device priced for an ordinary consumer. Pre-recorded videotapes followed in 1976. A year later, JVC's competing VHS format joined the battle for the family den, introducing con-fusion but also driving down prices. In 1978, only a tiny fraction of American households—roughly 150,000 early adopters—owned a VCR. By the time of Reagan's inauguration, some 2 million units were selling annually.[31]

Would-be home consumers of pornography drove the technol-ogy's rapid adoption. In 1979, X-rated videocassettes outsold refor-matted Hollywood films by a margin of 3 to 1, with a million tapes purchased. Industry analysts expected the number to triple by 1982. Porn shaped the evolution of cable programming as well. More than two hundred explicit stations plied the airwaves by the end of Reagan's first year. The number of theaters regularly showing hardcore films began to decline.[32]

Women Against Pornography's tours of Times Square met the sex industry where it lived most concretely, in movie houses and peep booths and live sex shows. But for all their gut-level effect, the tours had the emerging dynamics of the industry exactly backward. If WAP wanted to pull back the curtain on the heart of pornography's dark-ness, they should have sold tickets to rec rooms in Ramapo, to watch couples canoodling on their couches. These were the kinds of spaces Candice would colonize in the years ahead.

As porn headed home, children came to dominate the discourse about victimization and remedies. From Carter to Reagan through Clinton and beyond, Congress's discussions about pornography would be framed around the prevention of child sexual abuse and exploita-tion, a problem that began to obsess mass media quite suddenly in 1977 and quickly acquired the proportions of an all-out moral panic.[33]

At a news conference following WAP's big demonstration in support of *Ordeal*, Linda Lovelace asked, "Does a person become any less of a victim at age eleven or thirteen or nineteen? Or ever?" A photograph shows her before the microphone, eyes heavenward, a fuzzy white teddy bear in her lap.[34]

———

"ELECTION DAY IN U.S.A." Candice headlined her diary entry on November 4, 1980, a couple weeks after she turned "that traumatic age of 30" and several months into her marriage. "Will it be Carter or Reagan? Does it really matter?" She knew it did—knew it was "the most important election for our country," knew "how directly my life is affected by it." So many of her friends were sex radicals and gay men, now squarely in the crosshairs of the ascendant Right. Her own choices, too, had been shaped by freedoms imperiled by this New Beginning, the expansion of abortion rights, for one. Candice would soon terminate her fourth unplanned pregnancy. Yet she hadn't voted. Like a "big jerk," she "forgot to register on time," unaware, in the heroin-fueled haze of another personal appearance, that there was "any damned deadline."[35]

If Candice's appetite for organized politics was minimal, she was keenly aware that sensational stories like the sordid tale told in *Ordeal* had captured the public imagination. "Word has it that Linda Lovelace is going to use your show as a platform to make some strong statements about herself and other women in the erotic film industry," Candice wrote to one producer shortly after Reagan's inauguration. While she admitted she knew nothing of "Miss Lovelace's actual experiences," they hardly mirrored her own. "I resent her ridiculous accusations that all erotic film actresses are working under force," she continued. "It is not only untrue, it is degrading." She would "not pretend that this business is perfectly fair to women." But nor could anybody convincingly advance "such a claim about any business in our present society." Candida Royalle did not need "anyone, particularly one who so insults my intelligence, to be my self-proclaimed spokeswoman." Candida Royalle sought nothing more than "to publicly voice my opinion."[36]

Candice knew her voice, her arguments, and her sensibility were distinctive. She had a story to tell, and to sell. "My writing has been a great source of fulfillment," she had noted in her journal earlier in the year, while she was using her "creating pen" to doctor a film script. She wondered if "all those years of keeping diaries & journals" might have honed talents she was only beginning to use.[37]

18 Ink

Candice at work, c1982.

C andice had not held a straight, steady job since working as a salesgirl at Bergdorf's after high school. She owned little beyond the bric-a-brac she salvaged to decorate the apartment on Sackett Street. In 1980, she pulled in roughly $12,000—about $37,500 in today's dollars—her earnings split between acting and live performances. The money wasn't terrible; she was making a bit more than the median personal income in the United States. But it wasn't predictable. In April, she earned a grand total of $375; in August, nothing. You couldn't save for a rainy day on an income like that. And lately, it seemed that every day was rainy.[1]

The personal-appearance circuit, especially, ground her down to nothing. On the road, she forced herself "to become a character I have always flirted with, pretended to be for financial reward, and deep down inside, did not identify with." She "rationalized it away—everybody needs to make a living." But when the floodlights came up, snorting heroin was the "only thing that helps quell the agony," she confessed to her diary. Yet the fix was always temporary. By December—after seeing her name in lights at New York's Melody Burlesque and Pittsburgh's Casino Royale, and the Gayety Theater and Benny's Rebel in D.C.; and after Reagan's victory; and after John Lennon's murder, right there in New York; and good lord, what was next?—she found she could barely leave the house. "So what if I do want to lay in bed late and read magazines and write in my journal," she wrote, days blurring in a "nonstop flood of tears." Per was "working hard" to give her "the luxury of time" to regroup "with no financial worry." He was "strong-willed," she wrote, and did "not want to see me deteriorate into a junkie." He prevailed. By year's end, they had become "basically a no drug family, other than grass." Candice decided the time had come to focus on "more legit career goals," and forecast that "the career of Candida Royalle is seeing its end, other than articles."[2]

If Candice Vadala had outgrown *Candida Royalle*, she also knew that Royalle's name, and her biography, with all its hard-won naked truths, was a kind of commodity. Though she bemoaned Reagan's election, she had nonetheless absorbed the dawning neoliberal ethos: Let freedom reign. Every woman for herself. If you've got it, sell it. The administration and its Christian allies abhorred pornography. Yet the Reaganites shared what one journalist called the "liberation spirit" and "glib sense of rights" that defined the "New Porn style" of the era.[3] And so, for the first time, in that new beginning of 1980, *Candida Royalle* became a different kind of *nom de porn* than the name that scrolled by in screen credits or blinked on a burlesque club marquee. *Candida Royalle* became a byline.

THE SEX PRESS WAS BOOMING. The leading glossies, *Playboy* and *Penthouse*, had grown downright upstanding, with circulations to match, each hovering near the 5 million mark. *Hustler*, with its ethos of lowbrow, redneck raunch, had expanded from a two-page newsletter to a four-color glossy selling 1.6 million copies each month. Sales of the most popular titles had softened some since the porno-chic era, but if their slices were smaller, the pie was still growing apace. Each passing year saw the launch of new magazines, subsidiaries, and competitors, which catered to existing kinks and tried to invent new ones. *Hustler* begat *Chic*. *Screw* begat *Death*. *Playboy* begat *Oui*. *Penthouse* spun off *Letters*, *Forum*, and *Variations*. By 1980, the American adult press comprised nearly four hundred periodical titles, from *Adam* to *Velvet*.[4] Most were owned by privately held companies, which gave them broad editorial latitude. Gloria Leonard, the pornographic actress who had become the publisher of *High Society* in 1977, complained that she felt hemmed in after CBS bought Fawcett Books, which published the magazine. Leonard described herself as a "staunch feminist," and pitched *High Society* as vehicle of female liberation. "We want to stimulate people both above the waist as well as below," she said. "So far, we have been very successful." This was an understatement: *High Society* claimed a monthly circulation of 3 million readers.[5] Ink flowed out and money flowed in.

Committed to growing and segmenting a market that seemed nearly inexhaustible, adult periodicals spanned an enormous gamut in taste and quality. What they shared, as one business reporter explained, were steep cover prices, "the highest prices ever charged by large circulation magazines in publishing history," two to four times as much as *Time* or *Newsweek* or *Life*. Vendors typically kept 30 percent of a magazine's selling price, which meant that X periodicals claimed prime real estate on newsstands. Annual sales of monthly heterosexual softcore sex magazines—those showing full nudity but only simulated sex—reached $450 million in 1979. And that statistic doesn't encompass the publications' advertising revenues, or capture the earnings income of some two hundred hardcore periodicals, or the smaller group of explicit gay and lesbian magazines.[6]

Paper pornography had an incestuous relationship with the moving image. The magazines covered the movies; the movies ginned up the stars and backstage gossip that filled the magazines. Most of the photos in all but the highest budget skin mags came directly from the blue screen, in the form of "chromes": Kodachrome slides of sex scenes or stills documenting (and sometimes staging) the making of a hardcore film. Chromes were meant to titillate. As the publisher of *Fling* told one prospective freelancer, "We would need only reviews (and color slides) of pictures that feature BIG TITTED women, even though the parts might not be leading roles. If only one big titter appears (and we have some slides showing her) then it's OK for FLING."[7] As adult films proliferated on videotape, so, too, did explicit magazines devoted to reporting on, reviewing, and repackaging them. The year 1980, when Royalle's byline began appearing in the sex press, saw the launch of *Cinema X* and *Video X*. *Adult Video News* would join them two years later.[8]

Per shot Candice's debut chromes, provocative nude beach shots from their "horny honeymoon," for *Cinema X*, which was negotiating with her about a regular writing assignment. Sture Sjöstedt had paid for the trip, after originally suggesting Vegas, "in order to be able to obtain a quick & easy divorce there," Candice later wrote in her diary. She wangled the Caribbean instead. "Outsmarted the old buzzard that time."[9] The islands made for hotter copy too.

Candice on her honeymoon in Jamaica, March 1980.

The images illustrated the debut installment of Candice's new column, "The Royalle Treatment." In addition to offering up "the spiciest details" of her own "wildest adventures," she would interview other industry players and "do some promotional publicity." She was working on a reported piece for *High Society*, too; by year's end, her byline would appear there regularly. She tried her hand at a film script, for Larry Revene's *Blue Magic*, one of the last movies in which she acted in a sex role. She still went on the occasional casting call, but found those efforts increasingly "futile . . . If it's not a blond they're looking for it's a 5'8" bathing beauty," she wrote of hardcore's shifting standards.[10]

Writing sex wasn't nearly as lucrative as having it onscreen. In those first years, Candice's columns paid $125 to $150 apiece. A personal appearance could command twice that or more, and her day rate on films sometimes reached $500. But if writing earned her less, it also cost her less, and opportunities were plentiful. In 1980, she took in $1,150 for a half dozen columns and the *Blue Magic* screenplay: about 10 percent of her income. By 1982, she was earning more than three times that on her writing; the following year, she made nearly $9,000 for a combination of articles, chromes, and short scripts for *High Society Live*, Gloria

Leonard's pioneering pay-per-call phone-sex line. (The recorded phone messages were especially lucrative, paying $50 each for a few minutes' clothed work.) The Candida Royalle byline appeared in at least eight different publications that year. "Now I am a journalist, in the industry," Candice told a scantily clad Robin Byrd on Byrd's eponymous late-night X-rated cable show in November 1981. She described herself as "the new Hedda Hopper."[11]

Royalle's writings had twang and sass, though the skin-mag blueprint meant that her reporting was meant to titillate. She was, as she put it in a column for *Velvet*, "your thrill-seeking pleasure baby . . . with all the news that's unfit to print": Bedda Hopper. The first "Royalle Treatment" column detailed her preparations to attend the theatrical premier of *October Silk*, lingering on descriptions of toilette—lotion gets applied, self-lovingly—and costume—stockings rise slowly to meet garter belts. Royalle assures the reader that watching her film seated next to her handsome man had excited her, and recommends viewing porn with a lover. Then she narrates, in explicit detail, the scenes that aroused her the most. The column thus functions as complimentary copy for *October Silk*, reviewed (glowingly) elsewhere in the issue. While Candice pointed her readers, breathlessly, toward the theater, an advertisement on the magazine's back cover hinted at a dawning future: International Home Video Club promised that members could "Watch What You Want When You Want to Watch It!"[12]

Many of the articles under Royalle's byline packaged obvious fantasy with reality effects. "Fuckerware Party," which she offered to *Velvet*, describes a coterie of accomplished professional women gathering to try out sex toys, oils, and revealing lingerie. "I was the token porn star," the narrator mock-confesses, weaving a plot that ends in a threesome in an apartment bathroom. For "Royalle Audience," a short-lived advice column in *Harvey*, Candice wrote both the readers' letters and her responses. Most queries purported to be from married men lamenting sex lives grown dull with familiarity.[13]

In other features, Royalle offered readers a kind of documentary access to the industry. One behind-the-scenes article finds our roving reporter, with "note pad and tape recorder" in hand, observing the filming of *Nasty Girls*, whose director, Henri Pachard, aka Ron

Sullivan, had been Candice's lover the summer before she met Per. She describes the movie's sex scenes in explicit detail. But she also captures the actors on their downtime, in the staff kitchen, guzzling coffee and goofing around to blow off some of the tension of filming. "For scenes that must end with a man's orgasm, this is truly the most tense moment of a shoot," she instructs. She emphasizes the expertise marshalled on-set, quoting the young journalist E. Jean Carroll, who covered the same shoot for the upscale, softcore *Playgirl*: "What a fascinating business!" Carroll declares. "I've never seen anything like it! And so professional!"[14]

In all these ways, Royalle's reporting hewed to the conventions of a rigid genre. Yet the drafts of her published pieces also show a creative talent chafing against those strictures. Her writings about her experiences on the personal-appearance circuit, especially, defied formula. She tested out multiple versions, inching from the raw and addled pain of her diaries into a narrative as carefully airbrushed as the nudes that ran alongside her columns. She submitted long, searing reports of life on the road, "a way of living so different from anything I've ever experienced that I bring pictures taken at home with me to remind myself who I am." The toughest part, she explained, "was coming face to face with this character, Candida Royalle, that I have created . . . and having to honestly like and respect her so that I may go out there in front of all those people and be her."[15]

No editor wanted to run that story, not the general-interest magazines she pitched it to, and not the skin mags either.

She sent *Velvet* a sexier, sunnier cut, in which she wasn't "just trying to look hot up there anymore. I am hot!" Yet she admitted that she "felt vulnerable" onstage, with the men so close that "any moment any one of them could make a dive for me." In her diary, she made clear she had found that exposure terrifying. Here, she merely "giggled" at the thought that they "might all go nuts and start grabbing for me." Still, *Velvet* passed.[16]

She found the formula that worked. "I particularly love doing these engagements because I get to show off all my talents as well as my natural endowments," she wrote of a weeklong run of appearances at Times Square's Melody Burlesque. "It's so great to see all these guys (and sometimes girls!) on the edge of their seats, just begging to see more." She said their attention made her feel like "a cat in heat getting ready to pounce." That she particularly loved giving special customers—the ones who reached out with money in hand—"a private little show, . . . raising and parting my legs, getting on all fours and arching my back, exposing myself to them fully, while my face took on a look of lust." She promised, "it was all real!"

Cinema X spread that version of the story over two issues, saving the "dirtiest details" for last.[17]

———

IT IS PERHAPS too simple to say that Candice wrote her way clean. But one way and another, the detox from heroin held. There were stumbles, as in early 1981, when she tried "doing it 'just once,'" as she told Cinthea, with whom she'd begun to repair her relationship. But each relapse offered enough fresh horror to forestall the next one. Kirby Lowe, the bassist with whom she'd performed, and shared needles, in San Francisco, overdosed and died. "That could have been me," she wrote. She found a counselor at the New York State Office of Alcoholism and Substance Abuse Specialized Treatment Services and told him she knew she had to "just totally stop. He said 'when?' I took a deep breath and said 'now.'" That was April 11, 1981: "decision date," she called it. The "beginning of my rebuilding of my self."[18]

Candice worked to understand the connection between her addiction, her career in porn, and her ambitions for the future. Her counselor showed her that she'd been "indoctrinated to be a failure." Heroin had blunted her dreams, rubbed smooth her grit. Faced with hard choices, she had taken "an easy route to $ via porn films," she wrote to Cinthea. For all their father's talk of tramps and sin, "sex was always 'condoned' at home, was it not? Think about it . . ."

Eight weeks, four days, and counting since her last hit, Candice was working a mantra: "TIME & DETERMINATION."[19]

She turned down appearances, telling an agent who solicited her for a theatrical act in Vegas that she was planning "to resume my stage career on a more legit level," which excluded "most burlesque clubs, or anything hard-core."²⁰ She drafted essays and query letters for mainstream publications: *New York Magazine*, the *Times*. The pitch: she would take readers—serious readers—into sex clubs, from the performer's perspective, to give them an "understanding into the mind behind the body. Women in the sex industry have long been misunderstood & put down," she said. "I would like to help change that." Or she would report on the spread of heroin through the city. "I want to take the readers to the streets and alleys that are now marketplaces for illegal drugs, and into the gutted-out buildings that house 'shooting galleries.'" She wrote lighter fare: an essay for *Cat Fancy*—her first "major feature article" for "a magazine not in the sex industry," she crowed in her diary. It ran under her married name, Candice Vadala-Sjöstedt.²¹

"Candida Royalle" kept publishing too. But she grew bored with the fake and the fizz. Instead, she was increasingly interested in portraying the real lives of real women in the industry, and especially the lives of those who had gotten out. "Everyone hears the horror stories," she wrote in an article for *High Society* that pondered a question she often asked herself: "Is there Life After Porn?" She acknowledged the well-known tragedies: Lovelace's ordeal, of course, and the death of porn queen Tina Russell from alcohol-induced liver failure in May 1981, and the overdose of the "precedent-setting transsexual star" Jill Monro the following year. But tragedy wasn't the only story, and it wasn't hers. Readers "have these traditional views of women coming out" of the industry "and being totally strung-out whores or something," she told one interviewer in 1982. "I think we're some of the strongest, most together women I know."²²

But the pre-written scripts of mainstream and adult magazines alike meant that Candice did not have much success publishing such pieces. A few years later, after she'd become post-porn famous, she got an angry directive from her editor at *Cheri*, offering to "clarify any questions . . . as to what content and tone your column should have." She had written, alas, about "subjects that we try hard to avoid": pregnancies and families and everyday life. "I would prefer not to tell about people leaving the business, but rather of people entering the business," he scolded. Subscribers wanted to read about "porn stars getting involved and fooling around, but not of them getting married! In general, CHERI tries to talk about fun things and to give the impression that the people in the porn world . . . are having wild times out there."[23]

Life had gotten too serious for Candice to focus on *fun things* and *wild times*. "The issue of pornography, in my opinion, gets far too much attention anyway," she wrote in her diary in 1982, as the long-simmering tension on the subject among feminists boiled into open warfare. "Our energies could be better spent focusing on nuclear proliferation, how to make real peace, how to feed the hungry . . . the real moral issues."[24] Those were the battles she wanted to fight. Those were the stories she wanted to write, if only pornography would stop writing her.

———

"WHENEVER I HEAR SOMEONE talking about the sexual revolution or the new freedom, I don't look on that as progress," Linda Lovelace wrote in *Ordeal.*[25] While the actress's suffering at the hands of "the new freedom" was extreme by any measure, an increasing number of ordinary women shared her sense that the so-called revolution had let them down. In 1981, *Cosmopolitan* released the results of what it claimed was "the largest sex survey ever conducted": a magazine questionnaire netting 106,000 responses of great length and intimacy. *Cosmo* readers might have been expected to embrace the redemptive joys of sex that the magazine peddled. Yet more than half of the respondents felt that "things had gone too far. . . . that sex today had become too casual and too difficult to avoid, and that they themselves, and perhaps all women, had become pawns in a revolution chiefly engineered by men." In this way, the legatees of sexual revolution were much "like the heirs to political revolutions," the editor of *The Cosmo Report* supposed: "they had participated in the overthrow of one tyranny only to see another installed." They had lost their inhibitions and located their orgasms. But they had not found happiness. One young woman from Illinois admitted, "there are times when I envy my mom."[26]

She was hardly alone. A popular self-help text promoted a "new celibacy."[27] George Leonard, a leader in the human potential movement based in Esalen, California, said that cheap sex had outlived its conceptual usefulness. He advocated the pursuit of "High Monogamy."

Esquire ran Leonard's essay, "The End of Sex," on its December 1982 cover, over the image of a funeral wreath.[28]

The dying had already begun, though few news outlets were reporting on it. As early as 1979, a doctor in New York had noted a group of unusual deaths in healthy young gay men, who succumbed to opportunistic infections that typically claimed only the old and the sick. In June 1981, the Centers for Disease Control sounded the alarm about a similar cluster of deaths in Los Angeles. By the end of that year, the CDC had begun labeling the underlying disease as GRID: gay-related immune deficiency. National Public Radio, the *New York Times*, and the increasingly popular Cable News Network carried the story, at the bottom of the hour or in the back of the first section. But gay men, sex radicals, and others on the frontlines of the erstwhile revolution paid close attention.[29]

Patrick Cowley, Candice's musical soulmate and sometime lover, was hospitalized, in failing health, at the end of 1981, suffering from what "they're calling 'gay cancer,'" Candice wrote. She and Patrick had once "made wonderful love." But she assumed—as others then did—that women and straight men would be spared.[30]

By the time Cowley perished, in November 1982, the CDC had named the new disease Acquired Immune Deficiency Syndrome, or AIDS. Bodily fluids seemed to carry it, needles and sex to spread it. Gayle Rubin, a young ethnographer working in the San Francisco leather community, saw the dry tinder of an incipient moral panic. "When fears of incurable disease mingle with sexual terror," she warned, "the resulting brew is extremely volatile." The new plague intersected older feminist fault-lines at those vexed points where pleasure and danger crossed. Rubin urged: "The time has come to think about sex."[31]

———

RUBIN, one of the founders of the San Francisco-based lesbian feminist S/M collective SAMOIS, delivered remarks on "thinking sex" at a conference at Barnard College in April 1982. The ninth installment of an annual series called "The Scholar and the Feminist," sponsored by Barnard's Women Center, was themed around female desire. "Towards a Politics of Sexuality," the formal title ran, acknowledging the pre-liminary nature of the exploration. The conference organizers set out to explore many questions, but the first, the largest frame, was plea-sure: "How do women get sexual pleasure in patriarchy?" The "sexual domain" had long been, and remained, "a dangerous one for women," the anthropologist Carole S. Vance, the conference's academic coordi-nator, acknowledged in a letter to attendees. The ongoing "controversy about pornography in the feminist community" had made sexuality "a particularly timely and appropriate topic"—indeed, an urgent one. So, too, did "the intense self-consciousness and silence among het-erosexual women . . . about personal pleasure."[32] Rubin worried that many feminists had deferred even a theory of pleasure until "after the revolution," when the state withered away, and the heat and mess of "this earthly, fleshy existence" would recede, revealing "a transcendent image of celestial delight." In the meantime, feminist conversation around pornography had grown lopsided. "I have never seen a position become dogma with so little debate," Rubin said of the antis.[33]

The organizers of the Barnard Conference, as the 1982 event came to be known, were concerned that, rather than emboldening women, the feminist anti-pornography line "heightens fears of male violence and male danger." Arguments like the ones WAP made during its sex tours and in its slideshows overlapped to an uncomfortable degree with the New Right's understanding of women—especially white women—as vessels in need of protection. The conservative view had at least the virtue of intellectual coherence.[34] But feminists, as the jour-nalist and conference co-planner Ellen Willis noted, were "ambiva-lent, confused, and divided in their views on sexual freedom." Some of the emerging "feminist sexual orthodoxies," she said, might "best be described as neo-Victorian."[35]

The Barnard Conference organizers weren't the first feminists to articulate what came to be known as a sex-positive or pro-sex argu-ment within the women's movement. There had been, at the turn of the new decade, several niche publications trumpeting a feminist pleasure politics. Two volumes orienting readers to the San Francisco lesbian leather scene went through multiple printings, selling out at local feminist bookstores, parades, and festivals.[36] In late 1981, the New

York-based quarterly *Heresies* published a dedicated "Sex Issue" that cast a somewhat wider net around the topic of female pleasure, with a range of writings, from interviews and poetry to erotic fiction. The anthropologist Paula Webster tackled the battle over pornography in her contribution, which challenged feminists to invent "a truly radical pornography that spoke of female desire as we are beginning to know it and as we would like to see it acted out."[37]

But for all the new ground they broke, such works amounted to so many discussions around a family dinner table.[38] The fight over the Barnard Conference both intensified the debates and pushed an internecine disagreement more forcefully into the public sphere. A group calling itself the Coalition for a Feminist Sexuality and against Sadomasochism, a WAP front, picketed the gathering, massing at Barnard's gates to distribute a flyer that called out speakers and their organizations, accusing them of condoning pedophilia, mocking genocide, and internalizing misogyny. Nonetheless, some eight hundred people pushed past the demonstrators to attend.[39]

The conference itself was brief, the work of a spring Saturday.[40] But its aftershocks rippled for years, even decades. Coalition members had successfully lobbied the college administration to confiscate the seventy-two-page *Diary of a Conference*, in which the organizers described the year of study and debate that had shaped the program. But the proceedings were published in 1984, not in an obscure mimeographed journal but as a freestanding anthology by Routledge. *Pleasure and Danger: Exploring Female Sexuality* was widely reviewed in mainstream publications, including the *Times Book Review*, which headlined its appraisal "Sex Still Not Simple," surely the understatement of the century.[41] Those books, and new periodicals, like the lesbian erotica magazine *On Our Backs*, spread the gospel of "free speech and sex-positivity" far and wide. Until Barnard, the Bay Area sex radical Carol Queen recalls, "anti-porn and sex-nervous feminists" had possessed a near "monopoly on the paper stack." She picked up *Pleasure and Danger* and *On Our Backs* at a feminist bookstore, and discovered "how Barnard proved to be the flashpoint," revealing a disparate set of experiences, and weaving loose "threads of rhetoric" into "an active, other kind of feminism."[42]

But if the Barnard Conference functioned as a noisy coming-out party for sex-positive feminists, it also revealed the limitations of their framework. The speakers were skeptical of the anti-pornography movement, but had no shared position about pornography itself, nor about pleasure more broadly. Indeed, where most antis theorized a female universal, their opponents embraced, and even fetishized, axes of difference, from race and class to kinks and queerness. Collectively, they were anti-anti-porn, not pro-porn. They were also, in a literal sense, reactionary, fighting a rear-guard not-quite-campaign against far better organized and more single-minded opponents. WAP members, not conference speakers, had the newsletters, the tours, the slogans, the T-shirts. Many of the antis were movement people, some with long experience in New Left and Civil Rights circles. The anti-antis, self-proclaimed outsiders, even perverts, were in many ways anti-institutional, and sometimes anti-identity altogether. As the queer legal theorist Janet Halley notes, "supporters of deviance are hard to rope into a unit," much less to fund and brand. In the years ahead, pro-sex solidarities would tend to coalesce around particular occasions or threats, and then to evanesce just as rapidly.[43]

More an anthology of viewpoints than a social movement, it is fitting that sex-positive feminism's emerging voices were best organized on paper. Since 1984, *Pleasure and Danger* has gone through three English-language editions and a Spanish translation. It remains widely taught, appearing in recent years on hundreds of syllabi; it has been cited more than six thousand times. Together with *Powers of Desire,* a collection of scholarly contributions to a "countervailing feminist politics that stresses sexual variety and pleasure," which appeared at nearly the same time and featured many of the same writers, *Pleasure and Danger* marked the entrance of sex into new corners of the modern university and American public life.[44]

––––––

BARNARD WAS A SPACE for thinking sex, not working sex; the program featured no adult-industry professionals. Certainly not Candice, who did not read feminist newsletters or scholarly journals, and could scarcely have imagined that she would, within a few short years, appear alongside some of the organizers *and* some of the protesters. When the barricades went up in Morningside Heights, she was in Brooklyn, pondering her next moves. "Realization: I don't have to please men to survive!" she wrote in her diary the week of the conference. She had come to believe that "women are innately more intelligent, more tied into the world, the elements, the universe" than men, and thought the "future of our planet depends on women taking hold of the reins."[45]

The anti-porn feminists protesting at Barnard shared Candice's understanding of the essential differences between the sexes: the belief that men were often violent and predatory, and women innately nurturing and vulnerable. Candice acknowledged, in her private writings, that some of their arguments chimed with her experiences. That June, she saw the acclaimed Canadian documentary *Not a Love Story: A Film about Pornography*. "My feelings about porn going thru many radical changes due to intense realizations now that I'm free to really look at it," she wrote in her diary afterward. Parts of the movie "hit home hard & released another whole set of feelings not previously surfaced": embarrassment, even "humiliation. . . . Awful feelings I ignored by failing to be conscious."[46]

Shortly after Candice saw *Not a Love Story*, she published one of her hardest-hitting articles, "Vertical Smiles and Cum-Soaked Aisles," in *High Times*. Perhaps because the magazine featured more drug than sex content, or perhaps because the editor, Larry Sloman, was, as Candice wrote, a cut above "the schmucks at most men's magazines," her critique was allowed to bleed through the gossip and titillation. She was candid about having gotten into the industry "for the same reason anyone else gets into the sex business—money." She reprised her first experiences making "fuck and suck loops . . . the bottom rung" of the porn hierarchy, for an ugly, callous, conniving director. She proclaimed, proudly, that she was now off the set, and out of the burlesque theaters, which she called "bargain basement whorehouse[s] run by low-life swine."[47]

In her diaries, the reckoning was rawer still. "It creates an actual physical pain for me to think about doing those films," she wrote in November 1982, the month the Playboy Channel debuted on cable and

Patrick Cowley died of AIDS. "What must I have thought of myself to think I had to do that to get by?"[48] Her recent discovery, through a blood test during a routine check-up, that she had been carrying hepatitis C since those drug-shooting, porn-shooting days, only heightened her regret.[49]

Yet Candice was nobody's victim. She had chosen badly, and from a limited field of options. But she had chosen nonetheless. This was not the way anti-pornography feminists would have her understand her own life. That October, when WAP members picketed Sexpo '82—"the first unofficial World's Fair of Erotica"—they were picketing Candice. In an article for *Velvet*, she decried "all the noisy hullabaloo being tossed around by groups like 'Women Against Porn.'" She found the opposition cynical. Pornography was "everyone's fave pet peeve": an "easy dumping ground" for politicians, allowing them to "stir up trouble," cement alliances with powerful church groups, and rake in votes. Porn had been demanding and demeaning, but anti-porn was, she said, a "sham."[50]

But how to fight back? At Sexpo, counterprotesters—some of them dressed as sexy colonists in mob caps, carrying signs bearing slogans like, "WAP! CALL OFF YOUR NEO-PURITAN WITCH HUNT," and "WOMEN

Anti-WAP protest at Sexpo '82.

AGAINST PORNOGRAPHY OBJECTIFY MEN"—confronted WAP marchers who lofted signs with slogans like "PORN IS RAPE ON PAPER," and blow-ups of *Hustler* covers, including the infamous meat-grinder image. Candice told *Velvet* readers that "women in porn" had formed "a new organization called 'FREE': Feminine Rights to Erotic Expression." There was plenty of stagecraft on both sides. FREE, like the coalition protesting at Barnard, was a front—in this case for the adult industry. The group's signs appear to have been professionally lettered. Nor was WAP immune to a bit of camp; one image shows a black-clad WAP picketer holding a sign reading "'MISS NUDE' PROMOTES VIOLENCE AGAINST WOMEN" while smiling broadly, arm in arm, with a towering starlet in lingerie—perhaps Miss Nude resplendent in the flesh.[51]

Candice began to wonder, that fall, whether the answer to porn's obvious deficits—and to WAP's gauntlet—was better porn. The pro-testers at Barnard had mocked the very idea that "instead of chal-lenging a six-billion-dollar-a-year industry that traffics in women's bodies, feminists should simply make their own pornography."[52] But recent changes in the industry and its technologies seemed to offer fresh possibilities. Candice noted the "growing accessibility of eroti-cism on pay TV," which she called "the blue screen." "It's good to see more women getting involved," she wrote. "Maybe us gals will finally begin to see movies that turn us on as well." Certainly, women were watching. "One of the largest growing audiences for porn films is the middle-class suburban housewife who's left to her own amusement all day while hubbie's out at work," she maintained in one column draft.[53]

What might those suburban housewives wish to see? Candice shared some ideas with Rick Marx, an adult screenwriter who freelanced for *Porn Stars* magazine, when he interviewed her for a feature entitled "Five Sluts Who Split." "Women are going to be making their own pornography," she predicted. She expected that female creators would insist on "a lot more foreplay" than the conventional male-directed sex scene, which she lampooned as "a woman entering a room and say-ing 'fuck me.'" There was a market as well as a moral angle: Candice pointed out that if "films were more realistic, men might find out just what women like, and you'd have women liking the films more, too." When the interview ran, in November 1982, Marx cut those lines.[54]

19 Deep Inside

Carnival Knowledge, Second Coming, *Franklin Furnace,*
New York, January 1984. Candice (left), Gloria Leonard
(center), and Janie Hamilton (right) kneel; Annie Sprinkle and
Veronica Vera stand, third from left and second from right.

andice and Per had civilian friends, neighbors, cousins. But most of the joyous and convivial set who dined and drank and smoked and laughed in the Sjöstedts' home in Brooklyn worked in porn. The women Annie Sprinkle calls the "long-haulers"— writers and actors and technicians who plied the trades steadily, as opposed to those who were "out for a quick buck," or a thrill, or a dare—comprised a small tribe, a family. In the early '70s, they'd been bona fide "outlaws," as Sprinkle says. "If you got caught, you were risking jail."[1] A decade later, their work was generally legal but hardly legitimate—demonized, increasingly, by a new Right and a new feminism alike. Pushed to the margins, they bonded and reveled there.

Candice had appeared with Janie Hamilton, who performed as Veronica Hart, in a couple of Larry Revene's movies: *Fascination* (1980), and *Blue Magic* (1981).[2] Six years Candice's junior, Janie was the baby of the group, as well as the only one with training as an actor: a degree in theatre from the University of Nevada. Her path to New York routed through London, where she'd modeled nude and worked as a stripper. She hit it big as the title character in Revene's *Wanda Whips Wall Street* (1982), one of the last porn films to gain huge success in theatrical release, in the *Deep Throat* model. "She was the big star," Sprinkle recalls, "big, big, *big* star. She was very loved."[3]

Janie, like everybody else, knew Gloria Leonard. Born in 1940, Leonard was the elder stateswoman. A New Yorker first, last, and in between, she'd worked as a stockbroker before venturing into blue movies. *The Opening of Misty Beethoven* (1976), one of the biggest box-office hits of porn's theatrical age, had made Leonard famous. The following year, she became the publisher of *High Society*, which threw many of the parties that Candice covered as a columnist. Gloria had acted with Janie in Chuck Vincent's *Roommates* (1981). Per and Candice had met on Vincent's set and celebrated their marriage in his loft.

Gloria and Janie knew Annie Sprinkle, who was beginning to carve out a different kind of celebrity, as a performance artist. Born Ellen Steinberg in Philadelphia in 1954, Sprinkle had worked her way west, carried in the slipstream of the counterculture. In 1972, she was busted in a raid on an Arizona theater screening *Deep Throat*, where she sold popcorn. When she testified at the ensuing obscenity trial, she caught the eye of the film's director, Gerard Damiano. "He was forty-six and married with two children," she later wrote. "I was eighteen and ready for anything. I eagerly became his mistress and followed him back to New York City." There she found work on porn sets, operating the boom, changing the sheets, shooting chromes. Sometimes she did a little fluffing. She soon realized that acting paid better than crew work. By the end of 1973, Annie had appeared in several films and dozens of loops. People assumed she'd done it because she'd been "coerced," or was "desperate for money," or wanted to lash out at her middle-class parents. She countered: "Porn combined my two big loves: filmmaking and sex."[4]

Along the increasingly porous border between pornography and conceptual art, the publishers of a zine called *LOVE*, for whom Annie took pictures, were friendly with Willem de Ridder, who was part of Fluxus, the international neo-Dadaist anti-art movement.[5] Comprised of denizens of the avant-garde as diverse as John Cage, Yoko Ono, Joseph Beuys, and Nam June Paik, Fluxus deliberately blurred the boundaries between creator and audience, art and commerce. Shortly before Women Against Pornography began its earnest tours of Times Square, Fluxus parodied such forms by staging "Fluxtours" of gutters and public restrooms in New York's gentrifying post-industrial SoHo neighborhood.[6] Annie's first collaboration with de Ridder was to feature excerpts from her diary interspersed with explicit photographs, but they were arrested in Rhode Island on charges that included obscenity, depravity, and sodomy. When they got out of jail, she followed him to Italy.

Annie returned to New York in 1979, the same year Candice came east from Los Angeles. It was a giddy moment, after the Bronx burned but before the Disneyfication of Times Square. There were "a lot of artists exploring sex, and a lot of sex people exploring art," Annie says.

Her work morphed into a kind of meta-pornography, performed in underground spaces like Hellfire, a BDSM club in the Meatpacking District, part Fluxus installation, part San Francisco–style leather dungeon, with snakes and dogs and Nazi role-play and "foot-worshipping slaves": the kind of place WAP warned you about.[7]

Veronica Vera wanted to learn more about kink. Raised Catholic in New Jersey, she had made her way to Manhattan and found a job—like Gloria, like Janie's fictional Wanda—whipping Wall Street. But she felt called to be a writer, and the only person she knew in the print trades edited *Penthouse Variations*. So she started writing erotica. Research for a piece on S/M led her to the studio of photographer Charles Gatewood, who was collaborating with Annie on outdoor S/M-themed happenings that she termed "PVC picnics."[8] Annie and Veronica teamed up as the High-Heeled School of Journalism. They sold sex products with a Fluxus twist via a catalog designed by de Ridder, offering items including a Pubic Hair Ritual Kit and a Golden Shower by Mail, each "guaranteed 100 percent art."[9]

So Veronica knew Annie and Annie knew Gloria and Gloria knew Candice and everybody knew Janie. Sometimes the Venn diagrams overlapped, as at Sexpo, which Candice covered for *Velvet* and *Erotic Film Guide*, while Gloria repped *High Society*, Annie shot pictures, and Veronica wrote about the protests. A snapshot from the event puts Candice, Annie, and Veronica in the same frame, if not yet exactly together.[10]

Janie was pregnant when Sexpo opened, in October 1982. Annie hosted a shower for her early the following February, in her spacious apartment on Lexington Avenue, on the eastern edge of NoMad. "All kinds of women came," Candice later recalled. But it was the women in porn, or just out of porn, who hung around till the end, when somebody put the recording of *West Side Story* on the stereo, and they sang and danced like junior high schoolers, "all these frustrated ballerinas and girls who'd gone to tap-dancing school," feeling pretty and letting loose, Veronica said. They performed not only with but also "for each other," Candice wrote in her diary. And they talked, really talked, about life in the business, in all its splendor and tragedy.[11]

Several months later, Annie called Candice to ask for the phone number of the psychotherapist she had raved about that night. Candice shared the number. Annie mentioned an idea Gloria had floated: regathering the women from the after-party, to meet regularly in some kind of "talk group," in hopes that sharing their stories might help them to better understand where they'd been and what came next.[12]

CANDICE HAD BEEN in treatment for about a year with the therapist she recommended to Annie, a clinical social worker named Linda Hirsch. When Candice met Linda, she'd been clean for about six months and felt "finally ready to really look inside." The junk, after all, had been as much a symptom as a cause of her distress. She knew she needed to "dig away," deep enough to pull the roots out, or hard drugs would find her again.[13]

It's not clear how Candice happened upon Hirsch, her eighth therapist. But she could not have found a better partner in her search for self-knowledge. Hirsch had been an addict and a prostitute in her teen years. Annie remembers her as "sex positive and non-judgmental, and also very realistic about the issues and down sides of the industry."[14]

Hirsch pushed Candice to imagine the next chapters of a "long & pretty future." Candice framed the scene in her diary: Per would make a fortune directing action films. She would "become a noted speaker & journalist on the topic of women's sexuality." She would give birth to their first child, a girl, just before turning forty; a son would follow two years later. Per's success would allow them to move out of New York. Candice would stay home with the children and then launch a new career writing books and making music for young people. She would sing to the kids, who would follow their parents' artistic paths. She could almost smell the cookies baking.[15]

But if therapy meant dreaming forward, *digging away* also meant looking bravely back, poring over old journals, chiseling through the sedimentary layers of the Vadala family's secrets. Candice had a nightmare in which she discovered her father lurking in the room while she had sex with Per. A few days later, she removed her father's monogramed communion ring, which she'd worn stacked atop her simple wedding band, "to spruce it up." She called the gesture a "divorce from father," and wrote a poem to mark the moment. But the "divorce" didn't stop the nightmares.[16]

Cinthea moved back to New York for a while, but the sisters weren't close. They had recriminated each other too often and too bitterly, each documenting the other's betrayals. Their parents had pitted them against each other even while teaching them to band together for safety.[17]

Helen had divorced Louis Vadala nearly a decade before. She still lived in Florida, a "ticky tacky life," Candice said. She visited Brooklyn once a year or so, which Candice generally dreaded. Louis had likewise stayed in Largo, and never ventured north. "He might as well be in Hong Kong," Candice wrote. He was older now, living alone in a trailer park, collecting Social Security, not enough to make ends meet. He gave drum lessons at a music store in Clearwater, teaching little boys and girls, kids far less talented than his daughters. It was the kind of work he had always hated, the very "shape of death" for a musician, as Cinthea put it.[18]

In late 1983, as the talking circle that Annie and Candice assembled hit its stride, Louis sexually assaulted a six-year-old girl, exposing himself to her, licking and fondling her, making her do the same. He gave her small gifts—lipstick, for one—and warned her not to share their secret. His moves sound practiced; it seems unlikely that this was the first time he acted on the urges he had directed, in more muted fashion, toward his daughters during their adolescence. The little girl's mother told the sheriff that Louis had molested her daughter somewhere between twenty and thirty times.[19]

By the time Louis faced a grand jury the following spring, charged with four counts of sexual battery, the United States was in the grip of a child-abuse panic, as ever more fantastical accusations of satanic sex rituals in the basement of the McMartin Preschool, a family-run daycare center in Orange County, California, overspread the national news. Eventually, most of those cases collapsed, and the concept of recovered memory, crucial to the incest-survivor movement from its inception, faced grave challenges in courtrooms and psychology labs alike.[20] The allegations against Louis, though, were as pedestrian as they were appalling. He pled no contest to reduced charges of lewd and lascivious acts in the presence of a minor under the age of fourteen, for which he was sentenced to twenty-five years of probation and mandatory counseling. Neither Candice nor Cinthea would learn what he had done for more than a decade.[21]

Candice danced one of her last stage shows, in Roanoke, about six months after her treatment with Linda Hirsch began. It had been, she said, a classy affair, a real burlesque act with "no spread shots, not even floor work." Her set had included, as usual, a naughty Cole Porter favorite, "My Heart Belongs to Daddy."[22]

———

CANDICE CAME TO THINK of the biweekly post-porn talking circle as a "support group." Club 90 took its name from Annie's address, 90 Lexington Avenue, where they held most of their meetings. Annie, Candice, Gloria, Janie (with her baby son, the "honorary male of the group"), and Veronica were the core members; Kelly Nichols and Sharon Mitchell came often; others dropped in occasionally. By September 1983, the docket was getting crowded. "I think we're deciding to close the door on admissions," Candice wrote in her diary. "Already it was getting difficult to get a word in edgewise."[23]

Club 90 gathered at dinnertime. Annie cooked, and the others brought snacks, wine, some grass. ("Gloria & I are the 'heads,'" Candice wrote.) Meetings sometimes lasted till midnight. They sat in a circle and shared in turn, like a feminist consciousness-raising group, each one's narrative igniting a *click!* of recognition in the others. But unlike classic second-wave feminist C-R, or the twelve-step programs to which C-R bore more than a passing resemblance, Club 90 was focused on the future. "We were all kind of similarly ambitious," Annie says, when asked what made the group gel. Their goal was "not to be rich and famous, but to do something in the world," something of substance, something "of meaning."[24]

Club 90 had been meeting for about six months when Candice received an inquiry from an arts group called Carnival Knowledge, a feminist collective formed by women in the downtown arts scene, in direct response to the founding of the Moral Majority. They were installation makers, performers, and activist-artists who made reproductive rights their theme. Like Annie, they practiced the conceptual art of the body. Carnival Knowledge meant upside-down knowledge, the lowly elevated and the high brought low. The collective's first happening, staged at the New School, had been an actual carnival. "See Women, Men & Children Fight the Moral Majority!" shouted the Barnumesque handbill.[25]

The next major Carnival Knowledge production, with the punning title "Second Coming," was to be far more extensive and ambitious, thanks to funds from the National Endowment for the Arts and the New York State Arts Council. Second Coming would take place at Franklin Furnace, on Franklin Street off West Broadway, in a derelict warehouse converted into a pioneering alternative arts venue.

By the '80s, these once-frontier spaces—"demi-institutions," as some called them—had forged a trendy mainstream. Uptown art patrons flocked to purchase the frisson of counterculture in the enclaves of SoHo (already pricey), TriBeCa (still edgy), and the East Village (the latest vanguard). The *New York Times* ran several articles explaining the claims of "performance art."[26] Major granting agencies, including the NEA, began to underwrite programs that once might have seemed beyond—or beneath—their scope. Support from the NEA acted like "the Good Housekeeping Seal of Approval" for other deep-pocketed funders, Franklin Furnace founder Martha Wilson said.[27]

For its Franklin Furnace happening, Carnival Knowledge decided to tackle the topic of pornography. The call to performers asked a single, provocative question: "Could there be a feminist porn?" In January 1984, the answers would occupy a month's worth of discussions, screenings, and performances ranging from poetry readings to mud wrestling. "Why a Porn Show?" The Collective answered: "In the eighties, sexuality remains overvalued and repressed." They rued the deepening chasm between "anti-porn" and "pro-sex" feminists, finding merits and deficits in both arguments. The pro-sex side had made "room for pleasure, privacy, fantasy and freedom." The antis rightfully called attention to "the demeaning effect" of conventional porn. Was there no middle ground? "Why should we have to choose between the Pope and *Playboy*?" the organizers asked.[28]

Club 90's response to this question served as the last major performance of the Second Coming series. The core members decided they would dramatize one of their meetings, using costumes and slides to craft a multi-media spectacle. They chose the name *Deep Inside Porn Stars*, winking at Annie's hugely popular 1982 explicit film, *Deep Inside Annie Sprinkle*, which itself had winked at other X-movies that promised to take viewers "inside" leading actresses. But Club 90's *Deep Inside* was only emotionally explicit. Each of the support group's core members would take the mic, explaining why she'd bared all onscreen. Annie said she'd done it for art; Candice "for feminism"; Janie "for theater"; Gloria to flex her "First Amendment rights"; and Veronica "for God." Not every Club 90 sister was so high-minded. Kelly Nichols said she'd done porn because it was a slightly better crappy job than any of the other crappy jobs she'd worked.[29]

Taking turns in the spotlight on a stage furnished as an ordinary living room, the women of Club 90 peeled back their layers. "I'm Jane, and I'm still very much Veronica Hart," Janie said. There were sight gags and wordplay. There were truths without tears. Candice described her childhood as "so-so," not "always stable" or "always happy." "Nothing is black and white," she said. "I made the choice." And "Candida paid the bills very well."[30]

"Do you think people are really interested in what porn stars talk about?" Candice asked, the last line of the *Deep Inside* script. She knew the answer. Tickets had sold out weeks in advance. *Deep Inside* wasn't a "big happening," Annie recalls, but it was certainly "a cool happening." The packed house held about a hundred people, a diverse group of feminists and artists and adult industry veterans, including *Penthouse*'s Bob Guccione, all on hard vinyl folding chairs.[31]

Critics were interested too. *Artforum* devoted a full page to Second Coming—with allusions to Foucault, Sontag, and Dickens—and several columns to *Deep Inside*, "a kind of Canterbury Tales," a play "fraught with ambivalences which reflected those of society's attitudes to the commodification of sex." Critic Jean Fisher reflected that the "cast of victims of uncertain sociosexual identities included us all." Our porn stars, ourselves: *Deep Inside* seemed, for a moment, to augur the career in art that Candice so long had dreamed of.[32]

The writer assigned by *High Performance: A Quarterly Magazine for the New Arts Audience*, appended a half-page "Feminist Preface" to her review of *Deep Inside*, noting, "Editorial readers questioned my current feminist values because I had not made a case against pornography and appeared to be neutral in this piece." The preface was bordered in black, like a funeral notice.[33]

———

TO BE NEUTRAL in the feminist debate over pornography was increasingly impossible. Just when the Barnard Conference had marked the emergence of a vocal if not quite coherent feminist rebuttal to anti-pornography activism, the anti-porn movement opened a new front, allying more closely with law and government. In December 1983, while Club 90 was rehearsing *Deep Inside*, the Minneapolis City Council held hearings on a proposal to amend to its municipal code, to define sexually explicit materials that subordinated women—or used men in the position of women—as gendered violations of civil rights. Under the proposed ordinance, those victimized by pornography's production, consumption, or display could sue for damages. The activist Andrea Dworkin and the political theorist and law professor Catharine MacKinnon had framed the approach and drafted the text. "We're going to use the courts as our theater, and we're going to try you for your crimes against women," Dworkin later said of the ordinance strategy.[34] (It was at about this time that *Hustler* publisher Larry Flynt, who had answered his latest round of obscenity charges by showing up to his court date wearing an American flag as a diaper, announced that he would run for the presidency of the United States.[35])

That fall, Dworkin and MacKinnon had co-taught a course at the University of Minnesota Law School on pornography as a form of sex discrimination. The class was rigorous, with a syllabus covering twenty-one single-spaced pages and a binder of readings as thick as the Bible. Students learned to see pornography everywhere. They watched *Snuff* and *Deep Throat*; they read *Ordeal*; they witnessed live sex shows. They deconstructed issues of *Playboy*, *Penthouse*, and *Hustler*; and they critiqued glossy magazine advertisements, including an infamous Calvin Klein jeans campaign featuring a very young and highly sexualized Brooke Shields.[36] The course was, by all accounts, transformative, even, some said, "traumatic." "I feel so overcome that it's hard to enter into daily normal conversations," one student told the *Sunday Pioneer Press*.[37] While teaching that semester, MacKinnon also forged alliances with several city council members long concerned with urban vice and increasingly worried about gender inequality. She persuaded them that a new approach was needed: "a statutory scheme" meant to "situate pornography as a central practice in the inequality of the sexes."[38]

Hearings on the proposed municipal ordinance featured the impassioned testimony of scores of self-proclaimed pornography victims, including Linda Boreman, who had remarried and now used her husband's surname, Marchiano, and who spoke, in the third person, about her torture, imprisonment, and coercion when performing in *Deep Throat* as Linda Lovelace. Gloria Steinem sent a telegram to be read into evidence, urging Minneapolis to demonstrate its customary leadership forging the "path to progress." The city council passed the ordinance by a single vote. But despite a week of rallies and vigils organized by the antis, Minneapolis mayor Donald Fraser vetoed the measure at a press conference packed with scores of women, many of them weeping. He appointed a task force to scrutinize its constitutionality and recommend alternative approaches. A new vote on a revised ordinance was promised by summer.[39]

The force of Dworkin's rhetoric and MacKinnon's intellect, coupled with WAP's genius for publicity, ensured that the struggle over the Minneapolis ordinance would be anything but a local affair. The wire services covered it, and the *New York Times* and the *Washington Post* both put stringers on the story, which inched closer to the front page in January, the month of Fraser's veto, the month the curtain went up on *Deep Inside*. In March, the battle reached *Time* magazine.[40]

Temperatures rose in frozen Minneapolis. About a hundred protesters stormed the Rialto, an adult theater and bookstore, chanting and singing as they slashed seats and pitched racks full of skin mags onto the floor. Rallies continued through the spring. In May, Dworkin flew in from New York to headline a particularly stirring assembly.[41]

In June, Phyllis Schlafly, who had once debated MacKinnon on the ERA, lauded the ordinance strategy, among other "new weapons" in the battle against pornography.[42]

Demonstrations lasted into the summer. And then, in July, shortly before the re-vote, Ruth Christenson, a twenty-three-year-old anti-pornography advocate who had first surfaced, sobbing, at Dworkin's rally, entered a downtown Minneapolis newsstand that carried adult publications, doused herself with gasoline, and lit her own pyre. Flames touched the roof of the store.[43] "Sexism has shattered my life—psychologically, economically and spiritually," Christenson explained in a letter sent to city officials before the burning. "I do not know if any of this will have any impact on your civil rights legislation, but at least someone will have done something about this nightmare of racism and sexism that most pornography involves."[44]

Thanks to quick-thinking patrons who blanketed her with rugs, Christenson survived, with third-degree burns over 65 percent of her body. Rushing to the County Medical Center "to comfort family members," who declined to see her, Terese Stanton, a leader of the local Pornography Resource Center, compared the spectacular protest to clerics' self-immolations during the Vietnam War, when people "had to burn themselves to be heard." Catharine MacKinnon, who likewise paid a late-night visit to the burn unit, told the *Star and Tribune*, "Women feel very desperate about the existence of pornography. . . . People make choices on how" to express their pain and fury.[45]

Years later, when MacKinnon and Dworkin published the transcripts of the Minneapolis hearings, they would dedicate the volume to Christenson, who recovered from her injuries only to die by suicide six years later.[46] But readers of the local papers were aghast at the antis' comments. "This disturbed young woman deserves all the help that society can give her," a woman from a farm town near the South Dakota border told the editors of the *Star and Tribune*. "However, if the antiporn group sees suicide as a viable means of protest, then they should not be surprised if a great many people do not take them seriously." Local officials had the opposite worry: that the antis would be taken all too seriously, by copy-cat victims. Stanton's Resource Center quickly issued a statement: "We don't want women to harm themselves, we need women to stay alive and intact for the struggle." They vowed, "This will not be in vain."[47]

Christenson burned in vain. The council passed a watered-down bill, by the same one-vote margin, and Mayor Fraser again vetoed it.[48]

Nonetheless, the ordinance strategy was igniting elsewhere, with Dworkin and MacKinnon's help. In Indianapolis, where Christian evangelicals had been organizing against pornography for several years, the city council had passed a version nearly identical to Minneapolis's in April. There, the mayor, William Hudnut, eagerly approved.[49] National politicians took notice too. Opposing pornography was a winning stance for Republicans in an election year. Reagan, who had publicly mentioned pornography only four times in the first three years of his presidency, returned to the topic, with increasing vehemence, nine times in 1984 alone, including during his State of the Union Address. In May, at a signing ceremony for the Child Protection Act of 1984, the president inveighed against the rise of "ugly and dangerous" pornography, which he said was becoming "increasingly more extreme." He directed his attorney general, William French Smith, to empanel a "new national commission to study the effects of pornography on our society."[50]

As the 1984 election approached, public discourse around pornography grew ever more "messianic and apocalyptic," as one scholar puts it.[51] Pornographers were likened to Nazis and slaveholders. In much of the country, the response to Carnival Knowledge's question—*could there be a feminist porn?*—seemed axiomatic: there could not.

But Candice, who had probed the question with her body as well as her pen, was looking for a new answer. After *Deep Inside*'s success, she and the other Club 90 sisters met with producers to discuss the possibility of taking the show from downtown to Off-Broadway. She felt further along in the process "exorcising Candida Royalle," as she wrote in her journal. "I am Candice. Candida is a character I've encompassed in my repertoire. If I look hard, I might find others as well."[52]

20 Tastefully Hardcore

Filming Urban Heat, *July 1984. Candice stands at right; Lauren is second from right.*

auren Niemi had the idea. A middle-class Midwesterner with dreams of city life, she had left a small-town Catholic college to study the brand-new medium of video at the University of Minnesota. She worked for a few years in Chicago, including a stint at the printer that produced both *Playboy* and the Sears catalogue. Around 1980, she returned to Minneapolis and took a job in the production department of Campbell-Mithun, the largest midwestern ad agency.[1] There she met Richard Cole, an adman turned poet. Together, they lit out for Manhattan in the summer 1983, just before the ordinance campaigns ignited Minneapolis politics. They found an apartment in the East Village, just below Tompkins Square Park, a neighborhood still filthy and crime-riddled. Richard got a job on Madison Avenue. Lauren had trouble finding work. She spent her days job-hunting and her nights trying "not to show that I was completely out of my depth every second."[2]

Lauren worked the occasional shift as an office temp, and it was during one of those gigs that the lightbulb went on. As she beavered away in a huge room filled with the cubicles that were the new face of clerical work, she and some of the other women started talking about the increasing ubiquity of VCRs. "You know, the only things you can watch on these home video machines are porn and Hollywood movies," one of the secretaries said. And of course, all the porn, as Lauren responded, was "hideous." Her radical question: what would it mean to create explicit videos for female viewers, featuring "things that women would like"? Hers was a version of Carnival Knowledge's question, *Could there be a feminist porn?* Which itself was a version of the Barnard Conference's question, *How do women get sexual pleasure in patriarchy?* But Lauren's interest was not theoretical. She figured that, if you could figure out what women liked to watch, you might get rich.[3]

She thought, first, of rock videos. In November, some executives from MTV, the two-year-old cable station that had pioneered that format, took a meeting with her. She pitched the idea of explicit shorts for the female viewer. A woman in MTV's offices gave her Candice's name. In late January 1984, a couple days after *Deep Inside Porn Stars* peeled back the curtain to offer a glimpse into the private lives of porn-star feminists, Lauren made her way to Sackett Street.[4]

When Candice opened the door, Lauren recalls, it felt as if "angels were singing." Smiling and sunny, like a Disney heroine with bluebirds twittering around her head, Candice utterly confounded whatever Lauren expected a former porn star to be. They sparked a joint and started brainstorming. (It helped, Lauren says, that they were so often "stoned to our eyeballs" in those first months.) In a letter dashed off the next morning, basking "in the glow of the day after," Lauren told Candice, "I was absolutely *crammed* with ideas by the time I got home and couldn't write them down fast enough." She attached her résumé and wound up her pitch: she needed introductions to "the right people," from "someone who knows the business and can steer me around disasters"—a real "partner." They agreed to meet again in a week. In the meantime, Lauren promised not to talk the idea around too much, lest it seem good enough to steal before it was ready to launch.[5]

Lauren and Candice had good reason to hold their idea close. Pornography for the female viewer had lately become something of a holy grail for cable executives seeking what one self-described "feminist porn programmer" called the "sleaze to please." Surveys told her network that "over 60% of our viewers were female."[6] That audience was ill-served and increasingly vocal. "The biggest complaint we get about our adult films is from women, who say they're not female-oriented enough," a cable programming VP had told the *New York Times* back in 1981. Over the next two years, creators raced everything from pornographic sitcoms to avant-garde erotic films to market, to satisfy those elusive female viewers.[7] In 1983, its second year on the air, the Playboy Channel, which faced the highest monthly turnover of any subscription service, piloted *4Play*, a scripted comedy, and *The Friday Files*, hosted by Nancy Friday, who had written bestsellers about men's and women's sexual fantasies. Nothing broke through. As one Playboy

Channel executive put it, "We do a lot of shows for women. But they still complain."[8]

The adult videotape market was also growing rapidly. By the end of 1982, *Playgirl* reported, at least 3 million American homes had a VCR, and racy cassettes—with an R or an X rating—had "captured 45 to 60 percent of the total tape market." As with adult cable, couples often watched explicit tapes together. What happened when they paused the video was their own business. A year before Candice met Lauren, *Cosmopolitan* had noted a "spate of new-wave porno films" for the home market. "If the Nobel Prize were awarded for contributions to human sexuality," the writer joked, the award should go to the inventor of the VCR, for having "put pornography in the bedroom, where it belongs." Acknowledging that porn had "long been controversial," *Cosmo* turned the family values argument on its head, touting it as a marital aid.[9]

In her diary, weeks after that first meeting, Candice noted her growing excitement at the prospects of "my video project—'women's fantasies'—with Lauren."[10] Lauren makes those early months, in the winter and spring of 1984, sound like an old Mickey Rooney/Judy Garland movie, where Lauren had the concept, and Candice had the Rolodex, and they were trying to figure out who on earth had the costumes, the instruments, the barn, and above all, the money. They spent long days brainstorming with Per. Lauren recalls showing up at eight in the morning to find Per already stoned and rolling joints for the trio. "That anything ever got done was amazing," she says. They kicked ideas around, moving their meetings into the garden as soon as the weather allowed. They played music on a boombox; Candice would often get up and dance. They spent a lot of time talking about how their company would treat the talent, with a level of professionalism, integrity, and respect that Candice hadn't always experienced in her own acting career. They felt like the three musketeers of feminist porn, Lauren says.

They were also, as Lauren puts it, "the blind leading the blind." Each of them had a bit of domain experience—Lauren as videographer, Per as producer, Candice as actress and writer—but none had ever made a feature-length film. Lauren's partner, Richard, with his

Madison Avenue job, peppered them with practical questions: *What is the business plan?* His doubts annoyed Candice. But Lauren knew that Richard had a point.[11]

The three stoned musketeers started to call their venture Femme. In April, Lauren and Candice incorporated as Femme Productions, agreeing to a fifty-fifty split of their profits.[12] To make the paper corporation a reality, they leveraged all the connections they had. Saga Film AB, the Swedish production company owned by the Sjöstedts; and Lunarex, the New York–based joint venture between Saga and the directors Larry Revene and Chuck Vincent, together invested $25,000 in Femme's first feature.[13] Lauren recalls that Richard Cole's mother, Janice—a prim Southern lady who wore white gloves and knew exactly what she was getting into—also put money into that initial film. "We thought we were all going to be rich," Lauren says.

Like most independent filmmakers, they had some industry backers. But anti-porn feminists' arguments to the contrary, Lauren and Candice were not pimped, by anyone. What they made was theirs. In those days, Lauren recalls, Femme felt "like a movement."[14]

CANDICE AND LAUREN shot Femme's first feature, the eponymous *Femme*, just days after they signed their partnership agreement. Lauren directed and Candice served as her assistant. Many among the cast of ten and crew of fourteen were friends. Even the location, a former printing factory in Park Slope, came through personal connections: Jerry Vitucci, an old pal from the High School of Art and Design, had become a union soundman, who re-encountered Candice while working the boom mic for *October Silk*, back in 1979. He and his wife, Susan, grew close to Per and Candice. They loaned out their loft for the taping.[15]

Shot on videotape, *Femme* combined aspects of feature-length porn films and one-act loops. Its six vignettes, each a little over ten minutes long, build toward sexual climax. The episodes—roughly sketched scenarios, with short evocative titles—are nearly wordless; the dialogue list for the entire film runs a scant five pages. The characters are nameless, mere types. The miniatures vary in mood as well as conceit. "Rock Erotica," the first and most MTV-like of the group, is also the darkest, featuring a leather-clad male lead and an actress got up like early Madonna. Their semi-clad encounter on the stairs, above a driving electronic track that Candice, in her workbook, called "Je Suis le Masturbateur," reaches almost parodic intensity. "Sales Pitch," by contrast, is lace-trimmed and gauzy, a lesbian encounter between a door-to-door cosmetics saleswoman and her customer: Avon coming. In "TV Idol," a male soap-opera star emerges from a television to bed the watcher, a fantasy sprung to life. (Royalle has a cameo, clothed, in the video within the video.)[16]

How different was *Femme* from the established grammar of pornography? In some respects, not very. The film features the same number of orgasms as the typical porno—though the first is delayed well beyond the usual two-minute mark. The day rates paid to the talent, ranging from $200 at the low end to $600 for Michael Knight, the bankable male star of the "Rock Erotica" and "Gallery" vignettes, were no higher than industry standard. Lauren and her crew shot *Femme* in two days, three scenes per day, which was about the pace Candice had experienced in her very first porn acting, in the summer of 1975, when she filmed two loops before lunch.[17]

Yet in other ways, *Femme* marked a distinct departure. It shifts priorities from intercourse to foreplay and, to a lesser extent, toward what Candice called "afterglow," which would become a key part of Femme Productions messaging. *Femme*'s vignettes devote time to kissing, undressing, even spooning. The actors, lit warmly, wear neatly tailored clothing and tasteful lingerie; their makeup is muted; the camera zooms in on their manicures. The male performers often seem focused on their female partners, a direct inversion of conventional porn's blueprint.

The most striking and deliberate contravention of genre, though, was *Femme*'s portrayal of sexual climax, which did not include even one external male orgasm. Lauren says Sture Sjöstedt didn't think an explicit film could be financially viable without the "money shot." But Candice had long found that convention both distasteful and contrived. Her 1982 exposé for *High Times* had mocked the absurdity of asking performers flecked with semen to act "as if they've just received a magic potion for eternal life."[18] *Femme* and its successors shaped her distaste into a brand. Without proof of climax, the performers would need convincing passion. Femme films promised to create "real heat by matching up people who are genuinely hot for each other, in some instances pairing off real-life lovers and married couples."[19]

By the time *Femme* wrapped, Candice felt sure their concept was going to sell. But to launch, they needed a product line, not just a single movie. She started sketching a second film, initially called *Femme II: Summer in the City*, but released as *Urban Heat*.[20] Sture Sjöstedt must have seen the initial footage from *Femme* as proof of concept; Saga and Lunarex together invested an additional $60,000—more than double *Femme*'s budget—to produce new entries in the series.[21]

Candice also began a publicity blitz. In the late spring, she circulated screener tapes of the *Femme* rough cut, with such pride in the work that she refused an offer to preview the film at the popular lower Manhattan nightclub Area, an Andy Warhol haunt, explaining that the venue's projection system simply didn't achieve "the level of quality we are striving for."[22] Sometimes, in print, she acknowledged Lauren's formative role, seeing the "unpredictable hand" of fate in the appearance of a "highly charged woman from Minnesota," who had turned up at her door "with a portfolio full of the sexiest pictures and video tapes I'd ever seen." But Candida Royalle was the bankable name, and most of Candice's early writings on Femme erased Lauren entirely. "I produced my first and very own erotic video tape," she boasted in a column sent *Velvet* in May. She carefully distinguished *Femme* from pornography, which, she wrote, as if paraphrasing Dworkin, "actually means the 'depiction of harlots.'" But she also defended the film's explicitness. "Women are just as lusty as men, and just as into the real nitty-gritty as any male viewer out there." Club 90 enlisted in the project's success: Veronica Vera worked on a long profile about Candice and Femme that ran in *Adam* in September.[23]

Candice also appeared on television a couple of times as she readied to launch Femme. Though she later told an interviewer she had studied and excelled at public speaking in college, those skills don't much show in her first TV appearances, on local network affiliate stations. She was still early in her media training, with a thick Bronx accent and makeup applied by her own heavy hand. She demonstrates a canniness about the industry, but she baby-voices her pronouncements. "Theaters are dinosaurs right now. . . . It's all home video," she says, looking up at the host of the Boston-based midday show *People Are Talking*, with the round, pleading eyes of a little girl.[24]

On television as in print, Candice's voice remained, in 1984, largely confined to adult industry conduits like *The Leonard Report*, a late-night cable show where Gloria Leonard interviewed adult industry veterans, and Al Goldstein's *Midnight Blue*, where Candice talked about her approach in *Femme*. "I don't fool around with plots," she said emphatically. "I really think it's silly, to be making these movies and trying to imitate Hollywood." Getting couples lathered up to have sex in front of their televisions was the "whole point." *Midnight Blue* was no feminist platform. Candice's segment was peppered with advertisements for escort services, sex shops, and gambling parlors. This, for now, was her niche. "I'm probably more in the business than I was when I was doing films," she said. Acting had always been on and off. Now she was embedded, part of the industry.[25]

THE TWO FILMS Candice and Lauren shot that summer were costlier and more ambitious than *Femme*. There was already some buzz in the performing community, about Femme being a great outfit to work with, so they had their pick of talent. An anthology of almost wordless vignettes, *Urban Heat* followed the *Femme* formula, but loosely tied all six together through their mise-en-scène: the steamy feeling of summer in New York. Shooting, in several different locations, took four days, some of them twelve hours long. There was a crowd scene, filmed at a nightclub in Chelsea. "Dress up in your finest heat-waveware and dance, drink, socialize, or just pose for the cameras!" teased a flyer Candice drew, seeking extras by promising "a whole new concept in entertainment called 'Progressive Rock Erotica.' . . . Come be a part of the future!"[26] Another episode centers on a spontaneous sexual encounter in a freight elevator between a middle-aged businesswoman and a younger male laborer. (She retains her red high heels, and he his tube socks.) But most of the action takes place in apartments: couples having sex in their kitchen, or sweating on the couch, with a small fan that can barely dent the heat, watching porn on television and hitting the Pause button to tear each other's clothes off. All the to-ing and fro-ing raised the budget to nearly $35,000. The musical scoring and performances, including an original song by Candice's friend Jorgé Socarras, cost almost twice as much as the actors.[27]

Shortly after they finished *Urban Heat*, Lauren and Candice headed to the Pennsylvania countryside to film their third feature. *Christine's Secret*, the first project on which Candice served as co-director, was a far more complex production, with thirty-five scenes shot over five days.[28] It was to be "a love story," and so "much sweeter & more romantic" than the MTV-inspired first efforts, Candice explained. The film traces a single narrative, just enough of a plot, as Candice later told Kathy Keeton of *Penthouse*, that "if you wanted a storyline there was one, but if you didn't want to pay attention to it you wouldn't miss anything." Christine, played by *Urban Heat* veteran Carol Cross, returns each year to "Love Inn," alone, for a mysterious reason. (Latter-day D. H. Lawrence spoiler alert: it's the property's caretaker, Jake, he of the sculpted pecs and rock-hard abs and an Eton crop evoking a young Hugh Grant.) Candice drilled the actors on their characters' motivations: "*Anna* and *Anthony* are young, sweet, happy honeymooners. They are upwardly mobile. He's in computers, she manages a small imported food business. She'll probably quit when she gets pregnant."[29]

The farmhouse where they filmed became a central character in the story. Behind-the-scenes snapshots show Lauren, Candice, Per, and their crew setting up tripods in meadows and perching on logs in the barn. "We were pure and dewy," Lauren remembers. Candice wears her glasses and a T-shirt, hair pulled back from her face.[30] She floods her shots with natural light, letting the camera linger on wide plank flooring, chenille bedspreads, gingham upholstery, and barn blankets: the kind of American country décor made newly fashionable by designer Ralph Lauren, né Lifshitz, who had grown up not far from Candice in the Bronx. The exterior B-roll showcases a lush surround: mist creeps over ponds and grass, flowers open in close-up worthy of

O'Keeffe, spider webs drip with morning dew, a puppy cavorts. (The credits list a dog trainer.)

There is also, it must also be said, a whole lot of fucking in and around Love Inn: six sex acts, per the standard adult-feature formula, build tension toward the long-anticipated encounter between Christine and her no-longer-secret amour. This climax of climaxes plays out over twelve minutes, with plenty of sweat and what reads as genuine ecstasy. What dialogue there is centers on commitment. "Move in with me," pleads the innkeepers' daughter's boyfriend, in scene twenty-two, after a roll in the literal hay. "We'll get married, have a couple of kids. Why not?"[31]

Why not indeed? "CHRISTINA'S [sic] SECRET is a lot like married sex," a reviewer for *Swank* would later opine. He did not mean this as praise.[32]

Candice was proud of her work on *Christine's Secret*, which she would call on, over the coming years, to demonstrate the Femme formula in full flower: long on beauty, slender on plot, devoid of sleaze. "Dirt with a difference," *Hustler* proclaimed.[33] When the shoot ended, she and Lauren booked time at Tapper Studios to do the cutting and mixing.[34] They would hold the film for later release, after *Femme* and *Urban Heat* established the Femme brand. The launch would prove consuming. After filming wrapped, in August 1984, Candice would not pick up a camera for almost two years.

———

WHILE THE COUPLES FROLICKING in *Christine's Secret* bathed in golden August light, some shade fell on Candice's real-life partnerships with Per and Lauren. During a weeklong getaway with the Club 90 girls, who were still working on the script for a bigger, bolder version of *Deep Inside Porn Stars*, Candice felt support and sisterhood, but also noticed jealousies surfacing. Janie Hamilton brought her husband and her baby son, triggering Candice's "old, old deep pain, way from the bottom of my gut," about Peggy, her own absconded birth mother. "I'm like a wounded animal," Candice journaled on loose-leaf pages at the retreat. She had vivid, unsettling dreams about giving birth and gentling a baby, noting that her "sub-conscious" seemed to be pointing her toward motherhood.[35]

Bunking with Janie's happy brood also made Candice see flaws in the family she had made. Per's desire for her seemed to have diminished. "I think the biggest problem is that he's feeling frustrated & dissatisfied with his own place in life right now—Only five years left till he reaches 30 and no sign of a million bucks yet!" Candice felt bad about the "heavy trip" Per was "laying on his head," but couldn't figure out a way to soothe him, like the baby in her dreams. His resentments made her "current projects & successes all the more difficult to enjoy."[36]

Candice calmed the roiling waters with Per by turning on her business partner. Tensions between her and Lauren had first surfaced during their work on *Urban Heat*, when Candice "became furious at her slowness & incompetence," while feeling that Lauren had blocked her "from any directorial duties whatsoever." Lauren had less experience than she had claimed, and Candice was mad at herself for failing to assert her own authority. When they got back to Brooklyn after filming *Christine's Secret*, she "decided it was my turn to take advantage of the investors I had found & learn how to direct."[37]

Lauren remembers the growing divide between them differently. The partners had competing ideas about what worked on film, with Lauren favoring atmosphere and Candice drawn increasingly to narrative. She had a "junior high idea of romance," Lauren says, commenting on *Christine's Secret*. Their diverging visions were hard to navigate, because Candice was brittle. "Everybody was a little afraid of Candice, all of the time," Lauren recalls. People tended to let her have her way; Lauren showed more backbone than most. She also thinks Candice was "extremely insecure about her lack of education"—intimidated by Lauren's and Richard's degrees. "She was like a Dickensian character, always wanting to rise above her class," Lauren says. But the adult industry tended to police its denizens. She offers a salty metaphor: "It was like the hundredth crab trying to crawl out of the bucket, and the other crabs pulling you back down." Lauren refused to play her part, neither building Candice up nor reining her in.[38]

Despite tensions on the set and in the editing room, when Lauren married Richard that October, she asked Candice to serve as her "entire wedding party." The strain in the relationship doesn't show in the pictures. Femme's co-founders walk side by side through the East Village toward the church, chins raised, strides matched. Lauren is resplendent in white satin, but Candice, a head shorter, in elegant gray, steals the scene. The camera loves her, and vice versa. She has bobbed her hair, a professional style for the work just ahead.

Looking at the wedding photos now, Lauren sees a vanished world: a friendship already foundering. A church filled with people who have since peeled away from traditional religion. "Richard converted, Per is living as a shaman in the desert, and I have returned to my Pagan roots," she writes. A reception attended by many later claimed by AIDS, which "hit big the following year." The CDC had recorded fewer than 7,000 cases in the United States, but government scientists had grown increasingly concerned about the rate of spread. There was some evidence, too, of "heterosexual transmission," the *Times* reported the next month, in a squib buried deep in the second section—news that would, in short order, rock the porn industry.[39]

A couple weeks after Lauren's wedding, Ronald Reagan was reelected in a historic landslide. At his second inauguration, he would declare a new birth for freedom. "Let history say of us, 'These were golden years—when the American Revolution was reborn, when freedom gained new life, and America reached for her best.'"[40] Though sexuality, as one scholar has written, "was the battlefield on which the 1984 presidential campaign . . . was fought and won," Reagan had never so much as uttered the plague's name. No mourning, only morning, in his America.[41]

———

THAT FALL, Candice found herself "doing Femme—living, thinking Femme—Everything is Femme these days."[42] After nearly a year of long days behind the camera or the editing deck, she and Lauren were getting ready for the line's official debut.

They had letterhead, hand-drawn and crudely duplicated, and a business address: Lauren's apartment on East Sixth Street.

They had a press release, distilling their brand on a single page. "Femme is trying to attract the vastly untapped women's market by presenting eroticism that is conceived and executed by women from a woman's point of view." Femme centered female pleasure. Femme also knew its place. "We believe people look at erotic films for the eroticism, not necessarily the plot," they wrote. "We also believe that our available talent is at its best in the department of eroticism rather than delivering lines convincingly." Femme films had "grit and passion" that was "softer and prettier." Femme films were, in a phrase, "tastefully hardcore."[43]

They had product. *Femme* and *Urban Heat* had been edited, duplicated, and shrink-wrapped. Candice mocked up the box design herself, with a logo based on her own cursive, as if written in lipstick. As she explained to her contact in the publicity department at VCA Pictures, a leading wholesaler of X-rated videotapes, "We need to put across right away that Femme is of a better quality and aesthetic."[44]

They had, at least provisionally, a distributor in VCA, though Candice was still shopping for a partner that better "understands what we're trying to do," as she told Bill Brown, her sometime housemate from the Haight-Ashbury days. In her diary, she lamented that VCA had "made a pretty lousy impression." When she and Per showed up, the company's founder and "his 'flunkies'" were openly snorting coke in their Hollywood office. Just like people in L.A. to "think of nothing but pleasures & self-gratification," Candice sniffed. Worse still was Russell Hampshire's "know-it-all pitch about how we should 'put more anal into Femme—that's what the guys wanna see now—so they can bring it home & show their wives & get them to do it!' Fuck you Russell . . . asshole," she wrote, accepting that they would stay in business together for the time being.[45]

And Femme had purpose. At the depths of Candice's exhaustion during the run-up to the launch, she had gone to see a conventional porn film, *Raw Talent*, at the Pussycat Theater in Times Square. Though the movie featured some of her friends, including Rhonda Jo Petty, who appeared in *Femme*, it was rotten enough to make her "remember exactly why we're doing Femme." But that realization came at a cost: "it makes me feel worse & worse about having performed in

Porn the more I grow to realize what crap it is," she wrote. Femme simply *had* to do the job better.[46]

Femme's pre-launch press, however meager, buoyed Candice. But it also meant that the family members who hadn't known of her adult-film work would now find out, since her backstory as an actress was an important part of Femme's narrative. She "came clean" to her Duffy cousins, Helen's kin. "I was so nervous—so anxious," she wrote in her diary. She needn't have worried. "Turns out they already knew," tipped off by E. Jean Carroll's snarky profile of the Club 90 sisters in *Playgirl*. Even nice Catholic cousins in Rochester read softcore porn for women.[47]

The first two Femme films premiered shortly after the election. Candice and Per had picked the venue carefully: Private Eyes, a buzzy new club in the Flatiron District. There were screens by the dozen, all showing *Urban Heat*. Candice dressed to fit her new role, as a "real businesswoman—career woman," in a blue strapless gown with a demure sweetheart neckline and just a hint of sparkle, a dress Princess Diana might have worn. In photos from the party, she carries a spray of pink carnations. Lauren is nowhere in sight. The club was so jammed, she recalls, that she and Richard never made it past the door.[48] Adult stars were there in force, including the casts of *Femme* and *Urban Heat*. But "lots of straight & x-rated press" had also shown up, Candice wrote: not only *Adam, Cheri, Erotic Film Guide, Puritan,* and *Swank*, but also the New York tabloids, along with staffers from *Ms., Newsweek, Variety, Vanity Fair,* and the *Village Voice*.[49]

Lauren watched the partygoers file in, convinced that the main-stream outlets had sent mere "gawkers . . . guys who were just mentally jacking off and trying to hit on all the women." The reporters were there, she says, to "sniff it up," and then head back to the newsroom to brag.[50]

Candice, though, took their presence in earnest. She sensed, from members of the "straight press," genuine "relief . . . over finally seeing a movie with 'joyful sex.'" And her adult industry friends, from whom she had expected "resistance," also cheered her on, "using words like 'revolutionary' and 'break-through.'" Candice could only "hope that middle America is as enthusiastic as progressive NYC!" If so, Femme would be "right on the mark, & hopefully the money." As she said in a column on Femme's debut for *Velvet*, "Let's hear it for the sexual revolution!"[51]

But in fact, the cheering in middle America had grown muted. Candice and Lauren filmed *Urban Heat* the same month Ruth Christenson set herself on fire in Minneapolis. The American Booksellers Association had won a speedy victory in a lawsuit against Indianapolis over the MacKinnon model ordinance. But the mayor planned to appeal.[52] Over the summer, the National Organization for Women had begun to test its members' support for the ordinance strategy, passing a resolution declaring that pornography "violates the civil rights of women and children" and urging "education and action by the chapters on this issue."[53] Numerous bills proposing to curb pornography had been introduced that year in Congress. In one snapshot from the making of *Urban Heat*, Candice and Lauren and their crew make merry around the opposition, mugging with a WAP-style placard reading "PORNO=WOMAN HATE." But in the press release that accompanied the launch, Femme pledged that "women are not placed in submissive positions" in its films, as if responding directly to MacKinnon's ordinance.[54] It was a canny move.

In November 1984, the month Candice and Lauren celebrated Femme's debut, *Harper's* magazine devoted thirteen pages to a roundtable of leading thinkers across a wide spectrum of opinion about the escalating controversy over pornography. All played their parts. Susan Brownmiller described pornography as a primer for rape. The head of the ACLU championed expressive freedom at almost any cost. Neoconservative pundit Midge Decter lamented the coarsening effects of a permissive culture. Most everyone agreed with *Harper's* publisher Lewis Lapham that "the increase in pornography . . . is a symptom of profound unhappiness in our society." Only Al Goldstein rejected the characterization of the industry and its customers as pitiable. "This joylessness everyone is making so much of—I don't see it around me," he said. "We always say, 'Fucking is only friction.' " Decrying "the elitism of this panel," Goldstein proudly proclaimed that pornography was "junk food," not haute cuisine.[55]

Candice, a self-proclaimed health nut, couldn't stand junk food. Unlike her friend Al, she insisted on the efficacy of better porn—in effect, accepting Brownmiller's (and MacKinnon's) argument about inputs and outcomes. But she also insisted that Femme was not peddling politics.

"Has Linda Lovelace hurt your cause or helped your cause?" one television presenter asked.

"There is no cause," Candice replied flatly.[56]

———

"PEOPLE CAN TALK UP a storm, but it's the press I need," Candice wrote after the launch party. For the concept to pay off, journalists had to print what they'd told her.[57]

But Lauren was right about the straight press: those reporters were all pheromones and no ink. The only coverage of Femme and Urban Heat came from skin mags, whose readers were not really the demographic Candice was looking for. An alphabetical list in an early press kit tells the story: Adam, Adult Cinema, Adults Only, Adult Video News, Cheri, Cinema Blue, Eros, Erotica, Erotic Film Guide, Gentleman's Companion, High Society, Local Swingers, Oui, Penthouse Forum, Penthouse Letters (twice), Screw, Swank, Swingers, Tux, VCA's Video Insider, and the new annual X-Rated Videotape Guide all ran reviews or features.[58] Their verdict was predictably mixed. AVN called Femme "something different," with "style to burn." But after the glowing feature Veronica Vera had written in Adam in the fall, the magazine's April 1985 review of Femme must have stung. Calling the direction "insipid," the videography "weak," and the sex sequences "lifeless," Adam's critic awarded the tape one star. Adult Cinema warned that male viewers of Femme might "end up hot under the collar—if not the crotch," because "the sex in FEMME is steamy, not seamy."[59] Puritan complained that the slides Candice and Lauren had sent did not meet the publication's specs. The "visuals supplied to PURITAN must be utterly 'X-rated.' As to their quality, they must (again) be explicit; they must be well lit and of a startling nature," scolded the editor who said she was "in charge of feminist-oriented projects."[60]

It is something of an irony that the highest early praise for Femme came from Al Goldstein, the merry prankster of sleaze. While other adult publications damned Royalle's efforts for their excessive respectability, *Screw* named *Urban Heat* "the most unique and exciting X-rated film of 1984," praising it for casting off "all the old formulas" while featuring "good sex" shot with "high technical quality, intense communication between its sexual participants and an outstanding musical score." Goldstein also touted the first two Femme titles in his X-Rated Video column in *Penthouse* in May 1985, calling the series "sizzling stuff." "I hope it gets the kind of support it deserves," he wrote. "If nothing else, it's good to wave in the face of the next pro-censorship right-wing feminist you meet."[61]

Femme was loath to trumpet Goldstein's endorsement in its press kits; Candice's customer didn't read *Screw*.[62] But events proved him right: the fight among feminists would make Femme matter.

21 A War Made for TV

Candice onstage at Donahue, *November 1985.*

S hortly before Femme's launch, the internecine feminist struggle over the issue of pornography was called, for the first time,
a "sex war." Writing in the academic journal *signs* in late 1984,
Anne Ferguson bemoaned the "increasing polarization of American feminists into two camps on issues of feminist sexual morality."
Those Ferguson labeled libertarians fought for "the primacy of pleasure" and sought to combat sexual repression. Their opponents, whom
she deemed radicals, organized around "the primacy of intimacy"
among true equals, and so opposed all forms of domination, including pornography. A philosopher by training, Ferguson bemoaned a
dichotomy that reduced the "possible feminist perspectives on sexual
pleasure, sexual freedom, and danger" to these two flawed and mutu-
ally limiting paradigms.[1]

Since the Barnard Conference, soldiers on each side in this new
sex war had become increasingly convinced of the malignity of their
opponents. Feminist "anti-porn rhetoric is a massive exercise in scape-
goating," a veritable "demonology," Gayle Rubin said of WAP and its
allies. And indeed the antis' statements grew increasingly categorical
and absolute. The "liberal defense of pornography as human sexual liberation," Catharine MacKinnon argued, "is a defense not only of force
and sexual terrorism, but of the subordination of women."[2] At a NOW
hearing on the subject, Dolores Alexander of WAP declared that "America is being gassed by the perfume of pornography," the opposition to
which she took as "one of the most worthy priorities for the women's
movement." Some considered eradicating porn to be more founda-
tional to women's equality than safeguarding reproductive rights.[3]

The feminist "sex war" opened a new front in a much older conflict: since at least the 1930s, politicians had declared "war against pornography." In 1966, for example, Karl Mundt, Republican of South
Dakota, read into the record of the Senate a "splendid article" from the

monthly magazine of the Knights of Columbus, urging "a full-scale war against pornography, with President Johnson himself mobilizing the forces of decency in the Nation," at the same time he waged war on poverty and, of course, war on Vietnam.[4] The phrase "porn war" was typically used to describe battles between government enforcers and obscenity purveyors, like "Porn War Rages on in Fun City," as one Tucson paper had reported in 1977.[5] Candice's friend Howie Gordon used the expression differently, to describe the toll the adult film scene exacted on its workers. It "feels like we met in Vietnam!" he wrote in a letter in July 1984. "I'm glad that you've come through the porn wars with your head screwed on straight. A lot of us get lost along the way."[6]

By the 1980s, though, the nature of the war on pornography had changed. Feminist organizing helped to shift the debate from decency to harm. In a speech that became a much-read law review article, MacKinnon distinguished the jurisprudence of obscenity, rooted in notions of "good and evil," from the feminist understanding of pornography as a concrete practice: "behaviors of violence and domination which define the treatment and status of half of the population."[7] When Orange County congressman Richard Dornan called, in late 1982, for "real progress . . . in the war against pornography," he advanced feminist arguments. "As a depiction of predatory and sadistic male sexuality, porn, they say, makes violence against women not only acceptable but exciting to men. 'Pornography is the theory; rape is the practice,'" Dornan offered, in what was surely the only time a conservative Republican has approvingly quoted Robin Morgan on the floor of the House.[8]

In 1985, Femme's first full year in business, the feminist sex war converged with the Reagan administration's war on pornography, the arguments of each intensifying the other.[9] That February, Edwin Meese III replaced William French Smith as attorney general. Where Smith had been a creature of the Republican establishment, minimally concerned with the social issues that animated the new Right, Meese was an unapologetic family values warrior.[10]

Two days before Meese was confirmed—with more negative votes than any previous nominee—the Attorney General's Commission on Pornography was formally established, its findings prefigured in its official charge: "to address the serious national problem of pornography."[11] The panel's eleven members would include Dr. James Dobson, president of Focus on the Family; Ellen Levine, the editor of the supermarket glossy *Woman's Day*; and a phalanx of child advocates, prosecutors, and Republican Party operatives. "I'm afraid there is a train marked 'censorship' which has just left the station," an ACLU spokesman told the *Times*.[12] With an appropriation of under a half million dollars—roughly a tenth of the resources afforded to Johnson's obscenity commission two decades earlier—Meese's commission would not be able to conduct original research. The budget was quite sufficient, however, to put on a coast-to-coast touring show.[13]

That spring, as the members of Meese's commission began their work, Indianapolis mayor William Hudnut's appeal of the district court's ruling against his city's anti-pornography law inched toward the Seventh Circuit Court of Appeals, in Chicago. A sizeable and eclectic group of feminists opposed to the ordinance came together under the name FACT, short for the Feminist Anti-Censorship Task Force, to file an amicus brief in the case. FACT's membership included thinkers as diverse as the pro-masturbation activist Betty Dodson; Barbara Smith of the Combahee River Collective of Black feminists; leading second-wavers Betty Friedan, Kate Millett, and Adrienne Rich; the pioneering historians of gay life John D'Emilio and Jonathan Ned Katz; and Barnard Conference veterans Carole Vance and Nan Hunter. "We believe that the ordinance reinforces rather than undercuts central sexist stereotypes in our society and would result in state suppression of sexually explicit speech, including feminist images and literature," FACT's brief argued.[14]

Having first gathered around universities in New York and Madison, Wisconsin, local FACT groups quickly sprang up in the Bay Area, and in Los Angeles and Cambridge, Massachusetts, where fresh ordinance campaigns were under way. MacKinnon later decried FACT's efforts as "an act of extraordinary horizontal hostility" within what remained of American feminism. The members of FACT, she said, worked "to keep out of women's hands, this law"—her law—"written in women's blood, in women's tears, in women's pain, in women's experience, out of women's silence." With FACT's founding, she reflected, "the women's movement that I had known came to an end."[15] MacKinnon saved leaflets comparing "the bad girls of FACT," aka "Factoids," to Holocaust deniers and tobacco executives.[16] Copies of notes from Bay Area FACT meetings landed in her files, suggesting that ordinance supporters had infiltrated that group.[17]

The task force, another fraught, evanescent, rear-guard sex positive formation, would love to have been half as powerful as MacKinnon imagined it to be. Candice's own take on the group was arguably more astute. "I'm a bit disappointed with FACT," she told the managing editor of *New Directions for Women*, in a note accompanying a Femme press packet. She thought FACT's speakers were too often "unavailable," and their arguments too "inaccessible" to make much difference. She'd "tried to get them on a few talk shows . . . to no avail." She lamented that nobody "knows of their existence out there in the heart of America! As a result, no one's hearing anyone but Women Against Porn about the issue of censorship." FACT's "exclusivity can only hurt their cause," Candice concluded. "It's not enough to get your views into a feminist newspaper, no matter how well read the newspaper." And of course, such publications weren't widely read. By the early '90s, *New Directions* would fold for lack of funds.[18]

The Seventh Circuit's opinion, handed down in August 1985, upheld the lower court's verdict resoundingly, though on First Amendment grounds rather than on the feminist principles of the amicus brief. Judge Frank Easterbrook, a Reagan appointee, stated baldly that the MacKinnon-Dworkin ordinance

discriminates on the ground of the content of the speech. Speech treating women in the approved way—in sexual encounters 'premised on equality' . . .—is lawful no matter how sexually explicit. Speech treating women in the disapproved way—as submissive in matters sexual or as enjoying humiliation—is unlawful no matter how significant the literary, artistic, or political qualities of the work taken as a whole. The state may not ordain preferred viewpoints in this way. The Constitution forbids the state to declare one perspective right and silence opponents.

Judge Easterbrook did not mince words. The Indianapolis ordinance, he said, was "thought control."[19]

Mayor Hudnut had vowed all along to carry his fight to Washington. In September, Indianapolis appealed Easterbrook's ruling to the Supreme Court.[20] With Hudnut's last stand, and the hearings of the Meese commission, the feminist anti-pornography agenda—previously advanced town by town—entered the arena of national policy. Like *Sunset Boulevard* running in reverse, the pictures got big.

———

AT FIRST, it was hard for Candice to fight her way to the front lines of the escalating war. In late 1984, *Newsweek* had put a team of reporters on the new "War against Pornography," and the lead writer on the story interviewed Candice, who crowed in her diary that she would soon be "known as a revolutionary women's erotic video producer." *Femme* touted the upcoming *Newsweek* feature in its early press materials.[21]

But when the issue hit newsstands, in late March 1985, Candice learned that her remarks hadn't made it into the magazine. Instead, the article praised the conceptual innovations of Dworkin and MacKinnon, photographed standing together, stone-faced, in Times Square. *Newsweek*'s investigation also brought to a mass readership the research of Edward Donnerstein, a young psychologist at the University of Wisconsin, whose experiments suggested that pornographic films desensitized their viewers. Donnerstein was cautious: "We can show a causal link between exposure to porn and effects on *attitudes*; but no one can show a causal link between exposure to porn and effects on behavior," he explained. Still, the scientist suspected that some kind of neural rewiring occurred when the erotic and the violent were mixed. (MacKinnon often drew on Donnerstein's early work, which he would later back away from.) Less than half a column of the lengthy story went to the views of "anti-abolitionists," feminist and otherwise. Al Goldstein offered the most quotably obnoxious line: "Frankly, I don't think it matters whether porn is degrading to women," he said.[22] By First Amendment standards, he was entirely correct.

Candice sent a long, outraged letter to the editors. "If you are sincerely trying to report on the adult entertainment industry as a whole, I think it only fair to include those of us who are trying to upgrade the medium," she wrote. Were the anti-pornography civil-rights ordinances to become law, she feared, "someone's grandmother can look at an actress receiving sexual pleasure (on a privately owned videotape), call her a 'whore by nature,' and sue me right out of business." Her understanding of the ways the model statute could be applied was not fantastical. And as she pointed out, Big Porn could easily weather nuisance lawsuits, while "small independents" like Femme faced an existential threat. She closed by offering "another fact that was left out from my interview, and probably all the other adult film actresses' whose statements were never mentioned": she had never, in her years as an actress, been "'forced' to do anything. . . . . But I guess that fact, along with the noble ambitions of 'Femme,' was not scandalous enough to include in your sensationalist portrayal of contemporary pornography.'"[23] *Newsweek* never ran the letter, or any other reflecting a similar perspective. The media, like the antis, retained its investment in a sex war with two distinct and well-bounded sides, neither of which was interested in a more complex story of sex-as-work.

The following month, the feminist battle over pornography made the cover of *Ms.* The meticulous, seven-page-long feature mapped the divisions between the ordinance proponents and FACT, reprinted the text of the model law, parsed several of its variants, and included numerous sidebars pitting statements by Dworkin or MacKinnon against counterpoints from FACT leaders Vance and Hunter. But the only voice from the adult industry was that of Linda Marchiano, whose ordeal, as Linda Lovelace, had become a synecdoche for the experience of all women in porn.[24]

Candice fired off another letter, asking why *Ms.* seemed to "want nothing to do with a woman who's been directly associated with the adult film industry unless she has a horror story to tell." Given "the way WAP parades Linda Lovelace Marchiano's tragic story around like a banner, you'd think they'd also be concerned about improving conditions for the women who still work in adult films." Dangers increased in illicit industries, Candice wrote—an argument of a piece with progressive campaigns to decriminalize prostitution and drug use, then and now. "Keeping sexually explicit material in the ghetto will keep it a low-class job devoid of any rights and protections." Femme was forging a different, more elevated path, yet *Ms.* had "ignored all press information and screening invitations sent to them."[25] The magazine proved her point by quietly filing the letter.

The reporters wouldn't quote her, and the editors wouldn't print her rebuttals. But television talk-show producers were increasingly eager to bring Candice to the table.

Talk shows were a postwar paradox: mass commodities, produced by cultural elites, that traded in intimacy and ordinariness. They were cheap to make, lucrative to syndicate, and easy to target to a segmented market—housewives by day, couples late at night. Phil Donahue had pioneered the daytime talk formula decades before, getting rid of the host's desk to pace the auditorium, and inviting the studio audience—and, via telephone, the home viewer—into direct and often pointed conversation with panelists. Some of Donahue's guests were experts in their fields, the sorts of people who appeared on Sunday-morning news programs. But more were celebrities, and many were everyday folks whose authority stemmed from personal experience. Combining aspects of journalism and consciousness-raising, talk shows made the personal political, and vice versa. They quickly supplanted soap operas as the genre of television most watched by American women.[26]

By the '80s, the profitable programming space had grown crowded and competitive. Daytime talk became, increasingly, a tabloid medium, with topics meant to shock, discussed by guests primed to clash. *Confrontalk*, some executives called it. Story arcs built toward catharses written in tears and snot and occasionally in blood—a kind of money shot.[27] Sex sold; fights sold; fights about sex sold best of all. Pornography as a subject, porn stars as guests: in the tabloid era, these were talk-show gold.

Gloria Leonard had plied the talk-show circuit for years, debating members of Women Against Pornography, especially founder Dolores Alexander, since 1980. (Off-camera, the two were friends.) Leonard's platform—as *High Society*'s publisher, she was a prominent civil libertarian—gave her a higher profile than Candice, at least at first.

But in the spring of 1985, in the wake of the *Newsweek* and *Ms.* cover stories, New York's local talk program *MidDay* scrambled a larger chorus to debate the Dworkin-MacKinnon ordinance campaign. Candice was invited to take the opposing position, alongside Eve Ziegler from *Swank* and Sylvia Law from FACT. On the supporting side sat Valerie Heller of WAP, Ceil Welch from NOW, and John Stoltenberg, the founder of Men Against Pornography and—though it was not widely known—Andrea Dworkin's life partner.[28]

The result was a free-for-all. Heller testified, tearfully, about the sexual molestation she had suffered as a child, at the hands of her uncle. Pornography, she said, taught the next generation of abusers and groomed their victims. Stoltenberg was the first to bring up Linda Marchiano, flagging her as a likely claimant for the injunctive relief the ordinance would provide. Royalle pointed out that the creators of *Deep Throat* were not the ones who had coerced Marchiano. Ziegler added, wryly, "Linda is still making her living from pornography, and from the retelling of her story." Welch, dressed turban to toe in white, castigated Royalle and Ziegler for exploiting women. The ordinances, she hoped, would give women whose "rights are violated by walking down 42nd Street" a remedy for their suffering.

Candice had grown enormously as a public presenter since the year before. She wore a burgundy suit and matching blouse with a high ruffled neck, the very image of professional respectability. She took up space. When Stoltenberg said that the pornography industry, fearful of the ordinance, "sends women out to speak on its behalf," Candice answered back, "I came here on my own." She nailed Femme's talking points: Women made choices, and working in the adult industry was one of them. Slasher films were more toxic than hardcore. The remedy for bad porn was better porn. "Let's change it from within!" she cheered, promising she could create—*had* created—"egalitarian" images, showing "regular, joyful lovemaking."[29]

As Candice proved her televisual mettle, a trickle of invitations became a steady stream and then a deluge. "I'm in great demand as a spokesperson on the right to view adult material," she told Mario Vassi, a reporter from *Penthouse Forum*. TV appearances became the chief means of publicizing her new films; VCA, the national distributor, was, she complained, "doing virtually no promotion." Vassi's July 1985 profile, "Finally, Feminist Porn," described Candida Royalle's predicament: caught between a conventional "male-owned porn industry" that "regards sex in the same way that Detroit looks upon automobiles—as a product"—and "guerrilla groups like Women Against Pornography and the Moral Majority," which treated sex as a struggle. Candice, though, sensed that her predicament was a gift. The porn wars, she told a friend, had given her a new way to "help sell Femme."[30]

⎯⎯⎯

OVER THE SUMMER OF 1985, the Meese commission began hosting public hearings across the United States. The goal, the commissioners proclaimed, was to air "as wide a range of perspectives as possible." All but the first hearing would explore a theme: law in Chicago in July, psychology in Houston in September, business in Los Angeles in October, and so on.[31]

But the breadth of perspectives was a mirage. At the opening session, held in Washington in June, vice cops, customs officials, FBI agents, and evangelical leaders took the stage, along with Republican politicians, including Mitch McConnell, a freshman senator from Kentucky swept into national office on the coattails of the Reagan landslide, trailing his experience as chairman of the Kentucky Task Force on Exploited and Missing Children. In D.C. and in every city afterward, anti-pornography voices outnumbered civil libertarians by roughly 3 to 1.

At each session, victims of sexual abuse and molestation spoke their truth, some of them testifying behind screens. At the Miami hearing, centered on child pornography, a man holding a Bible spoke of falling into sexual perdition during his teenage years, after seeing a deck of explicit playing cards.[32] Porn's marquee casualty, of course, was Linda Marchiano, who might have been docketed for Los Angeles, when the hearings were to focus on the "production side of the industry," but instead was reserved for the final session, themed around organized crime, to be held in New York in January 1986. Marchiano's attorney, Catharine MacKinnon, assured her client that New York was fitting placement, and prepared civil-rights filings in her name, to be submitted the moment any of the ordinance campaigns ended in success. The Los Angeles County Board of Supervisors defeated that city's version by one vote in June, but Cambridge would hold its referendum late in the fall.[33]

All told, some 230 men, women, and children answered the commission's invitation to appear or submit written testimony. More than a hundred others sent unsolicited statements. The largest contingent, nearly one-third of the speakers, came from the ranks of law enforcement. Victims, psychologists, and representatives of religious or decency organizations comprised the next largest groups. Civil libertarians amounted to a baker's dozen; nine adult-industry representatives testified; the same number of sex workers came forward, most of them as victims of abuse. Among this chorus of witnesses, you can count the anti-censorship feminists on one hand, and the FACT members on one finger: Nan Hunter offered remarks, in Chicago, right after a sexual abuse victim and two slots before star witness Catharine MacKinnon.[34]

The commission reached out to Candice over the summer, inviting her to appear in New York in January, which would have seemed easy enough, a subway ride from Femme's offices. But she demurred, requesting a slot in Los Angeles instead. It's not clear why she preferred the West Coast hearings. She was working frantically: Lauren had all but withdrawn from the company's operations, so in addition to doing all the promo, Candice had taken over most of the back-office duties. She promised herself, "I will no longer put Femme before Candice." Yet despite all her press work, the movies were selling poorly; she told an investor that Femme sales had "gotten off to a slow start," moving under 3,000 copies nationwide.[35] Maybe she wanted the earlier date to help promote the project sooner. Maybe L.A.'s industry theme appealed more than New York's Mafia framing.

Candice flew to Europe in September, first to Rome, where Per was serving as Chuck Vincent's assistant director on a pornographic epic about Pompeii, and then to Amsterdam. She had been invited to appear in the Fifth Annual International Women's Festival, held at an alternative performance space called Melkweg (Milky Way), a Dutch version of Franklin Furnace. She did her burlesque act, wearing the bodystocking made of string she had used in personal appearances, before an audience who greeted the performance as art rather than as an invitation to solitary sex. She also appeared on a panel, "What Do Women Want?" alongside the sex-worker-rights activist Gail Pheterson, the experimental writer Kathy Acker, and SAMOIS co-founder Pat (now Patrick) Califia. The audience largely consisted of "lesbian feminists, and that can be a bit intimidating!" Candice wrote in her diary. But the events proved "really magical," as her co-panelists and the ecstatic Dutch press agreed. Califia wrote, soon after, a fan letter that smacked of a schoolboy crush: "If your movies don't take off like wildfire it will be because there really IS a conspiracy to keep women on the bottom."[36] Candida Royalle was becoming an international sex-positive celebrity.

The commission's official invitation to speak in Los Angeles was waiting when Candice returned from Amsterdam. She would be allotted twenty minutes to deliver her remarks, a draft of which she had already shared. She would admit there were "sleazebags that hide out on the periphery of the industry," but emphasize that, in her experience, most people had been "kind and thoughtful in such an intimate and vulnerable setting"—far more so, in fact, than was typical in the "so called 'legit' film world." She would argue that pornography was a mass medium of sex education and could be constructive as the pendulum swung "away from the 'sexual revolution'" and toward "a balanced middle ground" between "rampant promiscuity" and "Victorian sexual repression." "It's high time we grew up," Candice planned to tell the assembly. "I don't need anyone protecting me from my own choices."[37]

Barely a week after she confirmed her participation, the arrangement unraveled. She asked the commission to pay her airfare to California, a request they seem to have declined. Yet she also resented the use of taxpayer funds for its work; in her draft statement, she had noted, trenchantly, that while the commission's experts claimed to be fighting sexual violence, "New York's Women against Rape could sure use that money."[38] Maybe digging into her own pockets to speak to a body that so obviously disdained her was more than she could stomach.

When the curtain went up in Los Angeles, Candice's allies were surprised to find her missing. "I was in L.A. for the Meese Commission, looking forward to hearing you testify," FACT's Carole Vance wrote. "It was a zoo," Vance said, featuring "zillions of vice cops, grisly slides, etc. The chairman is still looking for a single person to testify who has benefited from pornography!"[39]

Whether Candice fit that bill or not remained to be seen.

———

BY THE TIME the Meese commission gaveled its Los Angeles hearings to order, the October issue of *Glamour* had hit newsstands. "How Women Are Changing Porn Films" was buried deep in the book, but the feature was long, and much of it centered on Candida Royalle, who had pitched the story the winter before. "*Finally, there's* Femme," the article opens, a bit breathlessly, quoting *Femme*'s own "throaty, womanly, come-hither voiceover." Author Susan Squire treated the raging public debate "over pornography's role in society" as a sideshow. Instead, she focused on an industry "quietly undergoing an evolution" from within. Films like *Femme*'s were meeting the needs of "middle-class women" and "middle-class couples," who watched porn at home and wanted to see people, as Royalle said, "*making love* rather than just screwing."[40]

Candice later reflected that the *Glamour* story had been her "one big break." She thanked the magazine's editor in chief for "daring to broach a much feared and ignored topic . . . and for treating it in a fair and objective way." The article had "helped us through many valuable doors," she said.[41]

One of those doors opened onto Phil Donahue's soundstage. November was ratings sweeps month, which meant, as Candice told a friend, that "all the stations start running movies & shows with sexy themes, and the talk shows . . . all start trying to line up controversial guests for risqué topics."[42] Donahue was no stranger to frank sexual content. Married to the feminist celebrity Marlo Thomas, he had given airtime not only to porn stars and sexologists but also to issues central to the women's movement, including voluntary childlessness, rape, and employment discrimination.[43] The Meese commission's national tour combined politics, explicit sex, and fierce debate among feminists, making the hearings a natural topic for the sweeps in 1985. Donahue taped his episode on the topic before an audience at the Palace of Fine Arts in San Francisco, a city known for sexual license.[44]

Donahue was, as Candice wrote, "the crème de la crème," and it's easy to see why she leapt at the chance to participate. The producers flew her to San Francisco and put her up at the St. Francis. Everything that came before had amounted to mere "practice . . . so I was just in right form for this, the most important show yet," she wrote.[45]

It is less clear why Catharine MacKinnon accepted the invitation. The ordinance proponents loathed the air of the catfight that surrounded public debate with other feminists. The just-concluded Cambridge campaign had become especially ugly. FACT members charged that leaders of the Women's Alliance Against Pornography, the local organization sponsoring the ballot question, had "a group policy not to be in the same room" with them.[46]

No FACT members appeared on *Donahue*, but neither did any other supporters of the ordinance strategy. The sex therapist Lonnie Barbach, author of several popular books on sexual intimacy, affirmed the value of explicit erotica, which she feared would become actionable under the proposed law. Steffani Martin, who hosted the cable access program *Plain Brown Wrap-Up* and was trying to make it as a distributor of erotica for women, spoke as an industry representative. Barbach, Royalle, and Martin smiled a lot, leaning back in their chairs, spilling into each other's space, with an easy rapport. MacKinnon, wearing a black suit reminiscent of judicial robes, sat stage right, a gap separating her from the rest of the group.

"There are some very lovely films out there," Martin offered.

"They make the rape and subordination of women look lovely," MacKinnon countered.

"I buy *Penthouse* and I rent cassettes and I think degradation is in the eye of the beholder," one caller, a self-described feminist, told the panelists.

MacKinnon asked the caller if she had enjoyed a *Penthouse* spread showing "Asian women bound, hanging from trees."

During the first half of the show, MacKinnon spoke nearly as much as the other panelists combined, as she decried the "circus quality" of the proceedings. Even Donahue struggled to enter the conversation. "Ms. MacKinnon let me just get this in," he pleaded at one point.

But during a break about two-thirds of the way through the program, the pro-sex panelists seem to have organized. When they went live again, Royalle, Barbach, and Martin took charge.

The "three of us are here because we want to present an alternative for women," Candice offered. "I'm making films I want women to get turned on by. . . . Do we now have to police and monitor our own fantasies because it is not politically correct?" she asked, using the Old Left term just recently adopted by the New Right.

MacKinnon answered that there was nothing new in what Femme was doing. "The pornographers have been trying to make a woman's market ever since day one."

"No, they have not," Candice spat back.

"Yes, they have," MacKinnon said, as the exchange descended toward the schoolyard.

"Not true," Martin rejoined.

"Their magazines have failed, their videos have failed," MacKinnon said, looking past her fellow panelists.

"No, they have not," answered Martin, who knew what sold, and how much.

"That's because women, in spite of everything do not enjoy being hurt," MacKinnon continued, speaking over her. But she seemed to have lost the momentum, the audience, and even, ostensibly, the host.

"Attorney-at-Law MacKinnon, you will acknowledge that the Right has co-opted this effort?" Donahue asked, suddenly prosecutorial.

"That is a myth that the press has invented," she answered. "What I would like is if some of you would hold the pornographers responsible for the consequences of their ideas like you're trying to hold me. We accept the responsibility for what people do with our ideas."[47]

The argument that ideas, words, films, even fantasies, had agentive force and tangible, physical consequences lay at the core of MacKinnon's intervention in the pornography debate.[48] Candice and many of her colleagues in the image industry believed otherwise.

"Fantasy is not reality," Steffani Martin had argued. "The President of the United States has all the freedom in the world to have his sexual fantasies when he goes home and is no less of a President," no "less of a man."[49]

It was a prescient remark, two presidents too soon.

22 Pornography of the People

Candice with trophies from the Critics' Adult Film Awards, 1987.

crew said porn was dying. Thanks to WAP and Meese and the Christian conservatives, the industry's image had become ever more "vile and repugnant," critic Rick Marx lamented, right around the time Candice appeared on *Donahue*. Adult theaters were closing, victims of politics, economics, and technology alike. Almost nobody was shooting on film anymore. And hardcore videos—some 1,700 of them released that year—generally stunk.[1]

Despair stalked the porn set. Shauna Grant, a fresh-faced star from Minnesota, had taken her own life in 1984, after only a couple years in the business. Her death by overdose would become the subject of a *Frontline* investigation and, soon after, a feature-length documentary. Matinee idol Rock Hudson had succumbed to AIDS in October 1985, soon after revealing both his diagnosis and his sexuality. ("Can you believe the whole thing with Rock Hudson?!" Candice asked the Belveweirds' Bill Brown. She figured his suffering was "good for people to see.") And Hudson hadn't fucked for a living. The adult industry had to know what was coming; "everyone waits for the first porn star to get AIDS," Marx said.[2]

But even *Screw* had to admit that Candida Royalle was flourishing. Her films, Marx said, demonstrated the impact of a "woman's movement with its own values and ideas about what sex and eroticism should be." If Marx mourned the glory days of 1970s hardcore, he glimpsed in Femme porn's future, in which the genre must "shed its outlaw image and begin appealing more to educated women, housewives and mothers." For better or worse, Royalle and Femme represented "The Next Degeneration," which would not be so degenerate after all.[3]

By the end of 1985, it seemed as if Femme's audacious gambit might just work. *Urban Heat* reached number three in adult video sales and had been nominated for several *AVN* awards. Candice had played *Donahue*, the Franklin Furnace, and the Dutch *Melkweg*. Femme's press kit included glowing clips from *Glamour* as well as *Oui*. Especially after the *Melkweg* appearance, coverage of the Femme project had also begun to appear in the foreign press. *Photo* magazine, in France, included Candida Royalle in a photo spread entitled "*Stars Porno: des Femmes Comme les Autres*," part of an international "special stars" issue that also portrayed Brooke Shields, Isabel Huppert, and Nastassja Kinski.[4] "My movies are causing quite a sensation in the media and talk show circuit, so I'm very busy these days," Candice told an industry contact who had written to pitch a script. She felt proud of Femme's body of work, which answered a real need, remedying some of the same gendered inequities that Catharine MacKinnon also abhorred. "My movies are my gift to women after partaking in films that exploit and degrade them," she said.[5]

Candice was also exhausted. In December, she and Per headed to Jamaica to spend a month on a yacht owned by their distributors at VCA, to recover from the frantic fall. Bill Brown flew from San Francisco to New York to stay with their cats. When the weeks of Brown's visit stretched into months, they put him to work in the office, where they desperately needed extra hands.[6]

Femme was on the cusp. Candice understood the adult world well enough—bottom to top, from the inside out—to feel, rightly, confident in the singularity of her vision and in the growing power of her voice. But unlike her anti-porn antagonists, she also understood the distance between words and things. Femme's tentative success could still "all fizzle out" and leave her mired in debt.[7] On New Year's Eve, Sture Sjöstedt sent a check for $2,000, the next tranche of Saga's investment. He had earned out on *Femme*, but they still owed him nearly $18,000 before *Urban Heat* recouped, bit by bit, netting $7.50 per unit sold. *Christine's Secret* would be released in April. All their efforts "MUST give a result soon," Sture believed, certain that 1986 "will be THE YEAR!"[8]

FROM THE START, *Femme*, and the broader Femme Productions project, had passionate followers. Just months after its release, the film won a Pornography of the People Award for Fans' Favorite Videotape, beating out *Romancing the Bone* and *The Year of Loving Dangerously*, among others, in a poll of the readers of five adult cinema magazines.[9]

Fan letters backed up the poll results. Candice kept them by the hundreds and responded to as many as she could. Some of the earliest came from the kinds of devotees who had been writing to her all along: men who had seen her '70s porn-star turns and wanted autographed photos, "preferable in the nude."[10] But especially after the release of *Christine's Secret*, a different kind of mail arrived, from women and couples living in seemingly every corner of the United States. They wrote in pencil and in Sharpie; they fed pin-holed paper through dot-matrix printers; they used corporate letterhead and Muppets memo pads. A mother from New Jersey wrote to say she and her husband had rented a Femme film and "enjoyed great love making the night we saw your tape." A man from a small town in Washington wrote in a shaky hand to say that he had enjoyed *Christine's Secret* with his wife, "the same beautiful girl" to whom he'd been married for forty-seven years. A woman from Petal, Mississippi sensed in Royalle a "kindred spirit," and described the discrimination she'd faced as one of the few female executives in a local bank.[11]

Some fans seemed eager to burnish their own feminist bona fides. A customer from Amherst, Massachusetts, described a conversation that Femme tapes had sparked with his partner, about "the complexity of distinguishing between the sexually explicit material we support and use and those that we want to let go of," and applauded Femme for avoiding "sexuality oppression." A frequent correspondent from Portland, Maine, compared Femme's aesthetic to the windows at Tiffany's. "When we visit New York we stay at the Plaza," he wrote. "We feel comfortable with Bach, Vivaldi, Chopin, Erte and Balanchine. We also feel comfortable with your films." But he didn't like reading about Femme in the sex magazines, and he didn't want to go "to the back room of a video store or to VCA to get the sort of film you are producing, just as I shouldn't go to Times Square to find a friend."[12]

Others wrote bashfully, seeking sex tips. "I am 32 years old, female, M.B.A., single, & don't like the 'other' porn movies," explained one fan who asked for "more 'instructions' for oral sex (fellatio)." Another, with a name suggesting Middle Eastern heritage, wrote in a loopy hand on notepaper flecked with pansies: "Are there any films containing lesbian themes?" By contrast, a Mrs. Peter Chang—one of many female fans in a marriage conventional enough to correspond under her husband's name—wrote from Florida to insist, "We like *straight sex* (male & female) *couples* (*not* homosexual, group or anal, S&M, etc.)."[13]

A few offered suggestions. An older viewer from California asked that Femme consider a project centered on "senior citizen sex tastefully done," to "help dispel some myths about senior sex." A writer who described herself as "a black female currently in a relationship with a white male" wanted "to see interracial couples." A "white female college graduate" from San Jose who had watched a Femme film with her mother recommended "better dialogue, better acting, more in-depth characterization, more foreplay, and good-looking actors!" A couple from Madison, Wisconsin sent a formal business letter praising Femme's aesthetic, but also urging, "try not to get too 'preachy.' "[14]

For all their variety, writers to Femme converged on two points: they had learned about Femme from Royalle's appearances on TV, and they had trouble finding the product. "After seeing you and other members of your company on a talk show, I rushed to my video club to try and rent one of your movies. NOTHING," complained one would-be viewer. A woman from Cleveland, unable to find Femme videos anywhere, suggested that Candice consign tapes to a local "gay/lesbian erotic hardware store called Body Language." Community standards sometimes played a role, as the *Miller* decision directed. "I look forward to viewing your films with my wife, when we can get to a city that is allowed to distribute them," wrote a man from Corpus Christi, which, he said, was "currently undergoing a tyrannical 'filth' exorcising by the puritanical-minded officials." But even in liberal markets, Femme films remained hard to rent, as Royalle herself became ubiquitous. A man from Rye, New York, had "asked the owner of our local video tape store if he could obtain a copy," only to be told that the film "would not have broad enough appeal to justify adding it."[15] A sex-positive feminist who had rechristened herself Lisa LaBia explained that even in Minneapolis—"otherwise known as

I-Hate-Everything-Dworkinland"—people remained either "unfamiliar with your work," or unable to find it.[16]

BY SUMMER, January's sense of imminent success had begun to evaporate. "It's amazing to discover how little money there is really in this genre," Candice told her onetime lover Martin Blinder. "We feel like we're working too hard for too little." *Femme* and *Urban Heat* were making modest profits. *Christine's Secret*, out three months, was still in the red.[17]

The porn wars remained national news, which was good for Candice, who had positioned herself, she noted in her diary, as "the only real answer to the porn problem." After *Donahue*, she had appeared with other adult industry veterans on Regis Philbin's *Morning Show* and on *Sally Jesse Raphael*, one of *Donahue*'s emerging national rivals. Both hosts expressed bemused skepticism about their guests' work, but the temperature was cooler and the stakes less existential than they had been on the *Donahue* episode. Candice was also called to join

National Writers' Union panel on Censorship and Pornography, January 1986. Candice is at the podium; FACT leaders Nan Hunter (center) and Carole Vance (left) are seated.

panels about the work of the Meese commission, with sponsors like the Gay and Lesbian Anti-Defamation League and the National Writers Union.[18] Sometimes, when she addressed these high-toned audiences, Candice traded her customary contact lenses for owlish horn-rimmed glasses, the kind of intellectual costume that would quickly be shed in a blue movie. A television crew from Dallas flew up to film separate segments with her, Bob Guccione, and Andrea Dworkin. The week-long "Porn Report" aired on Texas ABC affiliates in July, just as the Attorney General's Commission on Pornography released its findings. "Old Meese is making me very popular," Candice told a friend.[19]

The commission's two-volume, 1,960-page *Final Report* landed with a dull thud. The document, which asserted links between pornography and sex crime as well as tight connections between the adult industry and the Mafia, recommended various measures to curb the proliferation of explicit materials, including stepped-up enforcement of existing obscenity laws with, in some cases, mandatory minimum sentences. Edward Donnerstein, whose experiments the *Report* drew upon to buttress its arguments about causality, lambasted their use of his work. "These conclusions seem bizarre to me," he told the *New York Times*.[20] Two members of the commission, Columbia University psychologist Judith V. Becker and Ellen Levine of *Woman's Day*, issued a stinging joint dissent, alleging that "every member of the group brought suitcases full of prior bias" to the work. Deliberations had been short and shallow, and research underfunded. "No self-respecting investigator would accept conclusions based on such a study," they said.[21]

Nonetheless, feminist anti-pornography groups hailed many of the *Report*'s findings. Women Against Pornography commended "the Commission for being the first federal body to report on the systematic campaign of abuse, terror, and discrimination being waged against over half the citizens of this country." They were glad the *Report* had inventoried some 2,325 issues of pornographic magazines, their titles listed alphabetically, crawling over forty-two double-columned pages, from *A Cock Between Friends*, discovered in the nation's capital, to *69 Lesbians Munching*, which had apparently not been banned in Boston. ("It is a writer's dream to be anthologized in a prestigious, widely circulated publication bearing an official imprimatur," Al Goldstein joked in a *Times* op-ed.)[22]

WAP also found much to criticize. The organization rejected the commission's recommendation for tighter enforcement of obscenity laws, which "empower the state, not the victims, and in fact have repeatedly been used against the people most injured by pornography—the so-called performers." WAP also spurned the *Report*'s "division of pornography into three categories: violent, degrading, and non-violent/non-degrading." *All* pornography—every text and image that fed "an eight-billion-dollar-a-year traffic in the bodies, lives, and human possibilities of women and children"—was equally reprehensible, equally guilty of "the sexualization of women's subordination."[23]

John Stoltenberg of Men Against Pornography likewise welcomed the *Report* as evidence that the "analysis . . . first comprehended and put forth by radical feminists—people to whom the human rights of women matter fundamentally," had made its way into an important government document. He felt certain the commission's findings would "catapult the issue of pornography directly to the forefront of major issues confronting this country."[24]

The shortest, clearest response, four crystalline paragraphs, came from MacKinnon and Dworkin. "For the first time in history, women have succeeded in convincing a national governmental body of a truth women have long known: pornography harms women and children," they said. The *Report* was deeply "flawed" in the ways WAP and Stoltenberg had said; obscenity laws were "dangerously discretionary, anti-woman, anti-gay, beside the point and ineffectual." But the commission had also "recommended to Congress the civil rights legislation that women have sought": a federal statute based on their model municipal ordinance. Dworkin and MacKinnon urged support for this proposed new federal law, in hopes that the national will would succeed where officials and ordinary people in city after city had come up short.[25]

By the time the Meese commission released its *Final Report*, the back of the anti-pornography civil rights ordinance movement had been broken. In February 1986, shortly after the commission's final public hearing, the U.S. Supreme Court summarily affirmed the Seventh Circuit's ruling, refusing even to docket *Hudnut v. American Booksellers*

Association. MacKinnon found the court's action—"without hearing arguments, reading briefs, or issuing an opinion"—outrageous, and pointed out that the affirmation did not preclude subsequent challenges.[26] But its impact was nonetheless profound. After the Supreme Court declined to take up *Hudnut,* Madison, Wisconsin, withdrew another proposed version of the model statute. The California chapters of NOW decided thenceforth to oppose "any content-based legislation to deal with problems associated with pornography," and chapters in other states prepared similar statements.[27]

"The ordinance is not law anywhere," MacKinnon wrote, looking back, a dozen years later. "For those who survived pornography," she said, the public hearings that accompanied municipal campaigns had felt "like coming up for air." But as defeat followed defeat, "the water has closed over their heads once again." The model statute had been rejected by city councilors in Minneapolis, by county supervisors in Los Angeles, and, resoundingly, by the voters themselves in Cambridge: three of the most politically progressive places in the United States. Conservative Indianapolis had approved it, and then wasted nearly a quarter of a million dollars in legal fees to defend its action. There would be two more campaigns, one in Bellingham, Washington, in 1988, and the last in Massachusetts, a statewide bill "to Protect the Civil Rights of Women and Children," debated in 1992. Both would end in quiet failure, out of the national press.[28]

By the time the Meese commission reported, many leading feminists had disavowed not only the ordinance strategy but also the consuming focus on pornography within the broader fight for women's rights. At NOW's national conference in 1986, a "substantial majority of the voting members" had defeated five separate resolutions introduced by WAP. MacKinnon's parliamentary maneuvers to extend the time for discussing the proposals had likewise been voted down. Betty Friedan issued a clarion call in the *Times,* urging the movement to abandon its paralyzing "obsession" with porn, a crippling "preoccupation" at a moment when women's equality remained woefully incomplete.[29] Margaret Atwood, whose dystopian novel *The Handmaid's Tale* was published in the United States as the Meese commission concluded its work, later said she'd based the theology of the sadistic Aunts in her fictional Gilead on the excesses of the anti-porn campaigns and other misbegotten centerpieces of the "1984 feminism" that surrounded her as she wrote.[30]

Candice saw the furor around the Meese commission chiefly as an opportunity to advance her distinctive feminism and, with it, her product. "Women were only recently able to admit we like sex," she told an interviewer for *Penthouse Forum* while the commission's *Report* was in press. "We only recently feel free to watch porn films." WAP and their conservative allies on the commission promised women safeguards. "I don't want to be protected, thank you," she said. "I want women to make the porn they like to see."[31]

She had recently marked five years "clean from hard drugs." She drew new boundaries, turning down a request from *Playboy* to illustrate a feature about Femme with naked portraits of her. The article "will still go, but sans nudies of me," she wrote in her diary.[32] Candida Royalle would no longer be displayed on satin sheets, as if for the taking. Now she held the clapperboard. Now she called the shots.

The antis still questioned her feminism; during a program on New York's WBAI radio, John Stoltenberg likened Candice to an apologist for slavery.[33] But as the cracks in the anti-pornography edifice widened, she piloted Femme through them. She wrote to NOW, of which she professed herself "a card-carrying member," affirming her longtime feminism, touting the "revolution in the adult industry" her work represented, and pleading with "the feminist community to wake up . . . and offer a little support for my efforts." She urged the organization's leadership to cast aside the "myth of the porno-bimbette," which had allowed anti-porn feminists "to write us off as victims."[34]

The letter struck enough of a chord that a delegation from NOW, including Florence Rush, a pioneering advocate for victims of childhood sexual abuse who frequently appeared with WAP, trooped out to Candice and Per's Brooklyn townhouse for dinner and a screening of *Christine's Secret.* "We appreciate your efforts and the direction your videos are taking, and the open way you shared your concerns and responded to ours," the visitors offered in a fulsome thank-you note. It had been, they said, an "interesting evening."[35]

In August 1986, Candice finally cracked the pages of *Ms.*—earning a single, tepid, and parenthetical sentence in an article about sex toys:

"(Some women report that the videos of Candida Royalle are a step in the right direction.)" She wrote to the editors—yet another of her letters that *Ms.* declined to run—to amplify the point, to disclaim compilations of her old loops that "certain unscrupulous people" had lately released on tape, and to document her feminism, which the magazine's fact-checkers had apparently questioned. "To set the record straight, I was an active member of the Bronx Women's Coalition from 1969 through '71," she wrote.[36]

Some months later, Candice finally received the endorsement she'd long been hunting. "If this porn is the new erotica that appeals to women, then I think it's terrific," Gloria Steinem told *Time.*[37] The testimonial was careful, conditional: *if/then.* Steinem offered no indication that she'd actually seen the films. But even so tepid a blessing would waive Femme past the gatekeepers, like "the *'nihil obstat* of America's feminist Popa," as one critic noted in *Columbia Film View,* the kind of publication where serious critics talked about serious movies in serious tones.[38]

Dinner Scene, Three Daughters, *dir. Candida Royalle, 1986.*

AS THE MEESE COMMISSION readied its *Report*, Candice found her way back behind the camera, after eighteen months talking and hawking. With additional investment from Saga and Lunarex to float a budget twice as large as that of *Christine's Secret*, *Three Daughters* would have, she told a woman who had written to ask after a part in the movie, "an Ingmar Bergmanesque look to it, very lush and natural." Still, she warned, while Femme films were "softer and more sensual" than standard adult fare, "I do expect true sexual participation and real heat from my talent."[39]

Three Daughters was in every way a family affair. Candice directed and Per produced. (That summer, the couple incorporated Femme Distribution, and Candice formally severed her partnership with Lauren.[40]) Club 90 joined in force: Gloria Leonard played the matriarch of the movie's fictional clan. Janie Hamilton managed the complicated production, with twenty-five scenes and a sixty-two-page-long script. Several performers from earlier Femme films acted. (*Swank* joked that there was now an unofficial "Candida Royalle Repertory Theater.") Bill Brown worked in the office. Janice Sukaitis, the creative force behind White Trash Boom Boom, catered meals for the cast of ten and crew of twenty.[41]

Like all pornographic films, and indeed, like all romance novels, *Three Daughters* peddles a fantasy. In this fourth Femme production, the fantasy has two main axes: wealth and domestic bliss. The Claytons, Candice offers in her script notes, are a "typical American family. Middle to Upper Middle class." That *typical* means white, Protestant, and suburban goes without saying. Filmed in a sprawling house in New Jersey, the sets are beautifully appointed. A considerable portion of the action consists, quite literally, of table-setting; script notes describe napkin folds, the placement of glasses, and the lighting of "candelabras." "Be sure to use the matching silverware!" Jane Clayton scolds her soon-to-be married eldest. Her "liberated" future son-in-law helps with the cooking.[42]

Beneath the linens and lace, family sets the pulse of *Three Daughters*. The Claytons glory in their accomplished daughters: the youngest, Heather, is college-bound, pre-med, and the eldest, Michelle, has a job at the American embassy in London. Parts of the story are plainly drawn from Candice's early life. Jennifer, the middle daughter, is a talented if undisciplined musician. Heather experiments sexually with a female friend, as Candice had in adolescence. But if *Three Daughters* picks up autobiographical details, it also represents Candice's therapeutic rescripting of her family history.[43]

By the time she made *Three Daughters*, Candice had reconciled with her father, after a breach she reckoned at nine years. "Nervous I was indeed!" she wrote in her diary, shortly after seeing him in Largo. Neither she nor her sister had any idea that, the very month of Candice's visit, Louis Vadala had begun the twenty-five years of probation resulting from his conviction for lewd and lascivious conduct.[44] It seemed to Candice that he had "really mellowed out," as she told Bill Brown. "My dad & I have gotten very expressive with each other," she said. Their time together, with Per in tow, had restored to her "the father I always loved, before things got screwy."[45]

Things got screwy: Candice, who wrote so frankly and lived so brazenly, now tended to this kind of indirection when meditating on her father's behavior. Early in her therapy with Linda Hirsch, she had seen Louis as a "sick" man who had "put me through so much hell." Now he was guilty merely of "acting improper." Describing their "re-union" to Cinthea, she said she felt certain Louis "loves & needs me as much as I do him."[46]

As she continued her therapy, Candice trained her scrutiny on other members of her family. "If there was any villain in this story, it was your grandmother," Hirsch declared just before Candice rolled tape on *Three Daughters*. Marion Vadala had "sabotaged" Louis's marriage to Peggy; she "probably had a lot to do with our birth-mother leaving," Candice wrote. Marion was guilty of "emasculating" Louis, which was "why Dad 'acted out' on Cyn," as he tried to "feel powerful" in the face of a mother who treated him like a boy. Hirsch's line of interpretation echoed Louis's own: his mother "was in her own small world full of love, affection, oh and that big monster 'possessiveness'!" he had once explained to Candice. "I can still hear her saying it, time & again, . . . 'I was just like my father' ": the lecher, the bigamist.[47]

Even so, Marion, already fifteen years dead, earned at least some pity from her granddaughter. Shortly after Candice reunited with her father, she and Per had gone in search of Marion's grave, only to discover it missing a headstone. "Devastated" by the unmarked plot, Candice resolved to set the gravesite to rights, but they ran into trouble coordinating with Louis's older brother, Charlie. He held the deed to the family plot, which also contained the remains of his stillborn daughter, a ghost baby nobody knew of: secrets piled upon moldering secrets. Candice lamented her "poor grandmother, to be 'remembered' in such a way."[48]

For stepmother Helen, though, she found only fury. Shortly after Candice wrapped *Three Daughters*, Helen made her yearly visit to Brooklyn. She had stopped drinking a couple years before, which only made her more demanding. Her trips north always left a "a deep sad emptiness" in their wake, Candice wrote. And this one was worse. After Helen went home, Candice poured out her frustrations in a long, furious letter, part prosecutor's brief, part wounded child's cry, probably a therapeutic exercise. Now grown-up and loved, publicly esteemed, she was *still* "trying to exorcise" it all.[49]

Three Daughters was part of the exorcism. The members of the Clayton family are frankly sexual, yet always respect boundaries. Though the film's title flirts with incest as much as with Chekhov, the Clayton sisters know only filial love. (While she was working on *Three Daughters*, Candice rejected a script a fan sent her because of its "use of incest as a stimulus," which, she told the writer, was "incredibly irresponsible at a time when the widespread occurrence of incest in our society is just being revealed.") Jane Clayton and her husband Bill have "a flourishing sex life," and Bill is "a good provider," Candice emphasized in her notes. The Claytons do not so much echo the Vadalas as invert them.[50]

Candice was also careful, in her script, to establish that Heather, the youngest Clayton, was eighteen, and careful, during casting, to ascertain that the performers were legally of age. In a first for Femme, the actors' deal memos included a line on which to document proof of their majority—likely a defense against several child protection acts making their way through Congress.[51]

While Candice and Per were rushing the raw footage from *Three Daughters* through post-production on their new video editing system, news broke that the porn starlet Traci Lords, whom Candice had cautioned against overexposure in an interview the year before, had been making adult films since she ran away from home at age fifteen, using a stolen birth certificate. Movies in which Lords had appeared, nearly a hundred in all, were pulled from theaters and video store shelves—instantly creating an under-the-counter market.[52] An investigation by the Los Angeles County sheriff quickly grew into a federal case, following the lines of interstate commerce. The first indictment came down in August. The U.S. Attorney put agents, producers, and publishers, including Bob Guccione of *Penthouse*, on notice: having filmed or photographed the underaged Lords—knowingly or not—exposed them to a $100,000 fine and a prison sentence as long as ten years.[53]

Femme's *Three Daughters* debuted at Private Eyes in October 1986, amidst the fallout from the Meese commission's *Report* and the Lords indictments. "Erotica is under siege," proclaimed Nicholas Kristof in the *New York Times.* Pickets and nuisance suits and Meese's threats were driving the adult slicks from retail outlets, some 17,000 of which had stopped selling skin magazines during Reagan's second term. *Playboy* and *Hustler* were hemorrhaging subscribers; *Playgirl* filed for bankruptcy. Fewer than four hundred adult theaters remained nationwide, a collapse of two-thirds since 1980, almost entirely driven by the shift to video. The annual number of adult tape rentals—100 million—roughly equaled the number of adult movie tickets sold at the dawn of the decade. But that market was increasingly glutted, with prices and quality falling. Kristof singled out the "growing interest among women in adult videos" as one positive trend in a declining industry. He lauded Femme, one of more than eighty small film companies struggling to eke out a profit in some underserved niche.[54]

Candice was proud of *Three Daughters*. With a run time of nearly two hours—the length of a Hollywood feature—it was meant to mimic the pacing of real erotic life. She had stuck to the blue movie template by including six completed sex scenes. But she hoped her next effort might break the adult formula altogether, and feature "only two or three really beautiful love scenes . . . and I don't care about those stupid standards," she told one interviewer. "Who's counting?"[55]

The sex press was counting. *Screw* titled its review "Soft Bore."[56]

But suburban dailies were appreciative. The *Bergen County Record* styled this latest Femme offering "Ladies' Home Hardcore." Journalists still trotted out anti-pornography feminists to speak against Royalle's work. "She's trafficking in women's bodies, just like Bob Guccione," a WAP spokeswoman told the *Record*. But such comments had come to sound obligatory against a swelling chorus of mainstream acceptance. In March 1987, *Time* called *Three Daughters* "a cross between *Debbie Does Dallas* and *The Waltons*."[57] That same month, ABC's evening news program *20/20* aired clips from *Three Daughters* as an exemplar of the new erotica, in a segment opposing censorship. Days later, Candice guested for the second time on *Sally Jesse Raphael*, an appearance that felt entirely different from the year before. She had not been called on "to 'defend' what I do, but rather to talk about creating 'women's erotica,'" she told a friend.[58] In April, she landed a slot on the nation's most widely viewed morning show, NBC's *Today*. Jane Pauley seemed nonplused by the interview, hinting that she'd prefer to talk to the cast of *Golden Girls*. But the anchor's curled lip notwithstanding, *Today*'s imprimatur was priceless.[59]

At the spring 1987 Critics' Adult Film Awards ceremony, *Christine's Secret* and *Three Daughters* took home a combined five trophies. Candice was so overwhelmed with the warmth of the reception that she busted out "The Tomato Song" at the podium, the Angel of Light meeting the "Yuppie with sex appeal," as *Screw* had called her.[60] She had earned the spotlight, had worked hard to hold it, and she basked in it.

But the elegant public face of Candida Royalle also masked gnawing doubts that seemed only to grow with success. "I wasn't at my party—It was the Candida Royalle persona," Candice had written in her diary after the *Three Daughters* premiere. "I want to run away from all this. I feel imprisoned. A robot—an empty robot . . . It's no fun in here.[61]

She had been chasing freedom for so long—nearly two decades now. Freedom from Helen and Louis, then from middle-class morality, then from drugs and want, from an industry that chewed women up, from class-based disdain, from sexism, even from some forms of feminism. Along the way, she had become, by her own reckoning, an avatar of liberty: "the spokesperson for the freedom for adults to choose & view what we want."[62]

Yet she still felt so beholden and behind. What did it mean to endure while so many perished, and still be looking for the revolution?

23 The Parting of the Red Sea

Gay Widows float, San Francisco, 1975.
Candice stands front left, holding her skirt.

Once upon a time, in the summer of 1975, when Candice's straight theater career was poised for launch, before she'd acted in her first porn loop, she had strolled, beside other members of Warped Floors and assorted Angels of Light and a few stray Cockettes, along the route of San Francisco's Gay Day parade. Amidst a riot of rainbows and glitter, the denizens of her float dressed head to toe in mourning weeds, faces whitened, expressions somber. They were costumed as Gay Widows, as the black felt banner on their flatbed truck explained. The performance was an inside joke about the sadness girls and gays felt when the sun rose on another bathhouse trick or one-night stand. "I feel like a gay widow after these meaningless encounters," one of the troupe had sighed, some morning after, and the theme took flight.[1] A snapshot shows Candice leading the line of march, her pose a mix of ballet and kabuki. A scarlet-lipped Joe Morocco walks a couple paces behind.

A decade later, many who walked or rode with the Gay Widows float, like hundreds of the other young revelers on Polk Street that day, were dead or dying. In 1982, when Patrick Cowley perished, he had been one among five hundred lost in the U.S. In 1986, more than twelve thousand Americans succumbed, a two-thousand-fold increase. "One of our highest public health priorities is going to continue to be finding a cure for AIDS," Ronald Reagan declared that February, uttering the disease's name publicly for the first time. He directed his surgeon general, C. Everett Koop, "to prepare a major report to the American people on AIDS."[2]

Koop's October report, issued the month *Three Daughters* launched, laid out in plain language, with clear and explicit illustrations, the known facts of the disease. Koop believed in science and urged condom use, putting him at odds with the president, who preached abstinence. At first, the *Report* was made available only upon request from

HHS. Then it was distributed to congressional offices in limited quantities, and finally, in May 1988, as Reagan's second term neared its end, shipped to every household in the United States, the largest mailing in the federal government's history.[3] By then, more than sixty thousand people, nine-tenths of them men and the great majority under fifty years old, had followed Patrick Cowley to the grave.[4]

The plague had come first for the angels of light who flickered through Candice's psychedelic life in San Francisco's "high camp underground." She had seen Patrick, golden god of the bathhouses south of Market Street and sweet lover of her youth, wither to a wisp. Watching him drain away, when she was newly clean, had bolstered her resolve to stay off heroin, even when Per started using—at first, in a kind of "Friday night party" way, and then, as such things go, more heavily.[5]

A few years later, the Belveweirds, the Cockettes, and the Angels were falling like so many green blades to the scythe. "How did your blood test turn out?" Candice had asked Bill Brown in July 1985, right after Rock Hudson went public with his diagnosis.[6] The news was bad. A Polaroid Candice took in the Sackett Street garden that fall shows Bill by a grape arbor sere with encroaching winter, a late-blooming rose tucked behind his ear.[7]

Bill wanted to go home to die, but most of his family had turned against him. When he returned to San Francisco, after *Three Daughters*, it was to an AIDS residence run by the Shanti Project, a city-funded nonprofit for the terminally ill.[8] Candice wrote to him there in the spring of 1987, to note the passing of another of their friends to the disease. She urged him to "keep up the spirits and don't give in!" By year-end, he was bedridden. He kept beside him some perfume Candice had sent; his sisters told her he took comfort from it right to the end.[9]

There were other victims, all too young, claimed by tangles of AIDS and drugs and despair. Candice lost Joe Morocco well before AIDS claimed him, to heroin and its knock-on effects. The more Joe used, the more he stole, and the more he stole, the more he lied. Sherry Falek, who had known Joe almost as long as the Vadala sisters had, and who loved him almost as much, remembers him lifting money from her sister's purse.[10] Jorgé occasionally ran into Joe in the East Village, as he slowly succumbed to the twin ravages of HIV and smack. "All the love that was sent Joe's way couldn't save him," Candice later wrote of his "slow and mysterious demise." The last time she saw him, he looked "like the pictures of the men in concentration camps."[11]

Candice had lost touch with her dark prince, Danny Isley, but Cinthea, who had moved to Napa, read about his death in a local newspaper. He had overdosed, a suicide, it seemed, after causing an accident that left his girlfriend's young son in the ICU. The *Santa Rosa Press Democrat* reported that Isley, a "strapping rocker," had been lately known as "Ogre." Candice hadn't cried when Cin told her. "I feel like a rock—stunned into hardness," she wrote in her journal. It was "becoming normal to hear of the death of one I once loved."[12]

The death that had hurt the most came early, after Patrick's but before the rest. In March 1986, just as Candice started work on *Three Daughters*, she got word that Lailani, who had performed with her in everything from jazz to underground theatre to porn, and who had been, in those drug-addled, love-addled San Francisco years, more sister to her than Cin, had perished at the age of twenty-nine. They had been the sweetest of friends, and briefly lovers, onscreen in *Hot Rackets*, and offscreen too. In a page of free writing, on which they alternated lines, they extolled each other's soft skin and "total voluptuousness." They had "brought each other out."[13]

Lailani meant flower of heaven, Candice said. Now wilted, withered, dust. "She's in a quiet spot now in the country," wrote the man who was living with her at the end, in a hand like a schoolchild's. He hadn't been able to save her; all Lailani had wanted to do was "drink about the past." He sent a snapshot of her propped in a nest of pillows, reading an encyclopedia-sized volume, *The Sixties: The Decade Remembered Now, By the People Who Lived It Then*. Lailani had "lived her life as one big party" and "died young and beautiful," Candice said in her eulogy. She dedicated *Three Daughters* to her memory.[14]

In her diary, Candice waxed elegiac. "Poor Lailani, you never really had much of a chance," she wrote, as if to her fallen friend. "The only thing we didn't do together was survive." Beside the entry, she pasted a picture of the two of them, beaming, in better times.

But Lailani's death was more than a loss; Candice took it as a portent. "It's like the parting of the red sea," she wrote. "On one side are the survivors," the ones who had managed, in time, "to change drastically."

Lailani's death filled Candice with sorrow. But she also felt "so very thankful" that she had saved herself. "That could have been me," she knew. "But it's not."[15]

THE QUESTION NOW was how to make meaning on the far shore, among the living. As they reckoned their dead by the dozens, Candice and her friends tried on different answers. She saw less of Jorgé Socarras but knew he was "doing great with his music, and all his other creative gigs," including the original track for Femme's *Urban Heat*. His post-punk band, Indoor Life, was making records and playing club gigs downtown.[16] But by 1985, Jorgé felt more like screaming than singing. He remembers "walking down Broadway toward Astor Place and having this irresistible impulse to throw myself on the sidewalk and pound my fists on the ground." He kept a list of friends who had succumbed to AIDS, until the tally reached one hundred. Then he started organizing. He met with a handful of other gay male friends, some HIV-positive, first to raise consciousness, and then to figure out how to raise hell. Artists all, they decided to make a poster, something startling enough to change the conversation: street art, in the mode of the Guerilla Girls, whose prints calling out sexism in the museum world went up by night on walls all over Manhattan.[17]

William F. Buckley, of all people, lit the way. In an op-ed published in the *Times* in March 1986, the conservative provocateur proposed that those infected with HIV be forcibly "tattooed in the upper forearm, to protect common-needle users, and on the buttocks, to prevent the victimization of other homosexuals."[18] The argument reeked of fascism, and that got Jorgé's little circle talking, and somebody mentioned the pink triangle the Nazis had used to identify gay men, a symbol lately reimagined as an emblem of gay pride. They debated the slogan to run beneath it—something to decry Reagan's longtime refusal to address the epidemic. They settled on SILENCE = DEATH. The following spring, a new organization, the AIDS Coalition to Unleash Power, or ACT-UP, adopted the motto for its direct-action campaigns, splashing it on T-shirts and buttons and stickers and banners, making the image Jorgé had helped to create into one of the century's most recognizable protest icons.[19]

In the spring of 1987, as ACT-UP planned its first zap actions and SILENCE = DEATH blazed from every street corner, Candice began to reckon with the threat of the virus to the adult industry. Performers in adult films engaged, "as a routine requirement of their profession," in "the entire repertoire of high-risk sexual behaviors," as one psychologist wrote. Greater Los Angeles, where 80 percent of pornographic films were, by then, produced, had become a viral hot spot.[20] Little data was available on industry-wide rates of infection, but there were whispers, retirements, even rumored suicides. In the summer of 1986, John C. Holmes, the industry's most prolific male star, had tested positive. Holmes had made, by some estimations, four thousand movies, including two with Candice. He filmed six shortly before his diagnosis and acted in at least one more, in Europe, after the positive test. About the fate of his costars, he was blithe, fatalist. "He just figured, if they don't get it from me or they don't already have it, they're going to end up with it anyway," his wife later recalled.[21]

As Holmes languished, the sheer profusion of his contacts, and their contacts, should have forced a broader reckoning. But instead, the industry demonized the notorious headliner, whose life of violence and wild excess made him an easy target, and a seeming outlier. An academic study of AIDS and porn published in 1988, the year Holmes died, found that little had changed in the adult film world. Its author recommended stochastic modeling, using such variables as the incidence of anal intercourse (which exacerbated risk), divided by the prevalence of external ejaculation (which mitigated it). He also urged safe-sex training for performers, along with incentives for widespread, frequent, voluntary, and confidential HIV testing.[22]

Remote from the larger West Coast scene, Femme was far ahead of the industry on the public health curve. As the news about Holmes's HIV status spread, Candice began not only requiring condoms on her sets but also thinking about ways to work safer sex into her story lines.

In part, her customers—the white, middle-class couples' market she had helped to create—demanded it. "I think that the AIDS situation adds impetus and special justification to directions you have already taken in your films: emphasis on one-to-one relationships and on relationships within the relatively safe haven of the family," one fan wrote. "Scenes of chance, casual encounters, and especially orgy scenes now remind me of the AIDS hazard; and I cannot help but be afraid for the actors in the real-life of making the film." No viewer felt sexy watching the equivalent of "a war movie done with live ammunition."[23]

Candice agreed. Privately, she considered "dropping explicit sex" from Femme films entirely. Going R wasn't something she was then "very happy about," she answered one correspondent in June 1987, "but it's a possibility based on economics, politics, and the AIDS crisis." A week later, she told the *Daily News* that her films would "show people taking responsibility for their lives because nowhere in mainstream TV or movies do you see the [AIDS] issue addressed." Unless "the talent refuses to make movies" under unsafe conditions, she warned, a "major tragedy" loomed.[24] Some of the talent was indeed balking. "Is there anyone else using safe sex techniques?" asked one sometime Femme actor, who had come to find "the health risk" on other sets "overwhelming." In July, Candice told a reporter for *Playgirl* that she felt "strongly enough about protecting my talent to now be shooting everything using condoms and safe-sex techniques."[25]

That summer, Femme launched the Star Directors series, a venture with aesthetic, ethical, and practical goals. Candice said her artistic inspiration came from the photographer Nan Goldin's *Ballad of Sexual Dependency*, a slideshow of haunting, sometimes explicit portraits rooted in gritty realities, including prostitution, heroin, and intimate-partner violence. These were works of great beauty, set to music and screened, in the early '80s, in alternative spaces in downtown Manhattan, then exhibited at the Whitney Museum and published as a coffee-table art book. AIDS hovers over the project; the last image in the book is a graffito of skeletons coupling. Candice initially pictured Goldin-like vignettes centered on Gloria, Annie, Janie, and herself, depicted before porn, and after.[26] The vignettes soon morphed into what she called a "mini-dramas" format: novella-length erotic films directed by rather than starring the Club 90 sisters. Star Directors was also an employment project, a way to bring the core of Club 90 into the work of Femme, and vice versa.[27]

Candice hoped the guest directors would lighten her burdens. "Femme has taken over my life," she lamented in September 1987, after she and co-director Janie Hamilton (as Veronica Hart) wrapped the first Star Directors video, *A Taste of Ambrosia*. The business office was in an uproar. A woman hired that year to serve as Femme's sales agent had misspent funds, leaving Candice and Per to cover sudden losses. "The dollar has become our God," she wrote, and "a cruel and elusive one at that." And it wasn't just the toil and trouble; she was sick of the "stupid people" she dealt with in the adult world. As she mixed the sound for *Taste of Ambrosia*, a day never passed that she didn't "fantasize about stopping all this." She was two weeks shy of her thirty-seventh birthday. "Am I going to have a child?" she wondered in her diary.[28]

The Star Directors venture also committed, visibly and loudly, to sexual health. Candice's only firm guidance to her sister-directors, she told the *Hollywood Trade Press*, "was that we address the current health crisis by using safe-sex practices."[29] In "The Pick-Up," Veronica Hart's segment of *Taste of Ambrosia*, what seems to be an encounter between a hooker and a john depicts negotiation over the use of a condom. The female protagonist fingers the condom packet with long, red nails and gnashes it open with her teeth. Before fellating her trick, she applies the prophylactic so slowly and meticulously that the scene could be used in a sex ed workshop. Indeed, "The Pick-Up" uses more genital close-ups than other Femme films, with both the scenario and the AIDS crisis inviting a safer-sex gloss on conventional porn's "meat" shots. Then the camera pulls back to reveal family photos, and the couple's apparent transaction is revealed as spicy role-play. "I'm so glad that your mother could spend the night with the baby," the female lead says to the man, who turns out to be her husband. The press release that launched the series trumpeted: "Candida Royalle's New STAR DIRECTOR SERIES Eroticizes SAFE SEX." After reading it, one distributor of educational films asked whether the installments might be appropriate for use in medical or nursing schools.[30] *Playboy*'s cable division, which had rejected *Femme*, *Urban Heat*, and *Christine's Secret*, licensed *Taste of Ambrosia*. The deal, long sought, paid Femme the grand sum of $5,000.[31]

By all appearances, Candida Royalle was flourishing as Star Directors launched. In October 1987, *Mademoiselle* magazine featured her as an expert in "Bedroom Eyes," a long article on the home erotica revolution, which praised her films for making the point that "feminism is compatible with sexuality." The reporter predicted that the public health crisis would be good for Femme's business, since "fears of AIDS and other diseases will lead to much greater private use of pornography as a way to infuse excitement into monogamous relationships."[32]

Femme was getting enough mainstream media coverage that the company dropped its early adult-magazine clips from new promotional materials. "I must say that I'm a mite miffed that you omitted *Adam* and *Adam Film World* from your list of Femme press credits," a contact from Knight Publishing wrote, noting that *Adam* had been "one of the first media of any kind to break the news about the Femme project." This was true, and Candice was grateful to the magazine in which Veronica Vera's column had forged the path. But she had a different platform now. In November, she sent copies of *Three Daughters* and *Taste of Ambrosia* to the booking staff of a year-old smash-hit television talk program, *The Oprah Winfrey Show*, insisting that "Oprah would be the best person to present what we do fairly and interestingly." Oprah's people asked her to circle back in a year.[33]

Instead, that fall, Candice appeared, alongside Gloria Leonard and the actress and adult bookstore owner Seka, on the debut episode of a new talk show filming in Secaucus, a program with a toothy, screaming mouth as its icon. The host, Morton Downey Jr., blew in from the west. In Sacramento, he'd pioneered the no-holds-barred format that would soon come to be called shock radio, a genre that flourished after 1987, when the Reagan administration finally achieved the long-held conservative goal of killing the Truman-era Fairness Doctrine, which had required broadcast media to air contrasting viewpoints around controversial issues of public importance.[34] Suspended by KFBK-AM after telling an ethnic joke on air, Downey headed east, offering his "cross-country conservatism" on the AM dial in the morning and via local-access TV at night. (Back in Sacramento, KFBK replaced the "controversial" Downey with a Kansas City disc jockey turned sports marketer turned political commentator named Rush Limbaugh.)[35]

Where *Donahue* and *Oprah* floated on a river of women's tears, *The Morton Downey Jr. Show* trafficked in spittle and rage.[36] And where Donahue, two years before, had brought Candice to the stage alongside Catharine MacKinnon, to debate a substantive issue, Downey sought only to entertain. He worried, loudly, about the "morality of this country," and sneered that "anybody who lies down for a buck is being abused." But as Gloria pointed out during that inaugural episode, Downey was just "trying to paint that stereotype because it's your first show and you want boffo ratings."

Downey reveled in his vileness. He condemned Seka as "someone who's laid down with everyone they can find in a porn film." When she walked off the set, he turned to the audience in mock perplexity, asking how somebody who'd appeared onscreen, with her "dripping, empty body accepting every penetration, can be insulted by me." Gloria said Downey was "exploiting" the panelists and the audience, so he hounded her off the stage too. Candice was left alone, spot-lit with a rosy gel to match her dress. Downey turned to her. She said Femme was different; her films were for couples. "It's basically monogamy," she offered. Downey nodded approvingly, and came close to admitting he'd staged a catfight. "I suppose it looks like I've sided with Candida Royalle, and indeed I have, because I don't think she's exploiting women," he said.[37]

In her diary, Candice insisted she'd emerged from the taping unscathed, enhaloed, sitting pretty in pink, "like a fairy princess," as the black-clad made-for-TV villains exited, stage right, under a cloud. Several months later, she would agree to appear on *Downey* again, jotting down a "flash realization": "I like dangerous men who adore me." She thought the debut episode had landed like "a full hour of prime-time promo," for Femme and its cultural significance.[38]

She was wrong.

But so was Downey. He had acted as if the Meese commission, whose authority he invoked several times, were still headline news. But the American public had moved on from the porn wars. In a nationwide survey asking five thousand households to rank eighteen social problems, pornography came in second to last. "Drug abuse, the cost of medical care and the Federal budget deficit are major concerns of people in virtually all age and income groups," offered a spokesman for the Conference Board, which conducted the polling, adding dryly, "the major concerns of the public are not always the same as those expressed by public officials."[39]

Indeed. On October 19, 1987—the very day Candice did *Downey* the first time—the Dow Jones Industrial Average plunged more than 500 points, losing nearly a quarter of its value: twice as big a one-day drop as the great crash of 1929. Neither Candice's camera nor Downey's big mouth could match the headlines.

The work of Femme remained "grueling" and the Sjöstedts' savings accounts at a low ebb. Per was taking freelance gigs "just to make us some money to live on." Candice found herself so stressed that she broke down in tears in her hairstylist's chair. By Christmas, she wanted nothing more than to be by herself. "Per & I are so on top of each other these days—24 hours a day—under nothing but stressful situations," she wrote in her diary. "No fun times together." She planned to sit out their annual visit to the elder Sjöstedts in Sweden, but wound up going for a week, deciding that she shouldn't refuse "a family offering some holiday love & belonging." A broken family, "just like with my parents," she wrote. She found the Sjöstedts' home "sterile & regimented." But even so, Candice and Per had eaten beautiful meals and traversed a sparkling, snow-covered landscape that made Christmas magic. On balance, she was glad she'd made the trip.[40]

She worried about Per, though. He was twenty-eight and looked twenty and acted sixteen. The trip home had left him "enraged with his parents—totally confused." He was increasingly dependent on hard drugs. When he wasn't nodding out, he was exhausted by New York and gutted by the AIDS crisis claiming so many of their friends. And he was growing tired of porn—his father's business, his own, his wife's. Femme was different, yes. But there was still so little room for art. He didn't know what he wanted to be when he grew up, or if he really wanted to grow up at all.[41]

Candice was inching toward forty, "fortified with 6 years of hardcore therapy," running a production company, making headlines, yearning, at least sporadically, for a baby. It was the age of *having it all*, the yuppie woman's mantra, the place liberal feminism had gone to die. "I have my own business, lots of wonderful friends, a terrific husband," she wrote in her diary. "My life is in my hands now, & it's a good life." Yet as she rang in the New Year, she worried about where Per's "terrible 20s" might lead them both.[42]

PART V

Mainstream

When all is stripped away, what & who is left inside me?
—Candice Vadala, 1997

24 Gypsy Feet

"Our 2nd [Eighth] Anniversary Party," Leap Day, 1988.

C andice strayed first, right before her eighth wedding anniversary.[1]

The setting for her seduction was made for a porn loop: the glare of Las Vegas, amidst the whirl of the Sixteenth Annual Consumer Electronics Show (CES), which saw an estimated 100,000 visitors to some 1,400 displays spread over a space the size of two dozen football fields. Femme was on exhibit there because the X industry had begun to coordinate its annual *Adult Video News* Awards with CES. And no wonder: CES and porn had grown up together. By 1988, the year Candice made her CES debut and risked her marriage, 60 percent of American households owned a VCR, an estimated 200 million adult tapes were being rented annually, and CES's "adult software" exhibitions had grown to become a substantial conference within a conference: the tail that wagged tech's dog. Candice headlined a panel on women in the adult industry. She urged video-store owners to "become more politically aware if they want to live in a progressive society," which was also, she hastened to add, good for business.[2]

In the halls, she happened on an acquaintance from a smaller trade show, back east. Frank was Per's opposite: tall, dark, powerful enough to pick Candice up and sling her over his shoulder. "When he walked over to me it was like Tony & Maria," she swooned in a lightly fictionalized version of the scene, which she called "Dreams Come True in Glitterland." Being with Frank was "like being five again & waking up in my daddy's arms," she wrote. When she flew back to gritty, snowy New York, Per took it well. "He always rises to the occasion," she said, as if of a prized employee.[3] After years of companionable if not besotted monogamy, their marriage was now officially open.

Per began an affair with Veronica Vera. It was all above board, and while Candice was besotted with Frank, it seemed to work, in polyamorous fashion: new loves, longtime partners, close friends. But by spring, the fire Candice felt with Frank had cooled, and the embers of jealousy ignited—a familiar burn, for Veronica was, after all, a kind of sister. There followed a deep, searching "talk about everything that happened between her & Per & me." Candice decided not to "lose a friend over it," this time choosing the fictive sibling over the man. "So much for open marriages," she wrote after a trial run of three scant months.[4]

Which left Per adrift, addicted, "depressed & negative," and Candice "dead inside." She had fleeting thoughts of getting pregnant, accidentally-on-purpose, to answer her own "pangs of motherhood" and in hope, like so many women before her and since, that a child would "solidify our faltering marriage."[5]

The advantages of the union with Per were undeniable. He came "from a well-off family," Candice wrote. He would, she believed, make a success of himself yet, "when he eventually applies himself to something." It was hard to let go of "the security of having a husband," however sad and unformed he was. But Per wanted out of Femme, which continued to generate more converts than profits. And their landlord on Sackett Street had just put the brownstone up for sale, so that even their "oasis" hung in the balance.[6]

That spring, the two of them went to Los Angeles on Femme business—a conference appearance by Candice—and Per stayed on, driving up the California coast in search of peace. He wrote some weeks later, from "the middle of the most beautiful nowhere," near Mendocino. "It is all still very confusing but I am working on getting totally calm inside so I can feel what I'm to do next," he told her, sounding not unlike Candice in the Haight in 1972.[7]

"He's got gypsy feet," Candice explained to her friend Pauline, a former adult star who had left the business for good. But she insisted that she and Per remained each other's anchors, even as he roamed. "Even if another man came into my life, my home is his home," she wrote. There was indeed another man: she'd started seeing a guy I'll call Alan, "a dark, mysterious & handsome jazz pianist" who played with the chorus Candice had recently joined. The sex was good, though she wasn't sure where the relationship was headed.[8]

"Every aspect of my life is upturned—My marriage, my home, my business looks shaky," Candice wrote in June. Customs officials had confiscated a container of adult video tapes, impounding copies of *Urban Heat* with the haul. Candice sued to defend the redeeming value of her work, hiring a Washington, DC, law firm that often worked First Amendment cases for the ACLU. The charges touching Femme were dismissed on July 6, the same day that Attorney General Edwin Meese announced his resignation, a coincidence Candice's legal team found fitting.[9]

But the ordeal, however brief, had reminded Candice of the precarity of her business. It was hard to demand respect just inside the boundaries of law, harder still to find fortune amidst the glut of low-cost competitors. Despite revenues of over a quarter of a million dollars, Femme ended the fiscal year in the red. Per's dad—their chief investor—was reassuring. "Compare[d] to many big American film companies," he said, "your loss is very small." But then again, Femme's sales "were not so very big either." Sture Sjöstedt still believed in the "big HIT" right around the corner. He was willing to let Candice keep the money she owed him, even as her marriage to his son crumbled. But he wouldn't write another check.[10]

One evening shortly after the judge threw out the charges against Femme, Candice visited the Seventy-Ninth Street Boat Basin, to see her friend Michele on his houseboat. On her way home, she caught sight of the "new monster yacht" owned by the city's brash, headline-hogging, megamillionaire real estate developer as it glided down the Hudson. She was snide about it in her diary, where she called the *Trump Princess* "a hand-me-down" from Adnan Khashoggi, the Saudi billionaire who had been implicated, along with Edwin Meese, in the covert arms-for-hostages scandal known as Iran-Contra. But such wealth also made Candice envious. She hadn't become rich, or anything close to it. She was kind of famous, but her notoriety was complex. Dating Alan made her think, as she hadn't for years, about pursuing a career in music. Then she had a nightmare that she took as a sign that singing would leave her addicted and "destitute."[11]

Losing her home of eight years was nearly as hard as losing Per. Candice found a smaller apartment on the second floor of a modest brick row house a couple blocks down Sackett Street, close enough to the Brooklyn-Queens Expressway to feel the rumble of traffic. In

September, after a last brunch under the grape arbor with Per and their friends, she held a stoop sale to offload things she no longer had room for. Per filmed the scene: stacks of books and videos for sale. Candice with a new flat-topped buzz cut, her chestnut hair now flecked with gray. Friends and strangers pawing through old props and costumes. Somebody, maybe Alan, plays a piano heaped high with clothes priced to move. Another friend collects the sale's modest proceeds, stuffing dollar bills into a tin commemorating the wedding of Prince Charles and Lady Diana, whose fairy-tale marriage began the year after Candice's and was, by then, very publicly unraveling.[12]

As Candice settled into the new apartment, Per took off again, bound for New Mexico by train. In Albuquerque, he fell in with some Brits on a world budget tour. They met a German travel agent, who said that Mexico was what their hungry souls craved, and so the new friends boarded a bus for El Paso, and thence to Chihuahua and on to the Pacific. Per told Candice that he looked at her picture every day, and he showed the photos around, too, because her beauty burnished his standing with guys on the road. He kept writing, every couple weeks, as he worked his way down the coast to Guatemala, moving from one "ex-hippie paradise" to the next. Candice answered with dispatches from her own travels—San Francisco, New Orleans, Paris, Toronto, with Sydney and Maui in the offing—all pushing product, each trip evidence of Femme's perpetually imminent success. "It really feels like we're on the verge," she wrote in December.[13]

Candice said nothing of Alan, but she told Per a great deal about her recent trip to see her parents in Florida: a disastrous visit with Helen, followed by a much nicer one with Louis. "I spent the first time ever alone with my dad hanging out & getting to know him better," she wrote. In her diary, she elaborated: Louis had "shared many personal things with me—His own drug history, an ill-fated romance early in his life that he sadly never got to fulfill," the vicissitudes of a career in music. Louis had also "talked openly about sexual matters" with her. "I was so surprised. And we relate on such an intelligent & equal level. It's really a terrific father daughter relationship," she said.[14]

Candice still did not know of her father's sex offense in Florida in 1984, nor that he had recently violated his probation by failing to get the court-mandated counseling, and by driving under the influence. He had pleaded no contest, receiving a one-year sentence under what the state called "community control."[15] Louis and Candice had hung out in his trailer, getting to know each other better, talking all day rather than moving about because, unbeknownst to his daughter, he was midway through a prolonged period of house arrest.

———

BY MAY 1989, Per and Candice had decided it was well and truly over. "It was more than a relationship," Per wrote from "somewhere in the woods" in Sweden, lilies of the valley blooming all around. The marriage had been "a family substitute," he said. "Now we have left home." Though she felt torn between "a clean break" and a paper husband, Candice decided that a formal, legal, forever split would "ultimately free us up to be better friends" in the years ahead. "The fact that it's better for me tax-wise only adds to that side of reasoning," she continued, explaining that she'd initiated divorce proceedings.[16]

"Nothing prepares you for the sadness that accompanies a divorce," she wrote two weeks later. The papers were winging their way to Sweden, and she wanted to warn Per about the terms under which she'd filed, for in New York, divorce could only be granted for cause. (New York would not allow no-fault divorce until 2010, the last state in the nation to do so.) "The wording of the divorce is really kind of creepy," Candice said. "Downright traumatizing for me actually considering my history." The petition stated that Per had abandoned his wife and refused to return, despite her entreaties. "Pretty awful, huh?" Though, as Candice noted, he really *had* left and he really *didn't* want to come back. Abandonment promised the most "simple, painless & relatively quick & inexpensive divorce" to be obtained in the state. And maybe—though she knew it might sound "off the wall"—they would one day choose each other again, with "a real marriage ceremony, the way we'd really want it." No green card, yes white dress. Elizabeth Taylor and Richard Burton had done it, hadn't they? Meanwhile, she hoped Per wouldn't contest. He didn't; everything was signed before the summer was over.[17]

The state formally dissolved the marriage in January 1990. Two months later, the official papers found Per back in Marin County, where, he told Candice, he was "working on myself like a crazed mechanic on an old VW." That big manila envelope, with the lawyer's return address, hit him "like a Mike Tyson punch." He staggered, but he stood. "I will always carry you with me," he said.[18]

CANDICE AND PER remained close, but the divorce rippled through her family.

She told her father she had "ended up out-growing Per," who was still forging an outer man to shield his inner child. She worried that Louis would compare her to Peggy, his first bride, her absconded birth mother. "I don't want to be put into the category of 'bad wife,'" she pleaded. But Candice needed a different sort of partner, and fast, while there was still "a chance to have a child" of her own. She would soon turn thirty-nine, and her biological clock—a phrase whose meaning had lately shifted from the circadian rhythms of animals to the plight of middle-aged female professionals—was ticking louder.[19]

Candice feared that the sisterhood she'd forged with Gloria and Veronica and Annie and Janie wouldn't survive the split. She told Per that the "Club 90 gals" seemed to be "moving on in our own directions." Janie was in Europe, Gloria bound for Los Angeles. Annie and Veronica remained in the city, and the three of them got together sometimes, but it wasn't like the old days.[20] The women of Club 90 would remain a powerful force in each other's lives, though they became less of a quintet. Candice and Veronica recovered their sisterly bond. As time passed, the group tended to convene over email, or at reunions.

Candice went back to Alan after a rocky patch between them. "I have come home to daddy," she wrote. But she also sensed that he was rather more like her actual father than she could easily admit or accept. Maybe he acted the top in bed because he was so often the bottom in life. A musician's career was precarious, as Candice knew from bitter family experience. Was Candice again "playing mommy" to a man who needed her help to grow up? Or maybe *she* was still the wounded child, even now, after having achieved such public renown, after so many men and so much therapy. In her diary and with Linda Hirsch, Candice pondered the craving for attention, and the fantasies of rescue, that ran like a bright red thread through her nearly four decades.[21]

Yet in December 1989, when a columnist for a San Francisco alt-weekly cautioned readers against dating women in the adult industry, because too many of them were too badly broken, and asserted that "virtually every woman I've known in the sex business admitted to being molested," Candice fired off a long, furious response. "Yes, women in the sex biz are the products of a sex-negative culture," she wrote. But "molestation and child abuse happens tragically to probably a majority of children . . . far more than end up in the sex biz." She cautioned the writer not to "generalize" about what brought people "into the sex industry. We all have our own unique stories and we all feel our own particular way about what we have done with our lives." She touted her contentment, during a decade-long "monogamous marriage that was for the most part happy and loving," in her soaring "new career as a film-maker," and in her current "positive, loving and monogamous relationship that's still going strong after a year and a half."[22]

One of those things was true.

———

CANDICE AND ALAN spent a quiet Christmas at home, watching the simulcast of Leonard Bernstein conducting Beethoven's Ninth Symphony, humanity's hymn to joy, amidst the rubble of the Berlin Wall, which protesters had pulled down, block by concrete block, the month before.[23] The '80s were done. The world of the Cold War lay in ruins.

"Many incredible changes have occurred in my life in these last 10 years," Candice wrote on New Year's Day, 1990. She had embarked on the previous decade "still a drug addict." She ended it a celebrity, with her own film company, a catalogue of seven movies, a fat library of clippings, a cabinet full of videotaped television appearances, and "the respect of my peers. . . . let's not minimalize," she wrote: "I created women's erotic movies!"[24]

Why, then, did she still feel "so inadequate," so "ambivalent," and so often "insecure"? "I'm all shook up—My whole foundation," she wrote several months later. Her marriage had faded to friendship. The relationship with Alan was all but over. Femme still barely eked out.[25] It was hard to find one's center in a world built on pleasure, a world with so many open doors and so few walls to hold them.

25 Sex in the '90s

Candice with Diana Wiley, MFT, PhD. March 1992.

n October 1990, HBO premiered *Real Sex*, an hour-long compilation of titillating news segments. "Sex with a documentary beard,"
one media studies scholar calls it.[1] "*The sexual revolution is being rede-
fined*," proclaimed the opening titles. "*In the 1990s, the ground rules have
changed.*" Or so premium cable stations hoped. They were fighting for
their lives: more than two-thirds of American households owned a
VCR. Even as the range of videotaped offerings expanded, porn continued to engross a hefty slice of the market, perhaps 15 percent. Ordinary people were beginning to create their own explicit content. In
1983, SONY had introduced a handheld video camera for the home
market, complete with sound, auto-focus, and the capacity to adjust
for low light. By 1990, American consumers were buying 3 million
camcorders a year. Together, the two technologies revolutionized not
only porn viewing, but also porn-making.[2]

Daring a new level of explicitness in the struggle to retain viewers, *Real Sex* featured real people. In the first episode, a dance teacher
instructs women to strip for men who "want a whore in the bedroom";
a thirty-one-year-old virgin talks about celibacy as an identity; men
on the street answer sex questions for the camera. Technology often
takes center stage: one vignette centers on a couple who plot, costume,
and shoot their own sex scenes, one of which involves Groucho Marx
glasses; another explores the $400-million annual business of phone sex.

But the headliners in the debut of *Real Sex* were well-known sex-
perts seizing a new platform in a new decade. In the episode's longest
segment, "An Actress Turns Director," Candida Royalle talked about
Femme. "I don't like to call my work pornography," she purrs. "My
work is all about sexual love." The directors intersperse shots of Candice hunched over her editing deck with short clips from *Urban Heat*
and *The Tunnel*: sex scenes centered on breasts and butts, establishing
the premium cable formula that would endure for decades.[3]

"The point of the movies is definitely to turn people on," Candice states flatly. Pleasure needed no apology, not anymore. But where porn shouted SEX, Femme whispered *class*. Femme films never featured "breast jobs, fake nails, [or] bleached, teased hair." Candice herself dressed the part, looking "more like a chic entertainment executive than a glittery porn star," as *Mother Jones* had recently noted in a feature titled "Nasty Girls." And now here she was, headlining on HBO, the channel that, barely two years before, had rejected Femme's *Sensual Escape*, explaining that viewers wanted less sex and more plot.[4] "I wanted to put dignity back in the name Candida Royalle," Candice says, tilting her jaw proudly upward. And hadn't she? HBO, like so many others, had come to her.

CANDICE FLUSHED ALAN in April, the moment each year she felt herself coming back to life. Her fortieth birthday loomed, a prod, a cliff. "There's no time for bullshit," she wrote. She sketched the concept for a new film centered on that spring-fling feeling, *All About April*. A few months later, Per roared through town at the end of a cross-country motorcycle trip. They decided to work on the project together.[5]

That summer Candice took a share in a ramshackle house called the Ark, in Fair Harbor, at the western end of Fire Island. She played the field, meeting hot men at parties. AIDS stalked the Pines, a couple miles east, literally decimating the island's gay male scene, and even straight men had grown careful, and sometimes cruel. Men like Brandon, who told her "he wanted to keep things on a touching level," fearing disease from sex with a former porn star. "This is a man who washes himself with hydrogen peroxide afterwards!" she wrote in her diary. When one romantic prospect told her he wanted to "get to know Candida Royalle better," she answered: "There is no Candida Royalle. Candice is the only one home here!"[6]

But for all her visibility, Candice still earned, as she said, only "the salary of a decently paid clerical worker." After nearly a decade of frenetic work and careful saving, she had $14,000 in the bank. "Must I be confined to this world?" she asked. "Sometimes I feel like a prisoner still to a decision I made 15 years ago." The clash between her profile and her savings balance amazed her. "My life is full of glamour," she noted in her diary, after a whirlwind few weeks during which she sat for twenty interviews promoting a sex conference in Holland, flew to Los Angeles to shoot Ron Reagan Jr.'s debut show on Fox TV, and posed at the Carlyle Hotel for portraits to accompany a six-page feature in *Details* magazine called "Sexual Healing." She loved seeing the profile touted on the cover, beside a photo of her hero David Bowie, "my name sitting right on his shoulder." But the numbers didn't lie: Candice was nearly as broke as she was famous.[7]

And still calls for *Candida* kept coming, from novel quarters every day, as sex in the '90s found a new equilibrium, well past the untrammeled hedonism of the '70s and early '80s, out of the dark corners of peep shows and bathhouses, out of the shadows, into the doctor's office, the classroom, and the broader marketplace of ideas.

———

PORN HAD ALWAYS BEEN in school, of course. Sexuality educators and therapists had relied on explicit media since the hygiene films of the World War I era. Alfred Kinsey used movies to teach Indiana University students about the biology of human sexual response in the '40s. By the late '60s, a more public-facing version of such instruction was reaching adult learners through the San Francisco–based National Sex Forum, which morphed into the Institute for Advanced Study of Human Sexuality (IASHS), a pioneer in the promotion of "humanistic sexology," which fused the empiricism of Kinsey with the inward direction of the human potential movement. In 1976, while Candice was living in San Francisco, IASHS began offering unaccredited graduate degrees, as well as marathon, sometimes weekend-long seminars on "Sexual Attitude Re-assessment," or SAR, and hands-on, clothing-off workshops on erotic massage. Such meetings, as Virginia Johnson tutted in 1978, had "an underlying orgy atmosphere" that seemed inimical to science. SAR earned the nickname Fuck U. On the East Coast, the graduate program in Human Sexuality at New York University's School of Education, among others, adopted aspects of the

SAR method, which centered on viewing, discussing, and physically responding to explicit films.[8]

Therapists, too, used a range of explicit tapes in their work, some gleaned from sex shops and others produced by and for the clinic. Femme films offered something in between, and Candice, who believed enormously in the project of human perfection, was eager to meet the sexologists in their market. A breakthrough had occurred in late 1986, when she appeared on *The Dr. Ruth Show*. Ruth Westheimer, child survivor of Auschwitz, had become the country's leading TV sexologist. She treated Candice with the same plainspoken respect she offered to all guests. The doctor asked about her porn-star years: How had her body tolerated it? "Did you use lubricants, as I suggest?" she inquired in her chirpy middle-European accent. Did Femme illustrate different positions? Oh yes, absolutely, Candice answered. "I believe in educating as well as entertaining," she said of Femme's mission. "I approve of zat!" the elfin doctor twinkled. A week later, the Kinsey Institute, the nation's premiere sexology research center, requested copies of all Femme materials for their archive.[9]

Femme's fans noticed the sexological opportunity too. A frequent correspondent from Maine asked: "Is it possible that there is an overlapping of the sex-therapy market and the commercial-entertainment female/couples market you have been targeting?" "Know that my wife and I appreciate your efforts to find an acceptable Rx—middle ground—between R and X," wrote a customer from the hamlet of Bondville, Vermont.[10] Candice picked up his clever coinage immediately, crafting a press release hailing her films' educational properties. A new tagline appeared in Femme merchandising in 1988: *Candida Royalle's FEMME: the 'RX' for couples who like to watch*. In addition to the fan's letter, the press release touted an upcoming screening of *Three Daughters* at the annual convention of the American Association of Sex Educators, Counselors, and Therapists (or AASECT), a national professional association founded in 1967, which had been training teachers to improve sex education in American schools.[11]

The AIDS epidemic meant that sex literacy was having a cultural moment; that May, *The Phil Donahue Show* taped two episodes with a studio audience comprised entirely of AASECT members, whom he urged to become "more politically involved." Pornography gained legitimacy as part of this thickening therapeutic armature. *Sexuality Today* reported that a "growing majority of sexuality professionals"— some 62.8 percent of survey respondents—used "sexually explicit professionally developed videos" in the clinic, the classroom, or both. "As the saying goes, 'One picture equals a thousand words,'" said a college sexuality instructor from Minnesota.[12]

To Femme, therapists and their clients represented a whole new market, one that favored direct mail and avoided the back rooms of video-rental stores, which stocked feminist product spottily at best. Candice began tracking the publications of sexology researchers who described the use of explicit films in their practices. After Dr. Michael Schwartz, a professor of adolescent psychiatry, praised Femme during a presentation at a conference of the American Association of Marriage and Family Therapists (AAMFT), an older, more staid organization than the '6os-inflected AASECT, Candice sent him a full library of her titles and asked for an endorsement. He offered a testimonial about their *educational* quality but said he lacked evidence to tout their scientific value. He wondered, though, if Candice might present with him at a future conference.[13] They hatched a plan for a workshop with film clips at AAMFT's 1988 annual convention, which the association's leadership scuttled, citing "an injunction which prohibits the showing of sexually explicit materials." Ultimately, the board ruled that Royalle and Schwartz could describe but not screen examples of Femme's work, which made the session a flop.[14]

But in the coming months and years, Candice would deepen her ties with therapists' organizations and sharpen Femme's sexological talking points, which centered on elevating women's voices, on positive role modeling, on safe sex and foreplay and "afterglow"—a visual politics said to be as much "humanist" as feminist. Femme films, Candice told members of the Society for the Scientific Study of Sexuality, or Quad-S, the youngest and least hidebound of the three major sex-therapy associations, were "a self-help product." Therapeutic audiences lapped it up. "I was a real curiosity to people," Candice wrote after a session at AASECT's annual meeting. A spate of new orders quickly followed the panel.[15]

Letters and invitations piled up. An AIDS educator in Toronto sought a commercial film that featured proper condom use. A self-described "sexological scientist . . . concerned with social policy" was launching a research project "to study your new genre of films by comparing and contrasting responses in men and women to the more common X-rated films produced for a male market"; writing on university letterhead, he sought a free set of tapes. (Femme obliged.) A clinical psychologist from the Netherlands reported that Femme films were being used by Dutch gynecologists to treat "inhibited sexual desire," and by urologists in "a diagnostic protocol for erectile dysfunctions." A doctor from Guy's Hospital in London sought to include Femme materials in a "resource pack" connected to his research on "sexual adaptation with the physically disabled." A rabbi from New Haven followed the suggestion of a "sex therapist at Yale University" when she wrote in search of films for her Jewish women's group. An apostate priest, founder of a splinter sect called the Free Catholic Church of Saints Mary Magdalene and Thomas, asked Femme to donate a copy of *Sensual Escape* "to assist in the enlightenment of individuals in their own sexuality and views of sex as an acceptable part of their own spirituality."[16]

By 1990, Femme was offering special pricing to attendees of the major conferences for sex therapists and educators and touting their support on its brochures. Candice also began to imagine films created specifically for that educated and affluent audience. She worked up a treatment for an anthology series called "Sonia the Sex Therapist," a "real albeit lighthearted look at the life and experiences of Dr. Sonia Charell, a certified sex therapist with a private practice as well as her call-in radio show." She also hoped her "association with the sexology community" would lead to "an endorsement from AASECT or a prominent therapist."[17]

A year or so later, Diana Wiley, a respected couples therapist based in the Bay Area, contacted Candice to pitch a related concept. Wiley recalls that they first traded ideas at the World Conference for Sexology in Amsterdam in 1991. By the following summer, they were calling their series "Case Studies: An Educational Line for Femme Films." Wiley thought she should play herself; Candice favored a professional actress for that crucial role. Both agreed that the cast dramatizing such topics as trouble reaching orgasm, the role of fantasy, and safer sex must reflect the diversity of contemporary society, including "some average looking people," some "older middle-age, and even an elderly couple," as well as Black and Asian Americans, whose presence would expand the potential for adoption in Japan.[18]

The two were hard at work honing the concept in the fall of 1992 when Wiley received a flurry of national news coverage as the long-ago girlfriend of Democratic presidential candidate William Jefferson Clinton, during the years he spent at Oxford. "She showed me letters he had written to her that showed him to be a very nice & thoughtful person, with progressive attitudes, or at least liberal," Candice wrote in her diary shortly before Election Day. Wiley, she said, had also told her "some very intimate details about the Clintons' sex life that I haven't shared with anyone else."[19]

Candice and Wiley shopped the Case Studies concept to an outfit called the Research Venture Group, which collaborated with the Masters and Johnson Institute on for-profit projects. They proposed a first volume on sex and aging, a research specialty of Wiley's and a huge potential market, as America's Baby Boomers neared fifty.[20] Though the talks fizzled, Wiley and Candice remained fast friends, and the sexology conference circuit continued to be a vital market for Femme's work.

Candice was enormously proud of her associations with the therapists' organizations, AAMFT, AASECT, and Quad-S. She loved their conferences, a tonic compared to the adult-industry trade shows, which she had come to dread. She kept albums of snapshots from the sexology gatherings, where she hung out with Wiley and other clinicians. This, she felt, was her tribe, respectable and educated, sex people in the classiest possible way.[21]

But how fully did the sexologists return her esteem? There is no doubt that her talks and screenings were popular attractions. Diana Wiley recalls seeing Candice take the stage with the renowned Viennese psychologist Helen Singer Kaplan. Kaplan presented first, about her research, in quite technical terms. And then came Candice. "You could have heard a pin drop," Wiley says. Those psychiatrists, mostly men, were "totally enthralled." One of Candice's early appearances at Quad-S, the first time that society allowed screened pornography, had played "to a packed house," *Behavior Today* reported. But the newsletter also noted that the session "was not without controversy," and had been "intentionally left off the preliminary program mailed to Society members."[22] A whiff of the circus hangs over these professors-and-the-porn-star moments. But while the sexologists could be sniffy, perhaps because of their own somewhat fragile status in the discipline of psychology, Royalle's work had already moved into corners of learned culture well beyond the psych lab and the health center.

IT'S HARD TO PINPOINT the moment when pornography became *text*. Academic humanists had troubled the category of literature since the early twentieth century, when poet and critic Van Wyck Brooks blurred the too-bright line between the canon taught in universities and the "richly-rewarded trash" atop bestseller lists. "The very accent of the words Highbrow and Lowbrow implies an instinctive perception that this is a very unsatisfactory state of affairs," Brooks wrote in in 1915, in the kind of small magazine that had large impact among the chattering classes.[23] By midcentury, the highbrow/lowbrow distinction was nearing collapse, as intellectuals in many disciplines plumbed the aesthetics, economics, and sociology of consumer culture. Everything from comic books to product packaging became fit objects for literary analysis and, indeed, for art.[24]

If consumer culture was good to think with, why not pornography—sex, sold? In 1967, Susan Sontag argued for treating "pornography as an item of social history": a "literary genre" no more debased than science fiction. "But nowhere in the Anglo-American community of letters have I seen it argued that some pornographic books are interesting and important works of art," she wrote. Sontag proceeded to do just that, parsing with high critical seriousness such ostensibly low works as *The Story of O* (1954) and *Candy* (1958). The "pornographic imagination says something worth listening to, albeit in a degraded and often unrecognizable form," she declared, insisting that "this spectacularly cramped form of the human imagination has, nevertheless, its peculiar access to some truth."[25]

By 1980, a handful of eminent historians and literary scholars had begun seeking out those very truths. The publication of the first volume of French philosopher Michel Foucault's *History of Sexuality* (1976, English translation 1978) placed the regulation of sex at the very heart of capitalism and modernity. Foucault posited a prelapsarian early modern world in which "the coarse, the obscene, and the indecent" were gleefully expressed and minimally policed, a "bright day" before Victorian "twilight" and twentieth-century darkness. His taxonomy served as an intellectual watershed of the first magnitude; new, more rigorously empirical histories of sex, sexuality, and pornography quickly followed. In 1982, Robert Darnton published the opening salvo of what would become a decades-long study of the underground literature of ancien régime France, including its pornography; Lynn Hunt began her exploration of the political uses of pornography during the French Revolution shortly thereafter.[26]

With the publication of *The Secret Museum: Pornography in Modern Culture* (1987), Fordham University literature professor Walter Kendrick brought these histories into the contemporary period, casting the MacKinnon-Dworkin ordinance campaigns, along with the Meese commission's *Report*, as merely "the latest in a long series of paroxysms" over sexual morality. Kendrick found in these repeated attempts to slay the "pornographic vampire" evidence of a peculiarly American "cultural neurosis," one that was intensifying as the millennium approached. He analyzed the literary works—*Lady Chatterley's Lover*, *Finnegan's Wake*, and *Lolita*—whose bans had provoked the liberalization of obscenity jurisprudence in the '50s and '60s. But his attention, like Sontag's, remained "far removed from the semen-stained squalor of the peep show, the strip joint, the video arcade, and other sites of popular pornotopian fantasy," as one critic later noted.[27] Kendrick's only mention of *Hustler* falls within an exegesis of Andrea Dworkin's *Pornography*; the phrase "hard core" appears only via the *Roth-Alberts* decisions of 1957; *Deep Throat* gets no mention at all.

But by the time Viking published Kendrick's high-toned analysis, other scholars were hard at work on a second generation of sexuality studies that would not only stretch but finally break the boundaries of the literary canon, much as Nan Goldin and Robert Mapplethorpe were then exploding the frame of the photographic nude. In the spring of 1988, shortly after Candice returned from screening *Three Daughters* at AASECT's conference in San Francisco, she received a query from Linda Williams, an associate professor of English at the University of Illinois, who was completing the first serious book-length study of the visual grammar of pornographic film. As Williams explained in her letter, she had begun her research "with the idea that film and video pornography would illustrate all my previously held ideas about the objectification of women. The genre has surprised me. Your work has delighted me." Williams praised, in particular, Femme's Star Directors Series, for "quietly dispelling many of the myths of pornography's supposedly intrinsic antipathy to women." She wondered about filmmakers who had influenced Femme's aesthetic. In the margins of Williams's letter, Candice jotted, "Bertolucci, Scorsese."[28]

The following year, Williams published *Hard Core: Power, Pleasure, and the "Frenzy of the Visible"* with University of California Press. Drawing on Foucault, Sontag, and Kendrick to establish the historicity of sexual expression, Williams took aim at anti-porn feminism, which, she said, "has impeded discussion of everything but the question of whether pornography deserves to exist at all." Her analysis revealed many of the "pat polar oppositions" that organized thinking about sexually explicit media—hard versus soft, pornography versus erotica—to be facile and obfuscating. She lauded new voices, including the efforts of "women directors like Candida Royalle . . . to make a decidedly different kind of heterosexual hardcore video." Williams linked Royalle to the poet Adrienne Rich: feminist artists "seeing again with fresh eyes from an entirely different, woman's point of view." She found, in Femme's *Urban Heat*, a "spatial-temporal 'integrity'" unheard of in the genre, and pronounced *Three Daughters* simply "unparalleled in hard core."[29]

Williams's work met with glowing reviews both within and beyond the academy. Calling *Hard Core* "daring" and "brilliant," *Discourse*, a literary studies quarterly out of Berkeley, recommended the book "to anybody interested not only in film pornography in particular but in the problematics of discourses on twentieth-century culture in general." The *Times* paid attention, too, giving *Hard Core* a full page in the Book Review, praising Williams for "thinking that leaves polemics behind."[30]

Before the *Times* review ran, Williams had moved, with promotion, from Illinois to the University of California, first to Irvine, where she launched a new program in Film Studies, and then to Berkeley, where she assumed a similarly august role. And she had company—still small but rarefied—in the elevated study of underground media. Andrew Ross, then an enfant terrible of cultural studies, untenured in the English Department at Princeton, featured Royalle's work in a chapter of his breakout book *No Respect: Intellectuals and Popular Culture*, released the same year as *Hard Core*. Using *Playboy*, *Deep Throat*, and Royalle's *Christine's Secret* (which he mislabeled, on occasion, *Christine's Dream*) as core texts, Ross theorized what he called "the *liberatory imagination*." "Pornography, it could be argued, is the lowest of the low, because it aims below the belt, . . . at the psychosexual substratum of subjective life," he wrote. Yet the genre was "not at all inattentive to narrative." Even so, much like a reviewer in *Swank* or *Screw*, Ross pronounced some of Femme's plots didactic to the point of "overkill . . . a turn-off."[31]

Works like Ross's and Williams's—and the wave of what came to be called not just postmodernist but also *post-feminist* analyses that followed—were highly mediagenic, slipping easily from the classroom to the popular press and back. "Not all prudes are feminists, but almost all boilerplate modern feminists have been prudes," quipped a column in the *Wall Street Journal* praising Williams, Camille Paglia, and other such provocateurs for their "postfeminist re-embrace of traditional sensuality."[32]

By 1991, reporting on the bad boys and girls of sex-as-literature had migrated from the Book Review and the education supplement to the glossier precincts of the *New York Times Magazine*, which ran a lengthy and, it must be said, borderline parodic feature on the annual convention of the Modern Language Association, entitled "Deciphering Victorian Underwear," and centered on Ross, with his "saturnine good looks" and "mango wool-and-silk Comme des Garcons blazer," which, the professor explained, was "a sendup of the academic male convention of yellow polyester." Ross's flash and sizzle, reporter Annie Matthews argued, quite literally embodied the broader struggle of the humanities at a "heady (and dangerous) moment for literary criticism," as the guardrails came off the canon and self-proclaimed radicals celebrated "the overdue fall of high culture's Bastille." Ross embraced the role of Jacobin: "I teach in the Ivy League in order to have direct access to the minds of the children of the ruling classes," he said.[33]

It has become clear, in the intervening decades, that this outré turn in literary and cultural studies would prove costly to humanities departments, and indeed, to American politics. If the anti-canon failed to draw students—the number of English majors continues to plummet—it has proved, over decades, a durable and effective stalking horse for conservatives.[34] But in the heady days of the early '90s, campuses celebrated the fall of high culture's Bastille as a democratizing intellectual revolution.

Among its other affordances, the new low-culture studies begat a wave of campus appearances by Candida Royalle. A month after the *Times* profiled Ross, she headlined Princeton's fourth annual Women and Film Series: Both Sides of the Camera. Other presenters included the decorated avant-garde filmmaker Barbara Hammer and Princeton's Anne McClintock, who had interviewed Candice for an essay that would eventually appear as "Porn in the USA," in a special issue of the haute-theory journal *Social Text*. Hammer's growing eminence notwithstanding, Royalle was the festival's star attraction, speaking to an overflow crowd. *The Daily Princetonian* covered the appearance of the "Former X-Rated Star" worshipfully.[35]

Requests for interviews poured in from graduate students conducting research on Femme in their programs in women's studies and sociology and communications, in Wisconsin and Massachusetts and Illinois and in the UK and on and on, until Candice had to holler stop. By 1993, she had a template reply. As she told one doctoral student at the University of Texas, she'd be happy to talk, but the "overwhelming number of demands" on her time meant that she now charged a standard interview fee of $250.[36] In any case, Femme was already on the syllabus. Candice lectured at University of California, Santa Barbara, where Constance Penley's course, "Pornographic Film," analyzed three Femme titles. That fall, "A Porn of Our Own," the first academic journal article centered on Femme, rhetorically placed Royalle's opus in the lineage of Virginia Woolf. At year's end, Princeton invited Candice for a repeat appearance at the Women and Film Series, in a lineup that included bell hooks, Cornel West, and the ubiquitous Andrew Ross.[37]

Candice was flattered by the elevation of her films. But in the '90s—her forties—she felt ever less certain about the centrality of sex to her actual life. She had given up on casual flings, which she compared to "settling for an array of hot-dogs after feasting on a 4-star meal." Instead, she poured her energies into work, and a new apartment in the Cobble Hill section of Brooklyn, her "very own pink palace." The rent was a little higher, but it felt like a worthwhile investment, "part of my upward mobility," she wrote. Yet she continued to pick terrible men, and to know they were terrible, and to ponder why she did it, and to do it again. She went back to Alan, about which she felt so ashamed that she stopped writing in her diary for months.[38]

But even as she backslid, she mapped her climb, "from slut-drug addict to politically correct successful entrepreneur spokeswoman for women's sexuality." "The Only Erotic Film Series to Meet Ivy League Standards" read an advertisement for Femme in AASECT's 1994 annual meeting program. Candice had become "something of a 'hero' amongst university students these days, as well as in the sex-therapy community!" she told her ex-father-in-law. She scribbled her note to him on the train home from Wellesley College, where she'd given a lecture to four hundred enraptured young women, who broke off studying for finals to trudge through the snow to her talk. Shortly before that, she'd spoken at the Smithsonian. "Not bad for a gal who was once a 'porno-queen' eh?"[39]

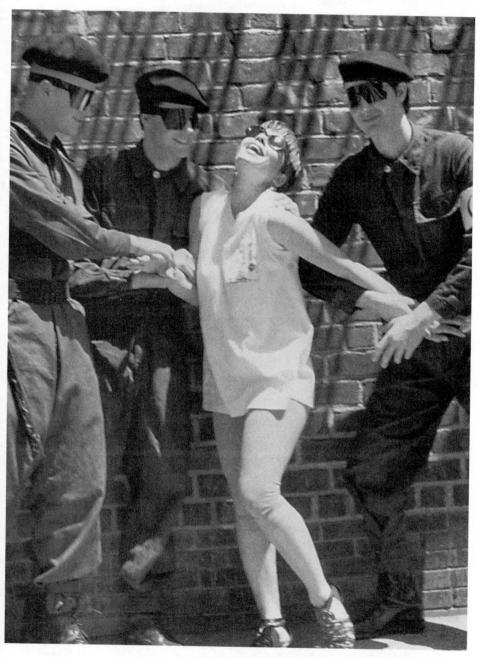

26 Revelations

"New Order" soldiers clowning with Candice on the set of Revelations, *c1992.*

*H*ave I told you how I got here? About what life is like outside
of here?

Ariel addresses the camera, her voice a whisper. She is
ashen, pale as the walls. She is imprisoned, caged, somewhere, by
someone, for some sin. We hear talk of a New Order and its tireless
efforts to combat "decadence," which clearly means desire.[1]

Revelations, released in 1993, was the first movie Candice had made
in half a decade. Fans were itchy, and she was sick of hearing *"what,
still no new movie?!"* This would answer the doubters. The "big one,"
she called it when she first hatched the idea, dreaming of a project
orders of magnitude more ambitious, and more costly, than anything
she'd undertaken before. She expected to lavish anywhere from half
a million to 2 million dollars on the film. She planned to market the
"psychological erotic drama" as the work of Candice Vadala—"my real
name," she had explained to one potential funder.[2]

Per and Candice worked on it together, she as writer and director,
he as producer. She wanted to make a real movie, shot, for the first
time, on 35mm film. Femme argued that *Revelations* and future projects like it would "enable the company to expand into the theatrical
market worldwide." The whole industry was trending the other way,
shrinking its ambitions to the size of the television screen. But Femme
was different, the darling of sexologists and theorists. Candice meant
to create something she could take on the "film festival circuit."[3]

SAGA films, Per's father's company, agreed to kick in some funds,
but *Revelations* demanded more. Candice and Per reached out to contacts beyond the adult industry, including Miriam Stern, a lawyer
they'd met through New York Women in Film. ("New York Women
in Filth," joked the hosts of a Town Hall event Candice had done with
them couple of years before, a controversial porn panel, closed to the
public after threats that Women Against Pornography would picket.)

They wound up contracting with Stern to raise a million dollars of operating capital for the project, and they hired a new sales director, an ambitious young man, who worked up a proposal for *Revelations* and its successors. Femme promised four new feature-length movies per year, each with a budget in the quarter-million-dollar range, shot on film, over four weeks rather than the four days more customary for pornography: "softer features" for an ever-harder mainstream market.[4]

———

IN THE SUMMER OF 1990, when Candice had first imagined *Revelations*, the Sacramento shock jockey turned national radio phenom Rush Limbaugh declared that America was "in the midst of a culture war." Limbaugh said he spoke in the name of *"real people,"* the "people who make the country work . . . believers in the traditional American values." They were concerned—indeed "repulsed"—by a new "counter-culture rising up," burning flags, pissing on the cross, spewing obscenity, making claims that porn was art. There was a "battle being waged for the American public and its mind," Limbaugh said, confident that conservatives would win it.[5]

This was a new style of politics, waged in a new media landscape. Limbaugh delivered his pronouncement on televangelist Pat Robertson's *700 Club*, aired by the ever-more-powerful Christian Broadcast Network. He and other culture warriors divided the electorate morally as much as politically, outlining worldviews as absolute and as passionately held as they were incompatible. In culture wars, coalition-building and conventional arguments were cast aside in favor of a "deliberate, systematic effort to discredit the opposition," as James Davidson Hunter wrote the following year, in the first book to anatomize the emerging politics of schism.[6]

There was an irony to this 1990s culture war: its opening salvos came from the Right. For a generation, transforming politics and society by reorienting American culture had been a central commitment of thinkers and activists of the Left, who had supplanted the economic materialism of the 1930s with faith in the notion that culture was the ultimate locus of power. The progressive cultural turn had been especially pronounced among feminists. Anti-pornography feminists, in particular, insisted on the world-shaping power of images. Pornography did not merely *reflect* women's subordination; it structured and enforced it; it *was* subordination, in MacKinnon's analysis. On this critique of a decadent American culture, a new Right had come to agree.[7]

Contests over obscenity occupied the front line of Limbaugh's newly declared conservative culture war. The American Family Association, the Christian Coalition, and other organizations on the Christian right created a public furor over exhibitions of the work of Robert Mapplethorpe, Andres Serrano, David Wojnarowicz, and other contemporary artists who took the body and its desires as their central subject. Orange County Republican representative Dana Rohrbacher sent an open letter to Congress singling out Annie Sprinkle's "Post Porn Modernist," produced in early 1990 in a New York performance space that received funding from the National Endowment for the Arts. Later that spring, the NEA overturned the recommendations of an expert selection panel and rescinded grants to several artists said to have flouted Public Law 101–121, preventing the use of government funds to support works which "may be considered obscene." The artists—performers like Karen Finley and Holly Hughes, who, like Sprinkle, exhibited their bodies, but who, unlike Sprinkle, had clung obscurely to the cutting edge—attracted enormous media attention in their 1990 reincarnation as the NEA Four.[8]

As Candice worked on *Revelations,* Patrick J. Buchanan, right-wing challenger to the re-nomination of President George H. W. Bush, addressed the 1992 Republican National Convention in Houston, proclaiming the "cultural war, as critical to the kind of nation we shall be as the Cold War itself." That year's election was, Buchanan said, nothing less than a "war . . . for the soul of America": a struggle between "our side"—the side of God and flag and family—and "the other side": the side of "unrestricted abortion on demand" and gay rights and "radical feminism." The side of "the raw sewage of pornography that so terribly pollutes our popular culture," a subject to which the party's platform, for the second election cycle in a row, devoted an entire paragraph.[9]

Femme's *Revelations* translates the 1990s culture war into the language of pornography. The battle becomes literal; the New Order's security forces fight house-to-house in a crusade to "ferret out remaining pockets of decadence and subversion." Pockets like the subterranean apartment of Ariel's neighbor, a shuffling old man whom she watches a New Order squadron drag away. They wear black berets and mirrored wrap-around shades, like mini-Terminators. But in their haste to extirpate sin, the squadron leaves the detainee's battered door ajar, beckoning.

Stepping through that portal, Ariel discovers an oasis "full of color." And then, behind a cupboard, a "secret little room, full of pictures of naked bodies, and people having . . . *sex.*"

On a small table sits a forbidden television, gleaming, and a VCR, its empty mouth all but whispering, *Watch me.*

PATRICK BUCHANAN'S CULTURAL WAR was Susan Faludi's war on women. The *Wall Street Journal* reporter's blockbuster book *Backlash* was published in November 1991, just after Anita Hill's testimony at Supreme Court nominee Clarence Thomas's Senate confirmation hearings riveted the nation and prompted women in Congress to declare an electoral war of their own. As Faludi demonstrated in some five hundred closely reported and vehemently argued pages, the '80s had been anything but liberatory. She cast "post-feminism" as a disinformation campaign. Journalists trumpeted pseudo-statistics claiming that high-achieving women were late to marry, that late-marrying women were helpless to procreate, and that child-bearing women couldn't in fact *have it all.* Merchants of backlash declared that second-wave feminism and its close cousin, the sexual revolution, had sold women a bill of shoddy goods. "You may be free and equal now," the typical backlash news item ran, "but you have never been more miserable." Many of the stories were simply lies.[10]

Yet when *Backlash* was released, Candice was indeed free and equal—and miserable. She had spent much of that summer shooting *Revelations,* burning money, while the fundraising strategy deployed by Femme's new sales manager imploded. The company plunged into financial chaos, and the employee was sacked.[11] She put down her diary for the better part of a year, a sign of the "crisis" she described in faxes to Per and their friend Michele Capozzi, who had done a cameo as the shuffling detainee. "Traumatized" by the struggle in her company, Candice thought about quitting. But she picked herself up, as she usually did, and decided to soldier on. She had rivers of film in the can and needed to figure out what she could make of it.[12]

As *Revelations* languished, *Backlash* soared, winning the National Book Critics' Circle Award and climbing the *New York Times* best-seller list.[13] The following spring, Gloria Steinem published *A Revolution from Within: A Book of Self-Esteem*. The analyses were in many ways opposed: Faludi's broad and structural, and Steinem's narrow and personal. One reviewer called Steinem's book a "blender treatise on the inner child." But both books' publishers knew synergy when they saw it, and they launched what they called "an unprecedented joint venture" in the form of a tandem national tour. In March 1992, Faludi and Steinem landed on the cover of *Time*, with a soulful and defiant double profile entitled "How to Revive a Revolution."[14]

In the world of *Revelations*, counterrevolution has triumphed. Hidden in her neighbor's subterranean lair, Ariel pops a tape into the VCR and experiences the redemptive power of porn. "How cheated I felt," she says in voiceover. "I had no idea sex could be that way." She knows only "the act of procreation," its purpose to create "a soldier for the New Order." Ariel and her husband couple, as instructed, in uniform. "Rear-entry position!" He barks; she pivots. Both cry out, "for the New Order!" as he climaxes.

———

IN THE SUMMER OF 1991, as Candice continued her work on *Revelations*, Kentucky's freshman senator, Mitch McConnell, introduced a new, streamlined version of legislation colloquially known as the "Bundy Bill." Named after the serial killer Ted Bundy—who had claimed, before his execution, that porn made him do it, the bill, S.B. 1521, would create a tort action through which victims of sex crimes could recover damages from producers or distributors of pornography in cases where explicit material was judged "a direct motivating factor in causing the offender to commit the offense." The Bundy Bill bore more than a passing resemblance to the Dworkin-MacKinnon model ordinances of the previous decade. But the Senate's proposed tort, which could be triggered only after a felony conviction and only by materials already deemed obscene, cared about violent criminality rather than women's equality.[15]

Sponsored almost exclusively by Republicans from the heartland, the bill might well, like its predecessors, have died in committee, had it not been for the pubic hair that Anita Hill said that Clarence Thomas had joked about finding atop his can of Coke. In the wake of the Thomas confirmation hearings, mortified male politicians rushed to curry favor with female constituents, hoping to prevail against the record number of female candidates standing for office, in what some were calling "The Year of the Woman." The volatile political atmosphere energized new coalitions of anti-pornography activists, ranging from evangelicals outraged by a floodtide of filth swelling into a tsunami on the newborn Internet, to MacKinnon and her allies, whose harm-based ordinance approach, repeatedly defeated in U.S. courts, would soon be adopted by the Supreme Court of Canada. The moment made for even stranger bedfellows than the fight against porn usually assembled. When Senator McConnell had to cancel an appearance on *Larry King Live*, his staff recommended, in his stead, a spokeswoman from the radical New York collective Feminists Fighting Pornography.[16]

Concerned that the liberal chairman of the Senate Judiciary Committee, Delaware Democrat Joseph R. Biden, might go hard against porn to prove his pro-woman bona fides, several dozen First Amendment proponents gathered in the ACLU's conference room at New York Law School in January 1992. Marcia Pally, a civil libertarian, assembled the glittering roster of white feminists, which included notable attorneys and scholars, as well as an array of prominent creatives, among them the novelist Erica Jong, Holly Hughes of the "NEA Four," and the two New York–based members of Club 90, Veronica Vera and Candida Royalle. Candice suggested a name for the group, which they quickly adopted: Feminists for Free Expression, or FFE.[17]

FFE's first task was to draft an open letter to the Senate Judiciary Committee protesting the Pornography Victims' Compensation Act, a letter that ran in the *Washington Post* on Valentine's Day. Calling S.B. 1521 "book banning by bankruptcy," FFE warned that "the harms of censorship, legislative or monetary" had historically fallen heavily upon feminists themselves.[18] Enforcement of the Canadian Supreme Court's February 1992 decision in *Butler v. The Queen*, a sweeping victory for feminist anti-pornography advocates, would soon prove this point; the lesbian erotic magazine *Bad Attitude*, along with Andrea Dworkin's *Pornography* and *Woman Hating*, would number among the first items seized. Candida Royalle was one of the FFE letter's near-two hundred signatories, including feminist foremothers Betty Friedan and Adrienne Rich, as well as the novelist Jamaica Kincaid, the only Black woman among the headliners.[19] Perhaps Candice was playing up to the company when she listed her affiliation as the American Association of Sexuality Educators and Therapists, prompting what amounted to a cease-and-desist letter from AASECT's president.[20]

FFE was close kin to FACT, with whom it shared several prominent members. Like FACT, FFE formed to do a piece of legal advocacy. Which meant that FFE, like FACT, entered into pitched debate with anti-pornography feminists and courted, especially, the public enmity of Catharine MacKinnon, who championed the Senate bill and had had considerable influence upon the *Butler* decision. MacKinnon, Andrea Dworkin, and their allies had long reviled conventional liberal claims around expressive freedom. As early as 1981, Dworkin had excoriated the ACLU as an organization whose letterhead ought, in the interest of transparency, to feature "a woman tied, chained, strung up, and gagged."[21]

Libertarian and feminist ideas about speech had moved further apart since 1985, when FACT coalesced to support the American Booksellers Association in its case against the Indianapolis anti-pornography ordinance. Progressive legal thinkers increasingly elevated concerns of social justice—of civil rights—over mere expressive liberties. The *harm* framework that was radical when MacKinnon first articulated it around sex and gender had grown both broader and more commonplace as it was applied, especially on college campuses, to matters of race, under the flag of "hate speech."[22] Libertarian feminists were left behind with their whiteness. At a later FFE meeting held in Candice's apartment, a young Black staffer from the New Museum commented on the group's homogeneity and offered that "the porn/antiporn thing does not speak to women of color."[23]

The members of FFE, to a far greater degree than the feminist sex radicals of FACT, were ACLU liberals. And much as MacKinnon tended to hyperbolize about free expressionists as pornography's pimps, FFE really *was* in bed with the sex industry. Indeed, the group was *Playboy*'s brainchild. Two weeks before that first meeting, *Playboy* CEO Christie Hefner had written to the ACLU's president, Nadine Strossen, to highlight "the increasing credibility of Catherine [*sic*] MacKinnon and the attitudes she represents." Noting that "the best defense is a good offense," Hefner mused, "if we could put together some prominent feminist attorneys on the other side it would be particularly powerful." Marcia Pally, who organized FFE's first meeting, wrote frequently for *Penthouse*, and many of those she had assembled were, as FFE co-founder and Playboy Enterprises PR director Cindy Rakowitz put it, "old Playboy friends."[24] The morning after that first organizing session, Strossen's assistant faxed Hefner a briefing about the proceedings and promised to keep her apprised of the group's activities.[25]

The presence of sex-industry professionals within FFE was no secret. Yet within a month of its formation, the coalition came apart— "no surprise," one Playboy staffer wrote—over "the visibility of the ACLU, Playboy and Penthouse" on its roster. A clutch of former FACT members met, secretly, and decided to ask the group's ACLU-linked members to step away from the microphone and, more controversially, to request that its most visible sex-industry representatives, especially Pally, resign. Playboy's Cleo Wilson pointed out the multifold ironies of these demands to Christie Hefner: "Playboy has underwritten the costs of the mailings, and Marcia is the hardest working, most visible, and only spokesperson for the group." There was yet another layer to the intra-group drama: among those calling for Pally's ouster was Leanne Katz, head of the National Coalition Against Censorship, an ACLU offshoot that itself was apparently quietly taking money from Playboy and Penthouse.[26] The battle lines drawn, with a "delegated 'spy'" in place from each faction, reporting on the other, the dilemma resolved as internecine feminist disputes had done for decades: by schism. The former FACT members split off and formally reconstituted that group, with closed meetings and an invitation-only membership, to fight censorship without the taint, or the dollars, of the skin mags and their corporate parents.[27] And of course, as Candice had observed back in 1985, without their reach.

In the spring of 1992, as FFE splintered and S.B. 1521 occupied the Senate Judiciary Committee, journalists touted—indeed, seemed to long for—a renewed "Pornography War among Feminists," as Nat Hentoff put it in a column in the *Washington Post*. Later in the year, after the bill cleared committee and was remanded to the full Senate, where it languished and finally died, Dan Rather devoted an episode of the primetime news vehicle *48 Hours* to what the program teased as a "passionate fight" over pornography, "an industry at war." On Rather's set, the battle seems as staged as professional wrestling: McConnell touts the Pornography Victims' Compensation Act as woman-friendly; Dworkin argues that pornography serves as a "recipe book" for violent offenders; Ted Bundy, reanimated via file footage, concurs that porn plots had scripted his crimes; Royalle insists she makes "lovely, sexy, erotic movies"; and an ambitious young U.S. assistant attorney general, Robert Mueller, asserts that pornographers are "much like the Ku Klux Klan that tries to hide behind the American flag."[28]

MacKinnon did not appear on *48 Hours*, but she continued to beat the drum against the pornographers and their libertarian handmaidens. Of Femme and its founder, she told *Elle* magazine, "Any person who sells women as sex and for sex is a pimp."[29]

Candice remained part of FFE, which was led by the feminists most sympathetic to her work, including Pally, who had profiled her in *Penthouse Forum* soon after Femme released its first titles.[30] To Candice, FFE offered a formal feminist affiliation, the first she had joined since the Bronx Coalition in 1970. Because of the sex industry's backing, the group endured and evolved in a way that few sex-positive feminist solidarities had done. As it grew from an ad-hoc committee into a duly constituted nonprofit corporation, she climbed its ranks, taking a seat on the board and superintending the Speakers Network. She pushed the group to make its image "flashier and less stodgy." She hoped to connect FFE to the burgeoning college sex circuit through topics including "Women's Sexuality/Pro-sex Feminism" and, on the technological cutting edge, "Censorship in Cyberspace." She shared Femme's mailing list with the group, a sign of both devotion and trust.[31]

Taking full commercial advantage of this latest turn in the divisive politics of feminism and pornography, Candice also inaugurated a new column for *Playgirl* at the end of 1992, shortly after Americans elected Bill Clinton, the first president to belong to her own Baby Boom generation, and one who already had a reputation for sexual licentiousness. In an installment that winter, Candice took stock of the state of the sexual revolution. "It may not be a 'party' anymore, but then again, perhaps it shouldn't be," she wrote. "We all seem to be whining about our fun being ruined," by AIDS and aging and the latest neo-Puritan turn. But she also asked her reader to ponder: "what exactly is it that we've lost here? I think perhaps a little history lesson might be in order."[32]

Revelations was part of that history lesson. By the time Candice wrapped the film, after nearly three years of work, its costs had reached $125,000. No major investor ever materialized. But she kept on, for the message. The movie's final frames show the American flag encased in barbed wire. In an interview with the feminist erotica magazine *Libido*, she described *Revelations* as her "reaction to what is going on politically," and as a challenge to the consumers who watched hundreds of millions of adult video tapes every year, people who would "go out and rent these things, and get off on them, but will not stand up and defend their right to access this material."[33]

Revelations debuted in March 1993, at a benefit for FFE, co-hosted by Holly Hughes and Karen Finley, as well as post-punk superstar Debbie Harry. Candice worked the FFE roster to turn out other celebrity intellectuals, including the writer Nora Ephron and the fashion designer Betsey Johnson: artists and thinkers to toast a serious film about a subject of grave importance.[34]

THE STRAIGHT PRESS FAILED to take *Revelations* half as seriously it took itself. For all Candice's media connections, the *Times, New York, Glamour,* and other outlets that had featured her over the years said nothing at all about the project.

The sex press, perhaps predictably, was merciless. *Penthouse* was an exception; Al Goldstein, who had become Candice's close friend, named *Revelations* the Couples Tape of the Month, calling it a "sexually explicit variation on *The Handmaid's Tale.*" But *Adult Video News* slotted *Revelations* into its "Gonzo" section, noting that "political art" is "rarely very sexy."[35] And *Screw*, on brand, was still less polite: a lengthy column entitled "The Gook of Revelations" damned the film as "cloyingly pretentious entertainment that thinks it's something more."[36]

Even Femme's fans did not stand up. To the contrary, they responded to the film much as *Screw* had. "We looked forward to your new release, *Revelations*," wrote a couple from western New York who owned a shelf full of other Femme titles. Though they professed themselves "sympathetic to your concerns about censorship," having "recently moved to a county . . . in which it is illegal to rent adult-oriented materials," they also noted that it was "perhaps a truism of some sort that a *movie about censorship should itself be something worth censoring.*" Candice, who by then typically farmed Femme's fan mail out to her assistant, took the unusual step of answering the letter herself. "I knew I was taking a chance marrying adult erotica to a political message," she explained. "I'm sorry this displeases you," she told her frustrated fans, "but I am not sorry for doing it."[37]

But the price for that conviction was high. In October, Royalle licensed the film to the Playboy Channel, for $15,000, barely a tenth of its cost. Femme, which paid her, as president, an annual salary of $52,000, reported another loss that year.[38] When Helen Vadala asked for a loan, Candice explained that while she "put on a very good appearance of being successful," it was largely smoke and mirrors. As the '90s, and Candice's forties, approached their midpoint, she summed up, for her stepmother, her own painful revelations: "I'm a single woman alone who owns no property, no investments, nothing of any real value."[39]

27 Surrender

Candice and Kat Sunlove at the Consumer Electronics Show, Las Vegas, 1998.

She'd made the pledge at the dawn of the decade: two more years of round-the-clock work to "take Femme as far as I can take it. Then sell it or pass it on and get pregnant with or without a steady man in my life."[1] Then three years passed, and relief was nowhere in sight.

Prestige abounded. By 1993, Candice was lecturing less on her work as a porn star and filmmaker and more often on FFE-aligned topics, like "The Justice Department's War on Sex." That June, she addressed some 1,500 members of the American Psychiatric Association on "Pornography and the First Amendment." But reputation wasn't enough. Candice worried that she'd traded her "creative self for the sake of trying to secure my financial future," only to be left with neither integrity nor stability. With the failure of *Revelations*, the escape plan crumbled; she feared she would have to give Femme five more years, though she no longer cared enough about the enterprise. "If only there was something in my life I felt as impassioned about as I do over my affairs with men," she wrote.[2]

Alan had schooled her, once again, in the perils of loving "a man who's still a boy." Per, too, had been so young and so lost. Yet now he was married again, with a child and a quiet life, while Candice felt "the finite quality of that ticking biological clock," the drumbeat *Backlash* dismissed as anti-feminist propaganda, yet which seemed to grow louder and more insistent each year. She knew it was high time to "stop waiting for some false prince to rescue me."[3] But it was hard not to look for a glint of shining armor in a sea of flannel and drab.

Men still swarmed her "like flies," Candice wrote. It was a pheromonal thing, beyond beauty; she was "like champagne," sparkling, fizzy, and fun, one ex-lover says. Certainly she had no reason to look to the new online dating services like Kiss.com and Match.com.[4] Yet she found herself so often and so quickly disappointed. "Another troubled artist," she sighed, after a date with a man who said being with her was like "passing a car wreck & slowing down to look."[5] In fact, tall, handsome, one-night Warren had it backward. Candice was usually the one who fell in love by rubbernecking at a wreck of a man.

She met a man I'll call Jacob shortly after the debut of *Revelations*. Considerably younger than Candice, he was a brash and ruggedly handsome Jewish doctor who also had a band; during a press swing through San Francisco, Candice blared his demo tape as she drove the Pacific Coast Highway.[6] Ambitious in medicine and in music, Jacob also made time for the good life: for food and travel and rock 'n' roll. For cocaine, too, it turned out. While "hooked on his adoration," Candice fell back into old habits. Partying hard, she lost weight, which made her more confident. Confidence made her sexier. But she remained unsure whether Jacob could be a partner, much less a worthy father to the children for whom she sometimes longed.[7]

Candice knew that any story about the family she might create was also a story about her family of origin. She looked to her father. "I really treasure our relationship. It's very adult & very much a father-daughter relationship in the purest & most tender ways," Candice told Louis that spring. But then, over the summer, she tried to visit him, and he waved her off.[8] She blamed the ancient triangle that bound her, her father, and her sister. "There was no reason for my father not to love me—except that I wasn't Cinthea," she wrote. She steeled herself to keep her parents at bay, writing, on the flyleaf of a new diary, "I will not let my history ruin my future."[9]

But Candice's vision of that future remained cloudy. Jacob said she concentrated too much on "developing Candida Royalle and not Candice Vadala." How could she tune in to Candice? She sang some gigs with his band, at late-night shows in clubs including the fabled CBGBs, on the Bowery.[10] She thought about writing a book: Candida's story, but Candice's too. An editor at St. Martin's told her that the volume she was picturing—a bracing memoir centered on women's desires and sexual self-empowerment—wouldn't sell; "lingerie books" owned the sex market.[11]

When Candice got stuck on the page, Jacob encouraged her to speak her ideas into a tape recorder. The suggestion made her feel lousy, "as though he were questioning my writing ability." She did it, though, in late 1994, amidst a whirl of FFE meetings, some of them held in her new Manhattan apartment, on East Eighth Street, near Washington Square Park. There was much for FFE to protest, as an uncompromising new breed of Republicans and their "Contract with America" swept into Congress at the midterm, and Bill Clinton, making common cause with centrists in the face of a resurgent Right, fired the surgeon general, Jocelyn Elders, for saying that young people should learn about masturbation. Later, when Candice played back the tape of her book proposal, all she heard was "a useless babble of drug rap."[12]

Jacob was history by then. Their breakup, at the bitter end of 1995, had been spectacular, a screaming match. He compared Candice to Hitler. Candice shouted that he had insinuated himself with her music industry contacts. He raged back, "what contacts? I've been stuck in your slime world of fringe people." In her diary, Candice said she and her friends had "howled" at the line and joked about printing bumper stickers reading "SLIMEY FRINGE PEOPLE."[13]

But it stung, too, this verdict on her fitness for the fairy-tale future. Cinthea says Candice loved Jacob deeply and dreamed of marriage, until he told her something like, "*You know, honey, my father's a rabbi. There's no way I'm taking you home.*" His rejection "broke her badly." But Candice's despondency also drew the sisters together. "For that little wounded period," Cinthea remembers, "it allowed us to get very close."[14]

———

EVEN AS CANDICE FLEW around the country, lobbying for FFE and packing campus lecture halls, it was getting harder to squeeze money out of her brand. *Revelations* had flopped, epically. But the challenges Femme faced were broader. Innovations in media continued to unleash new forms of pornography, and new pornographies drove technological change in turn. Femme had found its niche, and its market, in large part because the VCR dethroned the XXX theater. But soon thereafter, the decreasing cost and increasing quality of the fully automatic camcorder threatened the dominance of the professionally produced, pre-recorded tape. By the early '90s, "DIY videosex" was no longer a cottage industry. There were annual conventions, a journal called the *Amateur Video Guide*, and tens of thousands of explicit homemade tapes flooding the retail market.[15]

At mid-decade, adult content began to migrate yet again, as pornography fueled Americans' nascent lives online, and vice-versa. "Cyberporn" was the neologism used to describe the spaces where people could interact sexually through their modems. In July 1995, *Time* devoted a cover story to what purported to be a study out of Carnegie Mellon, estimating that some 83.5 percent of images stored online were pornographic, many of them violent.[16] Four of the top ten Usenet bulletin boards, serving nearly two million people, were "sexually oriented." Such demand fueled product development; higher transmission speeds and better graphics were in the pipeline. "Pornography in cyberspace is pornography in society—just broader, deeper, worse, and more of it," Catharine MacKinnon wrote. The question the new medium begged was "the same as pornography poses everywhere else: whether anything will be done about it." Conservative politicians would try; Sen. Charles Grassley of Iowa had the *Time* story read into the official record as Congress debated a new Communications Decency Act.[17] But for the most part, the answer was no.

Some analysts declared the DIY trend empowering. Camille Paglia, the postfeminist critic and pundit who sometimes worked the lecture circuit with Candice, told the *Times* she found amateur videos "very positive," because they represented "people . . . taking into their own hands the redefinition of sexual conduct." But if DIY videosex augured a kind of hardcore populism, Big Porn was also happy. *Playboy* and *Penthouse*, whose circulation had fallen dramatically, saw hundreds of thousands of visits per day to their new websites, among the first with streaming speeds fast enough to feature moving images. Both quickly became top-ten Internet destinations. To economists, as the historian of technology Jonathan Coopersmith notes, cyberporn quickly revealed itself as an "ideal free good," with wide availability, minimal transaction costs, and seemingly inexhaustible demand.[18]

For a filmmaker committed to art and a brand built on elegance, an industry chasing scale meant a race to the bottom, a race she could not win if she wanted to. By 1994, Femme's per-tape wholesale prices were three to five times higher than those of most distributors. The perpetually undercapitalized company had only recently acquired a toll-free order number and the ability to accept credit cards. Candice thought about ways to combine the frisson of homemade product and the brand identity of Femme, working briefly with Ray Hörsch, an old-school pornographer and New Age sex radical, on a line of videos called *Lovers: An Intimate Portrait.* The series promised to curate "the best of amateur films," thereby marrying "the voyeuristic thrill & realism of real people having real sex with the quality & integrity Femme has become known for." Candice planned fifty thousand direct mailers and a glossy catalogue. *Penthouse* lauded the debut tape. But *Lovers* managed only one more installment.[19]

And if Femme couldn't ignore the downward pressure of amateur X, Candice increasingly found her concept squeezed from above as well. Hollywood studios edged ever closer to hardcore, with pictures like MGM's *Showgirls*, a $40 million extravaganza distributed under the MPAA's new NC-17 rating, designating films with enough nudity or violence to signal adults-only, yet enough prestige to claim a berth at the multiplex.[20] The film bombed, both critically and at the box office. But then it more than recouped its staggering cost in rentals and on cable, where it ran alongside an ever-growing docket of similar fare, all of it competing with Femme.[21]

In late 1994, as FFE and other civil-liberties organizations joined forces to protest yet another congressional effort to regulate explicit content on cable, Candice opened negotiations with Phil Harvey Enterprises, or PHE, a direct-to-consumer adult products conglomerate in North Carolina.[22] The eponymous Harvey, a global family planning and sexual-health advocate, financed his international aid work with revenues from a suite of domestic sex businesses, selling at first condoms and then a full gamut of adult products—costumes, toys, vitamins, videos—by mail. After eight years in court and $3 million in legal fees, Harvey had recently won a major victory against federal agents attempting to bankrupt vendors of explicit materials through simultaneous trials in multiple jurisdictions. The prosecution scheme, which followed on the Meese commission's recommendations, was known as Project Post Porn, a joint operation of the Department of Justice and the U.S. Postal Service.[23] Harvey, a civil-liberties hero to organizations like FFE, led several entities, including Adam & Eve, the adult entertainment core of PHE's domestic operations; and the Sinclair Institute, whose *Better Sex Video Series* brought explicit sex ed to respectable middle America. (Candice's conviction that she could do the *Better Sex* concept one better had inspired her "Case Studies" project with Diana Wiley.)[24]

Once Candice decided she needed a deep-pocketed partner to take over Femme's distribution, PHE was the obvious, essential choice: "the biggest & most reputable game in town," as she told a friend. She pitched Sinclair, flying to Charlotte with a forty-page proposal touting her campus speeches, her membership in AASECT and leadership role in FFE, and her many television appearances and magazine profiles as evidence of Candida Royalle's "mainstream name-value." She hoped that a corporate backer with real muscle would allow her to build Femme's library to a healthy multiple of the eight extant films. She envisioned producing each year several "small-budget debuts from new directors," two or three "medium-budget, nicer couples' features," and directing an additional high-end film herself. "Candida" would serve as chief spokesperson, creative director, and talent-spotter; Sinclair would become her "distribution arm" and banker. "What's in it for all of us?" she asked at the end of the presentation. "Money!"[25]

Despite the cogency of her arguments, talks moved slowly, weeks dragging into months. "Where is paradise? How many years does it take to get there?" Candice doodled over drawings of herself in September 1995, exhausted, with the "grand prize" still just out of reach. A couple times she found herself "pretending there were competitive bidders"—the kind of coyness she might have rejected in a film script. Marianne Macy, a magazine writer who had interviewed Candice extensively for a book in progress, *Working Sex*, urged her to hang in. "If Phil Harvey isn't your guy, I don't know who is," Macy wrote.[26]

Candice hung in, and at the end of 1995, Femme and PHE passed papers. She contracted to create six new movies over a two-year period, with PHE covering healthy budgets of $65,000 per film, from which Candice was to take her own salary and all other costs. She didn't have to direct, "just be the executive producer," she told her ex-father-in-law, who knew the business as well as anyone. "As long as it has my name and look to it & is delivered on time, they're happy." PHE also agreed to underwrite the development of a new line of " 'intimate products' for women": vibrators bearing the Royalle name. Candice quickly approved two prototypes, which she said looked "like little cellular phones more than sex toys. Like my films," she told Sture, "they are discreet, tasteful, high-quality—perfect for the sexual woman who wants her erotica with class!"[27]

PHE paid Candice a lump sum to purchase distribution rights and cover her administrative expenses until the royalty checks started rolling in, "a near six-figure amount," she boasted to a friend. It was more money than she had ever seen at one time in her life. She paid off Femme's debt to her father-in-law. She trimmed her staff, retaining only a half-time personal assistant and a freelance bookkeeper. She terminated her office lease and rented a larger apartment in her building, where she could carve out a production space. She envisioned simpler movies, made on somebody else's dime, with "an emphasis on image and sound" and "as little dialogue as possible," as she told a writer whose ambitious script she declined that January.[28]

The agreement promised to inaugurate a "new, more lucrative phase" of work and life. "One day I will sit back & simply collect royalties on all the films & products with my name on them while I move on to my next creative idea," she told Sture. She fantasized about a line of gemstone jewelry bearing her name, though whether she meant Candice or Candida, she didn't say.[29]

THE NEW YEAR, 1996, dawned bright and cold. The Boomer president, Bill Clinton, who had begun an affair with an impressionable young intern during the government shutdown the previous November, declared, in his State of the Union Address, that the "era of big Government is over," and promised a "new, smaller Government" that would "work in an old-fashioned American way."[30]

Candice, long a boot-strapper in the old-fashioned American way, likewise looked forward to "new beginnings." She started dating again: a painter here, a comic there. "I want to learn how to have affairs without having to worry about falling in love," she wrote in her diary, still seeking to make good a core promise of the sexual revolution, yet unrealized, for her as for many women, if not for the president.[31]

In February, she flew to L.A. to cast and shoot the first of her six pictures with PHE, which she would call *My Surrender*. The filming went smoothly, but off-camera, the fit between Femme and its new corporate parent felt awkward. Candice wrote to Mary Gates, the PHE executive in charge of new business development, to complain about a litany of "problems and kinks." No sooner had Candice turned over her company's mailing lists than the line's longtime fans, used to receiving "woman-sensitive" materials, found their mailboxes stuffed with Adam & Eve brochures that buried the eight gauzy Femme titles beneath a mountain of conventional raunch. Such glitches threatened Femme's most precious asset. "My reputation is the foundation of my success and my future," Candice insisted. She expected to "be treated as something special like Sinclair . . . not simply to be turned into one page of the Adam & Eve catalogue."[32]

PHE responded by bringing in Bob Christian, who ran the company's nutritional supplement business, to mediate between Royalle and Gates, two exacting, strong-willed, and "fiercely independent" female executives, he recalls. Together, they rolled out a new marketing campaign, to debut at the big Video Software Dealers Association (VSDA) show in Vegas. PHE also set up a special toll-free number for Femme films: 1-800-456-LOVE, in anticipation of the release of the first Femme/Adam & Eve title in the fall.[33]

My Surrender ties together a series of hardcore vignettes with the slackest of narrative threads: the stock scenarios—bow-tied professor disciplines kilt-wearing college girl, cigar-chomping "lady pornographer" auditions male talent—are films-within-the-film, directed by protagonist April Hunter, who looks, for all the world, like Candice in the '80s. April offers loving couples expertly filmed versions of their fantasies, to add "a new dimension to their marriage." Clients are sometimes referred to the service by their therapists. "This is definitely something you'll be able to enjoy on your fiftieth wedding anniversary," April tells one couple, who go on to act out the naughty classroom scene, in which their wedding rings are visible, and an American flag stands in the background.

But it soon becomes apparent that April Hunter is her own worst customer, unable to sanction intimacy, let alone fantasy. She has been wounded, too many times unlucky in love. The movie culminates when she conquers her fear of "letting anyone in again," and gives in to lust on a bed draped in satin and curtained in tulle. Candice wrote and performed the title song, which plays during the climactic scene:

> *Let me surrender,*
> *Let it go. . . . .*
> *Surrender, sweet and tender.*[34]

Candice was proud of the film, which she called, in her diary, "the finest movie I've ever made," much as she'd said of *Revelations*, and other Femme films before it. But it's hard not to see in the tape a different capitulation than the one intended by the title. The film, like everything Candice would produce with PHE, relies more on the conventional grammar of pornography than the first eight Femme films had. The fantasy scenarios April films authorize bondage, spanking, gynecological closeups, even money shots. There is more meat and more pounding, less story and less "after-play" than, for example, in the languid *Three Daughters*, which remained, a full decade after its release, Femme's top seller.[35] The song "Surrender," a flicker of the musical career Candice dreamed of, is an amateur's earnest work, sung in an uneven alto. It is also a tree falling in a shabby forest: who but a biographer listens to the song playing over the closing credits of a porno?

––––––

"I'M SO SORRY, for all the broken hearts and the broken dreams," April addresses her own camera in the penultimate scene of *My Surrender*.

She regrets having approached love "from the wounded heart of a little girl," who measured every man against her "daddy, who can fix anything, and then make it all better." Like April, her creation, Candice felt ready to "find out, what it's like, to love from the heart of a woman."[36] But Candice had never had a daddy who could make it all better. She spent session after session with Linda Hirsch envisioning how to hold Louis accountable for his failures.

And then, in the summer of 1996, Candice's uncle Charlie got the call: his younger brother had been picked up wandering the streets of Largo. Charlie hospitalized Louis, now almost seventy-seven years old, and asked Candice and Cinthea to fly down. The sisters found their father retreating "into a delusional world of dementia," Candice wrote, a bitter sequel to "all his years of regret." Her father would disappear, again, before she had her chance "to ask him how he could treat a beautiful, lovable young daughter the way he did & still live with himself." In the hospital, Louis spoke only of his own childhood pain: how his mother had abandoned him for long hours when she worked in the sweatshops, making hats. "And he never got over it," Candice marveled. "He's still waiting for mommy to return."[37]

Which, of course, was a feeling she knew all too well.

Charlie and his nieces went to box up Louis's things to move him to a care home in Brooklyn, where Candice could easily visit. In the chaos of the trailer, they discovered papers documenting the 1985 conviction and quarter-century-long sentence of probation. Cinthea remembers emerging from the cramped bathroom to find Candice and Charlie whispering. She heard her uncle say, "Don't tell her." But then Cin found more documents, and Candice called the court, and the whole sordid story dribbled out.[38]

Cinthea thinks that Helen, their stepmother—Louis's ex-wife by the time it all happened—had known all along. "She believed he was innocent." Cinthea, too, has her doubts about her father's guilt. "It could be exaggerated," she says. She wonders about the setup: "why was this little girl . . . having so much freedom with my father?" Maybe the victim's mother wanted a payoff, she muses. But of course, Louis had pled no contest. And, Cinthea recalls, even on the flight back to New York, in his demented fog, her father had "acted like he was flirting with me. . . . He was giving me those looks again." Louis was hollowed out, "deranged," a shell of himself, she says. But he once had been so dashing. She still remembers the thrill of seeing his band on television. She keeps framed pictures of him close at hand, even now. She keeps, in a little dish, a few fragments of his bones.[39]

No sooner had Candice settled Louis into a memory-care facility than Helen was hospitalized in Albany, her third stay that year on a psych ward. "This time is very serious," Candice wrote.

Delusions sharpened Helen's tongue. "You want to slap me, don't you?" she asked Candice when she visited.

Candice let fly: "I'd like to punch your face in, just like you used to do to me when I was a kid." She felt awful about the outburst, noting that Helen was "a helpless old lady." But it was also "cathartic," a relief "to let her have it."[40]

Candice—"the daughter he rejected"—visited Louis often. In her diary, she plumbed the bitter irony that he consistently mistook her for Cinthea, "the chosen daughter."[41]

She practiced letting them go. "My parents are leaving," she wrote, "withering away under the weight of their own self-torture. Lives over. Amounted to so little."[42]

―――――

CANDICE MEANT TO add up to more. As PHE released *My Surrender*, she got to work shooting *The Game*. She thought it would be "the most beautiful Femme movie yet," better than *My Surrender*, which had been "better than ever" in its turn. Freed of responsibilities for distribution, she had rediscovered her love of making movies.[43]

But the pace of production laid out in the PHE contract was relentless, a factory discipline. Before Candice finished editing *The Game*, she readied the scripts for the next pictures in the series, shot in Los Angeles in the spring of 1997, two movies in eight days. And while she teed those up for editing, she began pre-production for the two after that, to be filmed in August. They had slender concepts, minimal scripts, shifting titles: *The Game* became *The Gift*; *Girls Night In* morphed into *The Bridal Shower*; *The Dress* got the racier label

One Size Fits All. Still, Candice fell behind. "Things have moved very slowly on all fronts," she admitted to Phil Harvey. "I have been slow to deliver films and now picking up speed and getting them done more quickly."[44] But *more quickly* was not fast enough.

There seems to have been pressure, too, to increase the proportion of explicit content in the films. Late that year, Candice fired off an angry email to Luke Ford, a writer working on a history of erotic films, insisting that PHE "did not demand that I make 'harder films.' They have given me complete artistic freedom." Yet she also assured Mary Gates that the third and fourth Femme/PHE movies would have "five complete sex scenes," where *My Surrender* and *The Gift* each had only four. Though still shy of the industry standard, five consummated sex acts meant higher production costs, which cut into what Candice could pay herself. She had earned a mere $4,000 for writing, directing, and editing *The Gift*: a whole season of work yielding less than enough to cover a single month's expenses. More than a year into her agreement with PHE, she estimated that Femme was running an annual deficit of $70,000.[45]

Sales of the Femme line were mixed. Couples' films, Bob Christian explains, tended to move only half as many units upon a movie's initial release, but were also longer-lived and more often reordered. Still, both parties in the new partnership were impatient for a quicker takeoff. Candice expressed continual frustration about marketing; Mary Gates worried that Femme titles weren't earning enough to justify their costs. She urged Candice to trim expenses, drawing an outraged response when she questioned her need for a personal assistant.[46] Candice took business matters personally. "I am very sorry for letting you down," she wrote after missing a deadline to get the fifth and sixth films—a two-parter, voyeur-themed—into the latest Adam & Eve catalogue. She floated new ideas, like a "lesbian line under the Femme label," while still struggling to execute the old ones. Gates responded coolly, with requests for data and market research.[47]

In those frantic years in the late '90s, while Candice mowed down the films she owed PHE like so many bowling pins, she also tried to bring discipline to her dating life. There was sex after Jacob, but where was the One? She rated the prospects of Randall, James, Chris,

Steven, John, Alex, Stoller, Jeff, Danny, David, Jon, Kramer, Dermot. "I'm practicing the 'Rules' now on these guys," she wrote, referencing the self-help sensation offering *Time-Tested Secrets for Capturing the Heart of Mr. Right*. Rules like: never split the check, or the counter-revolutionary mantra: *Don't rush into sex*. Aer followed, then Mike, then another Alex, one of her actors. As trysts and flings accumulated, Candice struggled, as she had for decades, "to view myself through my own eyes. . . . Rather than through the eyes of some guy."[48]

In the summer of 1997, while Candice was in Sacramento to testify, on FFE's behalf, against a proposed state sin tax on explicit media, she met the First Amendment lawyer Jeffrey Douglas. He was as smitten as she was impressed. They spent time together in the spaces where free-speech activism rubbed shoulders with the adult industry: in Vegas, where she headlined the PHE booth at VSDA, and in Los Angeles, where Candida Royalle received a Lifetime Achievement Award from the Free Speech Coalition, an adult-industry legal defense organization on whose board Douglas served. "He touches my heart & my intellect & my sense of fun," she wrote, wondering if they might get "serious." But she also wished Jeffrey had Jacob's body; male beauty had become more important to her as she watched her "own youthful beauty fade." When summer ended, Candice broke it off.[49]

Always a dedicated student of her own body, she tracked the first signs of menopause. Diana, Princess of Wales, died that September, in a hail of flashbulbs and shattered glass, and Candice watched the funeral, sobbing, both for the "tragedy of princess Diana" and for her "own grief," not least over the children she might have, "had I carried those pregnancies to term all those years ago." She tried "to adjust and accept" aging, giving away old clothes: sized 4, from the '80s, sized 2, from the "skinny," frantic, coke-fueled "party years" with Jacob.[50]

There were plenty of hot dates. Alexander, Jeff, Kevin, Mark, Joe— "So many men, so little time"—and briefly Mary Dorman, "the hot First Amendment lawyer" and FFE leader who looked, Candice said, like the singer K. D. Lang, and made "straight girls" weak in the knees. But there were also too many nights wasted on men who were just "killing time" before "shopping for a young bride with many birthing years to go." Candice had "no knight, no prince," no real estate. She had "no family to fall back on"; to the contrary, her father and step-mother had both fallen back on her.[51] She felt the Janus-faced grief of having known neither mother nor child.

Still, she insisted, there was much to celebrate. "I like my life. I have so much freedom," she wrote.[52] She lived the freedom the sexual revolution had promised decades before, freedom she bought dear and then sold to other women, the profit uncertain on both sides.

Much as she tried to look around and ahead, Candice found herself raking the past. Nearing fifty, she felt, looking back, that she'd managed only one decade with "any real sense of stability, flourishing, excitement": her thirties, when she and Per were married, when she and Lauren launched Femme. Until then, and sometimes since, she'd lived with what she called "wreckless abandon," a misspelling that captured both her wanton youth and her improbable survival. "I trashed myself," she wrote, grateful to have emerged mostly intact.[53]

On a speaking trip to San Francisco, she wandered through the Haight, where she had "blossomed and secretly suffered" half a lifetime before. She sensed, as she walked down Belvedere Street, the rustling of ghosts, as if the shades of "Joe Morocco and our gang of circus-colored freaky young things" had "come pouring out onto the street," laughing and tripping, "music blaring." But as she fended off the neighborhood's "drug-ridden pan-handlers," she couldn't help wondering: had some of the "burnt out street beggars" who asked her for change been part of the youthquake a quarter century before? "How many survived, how many fell prey to our misguided utopian dream of free love that deteriorated into drug abuse and killer disease?" She gave thanks for her "inner strength and self-love," the qualities that had allowed her to "move up and out," and finally to put her "life together in a way that works."[54]

And it did seem to work: career accolades accumulated. At the CES winter extravaganza in January 1998, the X-Rated Critics Organization inducted Candida Royalle into its Hall of Fame, not as an actress but as a "film creator," the first woman so honored. Candice found herself moved by the industry's "surprisingly wonderful tribute." But the expo that feted her also gutted her. "I felt like I was stuck in an airless world of tawdry trash," one she "felt ashamed to still be around."

Scribbling her thoughts on looseleaf pages while she filmed for PHE in Malibu, working nine days straight, sixteen or seventeen hours a day, she asked herself: "Why was I still here?"[55]

Stigma—evidence of the partial victories of feminism, not to mention the incompleteness of sexual revolution—was part of the answer. As Candice later told a reporter for *Complete Woman* magazine, a sort of *Cosmopolitan*-meets-*Redbook* supermarket glossy, actors willing to have sex on-camera could expect to make decent money. But she also offered a warning to those who would answer casting calls: "Make sure this is something that you really want to do because it's a career choice you will live with forever."[56]

———

WHILE CANDICE WONDERED how she'd gotten stuck in porn, wider swathes of American culture joined her there. Two major studio films from auteur directors centered on the adult industry—*The People vs. Larry Flynt*, released in early 1997, and *Boogie Nights*, which debuted on the festival circuit late that year—had "made porn chic again," Candice wrote as she fielded a fresh wave of interview requests. Predictable feminists used predictable metaphors to express predictable outrage. "Let's be clear," Gloria Steinem wrote in a *Times* op-ed. "A pornographer is not a hero, no more than a publisher of Ku Klux Klan books or a Nazi on the Internet."[57] But those films did indeed mint new heroes and revive old ones, touching off a broader '70s revival in music and fashion. Both received multiple Oscar nominations.

Famously cautious, the major movie studios had followed as much as led what would come to be called a pornified popular culture. By 1998, nearly 9 in 10 American households owned a VCR. To feed those machines, the adult industry cranked out some ten thousand tapes per year.[58] Profit margins were slim, but the volume was enormous, and the industry had achieved a measure of legitimacy, or at least penetration, simply inconceivable in the *Deep Throat* era. In January, word of the president's affair with the intern went public. The very same week, *Variety* reported that adult video revenues had reached a new peak, over $4 billion per year. *New York Times* culture columnist Frank Rich mused that "these bicoastal stories, one from the nation's political capital and the other from its entertainment capital, were in some essential way the same story."[59]

The aesthetic of adult pushed the boundaries of primetime. That June, a new comedy called *Sex and the City* debuted on HBO. "Welcome to the age of un-innocence," our heroine, sex columnist Carrie Bradshaw, proclaims in the pilot episode. "No one has breakfast at Tiffany's and no one has affairs to remember." The first season themed episodes around anal sex, spanking, penis size, vibrators, and the "blowjob tug of war." Fans were passionate and critics, enchanted.[60] In a cover story that hit newsstands shortly after *Sex and the City* debuted, *Time* magazine asked, "Is Feminism Dead?"[61]

By the end of that surreal summer of 1998, the whole country was talking about the president's penis. The same month *Sex and the City* launched, the intern, now revealed to the public as Monica Lewinsky, posed for *Vanity Fair*, channeling, by turns, Jackie Onassis, Marilyn Monroe, and Gypsy Rose Lee. *Times* political columnist Maureen Dowd declared, "Monica Lewinsky's glamour shots in Vanity Fair are pornography." Dowd, like most feminists, stood behind the president; some declared themselves willing to kneel before him. The journalist Nina Burleigh told the *Washington Post* she would be "happy to give him a blowjob just to thank him for keeping abortion legal."[62] Candice dreamt about "an exciting event" where Jacob lurked in the background while she had dinner with Bill Clinton.[63]

In August, several weeks after Lewinsky delivered up her semen-stained navy-blue dress to the Office of the Independent Counsel, a grand jury heard her testimony, as explicit as it was tragic. The major TV networks spent more time covering Bill and Monica than all other major stories combined. "The Clinton Show," *Variety* joked, had succeeded by fusing unlike genres: the "raunchy sex comedy" and the "war story."[64]

That same month, the Center for Sex Research at Cal State Northridge—located in the San Fernando Valley, where most professional adult films were made—hosted a three-day-long World Pornography Conference, co-sponsored by the Free Speech Coalition. It was a glitzy affair, timed to coincide with the Adult Video Association's annual "Night of the Stars." Howie Gordon, Candice's longtime friend, praised the way the program "completely cross-pollinated the porn stars with the mental health professionals and the First Amendment attorneys." Club 90 appeared in force. Candice and Annie opened the proceedings with a multimedia performance called "Pornocopia: Our Body of Work." The two of them, along with Janie, also headlined a panel entitled "Women in Pornography: Victims or Visionaries?" The answer was baked into the question. Nobody on the anti side had even agreed to appear.[65]

But even in pornography's headline moment, Candice's triumph remained uneasy. A couple weeks after the Northridge conference, she received a message on her answering machine from a man threatening to bomb Femme's offices—her home—"because the Lord doesn't like what I do." She filed a police report, which didn't make her feel any safer. "I have chosen a life of my own defiant design," she wrote in her diary. She knew she had paid "a high price in the form of alienated family," as well as forfeiting, at least so far, "mate & offspring." Now her very survival seemed at risk. "I am marginalized," she wrote, even as the margins changed the course of the mainstream.[66]

In September, the Independent Counsel's office issued one of the most salacious books since the Meese commission's two-volume compendium a dozen years before. *The Starr Report*, its 3,183 pages word-searchable on news media websites, detailed nine occasions when Lewinsky had fellated the president, including two during which "he touched her genitals, both through her underwear and directly, bringing her to orgasm." The *Starr Report* offered enough mise-en-scène that Candice could easily have created a film treatment from it, were not the whole sorry spectacle already available online for free.[67]

As the news cycle churned through the *Starr Report*, the Republican-controlled House voted to open an impeachment investigation. But then "The Clinton Show" took a plot twist : the widely lampooned affair strengthened the president's approval ratings even as its wall-to-wall media coverage obliterated broadcast standards for sexual content.[68] "Ran out to vote . . . literally ran the two blocks to the voting center because I had so much energy coursing through my body," Candice wrote that November. She felt "determined to get the wretched Republicans out of office," and she wasn't alone. Democrats gained seats in the House, shattering norms for an off-year election in an incumbent president's second term.[69]

Candice watched the president's trial on television. She blamed Kenneth Starr for stirring pornography and politics into a narrative fit for the world of *Revelations*. At first, she blamed the intern too. But in the end, she decided that "Monica redeemed herself by standing up to those creeps," as she told Annie. The saga of the president and the ingénue made both Club 90 sisters reflect on the arcs of their lives as they dished the whole sorry spectacle by email. Annie thought that if she had it all to do over again, she might become a lawyer.[70]

Candice felt grateful to have reached a stage where she could "handle acknowledging my sadness and regrets about my life choices." The more she learned about hepatitis C, the more she worried that having injected "hard drugs" would end up shortening her life. She had a liver biopsy scheduled, the first since her diagnosis in 1982. She remained HIV negative—almost miraculously, given the extent of her exposure in the '70s. That astonishing luck notwithstanding, she wished she hadn't picked work "that would severely limit my career choices." But she also knew she had chosen as she had because of who she was. "I didn't have the drive to become a successful singer or dancer," she admitted to Annie. "And doing what I did has made me a celebrated and mostly respected person. . . . So it's OK. I can live with all of it."[71]

Business was going well enough. Candice had recently completed the last of the six pictures she owed; she thought she'd never make another "adult feature." The Natural Contours vibrator line had launched, and PHE agreed to move Candice into a role centered on the marketing and promotion of her products, duties she thought would be compatible with her plan to finally write a book.[72]

And she had a dashing new man in her life. She met Bart-Jan Brouwer, a handsome young Hollander who worked for Dutch *Penthouse*, porn-cute, at the thirtieth anniversary party Al Goldstein threw for *Screw*. Separated by an ocean, they fed their longing into the fax machine, like primitive sexting. For months, the whirring of the console was the music that started Candice's day. Though they saw each other only occasionally, it felt like a deep and durable connection. "Will he still love me next year?" she asked her diary, much as she had at thirteen. "Could I really be this fortunate?"[73]

28 The Book of Life

Candice, c1999, in Brooklyn.

There had been fleeting moments, late in the American century, when Candice felt "fertile & ripe," as if she might yet complete a pregnancy. But blood tests revealed that it was all but impossible.[1] And other lab results gave her more to worry about. Her assistant, the one for whose meager hours Candice had to fight the bean counters at PHE, faxed her the kind of message that strikes dread even years later, lying inert in an acid-free box in an archive: "Dr. Presser called and wants you to call her regarding the results of your biopsy. She said to ask that she be interrupted from whatever she's doing to talk to you." Cells taken from Candice's left breast had shown irregularities. She'd need surgery to remove a lobular carcinoma in situ, which often presaged breast cancer. Afterward, she'd have to be followed as a "high-risk" patient.[2]

The carcinoma diagnosis also precluded estrogen supplements to cushion the impacts of menopause, which in turn meant declining libido. Candice put a positive spin on her symptoms. "I'm glad I'm doing it au natural," she wrote. "It gives me a window into what our culture is coaxing women out of discovering . . . when our energy begins to turn toward higher goals besides chasing men and scratching our sexual itch." But there was a cost too. "I'm sure it's why I care little now about making sex movies," she said.[3]

In October 2000, she threw herself a small party for her fiftieth birthday—"a 'Candice' party, not a 'Candida' party," she warned everyone, though Janie sent a stripper anyway. Bart-Jan flew over, but it had become clear that they imagined different futures. She felt not only middle-aged but out of sync. "Gone is the first 50 years of my life," Candice wrote a couple weeks later. "Gone is the 20th century." Though she reflected often on the drug-addled '70s, she had come to believe it was not the decade that had defined her. "We really were children of the Fifties," she reflected. She recalled that era as one of "idealism & innocence," a cliché which belied her own experience.[4]

She had a basal-cell tumor cut from her nose—more cancer, more stitches, more scarring. "And what have I but my beauty?" she asked. Loss was everywhere: foregone fertility, faltering lust, fading hopes, the remnants, she wrote, of a "strange, sad little life. So now, after years of struggling & working hard, what am I left with? C for Candice, C for Carcinoma. C for Hep C."[5]

————

WHAT HAD SHE MADE and what had made her?

About her career in pornography, she vacillated. "I am an innovator. I have changed the world!" she wrote after yet another award presentation. Her body of work had "helped so many & set cultural trends in motion." Yet those trends were mere eddies in the fast-flowing river of the adult industry. For all her efforts, the common run of product was getting worse. A marathon of viewing as an awards juror left her bemoaning the industry standard: "big-boobed babes having meaningless, passionless sex with some perfectly buffed 'stunt-cocks.'" "I HATE PORNO!!!!!!!" she faxed Bart-Jan. "And I fear the young men being brought up on this latest crop of feelingless mechanical crap are learning some terrible things about sex and women."[6]

A new wave of women directors was trying to make its mark in erotica, evidence of Femme's "real impact on our culture," Candice said. The baton, such as it was, had been passed. "My work is done," she wrote in early 2001. She tried to picture an alternate life, one spent "tapping into my real dreams, not just making the best of what I've done with myself."[7]

Dating in her fifties felt awful, a masquerade. The men were new kinds of wrong. Still looking for her frog-prince, Candice felt herself "awash in a sea of toads." A filmmaker who came to see her about doing a TV movie of her life, a life marked by "all the signs of success most people strive for," was astonished to hear Candida Royalle express such regret.[8]

Nor had her efforts left Candice with much in the way of financial security. At one big adult trade expo, she estimated that she'd moved only a tenth as much product—videos, massagers—in 2000 as in 1999. Her income went down in turn. She panicked every time her lease came up for renegotiation.[9] She desperately wanted to buy her own place, but prices kept rising, even as the stock market slump following the bursting of the dot-com bubble ate away at her savings. Femme and Natural Contours would only support her if she continued to hustle, "day in & day out," to promote the product lines.[10]

"Sadness is like having an illness in your soul," Candice wrote that winter, after the Twin Towers fell. She had been in North Carolina, on Natural Contours business, when the planes hit. She returned, by car, to "a sadder and more nervous" New York, and a "world changed forever." From her apartment on Eighth Street, she could still smell the underground fire burning. "It's a strange new time," she wrote. "War has come home."[11]

————

HELEN AND LOUIS VADALA faded into shades of the shadow parents they long had been.

Helen went first, declining precipitously in 2002. "It's so sad to see someone give up on life," Candice said, surprised at the depth of her own grief about her stepmother's impending end. She tried to buck her up. "You're one tough cookie. . . . There's a reason that your nickname was Tuffy!" she wrote in a long fax from Paris. Candice was on her way home when Helen Duffy Vadala died, in hospital, of sepsis, at the age of eighty-two. She hadn't been "a perfect mother—far from it," Candice wrote in August. But she felt "eternally grateful for her having rescued me from a terrible, terrible fate."[12]

Louis died the next year. Candice spent a lot of time with him during his final month, in hospice. She kept Cinthea apprised by email, wishing that they might all now find peace. "You know, for all the horrible things Dad did to you and to me, Cin, there was always an under-layer of kindness and sweetness and love," Candice said. She could see that substratum now, shimmering, "underneath all his horrors," all the things that had "turned him into such a dark miserable person who unwittingly hurt so many in his path." She gentled the headphones of her Walkman over his ears to play Billie Holliday. "I just need a little rest," he rasped, last words. "Goodbye Dad. It's over. You're free," Candice wrote when he passed.[13]

Candice vowed to remember her father as a "young man full of hopes & dreams. A young jazz drummer ready to take on the world. A young soldier defending his country in WW2. A young husband & father. Young man with extraordinary beauty."[14]

Even though that beauty had cannibalized her own.

———

HER PARENTS GONE, Candice came to think that Peggy's abandonment had set the terms of her life as she lay in cradle: a Grimm tale, a Greek tragedy. "I used to think I had perhaps managed to do enough therapy . . . to have escaped the curse of not being able to share deep, lasting love," Candice wrote in her diary. But she had underestimated the strength of the wicked queen. "I now believe I have indeed been damaged," she said, diagnosing a lifelong attachment disorder, resistant if not immune to cure.[15]

As early as 1974—before heroin, before porn—she'd mused about looking up families named Thompson when a cross-country flight laid over in St. Louis.[16] A dozen years later, while there to tape an appearance on *Sally Jesse Raphael*, Candice jotted a blank verse, part Kaddish, part Disney:

Somewhere in this phone book
My mother is listed
Somewhere in this city
Half of my ancestry resides
including my Indian heritage
somewhere in St. Louis
the life I almost lived
Lies mysteriously in an abyss
And I cannot find it . . . [17]

But it was hard to picture knocking on a strange door or sending the unexpected letter. Thompson was such a common name, and probably not even the one Peggy now used. And Candice, as Candida Royalle, was so very visible, so *findable*. But her mother had never come looking.

As Candice aged, and the wound of her abandonment festered, the technology of staying lost and getting found changed. The whole nation, even the world, suffered from attachment disorder and yearned to needlepoint their family trees. Alex Haley had invigorated the age-old pastime in 1977, with the television miniseries *Roots*, which drew a larger audience than the Super Bowl.[18] Ancestry Publishing, founded in the early '80s, catered to a burgeoning market for family history. In 1996, the company launched Ancestry.com; by 2001, the website hosted more than a billion digitized genealogical records.[19] "Today Cinthea and I may have found our birth mother on the web," Candice wrote that August, having discovered a Missouri-born Peggy Thompson who had died a couple years before. But the birth dates didn't match.[20] After turning up that false lead, she let the matter lie.

In February 2003, Candice and her friends thronged the neighborhood around the United Nations, joining a coordinated set of massive demonstrations around the world to protest President George W. Bush's plan to invade Iraq. And then, "inspired by having taken part in this historic event," Candice and Larry Trepel, a gentle, unassuming man whom she knew from her summer share in Fire Island, dragged their placards back to her place, where they smoked some grass and wound up making out. "I felt like I was fourteen," she wrote in her diary. Just when she'd grown tired of "waiting for some unknown prince to show up," a known one had, "right under my nose all these years." A tenderhearted guy, a cartoonist and classic-car aficionado with a business selling custom wheels, Larry hadn't seen a single one of her films, or much porn at all, beyond *Playboy* which, he says earnestly, he read for the cartoons. "It's spring and I'm in love," Candice wrote. Nobody was "more shocked" than she.[21]

They were inseparable that summer, in the city, on Fire Island, on trips to California, Paris, Amsterdam. Larry was "a lover, a true friend, & a partner," Candice wrote.[22] Larry held Candice when her father died, a grown-up man worthy of a grown-up woman, a man she did not have to worry was Louis Vadala in disguise. Months became years. They made plans to share the time they had left, which turned out to be shorter than either of them imagined.

———

CANDICE HAD LONG KNOWN that her most enduring asset was her story. As early as 1982, she had pondered her boxes of "journals, writings, lyrics, tapes, letters, etc.," things she'd carried with her, against the odds, through her wanderings. These were the raw materials, she supposed, of "an interesting & possibly incredible book . . . about one woman's life and a rather unusual one at that."[23]

In the early '90s, she began to hope that an autobiography might also pay. She got an agent, a rising star who helped her to work up a proposal for a book to be called *Great Sex: A Woman's Guide to Sexual Self-Empowerment.* They shopped the project to several leading editors in late 1995. Candice sensed that the conversations had gone badly— that "their idea of what I should be writing is not quite what I want to write," as she told a friend. She was right. "Women don't seem to want to read about sex in book form," an editor from Doubleday wrote, explaining why the imprint had passed.[24]

Later in the decade, the booming '70s revival seemed to promise new interest, and Candice thought about titling her story *My Life in "Boogie Nights."* Then she tried out another frame: *Sex Tips and Tales from the Cutting Edge,* sometimes called *Candidaly Speaking,* would foreground the "traumatic" aspects of her youth, "which included witnessing inappropriate behavior at home on the part of my father" and "fighting off a near rape at the age of 13." "Gidget becomes an unwilling Lolita," she scrawled in the margins of one draft, which promised to review the psychological literature on "the makings of a sexual predator," a subject about which Candice had doubtless been reading since she learned of her father's crime. Her book would "show how this trauma led in part to my performing in adult movies," and detail her triumph, through counseling, over her own "internal demons" as well as the "social constructs" that prevented American women from owning their authentic sexual desires. But no sooner would Candice rough out an outline than she wound up "slashing it to bits," unable to make the pages pile up half as quickly as the bills.[25]

Early in 2002, Candice wrapped another Femme film, the line's fifteenth: *Stud Hunters*, a comedy she felt, as she often did, was her "best production yet." She promised herself it would be the last. "It's time to grow & move on," she vowed in her diary.[26]

At some point that summer, Candice's agent found her a professional collaborator, Billie Fitzpatrick. Together she and Candice salvaged the proposal. By January 2003, Candice had a deal, "not a great one," she wrote in her diary, "but it's with Simon & Schuster & I'll have a book out!" The contract was indeed not great: an advance of $25,000, of which the collaborator would earn more than half, and from which the agent would take the customary fifteen percent. When the first payment came through that June, Candice's cut amounted to under $5,000.[27]

They would call the book *How to Tell a Naked Man What to Do: Sex Advice from a Woman Who Knows*. Fitzpatrick came up with the narrative frame, which organized Candida Royalle's musings as the life cycle of a film, from research through postproduction. Within a couple months, several chapters were ready for the publisher's review. "I love the casual namedropping," the editor responded. It "makes it feel like the reader is at a cool cocktail party with an eclectic guest list." She also urged more of the apparatus of conventional self-help: a narrative "more 'chunky' with sidebars," to-do lists, and key questions broken out, as in a textbook. The collaborators took the note, adding a range of boxed features, from "Director's Notes" ("Don't try sex in these places"!); to "Candida Close-Ups" (author Q&A); to lists of everything from sexy CDs to diet tips.[28]

Fitzpatrick knew that Candice, like many authors, had a lot riding on the book—or "the fantasy of the book." She'd collaborated on a number of sex titles and thought this one would really sell.[29] But their editor knew of a competing project that muddied the Royalle title's path. Adult movie sensation Jenna Jameson had a book in the works, too, to be called *How to Make Love Like a Porn Star: A Cautionary Tale*.

Jameson was a generation younger than Candice and orders of magnitude more famous. Instead of pushing the feminist margins, she had defined the industry center. While Candice railed against "starlets with big plastic torpedoes for breasts," Jameson got implants.[30] And while Candice and Femme struggled to eke out, Jameson signed with Wicked Pictures, which dominated the much larger market catering to straight male viewers. A canny businesswoman and a master of new media, Jameson had launched her own production company, Club Jenna, in 2000. A website available by monthly subscription followed, selling videos, advice, sex toys, coffee mugs, even bobble-head dolls. *Salon* soon reported that Jameson was making $60,000 per acting gig and had become "the top-selling porn star on the planet." Frequent appearances on shock media—Jameson did the Howard Stern Show regularly and Fox's *O'Reilly Factor* occasionally—allowed her to cross over from adult to the mainstream of an increasingly pornified culture. While Candice worried about her rent, Jameson owned a $2 million, seven-thousand-square-foot McMansion in Scottsdale.[31]

Jameson's *How to Make* was due out in the summer of 2003, and Simon & Schuster planned to publish Royalle's *How to Tell* six months later, for Valentine's Day, drafting in the wake of Jameson's hardcover and getting ahead of her paperback. But as Candice and Fitzpatrick were finalizing the manuscript, they learned that Jameson's publication date had been pushed back to January 2004, forcing a delay in the release of *How to Tell*. The editor explained, "when two similar books are published closely together, the media tends to focus on one, usually at the expense of the one published second." That the attention would go to Jameson was obvious to everyone but Candice. The best bet, the editor suggested, would be to tie the publication of *How to Tell* to "an event, such as the release of one of your films. Do you expect to release a film in that time period? If not, is there another event (release of a DVD?) that we might be able to hook on to?"[32]

The answer was no. *Stud Hunters* had shipped months before, Femme's "swan song," Candice called it. Focusing her energies on the Natural Contours product line made economic sense, and kept her out of the bowels of a business that increasingly disgusted her—not because, as the anti-porn feminists had argued, all porn was bad, but rather because bad porn had won. "The adult-porn industry is becoming a trash heap of over-the-top extremities of the most violating acts foist[ed] upon a girl," Candice wrote in her diary some months later. Her "stealth armor" had failed her during a taped interview at the *AVN* Expo in Vegas, where she broke into tears on camera while describing an exchange she'd overheard at the A&E booth. "You can cum in my ass 'cause I don't wanna get pregnant," a starlet had told a couple of drooling fans.[33] Such moments were not the peg on which Candice wanted to hang the launch of her book.

Jameson's *How to Make Love Like a Porn Star* is a dirty book, bursting with topless photos, masquerading as a "cautionary tale" packed with hard-won advice. It proved a juggernaut, spending weeks on the *Times* bestseller list in 2004. While it soared, Simon & Schuster restructured, laying off Candice's editor. That August, the house sent Candice and Fitzpatrick a stack of pre-publication copies of *How to Tell*, which had no pictures at all. Its initial press run would be fifteen thousand.[34] By then, Jameson's book, on its sixth printing, was selling 150,000 copies a month. The *New York Post* offered a side-by-side comparison. "It's the stuff of fantasy: two beautiful, blond porn stars size each other up, and then vie for your attention," reporter Sara Nelson joked in "Catfight in the Book Store." But it wasn't a fair contest. Jameson's *How to Make* featured explicit "fashion-magazine-quality color photographs." Its moral was flexible. "This book is about the pornification of our culture," celebrity editor Judith Regan told the *Post* gravely. At once lamenting and furthering that trend, Regan-Books sent the author on a coast-to-coast promotional tour. Most of those who came to her readings were men, fans of her movies.[35]

For Royalle's *How to Tell*, Simon & Schuster cobbled together a "Radio Media Tour," with interviews in markets like Indianapolis, Grand Rapids, and Portsmouth. Beyond that, Candice seems largely to have arranged her own publicity. Valentine's Day, 2005 found her signing books at the Borders on Jericho Turnpike in Syosset.[36]

Candice worked her press contacts hard, and *How to Tell* earned short notices in mainstream women's magazines.[37] But the most serious engagement came from the *Village Voice*, New York's venerable alternative weekly, where Tristan Taormino devoted a page-long installment of her regular sex column, "Pucker Up," to Royalle's book. Taormino was a second-generation feminist pornographer, educated at Wesleyan and fluent in the language of the cultural mainstream. She had first contacted Royalle in 1997, seeking a blurb for *The Ultimate Guide to Anal Sex for Women*. "Like many others, I am a HUGE fan," Taormino gushed. "Your work has informed, influenced, and inspired me," she said, the acolyte genuflecting to the mother superior.[38]

But by the time *How to Tell* came out, the tables had turned. Taormino spoke to the future, with fulsome appreciation for all Royalle had been and built. "To say she was ahead of her time (um, 20 years) is a grand understatement," the columnist noted, larding a polite review of the book with a generous interview. She referenced Jameson's competing title, already known to all but "those of you living under a rock." But Taormino also made clear that *How to Tell* wasn't just losing "in a field of two"; it had entered what she called the "much more crowded arena of self-help fucking guides." In that gaudy company, Royalle's title seemed muted and wan, less "snarky" than one, less "explicit" than another, less "titillating" than a third. Taormino hoped *How to Tell* might yet find its audience among "the millions of women for whom *Cosmo* sex tips seem empty but *Sex and the City* over-the-top, the ones who aren't ready to buy a dildo harness or embrace their inner slut just yet."[39]

That reader proved hard to find.

Candice had sent *How to Tell* into the world as "a sort of wrap-up," and had dared to imagine retiring on the royalties. But fewer than four thousand copies ever sold.[40]

Several years later, Candice made notes toward a new book, to be called *Sexualized No More: My Journey In and Out of the Porn Business*. She wanted, in the new therapeutic language of the twenty-first century, to "tell the truth. My truth": to open "the closed door of our modest apartment" in Riverdale, to reveal "the kinds of secrets that cause young people to run from their families in search of a better place." After decades as "a silent victim, an unspoken & unrecognized casualty," she would voice her pain. It would be a war story, a battle-field memoir of plunging from "nice girl" to "anything goes," through "addiction & pornography," and finally "back into the pseudo-respectable world."[41] With its focus on false dreams and brave fronts and silent suffering, on what it had felt like to mistake being wanted for wanting, she would spin an epic of sexual revolution.

No publisher wanted that book.

29 Home Again

Candice at the beach in Long Island, September 2012.

'm looking for the happy ending," Candice wrote in April 2010, month of renewal, her favorite. In the fall, she would turn sixty, but she still felt fifty, even, sometimes, fifteen. The *ending* seemed far away, and *happy* still eluded her.[1]

Work hadn't satisfied her for a decade, more if she was honest. A final Femme feature, *Under the Covers*, had been a source of embarrassment, even "shame," from the moment she shot it, in the spring of 2006.[2] Shortly afterward, Candice floated a new concept, the Femme Chocolat line, "aimed at tastefully serving the erotic needs of women of color . . . a much-neglected audience." The neglect was real enough. Black women, when they appeared in adult films at all, tended to be served up for white consumption as "brown sugar," a "sticky fetishism," as historian Mireille Miller-Young writes. As creators, they remained vanishingly few. Candice, who had worked in the predominantly white world of pornography and erotica for decades, took up the issue of race in belated and shallow fashion, chasing a market niche. She served as the producer of *Afrodite Superstar*, a spoof Blaxploitation feature directed by the young auteur Abiola Abrams under the pseudonym Venus Hottentot. An attempt to marry arthouse experimentalism and porn conventions, the film carried a tag line from Audre Lorde (ironically, one of the only Black feminist pioneers prominent in anti-pornography circles in the '70s). But Abrams found her vision hamstrung by porn's grammar, its talent pool, and its markets. Femme Chocolat died with its inaugural offering, probably a mercy for all concerned.[3]

The failure of *How to Tell* still stung. In late 2009, Candice had been prepping, at long last, to appear on *Oprah*, thinking, as she always did, that the "ultimate recognition" of her "groundbreaking work" had "finally come." Then the producers bumped her, at the last minute, for Jenna Jameson ("who else"?) and a starlet who performed as Violet

Blue—one of "the growing legions of young dirty girls" who, Candice wrote in her diary, "revels in nasty porno, the harder the better." Femme's brand of erotica, "serving up sex that was sensual & lovely to look at," seemed like black-and-white films in a lurid Technicolor world. "I'm a thing of the past," Candice knew.[4]

———

THE ENDING WITH LARRY, improbable prince with a vintage coupe instead of a white horse, held for a while. "We're very happy together," Candice wrote in early 2005, as they neared their two-year anniversary. They decided to move in together. Larry rented a place for the two of them in Battery Park, close enough to the ruins of the World Trade Center that they could watch what some called the Freedom Tower rising from the ashes. And they shared a country escape: in March of that year, Candice realized her lifelong dream of owning a home, purchasing a sweet, shingled 1930s cottage in Mattituck, on the North Fork of Long Island, about seventy miles east of the Hempstead tract house in which she was born. Through a lifetime of hard work, without a pension or an inheritance, she had exercised enough fiscal discipline to pull together a down payment of $75,000. "She was very proud that she had managed to do that," Larry recalls. (He helped with mortgage payments.) And she was keenly aware that few of her friends had planned as carefully.[5]

Al Goldstein, the creator of *Screw* magazine and the *Midnight Blue* cable TV empire, had declared bankruptcy. Shortly before Candice bought the Mattituck place, he had fished up in a men's shelter. General Media, whose flagship *Penthouse* made Bob Guccione one of the richest men in America in the '80s, had likewise filed for bankruptcy; as the assets were distributed, creditors chucked Guccione out of his Upper East Side townhouse.[6] The cutting-edge technologies with which the adult industry had long had such a symbiotic relationship were now devouring its profits. A few years later, amidst the financial crisis that saw the federal government pump money into the coffers of banks and automakers deemed too big to fail, Larry Flynt and other "porn barons" made a show of asking Congress for a $5 billion bailout, to help "rejuvenate the sexual appetite of America."[7] Candice had never made it Goldstein big, Guccione big, Flynt big. But she didn't need the government to rescue her either.

Candice and Larry doted on the cottage, which fronted the wetlands edging Mattituck Creek and had a sprawling backyard. They relished even lawn care. "The compost pile was her house of worship," Larry recalls. Their little lane was called Farmer Road, and working farms stretched around them for miles. Candice biked out to the produce stands, and they both loved walking the beaches lining Long Island Sound. Mattituck was far from her city friends, bleak and lonely in winter. But Candice loved *playing house* again, as she had often said of her marriage with Per. After a year of living together, Larry asked her to marry him, and she agreed.[8]

The engagement dragged on, a promissory note with no due date, one year becoming two. "My cats. My flowers. My birds. My lovely serene home. These are now my greatest joys in life," Candice wrote in 2007, just before Thanksgiving. Larry was missing from the roster. His business was tanking, and Candice worried that his attempts to right it would ruin them both. And then, in the summer of 2008, that baleful season of failures and bailouts, Larry was diagnosed with brain cancer. The surgery to remove the tumor was dramatic, and successful, but the recovery was hard on them both. "All the focus of attention was on Larry," Candice later reflected. She put her own "needs & feelings away, tried to stuff them down into my belly until I could somehow make my way out of this unbearable torturous mess!"[9]

Extricating herself took more than a year, "the last brutal climb up," Candice called it. In the spring of 2009, she moved out of the downtown apartment, packing the life she had so painstakingly curated, over decades, into "boxes & boxes & boxes," bound for Mattituck. She combed the wreckage of a love that had been true but not lasting. Looking out her back window at a strawberry moon that June, she asked her diary, as if it were the Magic 8-Ball of her girlhood: "Was it meant to go on longer? Five years is a good run, no?"[10]

Come autumn, still working to disentangle herself from Larry's life and fate, Candice wondered how, were she to be "suddenly told I have cancer," it might "shift the focus" of her remaining years.[11]

SHE DID HAVE CANCER.

It would take most of a year before Candice learned that the pain she'd begun to feel during intercourse was a relentless malignancy. She had an ultrasound in late 2009, which looked normal. Early the following year, she sought another consult, with her physician in Mattituck, for a dull pain that never seemed to leave her left side. The doctor ordered a CT scan, which showed nothing beyond the kinds of anomalies that tracked with the progression of hepatitis C, like fluid in the belly, which made the doctors suspect that Candice's liver was slowly, inexorably failing—hardly unexpected some four decades after infection, via a dirty needle, with that incurable virus.[12]

And then, in a matter of weeks, the pressure in her gut began to make Candice seriously uncomfortable, and she experienced some postmenopausal bleeding. Bloodwork showed elevated levels of CA-125, a protein used as a rough screen for several reproductive cancers. In July 2010, just as Candice was starting to think about how she wanted to celebrate her upcoming milestone birthday, her internist turned the case over to Dr. Beverly Hannah Ortiz, who describes herself as the "friendly local gynecological oncologist," the founder of a practice at the eastern end of Long Island that was meant to be kinder and gentler, as well as much closer at hand, than the palace of heroic medicine that is Memorial Sloan Kettering. (Ortiz was also my college classmate.)[13]

Dr. Ortiz tapped the fluid in Candice's belly and found cancerous cells. She ordered a PET scan, whose results quickly set in motion a "very aggressive" abdominal surgery. In early September 2010, a little more than month before Candice turned sixty, Dr. Ortiz removed her ovaries and uterus, resected parts of her colon, and scraped away suspect tissue throughout her abdomen. The pathology confirmed stage III-C ovarian cancer, which means, in lay terms, "disease all over the place." Even still, the surgery had been a success. It was, Dr. Ortiz says, "a perfect operation."[14]

"The monster has come home. And he lives in me," Candice wrote on the eve of the surgery. She'd lost friends to the insidious disease, including her beloved therapist Linda Hirsch, to whom she had dedicated *How to Tell*. "Everyone knows what ovarian cancer means," Candice wrote. She pledged to live "as fully & as gratefully" as she could, for all the time that remained.[15]

The surgery, however perfect, was also devastating, a military assault. Cinthea flew out to tend to her besieged sister. The medical team gave Candice a month to recover her strength before beginning chemotherapy, infused through a port in her abdomen: a nuclear bomb following the ground war. The next phase of treatment would be "more of an art than science," Candice jotted in her "Healing and Wellness Journal," after conferring with Dr. Ortiz. The hepatitis C meant that they had to find a cocktail of drugs that didn't concentrate in her already damaged liver. They flooded her with eight cycles of Taxotere and Carboplatin. Cinthea recorded the side effects: hair loss, mouth sores, a precipitous drop in Candice's white blood cell count that left her vulnerable to infections, neuropathy that made her stumble. There were days when she felt too sick to bathe or dress.[16]

"Is it spring?" Candice wrote in March 2011, the first time she'd taken up her diary since starting chemo. The previous five months had been "the longest, coldest, darkest frozen winter of my life," the season a "metaphor" for her treatment. She stirred the cauldron of her memories: of her grandmother's house on President Street, where the flicker of a holy candle beside a statue of the Virgin had served as her nightlight. Of the Carroll Gardens of her youth, then an Italian neighborhood, where "greasers" roamed in packs, and bigger houses were said to belong to "high-ranking Mafia." Yet more "actual bad things happened to me in Riverdale than ever happened in Brooklyn." She felt safer now, after the treatments were over, and the doctors pronounced her "cancer free." "I made it," she wrote. "Into the light I go. To warmth & safety," the "two things I have sought my entire life."[17]

Candice was still clear in September 2011, six months after her eighth infusion—a landmark in the standard of care at the time, Dr. Ortiz explains. The chemo had worked, proving that the cancer was "platinum sensitive." The plan was to follow the patient closely until she reached the next major milestone, at two years.[18]

But before year's end, a PET scan revealed new masses. Candice opted at that point for Sloan Kettering. Under their guidance, she began a second round of chemo: another long winter of body and soul.[19]

When Candice surfaced from the brain fog, in the summer of 2012, she reframed her thinking about the disease. "My cancer diagnosis is a *life sentence*," she wrote, embracing the kind of branded positivity that fills the self-help aisles. Greg Anderson's *Cancer: 50 Essential Things to Do*, perched somewhere between medical guide and twelve-step manual, became a bible as Candice reviewed the "stress events" that preceded her diagnosis. "For me, Cancer is an opportunity to finally get away from the things that no longer bring fulfillment into my life," she wrote. She thought about setting up an art studio in her cottage or fostering more stray cats. She made a bucket list: more laughing, more singing, a trip to Tahiti, that kind of thing. "I choose to be well," she wrote in July. "I am getting better in every way."[20]

The second remission lasted a scant three months. "Can I not get a break?" Candice asked in her wellness journal, where bromides like "*Laugh for Healing Power*" had fallen desperately short. She needed a kidney stent, and a growth on her bladder had to be removed—an operation she postponed for several weeks to fly to California, to bring Cinthea one of her cats. The delay proved costly, resulting in a more involved surgery. But the visit was delightful—the last time, it would happen, that the two sisters, whom life had done so much to pit against each other, would take joy in each other's company.[21]

After the surgery, Candice started a milder chemo, and came to terms with the fact that she'd cycle on and off the poisons throughout whatever time remained. "It's been a real challenge," she admitted, "not to fall into utter despair." The illness ravaged the beauty that had long been her stock in trade. Her relationship to her bathroom scale flipped. "Up to 120 lbs today!!" she wrote some months later, proud of the weight she'd gained since her third round of chemo, which had left her "looking like a cancer patient," an identity she found unbearable.[22]

Candice threw herself back into life that winter of 2013, subletting a friend's loft in the rapidly gentrifying East Village, to lessen the number of long trips from Mattituck to Sloan Kettering. After the isolation of the North Fork, city life felt full unto frantic, peopled with the chosen family she'd accumulated over decades: Jerome and Susan from high school, the Club 90 sisterhood of Veronica and Annie, Mary Dorman from the FFE gang, Jorgé and Teresa and other assorted survivors of the San Francisco days, several generations of Femme employees. She joined a chorus. She gathered friends weekly to watch *Mad Men*, and monthly for a "Dirty Book Club." Sloan Kettering asked her to give talks on subjects like "Getting Your Groove Back: Sex, Reproduction, and Body Image During and After Cancer."[23]

She also met with an increasing number of next-generation feminist pornographers. Tristan Taormino, Petra Joy, and Erika Lust all sought wisdom and paid tribute. Taormino featured Candida, as a founding mother, in *The Feminist Porn Book*, an edited collection that debuted that spring, trailing a starred review from *Publishers Weekly*, and soon earned a rave in the inaugural issue of *Porn Studies*, a new scholarly journal from Duke. The reviewer there praised Royalle's essay, "What's a Nice Girl Like You . . . ," as a "pointed reflection" on feminism by "the 'pioneer'" of couples' porn.[24]

Larry was part of Candice's support system in the city, and she saw him often, and happily. But dating him or anyone else seemed out of the question. "I must accept that I am destined to finish out my days alone," she wrote late that summer. She pictured herself in a long line of women thus consigned: her grandmother Marion, her stepmother Helen, Cinthea. She asked, with a sense of both disbelief and inevitability: "What happened to my happy ending?"[25]

———

BETRAYED BY HER ENDING, Candice's thoughts turned increasingly to her origin story. "I am still searching for the love of a mother who left me at the tender age of 18 months," she wrote in the summer of 2013, at the beginning of yet another cycle of chemo.[26]

Why hadn't she looked harder for Peggy? Too many people had asked her, over too many years, "too many times to count." Now the question took on fresh urgency. Candice learned that she carried the BRCA1 mutation, a defect in a key "surveillance gene" that helps healthy cells rout small cancers. Dr. Ortiz explains that Candice's history of lobular carcinoma in her breast, followed by the erumpent ovarian malignancy, sent up a "red flag for hereditary mutation." The new high-tech screening confirmed what that medical history suggested: Candice's incurable illness was, in part, an inheritance.[27]

Just when genetic testing revealed the role of Candice's family tree in the ontology of her cancer, another sympathetic storyteller entered her life. Sheona McDonald, a Canadian filmmaker whose work often focused on gender, was making a documentary on women and shame. Her production company had reached out to Candice the previous July, to schedule an interview about "the world of women and porn." It took Candice months to answer the query, and she first sat down with McDonald in June 2013, just ten days after receiving her genetic counseling results. Their interview ranged widely. Candice had been frank—perhaps, she worried, too frank—about what had become of feminist porn. "I began to feel that perhaps I was a bit too hard on the young women filmmakers here in the states," Candice emailed McDonald afterward. She didn't "want to hurt anyone's feelings or make enemies with the very women who I've heard credit me as their inspiration."[28]

In the months that followed that first interview, new treatments ravaged Candice, again. "I watch as my hair comes out by the handfuls," she wrote in January 2014, amidst the latest round of chemical attack. Her hands grew gnarled. Her skin thinned. She felt no "sign of desire," no "glimmer of sexual excitement," no intimation of the pleasures she'd long placed at the center of her vision of the good life.[29]

Conventional medicines failed, one after another. Candice scribbled notes about alternatives—"mushroom therapy," milk-thistle extract, graviola bark, cannabis oil, citrus pectin—on the tiny pages of her date book, too sick and too disoriented to keep up her lifelong diary habit. She investigated energy healing and pendulum work. She called Femme co-founder Lauren Niemi Cole, who had moved to Austin and become a psychic. Lauren told her she sensed the "ancestors . . . gathering" and heard "ancient Indian drumming," a signal from Candice's mother.[30]

In February, shortly after Club 90's Gloria Leonard died of a stroke, with no warning, at the age of seventy-three, Candice collected information about private investigators who might help her find her mother. She interviewed Lynne Friedman, of the local Valley Investigations LLC, and a principal from Kinsolving Investigations, based in North Carolina. Kinsolving's practice centered on prizing open closed adoptions, and they charged a flat fee, of $3,000, for successful searches. Friedman thought it would cost less than half that to deliver conclusive results within three or four weeks. She went with Friedman.[31]

As Friedman trawled the public record, Candice and Sheona McDonald scheduled additional interviews for the film on women and shame, which had come to be called *Inside Her Sex*. A crew shadowed Candice for two days in mid-March, at a variety of New York locations, though a plan to film at Sloan Kettering fell through. During those long days together, filmmaker and subject hit upon the idea for a spin-off project: a documentary framed by Candice's biography and centered on the search for her mother. Candice agreed to have Lynne Friedman announce her findings on-camera.[32]

Friedman did so in April, producing a report that included contact information for the Vadala sisters' long-lost half-brother, Jimmy Hume, and the birth and death certificates of Peggy Thompson Hume Vadala Frazier, who had died in 1991 at the age of sixty-two, of ovarian cancer. "No determination could be made about the native American ancestry of Peggy Frazier," Friedman concluded. The persistently unproven Cherokee legend notwithstanding, Friedman's report served up the story that Candice and McDonald alike longed for: a tale of hereditary fate. A few days after the taping, Candice dispatched an intimate and searching letter to Jimmy Hume, who lived in Florida. "Do you remember your two little sisters?" she asked, enclosing photos of the house they'd shared sixty years before, the house where Peggy had given birth to her.[33]

Within the month, Candice and her half-brother were talking by phone. Jimmy told Candice about the shadow family she had never known: Peggy's violent first husband, before Louis, and the nameless third and fourth after him. The kindly fifth had been with her at the end: John Frazier, a Black man more than a decade Peggy's junior, the best of all the husbands, Jimmy said. Peggy and John had a daughter, Susan, and Candice called this newly discovered half-sister, who told her their mother had been much beloved in the mostly Black hamlet where she lived out her golden years. Peggy "always had class," Susan said. Jimmy was more pointed: being a white woman in a Black community raised his mother's status and made her hardscrabble life a little easier.[34]

"We were loved," Candice jotted during one conversation with Jimmy. He said Peggy had kept photos of her and Cinthea on a stand in their living room: an altar to a long-ago life. Yet she had never tried to find them. Jimmy blamed the clannishness of the Vadalas, implying that Marion had scared Peggy off for good. Regardless of the reason, the Vadala branch had been lopped from the Hume family tree. Peggy's obituary mentioned only Jimmy and Susan. There was no funeral.[35]

Candice's condition worsened that summer. She started on oxycodone for the pain on the same late May day she first connected with Jimmy. Soon the medical team detected lesions on her spine, another remission ended, another round of chemo looming. There was talk of a new drug, Olaparib, specifically engineered for BRCA1 cancers, which had shown promising results in Europe. Candice hoped to enroll in a U.S. trial.[36]

As her health declined, her sense of urgency about the film grew. "Something's going on, Sheona," she wrote. "We're being swept up into some sort of bundle of energy." They planned to record her reunion with Jimmy Hume in Florida, after which the half-siblings would fly together to St. Louis. Candice hoped Cinthea would come with them. "The whole issue of nature vs. nurture, or genes versus upbringing really comes up here," Candice told Sheona. She also thought the family reunion angle would "set my story apart from the many porn stories coming out," mentioning Jenna Jameson's decade-old book, still rankling.[37] While McDonald worked on the budget and a fundraising plan, Candice met with her literary agent to pitch a memoir centered on the search for Peggy, and "how cards I was dealt led to my cancer." The saga of the motherless child was, she said, among the "most universal" stories. "It's very nuanced, like a novel."[38]

In July, Candice and Sheona launched a Kickstarter campaign to raise $135,000 (Canadian) to fund the documentary they were calling *While You Were Gone: The Untold Story of Candida Royalle.* The costs they outlined were in range of the more expensive Femme films, except that the talent exposing all in the documentary would work for free. Sheona warned of long odds: "I think the first thing to note is that the likelihood of making money once the film is complete is very, very low." To steer traffic to the month-long campaign, they created a WordPress site, featuring old Vadala family photos captioned as if young Candy had sent them to Peggy.[39] Candice worked her press contacts; the *New York Post* agreed to run a story. But she worried about how the *Post* would spin it, telling the Club 90 girls she was "beginning to wish I'd never started this f'ing project."[40] The *Post*'s feature, "Ex Porn Star Now Baring Her Soul in Search for Mother," traded on the salaciousness of Candice's past as a "onetime porn princess" and the bathos of her "cancer-stricken" present: everything she had feared.[41]

As contributions trickled in, Candice pondered what she might provide "as incentive" for her backers. She considered DVDs of Femme films, autographed photos, mini vibrators from the Natural Contours line, inscribed copies of her book: the remains of a remaindered life. A week before the Kickstarter was set to close, they had raised less than a third of their goal. Sheona expressed surprise that it had proven so difficult to reach an audience beyond Candice's "circles" in the sex industry. She was not "hugely optimistic about our chances." "Part of me feels like freeing myself of this whole thing," Candice told the filmmaker. But at the same time, she worried that if she met Jimmy without cameras rolling, she'd "be thinking the whole time about what a missed opportunity it was."[42]

In September, Candice started yet another round of chemo. Cinthea decided not to accompany her to meet Jimmy Hume. Creative differences between protagonist and filmmaker grew. Sheona suggested that they scale the project back to a documentary short. But Candice insisted that her biography amounted to "more than searching for my mother and fighting cancer." It was the saga of "a career, a vision, a movement, a legacy," not just a tragedy. Meeting Jimmy— seeing something of the life she might have had, with Peggy—could be a great way to "wrap up" that broader tale: "the final journey for me before I take my final bow," Candice called it. "But I didn't mean for it to be my only story."[43]

They persevered. Sheona found a Canadian nonprofit to which she could apply for grant support. Candice agreed to trim their itinerary, skipping Florida and bringing Jimmy to meet her in St. Louis. The day before she got on the plane, she had an infusion and filled her prescription for oxy. She would power through another session of chemo the day after she returned.[44]

The Midwest in November was spectacularly, suitably bleak—death-haunted. McDonald filmed Candice reuniting with Jimmy at the Holiday Inn Express, in Troy, Illinois, northeast of St. Louis: "the middle of nowhere," Candice comments in voiceover. "You are so beautiful," Jimmy says, embracing his long-lost sister, who has dyed her thinning hair an improbable fire-engine red.

"We better get outta the doorway before we get arrested," he jokes.

"They'll think we're shooting a porno film, a senior citizens' porno film," Candice answers awkwardly, offering that she hopes there's no such thing—when, in fact, she and Diana Wiley had spent years talking about the serious and potentially profitable subject of sex and aging.

Jimmy shows her old photographs. Then they drive together through the poorer precincts of St. Louis, past the vacant lots and burned-out blocks amidst which Jimmy spent what remained of his boyhood after he left Hempstead and lost his surname and the only father he'd known.

"It really seems depressing around here," Candice tells her brother. "I think I would have been very uncomfortable in this environment."

"She was searching for somebody to treat her right," Jimmy says of the years of abuse Peggy endured at the hands of one man after another.

"Well, I think she was a fool," Candice answers flatly, her family romance dissolving before her eyes.

Jimmy and Candice pay a call on Peggy's surviving brother, John Thompson, known as Uncle Tommy, who as a young man had driven to New York to rescue his sister from her second rotten marriage, at the price of leaving her daughters. Peggy never should have married Candice's father, Tommy says. He reckons that Louis "had been mothered real hard," leaving him a boy-man who could barely care for himself, let alone a bride. Tommy, a skilled carpenter, shows them the coffin he built for himself.

In the climactic scene of the film, Candice and Jimmy and an unseen Sheona search for Peggy's grave in the city cemetery in Bonne Terre, Missouri, a town whose main industry seems to be detention. The sky is the color of the granite headstones. Neither Candice nor her brother can find the plot—Jimmy can't recall, in fact, if his mother was buried intact, or cremated. Finally, they locate the marker on the snowy ground. Candice asks for a few minutes alone—with Sheona's camera rolling. She kneels to touch the inscription, brushing away a tear. In voiceover, though, she is furious that she "didn't get to have my mother, but I got her cancer." Why hadn't Peggy tried to find her girls, while there was still time for them to unpack her genetic baggage? "Woman to woman: fuck you. *Fuck. You*," Candice says. "I wish it was a happier ending, but it's not."

The screen fades to black, and the chronicle of Candice's own death scrolls past.[45]

———

THERE WAS, if not a different ending, at least another way to tell the story of Candice's illness, one that insisted on choice and made space for joy, as well as inheritance and calamity. Cinthea, for one, doesn't quite credit the simplicity of the BRCA1 account. She thinks it was important, so late in life, for Candice "to find her mother" (who was, of course, also Cinthea's mother), and to discover "that she had inherited the gene. Because otherwise, she was going to blame herself. She had hepatitis C. She had, you know, picked up all the various assortments of STDs." Cinthea believes that "all of those things can lead to ovarian cancer."[46]

I ask Dr. Ortiz about the conflict between these two narratives of Candice's disease: the tragic inheritance and the reckless choices. A complete story, she explains, needs both. Hepatitis C had confounded the diagnosis. By lowering Candice's overall immunities, it had also made her more vulnerable to cancers of all kinds. And then it compromised the success of her treatment, narrowing the possible options, and blunting what was normally a strong response by BRCA1 cancers to the chemotherapies then available. Ovarian cancer would kill her. But the "kiss of death for her was the hep-C," Ortiz surmises.[47]

McDonald had filmed pieces of that shadow narrative back in June 2014, in San Francisco, at Candice's urging. The documentary intersperses footage of the sick and aging Candice with clips from the porn movies she made in the '70s. We see her skateboarding through *Hot and Saucy Pizza Girls*, and then looking wistfully at her old house on Belvedere Street and her apartment in Pacific Heights, where she had once overdosed on heroin. We watch the excruciating rape scene from *Easy Alice* as Candice explains to the off-camera interviewer "the time of the so-called sexual revolution," which had given women "the right to say yes, but kind of took away our right to say no."[48]

But the film discloses nothing of what had brought Candice to the Bay Area that June, already so sick. She flew west, with McDonald in tow, for a weeklong celebration at the Institute for Advanced Study of Human Sexuality.[49] Candice and her surviving Club 90 sisters were feted there, at "Days of the Divas," during which she, Janie Hamilton, and Veronica Vera each gave feature-length illustrated lectures on their life and work. Then Annie Sprinkle, who had received her doctorate from IASHS in 2002, presided over the investiture of her chosen sisters as Doctors of Human Sexuality. The degree was bogus in the state's eyes. The certificate was laser printed on cheap stock. But it carried a golden seal, and it set "Candida Royalle" in blackletter, a *nom de porn* elevated to something fit for framing. "These Divas personify what has always been a primary goal of the Institute, which is to spread the truth of human sexual experience in all its complexities," its director told *Adult Video News*.[50]

It meant something to Candice to have that ceremony filmed. "I will insist that we be able to shoot it," she told Sheona.[51] But the footage of that giddy event was poorly lit. And told the wrong story, one that reveled in hedonism and reviled pity. After Candice died, it landed on the cutting-room floor.

Candice believed in that achievement, and others like it, as fully as in the truth of her abandonment and its genetic consequences. In the final days of 2014, she doodled in her datebook: Candice Vadala, DHS, *Doctor of Human Sexuality.*[52]

———

BY FEBRUARY 2015, Candice knew she was actively dying. She began seeing a social worker and made a note that she needed to write a will.[53]

In late March, she entered the long-awaited clinical trial for Olaparib. Within weeks, she dropped out, the experimental drug having failed to dent the progress of her disease. The friends of a lifetime gathered: Jorge and Michele making the trip often from Manhattan, Janie and Annie flying in from California. Veronica moved into the cottage in Mattituck for the duration. Sheona McDonald came, too, with her camera, for a last round of filming in April. Candice looks gaunt in those segments, pared to her essence.[54]

Candice reminded herself, in May, that she should read the work of Elisabeth Kübler-Ross, pop prophet of death, and in June, that she still needed to put her affairs in order. Even still, she could not give up the fight, enduring another course of steroids, twice-daily injections of blood thinners, and ten days of radiation to shrink new tumors in her belly.[55]

All failed.

In late July, Sloan Kettering admitted her for a week. Per came from Santa Fe, sneaking sushi into his ex-wife's hospital room and raising a ruckus. It would turn out to be their last time together. Only at the end of August, and after much prodding, did Candice finally sit down with Mary Dorman to ready her will, which left the bulk of her estate to the surviving Club 90 members and to Cinthea—her sisters, born and made.[56] She told Annie that she couldn't quite believe that she'd never get to wear any of her party dresses again.[57]

Days after the will was signed, a hospice team set up a hospital bed downstairs, in the sunny back room of Candice's home, and added Fentanyl patches to her palliative regimen. The meds got too heavy for her to hold a pen. The last words in her hand, about an herbal supplement said to bolster immune response, show her, even then, clinging to life. She thought she'd try the nostrum for a few weeks, which turned out to be more than she had left.[58]

Cinthea arrived in September, the first time she'd seen Candice, face-to-face, in two years. She barely recognized her sister.[59]

Soon it was hour by hour, a death watch. There was sacred music from many traditions, including jazz, holy to the Vadalas. Candice's intimates encircled the bed. They chanted and held her papery hands.

Out in Texas, Lauren had a vision. She saw Candice's departed kin drifting toward her across a night sky, like diamonds on indigo velvet. She saw Peggy wrap her daughter in a blanket, swaddled at last.[60]

Epilogue
Transparency

Self-portrait, c1973.

Cinthea found the cartons of diaries and letters in a closet of the Mattituck house after Candice's death. She felt certain she should destroy them. Her son was there, to help his mother and Veronica empty the place.

"Dig a hole in the garden so I can bury Candy's journals," she remembers telling him.

But he worried that some future owner of the cottage would put in a swimming pool and unearth the papers and peddle them online.

And so the pit remained undug, and the archive survived another day.[1] In time, Veronica Vera, Candice's executor, took the bold step of sending the remains of her friend's extraordinarily well-documented life into the world.

Much as she had wanted to share her story, Candice worried about the fate of her paper carapace. "What will become of it?" she asked in her journal. Would her diaries and photos "end up in junk stores & flea markets"? She had longed to speak her piece, her way, "rather than wait for strangers to paw at my memories without even knowing my name."[2]

What became of it is this.

The Papers of Candida Royalle now live among strangers, at the Schlesinger Library on the History of Women in America at Harvard Radcliffe Institute. I am but the first of those strangers to have sifted her archive, discovering her biography and her impact, but never having known her heart or her laugh—not privy, for example, to the mordant sense of humor that every person I've interviewed attests to but which is hard to glimpse on the page. You can follow me there; the collection is fully open to research, which is fitting: Candice Vadala lived a life of radical and agonized transparency. If she couldn't quite stomach a feminism that made the personal political, she practiced a pornography that made the private public. Her boundaries were porous, like the edges of a self-portrait she drew in San Francisco in 1973, in which she depicted herself as a woman reaching, arms wide enough to grab the world. The passions and perils of the twentieth century flow through her in that image, as in life.

Perhaps the greatest and most perilous of those passions was the quest for self-understanding as the center of a life well lived. Candice Vadala, like Candida Royalle, was both self-conscious and self-made. She may have looked at the sky rather than the ground, as she often told Cinthea. But mostly, she peered within. And the inward gaze never took her far enough. For even as she scoured herself, the very culture of introspection and self-perfection that inspired her quest proved, in the end, to be her prison.

"Still trying to unlock the key to myself," Candice scribbled in a makeshift journal, less than two inches square, in the summer of 2013. She was enduring her third round of chemo, following her second recurrence. And she felt trapped, in the closing act of her life, by the "dreaded, 'How did I get here?' conversation with myself."

"Myself. Myself, myself, myself, myself," she continued. She remembered wondering, as a girl, how her life might unfold, "if only Mom—or Dad—could turn all that energy outward, instead of peering deep back inside their own psyche."[3]

If only they had. If only she had: what then?

THIS BOOK HAS taken up the challenge to look outward at the sexual revolution—its achievements and its failures alike. Candice Vadala observed those seismic upheavals in technology, politics, and sensibility with the pitiless candor of a foot soldier slogging through the muck. And she insisted, against odds, on preserving the raw materials of that raw experience: a history from below. Hers was an ordinary extraordinary life, one that amply illustrated Marx's famous dictum about personal agency and impersonal forces: "Man makes his own history, but he does not make it out of the whole cloth; he does not make it out of conditions chosen by himself, but out of such as he finds close at hand."[4]

Biography asserts, at least implicitly, that if the protagonist did not fashion herself out of whole cloth, she nonetheless tailored the fabric of her world. And to be sure, Candida Royalle and Femme nudged the course of intimate life, or at least of explicit movies, toward marriage and home—toward the middle-class respectability that Candice Vadala had found, since her girlhood, just out of reach. Femme films aimed to teach their viewers less what women wanted, in Freud's tired formulation, than *that* women wanted, and should declare their desires. The company's fan mail makes clear that thousands of ordinary women leaned on Candice's voice and vision to bend the arc of their sex lives toward their own pleasure.

But pleasure turned out to be scant reward.

A history of the late twentieth century United States with Candice Vadala at its center belies the easy verities of pleasure- and danger-centered feminisms alike. Candida Royalle was no mere puppet of the adult industry, as anti-pornography absolutists would have it. She was no pimp (as MacKinnon called her), nor was she trafficked into sex work. Yet her father's perversions of the obsessions of mid-century America inflected the course of her life, encouraging her to battle with and through her body.

Candice fought for, and won, and defended, and modestly profited from, a freedom to express herself sexually that was all but unthinkable in her '50s girlhood. A person of boundless ambition and strong libido, she learned, after protracted struggle, what would make her orgasm, and she helped countless other women to do the same. But that expressive range failed to liberate her from the gendered oppressions that American women suffered then and suffer still.[5] Hungry all her life for a family founded in love, she terminated pregnancies she couldn't want, and then wanted children she couldn't have, having worked too hard and waited too long. Having wanted too much. Having failed, as she said, to find the prince Disney and *Seventeen* had promised. Consumed by body politics and the quest for equal pleasure, she largely sidestepped the American body politic and the quest for equal rights. Liberty without equality proved frail.

Still, Candice often gloried in her choices, which also contributed to her untimely death. Her most substantive contribution to women's liberation arguably came in her early twenties, during her stint with the Women's Liberation Collective of the Bronx Coalition, which offered life-saving pap smears to poor women in public housing and fought to end the war in Vietnam. It is a tragedy both of Candice's life and of second-wave feminism more broadly that the collective's aversion to lipstick and lace drove her west, toward a more hedonic and less material vision of revolution.

She knew that her victories were at best incomplete and at worst self-devouring. She was proud of having "brought porn into the homes of reluctant nice women," like the fans who wrote her abashed, adoring letters and found, in Femme's films, both a recipe for better sex and a voice with which to demand it. But it shocked her that the daughters of those *nice women* seemed "all too happy to watch the same plastic formulaic pounding dripping in your face porno that their boyfriends have been watching all along." Then they started uploading their own, outdoing each other in shamelessness and, in the process, "making it unnecessary for anyone to actually pay for work that's thoughtful and professionally made." As those brazen girls came of age with their smart phones, Femme became the victim of its own success. "We've all created a monster, me, the porno industry," Candice wrote in 2009.[6]

She had not, in fact, created the monster. But she hadn't much tamed it either. Nor had the anti-porn feminists and their sometime conservative allies. To the contrary, their media hunger fed the beast, which, as Candice wrote, had "an engine of its own." By the end of the Aughts, it was "pulling out of the station fast," moving at the speed of bytes and bots, bound for "destinations beyond our wildest imaginings."[7]

The Internet did not make pornography more profitable; best estimates put the size of the U.S. market for adult and pornographic websites at just under $1.1 billion in 2022: roughly the scale of the "billion-dollar industry" Robin Morgan had decried nearly fifty years before.[8] But the market segmentation fostered by the web has arguably made explicit material more extreme—more violent and more racist. And it has certainly made it more ubiquitous. Omnibus sites like

Pornhub and YouPorn, which stream amateur videos or pirated clips for free while raking in advertiser dollars, are among the most visited in the world. Feminist porn, fair-trade porn, ethical porn, indie porn: all loom larger as talking points than as economic forces. In the *new* Roaring Twenties, writes one critic of "raunch culture," the "United States has devolved into a *Hustler* fantasy."[9] Porn—the *plastic formulaic pounding dripping in your face* kind—won the sex wars. Handily.

"We are obsolete," Candice wrote of herself and her films around the time she first felt the symptoms of the cancer that would end her life.[10] She was self-pitying, but she was right: porn stars had faded with the twentieth century. During the brief big-screen era, she had experienced a kind of celebrity, and in the short VHS generation, she had engineered a distinctive, mediagenic career. But in the tube world, porn labor became naked gig work—a throwback to her earliest days, on the industry's bottom rung, shooting loops.[11]

While the technologies and economies of pornography have mutated wildly, the feminist critique of the world that makes porn, and the world porn makes, has changed little since the late '70s. Journalists and activists continue to be drawn to exploitation stories, long on trauma and short on subtlety. Today's anti-porn warriors, rebranded as opponents of human trafficking and sex addiction, make passionate, inflammatory, and often distorted arguments about the harms inflicted by making and by watching porn. But they have no more empathy with the flesh-and-blood lives of consenting performers than Andrea Dworkin or Catharine MacKinnon did. As sociologist Kelsy Burke notes in a recent study of the long battle over pornography in America, "Antipornography feminists must assume that they know what is best for women collectively," while imagining the particular women who choose differently as "little more than dupes."[12]

Candice thought a second generation's feminist anti-porn arguments amounted to old whine in new bottles. "Back! With a vengeance!" she scribbled in her datebook shortly before her death, after reading *Pornland* by Gail Dines, one of the neo-abolitionists, who sounded an awful lot like her foremothers.[13]

———

CANDICE'S FRIENDS ADORED HER enough to celebrate her life twice, first in New York and then in San Francisco. Stalking the archive, I went with a friend to the East Coast service, which packed the Judson Memorial Church in Greenwich Village, a pioneering space in queer and sex-positive activism through the AIDS crisis and beyond. Attendees were instructed to wear red. The only thing I owned that fit the bill was a pair of spectacles.

The crowd, several hundred strong, was as flamboyant as Candice's life would have predicted. Here were lovers and friends and family, sex radicals and pornographers, scholars and activists, neighbors and at least two complete outsiders. Dressed in dour black and gray, Claire and I stood out like a couple of dead pixels in a field of poppies.

A video montage made from Candice's photo albums traced the strange and stuttering arc of her life, over a soundtrack that included Sinatra singing "I'm Gonna Live Till I Die." The celebrants said she had done just that. Annie Sprinkle extolled the Club 90 sisterhood, "the original 'Sex and the City' girls, long before *Sex and the City*," she said. "Today most of our biggest, wildest dreams have come true." A breathy recording of Candice's voice closed the service, singing a cappella, the "Tomato Song" that she had once imagined as the opening act of a life of music. Then the mourners partook in a communion of cherry tomatoes, the last fruits of the last harvest from her last garden.[14]

As I passed out my Schlesinger Library business card, I felt a bit like a grave robber. Several testimonials had mentioned Candice's journals; Veronica Vera described folders filled with "long letters . . . beautiful letters." She took them as testimony to her friend's habits of gratitude and mindfulness.[15] To me, those unseen pages were not relics but historical documents: vital *evidence*. Even as I expressed my sympathies, I meant for the library to get the goods, so that researchers could dig Candice up and pin her down.

In the end, no skullduggery was needed; Candice refused the grave. At both memorials, the organizers gave out vials of her ashes, for friends to spread in their gardens to help grow new life, to seed the next story. The library declined the ashes. But Candice's diaries and letters and photos and films and business records are remains, too, of a life whose outlines refuse a regular shape, or an easy moral.

Janie Hamilton, the member of Club 90 who both stayed most firmly in the adult industry and who succeeded to a degree in straight films, suggested that I call this book "Victim to Victor."[16] But in truth, Candice wasn't either of those things. Like so many American inventions before her and since, she was always both.

Acknowledgments

This adult production has counted on the material and moral support of a large cast, whose efforts I gratefully acknowledge here, without shame or pseudonyms.

This is, in many ways, a story of the vital cultural work of libraries and archives. The expertise and diligence of the staff of the Schlesinger Library, and numerous others, has been as sustaining as it was crucial. Special thanks to Kathyrn Jacob, Mark Vassar, Jen Weintraub, Kelcy Shepherd, Diana Carey, Joanne Donovan, and finder-master-general Ellen Shea. Whispered thanks as well to Schlesinger's now retired and still magnificent Marilyn Dunn, friend and co-conspirator, who allowed me to live the lifelong *Mixed-Up Files of Mrs. Basil E. Frankweiler*–inspired dream of a private reading room in a shuttered library over many months of pandemic closure. Joshua Lupkin and Fred Burchsted at Harvard's Widener Library and Melinda Kent at the library of Harvard Law School provided crucial support. Staff members at the Missouri State Archives and the GLBT Historical Society in San Francisco also went above and beyond the call. Josh Cheon of Dark Materials Records supplied historic audio; Sheona MacDonald shared materials from the making of her film, *Candice.*

Fellowships from the John Simon Guggenheim Memorial Foundation, the Leon Levy Center for Biography at CUNY Graduate Center, and the Public Scholars Program of the National Endowment for the Humanities underwrote time away from the classroom to research and write.

Time *in* the classroom was generative too, and I thank especially my co-instructor Janet Halley and all the students in "Feminisms and Pornography," particularly Jordan Villegas and Martin Bernstein, who went on to provide vital research assistance and conduct generative scholarship of their own. Rachel Steely relentlessly checked quotes and citations and facts; Liz Hoveland helped with images.

I have shared parts of this work in lectures and workshops at Harvard's Program in History and Literature, Vassar College (where my older son endured the spectacle of his mother analyzing pornography), the University of Chicago, the University of Sydney, and the American Historical Association. Audience questions and feedback helped the project immensely.

Many colleagues lent their distinctive expertise to parts of the manuscript, reading drafts and answering queries: warm thanks to Beth Bailey, Tatiana Brailovskaya, John Demos, Nicholas Forester, Dan Horowitz, Kathy Jacob, Durba Mitra, Jennifer Ratner-Rosenhagen, Penny Russell, Avi Steinberg, Krithika Varagur, Laura Weinrib, and Lisa Weissman. Chris McNickle led me on a walking tour of Candice Vadala's Bronx, which lingers in memory.

Several stalwarts read the entire manuscript, some of them more than once. It is a special pleasure to acknowledge the wisdom and care of Alice Echols, Edward G. Gray, Janet Halley, Claire Bond Potter, Jill Lepore, and designated Millennial Abigail Mae MacCumber.

The astonishing kindness of Candice Vadala's survivors and friends is perhaps the greatest testament to her impact. I am grateful to everyone who sat down with me, and especially to those who shared materials from their own collections: Karen Dunaway, Richard Koldewyn, Annie Sprinkle, Janice Sukaitis, Cinthea Vadala, Veronica Vera, and the many people who told me to follow Candice's story wherever it led me.

The inimitable Tina Bennett shepherded this project to W. W. Norton and steered it over some rough ground along the way. The manuscript has benefitted immeasurably from the enthusiasm of Julia Reidhead, the acuity of Alane Mason and, at the close, from the boldness and extraordinary generosity of Melanie Tortoroli. Rachelle Mandik is the Platonic ideal of a copyeditor, and Annabel Brazaitis ably steered both book and author through the maze of production.

At its core, this book is about sisterhood: its promise, its pressures, and its peerless joys. I am grateful to Candice Vadala for having made me think so much about the sisters in my own life, born and chosen. I have leaned on Ann Kamensky since she first drew breath, and on Judith Weinstein since the seventh grade. Sue Lanser transformed my intellectual world at its sagging midpoint and has fed mind and soul ever since. I wrote much of this book, and others, in the company of Elise Broach and Jill Lepore, friends over more decades than I care to count. All these women have nourished far more than this book, which I dedicate to them, with fierce love.

Notes

ABBREVIATIONS

APP	Gerhard Peters and John T. Woolley, the American Presidency Project, https:// www.presidency.ucsb.edu/
AVN	*Adult Video News*
B-JB	Bart-Jan Brouwer
BAR	*Bay Area Reporter*
CAM Papers	Papers of Catharine A. MacKinnon, 1946–2008, SL, MC 703
CRP	Papers of Candida Royalle, 1920–2017, SL, MC 967
CR	Candida Royalle
CV	Candice Vadala
FFE Records	Records of Feminists for Free Expression, Joseph A. Labadie Collection, University of Michigan Library, Ann Arbor
GLBTHS-SF	Gay Lesbian Bisexual Trans Historical Society, San Francisco
HSUS	*Historical Statistics of the United States: Millennial Online Edition*
LAT	*Los Angeles Times*
LHJ	*Ladies' Home Journal*
MST	*Minneapolis Star and Tribune*
NOW Records	Records of the National Organization for Women, 1959–2002, SL, MC 496
NYT	*New York Times*
PS	Per Sjöstedt
SL	Arthur and Elizabeth Schlesinger Library on the History of Women in America, Harvard Radcliffe Institute, Cambridge, Massachusetts
WSJ	*Wall Street Journal*

PROLOGUE: PERSONAL APPEARANCES

1. Diary, 4 Nov 1980, CRP 45.5.
2. CR, "What's a Nice Girl Like You . . ." in Tristan Taormino et al., *The Feminist Porn Book: The Politics of Producing Pleasure* (Feminist Press, 2013), 58–69, quotation at 60.
3. Appointment book, 1979, CRP 2.3, 2–6 Oct, 11–17 Nov; Diary, 20 Feb, 11 Apr, 22–26 Oct 1980, CRP 45.5; Scrapbook, c1975–1984, CRP 54.16.
4. Diary entry, 2 Sept 1979, CRP 45.1; Diary, "Accounts" appendix, CRP 45.5; Diary, 17 Nov 1979, CRP 45.8; CV to Danny Isley, May 1980, CRP 36.9.
5. Diary, 12 Feb 1980, CRP 45.5.
6. Diary, 7 Sept 1979, CRP 45.1; *Chicago Sun-Times*, 5 Sept 1979, np, in CRP 66.1. Live shows followed screenings of *Hot and Saucy Pizza Girls*.

7. Diary, 17 Nov 1979, CRP 45.8; Diary, 4 Nov 1980, CRP 45.5; CV to PS, 12–18 Nov 1979, CRP 34.3.

8. "Theater Manager Aids Rescue," *Pittsburgh Press*, 30 May 1980, 15; "Dancer, Friend, Charged in Fires," *Pittsburgh Post-Gazette*, 17 Apr 1980, 12.

9. Diary, 6 Oct 1980, CRP 45.5.

10. Display ad, *Pittsburgh Post-Gazette*, 10 Oct 1980, 22.

11. Diary, 13 Oct 1980, CRP 45.5; author interview with Karen Dunaway.

12. Diary, 6–13 Oct 1980, CRP 45.5; author interview with Karen Dunaway; CR, "The Royalle Treatment," *Cinema X*, n.d. [Dec 1980?], CRP 106.11.

13. Diary, 19 Dec 1980, CRP 45.5.

14. Diary, 30 Nov 1980, CRP 45.5.

15. Diary, 4 Oct 1980, CRP 45.5; Diary, n.d. Jan 1981, CRP 45.9.

16. Diary, n.d. Jan 1981, CRP 45.9.

17. CV Notes for "Coming Out," unpublished essay c1979, CRP 109FB.

18. Chuck Kleinhans, "The Change from Film to Video Pornography: Implications for Analysis," in *Pornography: Film and Culture*, ed. Peter Lehman (Rutgers University Press, 2006), 157.

19. On the "sex wars," see Suzanna Danuta Walters, "Introduction: The Dangers of a Metaphor—Beyond the Battlefield in the Sex Wars," *signs* 42:1 (Sept 2016): 1–9, https://doi.org/10.1086/686750; Lisa Duggan and Nan D. Hunter, *Sex Wars: Sexual Dissent and Political Culture* (Routledge, 1995); Carolyn Bronstein and Whitney Strub, *Porno Chic and the Sex Wars: American Sexual Representation in the 1970s* (University of Massachusetts Press, 2016); and Carolyn Bronstein, *Battling Pornography: The American Feminist Anti-Pornography Movement, 1976–1986* (Cambridge University Press, 2011).

20. James Atlas, "The Loose Canon," *New Yorker*, 29 Mar 1999, 60–65.

21. John Leo, "The Revolution Is Over," *Time*, 9 Apr 1984, 74–78, 83–84.

22. Andrea Dworkin, *Woman Hating* (Dutton, 1974), 53–54. On the *Hustler* cover, see Andrea Dworkin, "Pornography and Grief" (1978), in Laura Lederer, ed., *Take Back the Night: Women on Pornography* (William Morrow, 1980), 288.

23. Deirdre English, Amber Hollibaugh, and Gayle Rubin, "Talking Sex: A Conversation on Sexuality and Feminism," *Feminist Review* 11:1 (1982): 48, https://doi.org/10.1057/fr.1982.15; Bronstein, *Battling Pornography*, 153–157.

24. Sam Roberts, "Candida Royalle, 64, Dies; Filmed Erotica for Women," *NYT*, 12 Sept 2015, A17, https://www.nytimes.com/2015/09/11/movies/candida-royalle-maker-of-x-rated-films-dies-at-64.html.

25. Tom Wolfe, "The 'Me' Decade and the Third Great Awakening," *New York*, 23 Aug 1976, 26–40, quotation at 32, ellipsis original.

26. Diary, 31 Dec 1965, CRP 41.2, emphasis mine. Royalle's sense of her diaries as proxy-selves tracks with studies of collectors: see Werner Muensterberger, *Collecting: An Unruly Passion* (Princeton University Press, 1994), 1–48; James O'Toole, "The Symbolic Significance of Archives," *American Archivist* 56:2 (1993): 234–255, https://doi.org/10.17723/aarc.56.2.e481x55xg3x04201; and Jennifer Douglas, "A Call to Rethink Archival Creation: Exploring Types of Creation in Personal Archives," *Archival Science* 18:2 (2018): 29–49, https://doi.org/10.1007/s10502-018-9285-8.

27. Diary, 3 Jul 1982, CRP 45.11.

28. "Transcript: Donald Trump's Taped Comments about Women," *NYT*, 8 Oct 2016, https://www.nytimes.com/2016/10/08/us/donald-trump-tape-transcript.html.

29. Ron Rosenbaum, "Sex Week at Yale," *The Atlantic*, Jan/Feb 2003, https://www.theatlantic.com/magazine/archive/2003/01/sex-week-at-yale/378517/.

30. Andrea O'Reilly et al., "Forum on SlutWalk," *Feminist Studies* 38:1 (2012): 245–266.
31. Andrea Dworkin, *Last Days at Hot Slit: The Radical Feminism of Andrea Dworkin*, eds. Johanna Fateman and Amy Scholder (Semiotexte, 2019).
32. Nona Willis Aronowitz, *Bad Sex: Truth, Pleasure, and an Unfinished Revolution* (Penguin Random House, 2022); Christine Emba, *Rethinking Sex: A Provocation* (Sentinel, 2022); Amia Srinivasan, *The Right to Sex: Feminism in the Twenty-First Century* (Farrar, Straus and Giroux, 2021); Lorna N. Bracewell, *Why We Lost the Sex Wars: Sexual Freedom in the #MeToo Era* (University of Minnesota Press, 2021); Maggie Nelson, *On Freedom: Four Songs of Care and Constraint* (Graywolf, 2021), esp. chapter 2.
33. Eileen Micheau to Priscilla Alexander and Paula Lichtenburg, 27 Feb 1986, NOW Records, 95.9.

CHAPTER 1: HOME

1. Diary, n.d. summer 2013, CRP 49.2; CV to Andrew James Hume, 28 Apr 2014, CRP 54.17.
2. Kenneth T. Jackson, *Crabgrass Frontier: The Suburbanization of the United States* (Oxford University Press, 1987), 232–238; Sylvia Katz, *A History of the Town of Hempstead: The 325th Anniversary of the Town of Hempstead, Nassau County, New York, 1644–1969* (Town of Hempstead, 1969).
3. Advertisement for Franklin Homes, 1941, in Paul D. Van Wie, *Franklin Square* (Arcadia Pub, 2011), 38; Leland E. Gartrell, *Profiles of Nassau County Communities: A Summary of Social, Economic, and Housing Characteristics of 94 Nassau County Communities, 1960*, vol. 1: Town of Hempstead (Protestant Council of the City of New York, 1964), 44–45.
4. CV to Andrew James Hume, 28 Apr 2014, CRP 54.17; email from Cinthea Vadala, 5 Dec 2018; author interview with Cinthea Vadala.
5. U.S. Census of 1940, Kings Cty, NY; Roll: m-t0627-02568; Page: 8A; Enumeration District: 24-877, via Ancestry.com.
6. U.S. Census of 1920, Kings Cty, NY, sheet 8572; U.S. Census of 1930, Kings Cty, NY; Page: 8B; Enumeration District: 1085; U.S. Census of 1940, Kings Cty, NY; Page: 8A; Enumeration District: 24-877, via Ancestry.com; author interview with Cinthea Vadala.
7. Author interview with Cinthea Vadala; will of Marion Vadala, 11 Apr 1970, CRP 61.10.
8. Cost: Van Wie, *Franklin Square*, 38; ownership: Nassau Cty Deeds 2309, page 189, 14 Dec 1940; and 8853, page 190, 27 Sept 1975; Office of the Nassau Cty Clerk, Mineola, NY.
9. Transcript of Jim Hume/CV conversation, 14 Nov 2014, courtesy of filmmaker Sheona McDonald.
10. Peggy June Thompson Vadala to Johnny Thompson, 29 Jan 1949, CRP 54.17.
11. Diary, n.d. summer 2013, CRP 49.2.
12. Elaine Tyler May, *Homeward Bound: American Families in the Cold War Era* (Basic Books, 1988), 135–161; Judith Walzer Leavitt, *Brought to Bed: Childbearing in America, 1750 to 1950* (Oxford University Press, 1986).
13. Grantly Dick-Read, *Childbirth without Fear: The Principles and Practice of Natural Childbirth* (Harper, 1944); "Childbirth without Fear: A Condensation from the Book," *Reader's Digest*, May 1947.
14. Peggy June Thompson Vadala to Johnny Thompson, 29 Jan 1949, CRP 54.17.
15. CV to Andrew James Hume, 28 Apr 2014, CRP 54.17.
16. Peggy Thompson birth certificate, CRP 54.17; U.S. Census of 1930, St. Louis (Independent City), MO; Page: 1A; Enumeration District: 0428, via Ancestry.com.
17. U.S. Census of 1940, St. Louis City, MO; Roll: m-t0627-02204; Page: 4B; Enumeration District: 96-575; via Ancestry.com.
18. CV notes on conversation with James Hume, 23 May 2014, CRP 54.17.

19. "Uncover Crimes after Accident," *Jefferson City Post-Tribune*, 23 Jul 1940, 1; "Charged with Driving Car without License," *Jefferson City Post-Tribune*, 27 Aug 1940, 1. On the postwar juvenile delinquency panic, see Jason Barnosky, "The Violent Years: Responses to Juvenile Crime in the 1950s," *Polity* 38:3 (2006): 314–344.

20. Theodore F. Hume's March 1943 enlistment and September 1943 separation: *U.S., World War II Army Enlistment Records, 1938–1946*, via Ancestry.com; *U.S., Department of Veterans Affairs BIRLS Death File, 1850–2010*, via Ancestry.com. For the auto theft, see "Two Stolen Autos Found; Drivers Held," *St. Louis Star and Times*, 15 Jul 1943, 25.

21. U.S. Census of 1940, St Louis City, MO; Roll: m-t0627-02204; Page: 8B; Enumeration District: 96-568, via Ancestry.com. Theodore Frank Hume and Peggy J. Thompson marriage license and bond, 15 Jan 1945, in "Arkansas, Cty Marriages, 1837–1957," FamilySearch (https://familysearch.org/ark:/61903/1:1:NMXG-BQM). On youthful marriage, see Alan Petigny, *The Permissive Society: America, 1941–1965* (Cambridge University Press, 2009), 107–115; and Beth L. Bailey, *From Front Porch to Back Seat: Courtship in Twentieth-Century America* (Johns Hopkins University Press, 1988), 43–47.

22. Hume was sentenced to four years in Algoa Intermediate Reformatory in April 1945 and transferred to the State Penitentiary in July 1946; Theodore Hume, #59588; vol. 11, p. 138; Register of Inmates Received; MO State Penitentiary, Record Group 213; MO State Archives, Jefferson City.

23. Helen Thompson, d. 22 Jul 1945, "Death Certificates 1910–1967," MO State Archives (https://www.sos.mo.gov/images/archives/deathcerts/1945/1945_00022656.PDF); Peggy June Hume vs. Theodore Frank Hume, case 92248, Oct 1945–Feb 1946, Circuit Court of St. Louis City, St. Louis City Recorder of Deeds.

CHAPTER 2: HEPCAT IN SQUARETOWN

1. "Swing Band Drummer in Bermuda Finds the Army Full of Characters," *Yank: The Army Weekly*, 2 Dec 1942, 8.

2. U.S. Census of 1940, Kings Cty, NY; Roll: m-t0627-02568; Page: 8A; Enumeration District: 24-877, via Ancestry.com. On Prima, see Garry Boulard, *Just a Gigolo: The Life and Times of Louis Prima* (Center for Louisiana Studies, University of Southwestern Louisiana). Searches of Prima discographies and of the archive maintained by the Prima estate have not turned up recordings featuring Vadala.

3. Boulard, *Just a Gigolo*, 72–75. On the selling of Italian culture more generally, see Philip Furia et al., "Frank Sinatra: Musician, Actor and Quintessential Ethnic," *Italian Americana* 19:1 (2001): 5–22; and John Gennari, "Passing for Italian," *Transition*, no. 72 (1996): 36–48, https://doi.org/10.2307/2935359.

4. "Swing Band Drummer in Bermuda Finds the Army Full of Characters."

5. Boulard, *Just a Gigolo*, 60.

6. "Swing Band Drummer in Bermuda Finds the Army Full of Characters."

7. "Lou, Fort Snelling," c1941, CRP PD.1; military service records for Louis R. Vadala in the *U.S., World War II Army Enlistment Records, 1938–1946*, via Ancestry.com.

8. Louis R. Vadala, Army discharge papers, CRP 61.9.

9. Louis Vadala to CV, 16 Jan 1976, courtesy of Cinthea Vadala.

10. "Swing Band Drummer in Bermuda Finds the Army Full of Characters."

11. Corey Goldberg, "Raymond Scott: Rediscovering the Forgotten Wit of Jazz" (MA thesis, Rutgers University, 2006), 7, 36.

12. "Music—As Written," *Billboard*, 16 Nov 1946, 31; "Music—As Written," *Billboard*, 18 Jan 1947, 30; "Music—As Written," *Billboard*, 8 Feb 1947, 34; "Television: Easter Bonnets Ogled by KSD in Forerunner of Huge Outdoor Plans," *Variety*, 9 Apr 1947, 31; "Nite Clubs—Cocktail: In Short," *Billboard*, 31 May 1947, 25.

13. Theodore Frank Hume was released from the State Penitentiary on 3 Apr 1948, Register of Inmates, #59588; vol. II, p. 138; Missouri State Penitentiary, Record Group 213; Missouri State Archives, Jefferson City.
14. "Swing Band Drummer in Bermuda Finds the Army Full of Characters."
15. Email from Cinthea Vadala, 5 Dec 2018.
16. Peggy Thompson and Louis Vadala, Affidavit for License to Marry, 14 Aug 1947; Marriage License, 14 Aug 1947; and Marriage Certificate, 18 Aug 1947; NYC Department of Records and Information Services, Municipal Archives, vol. 38, license 26179. Candice thought the marriage location signified that Peggy was pregnant; Diary, n.d. Aug 2013, CRP 49.2. But Cinthea was born in May 1948, fully nine months after the wedding. The witnesses, Angelo DiMauro and Stella Guglielmo, lived near Marion Vadala's house; DiMauro, who served in Louis's outfit in the Army, was Cinthea's godfather. Telephone conversation with Cinthea Vadala, 2 Jan 2019.
17. Peggy June Thompson Vadala to Johnny Thompson, 29 Jan 1949, CRP 54.17.
18. Transcript of Jim Hume/CV conversation, 14 Nov 2014, 27.
19. Gerald Gurin, Joseph Veroff, and Sheila Feld, *Americans View Their Mental Health* (Arno Press, 1979), 85–116.
20. Paul Goodman, *Growing up Absurd: Problems of Youth in the Organized System* (Random House, 1960), 120.
21. Rebecca L. Davis, *More Perfect Unions: The American Search for Marital Bliss* (Harvard University Press, 2010); Jill Lepore, "Fix That Marriage," *New Yorker*, 29 Mar 2010, https://www.newyorker.com/magazine/2010/03/29/fixed; Wini Breines, *Young, White, and Miserable: Growing up Female in the Fifties* (University of Chicago Press, 2001), 33–41; and May, *Homeward Bound*, 183–207.
22. Helen Gurley Brown, *Sex and the Single Girl* (Random House, 1962), 8.
23. Louis Vadala to CV, 16 Jan 1976, courtesy of Cinthea Vadala.
24. Arthur V. Dieli and Carlo Puleo, *Proverbi Siciliani/Sicilian Proverbs*, Sicilian Studies 28 (2014), 100.
25. Author interview with Cinthea Vadala.
26. CV notes on conversation with James Hume, 23 May 2014, CRP 54.17; transcript of Jim Hume/CV conversation, 14 Nov 2014, 35.
27. Author interview with Cinthea Vadala.
28. *NYT*, 29 May 1952, 45. Peggy took an apartment down the street to establish separate residences; "Agreement of Separation between Louis R. Vadala and Peggy Vadala," 13 Feb 1953, CRP 54.17.
29. CV notes on conversation with James Hume, 23 May 2014, CRP 54.17. Theodore F. Hume was sentenced to 1–10 years at the Indiana State Prison North in Mar 1955; see Indiana State Prison Prisoner's Record 28049, Volume Q, Department of Correction Indiana State Prison 1897–1966, Indianapolis, IN.
30. *Peggy Vadala vs. Louis R. Vadala, Decree of Divorce* 76704-D, October 1954, State of Missouri, City of St. Louis, CRP 54.17.
31. CV notes on conversation with James Hume, 23 May 2014, CRP 54.17.

CHAPTER 3: PETER PAN

1. Louis's residence at 325 President Street, Brooklyn, by 1952, is established by the New York Telephone Company Directory, http://archive.org/details/brooklynnewyorkc1952newy, 1367.
2. Diary, n.d. summer 2013, CRP 49.3; Diary, 20 Mar 2011, CRP 49.10.
3. Arthur V. Dieli and Carlo Puleo, *Proverbi Siciliani/Sicilian Proverbs*, Sicilian Studies 28 (2014), 72; Elaine Tyler May, *Homeward Bound: American Families in the Cold War*

Era (Basic Books, 1988), 5; Andrew J. Cherlin, *Marriage, Divorce, Remarriage* (Harvard University Press, 1992), 6, 20–23, 29.

4. Diary, 16 Jan 1970, CRP 42.3.
5. Dieli and Puleo, *Proverbi Siciliani/Sicilian Proverbs*, 118, 111.
6. Alan Petigny, *The Permissive Society: America, 1941–1965* (Cambridge University Press, 2009), 102–116; Beth L. Bailey, *Sex in the Heartland* (Harvard University Press, 1999).
7. By 1940, Helen, age twenty, was working as a typist and pulling in an estimated $1,000 a year. U.S. Census of 1940, New York, Queens, NY; Roll: m-t0627-02732; Page: 5A; Enumeration District: 41-600, via Ancestry.com; author interview with Cinthea Vadala.
8. Jim Hume/CV conversation, 14 Nov 2014, 37.
9. Diary, 20 Mar 2011, CRP 49.10.
10. Dieli and Puleo, *Proverbi Siciliani/Sicilian Proverbs*, 72.
11. Diary, 5 Sept 1990, CRP 47.4.
12. Author interview with Cinthea Vadala.
13. Author interview with Cinthea Vadala; Diary, 10 May 1969, CRP 42.1.
14. Diary entry, 19 Mar 1986, CRP 46.11; Diary, 9 Dec 1968, 10 May 1969, CRP 42.1.
15. Diary, 10 May 1969, CRP 42.1. Candice returned to the incident in later writings, and Cinthea corroborated the details. It remains unclear whether Mrs. Hennessy's home was an official foster placement or a private arrangement. For the boarding home system at midcentury, see Henrietta L. Gordon, *Casework Services for Children: Principles and Practices* (Houghton Mifflin, 1956).
16. Diary, 21 Mar 1990, CRP 47.2.
17. Author interview with Cinthea Vadala.
18. Diary entry, Mar 19, 1986, CRP 46.11.
19. Dieli and Puleo, *Proverbi Siciliani/Sicilian Proverbs*, 70–71.
20. Diary, 10 May 1969, CRP 42.1; Diary entry, 19 Mar 1986, CRP 46.11.
21. Author interview with Cinthea Vadala.
22. Marriage certificate, Louis R. Vadala and Helen F. Duffy, 15 May 1955; CRP 6.5. It is not clear how Louis and Helen were able to marry in the Church, unless he had his marriage to Peggy annulled. Marriage age: *HSUS*, Table Ae481-488.
23. Nat Hentoff, *At the Jazz Band Ball: Sixty Years on the Jazz Scene* (University of California Press, 2010), 133–135; Marc H. Miller's Queens Jazz Trail Map, http://ephemerapress .com/queens-jazz-trail.html.
24. The Vadalas' address from 1955 to 1962 is established by Queens phone books on microfilm at the NYPL. For the age of the building see https://streeteasy.com/building/20_53 -18-street-queens.
25. This demographic portrait comes from U.S. Census of 1950 data accessed through Social Explorer, http://www.socialexplorer.com/.
26. Alan Feuer, "Queens Generating Station Is a Real Hall of Power," *NYT*, 6 May 2009, https://www.nytimes.com/2009/05/07/nyregion/07rooms.html.
27. Author interview with Cinthea Vadala.
28. CV, "Something about You," 28 Feb 1961, CRP 31.7. The document is in an adult hand, perhaps dictated to a teacher.
29. CRP 35.4, CRP 35.5.
30. Author interview with Cinthea Vadala. See also Cinthea's drawing of the game in Candice's c1972 scrapbook, CRP 111FB.1.
31. Diary, 26 Sept 1966, CRP 41.4.

CHAPTER 4: AMERICAN GIRL

1. Diary, 2 Apr 1966, CRP 41.1.
2. Stephen J. Whitfield, *The Culture of the Cold War* (Johns Hopkins University Press, 1996), 89–90.
3. "Ike Urged to Ask Big A-Shelter Setup," *Newsday* (L.I.), 30 Nov 1956, 43.
4. Elaine Tyler May, *Homeward Bound: American Families in the Cold War Era* (Basic Books, 1988); Stephanie Coontz, *The Way We Never Were: American Families and the Nostalgia Trap* (Basic Books, 1992), 23–41; Andrew J. Cherlin, *Marriage, Divorce, Remarriage* (Harvard University Press, 1992), 34–43; Steven Mintz, *Huck's Raft: A History of American Childhood* (Harvard University Press, 2004), 275–308.
5. Mintz, *Huck's Raft*, 277–280; Alan Petigny, *The Permissive Society: America, 1941–1965* (Cambridge University Press, 2009), 40–44.
6. Constance J. Foster, "A Mother of Boys Says: Raise Your Girl to Be a Wife," *Parents' Magazine*, Sept 1956, 43, 44.
7. Foster, 43–44. Foster drew on the bestseller, Marynia F. Farnham and Ferdinand Lundberg, *Modern Woman: The Lost Sex* (Harper, 1947).
8. During the 1950s, Boy Scouts membership nearly quadrupled, and Girl Scouts membership more than doubled; Mintz, *Huck's Raft*, 282.
9. Survey Research Center, *Adolescent Girls: A Nation-Wide Study of Girls between Eleven and Eighteen Years of Age Made for Girls Scouts of the U.S.A* (Institute for Social Research, University of Michigan, 1957), 1–2, 6, 9, 15–16, 19, http://hdl.handle.net/2027/coo.31924013984103.
10. *Joseph Burstyn, Inc. v. Wilson*, 343 U.S. 495 (1952). On the Hays production code, see Thomas Doherty, *Pre-Code Hollywood: Sex, Immorality, and Insurrection in American Cinema, 1930–1934* (Columbia University Press, 1999); and Thomas Doherty, *Hollywood's Censor: Joseph I. Breen & the Production Code Administration* (Columbia University Press, 2007).
11. Beth L. Bailey, *Sex in the Heartland* (Harvard University Press, 1999), 39.
12. *Roth v. United States*, 354 U.S. 476 (1957), quotations at 487, 353–354. The precedent was *Thornhill v. Alabama*, 310 U.S. 88 (1940). For *Roth* elevating the "social importance" of sex, see Linda Williams, *Hard Core: Power, Pleasure, and the "Frenzy of the Visible"* (University of California Press, 1989), 95. On *Roth*, civil liberties, and national security, see Louis Menand, *The Free World: Art and Thought in the Cold War* (Farrar, Straus and Giroux, 2021), 352–354, 374–379.
13. Whitney Strub, "Perversion for Profit: Citizens for Decent Literature and the Arousal of an Antiporn Public in the 1960s," *Journal of the History of Sexuality* 15:2 (2006): 258–291, https://doi.org/10.1353/sex.2007.0013; *Dian Hanson's: The History of Men's Magazines* (Taschen, 2004), III: 12.
14. Vladimir Nabokov, *Lolita* (Putnam, 1958), 11, 18–19. Bear, *The #1 New York Times Bestseller*, 71. *Lolita* had been published in Paris in 1955.
15. Maxwell Kenton, Mason Hoffenberg, and Terry Southern, *Candy* (1958; repr., Daniel Publishing, 1965), frontispiece; Nile Southern, *The Candy Men: The Rollicking Life and Times of the Notorious Novel Candy* (Arcade, 2004).
16. Miriam Forman-Brunell, "Imagined Bobby-Soxer Babysitters and the Uses of Girls' Work Culture," in *The Girls' History and Culture Reader: The Twentieth Century*, ed. Miriam Forman-Brunell and Leslie Paris (University of Illinois Press, 2011), 242–265.
17. J. Edgar Hoover, "How Safe Is Your Daughter?" *American Magazine*, Jul 1947, 32–33, 103. Hoover's war on sex crime fueled a moral panic about homosexuality; see Gayle S. Rubin, "Thinking Sex: Notes for a Radical Theory of the Politics of Sexuality," in Carole

S. Vance, ed., *Pleasure and Danger: Exploring Female Sexuality* (Routledge, 1984), esp. 269–270. The panic about strangers obscured family sexual abuse; Lynn Sacco, *Unspeakable: Father-Daughter Incest in American History* (Johns Hopkins University Press, 2009), 214–215.

18. Elaine Tyler May, *America and the Pill: A History of Promise, Peril, and Liberation* (Basic Books, 2010); Bernard Asbell, *The Pill: A Biography of the Drug That Changed the World* (Random House, 1995).

19. Mrs. Starkey to CV, 26 Jun 1961, CRP 35.6.

CHAPTER 5: LOCK AND KEY

1. CV, "My Secret Desires," 14 Aug 1962, CRP 35.6.

2. Kim Phillips-Fein, *Fear City: New York's Fiscal Crisis and the Rise of Austerity Politics* (Metropolitan Books, 2017), 15–20; author interview with Cinthea Vadala. The building was constructed in 1961, per https://streeteasy.com/building/6485-broadway-bronx.

3. Social Explorer (https://www.socialexplorer.com/) allows comparison of the Vadalas' census tracts in Riverdale and Astoria. The average property value on their blocks was nearly equal, but in Riverdale, surrounding tracts were much wealthier. Incomes also averaged much higher Riverdale, with some 20 to 45 percent of families in adjacent tracts making over $15,000 per year, compared to no more than 4 percent of those in Astoria. In Astoria, about 50 percent of adults had completed high school; in Riverdale over 80 percent had.

4. Diary, 3 Oct 1963, CRP 40.3; Diary, 28 Sept 1969, CRP 42.2.

5. Diary, 4 Oct; 10, 11 Feb; 6 Jan; 25 Dec 1963, CRP 40.3; author interview with Cinthea Vadala.

6. Diary, 5, 12 Jan; 4 Dec 1963, CRP 40.3; Diary, 15, 18 Jan; 15, 20 Feb; 20 Dec 1964, CRP 40.5. Scheherazade role documented in a snapshot dated Jun 1963; CRP PD.3.

7. For a similar box, see advertisement for "My Private Life," *American Girl*, Jan 1954, 36; ephemera from 1964 and 1965 diaries, CRP 40.6, CRP 41.3.

8. On the daily diary, see Molly McCarthy, *The Accidental Diarist: A History of the Daily Planner in America* (University of Chicago Press, 2013). Joan Jacobs Brumberg relies on but does not analyze the genre in *The Body Project: An Intimate History of American Girls* (Random House, 1997). See also Shannon McFerran and Daniel George Scott, *The Girls' Diary Project: Writing Ourselves into Being* (University of Victoria Press, 2013).

9. *Seventeen*, Nov 1962, 197; Apr 1952, 35, among many others. Louis Menand estimates that *Seventeen* reached over 40 percent of American teen girls in the Fifties: Menand, *The Free World: Art and Thought in the Cold War* (Farrar, Straus and Giroux, 2021), 292.

10. *Seventeen*, Nov 1952, 11.

11. Bonnie J. Morris, "Before Harriet Blogged: Notes on Girls with Notebooks," *Frontiers* 38:3 (2017): 51–52.

12. Diary, 5 Feb 1963; see also 19 Mar, 2 May; CRP 40.3.

13. Martha Ravits, "To Work in the World: Anne Frank and American Literary History," *Women's Studies* 27:1 (1998): 1–30, https://doi.org/10.1080/00497878.1997.9979192.

14. Diary, 19 Mar 1964, CRP 40.5. When Candice backpacked through Europe, she made the requisite pilgrimage to the Anne Frank House in Amsterdam, Diary, 29 Jun 1971, CRP 43.3.

15. Diary, 22, 23, 24, 26 Nov 1963, CRP 40.3.

16. Diary, 7, 9, 10 Feb 1964, CRP 40.5.

17. Diary, 7 Jan; 8, 16 May (emphasis original); 7, 21, 27 Jun; 1 Aug; 19 Nov 1963, CRP 40.3.

18. Diary, 6 May 1963, CRP 40.3; Diary, 7 Feb 1964, CRP 40.5.

19. Diary, 12 Jan; 14, 20 Aug, 4, 19 Oct 1963, CRP 40.3; Diary, 6, 14 Feb; 7, 14 March 1964,

CRP 40.5. The scene reads like a postwar version of nineteenth-century "smashing" friendships; see Carroll Smith-Rosenberg, "The Female World of Love and Ritual: Relations between Women in Nineteenth-Century America," *signs* 1:1 (1975): 1–29, https://doi.org/10.1086/493203.

20. Diary, 7 Jun, 1 Aug 1963, CRP 40.3; Diary, 7, 14, 15 Mar 1964, CRP 40.5.
21. Diary, 1 Apr 1963, CRP 40.3; see also Diary, 3 Sept 1965, CRP 41.2.
22. Diary, 30 Jan; 5 May; 17, 23 Oct, 17 Dec 1963, CRP 40.3.
23. Arthur Gordon, "Six Good Reasons Why You Should Keep a Diary," *Woman's Day*, Jan 1966, 6–7.
24. Diary, 17 Mar, 27 Jun, 17 Jul 1965, CRP 41.2; Diary, 28 Apr 1969, CRP 42.1; Diary, 27 Nov 1967, CRP 41.6.
25. Autobiographical fragment, c1984, CRP 46.5.
26. Diary, 28 Sept 1963, CRP 40.3.
27. Diary, 21, 27 Jun; 1 Aug; 19, 22 Sept 1963, CRP 40.3.
28. Author interview with Cinthea Vadala, 16 Mar 2018.
29. Autobiographical fragment, c1984, CRP 46.5.
30. Sgt. Jordan Mazur, Records Access Appeals Officer at the NYPD, conducted a microform search of the Criminal Records Section's Complaint Report Index for the 50th Precinct, Sept 1963, and did not find a record. He writes, "Some of the reports were completely unreadable, and of those that could be deciphered, none were related to the incident that you inquired about. . . . It is entirely possible that the records from this incident were never turned over to the Criminal Records Section to be archived," by email to Ellen Shea, Schlesinger Library, 3 Jan 2019.
31. Diary, 16 Jul 1982, CRP 45.11; Diary, n.d. Feb 1977, CRP 44.14.
32. Diary, 26 Jan 1964, CRP 40.5.
33. Autobiographical fragment, c1984, CRP 46.5.
34. Diary, 9, 4, 12 Feb; 27, 28 March 1963, CRP 40.3.
35. Diary, 2 Feb 1966, CRP 41.4.
36. Diary, 25 Mar 1964, CRP 40.5.
37. Diary, 11 Feb 1963, CRP 40.3.
38. Louis Vadala to CV, 16 Jan 1976, courtesy of Cinthea Vadala.
39. Joan Didion, "Goodbye to All That" (1967), in *Slouching towards Bethlehem* (Farrar, Straus and Giroux, 1968), 231; see also Douglas Martin, "Lester Lanin, Bandleader of High Society, Dies at 97," *NYT*, 29 Oct 2004, C11.
40. Author interviews with Cinthea Vadala; Diary, 19 Nov 1967, CRP 41.6.
41. Diary, 10, 11 Feb; 20 Jul 1963, CRP 40.3.
42. Diary, 25 Mar 1964, CRP 40.5. For neighbors intervening, see "Candice Vadala Summary," typed report from therapist [Margo Machida?], n.d., c1972, CRP 44.3.
43. Diary, 8 Apr; 11, 13, 26, 28 May 1964, CRP 40.5.
44. For "bedroom eyes," see Maurice Zolotow, "Women and Immorality," *Cosmopolitan*, Jan 1963, 40. Cinthea comments on her resemblance to Peggy: "You know, it's almost frightening how much I looked like her growing up." Author interview with Cinthea Vadala. The daughter who resembles her absent mother is a stock figure in the literature of incestuous families: Judith Lewis Herman, *Father-Daughter Incest* (Harvard University Press, 1981), 2.
45. Diary, 8 Feb 1963, CRP 40.3.
46. Diary, 13 Jan, 6 Feb 1964, CRP 40.5; diary, 6 Apr, 22 Feb 1963, CRP 40.3.
47. Diary, 8 Jan, 2 Apr, 7 Feb 1964, CRP 40.5; Diary, 26 Dec 1963, CRP 40.3.
48. Author interview with Cinthea Vadala.
49. Diary, 13 Jan, 20 Apr 1964, CRP 40.5; author interview with Cinthea Vadala.

50. Author interview with Cinthea Vadala; Autobiographical fragment, c1984, CRP 46.5.
51. Diary, 5 Jun 1964, CRP 40.5.
52. Diary, 5 Jun 1964, CRP 40.5; author interview with Cinthea Vadala.
53. Diary, 5 Jun 1964, CRP 40.5; author interview with Cinthea Vadala.
54. Diary, 26 Jun 1964, CRP 40.5; see also Diary, 16 Oct 1970, CRP 42.5; draft, CV to Helen Vadala [unsent?], 30 Jul 1986, CRP 46.11.
55. Diary, n.d. Aug 1964; n.d., 20 Dec 1964, CRP 40.5.
56. Diary, 13 Aug 1982, CRP 45.11.
57. Helen Vadala to CV, 27 Oct 1964, CRP 35.2.
58. Diary, n.d. after Nov, 30 Dec 1964, CRP 40.5.
59. Diary, 30 Dec 1964, CRP 40.5; Jill Lepore, "The Meaning of Life," *New Yorker*, 14 May 2007.
60. Diary, n.d. Jan 1965, CRP 41.2 (emphasis original).
61. Diary, 1 Jan 1965, CRP 41.2.

CHAPTER 6: HELP!

1. Diary, 17 Sept 1965, CRP 41.2; Diary, 24 Mar 1964, CRP 40.5.
2. Diary, 8, 29 Jan; 6 Feb 1965, CRP 41.2.
3. Diary, 1 Jun 1964, CRP 40.5. When Yvonne turned up the next day with a book about "how to develop," Candy thought her prayer had been granted.
4. Notes removed from 1965 Diary, CRP 41.3.
5. Diary, 2 Jul 1965; also "Special Note," n.d., CRP 41.2.
6. Gerald Gurin, Joseph Veroff, and Sheila Feld, *Americans View Their Mental Health* (Arno Press, 1979), xx–xxiii, 255–344, esp. 278.
7. John E. Gibson, "How Neurotic Are You?" *LHJ*, Mar 1958, 47–48.
8. "Analyst's Diary," *Cosmopolitan*, May 1962, 38–43; Selma H. Fraiberg, "This Is the Way Psychotherapy Works," *Parents' Magazine*, Oct 1962, 84ff. Between 1945 and 1965, major North American women's magazines ran 975 articles on neurosis and/or psychoanalysis; search of ProQuest Women's Magazine Archive, accessed 16 Jan 2019.
9. Alan Petigny, *The Permissive Society: America, 1941–1965* (Cambridge University Press, 2009), 15–52; Nathan G. Hale, *The Rise and Crisis of Psychoanalysis in America: Freud and the Americans, 1917–1985* (Oxford University Press, 1995), II: 276–299.
10. *The Analyst* (1975), dir. Jerry Abrams, aka Zachary Strong.
11. Diary, 6 Feb, 21 Mar 1964, CRP 40.5.
12. Diary, 24 Mar 1965, CRP 41.2; CV to Liza, c Jun 1965, CRP 41.3.
13. Diary, 22 Jun 1967, CRP 41.6.
14. Autobiographical fragment, c1984, CRP 46.5.
15. Samuel Kirson Weinberg, *Incest Behavior* (Citadel Press, 1955), 38–40. Lynn Sacco notes that, "Between 1938 and 1962, not a single article examining the psychopathology of incestuous fathers appeared in the psychiatric literature," Sacco, *Unspeakable: Father-Daughter Incest in American History* (Johns Hopkins University Press, 2009), 214.
16. Autobiographical fragment, c1984, CRP 46.5. As late as the 1970s, textbooks discounted the prevalence of family sexual abuse documented in surveys and placed blame on mothers and daughters; Judith Lewis Herman, *Father-Daughter Incest* (Harvard University Press, 1981), 11–18, 36–49; Sacco, *Unspeakable*, 157–181, 189–195. For the shift from the "incest legal framework" to the notion of "father rape," see Aya Gruber, *The Feminist War on Crime: The Unexpected Role of Women's Liberation in Mass Incarceration* (University of California Press, 2020).
17. Diary, 22 Jun, 19 Nov 1967, CRP 41.6.

18. Rachel Devlin, *Relative Intimacy: Fathers, Adolescent Daughters, and Postwar American Culture*, Gender & American Culture (University of North Carolina Press, 2005).

19. Walter Neisser and Edith Neisser, *Making the Grade as Dad* (Public Affairs Committee, 1950), 1.

20. Devlin, *Relative Intimacy*, 11.

21. Neisser and Neisser, *Making the Grade*, 10, 21.

22. Devlin, *Relative Intimacy*, 141–170. Metalious published *Peyton Place* in 1956; the film adaptation was released in 1957, and the television soap opera debuted in 1964. CV loved the TV show; Diary, 16 Jan, 14 Mar, 20 Aug 1966, CRP 41.4; Diary, 10 Nov 1969, CRP 42.3.

23. Diary, 17 Dec 1971, CRP 44.1. In 1970, CV first wrote about searching for her father's approval because of having "lost him sexually": Diary, 16 Jan 1970, CRP 42.3.

24. Autobiographical fragment, c1984, CRP 46.5.

25. Diary, 12 Jul 1966, CRP 41.4.

26. Diary, 5 Sept, 24–23 Jan, 25 Feb, 24 Mar 1965, CRP 41.2.

27. Diary, 29 Jan 1965, CRP 41.2.

28. Diary, 15 Jul, 31 Dec 1965, CRP 41.2.

29. Diary, inside flyleaf and 1 Jan 1966, CRP 41.4.

30. Grace Hechinger and Fred M. Hechinger, *Teen-Age Tyranny* (William Morrow, 1963), 3; Other popular works about teen challenges included Lester D. Crow, *Adolescent Development and Adjustment* (McGraw-Hill, 1965); and James S. Coleman, *The Adolescent Society* (Free Press, 1961).

31. Louis Menand, *The Free World: Art and Thought in the Cold War* (Farrar, Straus and Giroux, 2021), 292–293.

32. John D. Black, "U.S. 'Generation Gap' Widened by Conflicts in Modern Society," *LAT*, 20 Nov 1966, F1. On the extent and timing of the change, compare Petigny, *Permissive Society*, 179–223; to Grace Palladino, *Teenagers: An American History* (Basic Books, 1996), 96–173.

33. Diary, 28 27 Jun 1965, CRP 41.2.

34. Diary, 17 Feb, 2 Apr 1966, CRP 41.4.

35. Diary, 17 Sept 1965, CRP 41.2; Diary, 12, 17 Feb; 2 Jul, 20 Aug 1966, CRP 41.4; Diary, 26 May 1967, CRP 41.6; Diary, 19 Sept 1968, CRP 42.1.

36. Diary, 19 Mar, 22 Jun, 24 Jul, 9 Nov 1967, CRP 41.6. On the downtown scene, see Steven Watson, *Factory Made: Warhol and the Sixties* (Pantheon, 2003), 250–251, 281–282.

37. Diary, 19 Apr 1966, CRP 41.4.

38. Diary, 3, 4, 6, 18 Sept; 21, 29 Oct; 19, 21 Nov 1963, CRP 40.3; Diary, 4 Apr 1964, CRP 40.5.

39. Diary, 17 Mar 1965, CRP 41.2.

40. Diary, 17 Apr 1964, CRP 40.5.

41. Diary, 17, 24 Mar; 6 Feb 1965, CRP 41.2. On the narrow channel separating prudishness from promiscuity, see Barbara Ehrenreich, *Re-Making Love: The Feminization of Sex* (Doubleday, 1986), 20; and Wini Breines, *Young, White, and Miserable: Growing up Female in the Fifties* (University of Chicago Press, 2001), 86–91.

42. Daniel Sugarman, "Love and Sex," *Seventeen*, Jul 1965, 94ff; Diary, 8 Aug 1965, CRP 41.2.

43. Diary, 29 Oct 1965, CRP 41.2; Diary, 14 Mar 1966, CRP 41.4.

44. Diary, 19 May 1966, CRP 41.4.

45. Diary, 15 Oct, 12 Nov 1966, CRP 41.4. On early computer dating, see Jill Lepore, "Fixed," *New Yorker*, 29 Mar 2010; and Rebecca L. Davis, *More Perfect Unions: The American Search for Marital Bliss* (Harvard University Press, 2010), 101–135.

46. Diary, 30 Dec 1966, CRP 41.4.

47. Diary, 1 Jan, 12 Jul 1966, CRP 41.4; Diary, 25 Feb 1967, CRP 41.6; Beth L. Bailey, *From Front Porch to Back Seat: Courtship in Twentieth-Century America* (Johns Hopkins University Press, 1988), 77–96.

48. Diary, 1 Jan 1967, CRP 41.4; "Should Birth Control Be Available to Unmarried Women?" *Good Housekeeping,* Feb 1967, 12ff; see also readers' responses, *Good Housekeeping,* May 1967, 55; and Beth L. Bailey, *Sex in the Heartland* (Harvard University Press, 1999), 110.

49. Diary, 9 Jun, 3 Jul, 29 Dec, 24 Jul, 25 Sept 1967, CRP 41.6.

50. Diary, 22 Jun, 3 Jul 1967, CRP 41.6.

51. "Anything Goes: Taboos in Twilight," *Newsweek,* 13 Nov 1967, 74.

52. Diary, 9, 27 Nov 1967, 2 Jan 1968, CRP 41.6.

53. Kathie [Amatniek] Sarachild, "Funeral Oration for the Burial of Traditional Womanhood," January 1968, in *Notes from the First Year* ([New York Radical Women], 1968), 21; see also Alice Echols, *Daring to Be Bad: Radical Feminism in America, 1967–1975* (University of Minnesota Press, 1989), 54–59.

54. Diary, 2 Jan 1968, CRP 41.6.

55. Diary, 10 Feb 1968, CRP 41.6.

CHAPTER 7: FREEDOM

1. Thomas A. Johnson, "12 Are Arrested Here," *NYT,* 5 Apr 1968, 1.

2. *voice of the women's liberation movement* 1:1 (1968); *Notes from the First Year* ([New York Radical Women], 1968).

3. Martha Weinman Lear, "The Second Feminist Wave," *NYT Magazine,* 10 Mar 1968, 24.

4. James S. Kunen, *The Strawberry Statement; Notes of a College Revolutionary* (Random House, 1969), 58. Candice pronounced the film version an "insult to James Kunen's book, which wasn't even that great in the first place"; Diary, 24 Jul 1971, CRP 43.3v.

5. Tuition in 1968–69: Diary, 24 Mar 1969, 42.1; odd jobs: Gay Pauley, "Design Duo Foresees Still Briefer Skirts, *The News* (Paterson, NJ), 3 Feb 1965, 32.

6. Diary, 19 Sept 1968, CRP 42.1; Diary, 4 Oct 1971, CRP 43.1. Average age at first marriage for white women was 20.8; *HSUS,* Table Ae481-488.

7. Diary, 11 Oct 1968, CRP 42.1; Diary, 13 Jun 1971, CRP 43.1.

8. Diary, 19 Sept 1968, reviewing the events of the summer, CRP 42.1.

9. Diary, 11 Oct 1968, CRP 42.1. On press coverage of the hippies, see Charles Perry, *The Haight Ashbury* (Wenner Books, 2005); and Terry H. Anderson, *The Movement and the Sixties* (Oxford University Press, 1996), 170–176, 242–251.

10. Diary, 19 Sept, 11 Oct 1968; 2 Jan 1969, CRP 42.1.

11. Diary, 11 Oct 1968, CRP 42.1.

12. Author interview with Joseph E. Kovacs; Scrapbook, CRP 110FB.1.

13. Diary, 11 Oct 1968, CRP 42.1.

14. Diary, 20 Oct, 6 Nov 1968, CRP 42.1.

15. Diary, 17 Oct 1968, CRP 42.1; CV to Joe Kovacs, n.d. [Oct 1968], CRP 42.2.

16. Diary, 20, 22, 27 Oct 1968, CRP 42.1.

17. Diary, 16 Nov 1968, CRP 42.1; Ilene Sondike, "Music . . . Into the Secret Places of the Soul," *The* [Stony Brook] *Statesman,* 19 Nov 1968, https://dspace.sunyconnect.suny.edu/bitstream/handle/1951/27660/Statesman, V.12, n. 19.pdf?sequence=1.

18. Diary, 16, 22 Nov; 1 Dec 1968, CRP 42.1.

19. Israel Shenker, "Good Grief—It's 'Candy' on Film," *NYT Magazine,* 11 Feb 1968, 50ff.

20. Diary, 19 Dec 1968, CRP 42.1.

21. Diary, 22 Dec 1968, CRP 42.1.

22. Diary, 11 Feb 1969, CRP 42.1.

23. Gael Green, "How Sexually Generous Should a Girl Be?" *Cosmopolitan*, May 1968. See also Alice Lake, "Teen-Agers and Sex: A Student Report," *Seventeen*, Jul 1967; and Amram Scheinfeld, "Does She or Doesn't She . . ." *Cosmopolitan*, Apr 1965, 18.

24. Diary, 11 Feb 1969, CRP 42.1.

25. Diary, 11 Feb, 19 Jan 1969, CRP 42.1.

26. James Thurber, *Is Sex Necessary? Or, Why You Feel the Way You Do* (Harper, 1929), 84–86. The digital *NYT* shows no uses of the phrase before 1937; Google ngram reveals isolated learned society journals using it in the late 1800s.

27. Wilhelm Reich, *The Sexual Revolution: Toward a Self-Regulating Character Structure* (1945; repr. Farrar, Straus and Giroux, 1974), 247, 281.

28. Christopher Turner, *Adventures in the Orgasmatron: How the Sexual Revolution Came to America* (Farrar, Straus and Giroux, 2011), 5–8, 221–224, 408–411.

29. Beth L. Bailey, *Sex in the Heartland* (Harvard University Press, 1999).

30. Whitney Strub, "Perversion for Profit: Citizens for Decent Literature and the Arousal of an Antiporn Public in the 1960s," *Journal of the History of Sexuality* 15:2 (2006): 258–291, https://doi.org/10.1353/sex.2007.0013; see also Alan Petigny, *The Permissive Society: America, 1941–1965* (Cambridge University Press, 2009), 100–133.

31. Philip Larkin, "Annus Mirabilis," *Michigan Quarterly Review* 9:3 (1970): 146; anthologized in Philip Larkin, *High Windows* (Faber and Faber, 1974), 34.

32. "David Susskind's Banned Program" (transcript), *Mademoiselle*, Oct 1963, 112, 160; Albert Ellis, *Sex without Guilt* (Wilshire Book Co, 1966), 51, 111–112.

33. Jack Gould, "Backstairs at 'Open End,'" *NYT*, 12 May 1963, X15. See also Val Adams, "'Open End' to Leave Channel 5," *NYT*, 29 April 1963, 45; Val Adams, "Channel 5 Rebuts Suskind Attack, Denies 'Harassment,'" *NYT*, 30 Apr 1963, 54.

34. Ervin Drake, "The Second Sexual Revolution," *Time*, 24 Jan 1964, 60.

35. Pearl S. Buck. "The Sexual Revolution," *LHJ*, Sept 1964, 43–45, 102; and readers' ensuing letters, "Progress and Reaction," *LHJ*, Nov 1964, 8.

36. Pearl S. Buck, "The Pill and the Teen-Age Girl," orig. pub. *Family Weekly*, Oct 1967; condensed in *Reader's Digest*, Apr 1968, 111–114.

37. "U.S. Backs Obscenity Panel," *NYT*, 25 Apr 1967, 32; Robert O. Self, *All in the Family: The Realignment of American Democracy since the 1960s* (Hill and Wang, 2012), 134–160, 189–218; and R. Marie Griffith, *Moral Combat: How Sex Divided American Christians and Fractured American Politics* (Basic Books, 2017), 121–200.

38. Quotations from U.S. Commission on Obscenity and Pornography, *Progress Report, July 1969* (1969), 1–2, 10–11, http://hdl.handle.net/2027/umn.31951d02427913r.

39. Alice Lake, "Teenagers and Sex: A Student Report," *Seventeen*, Jul 1967, 88-89. *Griswold v. Connecticut*, 381 U.S. 479 (1965) had made the discussion and distribution of contraceptives legal for married couples, but not until *Eisenstadt v. Baird*, 405 U.S.438 (1972) would unmarried women have the same constitutional protection for pregnancy limitation. The following year, the *Times* put the "Sex 'Revolution'" in scare quotes when reporting on a Kinsey Institute survey; John Leo, "Sex 'Revolution' Is Called a Myth," *NYT*, 15 Dec 1968, 82.

40. Dana Densmore, "On Celibacy," *No More Fun and Games*, Oct 1968, 25.

41. Dana Densmore, "Independence from the Sexual Revolution," in *Radical Feminism*, ed. Anne Koedt, Ellen Levine, and Anita Rapone (Quadrangle Books, 1973), 111. The essay was originally published in *Notes from the Third Year: Women's Liberation* ([New York Radical Women], [1971]), 56–61.

42. Diary, 11 Feb 1969, CRP 42.1.

43. Diary, 23 Feb 1969. CRP 42.1.

CHAPTER 8: LIBERATION

1. Joan Didion, *Slouching towards Bethlehem* (Farrar, Straus and Giroux, 1968), 84.
2. Diary, 16 Mar 1969, CRP 42.1.
3. *HSUS*, Table Bd639-652.
4. Diary, 24 Mar; 3, 4 May 1969, CRP 42.1.
5. Diary, 17 Jan, 2 Mar, 8 Apr 1969, CRP 42.1; Diary, 10 Nov 1969, CRP 42.3.
6. Diary, 15 Jan, 24 Mar 1969, CRP 42.1.
7. Diary, 24 Feb 1969, CRP 42.1. On the counterculture's opposition to the Protestant work ethic, see Sherri Cavan, *Hippies of the Haight* (New Critics Press, 1972), 85–91; Timothy Miller, *The Hippies and American Values* (University of Tennessee Press, 1991), 94–97.
8. Diary, 12, 19 Jun 1969, CRP 42.3; Scrapbook, 13 Jul 1969, CRP 110FB.1.
9. Robert O. Self, *All in the Family: The Realignment of American Democracy since the 1960s* (Hill and Wang, 2012), 25–26, 131–132; Reva Siegel, "Introduction: A Short History of Sexual Harassment," in *Directions in Sexual Harassment Law*, eds. Catharine A. MacKinnon and Reva B. Siegel (Yale University Press, 2003), 1–39; Catharine A. MacKinnon, *Sexual Harassment of Working Women: A Case of Sex Discrimination* (Yale University Press, 1979).
10. Scrapbook, 1, 5 Aug 1969, CRP 110FB.
11. Diary, 11 Aug, 26 Jun 1969, CRP 42.3; Diary, 4 May 1969, CRP 42.1. Dr. Galanter was probably Eugene H. Galanter, a cognitive psychologist who began an appointment at Columbia in 1966; https://almanac.upenn.edu/articles/eugene-galanter-psychology. He may have offered clinical hours at reduced rates to gain research data.
12. Diary, 28 Jan, 26 Feb 1969, CRP 42.1; Diary entries, n.d. Jun 1998, CRP 48.10.
13. Diary, 9, 12 Jun 1969, CRP 42.3; photographs, CRP PD.10.
14. Diary, 4 Oct 1971, CRP 43.1; Diary, n.d. Jan 1973, CRP 44.1.
15. Diary, 28 Sept 1969, CRP 42.3. For CV understanding her parents' departure as abandonment, see Diary, 4 Sept 1983, CRP 46.2.
16. CV to Helen and Louis Vadala, copied into Diary, 8 Oct 1969, CRP 42.3. On SEEK, see James Traub, *City on a Hill: Testing the American Dream at City College* (Addison-Wesley, 1994); contra Judith Summerfield et al., "The City University of New York and the Shaughnessy Legacy: Today's Scholars Talk Back," *Journal of Basic Writing* 26:2 (2007): 5–29.
17. Helen Vadala to CV, 27 Oct 1969, CRP 35.2.
18. Sketchbook, n.d. 1970, CRP 30.2.
19. Diary, 8 Apr 1969, CRP 42.1.
20. Vincent Canby, "'I Am Curious (Yellow)' from Sweden," *NYT*, 11 Mar 1969, 42; U.S. Court of Appeals for the Second Circuit, 404 F.2d 196 (2d Cir. 1968); Diary, 28 Apr 1969, CRP 42.1.
21. Diary, 20 Apr 1969, CRP 42.1.
22. Diary, 10 Mar, 8 Apr 1969, CRP 42.1.
23. Diary, 30 Apr; 18 May; 22, 24 June 1969, CRP 42.3.
24. Diary, 11 Jul 1969, 23 Jan 1970, CRP 42.3.
25. Diary, 15 Jul, 28 Sept 1969, CRP 42.3; scrapbook, 15–17, 24 Aug 1969, CRP 110FB.1.
26. Diary, 4 Sept 1969, CRP 42.3.
27. Diary, 28 Feb, 2 Mar 1970, CRP 42.3.
28. Diary, 23 Jan 1970, CRP 42.3.
29. Diary, 13, 16 Jan; 23, 28 Feb; 2 March 1970, CRP 42.3.
30. Diary, 2 Mar 1970, CRP 42.3.
31. Helen Dudar, "Women in Revolt," *Newsweek*, 23 Mar 1970. Ruth Rosen calls 1970 the

year of the "great media blitz": *The World Split Open: How the Modern Women's Movement Changed America* (Viking, 2000), xxi, 93.

32. "The Liberation of Kate Millett," *Time*, 31 Aug 1970, 20.
33. John Leonard, "Adam Takes a Ribbing; It Hurts," *NYT*, 29 Oct 1970, 41.
34. Marilyn Bender, "Books to Liberate Women," *NYT Book Review*, 8 Mar 1970, 6.
35. Diary, 11, 18 Mar 1970, CRP 42.3.
36. Vivian Gornick, "Women's Liberation: The Next Great Moment Is Theirs," *Village Voice*, 27 Nov 1969, 54. On feminisms ca 1970, see Alice Echols, *Daring to Be Bad: Radical Feminism in America, 1967–1975* (University of Minnesota Press, 1989); Rosen, *World Split Open*; and Susan Brownmiller, *In Our Time: Memoir of a Revolution* (Dial, 1999).
37. Kathie Sarachild, "A Program for Feminist 'Consciousness Raising,'" in *Notes from the Second Year: Women's Liberation* ([New York Radical Women], 1970), 78, https://repository.duke.edu/dc/wlmpc/wlmms01039.
38. Carol Hanisch, "The Personal Is Political," in *Notes from the Second Year*, 76. On the relationship between C-R and other "countercultural strategies for social revolution," see Debra Michals, "From 'Consciousness Expansion' to 'Consciousness Raising': Feminism and the Countercultural Politics of the Self," in *Imagine Nation: The American Counterculture of the 1960s and '70s*, ed. Peter Braunstein and Michael William Doyle (Routledge, 2002), 41–68.
39. Mark Naison, *White Boy: A Memoir* (Temple University Press, 2002), 134–141.
40. *CrossBronx Express*, issues 1 (Mar 1970, quoted); 3 (May 1970); 4 (Jun–Jul 1970); Amherst College Special Collections.
41. Naison, *White Boy*, 140.
42. "Women's Liberation," *CrossBronx Express*, 1 (Mar 1970), 8. The unsigned essay is likely the work of Susan Steinberg Danielson; see Barbara J. Love, *Feminists Who Changed America, 1963–1975* (University of Illinois Press, 2006), 108.
43. Virginia Blaisdell, "Freedom Is a Long Time Coming," *CrossBronx Express*, 4 (Jun–Jul 1970), 11.
44. Diary, 1 May 1970, CRP 42.3; reading list, CRP 35.6.
45. Sketchbook, n.d. 1970, CRP 30.2.
46. Diary, 1 Jan 1971; see also 13 Jun 1971, CRP 43.1; and photographs, CRP PD.10. For the feminist focus on consumer culture, see Rosen, *World Split Open*, 159–164.
47. Diary entry, 30 Jul 1970, CRP 42.4.
48. Diary, 22 May 1970, CRP 42.3.
49. Diary, 22 May 1970, CRP 42.3; Diary, 14 Jul 1970, CRP 42.4; Diary, 14 Sept 1970, CRP 43.1.
50. Diary, 22 Sept 1970, CRP 43.1; Diary, 16 Apr 1970, CRP 42.3. For SEEK's demographics, see Traub, *City on a Hill*, 69–70.
51. Diary, 1 Jan 1971, 20 Sept, 16 Oct 1970, CRP 43.1; Diary, 18 Mar 1970, CRP 42.3.
52. Dana R. Shugar, *Separatism and Women's Community* (University of Nebraska Press, 1995); and Marilyn Frye, *Some Reflections on Separatism and Power* (Tea Rose Press, 1981). Estelle Freedman mapped the long arc of separatist women's organizations in "Separatism as Strategy: Female Institution Building and American Feminism, 1870–1930," *Feminist Studies* 5:3 (1979): 512–529, https://doi.org/10.2307/3177511.
53. Diary, 1 Jan, 5 Mar, 20 Apr 1971, CRP 43.1.
54. Diary, 6, 9, 30 May 1971, CRP 43.1; Michael to CV, 15 May 1971, CRP 43.2.
55. Diary, 2 Mar 1970, CRP 42.3.
56. See, e.g., Diary, 12, 17 Feb 1966, CRP 41.4.

57. Diary, 17 Jul 1971, CRP 43.3v; Cynthia Vadala to CV, 1 Mar 1972, CRP 34.10; author interview with Joseph E. Kovacs.

58. Diary, 6 Oct 1969, CRP 42.3.

59. Bender, "Books to Liberate Women."

60. Rosen, *World Split Open*, 164–167; Echols, *Daring to Be Bad*, 210–214.

61. Self, *All in the Family*, 179.

62. Radicalesbians, "The Woman Identified Woman," in *Notes from the Third Year: Women's Liberation* ([New York Radical Women], [1971]), 81–84.

63. Ti-Grace Atkinson quoted in Anne Koedt, "Lesbianism and Feminism," in *Notes from the Third Year*, 84. On the unintended consequences of this essentialist version of female sexuality, see Echols, *Daring to Be Bad*, 218–220.

64. Diary, 23 Sept 1971.

65. Diary, 13 Jun, 30 May, 2 Sept 1971, CRP 43.1.

66. Author interview with Phyllis Rabine.

67. Author interview with Phyllis Rabine.

68. Diary, n.d. May 1971, CRP 43.1; Diary, 22 Jun 1971, CRP 43.3v.

69. Diary, 4 Oct 1971, CRP 43.1; Phyllis Rabine to CV, 12 Jul 1971, CRP 43.2; author interview with Phyllis Rabine.

70. Diary, 29 Jun 1971, CRP 43.3v.

71. Phyllis Rabine to CV, 12 Jul 1971, CRP 43.2; Diary, 6 Jul 1971, CRP 43.3v.

72. Diary, 17 Jul, 9 Aug 1971, CRP 43.3v; see also Diary, n.d. Jan 1971, CRP 44.1.

73. Diary, 2 Sept 1971, CRP 43.1; Diary, n.d. Aug 1971, CRP 43.3v.

74. Phyllis Rabine to CV, n.d. autumn 1971, CRP 43.2.

75. Diary, 2, 23 Sept; 9 Oct 1971, CRP 43.1.

76. Phyllis Rabine to CV, n.d. autumn 1971, CRP 43.2.

77. Echols, *Daring to Be Bad*, 203–242; Brownmiller, *In Our Time*, 59–80.

78. Diary, 8 Sept, n.d. Sept/Oct, 4 Oct 1971, CRP 43.1.

79. Diary, 6 Dec 1971; 24 [25] Jan, 5 Jan 1972, CRP 44.1.

80. Robin Morgan's "Goodbye to All That," which ran in *The Rat* in Feb 1970, was widely reprinted, including in Morgan's collection, *Going Too Far: The Personal Chronicle of a Feminist* (Random House, 1977), 126, 124.

CHAPTER 9: THE GOLDEN WEST AND THE GOLDEN AGE

1. Jack Kerouac, *On the Road* (Viking Press, 1957), 169–170, 205.

2. *East Village Other*, 15–30 Jul 1967, 7. Terry H. Anderson, *The Movement and the Sixties* (Oxford University Press, 1996), 176, estimates that roughly 75,000 people flocked to Haight-Ashbury in the summer of 1967. See also Charles Perry, *The Haight Ashbury* (Wenner Books, 2005), 116–235; and David Talbot, *Season of the Witch: Enchantment, Terror, and Deliverance in the City of Love* (Free Press, 2012), 90–97.

3. Joan Didion, *Slouching towards Bethlehem* (Farrar, Straus and Giroux, 1968), 85, 84; Talbot, *Season of the Witch*, 55.

4. Press release for the Human Be-In, January 1967, in Talbot, *Season of the Witch*, 22.

5. Diary, 19 Sept 1967, CRP 41.6; Diary, 10 Nov 1969, CRP 42.3.

6. Joe Kovacs to CV, n.d. Jul 1970, CRP 43.2; Diary, 2, 5, 6, 15 Aug 1970, CRP 43.1.

7. Diary, 15 Aug 1970; 7, 2 Sept 1971, CRP 43.1; Diary, 16 Oct, 1 Nov 1971, CRP 44.1. She misquotes Mitchell's "The River," from the album *Blue*, released in June 1971.

8. Diary, 5 Jan 1972, CRP 44.1; CV college transcripts, 1968–69 and 1971, CRP 50.11.

9. Diary, 3 Nov 1971, CRP 44.1; author interview with Joseph E. Kovacs; email from Joseph Kovacs, 4 Mar 2019.

10. Diary, 11 Jan 1972, CRP 44.1. Marion Vadala died 25 July 1970; see Diary, 30 Jul 1970, CRP 43.1; Marion Vadala Will, 11 Apr 1970, CRP 61.10.
11. Author interview with Sherry Falek; Diary, 22, 24–25 Jan 1972, CRP 44.1.
12. Armistead Maupin, *Tales of the City* (Harper, 1978), 56.
13. Adrian Brooks, *Flights of Angels: My Life with the Angels of Light* (Arsenal Pulp Press, 2008), 45–46; Alice Echols, *Hot Stuff: Disco and the Remaking of American Culture* (W. W. Norton, 2010).
14. Josh Sides, *Erotic City: Sexual Revolutions and the Making of Modern San Francisco* (Oxford University Press, 2009), 46–53; Peter Alilunas, *Smutty Little Movies: The Creation and Regulation of Adult Video* (University of California Press, 2016), 131.
15. *A Report on Non-Victim Crime in San Francisco* (San Francisco Committee on Crime, 1971), 5, 7, http://archive.org/details/reportonnonvicti1971sanf.
16. Sides, *Erotic City*, 70–73, 86–88; Talbot, *Season of the Witch*, 104; Nan Alamilla Boyd, *Wide Open Town: A History of Queer San Francisco to 1965* (University of California Press, 2003); and Joseph Lam Duong, "San Francisco and the Politics of Hardcore," in *Sex Scene: Media and the Sexual Revolution*, ed. Eric Schaefer (Duke University Press, 2014), 297–318.
17. *The Marketplace: The Industry*, vol. 3, Technical Report of the Commission on Obscenity and Pornography (U.S. Government Printing Office, 1968–70), 34, 23, 31. On the sexual exploitation genre, see Eric Schaefer, *"Bold! Daring! Shocking! True!": A History of Exploitation Films, 1919–1959* (Duke University Press, 1999).
18. *The Marketplace: The Industry*, 48–49.
19. William Murray, "The Porn Capital of America," *NYT Magazine*, 3 Jan 1971, 8ff.
20. Duong, "San Francisco and the Politics of Hardcore"; see also "Erotic Flicks for Erotic Heads," *Berkeley Barb*, 24–30 Jul 1970, 19.
21. "Pornography, 1970," Joseph L. Alioto Papers, 1958–1977, box 5, folder 38, SF History Center, SF Public Library. See also (Feinstein's?) unsigned report to the Board of Supervisors, 5 Feb 1971; copy in Arlene Elster Papers, box II, folder 14, GLBTHS-SF.
22. Sides, *Erotic City*, 51–53; and Whitney Strub, *Perversion for Profit: The Politics of Pornography and the Rise of the New Right* (Columbia University Press, 2011), 123ff. For Proposition 18 and related polling, see Paul Avery, "Poll Shows 1 in 4 Want Porno Ban," *SF Chronicle*, 26 Apr 1972, 2; "The People's Fight against Pornography" (full-page ad), *SF Chronicle*, 6 Nov 1972, 24; and the paper's report on the proposition's defeat, 8 Nov 1972, 5C.
23. *The Marketplace: Empirical Studies*, vol. 4, Technical Report of the Commission on Obscenity and Pornography (U.S. Government Printing Office, 1968–70), 219–220, 160, 163.
24. SF ["Non-Victim"] Crime Commission [1974], 4–6, Records of COYOTE, SL, box 9, folder 459.
25. Debra Michals, "From 'Consciousness Expansion' to 'Consciousness Raising': Feminism and the Countercultural Politics of the Self," in *Imagine Nation: The American Counterculture of the 1960s and '70s*, ed. Peter Braunstein and Michael William Doyle (Routledge, 2002); and Beth Bailey, "Sex as a Weapon: Underground Comix and the Paradox of Liberation," in *Imagine Nation*, 305–324.
26. *Mushroom Effect: A Directory of Women's Liberation* (1970); Directories Ephemera, GLBTHS-SF.
27. *The People's Yellow Pages*, second edition (1972), quotation at 12; Directories Ephemera, GLBTHS-SF. On the Therapeutic Abortion Act of 1967, see Brian Pendleton, "The California Therapeutic Abortion Act: An Analysis," *Hastings Law Journal* 19:1 (1967): 242–255; and Robert O. Self, *All in the Family: The Realignment of American Democracy since the 1960s* (Hill and Wang, 2012), 143.
28. Carolyn See, *Blue Money: Pornography and the Pornographers* (McKay, 1974), 109.

29. Joseph W. Slade, "The Porn Market and Porn Formulas: The Feature Film of the Seventies," *Journal of Popular Film* 6:2 (1977): 180, https://doi.org/10.1080/00472719.1977.10661833.

30. Ralph Blumenthal, "Porno Chic," *NYT Magazine*, 21 Jan 1973, 28.

31. "Picture Grosses," *Variety*, 14 Jun 1972, 8.

32. "Picture Grosses," *Variety*, 21 Jun 1972, 8; Andy Newman, "A Publisher Who Took the Romance Out of Sex, Dies at 77," *NYT*, 20 Dec 2013, A1.

33. "50 Top-Grossing Films, Week Ending June 21," *Variety*, 28 Jun 1972, 9; " 'The Candidate' Keeps No. 1 Status In New York," *Boxoffice*, 17 Jul 1972, E2. The *NY Daily News* advertised it only as *Throat*; see "N.Y. News Sticks to 'Deep Throat' Nix," *Variety*, 2 Aug 1972, 6.

34. Michael Gartner, "A Kind Word or Two about Smut," *WSJ*, 15 Sept 1972, 12.

35. Paul L. Montgomery, "Johns Hopkins Professor Lauds 'Throat' as a 'Cleansing' Film," *NYT*, 3 Jan 1973, 46.

36. Kathleen Carroll, "X-Rated Movies Lure G-Rated Audiences," *NY Daily News*, 25 Feb 1973, C25.

37. Vincent Canby, "What Are We to Think of 'Deep Throat'?" *NYT*, 21 Jan 1973, 1.

38. Blumenthal, "Porno Chic"; Eric Schlosser, *Reefer Madness: Sex, Drugs, and Cheap Labor in the American Black Market* (Houghton Mifflin, 2003), 131. Tom Wolfe's "Radical Chic: That Party at Lenny's," ran in *New York*, 8 Jun 1970.

39. Nora Ephron, "Women," *Esquire*, Feb 1973, 14. For feminist responses to *Deep Throat*, see also Carolyn Bronstein, *Battling Pornography: The American Feminist Anti-Pornography Movement, 1976–1986* (Cambridge University Press, 2011), 78–82.

40. See e.g., "Pastor Renews 'Deep Throat' Protest," *Pittsburgh Press*, 15 May 1973, 2; "Pickets Protest 'Deep Throat,' " *St. Petersburg Times* (FL), 9 Sept 1973, 1B.

41. John Hubner, *Bottom Feeders: From Free Love to Hard Core: The Rise and Fall of Counter-Culture Gurus Jim and Artie Mitchell* (Doubleday, 1993), 162–224.

42. Advertisement, *NYT*, 28 Mar 1973, 34.

43. Quoted in Devin Thomas McGeehan Muchmore, *The Business of Sex: A Queer History of Pornography and Commercial Culture in 1970s America* (PhD dissertation, Yale University, 2018), 15.

44. Richard Nixon, "Statement About the Report of the Commission on Obscenity and Pornography," 24 Oct 1970, APP, https://www.presidency.ucsb.edu/documents/statement-about-the-report-the-commission-obscenity-and-pornography.

45. Whitney Strub, "Perversion for Profit: Citizens for Decent Literature and the Arousal of an Antiporn Public in the 1960s," *Journal of the History of Sexuality* 15:2 (2006): 258–291, https://doi.org/10.1353/sex.2007.0013, esp. 284–287; see also, Earl M. Maltz, *The Coming of the Nixon Court: The 1972 Term and the Transformation of Constitutional Law* (University Press of Kansas, 2016); and Kevin J. McMahon, *Nixon's Court: His Challenge to Judicial Liberalism and Its Political Consequences* (University of Chicago Press, 2011).

46. The five cases were *Miller v. California, Paris Adult Theater I v. Slaton, Kaplan v. California, United States v. 12 200-ft Reels of Super 8mm Film*, and *United States v. Orito*. Opinions in each, and a sampling of oral arguments, can be found at https://www.oyez.org/.

47. Email from Janice Sukaitis, 11 Jul 2019 (quoted); email from Theresa McGinley, 5 Jul 2019; email from Jorgé Socarras, 5 Jul 2019.

CHAPTER 10: BECOMING

1. Diary, [27], 24–25 Jan 1972, CRP 44.1.

2. Diary, 10 Nov; 6 Dec 1971; [27, 28?] Jan, 4 Feb 1972, CRP 44.1.

3. Tuli Kupferberg, "The Coming Age of Catastrophic Leisure," in Joseph H. Berke, ed., *Counter Culture* (Peter Owen Ltd, 1969), 85.

4. Sherri Cavan, *Hippies of the Haight* (New Critics Press, 1972), 70 (quoted), 93–97, 106–107;

see also Timothy Miller, *The Hippies and American Values* (University of Tennessee Press, 1991), 95–97.

5. Diary, n.d. Feb/Mar, 4 Feb 1972, CRP 44.1. On hip costume, see Cavan, *Hippies of the Haight*, 49–50.

6. Author interview with Sherry Falek; "Hashbury" in Hunter S. Thompson, "The 'Hashbury' Is the Capital of the Hippies," *NYT Magazine*, 14 May 1967, 14.

7. On Buena Vista Park, see Allan Bérubé, "The History of Gay Bathhouses," *Journal of Homosexuality* 44: 3–4 (2003): 49, https://doi.org/10.1300/J082v44n03_03. Theresa McGinley says Candice and her friends hung out on the flats; by email, 26 Feb 2019.

8. Diary, 4 Feb 1972, CRP 44.1; "Belveweird Freakos" on postcard from Candice, summer 1972, Scrapbook, CRP 111FB.1

9. Diary, [27] Jan, 4 Feb, 3 Apr, 19 Mar 1972, CRP 44.1.

10. Diary, 19 Mar 1972, CRP 44.1; undated notes [Sept 1972?], in Scrapbook, CRP 111FB.1

11. Diary, n.d. Feb/Mar 1972, CRP 44.1.

12. Diary, n.d. summer 1972, CRP 44.1; author interview with Sherry Falek.

13. Diary, 17 Sept 1970, CRP 43.1.

14. Therapy summary, c1971–1972, CRP 44.3. The author was almost certainly Margo Machida, whom CV had started seeing in Nov 1971.

15. Diary, 24 Jan; 2, 17 Mar; 15, 22 Feb 1972, CRP 44.1.

16. Tom Wolfe, *The Electric Kool-Aid Acid Test* (Farrar, Straus and Giroux, 1968), 9.

17. Charles Perry, *The Haight Ashbury* (Wenner Books, 2005), 40–47.

18. "A Mind Drug Suddenly Spells Danger LSD," and Albert Rosenfeld, "The Vital Facts about the Drug and Its Effects," *Life*, 25 Mar 1966, 29, 30; Perry, *The Haight Ashbury*, 84; David Farber, "The Intoxicated State/Illegal Nation: Drugs in the Sixties Counterculture," in *Imagine Nation: The American Counterculture of the 1960s and '70s*, ed. Peter Braunstein and Michael William Doyle (Routledge, 2002), 17–40.

19. Author interviews with Sherry Falek, Richard "Scrumbly" Koldewyn, and Joseph E. Kovacs. See also Joshua Gamson, *The Fabulous Sylvester: The Legend, the Music, the Seventies in San Francisco* (Holt, 2005), 55.

20. Author interview with Jorgé Socarras; author interview with Richard Koldewyn; David Talbot, *Season of the Witch: Enchantment, Terror, and Deliverance in the City of Love* (Free Press, 2012), 107–126. The undated drawing appears in Diary, CRP 44.1.

21. Diary, 3, 22 Feb, n.d. Feb/Mar 1972, CRP 44.1; Scrapbook, CRP 111FB.1; Sketchbooks, 1972–1973, CRP 30.3–30.5.

22. Diary, 4 Oct 1971, CRP 43.1; Scrapbook, n.d. 1972–1973, CRP 111FB.1.

23. Diary, 19 Jun, 26 Dec, n.d. Apr, 15 Nov 1972, CRP 44.1; Cinthea Vadala to CV, 13 Nov 1972, CRP 34.10.

24. Author interview with Joseph E. Kovacs; author interview with Sherry Falek.

25. Diary, 26 December 1972, CRP 44.1. There has been almost no historical work done on Transactional Analysis. See Thomas A. Harris, *I'm OK, You're OK; a Practical Guide to Transactional Analysis* (Harper & Row, 1969), esp. xvi–xvii on the technique's growth in California. After two years of slow sales, the book achieved mass success when the paperback was issued in 1972, spending twenty-three weeks atop the *NYT* bestseller list; John Bear, *The #1 New York Times Bestseller: Intriguing Facts about the 484 Books That Have Been #1 New York Times Bestsellers since the First List in 1942* (Ten Speed Press, 1992), 124. For evidence Candice read Harris, see Diary, 3 Feb, n.d. Aug 1973, CRP 44.1; Cinthea Vadala to CV, 21 Nov 1975, CRP 34.11.

26. CV to Roseanne Slomowitz, in Diary, 14 Jan 1973, CRP 44.1; see also Roseanne Slomowitz to CV, 25 Nov 1972, CRP 35.7.

27. Sketchbook, 1972, CRP 30.4.

28. Wolfe, "The 'Me' Decade," 38.
29. Beth Bailey, "Sex as a Weapon: Underground Comix and the Paradox of Liberation," in *Imagine Nation*, 305–324; Gretchen Lemke-Santangelo, *Daughters of Aquarius: Women of the Sixties Counterculture* (University Press of Kansas, 2009), 59–85.
30. Diary, [28?] Jan 1972, CRP 44.1.
31. Diary, 22 Feb 1972, CRP 44.1. Cyn was also involved with Joe Merlino; see Helen Vadala to CV, 12 Mar 1972, CRP 35.2; Cinthea Vadala to CV, 1 Mar 1972, CRP 34.10; CV to Cinthea Vadala, 15 Nov 1980, CRP 34.12.
32. Author interview with Jorgé Socarras; author interview with Joseph E. Kovacs.
33. Diary, 2 Mar, 3 Apr 1972, CRP 44.1. On rape fantasies, see *ibid.*, 17, 19 Dec 1971; Diary, 6 May 1971, CRP 43.1.
34. Diary, 10 Apr 1972, CRP 44.1; Diary, 21 Oct 1970, CRP 43.1.
35. CDC, Family Planning Evaluation Division, *Abortion Surveillance: 1972, Issued April 1974* (CDC/U.S. Department of Health, Education, and Welfare, 1974).
36. Diary, 10, n.d. Apr 1972, CRP 44.1; *HSUS*, tables Ae481–488, Ab536–565.
37. Diary, n.d. summer 1972, CRP 44.1; author interview with Jorgé Socarras. For The Stud, see: https://markhfreeman.wordpress.com/the-stud-decade-by-decade/.
38. CV to Sari Goodman, 22 Apr 1973, CRP 36.1.
39. Diary, 15 Nov 1972, CRP 44.1.
40. Author interview with Phyllis Rabine.
41. Diary, 29 Dec 1972, CRP 44.1.
42. Diary, 5 Jan, 18 May, n.d. Aug, n.d. summer 1973, CRP 44.1.
43. Diary, 16, n.d. Oct 1973, CRP 44.1; Diary, 27 Jan 1974, CRP 44.7.
44. Diary, 10 Dec 1973, CRP 44.1; author interview with Richard Koldewyn; author interview with Jorgé Socarras; Danny Isley to CV, 10 Aug 1976, CRP 36.5.
45. Diary, 10, 28, 17 Dec 1973, CRP 44.1.
46. Diary, n.d. Oct 1973, CRP 44.1.

CHAPTER 11: MAKING ART AND GETTING BY
1. Author interview with Jorgé Socarras; email from Jorgé Socarras, 22 Mar 2019; author interview with Richard Koldewyn.
2. Diary, 30 Nov, 11 Dec 1971, CRP 44.1; see also Susan Sklar to CV, 10 Oct 1972, CRP 35.7.
3. Diary, 10 Sept 1972, 3 Feb 1973, CRP 44.1. On plans for art school, see also Helen Vadala to CV, 4 Sept 1972; Helen Vadala to CV, 15 Oct 1972; CRP 35.2. Helen's letters imply that CV also applied to Berkeley, though I have found no confirmation. On Engel, see https://web.archive.org/web/20050207131715/http://www.netropolitan.org/engel/engel_main.html.
4. Louis Vadala to CV, 16 Jan 1976, courtesy of Cinthea Valada.
5. Diary, essay draft, n.d. [Feb?] 1973, CRP 44.1.
6. Diary, n.d. summer 1973, 29 Dec 1972, 27 Jul 1973, CRP 44.1.
7. Diary, 18 Jul 1974, recalling the previous summer, CRP 44.4; Adrian Brooks, *Flights of Angels: My Life with the Angels of Light* (Arsenal Pulp Press, 2008), 18.
8. Diary, n.d. summer 1973, CRP 44.1; Janice Sukaitis, "The Tomato Song," in "Notes on Patrick Cowley & Candida Royalle," booklet accompanying *Candida Cosmica* (Dark Entries Records, 2016). Janice Sukaitis has shared with me her recollections of the Angels' sexism; personal communications. On camp, see Susan Sontag's germinal essay, "Notes on 'Camp,'" *Partisan Review* 31:4 (1964): 515–530, esp. 519.
9. Diary, 1 Aug, 2 Nov, 28 Dec 1973, see also 30 Nov 1973, CRP 44.1.
10. Author interview with Richard Koldewyn; author interview with Jorgé Socarras.
11. Patrick was likely part of the San Francisco Sinthetics, a group born in Candice's "very

own kitchen" in late 1973; Diary, 11 Dec 1973, CRP 44.1. Some of Candice's recordings with Cowley were released in 2016 as *Candida Cosmica*, https://patrickcowley.bandcamp .com/album/candida-cosmica.

12. Diary, 2, 13 Nov 1973, CRP 44.1. Laurie Ann Detgen had "survived on the streets since she was fourteen"; Delores DeLuce, *My Life, a Four-Letter Word: Confessions of a Counter Culture Diva* (Double Delinquent Press, 2013), 154.

13. Company list for *Rickets*, Jul 1974, CRP, 61.1.

14. Janice Sukaitis, "Notes on White Trash Boom Boom," ms shared with me; interview with Theresa McGinley; see also DeLuce, *My Life*, 154–156. Josh Cheon, a San Francisco DJ and the creator of the record label Dark Entries, shared digital copies of the tapes with me. Dolores DeLuce and Karen Dunaway were also part of White Trash Boom Boom.

15. Diary, 13 Nov 1973, CRP 44.1; Jon Sugar, "Cocaine for Christ: The Bobby Kent Story," *BAR*, 28 Mar 1985, 33–34.

16. Diary, 30 Nov 1973, CRP 44.1; photograph of the Gospel Pearls, c1973, in CRP PD.14.

17. Diary, n.d., 24 Dec 1973, CRP 44.1; author interview with Richard Koldewyn.

18. Diary, 29 Dec 1973, CRP 44.1; "New Year's Eve at Bimbo's," *BAR*, 9 Jan 1974, 16.

19. Diary, 1 Jan 1974, CRP 44.1.

20. Helen Vadala to CV, 12 Mar 1972, CRP 35.2.

21. In his *Chronicle* column of 13 Feb 1972, Herb Caen attributed the quote to Jerry Johnstone; *The Best of Herb Caen, 1960–1975* (Chronicle Books, 1991), 215.

22. For San Francisco homicides, see *San Francisco Police Department Annual Report: 1974* (SFPD, 1974); for New York, see Kim Phillips-Fein, *Fear City: New York's Fiscal Crisis and the Rise of Austerity Politics* (Metropolitan Books, 2017), 33.

23. Author interview with Jorgé Socarras; email from Jorgé Socarras, 30 Mar 2019.

24. Diary, n.d. Sept/Oct 1973, CRP 44.1; DeLuce, *My Life*, 137. For relative values of historical dollars, see https://www.measuringworth.com/index.php.

25. Raymond Mungo, *Total Loss Farm* (1970), 105, quoted in Timothy Miller, *The Hippies and American Values* (University of Tennessee Press, 1991), 95.

26. Sherri Cavan, *Hippies of the Haight* (New Critics Press, 1972), 87–91.

27. Diary, 10 Feb 1974, CRP 44.7; Diary, n.d. summer 1972; n.d. Sept/Oct, n.d. Jan/Feb 1973, CRP 44.1.

28. Author interview with Sherry Falek; author interview with Richard Koldewyn.

29. Diary, 4 May 1974, CRP 44.7; Diary, 18 Jul 1974, CRP 44.4.

30. DeLuce, *My Life*, 156; Janice Sukaitis, "Rickets, A Day in the Life of the Counter Culture," ms shared with me.

31. Author interview with Richard Koldewyn. A partial recording of *Rickets*, from a community radio program in 1978, is held in the Kevin Burke Collection of the GLBTHS-SF.

32. "Rickets Chases the Blues Away," *San Francisco Phoenix*, clipping, n.d. Nov 1974, from Scrumbly Koldewyn's collection.

33. Sukaitis, "Rickets"; "Rickets," *BAR*, 13 Nov 1974, 19.

34. Diary, 4 May 1974, CRP 44.7; Diary, 4 Jul 1974, CRP 44.4.

35. Eileen Boris, *Caring for America: Home Health Workers in the Shadow of the Welfare State* (Oxford University Press, 2012), 97–99. As governor, Reagan substantially continued the welfare policies of Pat Brown's liberal administration; see Peter Schrag, *California: America's High-Stakes Experiment* (University of California Press, 2006), 97–99.

36. Abbie Hoffman, *Steal This Book* (Pirate Editions; dist. Grove Press, 1971), chapter 10.

37. *San Francisco Survival Manual* ([Page Street Survival House], c1975, n.p.; in Directories Ephemera, GLBTHS-SF; John Waters quoted in Joshua Gamson, *The Fabulous Sylvester: The Legend, the Music, the Seventies in San Francisco* (Henry Holt, 2005), 55.

38. Author interview with Theresa McGinley; author interview with Richard Koldewyn.

39. Cynthia Vadala to CV, 23 Aug 1972, CRP 34.10.

40. Diagnosis signed by Lana Lincoln RN, Nov 1973, CRP, 54.2.

41. Email from Jorgé Socarras, 30 Mar 2019.

42. Diary, n.d. late Feb 1974, CRP 44.7; Diary, 21 Nov 1973, CRP 44.1; ATD benefits notices, 5 Feb, 25 Mar 1974, CRP 54.2.

43. Diary, 3, 24 Mar; 4 Apr; 27 Mar; 17 Apr 1974, CRP 44.7. On welfare politics in California, see Boris, *Caring for America* esp. chapter 5; and Sharon Perlman Krefetz, *Welfare Policy Making and City Politics* (Praeger, 1976), 152–184.

44. Diary, 17 Apr 1974, CRP 44.7.

45. Appointment book, 1974, 26 Mar, CRP 1.9.

46. Carol Leigh, aka Scarlot Harlot, "Inventing Sex Work," in Jill Nagle, ed., *Whores and Other Feminists* (Routledge, 1997), 230; see also Frédérique Delacoste and Priscilla Alexander, eds., *Sex Work: Writings by Women in the Sex Industry* (Cleis Press, 1987); and Heather Berg, *Porn Work: Sex, Labor, and Late Capitalism* (Duke University Press, 2021).

47. Candida Royalle, "Porn in the USA" (c1991–1993), in Drucilla Cornell, *Feminism and Pornography* (Oxford University Press, 2000), 542.

48. *A Report on Non-Victim Crime in San Francisco*, 13, 14, 45.

49. Ralph Craib, "Hookers of the World, Unite!" *SF Chronicle*, 29 May 1973, 2; Appointment book, 1975, CRP 1.10, 28 Oct. See also Valerie Jenness, "From Sex as Sin to Sex as Work: COYOTE and the Reorganization of Prostitution as a Social Problem," *Social Problems* 37:3 (1990): 403–420, https://doi.org/10.2307/800751.

50. David Haldane, "A Chance Encounter," *Berkeley Barb*, 8–14 Feb 1974, 15. Advertisements for Kitten's Nude Encounter Parlor, at 456 Broadway, first appeared in Mar 1973; see *Independent Voices: An Open Access Collection of an Alternative Press*, online database. Jackie D's, in the Tenderloin, also featured nude encounter; see *BAR*, 6 Feb 1974, 5.

51. Author interview with Jorgé Socarras.

52. Diary, n.d. Aug, n.d. Sept/Oct 1973, CRP 44.1; Helen Vadala to CV, 25 Oct 1973, CRP 35.2.

53. Diary, 16 Jan, n.d. Jan 1974, CRP 44.7. See also Cynthia Vadala to CV, 21 Nov 1973; Cynthia Vadala to CV, 18 Dec 1973, CRP 34.10.

54. Diary, 3 Feb, n.d. spring 1974, CRP 44.7. For documentation of the marriage, see CRP 31.8. Candice petitioned the INS to naturalize her husband in April 1974.

55. Thadeusz S. Puchacz to CV, 4 Nov 1974; CV to Thadeusz S. Puchacz, 5 Dec 1974, CRP 36.3. The divorce was granted on 23 Jan 1975; see CRP 31.8. Candice had stayed with Sherry Falek in New York when she came for the failed interview; author interview with Sherry Falek.

56. See e.g., Diary, 18 Apr; 4, 13 May 1974, CRP 44.7. CV's datebooks from 1974 and 1975 show regular modeling appointments, some at night; CRP 1.9, 1.10.

57. Diary, 28 Jan 1974, CRP 44.7; Helen Vadala to CV, 12 Mar 1974, CRP 35.2; see also Cinthea Vadala to CV, 15 Jan 1974, CRP 34.11.

58. Email from Janice Sukaitis, 31 Mar 2019.

59. Author interview with Jorgé Socarras; see also Allan Bérubé, "The History of Gay Bathhouses," *Journal of Homosexuality* 44: 3–4 (2003). On gay male "public sex" more broadly, see Patrick Califia, *Public Sex: The Culture of Radical Sex* (Cleis Press, 2000), 14–27.

60. Author interview with Sherry Falek; author interview with Richard Koldewyn.

61. Diary, n.d. summer 1972, CRP 44.1.

62. Helen Vadala to CV, 30 Jun 1974, CRP 35.2; see also Peter Schweingruber to CV, 15 Dec 1973, CRP 36.2.

63. "Underground Explosion," *Vector* [December 1973?], 38, in Scrapbook, CRP 111FB.1; author interview with Janice Sukaitis; author interview with Richard Koldweyn.
64. Appointment book, 1974, 26 Mar, CRP 1.9.
65. "Game of Lust," n.d. (1975?), Debauchery Films #2, collected in Blue Vanities, DVD 257: *Peepshow Loops, c1970s*. Loops are audio visual ephemera, without theatrical release, reviews, or credits, and so rarely can be dated.
66. CR, "Vertical Smiles and Cum-Soaked Aisles: Confessions of a Porn Queen," *High Times*, Jul 1982, 40–41, 67; "Making Dirty Movies for Fun and Profit," *Washington Post*, 6 Jun 1971, K3. On the history and technology of loops, see also William Rotsler, *Contemporary Erotic Cinema* (Ballantine Books, 1973), 69–70; Peter Alilunas, *Smutty Little Movies: The Creation and Regulation of Adult Video* (University of California Press, 2016), 43–48; Patchen Barss, *The Erotic Engine* (Doubleday Canada, 2010), 79–80.
67. Appointment book, 1975, 6, 14, 17, 21–23, 27, 29 Aug; see also 28 Oct, 24 Nov, CRP 1.10.
68. *The Analyst* (also *The Analist* or *Fill All My Holes*) (1975), dir. Jerry Abrams; Alilunas, *Smutty Little Movies*, 133–135.
69. CV letter to Carl Esser, 2 Feb 1981, CRP 36.10. In later interviews, Royalle refused to talk about *The Analyst*, because she didn't "like to give the movie any promotion"; "Candida Royalle: Femme," in Jill C. Nelson, *Golden Goddesses: 25 Legendary Women of Classic Erotic Cinema 1968–1985* (Bear Manor Media, 2012), 236.
70. William Murray, "The Porn Capital of America," *NYT Magazine*, 3 Jan 1971, 22–23; *SF Chronicle*, 28 May 1976, 51, among many others. See also Eric Schaefer and Eithne Johnson, "Open Your Golden Gates: Sexually Oriented Film and Video," in *Radical Light: Alternative Film & Video in the San Francisco Bay Area, 1945–2000* (University of California Press, 2010), 192.
71. Diary, n.d. 1975, CRP 44.9; Appointment book, 1975, 15–16 Sept, CRP 1.10.

CHAPTER 12: HEARTBREAK

1. Diary, 10 Aug 1974, CRP 44.6.
2. Author interview with Janice Sukaitis.
3. Diary, n.d. May–Jun 1974, CRP 44.7.
4. Diary, n.d. Feb, 13 May, 18 Jul, n.d. May 1974, CRP 44.7.
5. Diary, 10 Aug 1974, CRP 44.6; Diary, 27 Sept 1974, CRP 44.9.
6. *Cry for Cindy* (1976), dir. Wendy Lions (pseud. for Anthony Spinelli).
7. *Bay Area Guardian*, 14 Nov 1975.
8. Author interviews with Scrumbly Koldewyn, Janice Sukaitis, and Karen Dunaway.
9. Diary, 22 May 1975, CRP 44.9.
10. Diary, 27 Sept 1974, CRP 44.9.
11. Diary, n.d. May–Jun 1974, CRP 44.7. In a later hand, "faggots" is crossed out and "gay men" substituted.
12. Author interview with Janice Sukaitis.
13. Diary, 27–28 Sept, 16 Dec 1974, CRP 44.9; Diary, 17 Dec 1974, CRP 44.6.
14. Diary, 2 Oct 1974, 11 Jan 1975, CRP 44.6; Diary entry, 10 Aug 1976, CRP 44.12.
15. Author interview with Jorgé Socarras.
16. Danny Isley to CV, 24 Nov 1974, CRP 36.3.
17. Diary, 16 Dec 1974, CRP 44.9.
18. Diary, 16, 17, 29 Dec 1974, CRP 44.6.
19. Diary, 11 Jan (draft of letter to Sherry Falek), 2 May 1975, CRP 44.6.
20. Author interviews with Karen Dunaway, Janice Sukaitis.
21. Author interview with Karen Dunaway; Diary, 2 May 1975, CRP 44.6.

22. Diary, 28 Jan, 25 May 1974, CRP 44.7; email from Jorgé Socarras, 15 Apr 2019; author interview with Janice Sukaitis.

23. Diary, 2 May 1975, CRP 44.6; Diary entry, 10 Aug 1976, CRP 44.12; author interview with Scrumbly Koldewyn.

24. Diary, 29 Dec 1974, 10, 11 Jan; n.d. Feb 1975, CRP 44.6; Diary, 2 Jan 1975, CRP 44.9.

25. CRP Diary, 2, 22 May; 6 Jul 1975, CRP 44.6; Bernard Jay, *Not Simply Divine: Beneath the Make-up, above the Heels and behind the Scenes with a Cult Superstar* (Simon & Schuster, 1993), 31–33. For the auditions, see *SF Examiner*, 24 Apr 1975, 29. On Danny and the Cockettes: author interviews with Scrumbly Koldewyn and Janice Sukaitis. Images of Danny with the Cockettes appear in "Cockettes: Historical Essay," http://www.foundsf .org/index.php?title=Cockettes.

26. *Heartbreak of Psoriasis* playbill, Jun 1975, courtesy of Janice Sukaitis; Natilee Duning, "A Song-and-Dance Duo with Sense of Humor," *The Tennessean* (Nashville), 15 Sept 1976, 39. The "economy cost" of $75,000 1975 dollars in 2018 is $916,000; https://www .measuringworth.com/calculators/uscompare/relativevalue.php.

27. Diary, n.d. Jun–Jul 1975, CRP 44.9.

28. Stanley Eichelbaum, "A Musical Comedy that's Sheer Agony," *SF Examiner*, 20 Jun 1975, 30; "Stage: The Heartbreak of Psoriasis," *BAR*, 26 Jun 1975, 22–23; Diary, n.d. Jun–Jul 1975, CRP 44.9.

29. Sukaitis quoted in "Out There," *BAR*, 20 Apr 2000, 30.

30. Champagne Flutes Intoxicating Entertainment to the cast and crew of *Heartbreak*, 21 Jun 1975, courtesy of Janice Sukaitis.

CHAPTER 13: PORN, INC.

1. David Foster Wallace, "Big Red Son" (1998), repr. in *Consider the Lobster and Other Essays* (Little, Brown, 2005), 44 *n*46.

2. *Abortion Surveillance 1974, issued April 1976* (CDC/U.S. Department of Health, Education, and Welfare, 1974), 1.

3. Lane V. Sunderland, *Obscenity: The Court, the Congress and the President's Commission* (American Enterprise Institute, 1975), 81. On conservative anti-pornography more broadly, see Whitney Strub, *Perversion for Profit: The Politics of Pornography and the Rise of the New Right* (Columbia University Press, 2011).

4. The CDL film, *Perversion for Profit*, quoted in Whitney Strub, "Perversion for Profit: Citizens for Decent Literature and the Arousal of an Antiporn Public in the 1960s," *Journal of the History of Sexuality* 15:2 (2006), https://doi.org/10.1353/sex.2007.0013, 258.

5. Carolyn See, *Blue Money: Pornography and the Pornographers* (McKay, 1974), 10–43.

6. *United States v. Hamling*, 481 F.2d 307 (9th Cir. 1973); *Hamling v. United States*, 418 U.S. 87 (1974).

7. Goldstein quoted in James Cook, "The X-Rated Economy," *Forbes*, 18 Sept 1978, 82.

8. *The Report of the Commission on Obscenity and Pornography* (Bantam Books, 1970), 110; compare to *Dian Hanson's: The History of Men's Magazines* (Taschen, 2004), V: 9–14, 40–51; see also Mike Edison, *Dirty!, Dirty!, Dirty!: Of Playboys, Pigs, and Penthouse Paupers* (Soft Skull Press, 2011), 166–169. The commission's count did not include the then-enormous subscription bases of *Playboy* and *Penthouse*, classed as "special magazines," for their literary quality.

9. Goldstein quoted in Cook, "The X-Rated Economy," 82.

10. Joseph W. Slade, "The Porn Market and Porn Formulas: The Feature Film of the Seventies," *Journal of Popular Film* 6:2 (1977): 168.

11. Cook, "The X-Rated Economy," 81–84.

12. Slade, "Porn Market and Porn Formulas," 175, 173. On *Hustler*, see Laura Kipnis, *Bound and Gagged: Pornography and the Politics of Fantasy in America* (Grove Press, 1996), 122–160.

13. *Young v. American Mini Theatres, Inc.*, 427 U.S. 50 (1976).

14. "Feelings About Pornography Laws," NORC survey, https://gssdataexplorer.norc.org/variables/640/vshow.

15. CV to Cinthea Vadala, 15 Nov 1980, CRP 34.12.

16. *Miller v. California*, https://supreme.justia.com/cases/federal/us/413/15/#tab-opinion-1950401.

17. CV to Cinthea Vadala, 1 Jun 1981, CRP 34.12.

18. Diary, n.d. Jun–Jul 1975, CRP 44.9.

19. Average 1975 unemployment, per Bureau of Labor Statistics, https://data.bls.gov/pdq/SurveyOutputServlet. The rate got as high as 11 percent; see Robert O. Self, *All in the Family: The Realignment of American Democracy since the 1960s* (Hill and Wang, 2012), 311.

20. Sherry Falek to CV, 6 Jan 1975; Roseanne Slomowitz to CV, 13 Mar 1975, both CRP 36.4; Rhonda Katz to CV, 15 Feb 1976, CRP 36.5.

21. Diary, 17 Jan 1974, CRP 44.7.

22. Appointment book, 1975, 27 Jul; 6, 14, 21–22, 23, 27, 29 Aug; 15–16, 22–23 Sept; 14, 28 Oct; 7, 9, 10, 24 Nov, CRP 1.10. The movies were *The Analyst*, in which Candice played a leading role, and *Carnal Haven* (1975), dir. Carlos Tobalina, in which she appeared uncredited.

23. CR, "Vertical Smiles and Cum-Soaked Aisles: Confessions of a Porn Queen," *High Times*, Jul 1982, 38.

24. Diary, n.d. Jun–Jul 1975, CRP 44.9.

25. Rhonda Katz to CV, 8 Oct 1975, CRP 36.4.

26. Louis Vadala to CV, 16 Jan 1976, courtesy of Cinthea Vadala.

27. Helen Vadala to CV, 12 Oct 1975, CRP 35.2. On the separation and divorce, see Helen Vadala to CV, 14 Sept 1974; Helen Vadala to CV, 14 Feb 1976, in *ibid.*

28. Appointment book, 1975, 31 Dec, CRP 1.10.

29. Appointment book, 1976, 2, 3 Jan, CRP 1.12.

30. Appointment book, 1976, 16, 17 Feb; 25, 26 Mar; 10 Apr, CRP 1.12. For the apartment loss, see Rhonda Katz to CV, 15 Feb 1976, CRP 36.5.

31. CRP 36.5 (address); Diary entry, 27, 11 Aug 1976, CRP 44.12; author interview with Karen Dunaway.

32. Appointment book, 1976, 28 May; 11, 17, 18, 19, 30 Aug; 4, 11, 22, 26 Sept; 19–22, 25, 28 Oct; 1, 11, 12, 10 Nov; 28 Nov–2 Dec, CRP 1.12.

33. *Easy Alice* (1976), dir. Tom Hoffman aka Joey Silvera; see also Joe Rubin, "Easy Alice (Joey Silvera, 1975 [*sic*])," *Porn Studies* 4:3 (2017): 305–310, https://doi.org/10.1080/23268743.2017.1333029.

34. Danny Isley to CV, 10 Aug 1976, CRP 36.5.

35. Diary entry, 26 Aug 1976, CRP 44.12; SF Dept. of Public Health report, 25 Aug 1976, CRP 54.2.

36. Diary entry, 26 Aug 1976, CRP 44.12; CV to Karen Dunaway, 1 Sept 1976, CRP 36.5; Diary, 9 Sept, n.d. Nov 1976, CRP 44.14.

37. Diary entry, 27 Aug 1976, CRP 44.12; Diary entry, 31 Aug 1976, CRP 44.13. Candice contrasted the optimistic tone of her letters with her despair-filled journals: Diary, 5 Feb 1977, CRP 44.14.

38. Diary entry, 27 Aug 1976, emphasis Mine, CRP 44.12.

39. Diary entry, 26 Aug 1976, CRP 44.12; Diary, 16 Sept 1976, CRP 44.14.

40. Diary, n.d. Nov 1976, CRP 44.14. Candice had moved into the Nineteenth Street apartment on 8 Nov, Appointment book, 1976, CRP 1.12.

41. Diary, Sept; 15, 14, n.d. Nov 1976, CRP 44.14.
42. Diary, 25 Sept 1976, 21 Jan 1977, 27 Dec 1976; see n.d. Oct 1976, for orders for drugs; CRP 44.14.
43. Diary, 21, 25 Jan 1977, CRP 44.14; draft of CV to Danny Isley, 7 Jun 1977, in Sketchbook, CRP 109FB.1.
44. Diary, 25 Jan, 19 Mar, n.d. Jan 1977, CRP 44.14; author interview with Karen Dunaway.
45. Cook, "X-Rated Economy," 84; Addison Verrill, "Porno Chic Fades," *Variety*, 30 January 1974, 1, 63.
46. Matt Cimber quoted in See, *Blue Money*, 60.
47. Slade, "Porn Market and Porn Formulas," 175, 174. On race in the adult industry in the Seventies, see Mireille Miller-Young, *A Taste for Brown Sugar: Black Women in Pornography* (Duke University Press, 2014), esp. 66–103.
48. Diary, 8 Oct 1976, CRP 44.14. *Hard Soap, Hard Soap* appears to have been shot 19–22 Oct; Appointment book, 1976, CRP 1.12.
49. Diary, 8 Oct, 25 Sept 1976, CRP 44.14.
50. ProQuest databases *Entertainment Industry Magazine Archive, Women's Magazine Archive, America's Historical Newspapers*; and Newspapers.com, searched 6 May 2019.
51. "Personal Appearances: Porn Star Lovelace Wrapped Up in Suits," *Variety*, 19 Dec 1973, 36; "Another Porno Flick Star Tries Café Turn," *Variety*, 6 Mar 1974, 2.
52. "Porn Queen Scores with Disco Single, 'More, More, More,'" *Variety*, 17 Mar 1976, 82.
53. Sam Chernoff, "AFAA Formed to Check Irresponsible 'Heat Artists,'" *Independent Film Journal*, 14 Oct 1969, 18; Devin Thomas McGeehan Muchmore, *The Business of Sex: A Queer History of Pornography and Commercial Culture in 1970s America* (PhD dissertation, Yale University, 2018).
54. "The Sex Exploitation Explosion," *Independent Film Journal*, 14 Oct 1969, 26.
55. Appointment book, 1976, 4, 5 Feb, CRP 1.12. *Easy Alice* also premiered at the Presidio; see *SF Examiner*, 23 Jul 1976; see also "Blue Film Festival in S.F.," *LAT*, 4 Dec 1970, J34.
56. Appointment book, 1976, 29 Jul, 19 Aug, CRP 1.12. For *Variety* reviews, see 5 May 1976, 18 (*Femmes de Sade*), 11 Aug 1976, 19 (*Baby Rosemary*).
57. *Dian Hanson's: The History of Men's Magazines*, V: 9–14, 40–51; Edison, *Dirty!, Dirty!, Dirty!*, 166–169.
58. Diary, 4 [8] Sept 1976, CRP 44.14.
59. Sarah E. Igo, *The Known Citizen: A History of Privacy in Modern America* (Harvard University Press, 2018), 315–324.
60. Xaviera Hollander with Yvonne Dunleavy, *The Happy Hooker* (Dell, 1972); Fanne Foxe with Yvonne Dunleavy, *Fanne Fox* (Pinnacle Books, 1975).
61. Diary, 17 Apr 1974, CRP 44.7; Diary, 6 Sept 1976, CRP 44.14.
62. Appointment book, 1976, 29 Oct, CRP 1.12; "Daffy Hookers Ball: It Was Coyote's Night to Howl," *SF Examiner*, 30 Oct 1976, 1, 11.
63. Sege, "Teenage Cowgirls," *Variety*, 21 Feb 1973, 24; Kenneth Turan and Stephen F. Zito, *Sinema: American Pornographic Films and the People Who Make Them* (Praeger, 1974), 114–115.
64. Legs McNeil, *The Other Hollywood: The Uncensored Oral History of the Porn Film Industry* (Regan Books, 2005), 88.
65. Author interview with Jerome Vitucci.
66. Steven Ziplow, *The Film Maker's Guide to Pornography* (Drake, 1977), 77. For women's experiences on porn shoots, see Shira Tarrant, *The Pornography Industry: What Everyone Needs to Know* (Oxford University Press, 2016), 35–39, 56–58.

67. Ziplow, *Film Maker's Guide to Pornography*, 34, 82–87, 76–77, 39; Clay McCord quoted in William Rotsler, *Contemporary Erotic Cinema* (Ballantine Books, 1973), 151–152.

68. Jill C. Nelson, *Golden Goddesses: 25 Legendary Women of Classic Erotic Cinema 1968–1985* (Bear Manor Media, 2012), 237–238, 240; Diary, 25 Sept 1976, CRP 44.14.

69. Diary, 1 Apr 1978, CRP 45.3; Nelson, *Golden Goddesses*, 236–237, 239.

70. Howie Gordon, *Hindsight: True Love & Mischief in the Golden Age of Porn* (Bear Manor Media, 2013), 315, 137.

71. Diary, 6 Jul 1975, CRP 44.9; CR, "Vertical Smiles," 40.

72. CV notes, "Close Call with the Male Power Game," cDec 1976, CRP 44.12.

CHAPTER 14: ANTI-PORN, INC.

1. Bronx Coalition Feminist Collective reading list, n.d. [1970–1971], CRP 35.6.

2. Marjorie J. Spruill, *Divided We Stand: The Battle over Women's Rights and Family Values That Polarized American Politics* (Bloomsbury, 2017), 14–41.

3. Roxanne Dunbar, "'Sexual Liberation': More of the Same Thing," *No More Fun and Games*, November 1969, 49, 55, 52–53; Alice Echols, *Daring to Be Bad: Radical Feminism in America, 1967–1975* (University of Minnesota Press, 1989), 10–11, 165.

4. Morgan, "Goodbye to All That," 122.

5. Anselma Dell'Oilo, "The Sexual Revolution Wasn't Our War," *Ms.*, Spring 1972, 104. *Ms.* would not run an article on pornography until Robin Morgan's "Rights of Passage," Sept 1975.

6. See for examples Joseph N. Bell, "Danger: Smut," *Good Housekeeping*, Apr 1971, 85; Margaret Mead, "Can We Protect Children from Pornography?" *Redbook*, Mar 1972, 74; "Sexual Expertise and How to Get It," *Cosmopolitan*, Jul 1971, 42.

7. Ray C. Rist, *The Pornography Controversy: Changing Moral Standards in American Life* (Transaction Books, 1974).

8. Susan Griffin, "Rape: The All-American Crime," *Ramparts*, Sept 1971, 26–35.

9. Carolyn Bronstein, *Battling Pornography: The American Feminist Anti-Pornography Movement, 1976–1986* (Cambridge University Press, 2011), 44–50.

10. *The Report of the Commission on Obscenity and Pornography* (Bantam Books, 1970), 31–32, see also 169–309.

11. Susan Brownmiller, *Against Our Will: Men, Women, and Rape* (Simon & Schuster, 1975), 438, 441–444.

12. "Book Ends," *NYT Book Review*, 21 Dec 1975, 21; radio and television listings in *NYT*, 8 Oct 1975, 83; 15 Oct 1975, 87; 22 Oct 1975, 91.

13. "Editors' Choice 1975," *NYT Book Review*, 28 Dec 1975, 1.

14. Robin Morgan, "Theory and Practice," in *Going Too Far: The Personal Chronicle of a Feminist* (Random House, 1977), 165–166, 168, 169. Morgan dates the essay 1974, but I have found no printing of it that year; internal evidence suggests Brownmiller published first.

15. Quoted in Eithne Johnson and Eric Schaefer, "Soft-Core/Hard-Gore: Snuff as a Crisis in Meaning," *Journal of Film and Video* 45:2–3 (1993): 42.

16. Edward Kirkman, "Last Picture Show: Sex and Real Murder," *NY Daily News*, 3 Oct 1975, 16.

17. "Reel Scene of Murder in Porno Proves Real," *Orlando Sentinel Star*, 3 Oct 1975, 8; "Porno Movie Murders under Probe by FBI," *Cincinnati Enquirer*, 3 Oct 1975, 8. The database Newspapers.com turns up stories in twenty-six papers on the East Coast and Midwest the day the *Daily News* original ran.

18. "Deaths Linked to 'Snuff' Films," *Windsor Star* (Ontario), 4 Oct 1975, 2.

19. "'Snuff' (Sex Murders) Film Now Thought Hoax from Argentina," *Variety*, 17 Dec 1975, 4. Johnson and Shaefer identify numerous continuity errors in the murder sequence: "Soft-Core/Hard-Gore," 40.

20. "'Snuff' Premieres in Indy," *Boxoffice*, 9 Feb 1976, C1; "'Snuff' Shown in Wichita; Violence Labeled 'Fake,'" *Boxoffice*, 9 Feb 1976, C4.

21. "'Snuff' Protested in Philly," *Boxoffice*, 16 Feb 1976, E1.

22. John Leonard, "Cretin's Delight on Film," *NYT*, 27 Feb 1976, 21; "Morgenthau Finds Film Dismembering Was Indeed a Hoax," *NYT*, 10 Mar 1976, 37.

23. Leonard, "Cretin's Delight on Film."

24. WAVAW fact sheet quoted in Bronstein, *Battling Pornography*, 89.

25. Johnson and Schaefer, "Soft-Core/Hard-Gore," 44–45; Shackleton quoted in Beverly LaBelle, "The Ultimate in Woman-Hating," in Laura Lederer, ed., *Take Back the Night: Women on Pornography* (William Morrow, 1980), 276.

26. Bronstein, *Battling Pornography*, 93–126.

27. Minutes and organizational document, WAVPM Records, GLBTHS, box 1.

28. Draft of a letter to Sherry Falek, 11 Jan 1975, in Diary, CRP 44.6; Bronstein, 127–172.

29. Bronstein, *Battling Pornography*, 146–153, 157–165.

30. Andrea Dworkin, "Pornography and Grief" (Nov 1978), in Lederer, ed., *Take Back the Night*, 286–291, quotations at 288, 289, 291.

31. Bronstein, *Battling Pornography*, 166–169; Ariadne: A Social Art Network, "We Took Back the Night," https://www.againstviolence.art/more-take-back-the-night.

CHAPTER 15: PROJECT LOS ANGELES, U.S.A.!

1. Diary, 13 May 1974, CRP 44.7; Diary, 14 Jun 1977, CRP 44.7.

2. Diary, n.d. May 1975, CRP 44.6.

3. Howie Gordon, *Hindsight: True Love & Mischief in the Golden Age of Porn* (Bear Manor Media, 2013), 112–113; Jon Lewis, *Hollywood v. Hard Core: How the Struggle over Censorship Saved the Modern Film Industry* (NYU Press, 2000); Joseph Lam Duong, *California Hard Core* (PhD dissertation, University of California–Berkeley, 2014), 3–7; Devin Thomas McGeehan Muchmore, *The Business of Sex: A Queer History of Pornography and Commercial Culture in 1970s America* (PhD dissertation, Yale University, 2018), 181–182; Legs McNeil, *The Other Hollywood: The Uncensored Oral History of the Porn Film Industry* (Regan Books, 2005), 133.

4. William Rotsler, *Contemporary Erotic Cinema* (Ballantine Books, 1973), 43.

5. Diary, n.d. Oct 1976, CRP 44.14; Gary W. Potter, *The Porn Merchants* (Kendall/Hunt PubCo, 1986), 18; Laura Kipnis, *Bound and Gagged: Pornography and the Politics of Fantasy in America* (Grove Press, 1996), 129.

6. Lisa McGirr, *Suburban Warriors: The Origins of the New American Right* (Princeton University Press, 2001), 226–237; Robert O. Self, "Sex in the City: The Politics of Sexual Liberalism in Los Angeles, 1963–79," *Gender & History* 20:2 (2008): 288–311, https://doi.org/10.1111/j.1468-0424.2008.00522.x.

7. McNeil, *The Other Hollywood*, 349.

8. Diary entries, 16 Feb, 2 Apr 1977, CRP 45.1; Diary, n.d. Apr/May 1977, CRP 44.14.

9. Sketchbook, 1, 7, 6 Jun 1977, CRP 109FB.

10. Diary entry, 19–20 May [1977], CRP 44.15; email from Karen Dunaway, 4 May 2019.

11. Diary, 8 Jul 1977, CRP 44.14.

12. Sketchbook, 7 Jun 1977, CRP 109FB.1; SSI, decision on CV appeal, 26 Jul 1977, CRP 54.2.

13. Sketchbook, n.d. Jul 1977, CRP 109FB.1; Appointment book, 1977, 22, 25–27 Aug, CRP 2.1.

14. Diary, 2 Aug, 8 Jul, 25 Sept 1977, CRP 44.14; Appointment book, 1977, 25 Aug, CRP 2.1; CV to Karen Dunaway, 31 May 1977, courtesy of Karen Dunaway; author interview with Karen Dunaway.
15. Diary, 23 Jul, 25 Sept 1977, CRP 44.14.
16. Quoted in Muchmore, *Business of Sex*, 89–90, see also 82, 254–260. The AFAA exposed the role of Citizens for Decency in starting the rumors.
17. Tony Crawley, "Hollywood Extra," *Screen International*, 2 Apr 1977, 18.
18. "Ann Perry, First Lady," in Jill C. Nelson, *Golden Goddesses: 25 Legendary Women of Classic Erotic Cinema 1968–1985* (Bear Manor Media, 2012), 22–53, quotations at 46, 44.
19. Perry quoted in Muchmore, *Business of Sex*, 90–91; Crawley, "Hollywood Extra."
20. "Skin Flicks: Their Own Oscars," *Philadelphia Enquirer*, 16 Apr 1977, 17.
21. Diary, 8 Jul 1977, CRP 44.14; Ann Perry to CR, 19 Jul 1977, CRP 66.1.
22. Fred Pleibel, "Warsaw Quintet at Wilshire Ebell," *LAT*, 21 Jan 1977, F1; Ara Guzelimian, "Youth Symphony Heralds Its Own, *LAT*, 31 May 1977, G8.
23. William Knoedelseder, "Pioneer Theme: Erotic Film Awards Presented," *LAT*, 16 Jul 1977, B7; Erotica Awards Program, 14 Jul 1977, CPR 66.1. See also " 'Oscars' for the Porn Pictures," *The Guardian*, 16 Jul 1977; Muchmore, *Business of Sex*, 91–95.
24. Diary, 8 Jul 1977, CRP 44.14.
25. Diary, 2 Aug 1977, CRP 44.14; Appointment book, 1977, 16 Aug, CRP 2.1. On Eposito, see John L. Smith, *The Animal in Hollywood: Anthony Fiato's Life in the Mafia* (Barricade Books, 1998), 101–102, 124–125. I have not discovered the name of the movie.
26. Eve Babitz, *Slow Days, Fast Company: The World, the Flesh, and L.A.* (1977; repr. New York Review Books, 2016), 7.
27. Diary, 2 Aug 1977, CRP 44.14.
28. Diary, 25 Sept 1977, CRP 44.14; Diary, 1 Jul 1978. CRP 45.3; Diary entry, 29 Nov 1978, CRP 45.1.
29. Diary, n.d. late Jan, 23 Jul 1977 (quoted), CRP 44.14; Diary, 24 Feb 1978, CRP 45.3; author interview with Karen Dunaway. Date of the move to 1134 Alta Loma Road by forwarded letters, CRP 36.7.
30. Diary, 1 Jul, 21 Aug 1978, CRP 45.3; Diary, 26–27 Nov 1979, CRP 45.8; author interview with Karen Dunaway; email from Karen Dunaway, 2 May 2019. For Princess Jawahir's relationship with Vicki Morgan, see Joyce Milton and Ann Louise Bardach, *Vicki* (St. Martin's, 1986), 157–163.
31. Diary, 21 Aug 1978, CRP 45.3; author interview with Karen Dunaway; email from Karen Dunaway, 2 May 2019.
32. Diary, 29 Jun, 24 Feb, 1 Apr, 29 Jun 1978, CRP 45.3.
33. Diary, 13, 5 Apr 1978, CRP 45.3; Sketchbook, n.d. Jan–Feb 1978, CRP 31.2.
34. Diary, n.d. Apr–Jun, n.d. Jan 1978, CRP 45.3; Sketchbook, early Feb 1978, CRP 31.2.
35. Diary, 13 Apr 1978, CRP 45.3.
36. Diary, n.d. Apr–Jun 1978, CRP 45.3.
37. Diary, 1, 2 Apr 1978; see also 13 Apr 1978, CRP 45.3.
38. *Hot and Saucy Pizza Girls* (1978), dir. Bob Chinn; Gordon, *Hindsight*, 123–129.
39. Diary, n.d. Jun 1978, CRP 45.3.
40. Howie Gordon to CR, 31 Jul 1984; CR to Howie Gordon, 3 Dec 1984, both CRP 67.13; costume, CRP 115OB.10m.
41. Author interview with Martin Blinder.
42. Diary, 29 Jun 1978, 9 Feb 1979, CRP 45.3.
43. See among many others, Duffy Jennings, "Jury Told of the Turmoil within White," *SF Chronicle*, 9 May 1979, 1.

44. Diary, 15 Aug, 9–10 Jul 1978, CRP 45.3.
45. CV to Karen Dunaway, 21 Jul 1978, Diary, 1 Jul 1978, CRP 45.3; *Hot Rackets* (1979), dir. Gary Graver [pseud. for Robert McCallum].
46. Diary, 29 Jun 1978, CRP 45.3.
47. CV to Karen Dunaway, 21 Jul 1978; "Porno Fame Roster," *Variety*, 12 Jul 1978, 6.
48. Diary, 1 Jul, 15 Aug 1978, CRP 45.3; CV to Karen Dunaway, 21 Jul 1978.
49. Mrs. Fox to CV, n.d. c1978–1979, CRP 36.6.
50. CV to Karen Dunaway, 21 Jul 1978.
51. Diary, 14, 17 Oct; 5, 8 Nov 1978, CRP 45.3.
52. Draft of CV to Cinthea in Diary, n.d. Nov 1979, CRP 45.8.
53. Author interview with Janice Sukaitis.
54. CV to Cinthea Vadala, 15 Nov 1980, CRP 34.12.
55. Diary, 14 Oct 1978, CRP 45.3.
56. CV to Karen Dunaway, 21 Jul 1978; Diary entry, 29 Nov 1978, CRP 45.1.
57. Diary, 14 Oct 1978, CRP 45.3.
58. CV to Karen Dunaway, 21 Jul 1978; Appointment book, 1979, 7, 16 Aug, CRP 2.3; CV checking account (California), 1979, CRP 51.13. See e.g. the display ad for *Pizza Girls*, *Detroit Free Press*, 23 May 1979, 9D.
59. Appointment book, 1979, 15–18 Jan, CRP 2.3; CR, "Vertical Smiles and Cum-Soaked Aisles: Confessions of a Porn Queen," *High Times*, Jul 1982, 86.
60. Diary, 9 Feb 1979, CRP 45.3.
61. Diary, 9 Feb 1979, CRP 45.3; CR, "Vertical Smiles," 38.

CHAPTER 16: RIPE AND READY

1. Diary entry, 28 Feb 1979, CRP 45.1; Diary, 14 Oct, 5 Nov 1978, CRP 45.3.
2. Steven Ziplow, *The Film Maker's Guide to Pornography* (Drake, 1977), 45.
3. Izzy Smith quoted in Robert Rosen, *Beaver Street* (Headpress, 2010), 91.
4. Diary entry, 15 Mar 1979, CRP 45.
5. Diary entry, n.d. [May 1979], CRP 45.1. *Taxi Girls*, filmed in March 1979, was also shot in L.A., as was Candice's scene in *Ball Game*, filmed December 1979.
6. *The Tale of Tiffany Lust* (1981), dir. Gerald Kikoine; *Champagne for Breakfast* (1980), dir. Chris Warfield; *Taxi Girls* (1979), dir. Jourdan Alexander, all filmed March 1979. A decade later, Candice stumbled on a copy of *Sissy's Hot Summer* (1980), dir. Alan Colberg, noting, "I don't even have a sex scene!" Diary, n.d. Sept 1987, CRP 46.14.
7. CR, "Vertical Smiles and Cum-Soaked Aisles: Confessions of a Porn Queen," *High Times*, Jul 1982, 87.
8. L. R. Goldman, "Interview: Candida Royalle," *AVN* 1:27 (1985), 38; CV to Danny Isley, May 1980, CRP 36.9.
9. Lisa Lerman et al., "Violent Pornography: Degradation of Women versus Right of Free Speech," *NYU Review of Law and Social Change* 8 (1978–1979): 287–289, 292; Carolyn Bronstein, *Battling Pornography: The American Feminist Anti-Pornography Movement, 1976–1986* (Cambridge University Press, 2011), 177–188. On Flynt's shooting, see Larry Flynt, *An Unseemly Man* (Dove Books, 1996), 170–177, 259.
10. Bronstein, *Battling Pornography*, 188–199.
11. Georgia Dullea, "In Feminists' Antipornography Drive, 42nd Street Is the Target," *NYT*, 6 Jul 1979, A12; Bronstein, *Battling Pornography*, 206–222.
12. "Women's War on Porn," *Time*, 27 August 1979, 64; *Off Our Backs*, Jul 1979, 9.
13. "Women's War on Porn."
14. Robert O. Self, *All in the Family: The Realignment of American Democracy since the 1960s* (Hill

and Wang, 2012), 352–360; "Reagan Talk Attacks 'Smiles and Rhetoric,'" *St. Louis Post-Dispatch*, 7 Jul 1976, 2A; James Gannon, "1976: The Year of the Family," *WSJ*, 15 Sept 1976, 26.

15. Molly Ivins, "Feminist Leaders Join Anti-Smut Campaign Despite Reservations," *NYT*, 2 Jul 1977, 31; Bronstein, *Battling Pornography*, 194–195.

16. Barbara Basler, "5,000 Join Feminist Group's Rally in Times Sq. Against Pornography," *NYT*, 21 Oct 1979, 41; "Women March against NYC Pornography," *Binghamton Press and Sun Bulletin* (AP), 21 Oct 1979, 11; slogans from Bettye Lane's photograph "Women Against Pornography" demonstration, 20 Oct 1979, SL, http://id.lib.harvard.edu/via/olvwork748180/catalog.

17. "Women March against NYC Pornography"; Freda Leinwand (photographer), "March against Pornography" (photographs), SL, http://id.lib.harvard.edu/via/8000906158/catalog, image 13.

18. Diary, 2, 13 Oct 1979, CRP 45.8; Appointment book, 1979, 7 Aug, 2 Sept, CRP 2.3.

19. Diary, 2 Oct, 28 Jul, 7 Aug 1979, CRP 45.3; Appointment book, 1979, n.d., 25, 31 Jul, CRP 2.3.

20. Kenneth Heffernan, "Many of Your Finer Nudie Films: Saga Film, Swedish National Cinema and Seventies Transnational Erotic Film," in *Swedish Cinema and the Sexual Revolution: Critical Essays*, ed. Elisabet Björklund and Mariah Larrson (McFarland, 2016), 216–232, quotation at 222.

21. Author interviews with PS.

22. Heffernan, "Many of Your Finer Nudie Films," 222–223; Peter Alilunas, *Smutty Little Movies: The Creation and Regulation of Adult Video* (University of California Press, 2016), 137–138; author interviews with PS.

23. Diary, 2 Oct 1979, CRP 45.8; Appointment book, 1979, 17, 20 Sept; 28 Sept–1 Oct, CRP 2.3.

24. Diary, 2, 11 Oct 1979, CRP 45.8; Appointment book, 1979, 21, 26 Sept; 6–9, 11, 26 Oct; 7 Nov, CRP 2.3.

25. Appointment book, 1979, 18, 28 Nov; 2, 8–11, 12, 14 Dec, CRP 2.3.a

26. Appointment book, 1979, 22 Dec, CRP 2.3.

27. Diary, 1 Jan 1980, CRP 45.8; author interview with PS.

28. Diary, 1 Jan 1980, 11 Nov 1979, CRP 45.8.

29. Diary, 1 Jan 1980, CRP 45.8.

CHAPTER 17: A NEW BEGINNING

1. Diary, 29 Feb 1980, CRP 45.5; snapshots, CRP 55.2v; Diary, 21 Aug 1983, CRP 46.2.

2. Photograph in "The Bride Went Pink," *High Society*, Jul 1980, 6–7; author interview with PS.

3. CV to Louis Vadala, 22 May 1988, CRP 35.4; Diary, 29 Feb 1980, CRP 45.5.

4. Diary, 10, 28, 31 Jan 1980, emphasis mine, CRP 45.5.

5. Diary, 6 Feb 1980, CRP 45.5.

6. Diary, 14 Feb 1980, CRP 45.5; author interview with PS.

7. Diary, 17, 6 Feb 1980, CRP 45.5.

8. Photographs by Joyce Jordan, CRP PD.53; and by Jill Lynne, CRP PD.52sl.

9. Diary, 29 Feb 1980, CRP 45.5; author interview with PS.

10. "The Bride Went Pink"; Diary, 5, 11–20 Mar 1980, CRP 45.5.

11. Diary, n.d. Aug, 16 Apr 1980, CRP 45.5.

12. Diary, 29 Feb 1980, CRP 45.5; author interview with PS.

13. Diary, 29 Feb 1980, CRP 45.5.

14. Jimmy Carter, "White House Conference on Families Remarks at a White House Reception," 20 Jul 1979, APP, https://www.presidency.ucsb.edu/node/249648.

15. White House Conference on Families, "Listening to America's Families" (U.S. Department of Health, Education, and Welfare, Jun 1980), 7, https://files.eric.ed.gov/fulltext/ED198914.pdf. Carter had promised while campaigning to hold the conference; Robert O. Self, *All in the Family: The Realignment of American Democracy since the 1960s* (Hill and Wang, 2012), 332–337.

16. Phyllis Schlafly, "Foreword," to Rosemary Thomson, *Withstanding Humanism's Challenge to Families: Anatomy of a White House Conference* (Traditional Publications, 1981), iv.

17. Nadine Brozan, "Second Day of Family Conference Workshops and a Walkout," *NYT*, 7 Jun 1980, B46.

18. Thomson, *Withstanding Humanism's Challenge to Families*, 127, 124, 129; Leslie Bennetts, "Conservatives Join on Social Concerns," *NYT*, 30 Jul 1980, A1. On Houston, see Marjorie J. Spruill, *Divided We Stand: The Battle over Women's Rights and Family Values That Polarized American Politics* (Bloomsbury, 2017).

19. David E. Rosenbaum, "On the Issues: Ronald Reagan," *NYT*, 22 Mar 1980, A8; Howell Raines, "Reagan's Campaign Style Is Creating a Varied Coalition of 'Shared Values,'" *NYT*, 12 Apr 1980, A10; Craig Shirley, *Rendezvous with Destiny: Ronald Reagan and the Campaign That Changed America* (ISI Books, 2009), 324–348; Rick Perlstein, *Reaganland: America's Right Turn 1976–1980* (Simon & Schuster, 2020), 792–828.

20. "Republican Party Platform of 1980," APP, https://www.presidency.ucsb.edu/node/273420.

21. "1980 Democratic Party Platform," APP, https://www.presidency.ucsb.edu/node/273253.

22. Ronald Reagan, "Address Accepting the Presidential Nomination at the Republican National Convention in Detroit," 17 Jul 1980, APP, https://www.presidency.ucsb.edu/node/251302.

23. Amitai Etzioni, "'Porn Is Here to Stay,'" *NYT*, 17 May 1977, A31; Bonnie Shane, "The White House Conference on Families Recommendations and Conclusions," *University of Baltimore Law Forum* 11: 1 (1981): 15; Martin Bernstein and Jane Kamensky, "What Politicians Talk about When They Talk about Porn*: A Tableau™ Vivant," *Public Seminar*, 27 May 2021, https://publicseminar.org/essays/what-politicians-talk-about-when-they-talk-about-porn/.

24. Carolyn Bronstein, *Battling Pornography: The American Feminist Anti-Pornography Movement, 1976–1986* (Cambridge University Press, 2011), 206–214, 219–224; Perlstein, *Reaganland*, 465–496.

25. Falwell, *Listen America* (1980) quoted in Robert E. Webber, *The Moral Majority: Right or Wrong?* (Cornerstone Books, 1981), 50.

26. Andrea Dworkin, *Pornography: Men Possessing Women* (Putnam, 1981), 208–209.

27. Linda Lovelace, *Ordeal* (1980; repr. Citadel, 2006), 70, 130–133, 217, 249.

28. "TV actress Valerie Harper among Women Against Pornography Demonstrators on 42nd Street," photograph by Bettye Lane, 31 May 1980, SL, http://id.lib.harvard.edu/via/olvwork748183/catalog; WAP press release, "Protest Deep Throat," 31 May 1980, quoted in Bronstein, *Battling Pornography*, 261.

29. "What Americans Are Reading," *The Paris News* (TX), 25 May 1980,10C; "Best Sellers," *NYT Book Review*, 15 Mar 1981, 32.

30. Patchen Barss, *The Erotic Engine* (Doubleday Canada, 2010), 108–109; Luke Stadel, "Cable, Pornography, and the Reinvention of Television, 1982–1989," *Cinema Journal* 53:3 (2014): 57, https://doi.org/10.1353/cj.2014.0026.

31. Eugene Secunda, "VCRs and Viewer Control over Programming: An Historical Perspective," in *Social and Cultural Aspects of VCR Use*, ed. Julie Dobrow (Routledge, 1990), 9–24, https://doi.org/10.4324/9780203052327.

32. Henry Schipper, "Filthy Lucre," *Mother Jones*, Apr 1980, 32; Chuck Kleinhans, "The Change from Film to Video Pornography: Implications for Analysis," in *Pornography:*

Film and Culture, ed. Peter Lehman (Rutgers University Press, 2006), 157; Stadel, "Cable, Pornography, and the Reinvention of Television," 58; Megumi Komiya and Barry Litman, "The Economics of the Prerecorded Videocassette Industry," in *Social and Cultural Aspects of VCR Use*, 25.

33. Bernstein and Kamensky, "What Politicians Talk About"; Philip Jenkins, *Decade of Nightmares: The End of the Sixties and the Making of Eighties America* (Oxford University Press, 2006), 109–133.

34. Photograph of Lovelace et al., 31 May 1980, Bettye Lane Photographs, SL, PC32-Neg-PornDemo5311980; Lovelace statement quoted in Bronstein, *Battling Pornography*, 260.

35. Diary, 4, 30 Nov 1980, CRP 45.5. On the pregnancy: Diary, 16 Dec 2001, CRP 49.3; and author interview with PS.

36. CR to Mr. Smith, 4 Feb 1981, CRP 104.2.

37. Diary, [13?] Apr 1980, CRP 45.5.

CHAPTER 18: INK

1. "Accounts Appendix," 1980, Diary, CRP 45.5. For median personal income in 1980, see https://fred.stlouisfed.org/series/MEPAINUSA646N, and for inflators to 2020 dollars, see https://www.measuringworth.com/calculators/uscompare/relativevalue.php.

2. Diary, 4, 30 Nov; n.d., 19, 31 Dec 1980, CRP 45.5.

3. Henry Schipper, "Filthy Lucre," *Mother Jones*, Apr 1980, 60.

4. James Cook, "The X-Rated Economy," *Forbes*, 18 Sept 1978, 82–83; John Heidenry, *What Wild Ecstasy: The Rise and Fall of the Sexual Revolution* (Simon & Schuster, 1997), 194–209; Schipper, "Filthy Lucre," 32.

5. Cook, "X-Rated Economy," 83; "High Society in 1977: Gloria Leonard Takes Over – An Issue by Issue Guide," *The Rialto Report*, https://www.therialtoreport.com/2019/07/14/high-society-2/; "Gloria Leonard Publisher of High Society," press release, n.d. c1978, in CRP 52.8. Robert Rosen disputes Leonard's figures; Rosen, *Beaver Street* (Headpress, 2010), 22–40.

6. Cook, "X-Rated Economy," 83; Schipper, "Filthy Lucre," 32.

7. Arv Miller to James Thompson, 26 Sept 1986, CRP 68.2.

8. Peter Alilunas, "Bridging the Gap: *Adult Video News* and the 'Long 1970s,'" in Carolyn Bronstein and Whitney Strub, *Porno Chic and the Sex Wars: American Sexual Representation in the 1970s* (University of Massachusetts Press, 2016), 306–308.

9. Diary, 11–20, 22 Mar; 7, 13 Apr; 21 Aug 1983, CRP 46.2.

10. "The Royalle Treatment," *Cinema X*, Nov 1980, 18–19, 34; Diary, 21 Mar 1980, CRP 45.5.

11. "Accounts Appendix," 1980, Diary, CRP 45.5; Payments for Articles 1982–1987, CRP 103.14; *The Robin Byrd Show*, n.d. Nov 1981, CRP Vt-299.7.

12. Untitled column draft, *Velvet*, Sept 1982; typescript, n.d. 1982, CRP 106.8; "Royalle Treatment," Nov 1980, 18–19, 34, in CRP 104.3, 106.11.

13. "Fuckerware Party, 1982," typescript sent (on spec?) to *Velvet*, Nov 1982, CRP 105.9; "Royalle Audience" typescripts and clips, 1983, CRP 106.10.

14. Article on *Nasty Girls*, typescript, for *Velvet*, Jan 1982, CRP 105.4.

15. Typescript, "Introducing Candida Royalle," n.d. c1981, CRP 105.15.

16. Typescript, "On the Road," 23 Nov 1982, with notation "On spec for *Velvet*. NO" CRP 105.19.

17. "Royalle Treatment," Nov 1980, 34; Dec[?] 1980, 21; clips in CRP 106.11.

18. CV to Cinthea Vadala, 1 Jun 1981, CRP 34.12; Diary, n.d. Jan 1981, CRP 45.5; Diary, 11 Jan 1981, CRP 45.9; CV to Dr. John Heslin, 10 Feb 1982, CRP 36.11; Diary, 30 Apr 1981, CRP 45.11.

19. CV to Cinthea Vadala, 1 Jun 1981, CRP 34.12.
20. CR to Jess Mack, n.d. May 1981, draft, CRP 104.2.
21. Drafts in Diary, n.d. Jan 1981, CRP 45.9; Diary, 5 Oct 1982, CRP 46.2; CV to Cinthea Vadala, 1 Aug 1983, CRP 34.12; see also CRP 105.1.
22. CV to PS, 28 Oct 1983, CRP 34.6; "Is There Life After Porn?" *High Society*, Dec 1984, 40–43, CRP 105.16; Rick [Marx] to CR, 20 Jul 1982, CRP 104.2.
23. Rob [Leung?] to CR, 4 Nov [1987], CRP 103.14.
24. Diary, 28 Nov 1982, ellipsis original, CRP 46.2.
25. Linda Lovelace, *Ordeal* (1980; repr. Citadel, 2006), 138.
26. Linda Wolfe, *The Cosmo Report* (Arbor House, 1981), 24–25, 302, 198, 201. The magazine's survey—unsystematic as it was—garnered orders of magnitude more responses than Kinsey in the 1950s or Shere Hite in the 1970s; *ibid*, 8.
27. Gabrielle Brown, *The New Celibacy: Why More Men and Women Are Abstaining from Sex—and Enjoying It* (McGraw-Hill, 1980), 1.
28. George Leonard, "The End of Sex," *Esquire*, Dec 1982.
29. CDC, "Pneumocystis Pneumonia—Los Angeles, *Morbidity and Mortality Weekly Report*, 5 Jun 1981, quoted in James Kinsella, *Covering the Plague: AIDS and the American Media* (Rutgers University Press, 1989), 9; see also 1–29.
30. CV to Eva [?], 12 Jan 1982, CRP 36.11. On Cowley's illness and death, see Joshua Gamson, *The Fabulous Sylvester: The Legend, the Music, the Seventies in San Francisco* (Henry Holt, 2005), 208–210.
31. Gayle S. Rubin, "Thinking Sex: Notes for a Radical Theory of the Politics of Sexuality," in Carole S. Vance, ed., *Pleasure and Danger: Exploring Female Sexuality* (Routledge, 1984), 299, 267; Kinsella, *Covering the Plague*, 18–21.
32. Carole S. Vance, et al., *Diary of a Conference on Sexuality* (Barnard College Women's Center, 1982), 1, 4.
33. Deirdre English, Amber Hollibaugh, and Gayle Rubin, "Talking Sex: A Conversation on Sexuality and Feminism," *Feminist Review* 11:1 (1982): 41, 44, 45, 47, https://doi.org/10.1057/fr.1982.15. The conversation was originally published in *Socialist Review*, summer 1981.
34. *Diary of a Conference on Sexuality*, 15–17, 13; "The Barnard Conference," *Feminist Studies* 9:1 (1983): 178.
35. Ellen Willis, "Toward a Feminist Sexual Revolution," *Social Text* 6 (1982): 3–21, quotations at 5, 7; https://doi.org/10.2307/466614.
36. SAMOIS, *Coming to Power: Writings and Graphics on Lesbian s/m.* (SAMOIS, 1981), 9; SAMOIS, *What Color Is Your Handkerchief: A Lesbian s/m Sexuality Reader* (SAMOIS, 1979).
37. Paula Webster, "Pornography and Pleasure," in *Heresies* #12, "The Sex Issue," fall 1981, 48–51, quotation at 51.
38. Carolyn Bronstein, *Battling Pornography: The American Feminist Anti-Pornography Movement, 1976–1986* (Cambridge University Press, 2011), 94–97.
39. Carole S. Vance, "Epilogue," in Vance, ed., *Pleasure and Danger*, 431–439. The Coalition leaflet was reprinted in "The Barnard Conference," 180–182.
40. "Program: The Scholar and the Feminist IX: Towards a Politics of Sexuality," 24 Apr 1982, http://sfonline.barnard.edu/sfxxx/programs/sf09.pdf.
41. Dale Spender, "Sex Still Not Simple," *NYT Book Review*, 14 Apr 1985, 13.
42. Carol Queen and Lynn Comella, "The Necessary Revolution: Sex-Positive Feminism in the Post-Barnard Era," *The Communication Review* 11:3 (2008), https://doi.org/10.1080/10714420802306783, 274–291, quotations at 278, 281.
43. Email from Janet E. Halley, 5 August 2022; see also Halley, *Split Decisions: How and*

Why to Take a Break from Feminism (Princeton University Press, 2006), 115–119. Lorna Bracewell documents that racial difference, and the voices of feminists of color, played a larger role in anti-pornography feminism than most analyses have allowed; *Why We Lost the Sex Wars: Sexual Freedom in the #MeToo Era* (University of Minnesota Press, 2021), 129–179. Yet many antis, especially Dworkin and MacKinnon, deployed race chiefly as "an intensifier" of their gender analytic; Jennifer Nash, *The Black Body in Ecstasy: Reading Race, Reading Pornography* (Duke University Press, 2014), 9–12.

44. Sharon Thompson, Christine Stansell, and Ann Barr Snitow, eds., *Powers of Desire: The Politics of Sexuality* (Monthly Review Press, 1983), 38. On the role of *Pleasure and Danger* in building feminist institutions, see Rachel Corbman, "The Scholars and the Feminists: The Barnard Sex Conference and the History of the Institutionalization of Feminism," *Feminist Formations* 27:3 (2015): 49–80, https://doi.org/10.1353/ff.2016.0010. Figures from the Open Syllabus project, https://opensyllabus.org/; and google scholar.

45. Diary, 26 Apr 1982, CRP 45.11.

46. Diary, 9 Jul 1982, CRP 45.11; *Not a Love Story: A Film about Pornography* (1982), dir. Bonnie Sherr Klein.

47. Diary, 15 Jul 1982, CRP 45.11; CR, "Vertical Smiles and Cum-Soaked Aisles: Confessions of a Porn Queen," *High Times*, Jul 1982.

48. Diary, 28 Nov 1982, CRP 46.2.

49. CV to Rama, 3 May 1999, CRP 33.2; CV to B-JB, 28 Apr 1999, CRP 33.1.

50. CR, "The Rise and Fall of Sexpo '82," *Velvet*, Apr 1983, 8–10, 19, CRP 105.25; Diary, 28 Nov 1982, CRP 46.2.

51. CR, "The Rise and Fall of Sexpo '82"; photographs in CRP PD.66sl.

52. "The Barnard Conference," 180.

53. Untitled typescript, Sept [1982]; typescript, *Velvet* column, Sept 1982, CRP 106.8; typescript, "Films and Other Fun for Femmes," n.d. 1983, CRP 105.7.

54. Rick [Marx] to CR, 20 Jul 1982, CRP 104.2; compare to Marx, "Five Sluts Who Split," *Porn Stars*, Nov 1982, clip in CRP 63.20. Marx wrote the screenplays for Chuck Vincent's *Roommates* (1981), and for Larry Revene's *Wanda Whips Wall Street* (1982).

CHAPTER 19: DEEP INSIDE

1. Author interview with Annie Sprinkle; Annie Sprinkle, *Annie Sprinkle: Post-Porn Modernist: My 25 Years as a Multi-Media Whore* (Cleis Press, 1998), 28.

2. Script, notes, and clippings for *Blue Magic* (1981), dir. Larry Revene, CRP 61.11; see also Diary, 13 Apr 1980, and accounts appendix, CRP 45.5.

3. Sprinkle interview in Legs McNeil, *The Other Hollywood: The Uncensored Oral History of the Porn Film Industry* (Regan Books, 2005), 372.

4. Sprinkle, *Post-Porn Modernist*, 24–28, quotations at 26, 27.

5. Fluxus "Manifesto," [1963], in Roslyn Bernstein, *Illegal Living: 80 Wooster Street and the Evolution of SoHo* (Jonas Mekas Fdn, 2010), 38. DeRidder had also done the graphic design for Germaine Greer's *Suck*; see Alison M. Gingeras, "Revisiting *Suck* Magazine's Experiment in Radical Feminist Pornography," *Document*, 28 Nov 2018, https://www.documentjournal.com/2018/11/revisiting-suck-magazines-experiment-in-radical-feminist-pornography/.

6. Owen F. Smith, "Fluxus: A Brief History and Other Fictions," in Elizabeth Armstrong, et al., *In the Spirit of Fluxus* (Walker Art Center, 1993), 35; James R. Hudson, *The Unanticipated City: Loft Conversions in Lower Manhattan* (U. Mass. Press, 1987), 23.

7. Sprinkle, *Post-Porn Modernist*, 46–55; author interview with Annie Sprinkle.

8. Sprinkle, *Post-Porn Modernist*, 113. On Gatewood, see Krissy Eliot, "Finding His Tribe:

The Art of Charles Gatewood," *California Magazine*, Spring 2017, https://alumni.berkeley
.edu/california-magazine/spring-2017-virtue-and-vice/finding-his-tribe-charles-gatewood
-bancroft.

9. Sprinkle, *Post-Porn Modernist*, 60–61; McNeil, *The Other Hollywood*, 371–372.
10. CRP PD.66sl, slide 78.
11. McNeil, *The Other Hollywood*, 371–372.
12. Diary, 9 Sept 1983, CRP 46.2; author interview with Annie Sprinkle.
13. CV to John [Heslin], 10 Feb 1982, CRP 36.11.
14. Annie Sprinkle, *Providing Educational Opportunities to Sex Workers* (PhD dissertation, Institute for Advanced Study of Human Sexuality, 2002), 51–52; author interview with Annie Sprinkle.
15. Diary, n.d. Dec 1982, CRP 46.2.
16. Diary, 16, 19 Jul 1982, CRP 45.11; Diary, n.d. Aug 1983, CRP 46.2.
17. Diary, 19 Nov 1982, CRP 46.2; CV to Cinthea Vadala, 10 Sept 1982, CRP 34.12.
18. Diary, 4 Sept 1983, 19 Nov 1982, CRP 46.2; author interview with Cinthea Vadala. Helen and Louis Vadala divorced in 1974, CRP 61.5.
19. Pinellas Cty, FL, case no. 8403876CF: Arrest record for Louis Vadala, 25 Apr 1984; Indictment, *State of Florida vs. Louis Reginald Vadala*, 23 Jun 1984; Judgment, *State of Florida vs. Louis Reginald Vadala*, 3 Jan 1985. Lipstick and victim's birth year from CV notes on conversation with probation officer Barbara Ferriter, [Jun 1996], CRP 61.9. See also "Largo Man Charged with Sexual Abuse of Six-Year-Old," *Tampa Bay Tribune*, 25 Apr 1984, 3b; Christopher Smart, "Man Indicted in Murder of Clearwater Woman," *St. Petersburg Times*, 21 Jun 1984, 8b. On the "moral careers" of pedophiles, see Doug W. Pryor, *Unspeakable Acts: Why Men Sexually Abuse Children* (NYU Press, 1996).
20. Debbie Nathan, *Satan's Silence: Ritual Abuse and the Making of a Modern American Witch Hunt* (Basic Books, 1995); Philip Jenkins, *Moral Panic: Changing Concepts of the Child Molester in Modern America* (Yale University Press, 1998), 164–188.
21. Judgment, *State of Florida vs. Louis Reginald Vadala*; author interview with Cinthea Vadala; CV notes on conversation with probation officer Barbara Ferriter, [Jun 1996]. Florida criminal code suggests that this sentence was for a first offense; Fla. Stat. § 800.04.
22. Diary entry, 8 Aug 1982, CRP 46.1; "My Heart Belongs to Daddy," lyrics and music by Cole Porter, 1938.
23. Diary, 9 Sept 1983, CRP 46.2.
24. Diary, 9 Sept 1983 CRP 46.2; author interview with Annie Sprinkle. On the "click," see Jane O'Reilly, "Click! The Housewife's Moment of Truth" (1972), repr. Jane O'Reilly, *The Girl I Left Behind* (Macmillan, 1980), 23–58. On feminism and the recovery movement, see Trysh Travis, *The Language of the Heart: A Cultural History of the Recovery Movement from Alcoholics Anonymous to Oprah Winfrey* (University of North Carolina Press, 2009), esp. 143–228.
25. "Carnival Knowledge" handbill, c1982, http://gallery.98bowery.com/2017/bazaar -conceptions-at-the-new-school/; see also Julie Ault and Social Text Collective, *Alternative Art, New York, 1965–1985* (U. Minnesota Press, 2002), 64.
26. Jennifer Dunning, "New Arts Flourish in New Spaces," *NYT*, 6 May 1983, C1; John Rockwell, "Is 'Performance' a New Form of Art?" *NYT*, 14 Aug 1983, H1. On Franklin Furnace, see Alan Moore and Debra Wacks, "Being There: The Tribeca Neighborhood of Franklin Furnace," *The Drama Review* 49:1 (2005): 62; and Lauren Rosati and Mary Anne Staniszewski, *Alternative Histories: New York Art Spaces, 1960 to 2010* (MIT Press, 2012), 87–90, 170–171, 176–177.
27. Toni Sant, "A Long Conversation with Martha Wilson," in *Martha Wilson Sourcebook: 40*

Years of Reconsidering Performance, Feminism, and Alternative Spaces, ed. Martha Wilson (Independent Curators International, 2011), 210.

28. Carnival Knowledge, "Second Coming" handbill, CRP 65.6; McNeil, *The Other Hollywood*, 374–375.

29. Sprinkle, *Post-Porn Modernist*, 150–151; author interview with Annie Sprinkle.

30. *Deep Inside Porn Stars* VHS recording, 26 Jan 1984, CRP Vt-299.7.

31. Author interview with Annie Sprinkle.

32. Jean Fischer, "Carnival Knowledge, 'The Second Coming,'" and "Club 90, Franklin Furnace," *Artforum*, May 1984, 86–87.

33. Arlene Raven, "Looking Beneath the Surface: Deep Inside Porn Stars," *High Performance: A Quarterly Magazine for the New Arts Audience* VII:28 (1984), 24–27, 90.

34. "Dirty Pictures, Dirty Word?" WNEV-TV Boston, 1 Jun 1987, CRP Vt-299.37.

35. Larry Flynt, *An Unseemly Man* (Dove Books, 1996), 203–205.

36. "Classes—Pornography, 1983," CAM Papers, 101.1–102.9.

37. Alicia M. Turner, "Feminist Resistance: An Oral History of the Dworkin-MacKinnon Anti-Pornography Civil Rights Ordinance" (B.A. thesis, Kalamazoo College, 1997), 14–24, quotation at 23, in CAM Papers, 216.11; Elaine Fletcher, "UM Class Finding Porn Violent and Disturbing," *St. Paul Sunday Pioneer Press*, 13 Nov 1983, 1D.

38. Catharine A. MacKinnon and Andrea Dworkin, eds., *In Harm's Way: The Pornography Civil Rights Hearings* (Harvard University Press, 1997), 40.

39. Mike Kaszuba, "Hallway Full of People Awaited Word of the Ordinance's Fate," *MST*, 6 Jan 1984; MacKinnon and Dworkin, *In Harm's Way*, 39–260, quotations at 40 (MacKinnon), 252 (Steinem); Marchiano's testimony appears at 60–66. See also Donald Alexander Downs, *The New Politics of Pornography* (University of Chicago Press, 1989), 34–94.

40. "Minneapolis Asked to Attack Pornography as Rights Issue," *NYT*, 18 Dec 1983, A44; "Minneapolis Gets Rights Law to Ban Pornography," *NYT*, 31 Dec 1984, A24; "Minneapolis Mayor Vetoes Plan Defining Pornography as Sex Bias," *NYT*, 6 Jan 1984, A11; "Smut Is Declared Illegal Sex Bias in Minneapolis," *Washington Post*, 31 Dec 1983, A3; Charles Krauthammer, "Pornography through the Looking Glass," *Time*, 12 Mar 1984, 82–83.

41. "Women Ransack Rialto Theater during Anti-Pornography Protest," *MST*, 3 Dec 1983, 8B; Kate Parry and Martha Allen, "Dworkin Ends Return to City with Rally," *MST*, 24 May 1984, 1B; Wendy Tai, "Antipornography Activists Plan to Dump Magazines at City Hall," *MST*, 7 Jun 1984, 1B; Martha Allen, "Antiporn Group Rallies at City Hall," *MST*, 22 Jun 1984, 1B.

42. Phyllis Schlafly, "New Weapons in the Battle against Pornography," *Phyllis Schlafly Report*, Jun 1984, 2. For the debate, see Catharine A. MacKinnon, "Excerpts from MacKinnon/ Schlafly Debate," *Law and Inequality* 1:2 (1983): 341–354.

43. Dennis McGrath, "Woman Sets Herself on Fire," *MST*, 11 Jul 1984, 1A, 13A; Chuck Haga, "Peace Came at an Awful Price to a Soul Pained by Injustice," *MST*, 14 Dec 1990, 1B, 13B.

44. Dennis McGrath et al., "Woman Who Set Herself Afire Blamed Troubles on Pornography," *MST*, 12 Jul 1984, 1A.

45. Dennis McGrath, "Woman Sets Herself on Fire," *MST*, 11 Jul 1984, 13A.

46. MacKinnon and Dworkin, *In Harm's Way*, dedication page.

47. Sharon Fitzgerald, "Suicide and Porn," *MST*, 19 Jul 1984, 18A; Martha Allen, "Officials Urge Women Not to Hurt Selves," *MST*, 12 Jul 1984, 8A; "Woman Burns Herself to Protest Pornography," *NYT* (via UPI), 12 Jul 1984, A12.

48. Downs, *New Politics of Pornography*, 62–65.

49. Rev. Dr. Jerry R. Kirk, et al., "Second National Consultation on Obscenity, Pornography, and Indecency" (National Consultation on Pornography, Inc., 1984), 108–111.

50. Ronald Reagan, "Remarks on Signing the Child Protection Act of 1984," 21 May 1984, APP, https://www.presidency.ucsb.edu/node/261320. See also Ronald Reagan, "Address Before a Joint Session of the Congress on the State of the Union," 25 Jan 1984, APP, https://www.presidency.ucsb.edu/node/261634.

51. Downs, *New Politics of Pornography*, 72.

52. Diary, 28 Jan 1984, CRP 46.2.

CHAPTER 20: TASTEFULLY HARDCORE

1. Résumé enclosed in R. Lauren Niemi to CV, 31 Jan 1984, CRP 67.13.

2. Author interview with R. Lauren Cole; text exchange with R. Lauren Cole, 7 Jan 2021.

3. Author interview with R. Lauren Cole; see also Megumi Komiya and Barry Litman, "The Economics of the Prerecorded Videocassette Industry," in *Social and Cultural Aspects of VCR Use*, ed. Julie Dobrow (Routledge, 1990).

4. Veronica Vera, "Femme: Porn by Women for Women and Men," *Adam*, Sept 1984, 20–24; author interview with R. Lauren Cole.

5. Author interview with R. Lauren Cole; R. Lauren Niemi to CV, 31 Jan 1984, CRP 67.13.

6. Karen Jaehne, "Confessions of a Feminist Porn Programmer," *Film Quarterly* 37:1 (1983): 10, 15.

7. Tony Schwartz, "The TV Pornography Boom," *NYT Magazine*, 13 Sept 1981, 4; Jean Callahan, "Women and Pornography," *American Film*, Mar 1982, 63.

8. Playboy Channel president Paul Klein quoted in Stadel, "Cable, Pornography, and the Reinvention of Television," 62.

9. Jean Callahan, "Video Erotica Comes Home," *Playgirl*, Nov 1982, 79; Leo Janos, "The Adult-Film Industry Goes Hollywood," *Cosmopolitan*, Jan 1983, 198, 199, 201.

10. Diary, 25 Feb 1984, CRP 46.2.

11. Author interview with R. Lauren Cole.

12. Femme Productions, New York State Business Certificate for Partners, 19 Apr 1984; and partnership agreement, both CRP 103.4.

13. Agreement between Lunarex, Saga Films AB, and Femme Productions, 15 May 1984, CRP 103.4. Peter Alilunas argues that such investments were a tax dodge for Saga, which could funnel Swedish profits into U.S. investments; Alilunas, *Smutty Little Movies: The Creation and Regulation of Adult Video* (University of California Press, 2016), 145.

14. Author interview with R. Lauren Cole.

15. Author interview with Jerome Vitucci; *Femme I*, independent contractors deal memos, CRP 83.9; *Femme I*, performers releases, CRP 83.10.

16. *Femme* (1984), dir. R. Lauren Niemi; *Femme I*, dialogue list and cue sheets, CRP 83.9; Planning Femme 1984 daily workbook, CRP 79.3.

17. *Femme I*, performers releases, CRP 83.10; Planning Femme 1984 daily workbook, CRP 79.3; compare to Appointment book, 1975, 14, 17, 23 Aug, CRP 1.10.

18. Author interview with R. Lauren Cole; CR, "Vertical Smiles and Cum-Soaked Aisles: Confessions of a Porn Queen," *High Times*, Jul 1982, 41, 67.

19. Femme concept statement, n.d. [c Oct 1984], CRP 103.10; Femme Productions workbook 1984, CRP 79.6.

20. Diary, CRP 46.2, places the initial concept for *Urban Heat* sometime in April 1984.

21. Agreement between Saga Film AB and Lunarex, 25 Jun 1984, CRP 103.4.

22. CR to Joe Dolce, 11 Jul 1984, CRP 67.13.

23. Draft of September 1984 *Velvet* column, May 1984; draft of August 1984 *Velvet* column, Mar 1984; both CRP 106.8; Vera, "Femme: Porn by Women for Women and Men," 20–24.

24. *People Are Talking* (WBZ Boston), 25 Apr 1984, CRP Vt 299.9. For public speaking in college, see "A Conversation with Candida Royalle, April 27, 1999," CRP 53.10.

25. *Midnight Blue*, episode 444, n.d. Jul 1984, CRP Vt 299.12

26. *Urban Heat* party scene flyer, CRP 103.10; *Urban Heat* performers' releases, CRP 95.5; author interview with R. Lauren Cole.

27. *Urban Heat* (1984), dir. Lauren Niemi. Femme Productions Daily Workbook, 1984, CRP 79.4 shows expenditures of $10,250 for music and $5,950 for performers.

28. Femme Productions Daily Workbooks, 1984, CRP 79.4 and 79.5; *Christine's Secret*, Independent contractors deal memos, Aug 1984, CRP 82.11.

29. CR to Richard Pacheco (Howie Gordon), 3 Dec 1984, CRP 67.13; CR to Kathy Keeton, 16 Nov 1987, CRP 69.1; *Christine's Secret*, revised script [Jul 1984], CRP 82.10, n.p.

30. Author interviews with R. Lauren Cole; making of *Christine's Secret* slides, CRP 83.3.

31. *Christine's Secret*, revised script [Jul 1984], CRP 82.10, 10, 8; *Christine's Secret* Dialogue List and Cue Sheet, CRP 82.10, 6; *Christine's Secret* (1985), dir. Candida Royalle and R. Lauren Niemi.

32. [Eve Ziegler], review of *Christine's Secret*, *Swank*, Aug 1986, 56.

33. CR to Kathy Keeton, 16 Nov 1987, CRP 69.1; "Review of *Christine's Secret*," *Hustler*, Jul 1986, 27, clip in CRP 82.4.

34. Femme Productions Daily Workbooks, 1984, CRP 79.4, 101–135.

35. Diary entry, 23 Jun 1984, CRP 65.6; Diary, 29 Feb, n.d. Mar, 8 Oct 1984, CRP 46.2.

36. Diary entry, 18–19 Jun 1984, CRP 65.6.

37. Diary, 30 Aug 1984, CRP 46.2.

38. Author interview with R. Lauren Cole.

39. Text message from R. Lauren Cole, 13 January 2021; Bayard Webster, "Increase in AIDS Cases Reported," *NYT*, 30 Nov 1984, B10; Howie Gordon, *Hindsight: True Love & Mischief in the Golden Age of Porn* (Bear Manor Media, 2013), 548.

40. Ronald Reagan, "Inaugural Address," 21 Jan 1985, APP, https://www.presidency.ucsb.edu/documents/inaugural-address-10.

41. Linda Grant, *Sexing the Millennium: A Political History of the Sexual Revolution* (HarperCollins, 1993), 8.

42. Diary, 1–2 Oct 1984, CRP 46.2.

43. Press release, n.d. 1984, CRP 103.10.

44. CR to Vince Crisp [VCA], 11 Sept 1984, CRP 67.13. Founded by Russ Hampshire and Walter Gernert in 1978, the Los Angeles–based VCA (Video Club of America) Pictures presumably benefitted from the similarity of its name to the New York–based VCA/Technicolor Duplicating Corporation, the industry distribution leader across genres. See Alilunas, *Smutty Little Movies*, 77; James Melanson, "Homevideo: X-Rated Vid Ain't Blue Over 1984 Sale," *Variety*, 30 Jan 1985, 40; and Komiya and Litman, "The Economics of the Prerecorded Videocassette Industry," 31–33.

45. CV to Bill Brown, 27 Jan 1985, CRP 37.2; Diary, 3 Feb 1985, ellipsis original, CRP 46.2.

46. Diary, 1–2 Oct 1984, CRP 46.2.

47. Diary, 30 Sept 1984, CRP 46.2; E. Jean Caroll, "How to Make $1,000 a Day," *Playgirl*, Aug 1983, 53ff.

48. Mitch Rosten, "Rosten's Review," *Canarsie Courier*, 27 Sept 1984, 37; *Urban Heat* chromes, CRP 95.8; author interview with R. Lauren Cole.

49. Draft column for *Velvet*, typescript dated Sept 1984, CRP 106.8.

50. Author interview with R. Lauren Cole.

51. Column for *Velvet*, typescript, Sept 1984, CRP 106.8; CV to Bill Brown, 23 Nov 1984, CRP 37.1.

52. *American Booksellers Association v. Hudnut*, 598 F. Supp. 1316 (S.D. Ind. 1984), 19 Nov 1984, https://law.justia.com/cases/federal/district-courts/FSupp/598/1316/1476351/.

53. NOW press release, 1 Jul 1984, in CAM Papers, 214.2.

54. *Urban Heat* chromes, CRP 95.8; Femme Press release, n.d. 1984, CRP 103.10.

55. Susan Brownmiller et al., "The Place of Pornography," *Harper's*, 1 Nov 1984, 33 ff.

56. *People Are Talking* (WBZ Boston), 25 Apr 1984, CRP Vt 299.9.

57. CV to Bill Brown, 23 Nov 1984, CRP 37.1.

58. "Press Already Generated by Femme Productions," [n.d., before May 1985], CRP 103.10.

59. *AVN*, Jan 1985, n.p.; *Adam*, Apr 1985, n.p., clippings in CRP 83.11; Dorothy Allen, "Review of *Femme*," *Adult Cinema*, Feb 1985, 70–75, in CRP 62.11.

60. Terri Hardin to Femme Productions, 29 May 1985, CRP 68.1.

61. Review of *Urban Heat*, *Screw*, Feb 1985, n.p., clipping in CRP 95.7; Al Goldstein, "X-Rated Video," *Penthouse*, May 1985, 50.

62. Femme publicity materials collating review quotations place *Screw* far down on the list and omit Goldstein's name from the *Penthouse* pull quote; CRP 103.10.

CHAPTER 21: A WAR MADE FOR TV

1. Ann Ferguson, "Sex War: The Debate between Radical and Libertarian Feminists," *signs* 10:1 (1984): 106–112, https://doi.org/10.1086/494117, quotations at 106–107; Lorna N. Bracewell, "Beyond Barnard: Liberalism, Antipornography Feminism, and the Sex Wars," *signs* 42:1 (2016): 23–48, https://doi.org/10.1086/686752.

2. Gayle S. Rubin, "Thinking Sex: Notes for a Radical Theory of the Politics of Sexuality," in Carole S. Vance, ed., *Pleasure and Danger: Exploring Female Sexuality* (Routledge, 1984), 301; Catharine A. MacKinnon, "Not a Moral Issue," *Yale Law & Policy Review* 2:2 (1984): 327; Lorna N. Bracewell, *Why We Lost the Sex Wars: Sexual Freedom in the #MeToo Era* (University of Minnesota Press, 2021), 12–29.

3. Dolores Alexander Testimony, Philadelphia, 23 Mar 1986, NOW Records, 95.7; Eileen Micheau to Priscilla Alexander and Paula Lichtenburg, 27 Feb 1986, NOW Records, 95.9.

4. *Congressional Record*, 89th Congress, 2nd sess., vol. 112:4 (28 Feb–9 Mar 1966), 5257–5259.

5. Robert Yoakum, "Porn War Rages on in Fun City," *Arizona Daily Star*, 15 Jun 1977, A15.

6. Richard Pacheco (Howie Gordon) to CR, 31 Jul 1984, CRP 67.13.

7. MacKinnon, "Not a Moral Issue," 323–324.

8. *Congressional Record*, 97th Congress, 2nd sess., vol. 128:22 (9–14 Dec 1982), 30379.

9. Jean Bethke Elshtain, "The New Porn Wars," *New Republic*, 25 Jun 1984, 15–20.

10. Sean Wilentz, *The Age of Reagan: A History, 1974–2008* (Harper, 2008), 177–181.

11. "Notice of Establishment: Attorney General's Commission on Pornography," 22 Feb 1985, *Federal Register* 50:42, 8684; Leslie Werner, "Senate Approves Meese to Become Attorney General," *NYT*, 24 Feb 1985, A1.

12. Philip Shenon, "Meese Commission Panel to Study How to Control Pornography," *NYT*, 21 May 1985, A21. Commissioner biographies in *Attorney General's Commission on Pornography, Final Report* [hereafter *Meese Commission Report*] (Government Printing Office, 1986), 1–21.

13. Hendrik Hertzberg, "Big Boobs," *New Republic*, 14 Jul 1986, 21 ff., https://newrepublic.com/article/90764/big-boobs.

14. Nan D. Hunter and Sylvia A. Law, "Brief Amici Curiae of Feminist Anti-Censorship

Taskforce, et al., in *American Booksellers Association v. Hudnut* [April 1985]," *University of Michigan Journal of Law Reform* 21:1–2 (1987): 89–98.

15. MacKinnon, "Liberalism and the Death of Feminism," in Dorchen Leidholdt and Janice G. Raymond, eds., *The Sexual Liberals and the Attack on Feminism* (Pergamon, 1990), 9–10, 12.

16. "F.A.C.T. or F.I.C.T.I.O.N.," c1985; FICTION faux press release, c1985, in CAM Papers, 219.10. The authorship of these satires is unclear.

17. CAM Papers, 219.11.

18. CR to Phyllis Kriegel, 4 Mar 1985, CRP, 68.1; http://www.phylliskriegel.com/537263/ biography/; *New Directions for Women* 22:5 (Sept–Oct 1993): back cover.

19. *American Booksellers Association v. Hudnut*, 771 F.2d 323 (1985), https://cite.case.law/ f2d/771/323/.

20. Donald Alexander Downs, *The New Politics of Pornography* (University of Chicago Press, 1989), 135–139.

21. Diary, 30 Dec 1984, CRP 46.2; "Press Already Generated by Femme Productions," cFeb 1985, CRP 103.10.

22. Aric Press et al., "The War Against Pornography: Feminists, Free Speech, and the Law," *Newsweek*, 18 Mar 1985. For MacKinnon citations of Donnerstein pre-1985, see "Not a Moral Issue," notes 8, 9, 20, 36, 60. For FACT on Donnerstein, see Hunter and Law, "FACT Brief," 112–15.

23. CR to the editors of *Newsweek*, 13 Mar 1985, CRP 68.1.

24. Mary Kay Blakely, "Is One Woman's Sexuality Another Woman's Pornography?" *Ms.*, Apr 1985, quotation at 40.

25. CR to the Editors of *Ms.* and Gloria Steinem, 6, 12 Jul 1985, CRP 68.1.

26. Bernard Timberg, *Television Talk: A History of the TV Talk Show* (University of Texas Press, 2002); Jane Shattuc, *The Talking Cure: TV Talk Shows and Women* (Routledge, 1997).

27. Laura Grindstaff, *The Money Shot: Trash, Class, and the Making of TV Talk Shows* (University of Chicago Press, 2002), 19–20, 52–53.

28. Jordan Villegas, " 'You Don't Want to Miss This Show': Pornography, Populism, and the Performance of Feminist Conflict on Daytime Television Talk Shows," unpublished seminar paper, 2017; John Stoltenberg, "Living with Andrea Dworkin," Andrea Dworkin Online Library, 1994, http://www.nostatusquo.com/ACLU/dworkin/ LivingWithAndrea.html.

29. *MidDay with Bill Boggs*, Channel 5 WNEW (NYC), n.d. spring 1985, CRP Vt 299.15.

30. CR to Marco Vassi, 6 Mar 1985, CRP 68.1; Marco Vassi, "Finally, Feminist Porn," *Penthouse Forum*, Jul 1985, 69–71, 74; CV to Bill Brown, 28 Feb 1985, CRP 37.2.

31. *Meese Commission Report*, 219–220.

32. *Meese Commission Report*, 1939; Hertzberg, "Big Boobs."

33. Catharine A. MacKinnon to Linda [Marchiano], n.d. [October 1985]; Catharine A. MacKinnon to Linda [Marchiano], 6 November 1985; CAM Papers, 214.10.

34. *Meese Commission Report*, 1845–1871.

35. CR to Joseph B. Haggerty, 27 Jul 1985, CRP 66.2; Diary, 30 Jun 1985, CRP 46.2; CR to Michael [?], 3 Jul 1985, CRP 68.1.

36. Diary, 12 Sept 1985, CRP 46.2; Pat Califia to CR, 17 Oct 1985, CRP 68.1. For the festival, see CRP 68.4.

37. Henry Hudson to CR, 23 Sept 1985; CR Draft Statement, 2, 4, 6, in CR to Joseph B. Haggerty, 27 Jul 1985, all CRP 66.2.

38. CR to Henry Hudson, 28 Sept 1985; CR to Henry Hudson, 4 Oct 1985, CRP 66.2; CR Draft Statement, 4, CRP 66.2.
39. Carole Vance to CR, 21 Oct 1985, CRP 68.1.
40. Susan Squire, "How Women Are Changing Porn Films," *Glamour*, Nov 1985, 283, 322, 325. Femme sent press materials to *Glamour* in February, after the magazine ran a reader survey on erotica: CR to Janet Chan, 19 Feb 1985, CRP 68.1.
41. "A Conversation with Candida Royalle, 27 April 1999," CRP 53.10; CR to Ruth Whitney, 12 Feb 1986, CRP 68.3.
42. CV to Suzanne [Deckert], 30 Dec 1985, CRP 68.1.
43. *The Phil Donahue Show*: #6208, aired 15 August 1975; #9191, aired 18 February 1976; #9150, aired 27 October 1976; #9106, aired 12 March 1976; #9125, aired 8 June 1976; and #9137, aired 10 August 1976; https://www.atvaudio.com/.
44. "Donahue Transcript #11185," CAM Papers, 219.8; *The Phil Donahue Show*, 18 Nov 1985, CRP Vt 299.19.
45. CV to Suzanne [Deckert], 30 Dec 1985, CRP 68.1; Diary, 5 Dec 1985, CRP 46.2.
46. Janice Irvine, "Getting the FACTs Out," *Cambridge Chronicle*, 10 Oct 1985, 4; "Bliss and Power," *Cambridge Chronicle*, 10 Oct 1985, 4. On the "catfight narrative," see Bracewell, "Beyond Barnard," 5–12.
47. "Donahue Transcript #11185," 5, 7, 8, 12, 14, 16.
48. Catharine A. MacKinnon, *Only Words* (Harvard University Press, 1993).
49. "Donahue Transcript #11185," 12.

CHAPTER 22: PORNOGRAPHY OF THE PEOPLE

1. Rick Marx, "The Death of Porn, Part I," *Screw*, 25 Nov 1985, 4, 6–7.
2. CV to Bill Brown, 28 Jul 1985, CRP 37.2; Marx, "Death of Porn, Part I." See also "Shauna Grant: Rare Photos and 'Death of a Porn Queen,' 1987," https://www.therialtoreport.com/2015/11/22/shauna-grant/.
3. Rick Marx, "The Death of Porn, Part II: The Next Degeneration," *Screw*, 2 Dec 1985, 9–11.
4. Barry Janoff, "Getting the Royalle Treatment," *Oui*, Dec 1985, 37–42, 96; "*Stars Porno: des Femmes Comme les Autres*," *Photo*, Dec 1985, clipping in CRP 64.1.
5. CR to Robert Leung, 15 Nov 1985, CRP 68.1.
6. Diary, n.d. Jun 1986, CRP 46.2.
7. CV to Helen Vadala, 5 Jan 1986, CRP 35.3.
8. Sture Sjöstedt to CV and PS, 31 Dec 1985, CRP 68.1; Femme Films Income, 1985–1987, CRP 96.7.
9. PoP Awards Program, CRP 82.5; see also Diary, 27 Feb 1985, CRP 46.2; Joyce James to CR, 13 Feb 1985; and CR to Marco [Vassi], 6 Mar 1985, both CRP 68.1. The PoP Awards tallied reader votes from *Adult Cinema Review, Cinema Blue, Erotica, Swank,* and *X-Rated Cinema*.
10. Daniel Carl Fedrickson to CR, 5 Aug 1987; Thomas to CR, 12 Jun 1986; CRP 74.8. Annie Sprinkle had done an installation of such letters in a Lower East Side gallery in 1984; Annie Sprinkle, *Annie Sprinkle: Post-Porn Modernist: My 25 Years as a Multi-Media Whore* (Cleis Press, 1998), 92.
11. Marie Blazek to CR, n.d. 1988, CRP 75.1; Edmund H. Brand to *Forum* magazine, cc to CR, 11 Apr 1989, CRP 75.5; Pam Shields to CR, [2 Dec 1988 postmark], CRP 75.2. Fan letters comprise fifteen folders of the Royalle Papers, CRP 74.8–76.5.
12. Eric Bohr to CR, 26 Oct 1987; Robert Taylor to CR, 2 November 1986; CRP 74.8.
13. Anonymous to CR, 3 Oct 1988; Ayesha Ibrahim to Femme, 24 Jul 1988; Mrs. Peter Chang to Femme, 23 Jul 1988, CRP 75.3.

14. Ralph Mowry to CR, 24 Jul 1988; Ed Allen, [May 1988], CRP 75.1; Rita Peterson to CR, 21 Jul 1989; Linda Edwards to CR, 28 Sept 1989, both CRP 75.5; Robin Heilprin and Carter Lusher to Femme, 6 Jun 1988, CRP 75.2.

15. Rita Peterson to CR, 21 Jul 1989; Cindy Illig to Femme, 4 Aug 1989, CRP 75.5; Mike (and Jill) Evans to CR, 1 Nov 1988; Leslie Firth to CR, [nd, Apr 1988?]; both CRP 75.1.

16. Lisa LaBia to CR, [nd, spring 1987], CRP 68.6.

17. CV to Martin Blinder, 7 Jul 1986, CRP 37.3; Femme Productions finances from 1985–1987 detailed in CRP 96.7.

18. Diary, 7 Sept 1986, CRP 46.2; *The Morning Show, Sally Jesse Raphael*, n.d. Feb 1986, CRP Vt 299.19; press release, n.d. 1986, CRP 103.10.

19. CV to Pauline, 12 Jun 1986; CV to Martin Blinder, 7 Jul 1986, both CRP 37.3. "Porn Report," WFAA-TV Dallas, aired 7-11 Jul 1986, CRP Vt-299.27.

20. Daniel Goleman, "Researchers Dispute Pornography Report on Its Use of Data," *NYT,* 17 May 1986, A1.

21. "Statement of Dr. Judith Becker and Ellen Levine," *Meese Commission Report*, 195–212, quotation at 197–198; Philip Shenon, "Two on U.S. Commission Dissent on a Pornography Link to Violence," *NYT,* 19 May 1986, A17.

22. *Meese Commission Report*, 1505–1547; Al Goldstein, "Pay Dirt, as It Were," *NYT,* 12 Jul 1986, A23. The *Report* called these "separate magazine titles," but in fact listings included numerous issues of the same magazines.

23. "Women Against Pornography's Response to the U.S. Attorney General's Commission on Pornography: July 9, 1986," CAM Papers, 220.10, quotations at 1–3.

24. "Statement by John Stoltenberg, Cofounder, Men Against Pornography, [Jul 1986], CAM Papers, 220.10.

25. Statement of MacKinnon and Dworkin, 9 Jul 1986, CAM Papers, 220.10.

26. *Hudnut v. American Booksellers Association*, 475 U.S. 1001 (1986), https://cite.case.law/us/475/1001/6211098/; Catharine A. MacKinnon, "The Roar on the Other Side of Silence," in MacKinnon and Andrea Dworkin, eds., *In Harm's Way: The Pornography Civil Rights Hearings* (Harvard University Press, 1997), 17–18.

27. Priscilla Alexander and Paula Lichtenberg to NOW National Board, 14 Jul 1986, NOW Records, 95.5. For broader impact, see Stuart Taylor, Jr., "Pornography Foes Lose New Weapon in Supreme Court," *NYT,* 25 Feb 1986, A1; "Long Island Anti-Porn Bill Defeated," *Off Our Backs*, Feb 1985, 2; Donald Alexander Downs, *The New Politics of Pornography* (University of Chicago Press, 1989), xiii, 140.

28. MacKinnon, "Roar on the Other Side," 17. For the impact of *Hudnut* on the Bellingham referendum, see *Village Books et al. v. City of Bellingham*, U.S. District Court at Seattle, W.D. Wash No. C88-147OD, 8 Feb 1989.

29. Alexander and Lichtenberg to NOW National Board, 14 Jul 1986; Betty Friedan, "How to Get the Women's Movement Moving Again," *NYT Magazine*, 3 Nov 1985, 26 ff., https://www.nytimes.com/1985/11/03/magazine/how-to-get-the-womens-movement-moving-again.html.

30. Margaret Atwood, "Handmaids Rising," *NYT Book Review*, 19 Mar 2017, 1.

31. Marcia Pally, "Getting Down with Candida Royalle," *Forum*, Apr 1986, 56.

32. Diary, 29 Apr 1986, CRP 46.2.

33. Sheldon Ranz (WBAI) to CR, 21 Dec 1986, CRP 68.2.

34. CR, "Letter to the National Organization for Women," May 1986, CRP 103.10.

35. Eight members of New York NOW to CV, 26 Jun 1986, CRP 68.4.

36. Lindsy Van Gelder, "Toys for Free Grown-Ups: A Consumer Guide to Sex Gadgets, Potions, and Videos," *Ms.*, Aug 1986, 95; CR to the Editors of *Ms.*, 30 Jul 1986, CRP 68.4.

37. John Leo and Scott Brown, "Romantic Porn in the Boudoir: The VCR Revolution Produces X-Rated Films for Women (and Men)," *Time*, 30 Mar 1987, 63–66.
38. Marta Balletbo-Coll, "Girls Just Wanna Have Fun," *Columbia Film View*, Fall 1987, 19.
39. CR to Jennifer, 12 Feb 1986, CRP 68.3; Leo and Brown, "Romantic Porn in the Boudoir."
40. Femme Distribution business certificate, 28 Jul 1986; and Femme Productions certificate of discontinuance of business as partners, 2 Jul 1986; CRP 103.4.
41. CV to Candelora [Versace], 6 Jul 1986, CRP 37.3; *Three Daughters* scripts, CRP 94.11; *Three Daughters* cast and crew list, CRP 94.6; review of *Christina's* [*sic*] *Secret*, *Swank*, August 1986, 56; author interview with Janice Sukaitis.
42. *Three Daughters* location contract, Apr 1986, CRP 94.7; script, CRP 94.11, 38; dialogue and cue sheets, CRP 94.5, 6–7, 17; shot list, CRP 95.1, scenes 6 and 7.
43. *Three Daughters* script, CRP 94.11.
44. Diary, 3 Feb 1985, CRP 46.2; see also interpolated letter to Louis Vadala, 6 Mar 1985; Judgment, State of Florida vs. Louis Reginald Vadala, Sixth Judicial Circuit, case number 8403876CF, 3 Jan 1985.
45. CV to Bill Brown, 27 Jan 1985, 28 Jul 1985, CRP 37.2.
46. Diary, 20 Jan 1984, CRP 46.2; draft, CV to Helen Vadala [unsent?], 30 Jul 1986, CRP 46.11; CV to Cinthea Vadala, 19 Aug 1985, CRP 34.12.
47. Diary entry, 19 Mar 1986, CRP 46.11; Louis Vadala to CV, 16 Jan 1976, courtesy of Cinthea Vadala.
48. CV to Bill Brown, 28 Jul 1985, CRP 37.2.
49. Draft, CV to Helen Vadala [unsent?], 30 Jul 1986, CRP 46.11; Diary, 4, 7 Sept 1986, CRP 46.2.
50. CR to Harvey Woods, 4 Mar 1986, CRP 68.3; *Three Daughters* script, CRP 94.11.
51. The Child Abuse Victims Rights Act of 1986, which increased penalties for the sexual exploitation of children, was introduced in February, before *Three Daughters* was filmed: https://www.congress.gov/bill/99th-congress/house-bill/4157. The related Child Sexual Abuse and Pornography Act of 1986, centered on the visual depiction of minors, was introduced in September and became law in November: https://www.congress.gov/bill/99th-congress/house-bill/5560/text.
52. Dave Palermo, "Sex Films Pulled, Star Allegedly Too Young," *LAT*, 18 Jul 1986, Metro 1; Ronald Soble and Paul Feldman, "Sex Film Star Not Facing Charges, Reiner Says," *LAT*, 19 Jul 1986, Metro 1; "Underground Traci," *LAT*, 25 Jul 1986, V22.
53. "Distributor Indicted over Sex Videotape," *LAT*, 15 Aug 1986, A27; John Kendall, "Investigation of Traci Lords Pornography Case Expanded," *LAT*, 4 Oct 1986, Metro 1; Kim Murphy, "Three in Traci Lords' Sex Case Indicted," *LAT*, 6 Mar 1987, Metro 6. See also Peter Alilunas, *Smutty Little Movies: The Creation and Regulation of Adult Video* (University of California Press, 2016), 248–249 n18; Robert Rosen, *Beaver Street* (Headpress, 2010), chapter 10.
54. Invitation to *Three Daughters* launch party, CRP 94.10; Nicholas D. Kristof, "X-Rated Industry in a Slump," *NYT*, 5 Oct 1986, C1, https://www.nytimes.com/1986/10/05/business/x-rated-industry-in-a-slump.html; Chuck Kleinhans, "The Change from Film to Video Pornography: Implications for Analysis," in *Pornography: Film and Culture*, ed. Peter Lehman (Rutgers University Press, 2006), 157. The *NYT* Style pages discussed the trend, quoting Royalle on the feminist sexual politics of *Three Daughters*; Georgia Dullea, "X-Rated 'Couples Films' Finding a New Market," *NYT*, 6 Oct 1986, B12.
55. Balletbo-Coll, "Girls Just Wanna Have Fun," 21.
56. Rick Marx, "Soft Bore," *Screw*, 26 Jan 1987, 21, clip in CRP 94.10.
57. Barbara Hoffman, "Ladies' Home Hard-Core," *Bergen County Record*, 20 Oct 1986, B3;

Leo and Brown, "Romantic Porn in the Boudoir." Candice found Leo's discussion of Femme "fair and unbiased": CV to John Leo, n.d. Apr 1987, CRP 68.6.
58. CV to Bill Brown, 31 Mar 1987, CRP 37.4.
59. Diary, n.d. May 1987, CRP 46.2; *TODAY*, 21 Apr 1987, CRP Vt-299.31; Femme press release, 23 Apr 1987, CRP 103.10. Cinthea Vadala says Candice called her appearance on TODAY "one of my worst experiences because I had to sit in the green room and listen to Jane Pauley screaming, 'Why do I have to interview the porn queen?'" Author interview with Cinthea Vadala.
60. Diary, n.d. May 1987, CRP 46.2; CAFA Awards program, CRP 82.5; Rick Marx, "The Death of Porn, Part II," 10.
61. Diary, 7 Sept 1986, CRP 46.2.
62. CV to Bill Brown, 28 Feb 1985, CRP 37.2.

CHAPTER 23: THE PARTING OF THE RED SEA
1. Dolores Deluce, "Gay Widows: A Memorial of Love," book proposal, 1993, 9–10, CRP 54.9.
2. Ronald Reagan, "Remarks to Employees of the Department of Health and Human Services," 5 Feb 1986, APP, https://www.presidency.ucsb.edu/node/258092.
3. C. Everett Koop, *Surgeon General's Report on Acquired Immune Deficiency Syndrome* (U.S. Department of Health and Human Services, 1986), http://hdl.handle.net/2027/ucbk.ark:/28722/h2k93171p. For the report's distribution, see "Limit on AIDS Booklet Lifted," *NYT*, 16 Jun 1987, A27; "U.S. Booklet on AIDS Is Expected Out Soon," *NYT*, 31 Aug 1987, A16; "U.S. Will Mail AIDS Advisory to All Households," *NYT*, 5 May 1988, B10; and Andrew Hartman, *A War for the Soul of America: A History of the Culture Wars* (2015; repr., University of Chicago Press, 2018), 160.
4. CDC, "HIV and AIDS—United States, 1981–2000" *Morbidity and Mortality Weekly Report*, 1 Jun 2001, https://www.cdc.gov/mmwr/preview/mmwrhtml/mm5021a2.htm; CDC, "Epidemiology of HIV/AIDS—United States, 1981–2005, *Morbidity and Mortality Weekly Report*, 2 Jun 2006, https://www.cdc.gov/mmwr/preview/mmwrhtml/mm5521a2.htm.
5. CV, Notes on friends lost to AIDS, n.d. 1993, CRP 54.9; author interview with PS.
6. CV to Bill Brown, 28 Jul 1985, CRP 37.2.
7. "Bill Models a Rose," Oct 1985, CRP 55.3v.
8. Herm [Chittka] to Bill Brown, 2 Mar 1986; CV to Herm [Chittka], 4 Mar 1986; CRP 37.3; "Shanti Projects: Histories of Shanti Project and the AIDS Crisis," https://shantiprojects.dash.umn.edu/.
9. CV to Bill Brown, 31 Mar 1987; Jane Chittka to CV and PS, 29 Dec 1987, CRP 37.4; Janey [Brown?] to CV and PS, 1 Jan 1989, CRP 37.6.
10. Email from Sherry Falek, 30 Mar 2021.
11. CV, Notes on friends lost to AIDS; CV to PS, 24 Aug 1989, CRP 34.8; Emails from Jorgé Socarras, 22 Feb 2019, 2 Apr 2021. I have not located a death record for Joe Merlino aka Morocco.
12. Chris Smith, "Musician Kills Self after Injuring Boy," *Santa Rosa Press Democrat*, 8 Oct 1987, B1; Diary entry, 8-9 Feb 1988, CRP 46.15.
13. CV and Lailani, "Saturday Nite(-Fever)," c Aug 1978, CRP 52.4.
14. Doug Williams to Candice Sjöstedt, 18 Jun 1987, and snapshot, CRP 52.4; CV Eulogy for Lailani, CRP 52.4; *Three Daughters* credits, CRP 94.6.
15. Diary, 23 Mar 1986, CRP 46.2.
16. Diary, 8 Jan 1985, CRP 46.2; "Music Specialties," *NY Daily News*, 8 Jun 1983, 13; "Clubs," *NY Daily News*, 4 Oct 1985, 38.

17. Theodore Kerr, "How Six NYC Activists Changed History With 'Silence=Death,'" *Village Voice*, 20 Jun 2017, https://www.villagevoice.com/2017/06/20/how-six-nyc-activists-changed-history-with-silence-death/.

18. William F. Buckley Jr., "Crucial Steps in Combatting the AIDS Epidemic: Identify All the Carriers," *NYT*, 18 Mar 1986, A27.

19. Kerr, "How Six NYC Activists Changed History"; David France, *How to Survive a Plague: The Inside Story of How Citizens and Science Tamed AIDS* (Knopf, 2016), 244, 268, 330, 403–404; Jack Lowery, *It Was Vulgar and It Was Beautiful: How AIDS Activists Used Art to Fight a Pandemic* (Bold Type, 2022), 26–44; Sarah Schulman, *Let the Record Show: A Political History of ACT UP New York, 1987–1993* (Farrar, Straus and Giroux, 2021), 319–327.

20. Paul Abramson, "AIDS and the Pornography Industry: Opportunities for Prevention, and Obstacles," in Richard A. Berk, ed., *The Social Impact of AIDS in the U.S.* (Abt, 1988), 38.

21. Laurie Holmes quoted in Legs McNeil, *The Other Hollywood: The Uncensored Oral History of the Porn Film Industry* (Regan Books, 2005), 449; Jennifer Sugar, *John Holmes: A Life Measured in Inches* (Bear Manor Media, 2008), 362–390.

22. Ryan Murphy, "The Strange Life and Times of John C. Holmes," *Miami Herald*, 1 Apr 1988, B16; Abramson, "AIDS and the Pornography Industry"; and "AIDS in Los Angeles County by Census Tract, 1982–1987," in Berk, *Social Impact of AIDS*, 37–50, 4–5.

23. Robert Taylor to CR, 17 May 1987, CRP 74.8.

24. CR to David Dever, 10 Jun 1987, CRP 68.9; Michael S. Weisberg, "AIDS and Pornography: Some Producers of Smut Are Cleaning Up Their Acts," *NY Daily News*, 16 Jun 1987, 12.

25. Tim Haft to CR, 5 Apr 1987, CRP 68.6; CR to Pat McGilligan, 16 Jul 1987, CRP 68.9. McGilligan's article came out under a pseudonym: Bette Noire, "Porn with a Difference," *Playgirl*, Oct 1987; clip in CRP 63.1.

26. Notes on a new Club 90 performance, c Jul 1987, CRP 79.8; Nan Goldin, *The Ballad of Sexual Dependency* (Aperture, 1986).

27. CR to Kathy Keeton [*Penthouse*], 16 Nov 1986; CR to Len Miller [*Hollywood Trade Press*], 20 Nov 1987; both CRP 69.1.

28. Diary, 3 Oct 1987, CRP 46.2; *Film World Reports*, 19 Jan 1987, clipping in CRP 63.1.

29. CR to Len Miller, 20 Nov 1987, copy CRP 69.1.

30. "The Pick-Up," in *A Taste of Ambrosia* [Femme 5, Star Director Series 1] (1987); Mark Schoen, PhD to Femme, 18 Nov 1987, CRP 69.1; Femme "News Flash," Nov 1987, CRP 103.10.

31. "Agreement between Playboy Cable Network and Femme Distribution," 10 Nov 1987. *Playboy* licensed the next two Star Directors offerings, *Rites of Passion* and *Sensual Escape*, under the same terms, 20 Jan 1988 and 14 Apr 1988. Robert J. Trip to Lindsay Flora, 28 May 1987, suggests that there may have been a prior arrangement to license *Three Daughters*; all CRP 76.10. For the rejection of *Femme, Urban Heat*, and *Christine's Secret*, see Denise Zietlow to Vivian Forlander, 16 Nov 1987, CRP 69.1.

32. Erica Abeel, "Bedroom Eyes: Erotic Movies Come Home," *Mademoiselle*, Oct 1987, 195, 234.

33. Jared to CR, 27 May 1987, CRP 68.9; CR to Chris Tardio, 12 Nov 1987, CRP 68.7.

34. Nicole Hemmer, *Messengers of the Right: Conservative Media and the Transformation of American Politics* (University of Pennsylvania Press, 2016), 115–125, 258–261.

35. "KFBK Host Suspended over Ethnic Term," *Sacramento Bee*, 24 Aug 1984, B1; "Downey Finds Job, KFBK Names Host," *Sacramento Bee*, 13 Oct 1984, B9; Patrick Goldstein, "Shock Radio: Is It Satire or Just Bad Taste?" *LAT*, 22 Feb 1987, Calendar, 3.

36. Morton Downey, *Mort! Mort! Mort!: No Place to Hide* (Delacorte, 1988), 6–7; Wayne

Munson, *All Talk* (Temple University Press, 1993), 64–72; Jane Shattuc, *The Talking Cure: TV Talk Shows and Women* (Routledge, 1997), 14–26.

37. *The Morton Downey Jr. Show*, season 1, episode 1, 19 Oct 1987, CRP Vt.299-17.
38. Diary, 19-20 Oct 1987, CRP 46.2; Diary entry, 5-6 Feb 1988, CRP 46.15. See also CR to Bill Abbott, 13 Nov 1987, CRP 68.7.
39. "To Americans, Pornography Is a Minor Problem," *Sexuality Today*, 13 Apr 1987, 1.
40. Diary, n.d. Sept, 30 Nov 1987; 1 January 1988, CRP 46.14.
41. Diary, 1 Jan 1988, CRP 46.14; author interviews with PS.
42. Diary, 1, 17 Jan; 19 Apr 1988, CRP 46.14.

CHAPTER 24: GYPSY FEET

1. Diary, 30 Jan 1988, CRP 46.14.
2. "Show Gives a Preview of Upcoming Gadgets," *Elmira Star-Gazette* (AP), 10 Jan 1988, 4C; "Women of the Adult Industry," *AVN*, Feb 1988, 12; Jami Bernard, "The Way of All Flesh: Porn Tape Industry under Attack, May Be Dying," *NY Post*, 9 May 1988. On CES, see Patchen Barss, *The Erotic Engine* (Doubleday Canada, 2010), 94; David Foster Wallace, "Big Red Son" (1998), repr. in *Consider the Lobster and Other Essays* (Little, Brown, 2005), 3–50; and "CES Past & Present," *Dealerscope* 44:10 (2002): 70–74.
3. Diary, 30 Jan; 23, 21 Feb 1988, CRP 46.14.
4. Diary, 8 May 1988, CRP 46.14; author interview with Veronica Vera.
5. Diary, 19 Apr, 8 May 1988, CRP 46.14.
6. Diary entry, 8 Apr 1989, CRP 47.1; Diary entry, 8-9 Feb 1988, CRP 46.15.
7. PS to CV, c May 1988, CRP 34.8.
8. CV to Pauline, 12 Jul 1988, CRP 37.5.
9. CR to David Ogden, 30 Jun 1988; Burton Joseph to CR, 22 Jul 1988, both CRP 95.5. The firm was Ennis, Friedman and Bersoff. Records of the case, EDNY 88 CV 1657, U.S. v. Various Articles of Obscene Merchandise, were transferred to NARA and then destroyed according to a standard disposal schedule.
10. Sture Sjöstedt to CV, 8 Sept 1988, CRP 37.5; see also CV to Sture Sjöstedt, 21 Sept 1988, CRP 37.5.
11. Diary, 10, 15 Jul 1988, CRP 46.14.
12. Home movie, 4 Sept 1988, CRP Vt 299.58; see also Diary, 28 Aug 1988, CRP 46.14; CV to Rika [Mead], 29 Oct 1988, CRP 37.5.
13. PS to CV, 3 Oct; 1, 16, 24–28 Nov 1988; CV to PS, 31 Dec 1988, all CRP 34.8.
14. CV to PS, 31 Dec 1988, CRP 34.8; Diary entry, 30 Dec 1988, CRP 47.1. See also CV to Louis Vadala, 24 Apr 1988, CRP 35.4.
15. *State of Florida vs. Louis Vadala*, case number CRC84-03876CFANO-K, Violation of Probation Affidavit, 8 Apr 1988; Judgment of Guilt Placing Defendant in Community Control, 10 Jun 1988.
16. PS to CV, n.d. May 1989; CV to PS, 25 Jun 1989, both CRP 34.8.
17. CV to PS, 16 Jul 1989, CRP 34.8.
18. PS to CV, [2 Mar 1990 postmark], CRP 34.8; CV and PS divorce papers, Jan 1990, CRP 50.2.
19. CV to Louis Vadala, 22 May 1989, CRP 35.4; see also CV to Rika [Mead], 29 Oct 1988, CRP 37.5. On the "biological clock," see Jenna Caitlin Healey, *Sooner or Later: Age, Pregnancy, and the Reproductive Revolution in Late Twentieth-Century America* (PhD dissertation, Yale University, 2016). The first major book on the conflict between motherhood and women's careers was Molly McKaughan, *The Biological Clock: Reconciling Careers and Motherhood in the 1980's* (Doubleday, 1987).

20. CV to PS, 25 Jun 1989, CRP 34.8; see also Diary, 29 Jun 1989, CRP 47.1.

21. Diary, 20, 22, 7 May 1989, CRP 46.14; Diary, 27 Jul 1989, CRP 47.2; see also Diary entry, 8 Apr 1989, CRP 47.1; Diary, 11, 21 Apr 1989, CRP 46.14.

22. Dave Patrick, "Beware, Brother, Beware," *Spectator*, n.d. c1989, clipping; CR to Dave Patrick, 4 Dec 1989, both CRP 69.6.

23. Diary, 26 Dec 1989, CRP 47.2.

24. Diary, 1 Jan 1990, CRP 47.2.

25. Diary, 21 Mar 1990, CRP 47.2.

CHAPTER 25: SEX IN THE '90S

1. Chuck Kleinhans, "The Change from Film to Video Pornography: Implications for Analysis," in *Pornography: Film and Culture*, ed. Peter Lehman (Rutgers University Press, 2006), 16.

2. Megumi Komiya and Barry Litman, "The Economics of the Prerecorded Videocassette Industry," in *Social and Cultural Aspects of VCR Use*, ed. Julie Dobrow (Routledge, 1990), 25–26; Catherine Tavel, "Surviving the Sex-Vid Explosion," *Playgirl*, Apr 1991, 72–74; Patchen Barss, *The Erotic Engine* (Doubleday Canada, 2010), 95–97.

3. *Real Sex* (HBO), S1, e1, 8 Oct 1990, CRP Vt-299.86. Enforcing a distinction between scripted high-budget series with lots of naked bodies and the sex-centric offerings of the early '90s, HBO deleted *Real Sex* from its catalogue in 2018; Claire Spellberg, "HBO Has Quietly Pulled Sexy Series Like 'Cathouse' and 'Real Sex' from HBO Go," *Decider* (blog), 29 Aug 2018, https://decider.com/2018/08/29/hbo-pulls-adult-shows-movies/.

4. Laura Fraser, "Nasty Girls," *Mother Jones*, Mar 1990, 34; Elisabeth Glass [HBO] to Vivian Forlander, 29 Jul 1988, CRP 69.3.

5. Diary, 15, 16, 19 Apr 1990, CRP 47.2; CV to Cinthea Vadala, n.d. Apr 1990, in *ibid*; Diary, 18 Aug 1990, CRP 47.4.

6. Diary, 30 Jul; 11, 26, 20, 25 Aug 1990, CRP 47.4.

7. Diary, 29 Jun 1989, CRP 47.2; Diary, 1 Aug 1991, CRP 47.4; CR to Kevin Bright, 2 Aug 1991, CRP 70.2.

8. Johnson quoted in Janice M. Irvine, *Disorders of Desire: Sexuality and Gender in Modern American Sexology* (1990; repr., Temple University Press, 2005), 76; Chuck Rhoades, "Ethical Considerations in the Use of Sexually Explicit Visuals as an Instructional Methodology in College Sexuality Courses," in Elizabeth Schroeder and Judy Kuriansky, eds., *Sexuality Education: Past, Present, and Future* (ABC-CLIO, 2009), IV: 178–193; Meagan Tyler, "A Prescription for Porn: Sexology, Sex Therapy and the Promotion of Pornified Sex," in *The Sexualized Body and the Medical Authority of Pornography: Performing Sexual Liberation*, ed. Heather Brunskell-Evans (Cambridge Scholars Publisher, 2016), 117–138. On NYU's program, see Ronald Moglia, EdD, to CR, 8 Aug 1994 [1995?], CRP 72.3.

9. *The Doctor Ruth Show*, 9 Oct 1986, CRP Vt-299.31; David Frasier, Kinsey Institute, to CR, 15 Oct 1986, CRP 68.2. On films used by sexologists, see Irvine, *Disorders of Desire*, 94–95.

10. Robert G. Taylor to CR, 19 Sept 1988, CRP 69.4; George Gardner to Femme, 21 Mar 1988, CRP 75.2.

11. Femme press release, n.d. 1988, CRP 103.10, draft in CRP 79.9; and https://www.aasect.org/about-us. On AASECT and sex education, see Konstance McCaffree and Jean Levitan, "Sexuality Education in the Ongoing Sexual Revolution of the 1970s," in Schroeder and Kuriansky, eds., *Sexuality Education*, I: 96–122.

12. "Two Hundred Sexologists Appear on the Donahue Show," *Sexuality Today*, 18 May 1987, 1–2; "A Majority of Respondents Reveal They Use Sexually Explicit Films as Educational or Therapeutic Tools," *Sexuality Today*, 2 Mar 1987, 2.

13. Dr. Michael Schwartz, "X-Rated VCR Films in Conjoint Sex Therapy: Preliminary Experience in a Single Case of Retarded Ejaculation and Secondary Impotence," presented to AAMFT, Apr 1987; Dr. Michael Schwartz to CR, 5 Jun 1987; CR to Dr. Michael Schwartz, 4 Sept 1987; Dr. Michael Schwartz to CR, 9 Nov 1987, Dr. Michael Schwartz to CR, 16 May 1988, all CRP 66.3.

14. Diane Sollee to Dr. Michael Schwartz, 22 Jun 1988; Dr. Michael Schwartz to CR, 29 Jun 1988; AAMFT feedback tabulation, Dec 1988, all CRP 66.3.

15. CV speech outline for Quad-S conference, Nov 1988, CRP 66.1; CV outline, "Sexually Explicit Erotic Movies," AASECT Conference, Feb 1990, CRP 66.7; Diary, 8 May 1988, CRP 46.14.

16. Ah-Yin Eng to CR, 10 Feb 1988; Dr. Donald Mosher to CR and Gloria Leonard, 9 May 1988; both CRP 79.2; Ellen Laan to CR, 14 Feb 1990; Dr. Simon Dupont to Femme, 15 May 1992; Rabbi Esther Adler-Rephanto CR, 9 Jan 1992; Fr. Thomas C. Clary to Femme Dist., 22 Oct 1992; all CRP 79.1.

17. Femme order form for AASECT members, 1990, CRP 66.7; CV film treatment: "Sonia the Sex Therapist," 17 Jul 1990, CRP 81.2.

18. "An Educational Line for Femme Films, Inc., by Diana Wiley," 1992; CV notes on "The Sex Therapist" [1992]; "Educational Erotica," 1992; all CRP 81.3.

19. Diary, 1 Nov 1992, CRP 47.8; author interview with Dr. Diana Wiley. Candice never did spill those details, nor would Wiley.

20. Correspondence between Wiley, CR, and Ted Farnsworth of Research Ventures Group, Jul through Oct, 1993, CRP 81.3.

21. Photograph album, 1990–1991, CRP 55.4v.

22. Author interview with Dr. Diana Wiley; *Behavior Today* newsletter, 29 Nov 1988, clip in CRP 66.1.

23. Van Wyck Brooks, "Highbrow and Lowbrow," *The Forum*, Apr 1915, 482–483; Peter Swirski and Tero Eljas Vanhanen, *When Highbrow Meets Lowbrow: Popular Culture and the Rise of Nobrow* (Palgrave, 2017), 1–9; Lawrence W. Levine, *Highbrow/Lowbrow: The Emergence of Cultural Hierarchy in America* (Harvard University Press, 1988).

24. Daniel Horowitz, *Consuming Pleasures: Intellectuals and Popular Culture in the Postwar World* (University of Pennsylvania Press, 2012); Louis Menand, *The Free World: Art and Thought in the Cold War* (Farrar, Straus and Giroux, 2021), 225–290, 422–451.

25. Susan Sontag, "The Pornographic Imagination" (1967), repr. in *Styles of Radical Will* (Farrar, Straus and Giroux, 1969), 35–73, quotations at 35, 36, 70–71.

26. Michel Foucault, *The History of Sexuality*, trans. Robert Hurley (Pantheon, 1978), 3; Robert Darnton, *The Literary Underground of the Old Regime* (Harvard University Press, 1982); Lynn Hunt, "Révolution française et vie privée," in Philippe Ariès and Georges Duby, eds., *Histoire de la vie privée* (Seuil, 1987), IV: 21–25; Lynn Hunt, *The Family Romance of the French Revolution* (University of California Press, 1992); Lynn Hunt, ed., *The Invention of Pornography: Obscenity and the Origins of Modernity, 1500–1800* (Zone Books, 1993).

27. Walter M. Kendrick, *The Secret Museum: Pornography in Modern Culture* (Viking, 1987), 241 (quoted), 197–198, 231; Andrew Ross, *No Respect: Intellectuals and Popular Culture* (Routledge, 1989), 184.

28. Linda Williams to CR, 30 Apr 1988, CRP 69.4.

29. Linda Williams, *Hard Core*, 4, 6, 246–247, 251–252, 255.

30. Danuta Zadworna-Fjellestad, "Review of '*Hard Core*,'" *Discourse* 12:2 (1990): 154–157; Kate Ellis, "Lights, Camera, Sex," *NYT Book Review*, 16 Sept 1990, 31.

31. Ross, *No Respect*, 171–207, quotations at 173, 177, 200, 195, 199.

32. Raymond Sokolov, "Beyond Prudery: The New Postfeminists," *WSJ*, 27 Mar 1991, A12; see also Tad Friend, "The Rise of 'Do Me' Feminism," *Esquire*, Feb 1994, 47–56.

33. Anne Matthews, "Deciphering Victorian Underwear, and Other Seminars," *NYT Magazine*, 10 Feb 1991, 43, https://www.nytimes.com/1991/02/10/magazine/deciphering -victorian-underwear-and-other-seminars.html.

34. Arguments about ideology and indoctrination in the classroom advanced in polemics of this period, including Allan Bloom, *The Closing of the American Mind: How Higher Education Has Failed Democracy and Impoverished the Souls of Today's Students* (Simon & Schuster, 1987); and Roger Kimball, *Tenured Radicals: How Politics Has Corrupted Our Higher Education* (Harper & Row, 1990), continue to energize conservative organizing about race and sex in education. On the "free fall" of humanities majors, see Nathan Heller, "The End of the English Major," *New Yorker*, 6 Mar 2023, https://www.newyorker .com/magazine/2023/03/06/the-end-of-the-english-major.

35. CR [and Anne McClintock], "Porn in the USA," *Social Text* 37 (1993): 23–32, https://doi .org/10.2307/466257; Nina S. Copaken, "Former X-Rated Star Backs Couples-Oriented Erotic Film," *Daily Princetonian*, 8 Mar 1991, 1; Carol S. Vance to CR, 12 Mar 1991, CRP 70.1.

36. CR to Eithne Johnson, 8 Oct 1993, CRP 71.1; see among many others CR to Shulamit Reinharz, 27 Mar 1991, CRP 70.1; Femme to Jane Juffer, 7 Oct 1995, CRP 72.3.

37. Penley syllabus in CRP 66.9; Caroline Clark, "A Porn of Our Own: Female-Authored, Woman-Identified Heterosexual Pornographic 'Film,'" *Canadian Journal of Human Sexuality* 2:2 (1993): 79–87; Women and Film Series invitation and program in CRP 70.6.

38. Diary, 22, 8 Dec 1990, 11 May 1991, 30 Aug 1991, CRP 47.4.

39. Diary, 30 Aug 1991, CRP 47.4; ad mockup in CRP 81.7; CV to Sture Sjöstedt, 8 Dec 1995, CRP 38.4. For Wellesley, see Isabella Askari to CR, 8 Dec 1995, CRP 38.4; for the Smithsonian, see CRP 66.13.

CHAPTER 26: REVELATIONS

1. *Revelations* (1993), dir. Candida Royalle.

2. Diary, 18 Aug 1990; see also 7 Jun, 1 Aug 1991, CRP 47.4; CR to Paul and Gene, 23 Oct 1990; CR to Laurie Pike, 9 Nov 1990, both CRP 69.8.

3. Dan Brookshire to Miriam Stern, 9 Aug 1991, CRP 70.2; Lawrence Cohn, "New Feature Brings Candida Royalle Full Circle," *Variety*, 3 Jun 1991, 8.

4. Jayne Loader to CR, n.d. May 1989, CRP 69.5; NYWF correspondence, CRP 66.1; PS to Miriam Stern, 10 Jan 1991; Miriam Stern to CV, 11 Jun 1991; Dan Brookshire to Miriam Stern, 9 Aug 1991, all CRP 70.2.

5. *The 700 Club*, 10 Jul 1990, via CBN.com, accessed 2 Aug 2021; Lewis Grossberger, "The Rush Hours," *NYT Magazine*, 16 Dec 1990, 58.

6. James Davison Hunter, *Culture Wars: The Struggle to Define America* (Basic Books, 1991), 42–43, 136; see also Nicole Hemmer, *Partisans: The Conservative Revolutionaries Who Remade American Politics in the 1990s* (Basic Books, 2022).

7. Andrew Hartman, *A War for the Soul of America: A History of the Culture Wars* (2015; repr., University of Chicago Press, 2018), 171; Nadine Strossen, "A Feminist Critique of 'the' Feminist Critique of Pornography," *Virginia Law Review* 79:5 (1993): 1099–1190.

8. Joseph Wesley Zeigler, *Arts in Crisis: The National Endowment for the Arts versus America* (A Cappella, 1994), 80–115; Hartman, *War for the Soul of America*, 171–199.

9. Patrick J. Buchanan, "Address to the Republican National Convention in Houston," 17 Aug 1992, APP, https://www.presidency.ucsb.edu/node/279089; "Republican Party

Platform of 1992," APP, https://www.presidency.ucsb.edu/node/273439; "Republican Party Platform of 1988," APP, https://www.presidency.ucsb.edu/node/273433.

10. Susan Faludi, *Backlash: The Undeclared War against American Women* (Crown, 1991), ix.

11. Diary, 21 Aug 1991, CRP 47.4. Shooting began 7 Jun and wrapped Aug 1, *ibid.* Her urgent need for funds is seen in CV to Bob Rimmer, 20 Sept 1991, CRP 70.2.

12. CV to PS, 4 Nov 1991; CV to Michele Capozzi, 6 Nov 1991, both CRP 70.2.

13. "Best Sellers," *NYT Book Review*, 8 Dec 1991, 40.

14. Joelle Attinger, "Steinem: Tying Politics to the Personal," *Time*, 9 Mar 1992, 55; Esther B. Fein, "Book Notes," *NYT*, 18 Mar 1992, C20; N. Gibbs and J. McDowell, "How to Revive a Revolution," *Time*, 9 Mar 1992, 56.

15. S.B. 1521, "Pornography Victims' Compensation Act of 1992," introduced 22 Jul 1991, https://www.congress.gov/bill/102nd-congress/senate-bill/1521?r=1&s=5; Morrison Torrey, "Resurrection of the Antipornography Ordinance, The 1992 Symposium on New Perspectives on Women and Violence," *Texas Journal of Women and the Law* 2:1 (1993): 113–124, esp. 117–118.

16. Strossen, "A Feminist Critique of 'the' Feminist Critique of Pornography," 1110; Richard L. Berke, "With Outsiders In, Female Candidates Come Forward," *NYT*, 30 Apr 1992, A18; Maureen Dezell, "Bundy's Revenge," *New Republic*, 9 Mar 1992, 15–16.

17. FFE sign-in sheet, 29 Jan 1992, FFE Records, box 10, folder: Pornography Victims' Compensation Act; Jennifer Maguire, "FFE Fifth Anniversary Agenda," box 9, folder: 1997.

18. Letter reprinted in Strossen, "A Feminist Critique of 'the' Feminist Critique of Pornography," 1188–1190, quotations at 1189. On *Butler*, see Thelma McCormack, "If Pornography Is the Theory, Is Inequality the Practice?," *Philosophy of the Social Sciences* 23:3 (1992): 298–326; Tamar Lewin, "Canada Court Says Pornography Harms Women," *NYT*, 28 Feb 1992, B7, https://www.nytimes.com/1992/02/28/news/canada-court-says-pornography-harms-women.html.

19. Carolyn Bronstein, *Battling Pornography: The American Feminist Anti-Pornography Movement, 1976–1986* (Cambridge University Press, 2011), 330; Nadine Strossen, *Defending Pornography: Free Speech, Sex, and the Fight for Women's Rights* (NYU Press, 2000), 229–236; and Brenda Cossman, Shannon Bell, and Lise Gotell, *Bad Attitude(s) on Trial: Pornography, Feminism, and the Butler Decision* (University of Toronto Press, 2016).

20. Sandra S. Cole, PhD to CR, 18 Mar 1992, CRP 74.5. Candice apologized and removed the reference from her byline, CR to Cole, 23 Mar 1992, CRP 74.5.

21. Andrea Dworkin, "The ACLU: Bait and Switch" (1981), in *Letters from a War Zone: Writings, 1976–1989* (Dutton, 1989), 210, 212; see also Catharine A. MacKinnon, *Feminism Unmodified: Discourses on Life and Law* (Harvard University Press, 1987), esp. 218, 221, 225, 235; Lorna N. Bracewell, *Why We Lost the Sex Wars: Sexual Freedom in the #MeToo Era* (University of Minnesota Press, 2021), 67–102.

22. Samuel Walker, *Hate Speech: The History of an American Controversy* (University of Nebraska Press, 1994), 134–158. MacKinnon classed porn as hate speech in Catharine A. MacKinnon, "Pornography as Defamation and Discrimination," *Boston University Law Review* 71:5 (1991): 793–815. The 1993 conference "Speech, Equality, and Harm," held at the University of Chicago, offers one marker of the fusion of antiracist and anti-pornography thought. Its proceedings, edited by WAVPM founder Laura Lederer and critical race theorist Richard Delgado, were published as *The Price We Pay: The Case against Racist Speech, Hate Propaganda, and Pornography* (Hill & Wang, 1995).

23. FFE meeting minutes, Oct 1995, FFE Records, box 1, folder: 1995 Board Meetings.

24. Christie Hefner to Nadine Strossen, 14 Jan 1992; Playboy Enterprises interoffice memo:

"Coalition Meeting—Feminists against McKinnon [*sic*]," 31 Jan 1992, both in FFE Records, box 9, folder: Playboy/FFE.

25. "Memorandum," Catherine Siemann to Christie Hefner, 30 Jan 1992; see also Cindy Rakowitz to Christie Hefner et al., 31 Jan 1992; FFE Records, box 9, folder: General 1992.

26. Playboy Enterprises interoffice memo: "Ad Hoc Committee of Feminists," Cleo Wilson to Christie Hefner et al., 6 Mar 1992, FFE Records, box 9, folder: Playboy/FFE.

27. Playboy Enterprises interoffice memo: "FFE Update," Jennifer Maguire to Cleo Wilson, 5 May 1992, FFE Records, box 9, folder: Playboy/FFE.

28. Nat Hentoff, "Pornography War among Feminists," *Washington Post*, 4 Apr 1992, A23; *48 Hours*, 18 Nov 1992, transcript in CRP 53.10.

29. Quoted in Jodie Gould, "Debbie Directs Dallas: Video Erotica Made by Women for Women," *Elle*, Apr 1992, 144.

30. Marcia Pally, "Getting Down with Candida Royalle," *Forum*, Apr 1986.

31. Meeting minutes, Sept 1994; Meeting minutes, Mar 1995; in FFE Records, box 1, folders: 1994 Board Meetings, 1995 Board Meetings.

32. CR, "Women Now," *Playgirl*, Dec 1992, 36; Jan 1993, 34, clippings in CRP 107.7.

33. Diary, 1, 24 Nov 1992, CRP 47.8; "An Interview with Candida Royalle," *Libido* 5:4 (1993), 51–59. Sharon Peters, the critic *Libido* assigned to *Revelations*, panned it, and CR appears to have had the piece killed; see Andrew Wilk and Sunyna Williams to CR, 28 Sept 1993; CR to Williams and Wilk, 6 Oct 1993, CRP 71.1.

34. FFE Records, box 1, folder: 1992–1993 materials; CRP 71.1.

35. *Penthouse*, Sept 1993, 18; *AVN*, Mar 1993, 84. Candice complained about the placement, CR to *AVN*, 3 Aug 1993, CRP 70.7.

36. David Aaron Clark, "The Gook of Revelations," *Screw*, 29 Mar 1993, 19.

37. Andrew Wilk and Sunyna Williams to CR, 28 Sept 1993, emph. original; CR to Williams and Wilk, 6 Oct 1993, both CRP 71.1.

38. Addendum, agreement between Playboy and Femme Distribution, 8 Oct 1993, CRP 77.1; Femme Productions Tax Returns, 1993, CRP 97.1; Femme Productions Tax Returns, 1992, CRP 96.16.

39. CV to Helen Vadala, 16 Sept 1994, CRP 35.5; see also Diary, 31 Jan 1993, CRP 47.8.

CHAPTER 27: SURRENDER

1. CV to Cinthea Vadala, 22 Jul 1990, CRP 35.1.

2. Diary, 25 May; 15, 23–26 Jun; 21, n.d. Jul 1993, CRP 47.10; see also CRP 66.9.

3. Diary, 5 Apr 1992, CRP 47.6; Diary, 14 Oct 1992, CRP 47.8.

4. Diary, 14 Nov 1993, CRP 47.10; author interview with B-JB; Azad Ali and Kustim Wibowo, "Online Dating Services—Chronology and Key Features Comparison with Traditional Dating," *Competition Forum* 9:2 (2011): 481–488.

5. Diary, 4 Apr 1993, CRP 47.8.

6. Diary, 11, 22 Apr; 26 May 1993, CRP 47.8; Diary, 14 Nov 1993, CRP 47.10.

7. Diary, 1 Feb, 6 Apr 1996, CRP 48.2; Diary, 15 Mar 1998, CRP 48.9; Diary, 13 Jul, 3 Oct 1993; 2 Feb 1994, CRP 47.10; author interview with PS.

8. CV to Louis Vadala, n.d. spring 1994, in Diary, n.d. early 1995, CRP 48.2; Diary, 2 Feb 1994, CRP 47.10.

9. Diary, 8 Feb 1996, 20 Aug 1994, CRP 48.2.

10. Diary, 13 Oct 1993, CRP 47.10; Diary, n.d. Jan, 6 Apr 1996, recalling engagements in 1995, CRP 48.2.

11. Jared Kieling [St. Martin's] to CR, 12 Sept 1993, CRP 70.6; see also CR to Kathleen Kinsolving, n.d. Jul 1994, CRP 71.4.

12. Diary, 1 Feb 1996, CRP 48.2; FFE Records, box 1, folder: 1994 Board Meetings; folder: Letters & Positions, 1994. For the move to Manhattan, see Diary, 14 Oct 1992, CRP 47.8.

13. Diary, 1 Jan 1996, CRP 48.2.

14. Author interview with Cinthea Vadala.

15. Lawrence Cohn, "Pornmakers Surface in Mainstream: HV Quickies Speed Demise of Genre," *Variety*, 9 Mar 1988, 3; Michael Decourcy Hinds, "Starring in Tonight's Erotic Video: The Couple Down the Street," *NYT*, 22 Mar 1991, A14.

16. Philip Elmer-Dewitt and Hannah Bloch, "Cyberporn: On a Screen Near You," *Time*, 3 Jul 1995, 38–45. The vaunted study was in fact an "undergraduate research paper, partly plagiarized"; Kelsy Burke, *The Pornography Wars: The Past, Present, and Future of America's Obscene Obsession* (Bloomsbury, 2023), 75–76. On the reciprocal relationship between explicit content and the Web, see Patchen Barss, *The Erotic Engine* (Doubleday Canada, 2010), 117–183; and Samantha Cole, *How Sex Changed the Internet and the Internet Changed Sex: An Unexpected History* (Workman, 2022), 1–87.

17. Jonathan Coopersmith, "Pornography, Technology and Progress," *Icon* 4 (1998): 94–125; Catharine A. MacKinnon, "Vindication and Resistance: A Response to the Carnegie Mellon Study of Pornography in Cyberspace," *Georgetown Law Journal* 83:5 (1995): 1959, 1967; Cole, *How the Internet Changed Sex*, 25.

18. Paglia quoted in Hinds, "Starring in Tonight's Erotic Video"; Jonathan Coopersmith, "Pornography, Technology and Progress," 111–112.

19. CR, "Presentation to Sinclair Institute," n.d. [autumn 1994], courtesy of Rachel Vigneaux, PHE, Inc., [10-11]; draft press release for "Lovers" video line, n.d. fall 1993, CRP 80.3; CR, "Presentation to Sinclair Institute," [16, 19]; Al Goldstein, "X-rated Video: Couples Tape of the Month," *Penthouse*, Sept 1994.

20. Kevin S. Sandler, *The Naked Truth: Why Hollywood Doesn't Make X-Rated Movies* (Rutgers University Press, 2007), 83–121, 170–199. The producers asked FFE to stump for *Showgirls*; FFE refused: Meeting minutes, Aug–Oct 1995, FFE Records, box 1, folder: 1995 Board Meetings.

21. Larry Getlen, "The 'Showgirls' Must Go On," *NY Post*, 13 Jun 2010, https://nypost .com/2010/06/13/the-showgirls-must-go-on/. The explicitness of cable was one reason *Showgirls* bombed in theaters; Sandler, *The Naked Truth*, 181–183.

22. FFE Records, box 1, folder: Letters & positions, 1994.

23. Pam Kelly, "Adam & Eve Survived Obscenity Charges and Protests to Become Mainstream," *Charlotte Observer*, 9 Aug 2014, https://www.charlotteobserver.com/news/ business/article9149087.html; Jay Cheshes, "Hard-Core Philanthropist," *Mother Jones*, Dec 2002, https://www.motherjones.com/politics/2002/09/hard-core-philanthropist -phil-harvey/. On Project Post Porn, see Philip D. Harvey, *The Government vs. Erotica: The Siege of Adam & Eve* (Prometheus Books, 2001), 125–151.

24. The parent company of Sinclair Institute is Townsend Enterprises, also controlled by Harvey; email from Bob Christian, 15 Dec 2021. For the influence of the Better Sex videos on the proposed Case Studies series, see "An Educational Line for Femme Films," n.d. 1992, CRP 81.3.

25. CV to Rika [Mead], 8 Dec 1995, CRP 38.4; CR, "Presentation to Sinclair Institute," [2–7, 9].

26. CV drawing, "Where Is Paradise?" 15 Sept 1995, CRP 29.17; CV to Rika [Mead], 8 Dec 1995; Marianne Macy to CR, 4 May 1995, CRP 76.8.

27. CV to Sture Sjöstedt, 8 Dec 1995, CRP 38.4.

28. CV to Rika [Mead], 8 Dec 1995; CR to Leonard Abrams, 2 Jan 1996, CRP 71.7.

29. CV to Sture Sjöstedt, 8 Dec 1995.

30. William J. Clinton, "Address Before a Joint Session of the Congress on the State of the Union," 23 Jan 1996; APP, https://www.presidency.ucsb.edu/node/223046.

31. Diary, 1 Jan, n.d. late Jan 1996, CRP 48.2.

32. CR to Sue Raye, 3 Feb 1996, CRP 38.6; CR to Mary Gates, 13 Feb 1996, CRP 76.6.

33. Author interview with Bob Christian; Bob Christian to CR et al., 18 Jul 1996, CRP 66.14; CR to Lee Brigham, 5 Aug 1996, CRP 71.8.

34. *My Surrender* (1996), dir. Candida Royalle.

35. Diary, 28 Apr 1996, CRP 48.2; CR to Gesine Stross, 6 Aug 1996, CRP 71.8.

36. *My Surrender.*

37. Author interview with Cinthea Vadala; Diary, 11 Jun 1996, CRP 48.2.

38. Author interview with Cinthea Vadala; CV notes on conversation with probation officer Barbara Ferriter, [Jun 1996], CRP 61.9; CV to B-JB, 15 Feb 2000, CRP 33.11.

39. Author interview with Cinthea Vadala.

40. Diary, 23 Oct 1996, CRP 48.2.

41. Diary, 5 Feb 1997, CRP 48.6.

42. Diary, 29 Jun 1996, CRP 48.2.

43. Diary, 1 Oct 1996, CRP 48.2.

44. Diary, n.d. Apr 1997, CRP 48.8; CR to Phil Harvey, 4 Mar 1997, CRP 76.7.

45. CR to Luke Ford, 30 Dec 1997, CRP 72.4; CR to Mary Gates, 10 Jun 1997, CRP 76.6; CR to Phil Harvey, 4 Mar 1997.

46. Email from Bob Christian, 16 Dec 2021; CR to Mary Gates, 3, 12 Mar 1997; CR to Mary Gates, 10 Jun 1997, all CRP 76.6; Femme Productions 1997 and 1998 tax returns, CRP 97.5–97.7.

47. CR to Mary Gates, 20 Nov 1998; Mary Gates to CR, 23 Nov 1998; CRP 76.6; Mary Gates to CR, 22 Aug 2000, CRP 73.5.

48. Diary, 16 Sept 1996, CRP 48.2; Diary, 17 Feb, 9 Mar, 1 Jul (quoted) 1997, CRP 48.6; Diary, 1, 2 Apr 1997, CRP 48.8. *The Rules*: Ellen Fein, *The Rules: Time-Tested Secrets for Capturing the Heart of Mr. Right* (Warner Books, 1995).

49. Diary, 22–23 Jun, 14 Jul, 2 Sept 1997, CRP 48.6; author interview with Jeffrey Douglas. For Candice's lobbying against California SB1013, see CRP 72.5 and CRP 67.1.

50. Diary, 14 Sept 1997, CRP 48.6; Diary, 15 Mar 1998, see also 3 Oct 1998, CRP 48.9.

51. Diary, 28 Nov, 18 Apr, 15 Mar, 25 Apr 1998, CRP 48.9.

52. Diary, 15 Mar 1998, CRP 48.9.

53. Diary, 3 Jan, 23 May 1998, CRP 48.9.

54. Diary entry, 5 Nov 1998, CRP 48.10.

55. Diary entry, 4 Feb 1998, CRP 48.10; Diary, 7 Mar 1998, CRP 48.9.

56. Josephine C. Sharif, "Naughty Money: Fully-Clothed Ways These Women Earn $$$ from Sex!" *Complete Woman*, Dec/Jan 2000, 12–13.

57. Diary entry, CRP 48.10, 4 Feb 1998; Gloria Steinem, "Hollywood Cleans Up Hustler," *NYT*, 7 Jan 1997, A17.

58. Barss, *Erotic Engine*, 94; Robert Rosen, *Beaver Street* (Headpress, 2010), 181. The term gained traction with the publication of Pamela Paul, *Pornified: How Pornography Is Transforming Our Lives, Our Relationships, and Our Families* (Times Books, 2005).

59. Frank Rich, "Naked Capitalists," *NYT Magazine*, 20 May 2001, 51, https://www.nytimes.com/2001/05/20/magazine/naked-capitalists.html.

60. *Sex and the City*, created by Darren Star, quotations from season 1, eps. 1, 8; Caryn James, "In Pursuit of Love, Romantically or Not," *NYT*, 5 Jun 1998, E32; Nancy Haas, " 'Sex' Sells, in the City and Elsewhere," *NYT*, 11 Jul 1999, Styles Section, 1.

61. Ginia Bellafante, "Feminism: It's All about ME!" *Time*, 29 Jun 1998.

62. Maureen Dowd, "Feathered and Tarred," *NYT*, 10 Jun 1998, A29, https://www.nytimes
    .com/1998/06/10/opinion/liberties-feathered-and-tarred.html; Nina Burleigh, "My Spin
    through the Cycle," *NY Observer*, 20 Jul 1998, https://observer.com/1998/07/my-spin
    -through-the-cycle/; Gloria Steinem, "Feminists and the Clinton Question," *NYT*, 22 Mar
    1998, WK15; https://www.nytimes.com/1998/03/22/opinion/feminists-and-the-clinton
    -question.html.

63. Diary, 19 Jun 1998, CRP 48.9.

64. Timothy M. Gray, " 'The Clinton Show': 2,406 Days Running," *Variety*, 24 Aug 1998, 4.

65. Howie Gordon, *Hindsight: True Love & Mischief in the Golden Age of Porn* (Bear Manor
    Media, 2013), 637; Diary entry, 1 Sept 1998, CRP 48.10; Patricia Ward Biederman, "Por-
    nography Conference Explores Eroticism, Freedom of Speech," *LAT*, 8 Aug 1998, https://
    www.latimes.com/archives/la-xpm-1998-aug-08-me-11190-story.html.

66. Diary, 18 Aug 1998, CRP 48.9; see CRP 67.11 for police filings.

67. *The Starr Report: The Independent Counsel's Complete Report to Congress on the Investigation
    of President Clinton* (Pocket Books, 1998), 55.

68. Jenny Hontz, "Media Blows Off Standards: TV Takes Up Bawdy-Building," *Variety*, 29
    Apr 1999; see also Toby Miller, "The First Penis Impeached," Lauren Berlant and Lisa
    Duggan, eds., *Our Monica, Ourselves: The Clinton Affair and the National Interest* (NYU
    Press, 2001), 116–133.

69. CV to B-JB, 3 Nov 1998, CRP 32.7.

70. CV to Annie Sprinkle, 8 Feb 1999, CRP 38.9; CR quoted in [Thomas Adams], "Subplot:
    Hey, You Got Politics in My Porn!" *New York Magazine*, 25 Jan 1999, 15.

71. CV to Annie Sprinkle, 8 Feb 1999, CRP 38.9; CV to Rama, 3 May 1999; CV to B-JB, 6
    May 1999, both CRP 33.2; HIV test results, Soho Ob-Gyn, Feb 1997, CRP 54.2.

72. Diary, 27 Nov, 4 Dec, 27 Mar 1998, CRP 48.9.

73. Diary, 19 Sept–15 Oct, 4 Dec 1998 (quoted), CRP 48.9. For the relationship conducted
    by fax, see CRP 32.5–34.2.

CHAPTER 28: THE BOOK OF LIFE

1. Diary, 23 Oct 1999, CRP 48.11; Diary, 26 Feb 1999, CRP 48.9.

2. Suzanne Delaney to CV, 28 Mar 2000, CRP 73.6; CV to B-JB, 2, 15 Mar 2000, CRP
   33.12; CV to B-JB, 13 Apr 2000, CRP 33.13; Diary, 30 Apr 2000, CRP 48.11.

3. CV to B-JB, 29 Apr 2001, CRP 34.2.

4. Diary, 15 Oct; 11–12, 18 Nov 2000, CRP 49.3; Diary entry, 7 Jul 2000, CRP 48.12.

5. Diary, 1 Mar 2001, CRP 49.3.

6. Diary, 7 Jul 1999, CRP 48.11; CV to B-JB, 22 Apr 2000, CRP 33.13.

7. CV to B-JB, 29 Apr 2001, CRP 34.2; Diary, 22 Apr 2001, CRP 49.3.

8. Diary, 30 Jan, 31 Dec 2002, CRP 49.3; Diary entry, 10 Apr 2001, CRP 49.4.

9. CV to B-JB, 19 Feb 2000, CRP 33.11; CV to B-JB, 17 Apr 2000, CRP 33.13; CV to B-JB,
   22 Jul 2000, CRP 34.1; Diary, 18 Apr 2000, CRP 48.11; Femme Productions tax returns,
   2001, CRP 98.1; Femme Productions tax returns, 2005, CRP 98.5.

10. Diary, 1 Mar 2001, CRP 49.3; CV to Jane Hamilton, 29 Nov 2002, CRP 49.4.

11. Diary, 16 Dec, 28 Sept, 12 Oct 2001, CRP 49.3.

12. CV to Helen Vadala, 31 Jul 2002, CRP 61.5; Diary, 13, 19 Aug 2002, CRP 49.5; Helen
    Duffy Vadala death certificate, 13 Aug 2002, CRP 61.5.

13. CV to Cinthea Vadala, 23 Oct 2003, CRP 61.7; Diary, 20 Nov 2003, CRP 49.3.

14. Diary, 20 Nov 2003, CRP 49.3.

15. Diary, 31 Mar 2002, CRP 49.3.
16. Diary, 3 Feb 1974, CRP 44.7.
17. CV verse fragment [Feb 1986], CRP 54.13.
18. Josef Adalian, "*Roots* Is Still One of the Biggest TV Success Stories Ever," *The Vulture*, 26 May 2016, https://www.vulture.com/2016/05/roots-miniseries-ratings-were-off-the-charts.html.
19. Ancestry.com Corporate, "Our History," https://www.ancestry.com/corporate/about-ancestry/our-story, accessed 3 Mar 2022; Maya Jasanoff, "Ancestor Worship," *New Yorker*, 2 May 2022, https://www.newyorker.com/magazine/2022/05/09/our-obsession-with-ancestry-has-some-twisted-roots-maud-newton-ancestor-trouble.
20. Diary, 11, 13 Aug 2002, CRP 49.5. Candice jotted down names of websites to locate family members c Mar 2000; CRP 54.17.
21. Diary, 18 Feb, 25 Mar 2003, CRP 49.3; author interview with Larry Trepel. On the protests, see Robert McFadden, "Threats and Responses: From New York to Melbourne, Cries for Peace," *NYT*, 16 Feb 2003, A1.
22. Diary, 6 Aug 2003, CRP 49.5; Diary, 15 Oct 2003, CRP 49.3.
23. Diary, 3 Jul 1982, CRP 45.11.
24. Chapter outline for "Great Sex" [1995], CRP 105.30; CV to Rika [Mead], 8 Dec 1995, CRP 38.4; Lori Lipsky to Kim Witherspoon, 28 Nov 1995, CRP 105.30.
25. Diary, 27 Mar 1998, CRP 48.9; outlines and drafts, "Candida Royalle's Tell All," c1998–1999, CRP 105.29; chapter outlines, "Sex Tips and Tales from the Cutting Edge" and "Candidally Speaking," c2000, CRP 106.3; CV to B-JB, 9, 19 Feb 2000, CRP 33.11.
26. Diary, 7 Apr 2002, CRP 49.3.
27. Diary, 3 Jan 2003, CRP 49.3; Alex Hurley to CR, 10 Jun 2003, CRP 105.31. Candice may have had a previous collaborator; see Diary, 28 Feb–1 Mar 2002, CRP 49.3.
28. Author interview with M. Billie Fitzpatrick; Marcela Landres to Billie Fitzpatrick, 28 Mar 2003, CRP 105.31; CR, *How to Tell a Naked Man What to Do: Sex Advice from a Woman Who Knows* (Simon & Schuster/Fireside, 2004), 97, 85, 137.
29. Author interview with M. Billie Fitzpatrick.
30. CV to B-JB, 25 Sept 1999, CRP 33.6.
31. Peter Keating, "Two Girls on Jenna," *Salon*, 17 Jan 2001, https://www.salon.com/2001/01/17/jenna_1/; Dinitia Smith, "At Home with Jenna Jameson," *NYT*, 15 Apr 2004, F8. In 2005, *Forbes* named Jameson to its Celebrity 100: Matthew Miller, "The (Porn) Player," *Forbes*, 4 Jul 2005.
32. Marcela Landres to CR, 10 May 2003, CRP 105.31.
33. CV to Candelora Versace, 28 Mar 2003, CRP 39.3; Diary, 6 Aug 2003, 17 Jan 2005 (quoted), CRP 49.5.
34. Edward Wyatt, "Sex, Sex, Sex: Up Front in Bookstores Near You," *NYT Book Review*, 24 Aug 2004, 1; Marcela Landres to CR and Billie Fitzpatrick, 22 Jul 2003, CRP 105.31.
35. Sara Nelson, "Catfight in the Bookstore: Porn Stars Hunt Readers," *NY Post*, 13 Sept 2004, https://nypost.com/2004/09/13/catfight-in-the-bookstore-porn-stars-hunt-readers/.
36. "Schedule: Radio Media Tour," Oct 2004; and promotional ephemera, CRP 105.31.
37. See e.g. *O, The Oprah Magazine*, Oct 2004, 264.
38. Tristan Taormino to CR, 22 Sept 1997, CRP 72.5. If Candice supplied a blurb, it didn't make the cover of Tristan Taormino, *The Ultimate Guide to Anal Sex for Women* (Cleis Press, 1998).
39. Tristan Taormino, "Candid Candida: The Porn Star as Educator," *Village Voice*, 20 Oct 2004, 145.

40. Diary, 7 Oct 2009, CRP 49.10; email from Emily Simonson, Simon & Schuster, 7 Aug 2018.

41. Diary, 7 Feb 2008, CRP 49.10.

CHAPTER 29: HOME AGAIN

1. Diary, 8 Apr 2010, CRP 49.10.

2. Diary, 7 Oct 2009, CRP 49.10; Diary, n.d. Jul 2012, CRP 49.13; author interview with Larry Trepel.

3. Materials from *Afrodite Superstar* (2007), dir. Venus Hottentot (Abiola Abrahams), CRP 82.1–82.3; Mireille Miller-Young, *A Taste for Brown Sugar: Black Women in Pornography* (Duke University Press, 2014), 4, 263, 275–277. For Lorde's antipornography stance, see Lorde, "Uses of the Erotic: The Erotic as Power," in Lederer, ed., *Take Back the Night*, 295–300; and Lorna N. Bracewell, "Beyond Barnard: Liberalism, Antipornography Feminism, and the Sex Wars," *signs* 42:1 (2016): 137–139.

4. Diary, 7 Oct 2009, CRP 49.10; see also CR to Kayla McCormick (*Oprah Winfrey Show*), 21 May 2009; Kayla McCormick to CR, 15 Oct 2009, both CRP 74.4.

5. Diary, 17 Jan 2005, CRP 49.5; Deed for 465 Farmer Road, Mattituck, 17 Mar 2005, liber D00012377, p. 096; Mortgages for 465 Farmer's Road, 17 Mar 2005, liber M00021001, pp. 708–709; Suffolk County NY Clerk's Office; email from Larry Trepel, 1 Feb 2022.

6. Andy Newman, "68 and Sleeping on Floor, Ex-Publisher Seeks Work," *NYT*, 12 Aug 2004, B6; Robert D. McFadden, "Bob Guccione, 79, Dies; Founded *Penthouse*," *NYT*, 21 Oct 2010, A34, https://www.nytimes.com/2010/10/21/business/media/21guccione.html.

7. Sam Jones, "U.S. Porn Barons Appeal for $5bn Bailout to Help Prop up Limp Industry," *The Guardian*, 8 Jan 2009, https://www.theguardian.com/business/2009/jan/08/larry-flynt-porn-industry-bailout; Patchen Barss, *The Erotic Engine* (Doubleday Canada, 2010), 273–274.

8. Email from Larry Trepel, 2 Feb 2022; author interview with Larry Trepel; Author interview with PS; author interview with Veronica Vera; Diary, n.d. Jul 2012, CRP 49.13.

9. Diary, 19 Nov 2007, CRP 49.10; 29 Jan, 6-7 Feb 2008; Diary, n.d. Jul 2012, CRP 49.13; email from Larry Trepel, 1 Feb 2022.

10. Diary, 23–24 Apr, 6–7 Jun 2009, CRP 49.8.

11. Diary, 3 Oct 2009, CRP 49.10.

12. Author interview with Dr. B. Hannah Ortiz.

13. Author interview with Dr. B. Hannah Ortiz.

14. Author interview with Dr. B. Hannah Ortiz.

15. Diary, 2 Sept 2010, CRP 49.10.

16. Diary, 29 Sept; 20 Oct; undated entries, Oct–Dec 2010, CRP 49.13; author interview with Cinthea Vadala.

17. Diary, 20 Mar 2011, CRP 49.10.

18. Author interview with Dr. B. Hannah Ortiz.

19. Author interview with Dr. B. Hannah Ortiz; Diary, n.d. Jul 2012, CRP 49.13.

20. Diary, 1, n.d., 3 Jul 2012, emphasis in original, CRP 49.13; Greg Anderson, *Cancer: 50 Essential Things to Do* (Penguin, 2012).

21. Diary, 3 Aug, n.d. summer 2012, CRP 49.13; author interview with Dr. B. Hannah Ortiz; author interview with Cinthea Vadala.

22. Diary, 12 Aug 2012, CRP 49.13; Appointment book, 8 Apr 2013, CRP 28.4.

23. Appointment book, CRP 28.4, *passim*, talk on 8 Apr 2014; author interview with Cinthea Vadala.

24. Appointment books, January through Mar 2013, CRP 28.1–28.3; Taormino et al., *The Feminist Porn Book*; *Publishers Weekly*, 1 Apr 2013, 61; Rachael Liberman, "Book Review: The Feminist Porn Book: The Politics of Producing Pleasure," *Porn Studies* 1: 1–2 (2014): 217–219, https://doi.org/10.1080/23268743.2013.873582.

25. Author interview with Larry Trepel; Diary, 1 Aug 2013, CRP 49.2.

26. Diary, 1 Aug 2013, CRP 49.2.

27. Diary, n.d. summer 2013, CRP 49.2; author interview with Dr. B. Hannah Ortiz; Appointment book, 3 Jun 2013, CRP 28.4.

28. Jonathan Walker email to CR, 2 Jul 2012, CRP.E.4; CR email to Sheona McDonald, 16 May 2013; Sheona McDonald email to CR, 5 Jun 2013; CR email to Sheona McDonald, 21 Jun 2013; all CRP.E.4; Appointment book, 12, 13 Jun 2013, CRP 28.4.

29. Appointment book, 8 Jan 2014, CRP 28.4.

30. Appointment book, n.d. [Jan 2014], CRP 28.4.

31. Appointment book, 21 Feb 2014, CRP 28.4; Daniel E. Slotni, "Gloria Leonard, Publisher, Pornography Star, and Advocate, Dies at 73," *NYT*, 7 Feb 2014, B19; CV Notes on investigators, 14 Mar 2014, CRP 54.17.

32. Sheona McDonald emails to CR, 14 Feb, 18 Mar 2014, CRP.E.4; Appointment book, 14–15 Mar 2014, CRP 28.4.

33. Report of Valley Investigations LLC, 11 Apr 2014; CV to Andrew James Hume, 28 Apr 2014, and drafts; all CRP 54.17.

34. CV Notes on conversations with Andrew James Hume, 23 May 2014; and Susan Frazier Ellis, 25 May 2014, CRP 54.17.

35. CV Notes on conversations with Andrew James Hume and Susan Frazier Ellis; "Peggy Frazier," *The Daily Journal* (Flat River, MO), 17 Jun 1991, 3.

36. Appointment book, 23 May 2014, CRP 28.6; Appointment book, 7 Jul 2014, CRP 28.8; Appointment book, n.d. Sept 2014, CRP 28.10; Appointment book, 1 May 2014, CRP 28.4.

37. CV emails to Sheona McDonald, 9, 29 May 2014, CRP.E.4.

38. Appointment book, 21 Jul 2014, CRP 28.8.

39. https://www.kickstarter.com/projects/whileyouweregone/while-you-were-gone-the-untold-story-of-candida-ro; Sheona McDonald emails to CV, 5, 12 Jul 2014, CRP.E.4; https://whileyouweregonefilm.wordpress.com/page/2/, posts dated 14–17 Jul 2014.

40. Dean Draznin email to Bruce Golding, 28 Jul 2014; CV email to Annie Sprinkle, Jane Hamilton, and Veronica Vera, 29 Jul 2014, both CRP.E.4.

41. Lorena Mongelli and Bruce Golding, "Ex Porn Star Now Baring Her Soul in Search for Birth Mother," *NY Post*, 4 Aug 2014, https://nypost.com/2014/08/04/ex-porn-star-now-baring-her-soul-in-search-for-birth-mother/.

42. CV Notes, n.d. Aug 2014, CRP 54.17; Sheona McDonald emails to CV, 4, 15 August 2014; CV email to Sheona McDonald, 4 Aug 2014, all CRP.E.4.

43. Appointment book, n.d. Sept 2014, CRP 28.10; CV emails to Sheona McDonald, 27, 28 Sept 2014; Sheona McDonald email to CV, 27 Sept 2014, all CRP.E.4.

44. Sheona McDonald email to CV, 2 Oct 2014, CRP.E.4; Appointment book, 12, 19 Nov 2014, CRP 29.1.

45. *Candice*, dir. Sheona McDonald (2019).

46. Author interview with Cinthea Vadala.

47. Author interview with Dr. B. Hannah Ortiz.

48. *Candice*.

49. Appointment book, 23–27 June 2014, CRP 28.6. The California Bureau for Private Postsecondary Education cited IASHS for accreditation violations in 2016, leading to its

closure two years later. The Institute's website has been archived: https://web.archive.org/web/20110709131638/http://www.iashs.edu/history.html.

50. "Candida Royalle to Be Awarded Doctorate in Human Sexuality," *AVN*, 19 Jun 2014, https://avn.com/business/articles/video/candida-royalle-to-be-awarded-doctorate-in-human-sexuality-564790.html. The diploma is preserved in CRP 124FB.11.

51. CV email to Sheona McDonald, 28 Apr 2014, CRP.E.4.

52. Appointment book, 18 Dec 2014, emphasis in original, CRP 29.2.

53. Appointment book, 6, 19 Feb 2015, CRP 29.4.

54. CV email to Jason A. Konner, MD, 27 Mar 2015; CV email to Sheona McDonald by email, 3 Mar 2015, both CRP.E.4; Notebook, n.d. Apr 2015, CRP 54.6; Appointment book, 1, 6–15, 27–30 Apr; 1–2 May 2015, CRP 29.6.

55. Appointment book, 8 May 2015, CRP 29.6; Appointment book, n.d., 19 Jun 2015, CRP 29.9; Appointment book, 6–10 Jul 2015, CRP 29.11; Notebook, CRP 54.6.

56. Author interview with PS; author interview with Lauren Niemi Cole; Last Will and Testament of Candice Vadala, a/k/a Candida Royalle, 27 Aug 2015, courtesy of Mary Dorman.

57. Jason Lyon, "New York Remembers Candida Royalle," *AVN*, 11 Dec 2015, https://avn.com/business/articles/video/new-york-remembers-candida-royalle-614937.html.

58. Notebook, 16, 27, 29 Aug; 2, 5 Sept 2015, CRP 54.6.

59. Author interview with Cinthea Vadala.

60. Author interview with Lauren Niemi Cole.

EPILOGUE: TRANSPARENCY

1. Author interview with Cinthea Vadala.

2. Diary, 23–24 Apr 2009, CRP 49.8; see also 6 Sept 2009.

3. Diary, 11 Jul 2013, CRP 49.2.

4. Karl Marx, *The Eighteenth Brumaire of Louis Bonaparte* (1848), trans. Daniel de Leon (Charles H. Kerr, 1907), 5.

5. Breanne Fahs, "'Freedom to' and 'Freedom from': A New Vision for Sex-Positive Politics," *Sexualities* 17:3 (2014): 267–290, https://doi.org/10.1177/1363460713516334.

6. Diary, 7 Oct 2009, CRP 49.10; see also CR to Kayla McCormick, 21 May 2009; Kayla McCormick to CR, 15 Octr 2009, both CRP 74.4.

7. Diary, 7 Oct 2009, CRP 49.10.

8. IbisWorld, "Adult & Pornographic Websites in the US: Market Size 2005–2028," 18 Jun 2022, https://www.ibisworld.com/industry-statistics/market-size/adult-pornographic-websites-united-states/; Robin Morgan, "Theory and Practice," in *Going Too Far: The Personal Chronicle of a Feminist* (Random House, 1977), 166.

9. Shira Tarrant, *The Pornography Industry: What Everyone Needs to Know* (Oxford University Press, 2016), 162–170; Kelsy Burke, *The Pornography Wars: The Past, Present, and Future of America's Obscene Obsession* (Bloomsbury, 2023), 73–80, 155–158; Bernadette Barton, *The Pornification of America: How Raunch Culture Is Ruining Our Society* (NYU Press, 2021), 2 (quoted); see also Ariel Levy, *Female Chauvinist Pigs: Women and the Rise of Raunch Culture* (Free Press, 2006).

10. Diary, 7 Oct 2009, CRP 49.10.

11. Heather Berg, *Porn Work: Sex, Labor, and Late Capitalism* (Duke University Press, 2021), esp. 95–125.

12. Burke, *Pornography Wars*, 108–119, quotation at 119. On porn "addiction," see Burke, 171–214; Tarrant, *Pornography Industry*, 141–144; and Taylor Kohut et al., "Surveying Pornography Use: A Shaky Science Resting on Poor Measurement Foundations," *Journal of Sex Research* 57:6 (2020): 722–742, https://doi.org/10.1080/00224499.2019.1695244.

13. Appointment book, n.d. Apr 2014, CRP 28.4, referring to Gail Dines, *Pornland: How Porn Has Hijacked Our Sexuality* (Beacon Press, 2010).

14. Colin Rowntree, "Candida Royalle Memorial Celebrates Industry Pioneer, Icon," *XBIZ*, 24 Nov 2015, https://www.xbiz.com/news/201508/candida-royalle-memorial-celebrates-industry-pioneer-icon.

15. Jason Lyon, "New York Remembers Candida Royalle," *AVN*, 11 Dec 2015, https://avn.com/business/articles/video/new-york-remembers-candida-royalle-614937.html.

16. Author interview with Jane Hamilton.

Interviews Conducted

Blinder, Martin	June 12, 2019, by telephone
Brouwer, Bart-Jan	December 7, 2021, by Zoom
Christian, Bob	December 14, 2021, by Zoom
Cole, R. Lauren [Niemi]	January 24, 2020, January 22, 2021, by telephone
Douglas, Jeffrey	December 17, 2021, by Zoom
Dunaway, Karen	April 10, 2019, by telephone
Falek, Sherry	February 11, 2019, by telephone
Fitzpatrick, M. Billie	February 25, 2020, by Zoom
Hamilton, Jane	May 18, 2018
Koldewyn, Richard ("Scrumbly")	February 26, 2019
Kovacs, Joseph	October 15, 2018, by telephone
McGinley, Theresa	March 27, 2019, by telephone
Ortiz, B. Hannah	March 17, 2022, by Zoom
Rabine, Phyllis	June 6, 2019, by telephone
Socarras, Jorgé	January 28, 2019, by telephone
Sjöstedt, Per	October 11, 2018, by telephone; March 3, 2019
Sprinkle, Annie	December 11, 2020, by Zoom
Sukaitis, Janice	April 14, 2019, by telephone
Trepel, Larry	October 25, 2018; February 10, 2022, by Zoom
Vadala, Cinthea	March 16, 2018
Vera, Veronica	October 25, 2018; May 5, 2022, by Zoom
Vitucci, Jerome	September 4, 2020, by Zoom
Wiley, Diana	April 5, 2021, by Zoom

Illustration Credits

Grateful acknowledgment to Veronica Vera for permission to reproduce the images on the cover and frontispiece, and figures 1, 3, 4, 7–12, 14–17, 19–25, 27, 30–32, 35–37, 39, 40, 42, 43, 45–48, and 51, from the Papers of Candida Royalle. Their locations within the collection are noted below.

Index

Page numbers in *italics* refer to illustrations.

Kupferberg, Tuli, 128

Labowitz, Leslie, 187, 196
Lacy, Suzanne, 187, 196
Ladies' Home Journal, 65, 89
LaHaye, Beverly, 236
Lailani (Laurie Ann Detgen), 146, 153, 156
  background of, 145
  death of, 330–31
  drug use of, 207
  in *Hard Soap, Hard Soap,* 179, 182, 184
  in *Hot and Saucy Pizza Girls, 209,* 210
  in *Hot Rackets,* 212, 330
  in Old Jazz, 146
  in *Rickets, 141,* 150
Laing, R. D., 120
Lanin, Lester, 56
Lapham, Lewis, 289
Larkin, Philip, 88
Larry King Live, 371
Last Days at Hot Slit (Dworkin), 13
Last Tango in Paris, 172
Lauren, Ralph, 283
Law, Sylvia, 301
Lear, Norman, 39, 179
Leary, Timothy, 132, 134
Leigh, Carol, 153
Lennon, John, 63, 244
Leonard, George, 252–53
Leonard, Gloria, 347
  Annie Sprinkle and, 263, 264
  background of, 262
  Club 90 and, *261,* 267, 269
  death of, 417
  High Society and, 245, 263, 264, 300
  High Society Live and, 247–48
  The Leonard Report and, 282
  The Morton Downey Jr. Show and, 335, 336
  in *Three Daughters,* 320
Leonard Report, The, 282
lesbian activists, 107–8
Levine, Ellen, 296, 315
Lewinsky, Monica, 393, 394, 395
Libido, 375

Life, 132, 246
Limbaugh, Rush, 336, 367, 368
Lindsay, John V., 80
literary studies of sexuality, 360–63
"Little Tomato, The," 143
Lolita (Nabokov), 47
Lorde, Audre, 196, 410
Lords, Traci, 323
Los Angeles, Calif., 8, 200, 201
Los Angeles Times, 196, 205
Loud, Pat, 181
Loud family, 181
LOVE, 263
Lovelace, Linda, 178, 251, 290
  abuse of, 238, 271, 301
  media coverage of, 122
  Ordeal, 238–39, 240, 252, 270
  payment for films, 121, 238–39
  see also Boreman, Linda
Lovelace Enterprises, 179
Lovers, 382
Love Secrets, 175
Lowe, Kirby, 176, 250
LSD, 132
Lunarex, 225, 279, 281, 320
Lust, Erika, 416

Machida, Margo, 131–32
MacKinnon, Catharine A., 13, 270–71,
    290, 311, 432
  Donahue and, 306–8, 336
  FACT and, 296–97, 372
  on Femme and Candice, 374, 430
  Meese commission and, 302–3, 316
  Minneapolis ordinance and, 270, 271, 272
  ordinances campaigns of, 207, 271, 272,
    273, 289, 297–98, 299, 301, 316–17,
    360
  papers of, in Schlesinger Library, 10
  on pornography and subordination of
    women, 294, 295, 368
  on pornography in cyberspace, 381
  Pornography Victims' Compensation
    Act and, 371, 372, 374
  Schlafly and, 272

Sylvester, 147

Take Back the Night marches, 13, *187*,
    196–97, 222
Tale of Tiffany Lust, The, 219
Tales of the City (Maupin), 117
talk shows, 180, 300–301, 306–8
    see also specific talk shows
Taormino, Tristan, 407, 416
Taste of Ambrosia, A, 334–35
Tate, Sharon, 207
Taxi Girls, 219
10, 215–16
Texas, 118
That Lucky Stiff, 224, 225
Therapeutic Abortion Act (California),
    120
Thomas, Clarence, 369, 371
Thomas, Marlo, 306
Thompson, Helen, 21, 23
Thompson, John, 422–22
Thompson, Peggy June, *see* Vadala, Peggy
    June Thompson Hume
Thompson, Rosemary, 237
Three Daughters, *319*, 320–21, 335
    AASECT's screening of, 356, 361
    awards to, 324
    Candice's family history in, 321–22
    Club 90 and, 320
    debut of, 323
    dedicated to memory of Lailani, 330
    investors in, 320
    Linda Williams praise for, 361
    media coverage of, 324
    post-production of, 322
    reviews of, 324
    as top seller for Femme, 386
Thurber, James, 87–88
Time, 246, 319
    cover on feminism, 393
    Faludi and Steinem on cover of, 370
    Millett on cover of, 101
    on Minneapolis ordinance, 271
    on online pornographic images, 381
    on sexual revolution, 8, 89

    on *Three Daughters,* 324
    on WAP's tours, 222
Today, 324
Tonight Show, The, 122
Transactional Analysis, 134
Transaction Books, 189
Traynor, Chuck, 238, 239
Trepel, Larry, 402–3, 411, 412, 416
Trips Festival, 132
True, Andrea, 179
Tunnel, The, 352
20/20, 324
Twinkie defense, 211

Ultra Flesh, 216
Under the Covers, 410
unemployment, 148, 173
University of Minnesota Law School,
    270–71
Urban Heat
    budget of, 283, 285
    filming, *275,* 283, 289
    impounded copies of, 343–44
    nomination for several *AVN* awards, 311
    Playboy and, 335
    premiere of, 288–89
    press coverage of, 290
    reviews of, 291
    sales, 310–11, 314
    Socarras's original song for, 283, 331
    Williams praise for, 361
U.S. Postal Service, 383

Vadala, Candice, 429–31
    in alternative theatre and music scene,
        142–47, 149, 150, 166
        in Gospel Pearls, 146–47, 151
        in *The Heartbreak of Psoriasis, 166,*
            167–68, 170, 173
        in Humbug Cantata, 146, 167
        in *Kitsch-On* show, 143–44, *144*
        in Old Jazz, 146, 147, 151
        in *Rickets, 141,* 150, 167, 168
        in White Trash Boom Boom, 145
    awards to, 212, *309,* 390, 423–24

with Cyn, *63*

with Diana Wiley, *351*

at *Donahue*, 293

filming *Urban Heat*, *275*

in first grade, *43*

at grandmother's house on seventeenth birthday, *74*

on honeymoon, *247*

Joe Kovacs and, *79*

in June 1973, *127*

counseling during, 64, 66
divorce, 174, 266
meeting, 35–36
separation, 59, 61, 66, 75, 96
wedding, *38,* 38–39
relationship with Candice, 147, 155, 165,
174, 400
after Candice graduated high school,
83, 95, 96–97
during Candice's childhood, 40–41,
51, 56, 57, 58, 59, 60–61, 70, 388
Candice's visits to, 345, 388
Vadala, Helen Frances Duffy (*continued*)
Helen's visits to, 211, 266, 322
letters to Candice, 154, 156
requesting loan from Candice in, 376
relationship with Cinthea, 56, 58, 59, 61,
213–14
singing and, 143
Vadala, Louis, *25,* 26, 61
alcohol use of, 56, 176, 346
in army, 26–27, 64
career as a drummer, 20, 26, 27, 53, 56,
143, 146, 266, 345
death of, 400, 403
dementia of, 387–88
drug use of, 345
family background of, 19
marriage to Helen, 39, 48, 50, 97
divorce, 174, 266
meeting, 35–36
separation, 59, 61, 66, 75, 96
wedding, *38,* 38–39
marriage to Peggy, 18, 19–20, 21, 27–30,
31, 34, 174, 421
relationship with Candice, 70, 83, 135,
162, 232, 264–65, 321, 345–46
advice to Candice on being an artist,
143, 174
Candice's insecurity and, 101, 347,
379
during dementia, 387, 388, 400–401
relationship with Cinthea, 57, 58–59,
61, 64, 66, 74–75, 96, 213–14, 321,
387–88

relationship with mother, 34–35, 321, 387
sexual assault of six-year-old girl, 266–
67, 321, 346–47, 387
Vadala, Marion, 19–20, 39, 61, 70
background of, 19
death of, 116
granddaughters living with, 34–35, 36,
57, 58, 59–60, 64
grave of, 321–22
health of, 36
job weaving straw bonnets in factory,
19, 21, 387
marriage of, 19, 34
relationship with Candice, 57, 60, 70,
116, 321–22
relationship with Louis, 34–35, 321,
387
as self-taught pianist, 143
treatment of Peggy, 29, 35, 321, 419
Vadala, Peggy June Thompson Hume, *17,*
46, 347
abandonment of daughters, 31, 419
Candice's search for, 402, 416, 417–19,
420–22
Cinthea's physical resemblance to, 57, 58
death of, 418
family background of, 21–22, *22,* 28, 31
Marion's treatment of, 29, 35, 321, 419
marriage to John Frazier, 418–19
marriage to Louis, 18, 19–20, 21, 27–30,
31, 34, 174, 421
marriage to Theodore Frank Hume,
21, 23
Vance, Carole S., 254, 296, 299, 305, *314*
Van Cortlandt Park, 50, 54
Vanity Fair, 288, 393
Variety
on adult video revenues, 392
on *Baby Rosemary,* 180
on Clinton and Lewinsky, 393
on *Deep Throat,* 121
on Holmes, 181–82
on *Snuff,* 193
at *Urban Heat*'s premiere, 288
Vassi, Mario, 301–2